Second Edition

COLOR ATLAS OF
FORENSIC
MEDICINE AND
PATHOLOGY

Edited by **Charles Catanese**

CRC Press
Taylor & Francis Group
Boca Raton London New York

CRC Press is an imprint of the
Taylor & Francis Group, an **informa** business

CRC Press
Taylor & Francis Group
6000 Broken Sound Parkway NW, Suite 300
Boca Raton, FL 33487-2742

© 2016 by Charles Catanese
CRC Press is an imprint of Taylor & Francis Group, an Informa business

No claim to original U.S. Government works

Printed on acid-free paper
Version Date: 20151111

Printed and bound in India by Replika Press Pvt. Ltd.

International Standard Book Number-13: 978-1-4665-8590-4 (Hardback)

Visit the Taylor & Francis Web site at
http://www.taylorandfrancis.com

and the CRC Press Web site at
http://www.crcpress.com

This atlas is dedicated to my family, including my father, S. John Catanese, my deceased mother, Helen J. Amendola-Catanese, and my older siblings, John Catanese PhD, BMF, Anthony Catanese MD, and Gerald Catanese MD.

Contents

Acknowledgments

I thank my father, S. John Catanese, my mother Helen Amendola-Catanese, and my older siblings, John Catanese PhD, Anthony Catanese MD, and Gerard Catanese MD.

I thank Dr. Laura LaBay for assisting with editing.

I give a special thanks to Peter Barrale MS and Matt Carr MS.

Another very special thanks for the endless amount of hours put into editing, organizing, and formulating data to Patrick Horan DO and Brendan Tanner OM.

Very special thanks to Caitlin Treuting, for her countless hours of her free time to help edit photographs and organize text. Without her help this work would not have been possible.

My sincerest thanks to all of you,

Charles A. Catanese

Editor

Charles A. Catanese, MD, completed his medical school education at SUNY Downstate and his residency training at State University Hospital–Kings County Hospital complex in Brooklyn, New York. He is board certified by the American Board of Pathology in anatomic pathology and forensic pathology. Following his forensic pathology fellowship training in New York City, Dr. Catanese was employed as a full-time medical examiner in the Brooklyn office of New York City for more than 10 years. He has performed in excess of 5000 autopsies, including more than 500 homicides, and has supervised many more. As educational coordinator of Brooklyn, he accumulated many academic images demonstrating a wide variety and spectrum of presentation for many forensic topics. The Brooklyn office is the busiest of the five boroughs and New York City has the largest medical examiner's system in the country. Dr. Catanese has also worked as a private consultant for many years and has provided locums coverage in the states of New Hampshire, New Jersey, Tennessee, Rhode Island, Vermont, and New York. He also worked through several disasters, including TWA Flight 800, AA Flight 587, and more than 9 months on the World Trade Center fatalities. He has been the chief medical examiner in the lower Hudson Valley of New York for more than 7 years.

Contributors

Michael J. Caplan
Chief Medical Examiner
Suffolk County, New York
Hauppauge, New York

and

Visiting Associate Professor
State University of Stony Brook
Stony Brook, New York

Gerard A. Catanese
Deputy Medical Examiner
Nassau County, New York
East Meadow, New York

Thomas Gilson
Chief Medical Examiner
Cuyahoga County, Ohio
Cleveland, Ohio

Zhongxue Hua
Private Forensic Pathologist
New York, New York

Laura M. Labay
Forensic Toxicologist
National Medical Services Laboratory
Willow Grove, Pennsylvania

Bruce Levy
Associate Professor of Clinical Pathology
University of Illinois at Chicago
Chicago, Illinois

Amy V. Rapkiewicz
Assistant Professor of Pathology
New York University Langone Medical Center
New York, New York

Gina Marie Santucci
Forensic Photographer
Department of Forensic Imagery
New York City Office of the Chief Medical
    Examiner
New York, New York

Alex Kent Williamson
Chief, Autopsy Service, North Shore–LIJ
    Health System
Division of Pediatric Pathology
Cohen Children's Medical Center
New York, New York

and

Assistant Professor
Hofstra North Shore–LIJ School of Medicine
Lake Success, New York

Research Assistants and Photo Imaging Contributors

Peter Barrale
Ross Medical School
Portsmouth, Dominica

Jowaly Camacho
Autopsy Assistant
New York, New York

Patrick Horan
Autopsy/Research Assistant
New York, New York

Brendan Tanner
Pennsylvania College of Osteopathic Medicine
Philadelphia, Pennsylvania

Caitlin Treuting
Autopsy Assistant
New York, New York

Sudden Natural Death in a Forensic Setting

1

CHARLES A. CATANESE AND AMY V. RAPKIEWICZ

Contents

Introduction

This chapter offers a brief overview of some common and some not-so-common natural deaths that typically may occur in a medical examiner system. Also demonstrated are examples that may alter the appearance of tissue, such as formaldehyde fixation and variation due to different types of photographic imagery. There are also examples of normal organs in both a fresh and a formaldehyde-fixed state that can be used by the reader to compare with diseased organs.

Deaths under this category are often unexpected, sometimes unwitnessed, and without documented medical history. There may be a suspicion of foul play. Families may say, "But Doctor, he was in fine health. I saw him an hour ago. It cannot be natural. Somebody must have harmed him," etc. Because of the sudden, unexpected nature of these deaths, it is best to do an autopsy to clarify exactly what happened. This decision to autopsy depends on many factors, including the decedent's age, medical history, family wishes, decedent's wishes (wills, etc.), religious beliefs, circumstances at the time of death, resources of a particular system, etc. As one becomes less certain of the cause of death, the level of suspicion will increase. At some point, the decision to autopsy becomes obvious and absolutely necessary. This decision is based on experience, knowledge, and sound judgment. Not infrequently, seemingly natural deaths can have unnatural or traumatic previous circumstances; therefore, when uncertain, an autopsy is best performed. In many medical examiner systems, the majority of deaths end up being certified as natural.

Sudden death may be defined in different ways. It may indicate a death that occurs within 24 hours of the onset of symptoms. It may also indicate a death that occurred within 1 hour or even within seconds. There are not many diseases that can cause death within minutes of the onset of symptoms.

In order to know what is natural, one must be able to differentiate it from other manners of death such as homicide, accident, suicide, undetermined, and possibly therapeutic complication (see Chapter 2). Natural deaths occur exclusively as a result of etiologically specific diseases such as cancer, chronic obstructive pulmonary disease, atherosclerosis, diabetes mellitus, lobar pneumonia, chronic environmental insults, etc. Natural death means the manner of death is exclusively 100% natural. Accidental deaths are caused by violent means, not by intentional or criminal acts of another. Homicides are defined as death at the hands of another, or that occurred during an illegal act. Suicidal deaths that occur as a result of self-murder where the decedent intended to kill themselves. Undetermined are deaths where a reasonable classification is not possible. If there is a 1% component of an unnatural event, which contributed to death, of another manner, it is no longer natural. If there are multiple components of different manners of death identified during a case investigation, the following rule will apply: a homicide overrides all, then an accident, then a therapeutic complication. For example, someone with end-stage metastatic liver cancer ingests 100 acetaminophen tablets to commit suicide. In the process of waiting to die, he decides to walk to a store. On the way, he trips in a pothole, falls in the street, strikes his head, and has an expanding subdural hemorrhage. While he is lying there groaning in pain, waiting for EMS, a stolen car fleeing the scene of a robbery runs him over, lacerates his heart in half, and he dies within seconds. The manner of death in this case would be homicide. The death occurred as a result of being run over by a car during an illegal act. A lacerated heart is universally fatal regardless of the other violent and natural processes. The death certificate should include only the trauma from the car. If the trauma from the car was not lethal by itself, one may add "other finding" to part two of the cause of death, but the manner would remain homicide.

Heart Disease

Heart disease leading to ventricular irritability and fatal cardiac arrhythmia is the most significant cause of death in this category. The most common arrhythmia leading to sudden cardiac death is ventricular fibrillation. Ventricular tachyarrhythmias are most commonly seen within 12 hours of a myocardial infarction. Critical coronary atherosclerosis and hypertension are by far the leading causes of these processes. Some diseases that contribute to atherosclerosis and arteriosclerosis formation include hyperlipidemia, high blood pressure, diabetes mellitus, obesity, cigarette smoking, stress, and sedentary lifestyle.

Having 75% or greater blockage in any of the epicardial vessels is considered critical stenosis and is consistent with being alive 1 second and having loss of consciousness leading to death the next. Hypertensive cardiovascular disease is usually essential in origin from an intrinsic abnormality of sodium metabolism. Other significant causes of hypertension include many types of kidney disease, including adult polycystic kidney disease and renal artery stenosis. Hypertension may be sporadic and missed on routine doctor appointments. High blood pressure is also associated with small-vessel coronary artery disease, as is diabetes mellitus, which is a reasonable cause of death by itself. Once people reach a pivotal point of myocardial irritability and go into ventricular fibrillation, they usually have approximately 15 seconds of consciousness left. Prior to losing consciousness, decedents may reach up to chest or neck and mention a fluttering sensation in the chest. They may have pressure, pain, or no expectation of what is to come. Ventricular irritability associated with coronary artery ischemia is due to lack of oxygen and nutrients reaching the conducting system of the heart. If the heart is not cardioverted back to a normal rhythm within 4–6 minutes, there is usually irreversible brain damage.

Another major cause of ventricular irritability leading to fatal arrhythmia is hypertension. Concentric left ventricular hypertrophy, usually defined at autopsy as having a left ventricular wall thickness greater than 1.5 cm for most average-sized adults, is a known risk factor for sudden cardiac death. Left ventricular thickness is best measured approximately 2 cm below the mitral valve annulus and excludes trabeculations and papillary muscles. As the disease process causing cardiac hypertrophy advances, heart failure may ensue with chamber dilatation. Although the overall heart size is enlarged, the left ventricle wall thickness may be less than 1.4 cm in cases of cardiac chamber dilatation with wall thinning due to failure. Although hypertensive cardiovascular disease is the major risk factor for the development of left ventricular hypertrophy, other risk factors include aortic stenosis, either congenital or acquired. The hearts of patients with hypertensive or arteriosclerotic cardiovascular disease typically show evidence of prior infarction and interstitial fibrosis. Both findings also predispose to abnormalities in the conduction system, predisposing to myocardial irritability and fatal arrhythmias.

Complications other than tachyarrhythmia and pump failure of myocardial infarctions can result in sudden cardiac death; the most common include the myocardial rupture syndromes, including ventricular wall and papillary wall rupture. Typically, these insults occur approximately 1 week following a myocardial infarction, the point at which there is removal of necrotic myocytes by macrophages. Hemopericardium with ensuing cardiac tamponade can occur following ventricular free wall rupture; this scenario is rapidly fatal in most cases, causing decreased venous return to the heart with jugular venous distention.

In young patients, hypertrophic cardiomyopathy is a common cause of sudden death. Fatal arrhythmia occurs during or following exercise. These patients can be asymptomatic prior to the sudden event or may have past episodes of palpitations or syncope. Typically, in the classical type, macroscopic heart evaluation shows cardiac hypertrophy with significant asymmetry of the subaortic septal region, which poses as an outflow obstruction. Microscopic sections from this region show variable degrees of myocyte disarray, fibrosis, myocyte hypertrophy, and small-vessel disease. The disease is due to an autosomal dominant mutation in the cardiac sarcomere apparatus, most commonly the myosin heavy chain, but many mutations have been described. As this disease process becomes more defined, it has been described with a spectrum of change ranging from asymmetry of the left ventricle, in classical presentation, to the rarely described variant with no cardiac hypertrophy at all.

Arrhythmogenic right ventricular cardiomyopathy can present with sudden unexpected death. At autopsy, the right ventricle is thinned, with microscopic evaluation showing significant transmural infiltration by fibrofatty tissue.

Myocarditis due to a variety of causes, including viral, bacterial, fungal, parasitic, autoimmune, and hypersensitivity, can present as sudden death. The degree of activity, myonecrosis, and the location of the inflammation (i.e., conduction system involvement) are important in determining the significance of the infiltrates. Notably, eosinophils are seen quite commonly in hypersensitivity myocarditis, which is a delayed type for hypersensitivity reaction and can be a clue to the underlying etiology, which begins around blood vessels and tracks into the parenchyma. The origin of this process is thought to be mostly autoimmune where the immune system produces an immune response against heart muscle components.

Some viruses have been identified in myocardial cultures, such as coxsackievirus. The presence of giant cells indicates chronicity of infection and should not lead to mistaken diagnosis of giant cell myocarditis. Giant cell myocarditis is associated with extensive necrosis and high mortality rate, and is of unknown etiology.

Dilated cardiomyopathy is common, and has many etiologies that include idiopathic arteriosclerotic disease, hypertensive cardiovascular disease, alcoholism, elevated catecholamines, myocarditis, postpartum, doxorubicin, endocrinopathies, and genetic diseases. The heart typically is enlarged with a globoid configuration. The microscopic analysis shows interstitial fibrosis.

Rare infiltrative cardiac diseases such as amyloidosis, hemochromatosis, primary or metastatic tumors, and sarcoidosis can result in sudden death. Microscopic evaluation in these cases is necessary, with particular attention to nodal tissues.

Staphylococcus aureus is the most common organism found in infective endocarditis (IE). *S. aureus* endocarditis is associated with the highest mortality and risk of embolism. Increasing age, periannular abscess, heart failure, and absence of surgical therapy were identified in multivariate analysis as independent poor prognostic factors for increased mortality in patients with *S. aureus* IE. Other risk factors for the development of IE include congenital or acquired anatomic valve abnormalities such as stenosis. Impaired cardiac conductivity and function with heart failure not infrequently develop in patients with multiple septic myocardial emboli and infarcts due to IE, particularly with paravalvular abscess formation. According to a recent study of a cohort of 606 cases of IE, 99 cases have embolization, of which 32 cases involve the central nervous system (CNS) with significantly higher mortality (65%) than those without CNS emboli.

Recently, genetic abnormalities have been found to underlie many of the intrinsic abnormalities of conducting systems, including Wolff–Parkinson–White syndrome (WPW) and long Q-T syndrome. Sudden death in WPW is thought to occur as a result of an induction of ventricular tachycardia via an atrioventricular re-entry pathway. Long-QT syndrome can also present with sudden death. Investigations are ongoing around the association of sudden infant death syndrome with long-QT syndrome. Recent data suggest a genetic basis for the arrhythmogenic disease with the identification of the long-QT genes.

Sudden death related to cardiac valve pathology other than endocarditis is relatively uncommon, as valve replacement surgery has become a standard therapy. Patients with aortic stenosis, especially when acutely symptomatic, can experience sudden cardiac death. Most cases of aortic stenosis are caused by either rheumatic heart disease or valve calcification, which can occur on trileaflet or congenitally (uni)bicuspid valves. The mechanism for death in severe aortic stenosis (valve area <1 cm²) appears to be through left ventricular hypertrophy and subsequent myocardial instability. In rare instances of severe aortic valve calcification, the deposits can erode the region and involve the conduction system. Mitral valve prolapse has long been associated with sudden cardiac death. The underlying etiology is not well understood, but seems to most frequently involve a severe valve deformity with a redundant, thickened, myxomatous mitral valve and ventricular arrhythmias such as ventricular fibrillation. On histologic sectioning, the mitral valve will show deposition of acid mucopolysaccharides.

Coronary artery anomalies are not uncommon but only certain anomalies result in ischemia, such as anomalous origin of a coronary artery from the opposite sinus (ACAOS), anomalous left coronary artery from the pulmonary artery (ALCAPA), ostial atresia/stenosis, and coronary artery fistulas. Left-sided ACAOS can result in acute takeoff angles with an increased risk of sudden death during or shortly after exercise. Besides the acute angle takeoff, there may be ridgelike defect at the coronary ostia, further decreasing blood flow in times of accelerated heart rates with increased oxygen demand. Myocardial tunneling is another anomalous coronary artery distribution that may be associated with increased arrhythmogenic potential. There is debate about the significance of this anomaly. Some still believe it may be significant when a large portion of the epicardial coronary artery dips deeply into the left ventricle wall for a considerable distance, during times of rapid muscle contraction.

Vascular Disease

Causes of sudden death associated with vascular disease include those that lead to occlusion, narrowing, or rupture of a blood vessel. Atherosclerotic aneurysms can rupture, leading to rapid loss of consciousness and death. These aneurysms can occur just about anywhere, but are by far most common in the abdominal aorta. Most abdominal aortic aneurysms occur below the renal artery. The risk of rupture increases with the size of the aneurysm, smoking history, and hypertension. The annual risk of rupture over 7 cm in size is 33%. Retroperitoneal rupture is typically associated with hematoma formation, whereas rupture into the abdominal cavity can be rapidly fatal, with hemoperitoneum and shock. Patients who have a ruptured aortic aneurysm and reach the hospital have a 50% mortality rate, with the overall mortality rate greater than 85%.

Aortic dissection is characterized by an intimal tear followed by a dissection of blood within the wall of the aorta, most commonly the tunica media. Rupture of this dissecting aortic hematoma may lead to hemothoraces, hemopericardium, or fatal arrhythmia. Aortic dissection is a major cause of sudden death, mostly in patients over 50 years of age with the underlying risk factor being essential hypertension. However, pregnant women and patients with connective-tissue diseases such as Marfan syndrome also make up a significantly affected patient population. Aortic dissection can also occur following accidental or iatrogenic trauma to the aortic intima. In younger patients and those with connective-tissue disease, microscopy may reveal cystic medial degeneration of the aortic media.

Most spontaneous subarachnoid hemorrhages (SAH) (90%) are caused by ruptured intracranial saccular (berry) aneurysms. SAH occurs at a peak age of 55–60 years. Rupture of an intracranial aneurysm is believed to account for 0.4%–0.6% of all deaths. SAH is associated with a greater than 50% mortality rate. Some hospital-based studies suggest that approximately 10% of patients with aneurismal SAH die prior to reaching the hospital, 25% die within 24 hours of SAH onset, and about 45% die within 30 days. It is not unusual to perform forensic autopsies where death was almost instantaneous and outside of a hospital. The mechanism of death in such cases is cardiac arrhythmia, which is described in greater depth later. Most intracranial aneurysms (approximately 85%) are located in the anterior circulation, predominately on the circle of Willis. Risk factors for both SAH and intracranial aneurysms are similar and include hypertension, cigarette smoking, and alcohol consumption. Atherosclerosis is an independent risk factor for the development of intracranial aneurysms. The natural history of subarachnoid hemorrhage shows that rupture often occurs when they reach a size over 7 mm. Rupture of an aneurysm releases blood directly into the cerebrospinal fluid (CSF) under arterial pressure. The blood spreads quickly within the CSF, rapidly increasing intracranial pressure. A major symptom associated with SAH includes patients describing the worst headache of one's life. Increased intracranial pressure is associated with the Cushing's triad (hypertension, bradycardia, and abnormal respiration). SAH is associated with cerebral edema and subsequent herniation. Tonsillar and central transtentorial herniation is associated with compression of cardiovascular and respiratory centers in the medulla and, as such, is rapidly fatal. Other less common causes of SAH include angiomas and arteriovenous malformations. Ruptured berry aneurysms are the most common natural cause of SAH, whereas trauma is the most common overall cause. Ruptured berry aneurysms are a leading cause of sudden death in women during sexual activity, whereas for men, it is heart disease.

Cerebrovascular accidents (episodes), which include ischemic or intracerebral hemorrhage, can lead to sudden death. I recommend not using the term "accident" because there is nothing accidental about this process and its use often adds confusion in forensic proceedings. The term "stroke" or "event" as an alternative is less confusing to nonmedical personnel. Thromboembolic events can underlie ischemic cerebral events and are associated with heart disease, valvular pathology, or carotid artery disease. Hypertension is a major risk factor for intraparenchymal hemorrhage and may lead to increased intracranial pressure, herniation, and death.

The greatest percentage of thrombi resulting in pulmonary embolism is thought to originate in the deep veins of the lower extremities. Deep venous thrombosis can also occur in the pelvis or other locations. Fragments of blood clot may break off and embolize to the pulmonary arteries. An occlusion greater than 50%–75% of the large pulmonary vessels results in a rise of the pulmonary artery pressure greater than 40 mmHg. This rise of pulmonary arterial pressure is accompanied by an increase in right ventricular diastolic, right atrial, and systemic venous pressures, with a decrease in cardiac output resulting in sudden death. Patients who have multiple small pulmonary emboli or in situ thrombus formation over time may present with increasing shortness of breath and right-sided heart failure. Because the lungs have dual circulation, infarctions are less common unless there is significant underlying natural disease with decreased cardiac function.

Various types of vasculitis or blood vessel inflammation can cause wall thickening, thrombosis, dissection, and rupture. Mesenteric thrombosis may be associated with polyarteritis nodosum and other autoimmune conditions.

Other Causes of Sudden Death

Rare undiagnosed brain tumors may present with sudden death. The mechanism may be infiltration, or edema formation, into the key respiratory/cardiac centers of the brain, with possible herniation. Early- or late-stage malignancies may sometimes metastasize to the heart and interfere with the conducting system, causing a fatal arrhythmia. Other causes of sudden death in patients with malignancies include cardiovascular events such as acute myocardial infarction, therapeutic complications (i.e., anaphylaxis), and metabolic derangements. Rare causes of sudden death in patients with tumors or malignancies include erosion of large vessels or visci with fatal hemorrhage. A colloid cyst of the third ventricle may lead to sudden death and is usually associated with premortem postural headaches. In certain positions, the cyst will act like a ball valve and suddenly block the flow of cerebral spinal fluid, resulting in acute obstructive hydrocephalus. One may be fine standing but develop symptoms when he or she lies down. This buildup of cerebral spinal fluid pressure can cause a fatal arrhythmia. Bacterial pneumonia with the combination of hypoxia and bacterial toxins and end products can cause sudden death.

Status asthmaticus and sudden asphyxic asthma are life-threatening forms of asthma. These cases are not unusual in a forensic setting. Status asthmaticus is defined as an acute attack of respiratory failure due to airway inflammation, edema, and mucous plugging. Sudden asphyxic asthma is due to bronchospasm rather than airway inflammation. Viral infections and other causes have been implicated as precipitants of these potentially fatal complications. Grossly in both cases, the lungs may appear so much hyperaerated that, at times, rib indentations will show. Thick mucous plugs may obstruct the upper airways. Sudden death in asthmatic patients is thought to be secondary to fatal arrhythmia, occurring as a consequence of global hypoxia and right-sided heart failure.

There is a condition known as sudden unexpected death in epilepsy (SUDEP). The mechanism is unclear, but this phenomenon occurs in up to 18% of patients with epilepsy, presumably in those with subtherapeutic levels of anticonvulsants. Autonomic dysfunction has been proposed as a mechanism. Other mechanisms for death in patients with epilepsy include accidental/traumatic incidents such as drowning and choking that occur during a seizure. Hypoxia as a result of respiratory compromise can result in ischemic cardiac events. This may be part of the final mechanism of death in epileptic patients experiencing status epilepticus. Another interesting point to remember is that there is often very rapid rigor mortis formation in deaths directly following static epilepticus due to substantial adenosine triphosphate (ATP) depletion associated with prolonged muscle contractions from prolonged convulsions. Usually there are few pathologic findings that explain the sudden death in epileptic patients. Autopsy findings may include bite marks to the tongue with hemorrhage or a voided urinary bladder. There may be no finding at all. These are nonspecific findings, and seizure activity may also occur prior to many other nonepilepsy-related deaths.

Fatal anaphylaxis can result from exposure to insect stings, foods, latex, drugs, chemicals, and exercise. This mast cell-mediated systemic reaction results in severe angioedema and bronchoconstriction of the upper respiratory tract along with hypotension, resulting in respiratory and circulatory collapse. Death caused by anaphylaxis is primarily due to airway obstruction

when laryngeal edema fills the rich lymphatic supply of the epiglottic folds. Increased mast cell tryptase levels in the patient's serum can be detected that peak approximately 15–60 minutes after the onset of anaphylaxis and then decline with a half-life of about 2 hours.

The mortality for gastrointestinal bleeding (GI) in the case of ruptured esophageal varices, most commonly encountered in patients with portal hypertension, is high. Intra-aortic balloon pumps are lifesaving procedures but only if the patient presents in a timely fashion. Other causes of fatal upper GI include stomach and duodenal ulcers; in this scenario, the source is arterial as opposed to venous in esophageal varices. Fatal lower GI can be seen in patients with angiodysplasia, diverticulitis, and carcinoma; however, this scenario is less common than upper GI bleeding.

Mostly complications of morbid obesity are thought to underlie the association with sudden death. Hypertension, left ventricular hypertrophy, and cardiomegaly are all independent risk factors for sudden death. Postural asphyxia may occur as a result of obesity. Morbid obesity is a reasonable cause of death by itself due to stress on the heart. An individual who is three times the expected body weight has roughly three times the vasculature with three times the blood volume to pump. In times of other stress, this can have devastating consequences on the heart, with death by arrhythmia.

Waterhouse–Friderichsen syndrome was first described as occurring in patients with meningococcemia, and is characterized by severe bacteremia and bilateral adrenal hemorrhages. This combination results in overwhelming shock and, if untreated, sudden death can occur. Organisms other than *Neisseria meningitidis*, such as *Escherichia coli*, have been reported to produce this syndrome.

Multiorgan failure and death can be seen in sickle cell anemia patients with an acute crisis. Precipitants may include infection, dehydration, hypoxia, physical excretion, vaso-occlusion, or fat embolus following bone infarction. This acute hemolytic sickling crisis results in severe hypoxemia with end organ failure. Patients with sickle cell anemia have auto-infarcted spleens and are much more susceptible to encapsulated organisms such as pneumococcal bacteria. Even patients with sickle cell trait may develop crisis in times of great physical exertion with dehydration, such as basic training in the army or boot camp.

Natural disease processes may weaken the body, making fatal traumatic injury more likely. Osteoporosis from aging, Cushing syndrome, steroid use, and other natural disease processes will make bones more fragile and allow fractures to occur more easily.

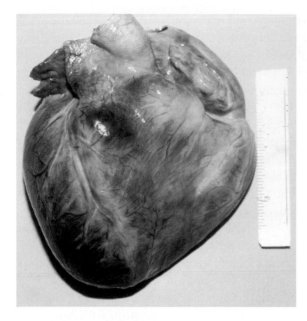

Figure 1.1 Normal heart from a recently deceased individual without formaldehyde fixation.

Figure 1.2 Sections of a normal heart from a recently deceased individual without formaldehyde fixation showing right and left ventricles.

Figures 1.4 and 1.5 Normal left lung demonstrating two lobes from a recently deceased individual without formaldehyde fixation. Right lungs have three lobes.

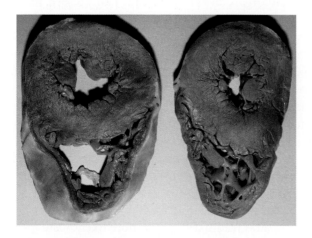

Figure 1.3 The same larger two sections, as depicted in Figure 1.2, after formaldehyde fixation, showing gray discoloration and slightly shrunken firm parenchyma.

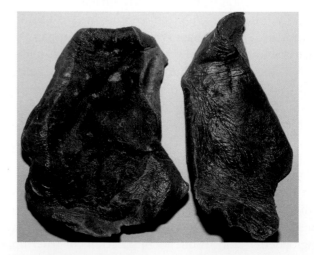

Figure 1.6 The same lungs, as in Figures 1.4 and 1.5, after formaldehyde fixation, showing gray discoloration and slightly shrunken firm parenchyma.

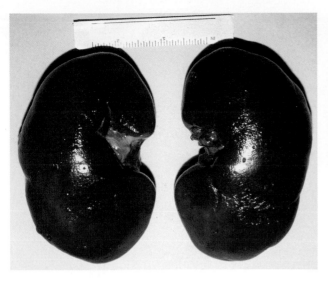

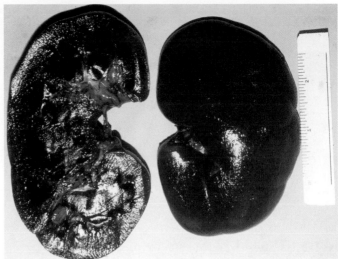

Figures 1.7 and 1.8 Normal kidneys.

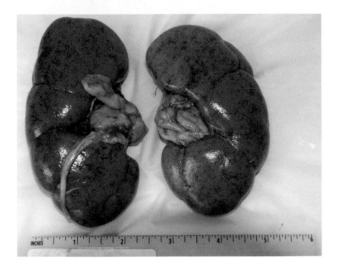

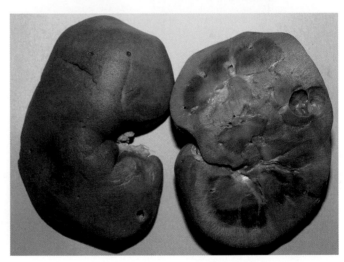

Figure 1.9 Nonfixed kidneys. Note the pale discoloration resulting from fatal blood loss prior to death due to a gunshot wound.

Figure 1.10 Normal bisected kidney fixed in formaldehyde.

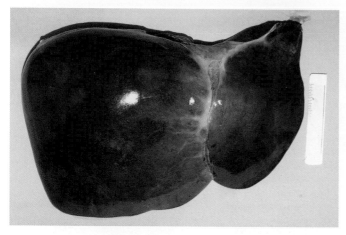

Figures 1.11 and 1.12 Normal liver.

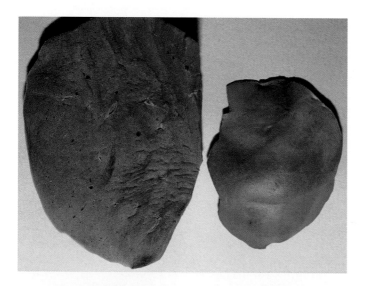

Figure 1.13 Normal liver fixed in formaldehyde.

Figure 1.14 Normal spleen.

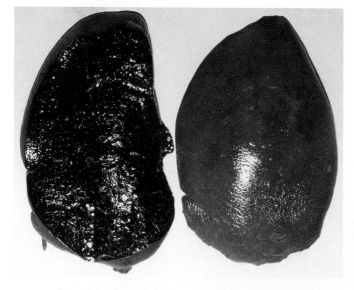

Figure 1.15 Normal spleen.

Figure 1.16 Normal spleen fixed in formaldehyde.

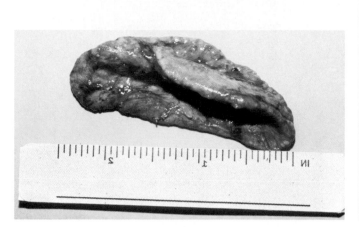

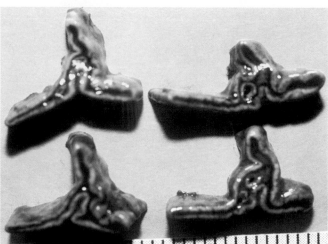

Figures 1.17 and 1.18 Normal adrenal gland intact and sectioned.

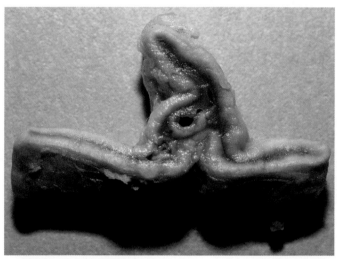

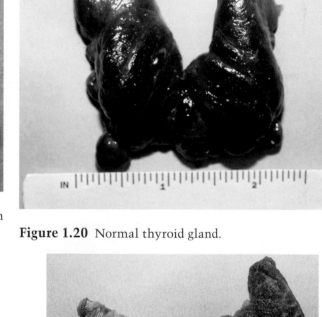

Figure 1.19 Normal adrenal gland section fixed in formaldehyde.

Figure 1.20 Normal thyroid gland.

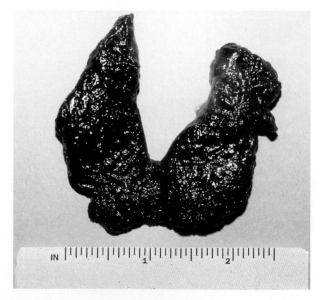

Figure 1.21 Normal thyroid gland.

Figure 1.22 Normal bisected thyroid gland fixed in formaldehyde.

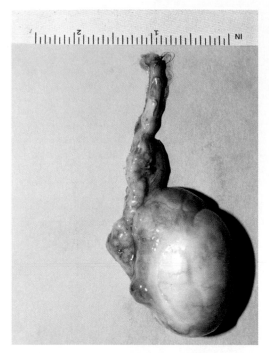
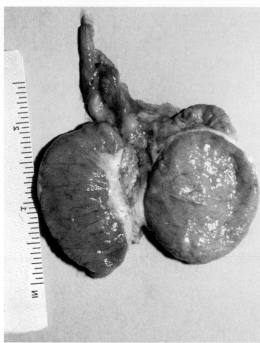

Figures 1.23 and 1.24 Normal testes.

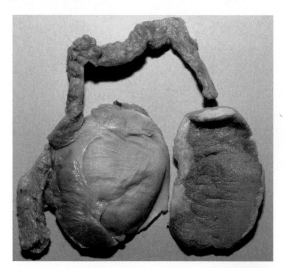

Figure 1.25 Normal testes fixed in formaldehyde.

Figure 1.26 Normal prostate.   **Figure 1.27** Normal prostate fixed in formaldehyde.

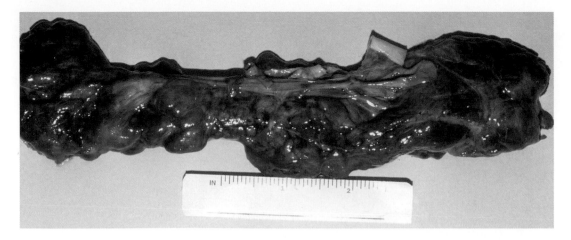

Figure 1.28 Normal pancreas.

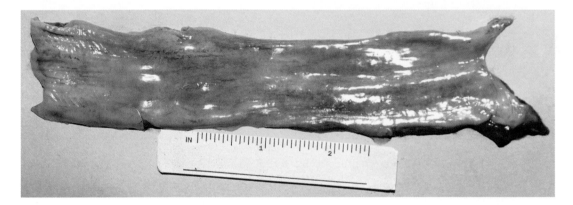

Figure 1.29 Normal esophagus.

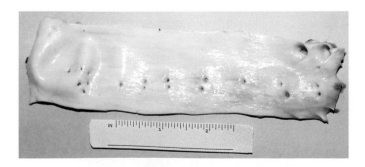

Figure 1.30 Aorta with slight atherosclerosis. Note the fatty streaks on the intimal surface from this individual in their early 20s.

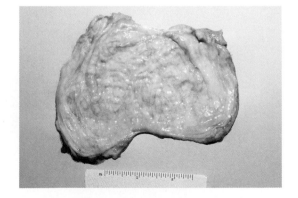

Figure 1.31 Normal bladder.

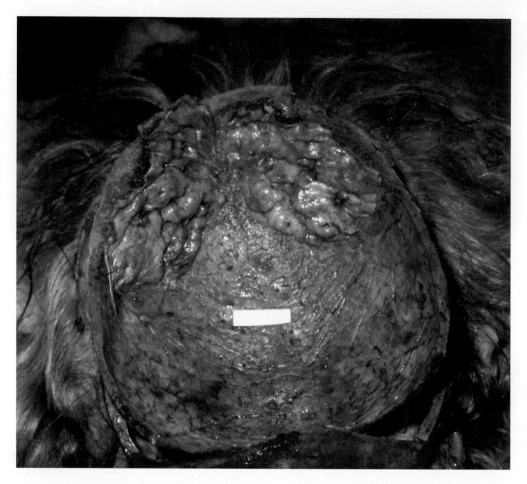

Figure 1.32 Hyperostosis frontalis is a benign process characterized by irregular thickening of the internal frontal bone that may help with identification.

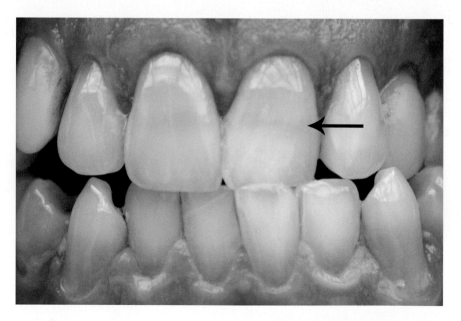

Figure 1.33 Tetracycline staining of the teeth due to exposure to this antibiotic as a child. This discoloration may be helpful as a feature for identification when other modalities are not possible. This discoloration, superior to the arrow, occurred during childhood when the teeth were still forming.

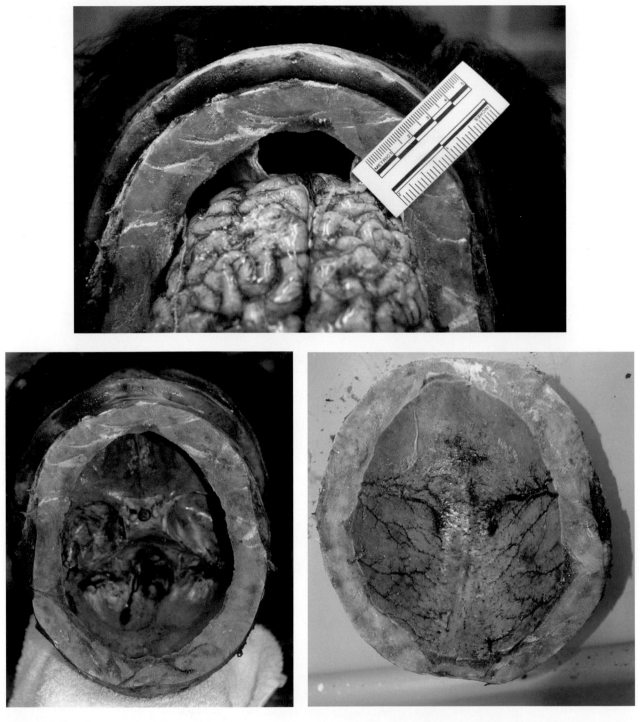

Figures 1.34–1.36 Paget disease is a disease involving the accelerated breakdown and formation of bone. Note the markedly thickened skull wall, which occurs gradually over time. See Figures 11.123–11.125 in the histology chapter.

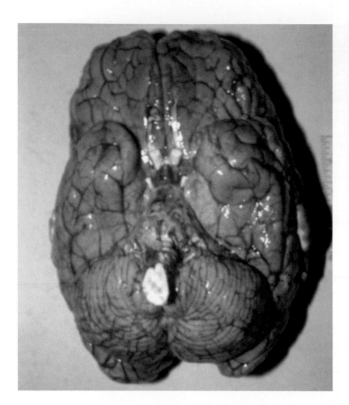 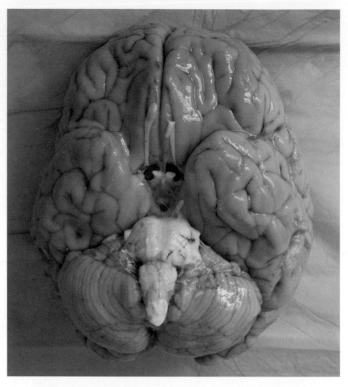

Figures 1.37 and 1.38 The first picture demonstrates congestion of non-formaldehyde-fixed brain. Note the slight pink color. The second picture demonstrates non-formaldehyde-fixed brain in an individual who exsanguinated from a ruptured aortic aneurysm. Note the pale discoloration due to blood loss.

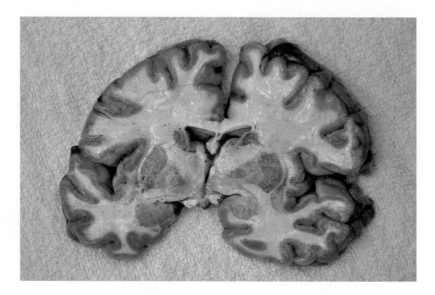

Figure 1.39 Note the green discoloration of the brain section from a person who died of hydrogen sulfide poisoning.

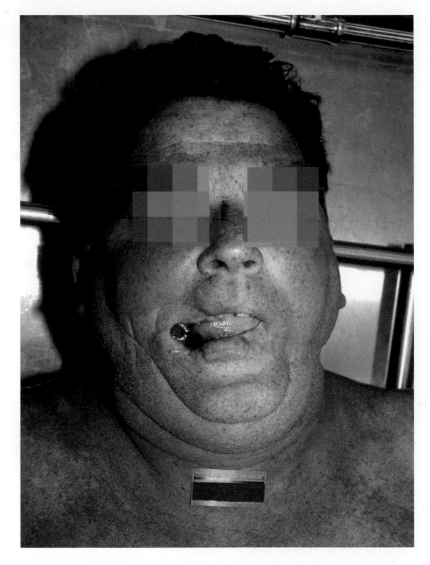

Figure 1.40 This picture depicts a decedent with an endotracheal tube in the right side of his mouth. It also demonstrates the "purple head sign," a common finding in victims of sudden death, particularly cardiac death. The explanation for this finding is not known in entirety but is attributed to uncontrolled terminal sympathetic nervous system discharges, which open free capillary sphincters and produce a gush of capillary blood.

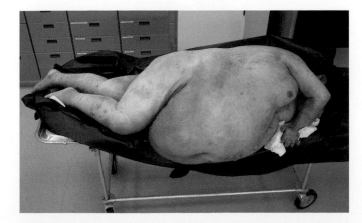

Figure 1.41 Morbid obesity. This is a legitimate cause of death and can stand alone on a death certificate.

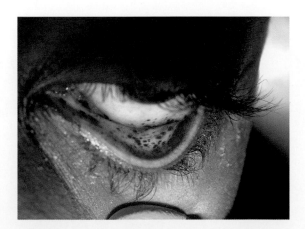

Figure 1.42 Petechiae associated with heart disease and resuscitation.

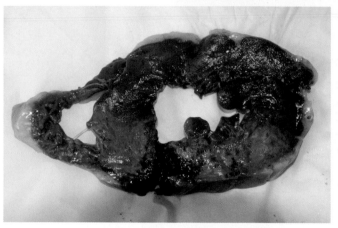

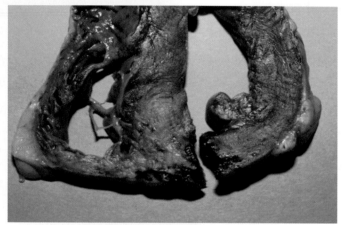

Figures 1.43–1.45 An acute myocardial infarction. Note the yellow discoloration due to necrosis. This infarction is approximately 3–6 days old. In Figure 1.45, there is a transmural acute myocardial infarction with rupture.

Figure 1.47 Epicardial vessel with complete occlusion by organizing thrombus. Note the adjacent epicardial hemorrhage.

Figure 1.46 Acute myocardial infarction.

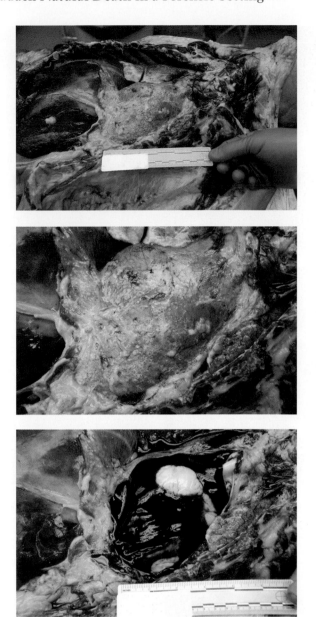

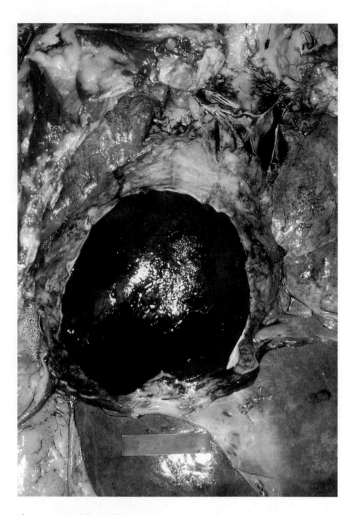

Figures 1.48–1.51 View of the thoracic cavity looking downward at the heart during autopsy. Note the purple discoloration of the pericardial sack due to underlying accumulation of blood. Note the two different examples with large blood clot encasing the heart after the pericardial sac was removed. This demonstrates a cardiac tamponade following an acute ruptured myocardial infarction.

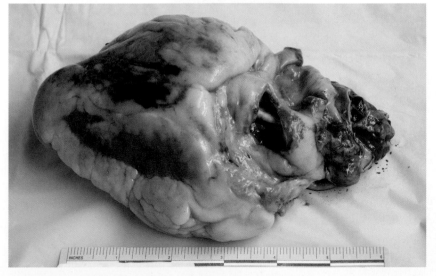

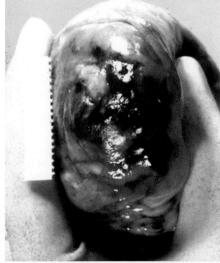

Figures 1.52 and 1.53 Two examples of hearts demonstrating acute ruptured myocardial infarction. Note the adjacent hemorrhage and perforation site. This resulted in cardiac tamponade and sudden death.

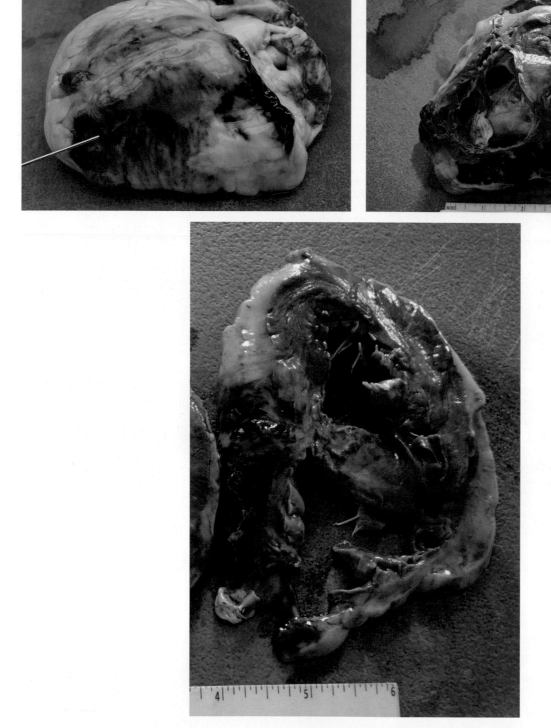

Figures 1.54–1.56 This individual had marked calcific atherosclerosis in all of his epicardial vessels with a ruptured acute myocardial infarction involving the posterior wall of the left ventricle, septum, and a large portion of the right ventricle. Note the hemorrhage to the right ventricle wall with the ruptured site indicated by the probe. Rupture of the right ventricle due to atherosclerosis is much less common than left ventricular rupture.

Figure 1.57 Early to moderate nephro-arteriosclerosis.

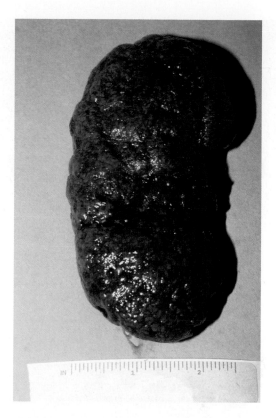

Figure 1.58 Moderate to marked nephro-arteriosclerosis.

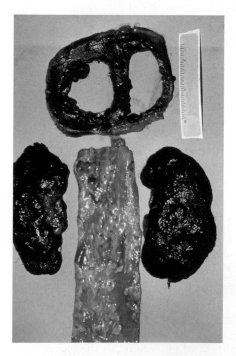

Figure 1.59 Nephro-arteriosclerosis with markedly granular subcapsular kidney surfaces and cortical scarring associated with hypertensive cardiovascular disease. Note the cardiac hypertrophy and biventricular dilatation in this failing heart. There is also moderate atherosclerosis of the aorta. Note the markedly granular subcapsular kidney surfaces and cortical scarring also associated with this process.

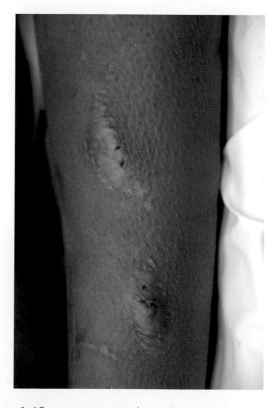

Figure 1.60 Arteriovenous hemodialysis grafts for treatment of chronic renal failure due to hypertensive cardiovascular disease. People receiving dialysis are more prone to hemorrhagic events during the time of treatment. Graphs may become infected and later rupture as well.

Figure 1.61 Normal cross sections of heart. Compare this image with the ones below.

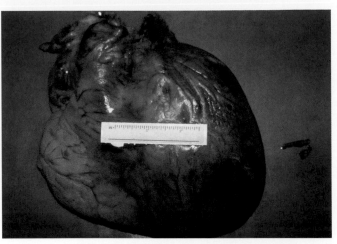

Figure 1.62 This is a markedly enlarged heart due to hypertensive cardiovascular disease. This heart is diffusely enlarged and shows cardiac hypertrophy.

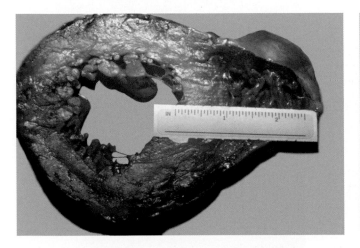

Figure 1.63 This is a markedly hypertrophied heart with extreme concentric left ventricle hypertrophy. This individual had severe hypertension.

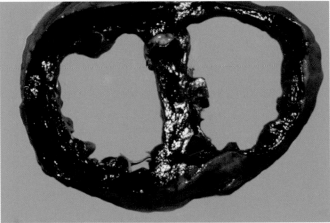

Figure 1.64 The right and left ventricles show marked dilatation. This individual died of a peripartum cardiomyopathy. A dilated cardiomyopathy or end-stage hypertensive cardiovascular disease with cardiac failure will appear the same grossly.

Figure 1.65 The sections of these ventricles reveal marked right ventricle hypertrophy. This individual had end-stage primary pulmonary fibrosis with cor pulmonale and cardiac failure.

Figure 1.66 The intimal lining of an aorta with marked atherosclerosis in a decedent with a long-standing history of smoking, diabetes, high cholesterol, and high blood pressure.

Figure 1.67 Abdominal aortic atherosclerotic aneurysm shown in its typical location inferior to the renal arteries and above the iliac bifurcation.

Figure 1.68 An abdominal atherosclerotic aneurysm with a rupture at its anterior aspect and visible thrombosis.

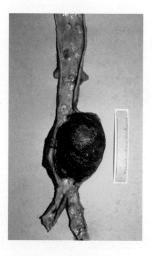

Figure 1.69 This abdominal aortic aneurysm has been opened to remove half of the vessel wall and show the underlying intimal surface with moderate atherosclerosis except for the region of the aneurysm that has marked atherosclerosis and a large overlying thrombus.

Figure 1.70 This abdominal aortic aneurysm has been cross sectioned to show the partial obstruction of the aneurysm by organizing thrombosis. The lumen is demonstrated by fresh red blood clot at its surface, and the thrombus is demonstrated by the light gray regions adjacent to the right and left wall.

Figure 1.71 Abdominal aortic aneurysm with vascular graft repair.

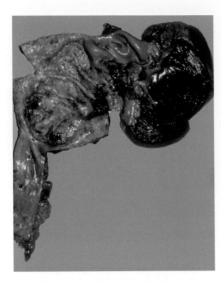

Figure 1.72 Thoracic aortic atherosclerotic aneurysm. This is not the typical location for such an aneurysm. Also note the aneurysm begins distal to the root of the aorta.

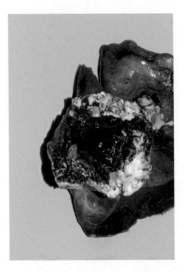

Figure 1.73 This demonstrates a decedent who had multiple atherosclerotic aneurysms including both iliac arteries.

Figure 1.74 Hemothorax from a ruptured thoracic atherosclerotic aneurysm.

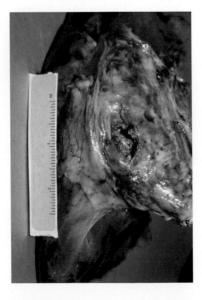

Figure 1.75 Thoracic atherosclerotic aortic aneurysm adherent to lung with rupture into the lung parenchyma causing massive hemoptysis. Note the second picture demonstrates the rupture site with adherent blood clot removed.

Figure 1.76 Thoracic atherosclerotic aortic aneurysm adherent to lung with rupture into the lung parenchyma causing massive hemoptysis. This picture demonstrates the rupture site with adherent blood clot removed.

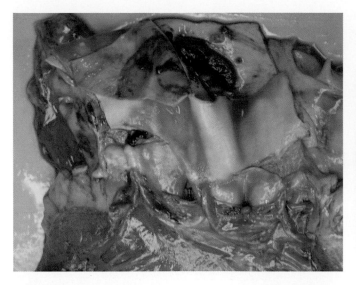

Figure 1.77 Intimal tear of the ascending aorta with dissection. Note blood tracking through the separated media.

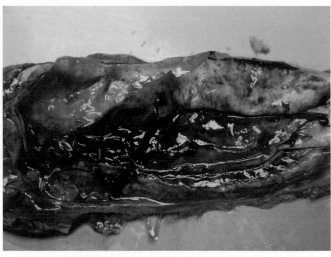

Figure 1.79 Aortic dissection with exposed separated media with blood clot in a person with Marfan syndrome.

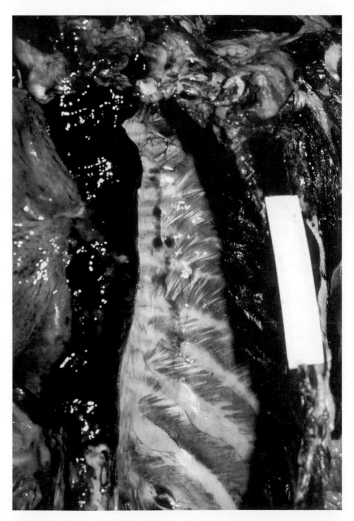

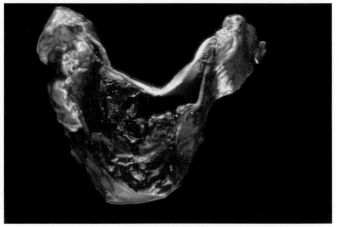

Figure 1.80 Cross section of aorta revealing a double barrel lumen. The superior aspect of this figure shows an opened aorta with the exposed lumen. Directly inferior to this is the separated media and adventitia with a second lumen that is partially thrombosed.

Figure 1.78 An in situ aortic dissection. Note the hemorrhage extending from the root of the aorta down the paravertebral region shown by dark red hemorrhagic discoloration. This decedent had severe hypertensive cardiovascular disease.

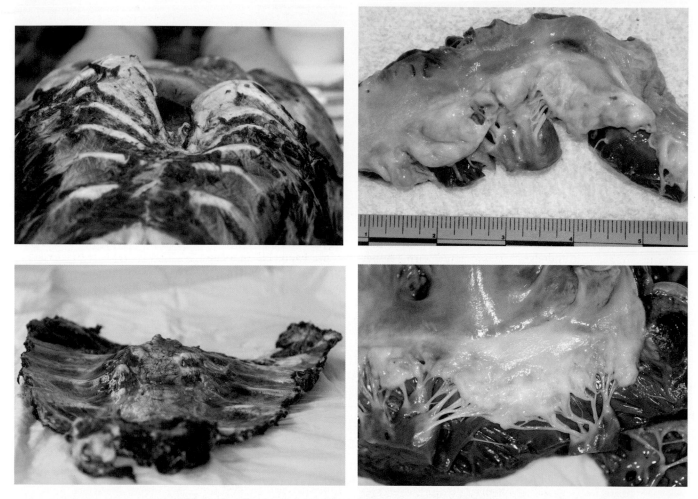

Figures 1.81–1.84 This demonstrates an individual with Marfan syndrome showing characteristics of pectus exca-vatum and mitral valve prolapse. Marfan syndrome is a connective-tissue disease associated with abnormality of the fibrillin gene on chromosome 15. This is also associated with aortic dissection. Mitral valve prolapse by itself may be associated with sudden cardiac death.

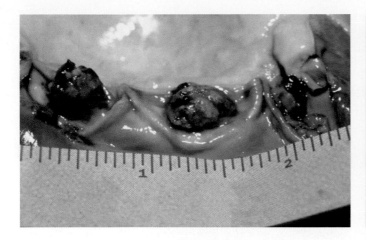

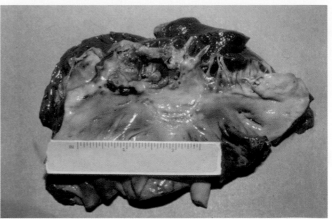

Figure 1.85 This endocardial surface shows large non-bacterial thrombotic endocarditis associated with a hypercoagulable state from metastatic adenocarcinoma. Special stains were negative for microorganisms.

Figure 1.86 This perforated mitral valve is secondary to acute bacterial endocarditis. This individual first went to the emergency room approximately a day and a half before with the complaint of fever and chest pain. He was sent home with antibiotics and later returned with severe pulmonary edema and died shortly after.

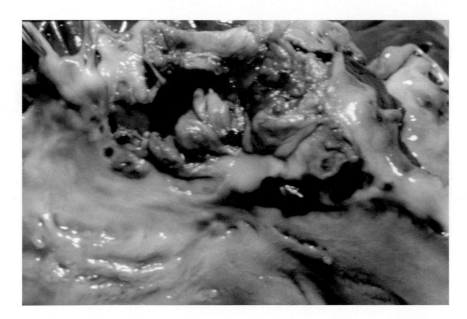

Figure 1.87 Close-up view of an acute infectious endocarditis with valve perforation. Gram stain revealed numerous Gram-positive organisms.

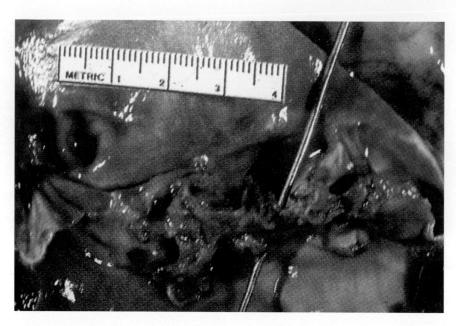

Figure 1.88 Acute infectious endocarditis with valve leaflet perforation.

Figure 1.89 Note the partially fused central aortic cusps with inferior displacement and subacute bacterial endocarditis vegetations. Also note the anomalies distribution of coronary arteries. This coronary artery anomaly may be associated with sudden cardiac death by itself. Note the left coronary artery is displaced adjacent to the right coronary artery with an acute angle takeoff and pass between the aorta and pulmonary trunk.

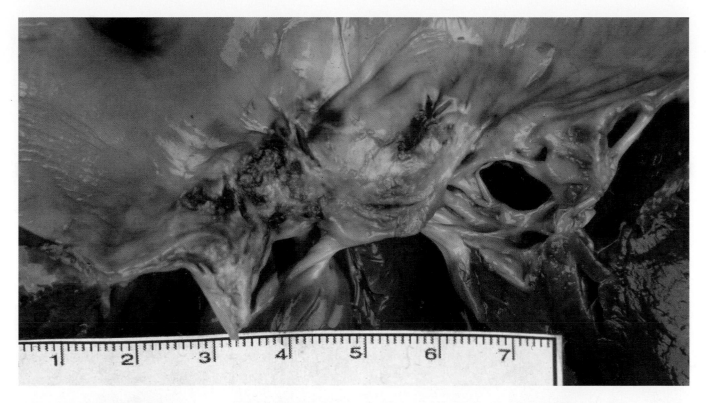

Figure 1.90 Remote cardiac valve damage from rheumatic fever.

Figures 1.91 and 1.92 These are views of a remotely damaged tricuspid valve secondary to chronic intravenous drug abuse and past endocarditis. Note the fibrosis of the adjacent endocardium secondary to regurgitative turbulent blood flow. The decedent was known to have a long-standing cardiac murmur.

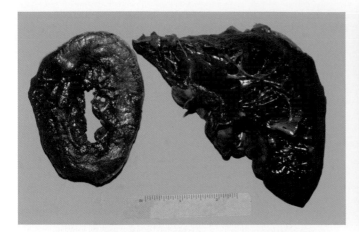
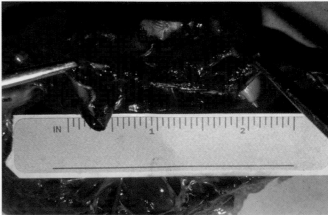

Figures 1.93 and 1.94 Markedly hypertrophic heart with concentric left ventricle hypertrophy and a congenital sub-aortic band causing marked aortic stenosis and sudden cardiac death at age 42 years. The decedent decided years earlier not to have a valve replacement.

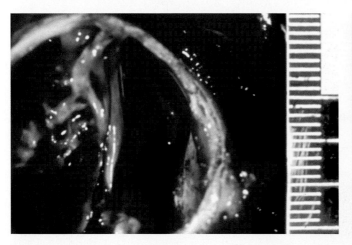
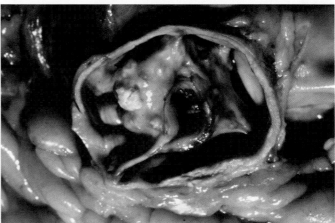

Figure 1.95 This is a bicuspid aortic valve. With advancing age and atherosclerosis, these valves may become markedly stenotic and increase one's risk for sudden cardiac death.

Figure 1.96 Markedly stenotic bicuspid aortic valve from an older individual with a long-standing history of athero-sclerotic cardiovascular disease.

Figure 1.97 Severely stenotic and insufficient aortic valve associated with childhood rheumatic fever. Correction of aortic stenosis will decrease the risk of sudden cardiac death.

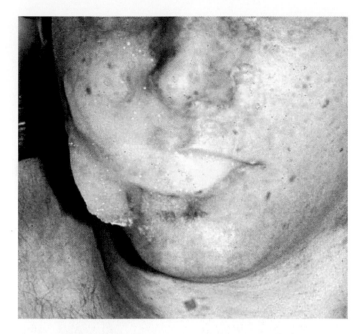

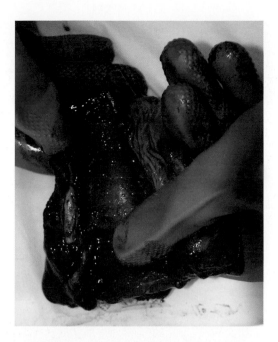

Figure 1.98 A fulminant pulmonary edema with foam extending from the mouth and nose due to congestive heart failure in this individual with past history of viral myocarditis. A foam cone in a younger individual should always first arouse the suspicion of opiate overdose in the absence of known heart disease.

Figure 1.100 Note the frothy fluid from pulmonary edema extending into the laryngeal airway.

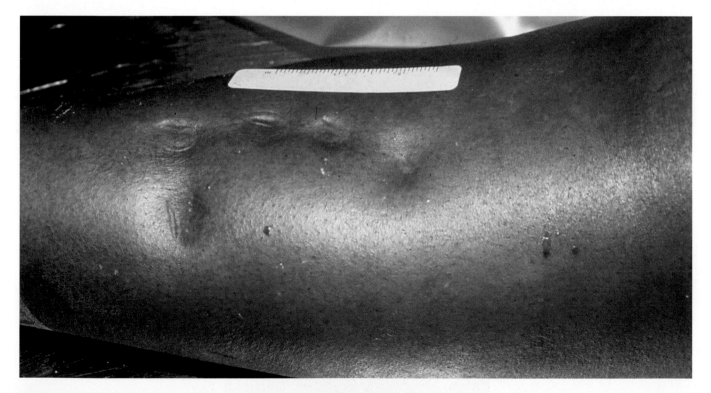

Figure 1.99 Pitting edema of the leg due to congestive heart failure.

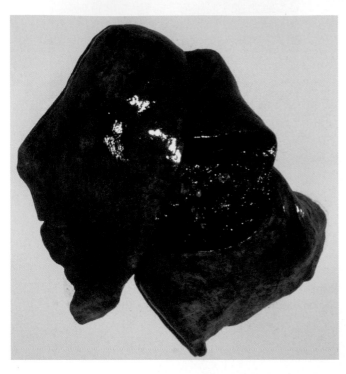

Figure 1.101 Lung with marked congestion and edema. Note the diffuse purple discoloration.

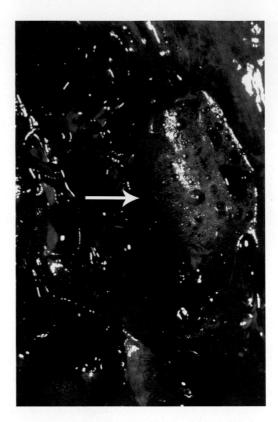

Figure 1.102 Marked pink to red frothy fluid extending from the cut parenchyma of a lung due to fulminant pulmonary edema.

Figure 1.103 Cut section of a lung with pulmonary edema.

Figure 1.104 Cardiac sclerosis due to pulmonary hypertension and right-sided heart failure. The subcapsular and perivenular fibrosis mimics micronodular cirrhosis.

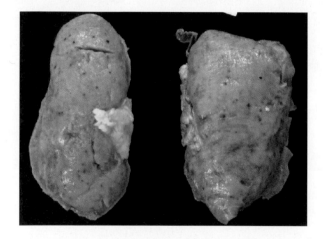

Figure 1.105 Amyloidosis, kidneys. The uniform pale waxy color of both kidneys is typical for organs involved by amyloidosis.

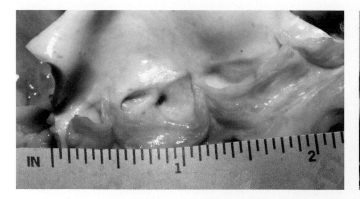
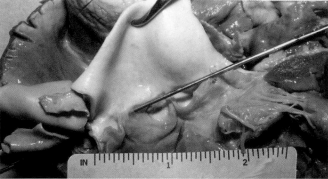

Figures 1.106 and 1.107 These figures demonstrate a coronary artery anomaly with acute angle takeoff and luminal narrowing in a 15-year-old who died suddenly during a basketball game. There was no history of blunt impacts to the chest during the game. There was no past history of syncopal episodes or chest discomfort.

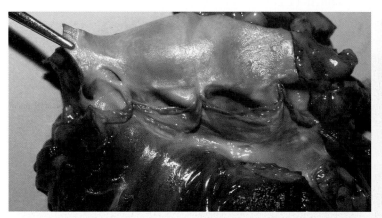

Figures 1.108 and 1.109 A coronary artery anomaly with acute angle takeoff and luminal narrowing where both coronary ostia rise from the right aorta sinus. This individual died of a sudden cardiac death shortly after exertion.

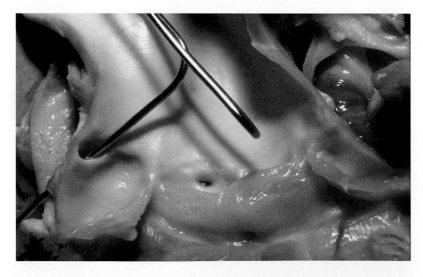

Figure 1.110 This coronary anomaly reveals a bicuspid aortic valve with superior displacement of one of the coronary ostia. This child died of trauma sustained in a motor vehicle accident and this finding was incidental.

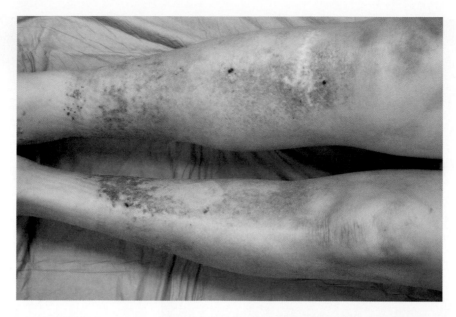

Figure 1.111 Note the large swelling of the right calf where deep venous thrombosis was found after incision.

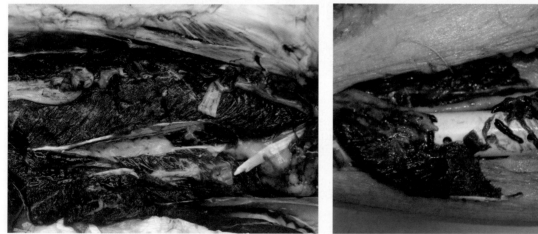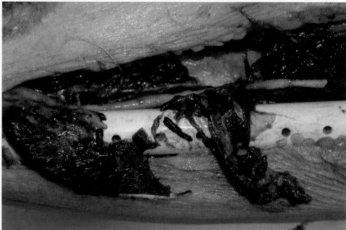

Figures 1.112 and 1.113 Incision of the lower leg with dissection of the gastrocnemius muscle demonstrating multiple deep venous thrombi from these individuals. Note the plastic tubing in Figure 1.113 associated with previous tissue donation with removal of bone and soft tissue.

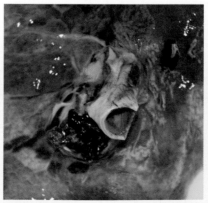

Figures 1.114–1.116 Pulmonary thromboembolus in an obese woman who was on birth control pills and smoked cigarettes. Note the dull granular tan to red overlapping thromboemboli that form branching casts of leg veins.

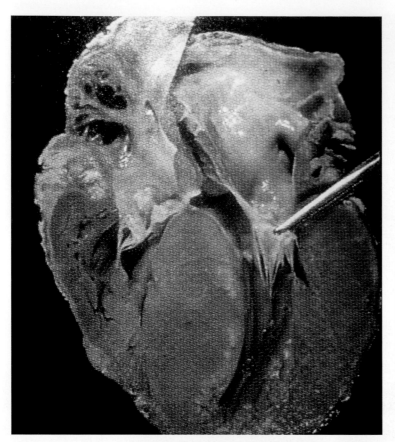

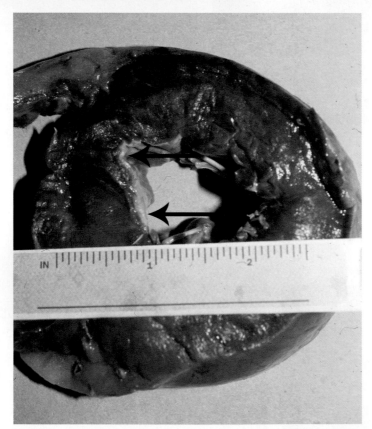

Figures 1.117–1.119 These are different views of two hearts with the classical type of hypertrophic cardiomyopathy. Note the large degree of asymmetric left ventricle hypertrophy.

Figures 1.120 and 1.121 Hypertrophic cardiomyopathy. Note the marked septal hypertrophy with asymmetry.

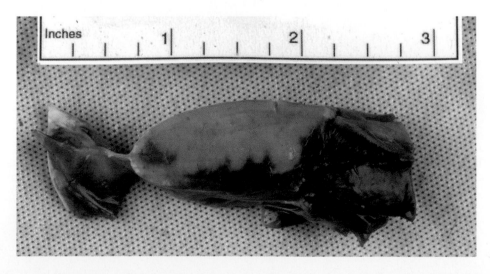

Figure 1.122 Gross autopsy section of myocardium from an individual who died of cardiac sarcoidosis.

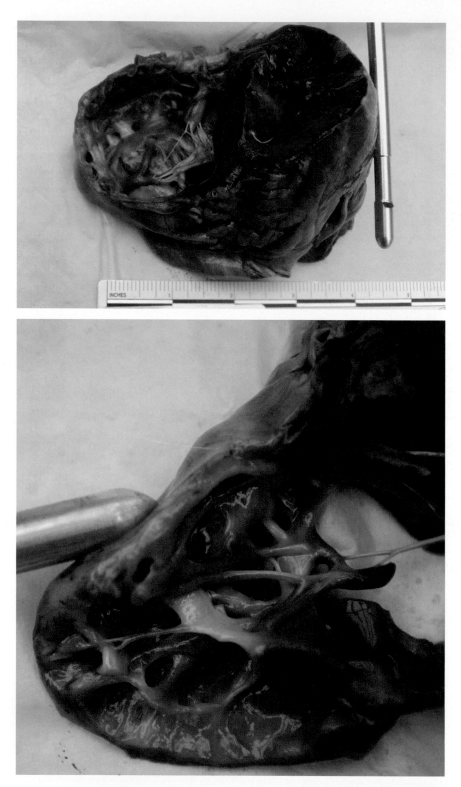

Figures 1.123 and 1.124 Arrhythmogenic right ventricular dysplasia. Note the transmural infiltration of fibro fatty tissue in regions of the right ventricle wall. This is a genetic defect of heart muscle involving desmosomes. This is usually an inherited autosomal dominant condition with variable expression that is associated with fatal arrhythmia.

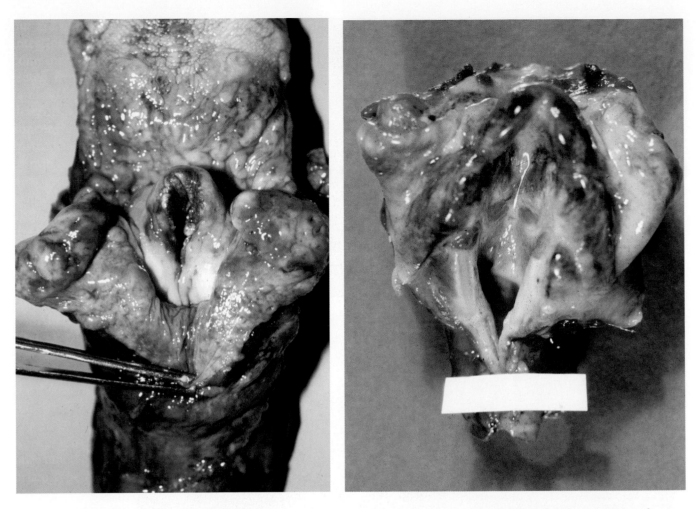

Figures 1.125 and 1.126 Acute epiglottis with airway obstruction due to *Haemophilus influenzae* type B infection. Note the swelling of the periepiglottic folds and the red/pink discoloration of the mucosa.

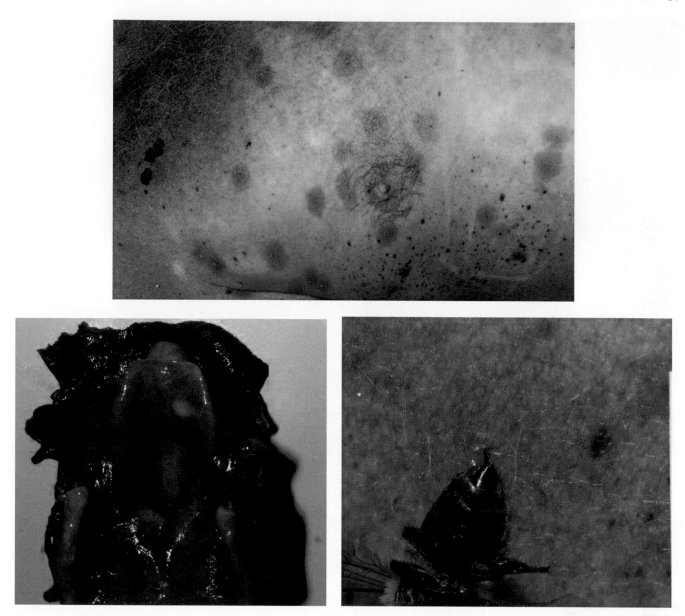

Figures 1.127–1.129 Bee envenomation associated with petechiae and laryngeal edema. Stung by over 100 bees, envenomation produced disseminated intravascular coagulation and anaphylaxis. Some of the bees had an "Africanized" profile.

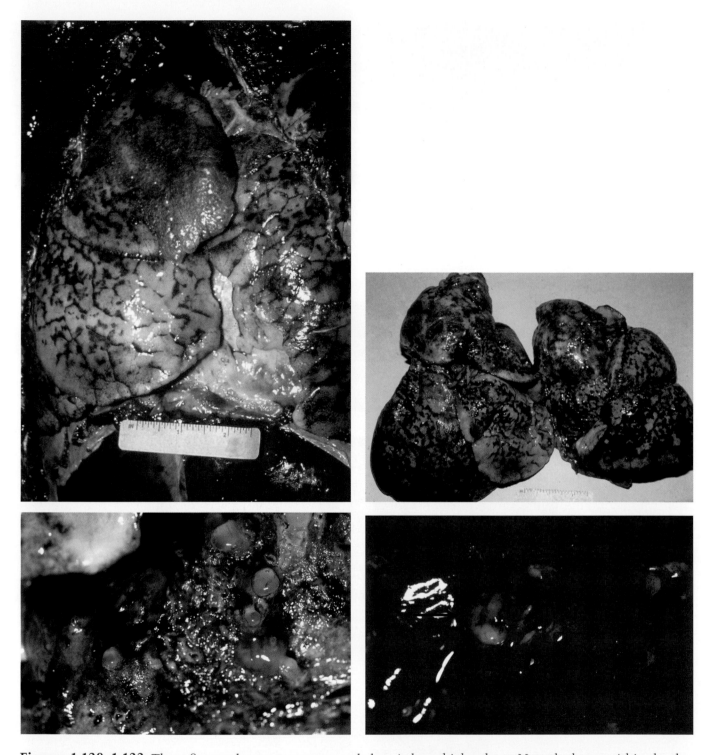

Figures 1.130–1.133 These figures demonstrate acute and chronic bronchial asthma. Note the lungs within the thoracic cavity are hyperaerated and expand to overlie the pericardial sac. Upon removal of the lung, they appear markedly hyperaerated. If these lungs were placed on a water bath, they would float almost entirely on the surface. Cut section through the parenchyma reveals thick copious mucoid secretions within the bronchial distribution. Note Figure 1.133 shows darker red discoloration with congestion and edema besides mucous plugging in an individual who had an acute asthma attack with heart failure.

Figures 1.134 and 1.135 Chronic obstructive pulmonary disease (COPD) with hyperaeration and emphysematous change.

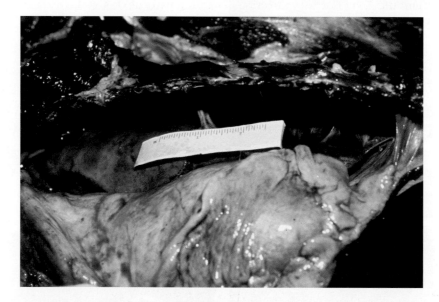

Figure 1.136 Pleural adhesions most likely due to past bouts of pneumonia.

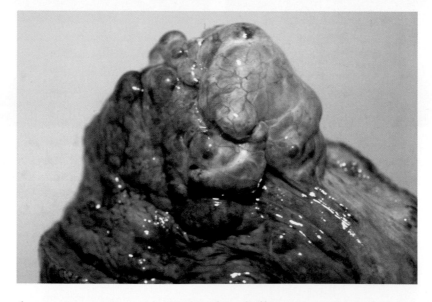

Figure 1.137 Bolus emphysema in a person with COPD. These bullae may occasionally rupture and cause a spontaneous pnuemothorax.

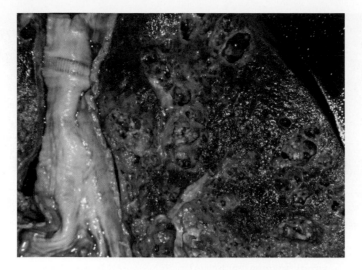

Figure 1.138 Acute or chronic *Pneumocystis* infection. The lung parenchyma is distorted by cysts filled with acute inflammation, fibrin, and organisms.

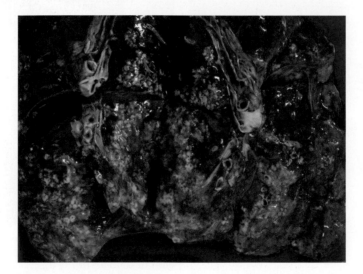

Figure 1.139 Disseminated tuberculosis, miliary pattern.

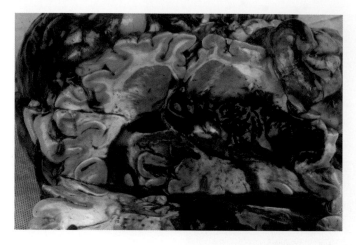

Figure 1.140 Hypertensive intracerebral hemorrhage. Mostly caused by rupture of a small intraparenchymal vessel.

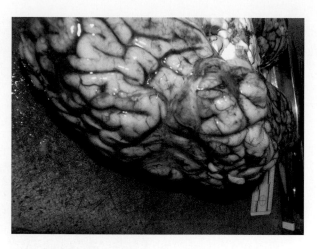

Figure 1.141 Old healed stroke. Note the indentation of the cerebral hemisphere.

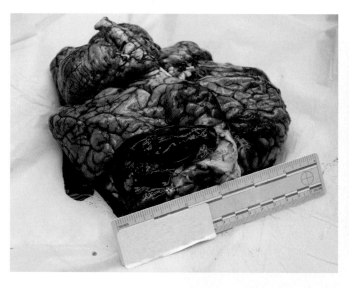

Figure 1.142 Intracerebral hemorrhage due to ruptured A-V malformation.

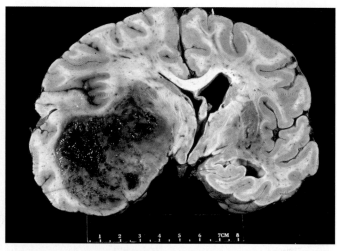

Figure 1.143 Astrocytoma causing significant compression of the surrounding structures.

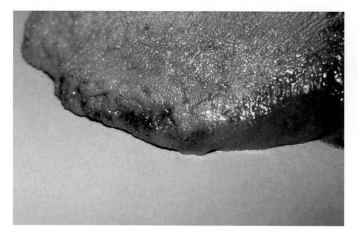

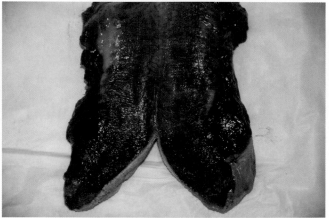

Figures 1.144 and 1.145 Bite marks to tongue with hemorrhage from an individual who died of epilepsy. This was the only finding at autopsy.

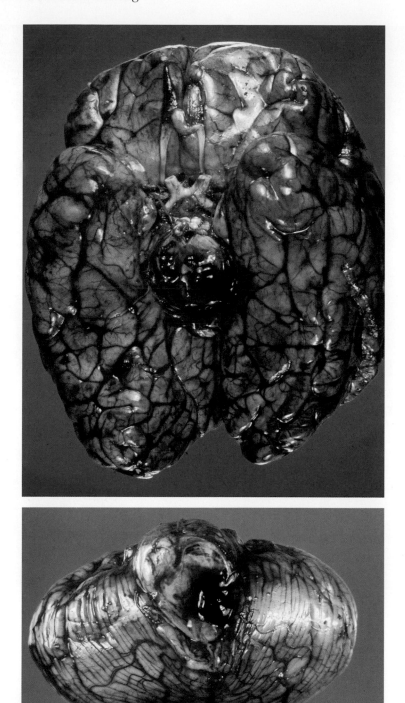

Figures 1.146 and 1.147 Pontine hemorrhage due to hypertensive cardiovascular disease. This may be associated with locked-in syndrome where the person loses all voluntary motor control, particularly when the ventral pons are involved.

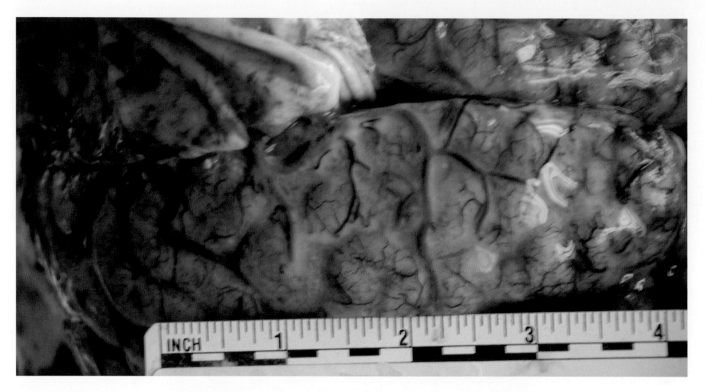

Figure 1.148 Bacterial meningitis. Note the yellow/green purulent exudate at the meninges.

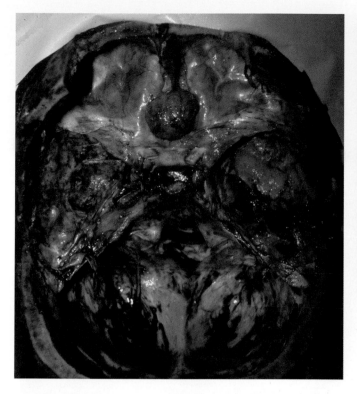

Figure 1.149 Anterior cranial fossa meningioma.

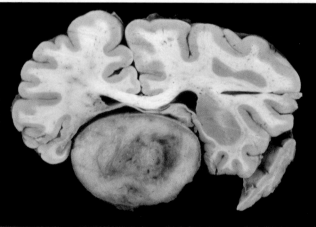

Figure 1.150 Pick disease. Note the asymmetric atrophy of the frontal, temporal, and parietal lobes. This form of chronic dementia occurs far less frequently than Alzheimer disease.

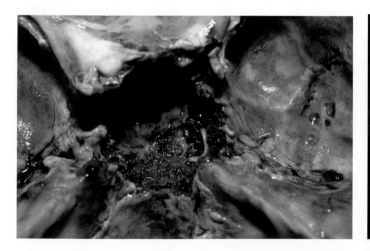

Figures 1.151 and 1.152 Two separate cases of pituitary adenoma. The first depicts a large erosion into the sella turcica. The second picture demonstrates a large adenoma viewed on a cross section of a cut formaldehyde-fixed brain. These adenomas may vary largely in size.

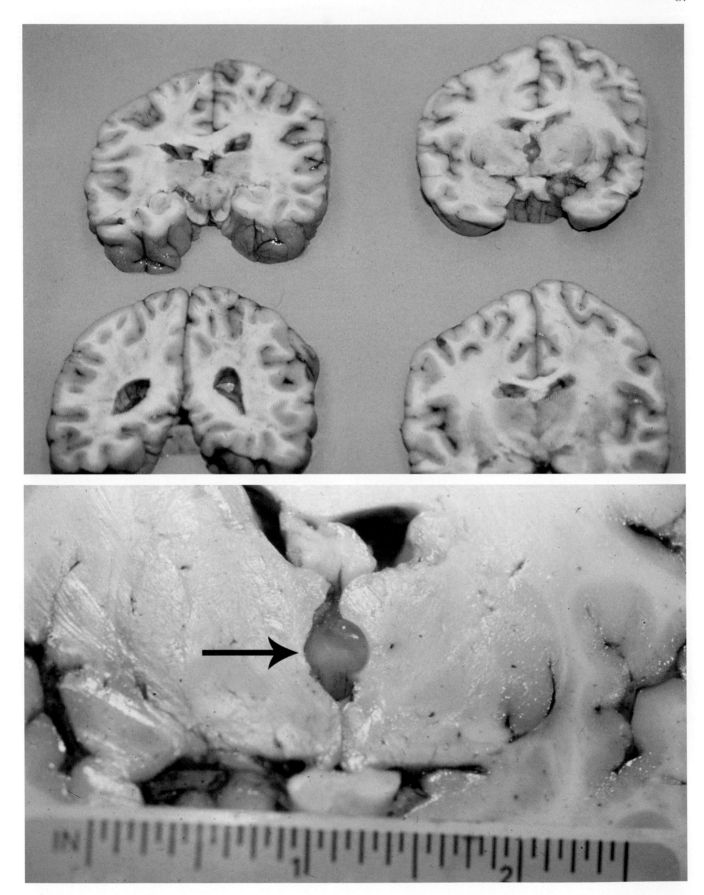

Figures 1.153 and 1.154 Colloid cyst of the third ventricle. This decedent had a history of severe headache with postural changes. This may be associated with sudden cardiac death following a buildup of cerebrospinal fluid pressures associated with central nervous system cardiac center disruption and fatal arrhythmia.

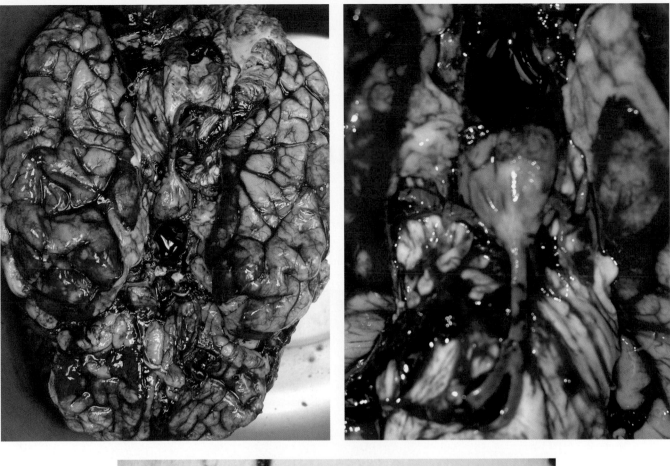

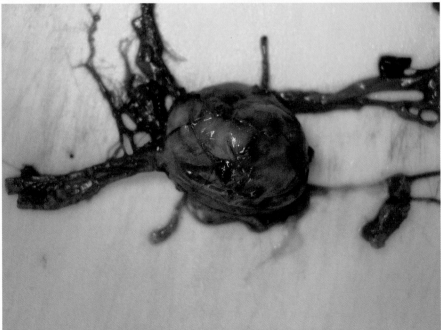

Figures 1.155–1.157 Sudden death associated with ruptured saccular cerebral artery aneurysm with subarachnoid hemorrhage. These are examples of giant berry aneurysms that are greater than 2.5 cm in greatest dimension. Small saccular aneurysms may rupture the same way. The jolt of increased pressure from arterial blood through the subarachnoid space at the base of the brain may disrupt the cardiac centers, causing fatal arrhythmia.

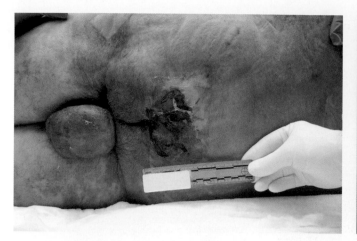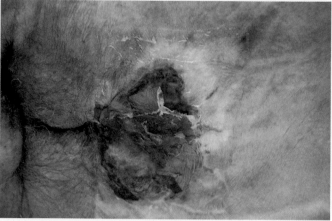

Figures 1.158 and 1.159 Decubital ulceration or pressure sore. This is often associated with poor nursing care but is also related to the degree of advancing disease associated with poor circulation and organ failure.

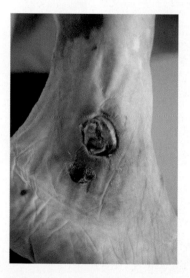

Figure 1.160 Healing ankle ulceration associated with peripheral vascular disease.

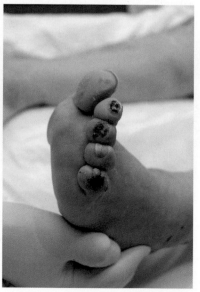

Figures 1.161 and 1.162 Dry gangrene associated with peripheral vascular disease due to long-term diabetes mellitus with pressure and/or rubbing from ill-fitting shoes or heavy blankets that further decrease blood flow.

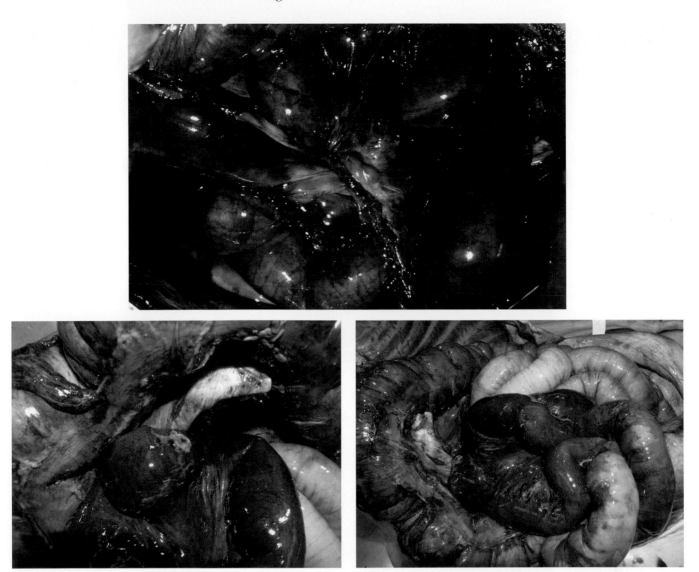

Figures 1.163–1.165 Ischemic bowel due to small intestine volvulus with vascular compromise. This segment of bowel twisted on itself and obstructed necessary blood flow. Note the early purulent exudate at the serosal surface.

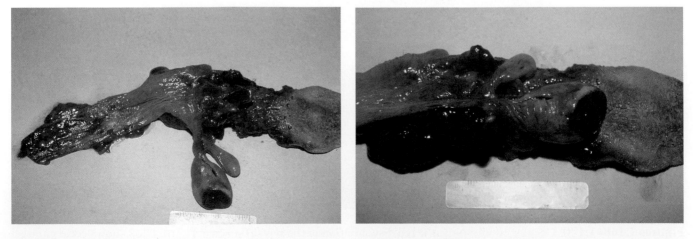

Figures 1.166 and 1.167 This decedent had a long-standing history of difficulty swallowing. They were witnessed to gesture as though they could not breathe and then collapsed. Autopsy revealed a large benign esophageal polyp that obstructed the upper airway. Note the ulceration at the tip of the polyp from constant rubbing. During this last episode she was unable to clear the obstruction.

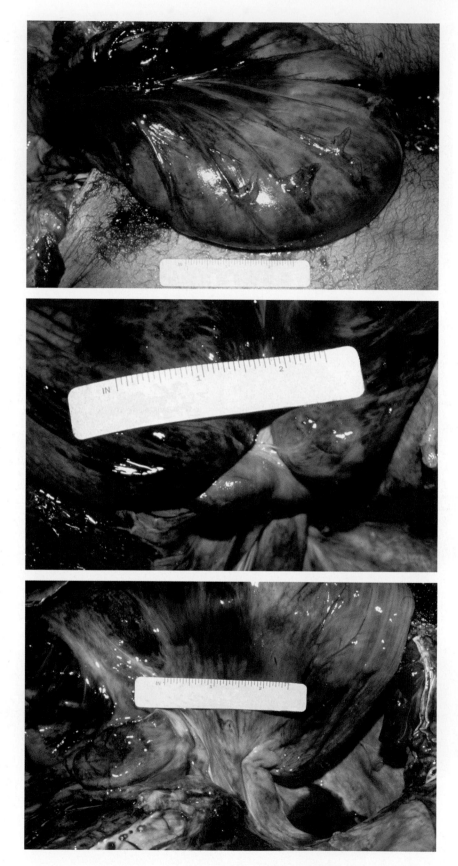

Figures 1.168–1.170 Cecal volvulus. Note the red discoloration of the serosal surface. Figure 1.168 shows cecal enlargement due to obstruction. Figure 1.169 shows the cecal volvulus with rotation and obstruction. Figure 1.170 shows this region untwisted.

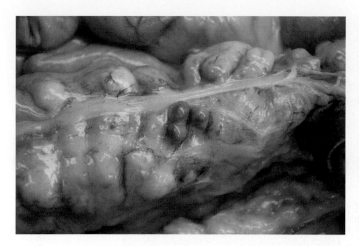
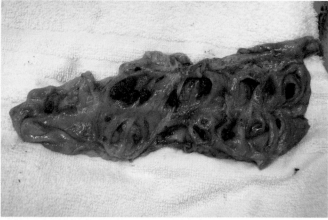

Figures 1.171 and 1.172 Diverticulosis, which is an outpocketing of large intestinal mucosa often with inspissated fecal material that may lead to infection as in diverticulitis with sepsis, peritonitis, or hemorrhage.

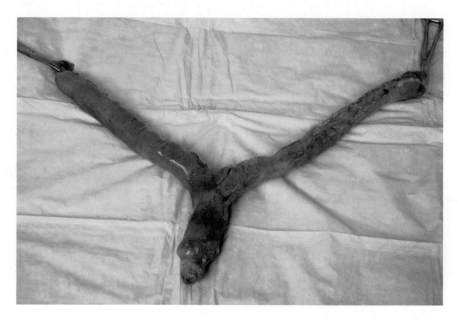

Figure 1.173 Meckel's diverticulum demonstrated here by tying off both ends of ileum and inflating the lumen with water. Meckel's diverticulum usually occurs within two feet from the ileocecal valve and may contain rests of gastric or pancreatic tissue that may lead to slow chronic blood loss. This is difficult to find clinically unless a radionucleotide study is performed.

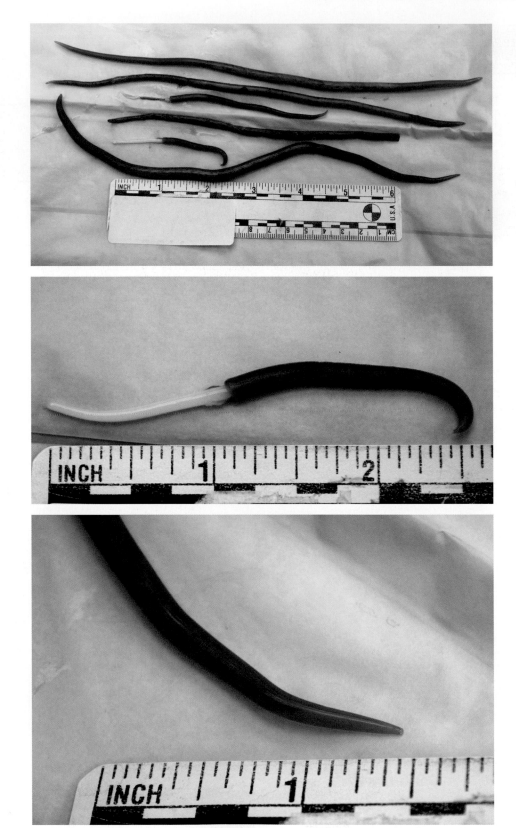

Figures 1.174–1.176 *Ascaris lumbricoides* may infect up to 1/6 of the world's population and is the largest and most common parasitic worm in humans. Typically worm eggs are ingested and the larvae travel to the lungs where they are coughed up and swallowed. Mature worms are found in the gastrointestinal tract. Often no symptoms are observed but infection may be associated with Löffler syndrome with systemic eosinophilia. These worms were an incidental finding at autopsy.

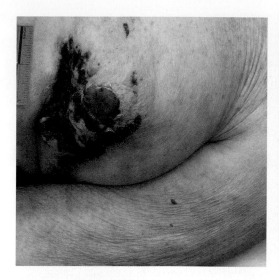
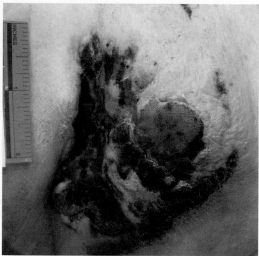

Figures 1.177 and 1.178 This individual never sought medical attention for her breast carcinoma and died at home.

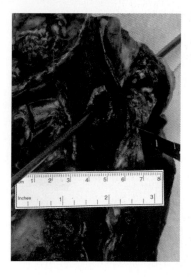

Figure 1.179 Bronchogenic carcinoma with erosion through the airway.

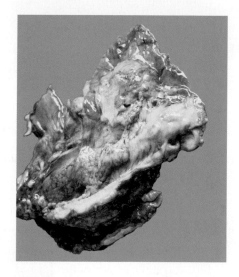

Figure 1.180 This individual never sought medical attention for his gastric cancer and died at home.

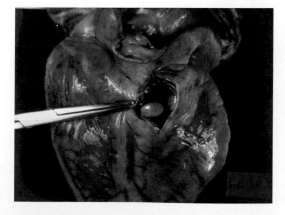

Figure 1.181 Metastatic bronchogenic carcinoma of the lung. Note the metastatic nodule in the heart muscle, causing fatal arrhythmia.

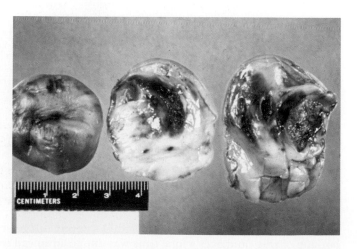

Figure 1.182 Primary rhabdomyosarcoma of the heart.

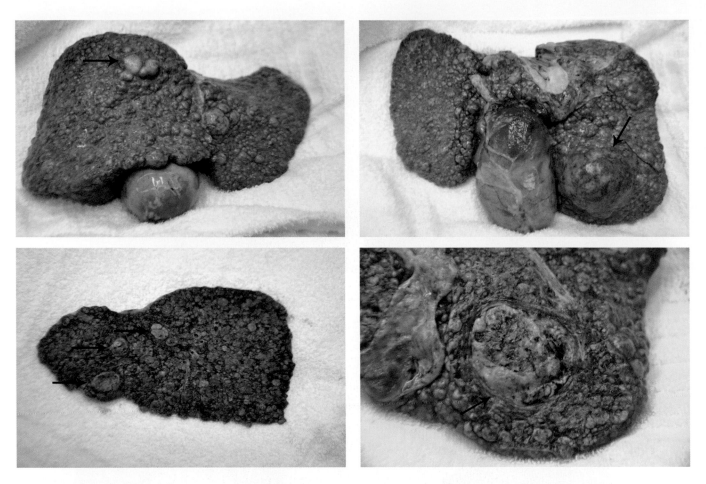

Figures 1.183–1.186 Hepatocellular carcinoma associated with hepatic cirrhosis due to hepatitis B infection. Note the macronodular cirrhosis and the larger tumor nodules.

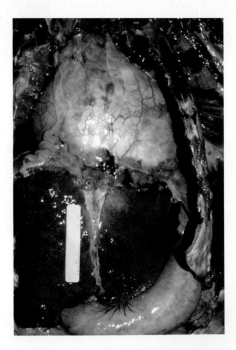

Figure 1.187 This decedent's pericardial sac was full of several hundred milliliters of yellow-pink fluid. The gradual buildup of this fluid over a long time was due to advanced secondary hemochromatosis. Note the hepatic cirrhosis with the bronze discoloration of the liver.

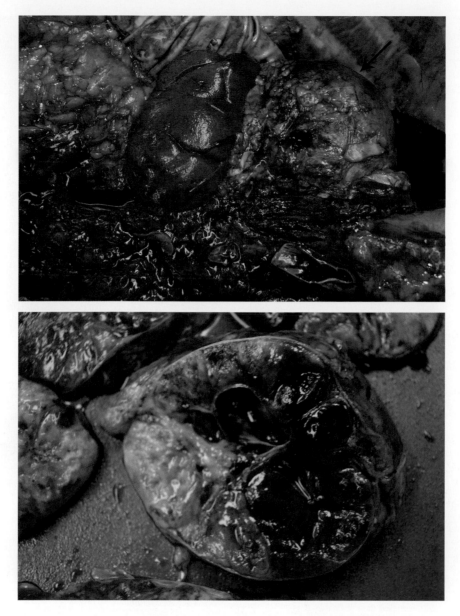

Figures 1.188 and 1.189 Pheochromocytoma is a neuroendocrine tumor of the adrenal gland medulla, which is known to secrete catecholamines and lead to fluctuations in blood pressure, elevated heart rate, syncopal episodes, and fatal arrhythmia. Note the mahogany appearance involving portions of the cut surface of this tumor mass. See Figures 11.206–11.208 in the Histology chapter.

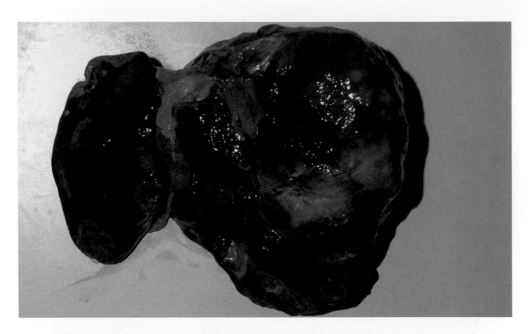

Figure 1.190 Metastatic pancreatic carcinoma with bile staining of the liver.

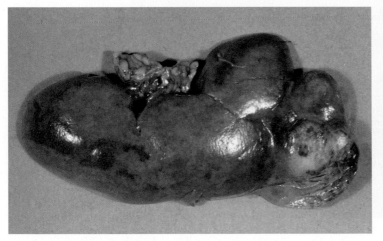 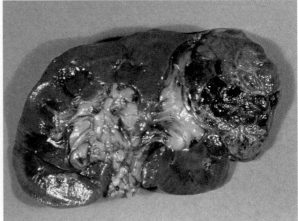

Figures 1.191 and 1.192 Renal cell carcinoma.

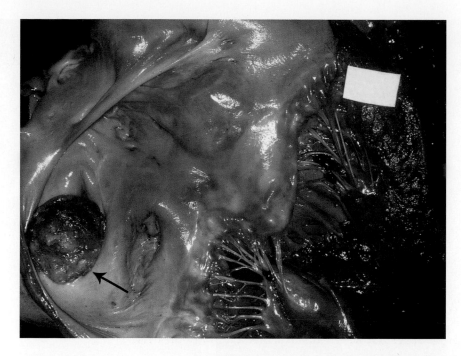

Figure 1.193 Atrial myxoma is a benign primary cardiac tumor usually growing from the wall of the left atrium, which may be associated with symptoms of mitral stenosis and fragmentation, causing stroke. It is the most common cardiac tumor and occurs more frequently on the left side.

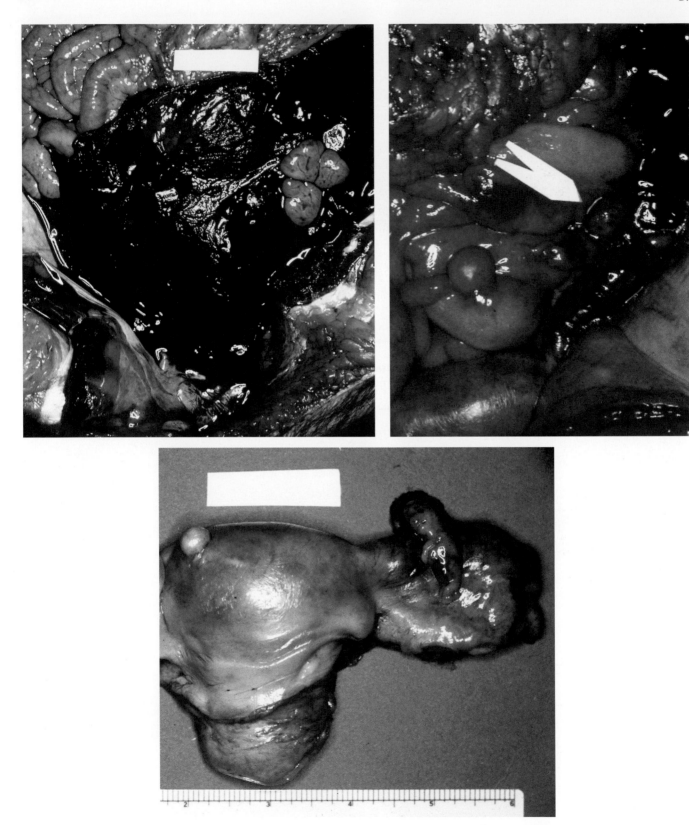

Figures 1.194–1.196 Death due to ruptured ectopic pregnancy with hemoperitoneum.

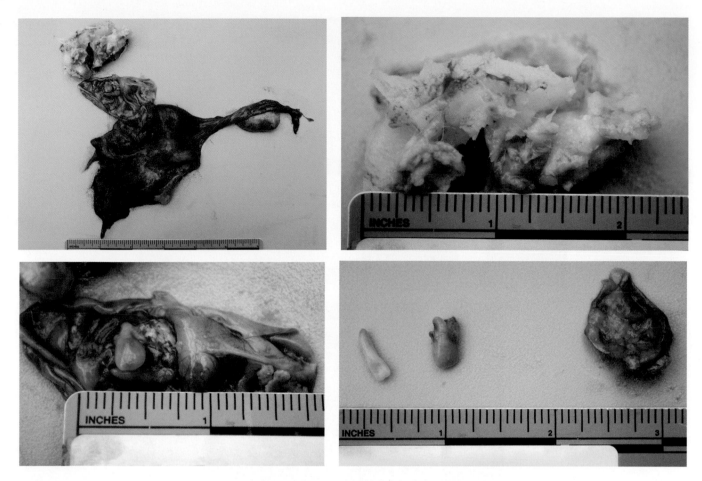

Figures 1.197–1.200 Incidental benign teratoma. Found during routine autopsy. A teratoma is in fact a germ cell tumor. Note the pieces of hair, teeth, bone, and semisolid material with sebum. During the middle ages it was believed it resulted from having coitus with the devil. During this time in history, witches may have been sentenced to death. It is interesting to see how advancements in science continue to result in more accurate legal proceedings as will continue to occur far into the future.

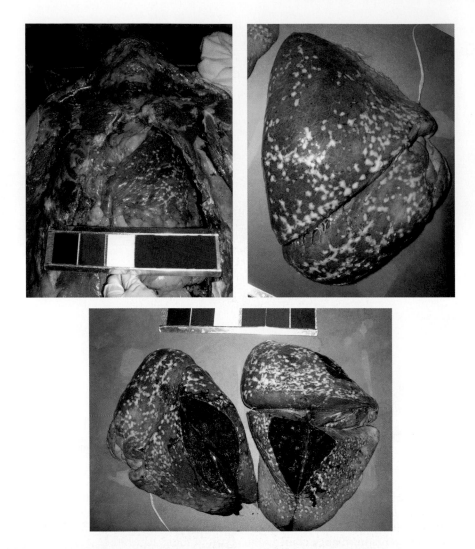

Figures 1.201–1.203 Multiple healed granulomas most likely from a past fungal infection.

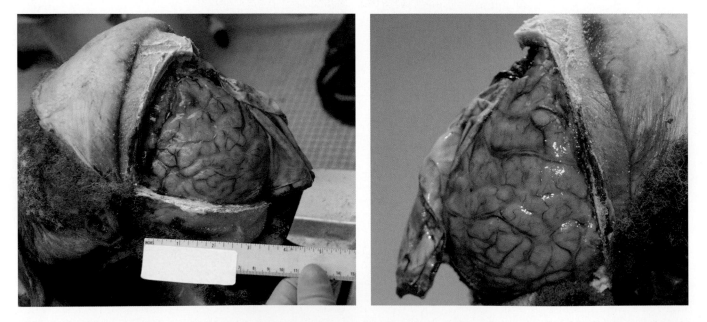

Figures 1.204 and 1.205 Cryptococcal meningitis in an individual with AIDS due to intravenous drug use. Note the cloudy meninges.

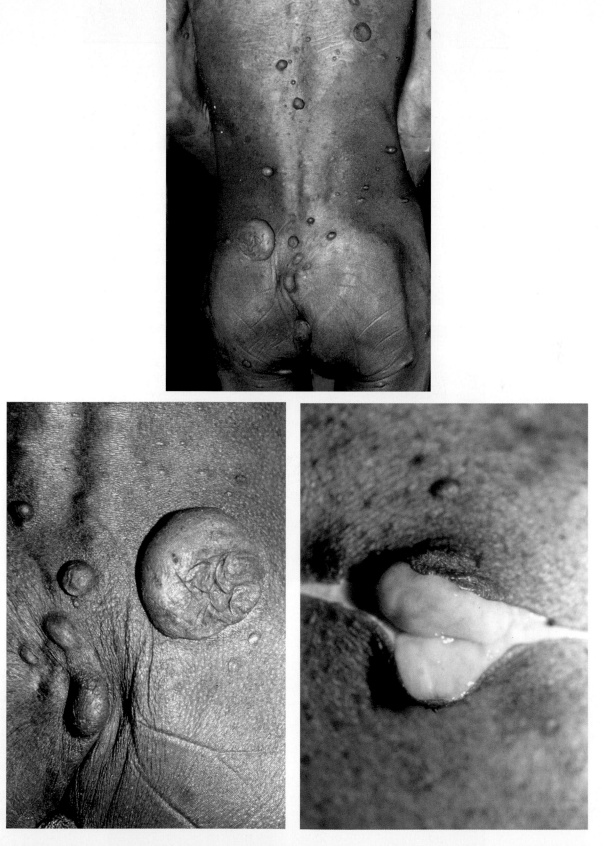

Figures 1.206–1.208 Neurofibromatosis type 1. Note the numerous neurofibromas at the surface of the body. These tumors may be found throughout the body. Death may occur by tumor growth leading to damage of adjacent structures such as the gastrointestinal tract with obstruction, central nervous system with compression, renal artery with hypertension, etc.

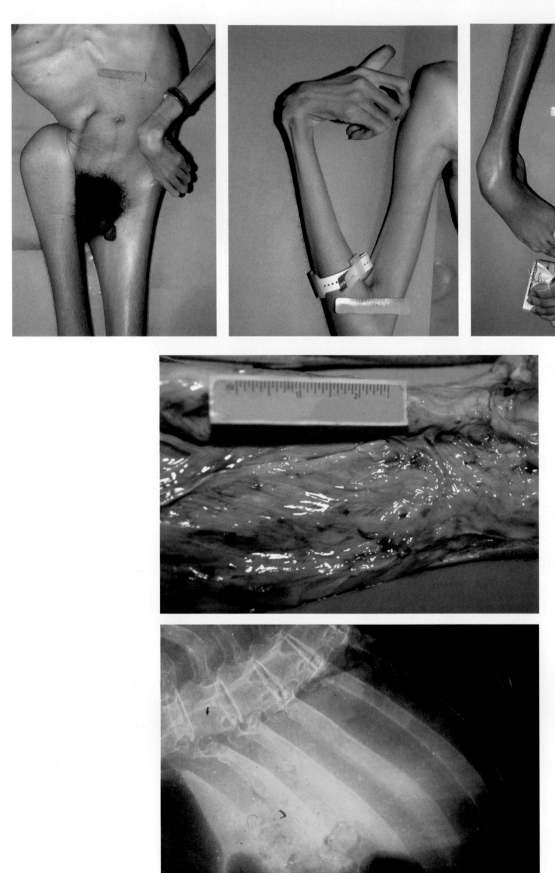

Figures 1.209–1.213 This decedent had Duchenne muscular dystrophy and was bedridden for many years. He developed severe osteoporosis. While being removed from bed one day by a new caregiver, he sustained bilateral femur fractures and died shortly after.

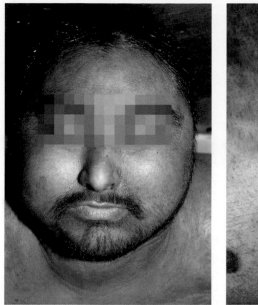
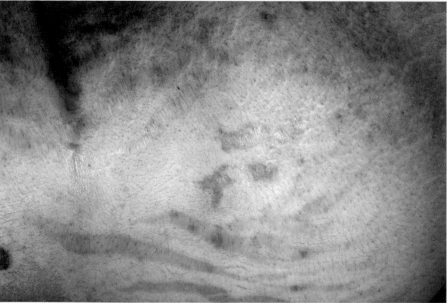

Figures 1.214 and 1.215 Cushing syndrome due to hypercortisolism. Note the "moon face," "truncal obesity," and purple striates at the lower abdomen. This syndrome is also associated with glucose intolerance. From a forensic standpoint and interpreting injuries, it is important to know whether this is associated with osteoporosis, increased bruisability, and poor healing.

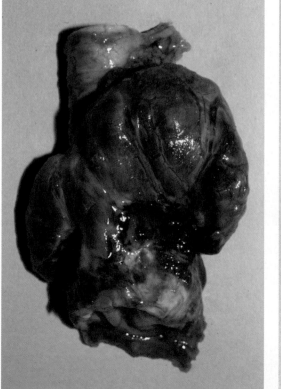
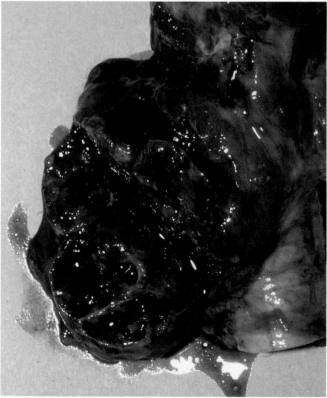

Figures 1.216 and 1.217 Multinodular goiter, in this case with hyperthyroidism, may lead to thyrotoxicosis and sudden cardiac death due to tachyarrhythymia. Multinodular goiters may also be associated with euthyroid or hypothyroid function.

Figures 1.218–1.223 This elderly woman was driving on a dark road and missed the last street turn and drove straight into the frigid water during winter. She was able to get out of the car and swim to shore, where she experienced marked hypothermia with hypothalamus malfunction, which is demonstrated by her paradoxical undressing. She walked disorientated from the scene of the accident and eventually froze to death before being found the next morning. Autopsy revealed acute gastritis with leopard skin pattern and acute pancreatitis. This death was certified as an accident.

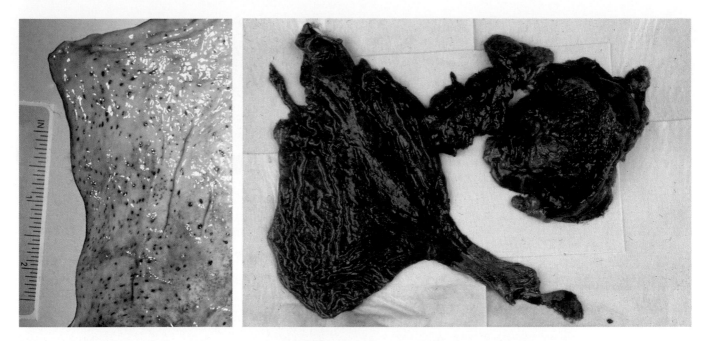

Figures 1.224 and 1.225 This portion of gastric mucosa reveals multiple small areas of hemorrhage in an individual with hypothermia. "Leopard skinning" of the gastric mucosa and acute pancreatitis are often seen with cases of marked hypothermia followed by short-term survival.

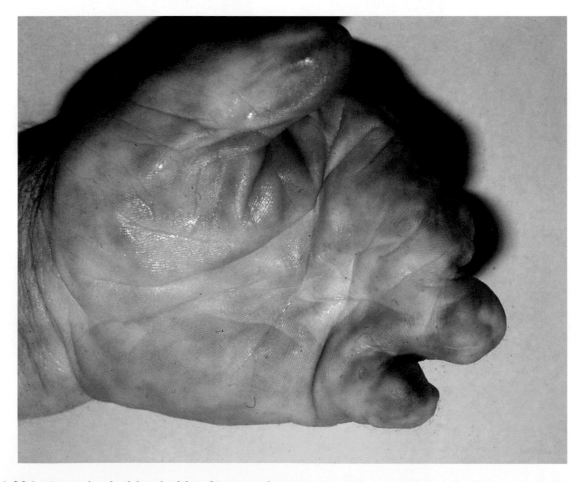

Figure 1.226 This individual has had his fingers and toes amputated years before following extensive hypothermic injury with frostbite.

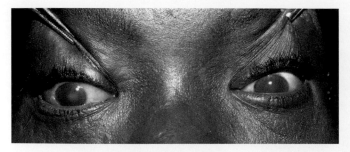

Figure 1.227 Jaundice due to hemolysis associated with sickle cell crisis.

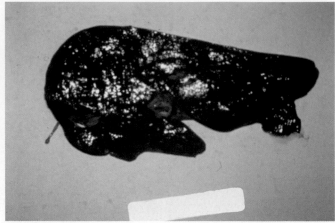

Figure 1.228 Sickle cell crisis. Note the dark red-black sludge within the gallbladder from hemolysis.

Figures 1.229 and 1.230 Auto-infarcted spleen due to multiple episodes of crisis in an adult with sickle cell anemia. Note in young children the spleen may actually be enlarged before this repeated damage.

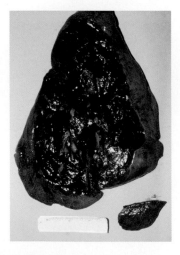
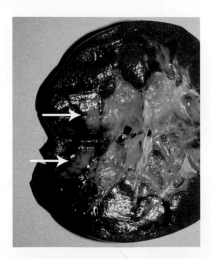

Figure 1.231 Sickle cell anemia with crisis. Lung with marked congestion and pulmonary edema.

Figure 1.232 Sickle cell anemia with crisis. Kidney with papillary necrosis and congestion.

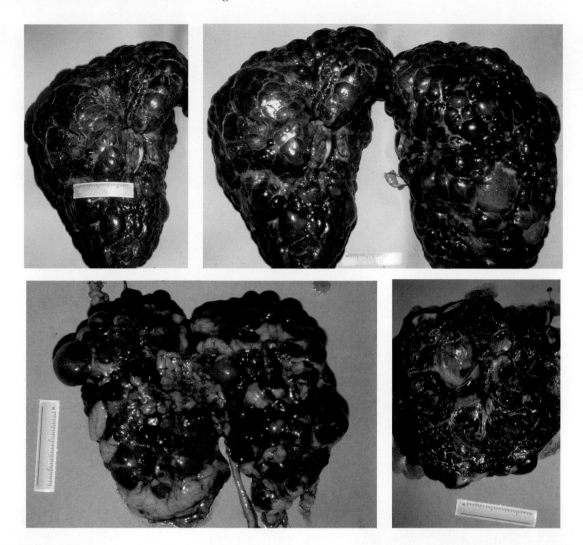

Figures 1.233–1.236 Adult polycystic kidney disease. This autosomal dominant disorder is another significant cause of hypertension. These kidneys weighed over 3000 g each. There is also an association with cysts in other organs and intracranial berry aneurysms.

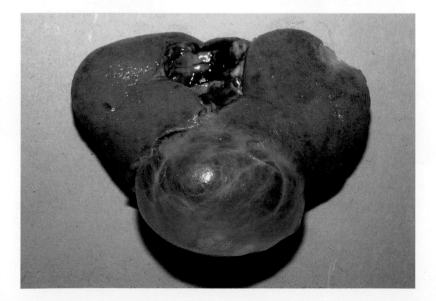

Figure 1.237 Simple benign cyst.

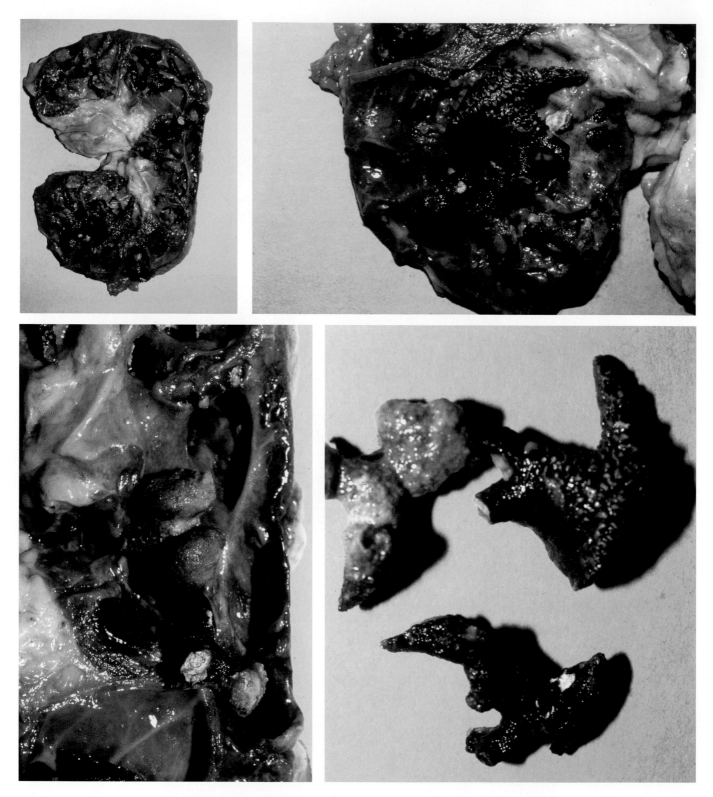

Figures 1.238–1.241 Chronic pyelonephritis with "stag horn calculi" associated with urea-splitting bacterial infection such as proteus or staphylococci causing magnesium ammonium phosphate salt precipitation. It is also important to know that acute obstructive urolithiasis with urosepsis can be rapidly fatal.

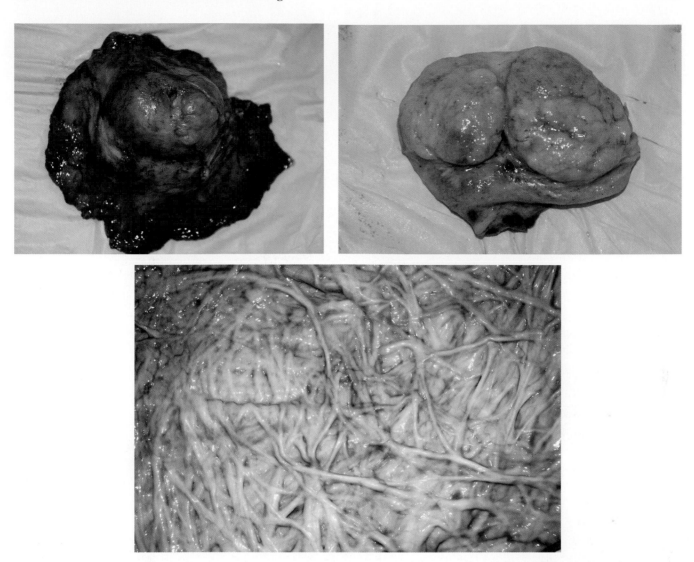

Figures 1.242–1.244 Benign prostatic hyperplasia. Note the markedly enlarged prostate gland with areas of central nodularity compressing the prostatic urethra. Note the trabeculations and thickening of the urinary bladder wall due to obstruction.

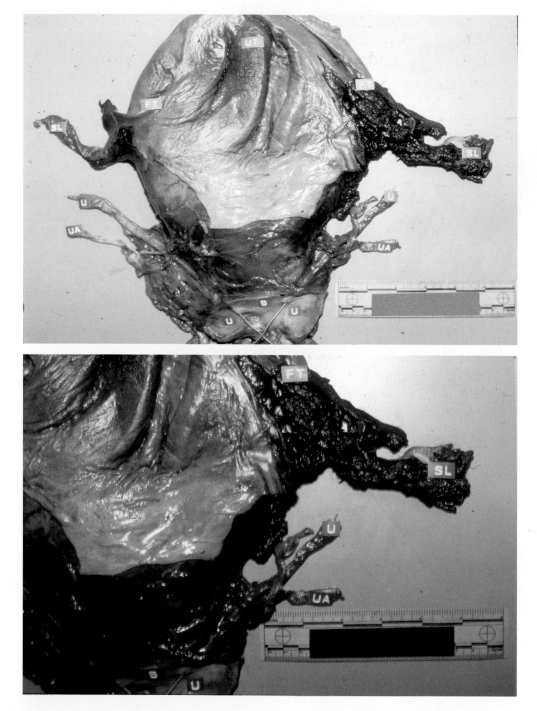

Figures 1.245 and 1.246 This is a postpartum death involving a 30-year-old nurse. This woman was known to be colonized by group A beta-hemolytic streptococcus (*Streptococcus pyogenes*). Approximately 8 hours following an uneventful delivery, she began to complain of back and pelvic pain. Within 4 hours she was in full-blown shock and was refractory to resuscitative measures. Death was pronounced approximately 14 hours following her delivery. This picture depicts the gravid uterus and confluent brown-black discoloration of the left adnexa, which proved microscopically to show areas of necrosis with numerous clusters of bacterial cocci and scant neutrophilic infiltrates. Postmortem cultures of multiple organs, including lungs, liver, spleen, uterus, and peritoneal fluid, all grew group A beta-hemolytic streptococcus beta-hemolytic streptococcus. This "toxic shock–like" death due to group A streptococcus has given rise to the term "flesh-eating bacteria."

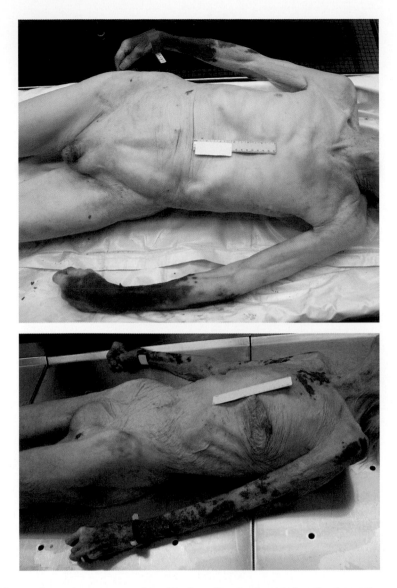

Figures 1.247 and 1.248 Senile ecchymosis in this elderly individual with fragile skin. These areas of hemorrhage may be caused by minimal trauma, which may or may not indicate neglect or elder abuse, depending upon the circumstances. This may also be seen in association with therapy including intravascular catheters and blood drawing.

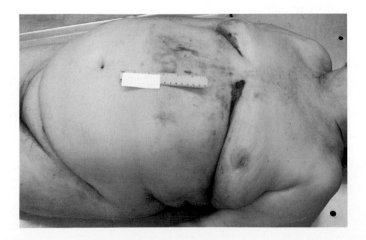

Figure 1.249 Note the areas of red discoloration due to fungal infection under the breasts where the skin was moist. This may be confused for trauma.

Therapeutic Interventions, Complications, and Accidents

2

MICHAEL J. CAPLAN AND CHARLES A. CATANESE

The evaluation of deaths related to complications of diagnostic and therapeutic procedures has traditionally been a problematic area for forensic pathologists and death investigators. The reasons for this are multiple: (1) these deaths often blur the boundaries dividing medicolegal and hospital death investigation; (2) many forensic pathologists do not feel comfortable approaching the often complex and highly technical issues present today in modern medicine; and (3) at least some forensic pathologists believe that these types of death belong more appropriately within the domain of the hospital autopsy. Despite this ongoing controversy, most forensic pathologists and death investigators will, at some point during their careers, be forced to handle these types of deaths.

If a patient dies either during or sometime following a diagnostic and therapeutic procedure, the first question in the diagnostic algorithm or decision tree becomes: Was the death in any way related to the procedure or was the procedure simply an artifact, with the death attributable to some underlying natural disease process or injury? For example, if a 65-year-old man who has stubbornly refused surgical intervention of a known 8-cm-diameter abdominal aortic aneurysm suddenly collapses and manages to make it to the operating room but dies before repair can be attempted, the "intraoperative death" is simply an artifact of modern medical resuscitation and transport technologies. In such a case, the medical intervention or procedure played no part in the death, and the cause of death would be worded as "ruptured abdominal aortic aneurysm due to atherosclerotic cardiovascular disease, manner: natural." On the other hand, if an otherwise healthy individual underwent an elective procedure, for example, a bunionectomy, and died on the operating table, to ascribe the death to "hallux valgus" would be as ridiculous as it was erroneous. It is for cases like this that the concept of therapeutic complication merits consideration for a place in manner-of-death certification.

Once it is determined that the death was related somehow to the procedure, the next question in the algorithm becomes: Was the death a result of a known or predictable (albeit rare or unusual) complication of a properly performed diagnostic procedure or appropriately administered therapy, or did it ensue from a procedural error? When the former scenario exists, the term *therapeutic complication* is preferred because that is a neutral designation, as opposed to the term *therapeutic misadventure*, which is inflammatory and prejudicial. When the latter situation is present, the manner of death is most accurately designated *accident*. Many examples of legitimate therapeutic complications exist. In the case of a 64-year-old man who sustained a non-ST (non–Q wave) segment elevation myocardial infarct, and who was treated with the antiplatelet drug eptifibatide (Integrilin), a platelet glycoprotein IIb–IIIa antagonist, he suffered intractable pulmonary hemorrhage and ultimately succumbed to respiratory failure. Pulmonary hemorrhage has been a recently reported complication of eptifibatide therapy. No error was committed in this case; rather, the decedent experienced an unusual yet known (documented) complication of appropriate therapy for his non-ST elevation MI. Therefore, the cause of death would be worded as: "Complications of pulmonary hemorrhage following eptifibatide (Integrilin) treatment for non-ST (non–Q wave) segment elevation myocardial infarct (due to atherosclerotic heart disease)" and the manner, "therapeutic complication." On the other hand, if a middle-aged woman underwent a surveillance colonoscopy and presented days later with peritoneal signs and was found to have *Escherichia coli* bacteremia and sepsis due to peritonitis resulting from inadvertent perforation of the colon during the procedure, the death certificate would read: "*E. coli* sepsis due to peritonitis due to colonic perforation complicating surveillance colonoscopy." However, because this complication is not an accepted sequela of an appropriately performed diagnostic or therapeutic procedure, but rather an unintentional error, the manner of death in this case is most accurately deemed accident. Admittedly, there are cases that fall within the murky zone between natural and therapeutic complication and between therapeutic complication and accident. In such cases, all that one can do is exercise one's best objective clinical judgment. It is important to recognize and remember that death certificates are not immutable documents that are "written in stone"; rather, they can be amended should more accurate information regarding the circumstances of death become available at a later time.

While the concept of therapeutic complication is an invaluable tool in the assessment of these types of deaths, the practical applicability of the term to the death certificate has enjoyed less success. Only two known jurisdictions—Cuyahoga County, Ohio, and New York City—include "therapeutic complication" as a choice in the manner of death on the death certificate. Therefore, when a death fits the criteria for therapeutic complication as the manner, but the particular jurisdiction does not include it on the death certificate, then the manner defaults to natural. One other option is to list "therapeutic complication" in parentheses after "natural," but this probably is not common practice. Thus, for the indefinite future, forensic pathologists will be resigned to use the term as a conceptual tool in the evaluation of these most challenging deaths.

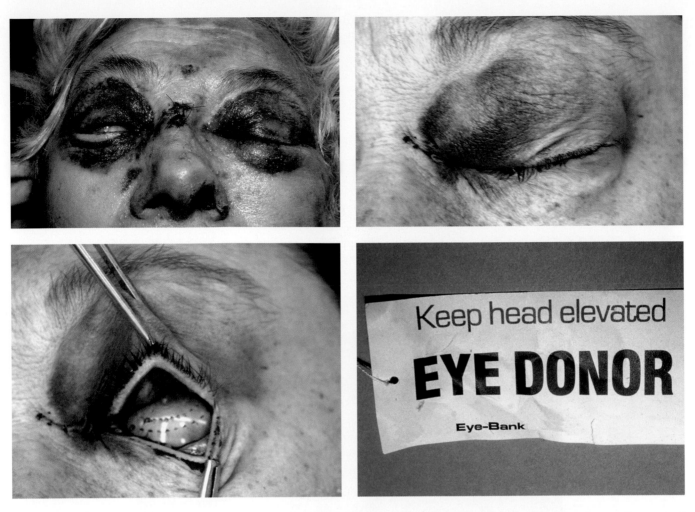

Figures 2.1–2.4 This shows one of many possible artifacts associated with organ donation that may be misinterpreted for injuries. Note the hemorrhagic discoloration around each eye (periorbital) and the plastic insert in the opened eye following tissue removal. Medical record review and clinician interview revealed that these periorbital hemorrhages were not present at the time of admission.

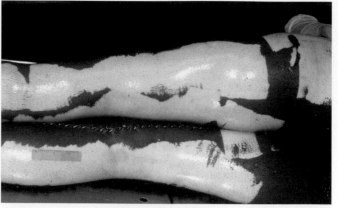

Figures 2.5 and 2.6 This shows tissue procurement of superficial skin layers in a dark-skinned individual.

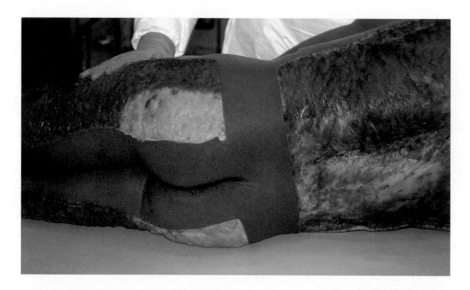

Figure 2.7 Full-thickness tissue procurement skin harvesting.

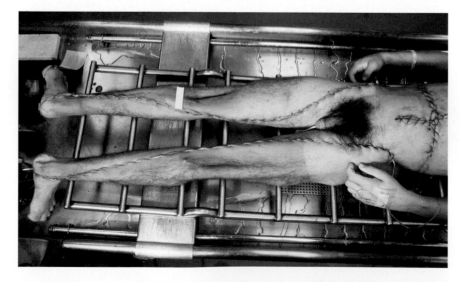

Figure 2.8 These sutured incisions of the lower extremities are seen commonly when long bones and saphenous veins are removed for postmortem procurement procedures.

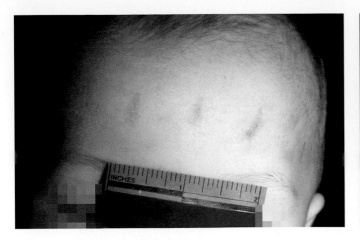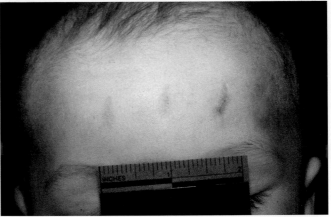

Figures 2.9 and 2.10 There are ill-defined, parallel, vertically oriented gray-brown marks on the forehead. These are artifacts of transport, caused by a strap to secure the child's head, as they were flown by helicopter from an outside hospital to a tertiary pediatric center.

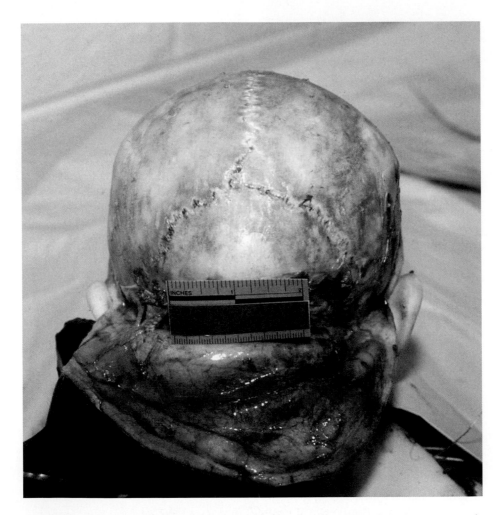

Figure 2.11 Same case depicting reflected scalp and well-defined sagittal and lambdoid sutures without features of subgaleal contusions or skull fractures.

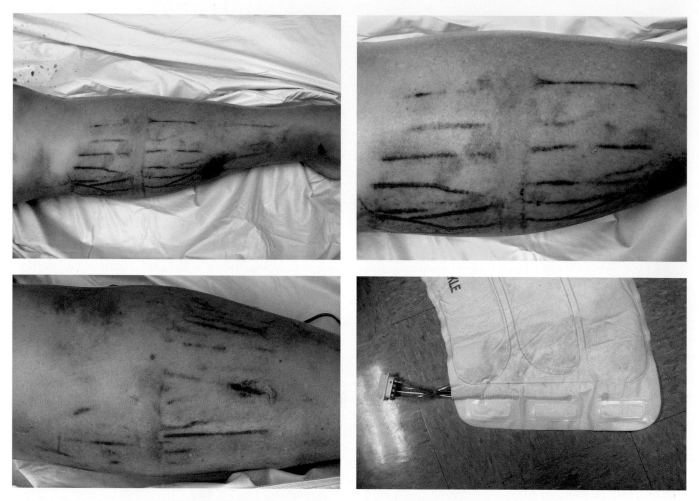

Figures 2.12–2.15 This individual was ejected from a car during a collision. He was taken to the hospital in an unconscious state and remained so until his death. There was initial speculation that he was struck by another motor vehicle due to the "tire-like" patterns on his legs. Further investigation revealed these injuries were not present at the time of arrival to the Emergency Department. He survived in the hospital for approximately 2 days. There was a pelvic fracture with blood seeping into the legs, extensive generalized edema, and disseminated intravascular coagulation. Pressure boots were placed to decrease the risk of deep venous thrombosis. This pattern of ecchymosis was caused by the pressure boots in conjunction with the complications of the injuries.

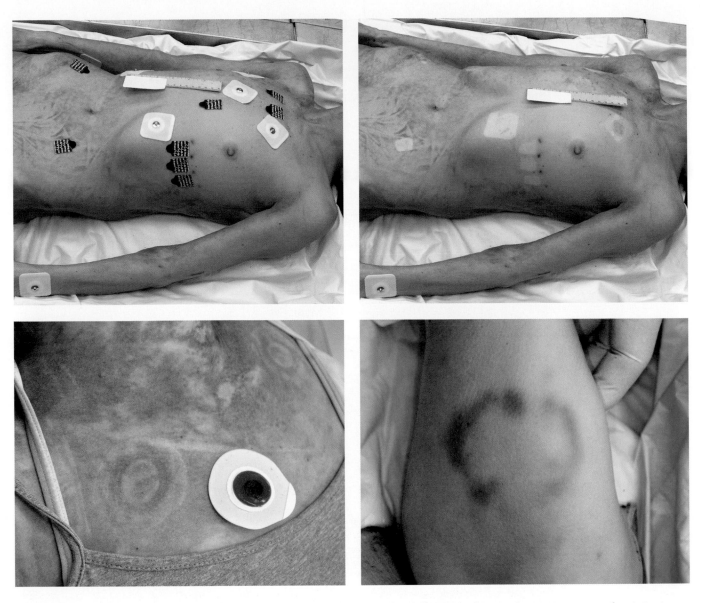

Figures 2.16–2.19 Note the marks left behind by therapeutic patches. These marks may be misinterpreted as injuries to the inexperienced eye. Note the similarity between the EKG patch outline and the antemortem bite mark to the forearm. It is important for therapy to be left on the body and examined by the pathologist before removal. Also note the early putrefactive change consisting of green coloration of the lower abdomen.

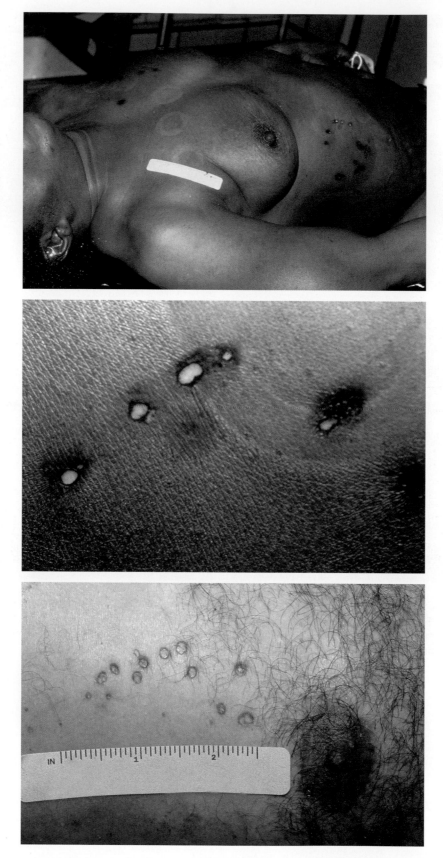

Figures 2.20–2.22 These are electrical burns caused by defibrillation with damaged cardioversion paddles during attempted resuscitation.

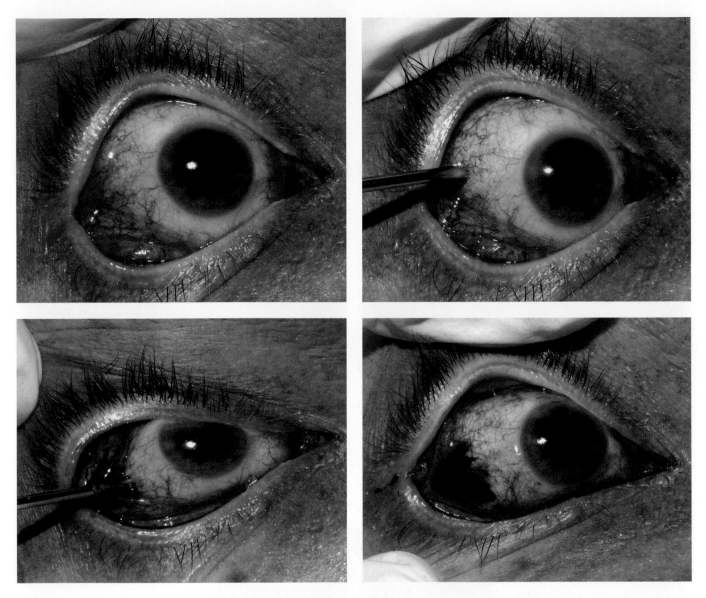

Figures 2.23–2.26 These images show an artificially created scleral hemorrhage associated with needle aspiration of vitreous fluid. Note there is no hemorrhage in the first image. It is absolutely essential for the pathologist to examine the eyes before vitreous fluid is obtained. Marks similar to petechial hemorrhage may also be created with tooth forceps.

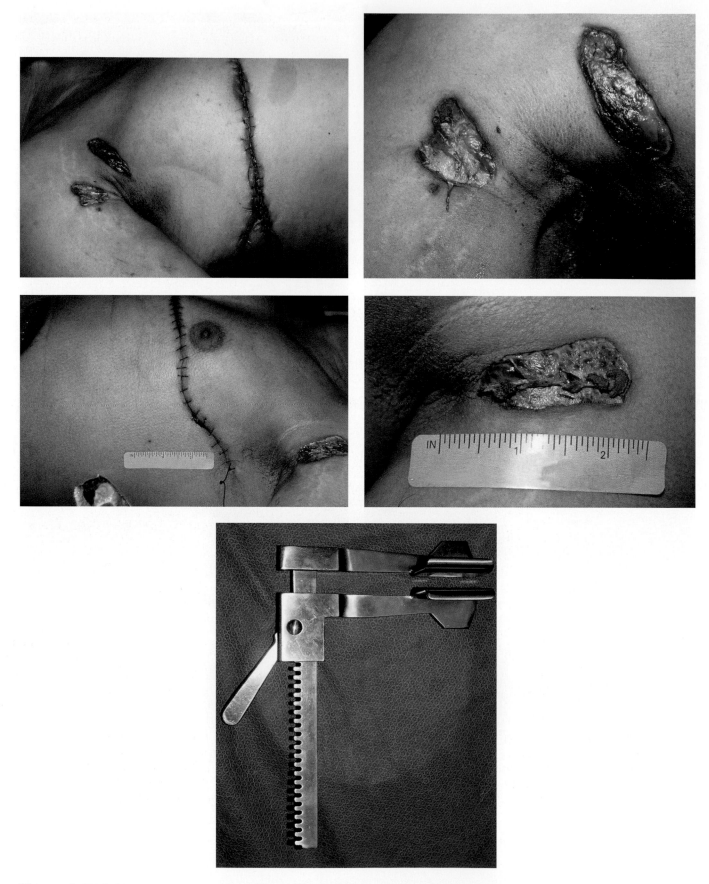

Figures 2.27–2.31 These figures show perimortem injuries to the anterior chest, the axillary regions, and the anterior aspects of the upper arms associated with incorrect placement of a rib splitter during a thoracotomy.

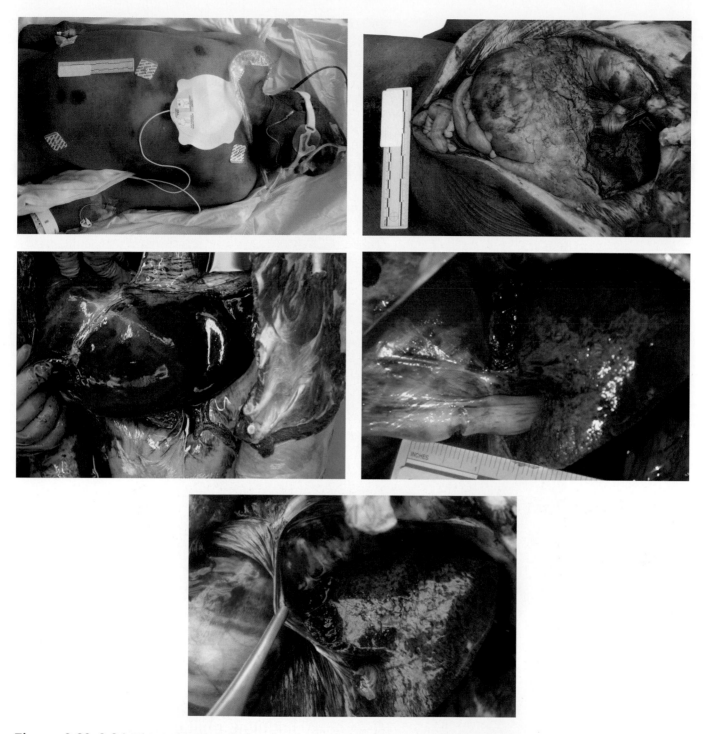

Figures 2.32–2.36 This individual was vigorously resuscitated by family members after suddenly going unresponsive. There was no trauma to his trunk except for the attempted resuscitation efforts by family and later by hospital personnel. He had hepatic parenchyma with lacerations and intact capsule and minimal sub Glisson's capsular hemorrhages. The two lower images show a similar case of hepatic injury due to improperly placed hands while performing chest compressions. Note the superficial laceration adjacent to the round ligament. There was a minimal amount of liquid blood in the peritoneal cavity.

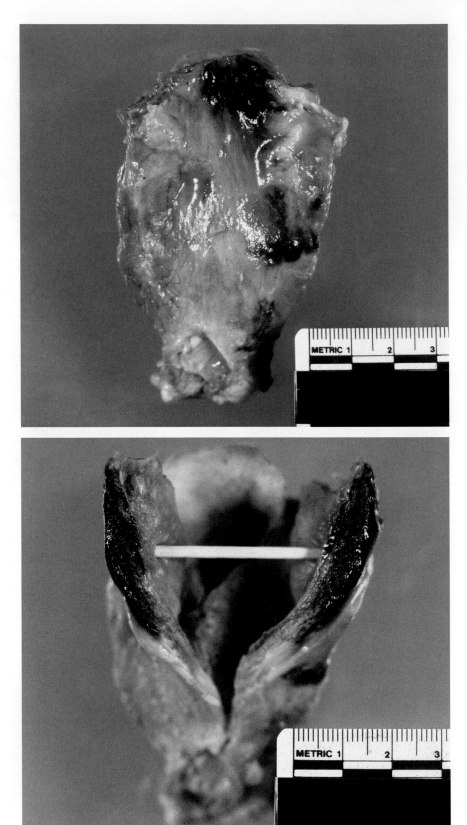

Figures 2.37 and 2.38 These pictures demonstrate the posterior pharyngeal/esophageal cut surface with intramural hemorrhage. This is an artifact encountered frequently during resuscitative measures, often referred to in forensic textbooks as the "Prinsloo and Gordon" artifact. Because of the rich esophageal venous plexus, this tends to be a very hemorrhagic area following intubation and therefore may be confused with stigmata of manual strangulation.

Figure 2.39 This demonstrates an esophageal intubation with the tip of the endotracheal tube protruding from the esophageal lumen. The epiglottis can be seen slightly behind the endotracheal tube, confirming an esophageal intubation.

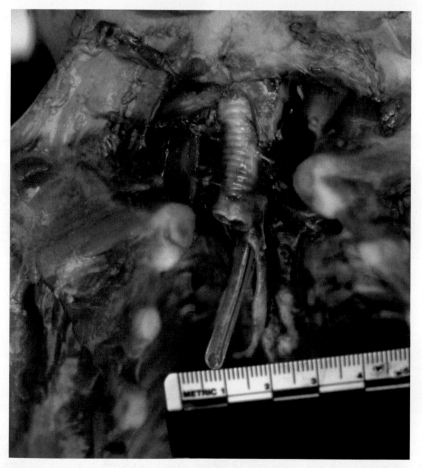

Figure 2.40 This autopsy involved an infant who succumbed to sudden infant death syndrome and was discovered at home asystolic. The close-up of this autopsy photograph depicts an esophageal intubation, with the endotracheal tube clearly within the esophageal lumen and the concentric tracheal rings visible slightly anterior to and (anatomically) to the right of the tube. Esophageal intubation is not an uncommon finding associated with resuscitation and usually plays no substantial contributory role in the death; however, it should always be documented as part of a complete autopsy and may, in some situations, be a quality control measure for Emergency Medical Services (EMS) personnel and paramedics. Esophageal intubations during an elective procedure, on the other hand, would be very important and potentially causal or contributory to the death.

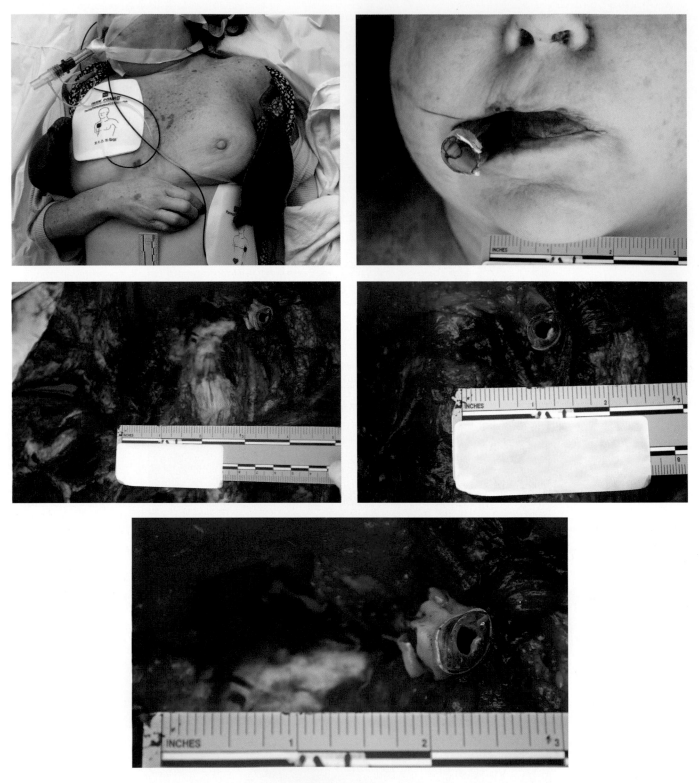

Figures 2.41–2.45 A 60-year-old woman found in cardiac arrest at home. Resuscitative efforts failed. Note the misplaced endotracheal tube that crossed from the right side of her mouth to the left pharyngeal region where it perforated and penetrated the soft tissues of the neck, completely missing the airway.

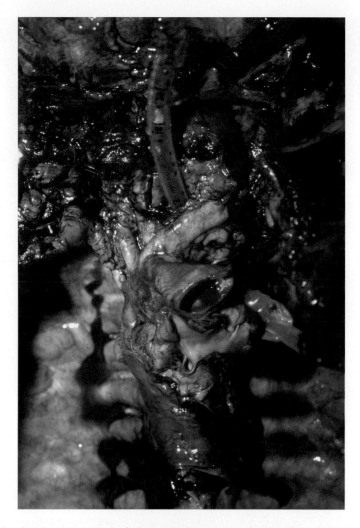

Figure 2.46 This endotracheal tube was inserted through the paratracheal soft tissues into the thoracic cavity during resuscitation.

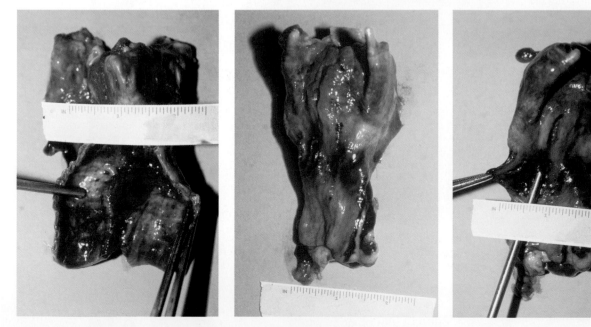

Figures 2.47–2.49 A tracheostomy tube was inserted through the posterior aspect of the trachea into the esophagus (traumatic tracheoesophageal fistula). Note the perforations on the posterior surface of the trachea and the anterior aspect of the esophagus.

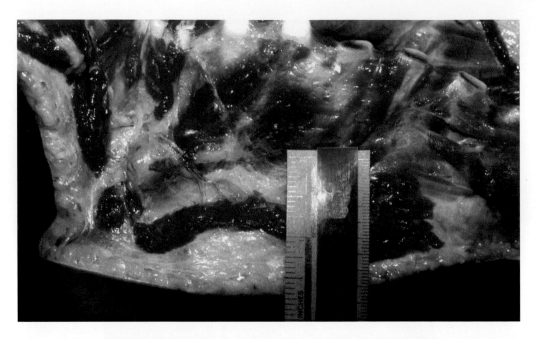

Figure 2.50 This is a view of the chest wall of an 18-month-old toddler with a history of tracheomalacia and sub-aortic stenosis, who required a tracheostomy. During a bout of crying, the tracheostomy tube became dislodged, and after nurses attempted to reposition it, she rapidly developed subcutaneous emphysema, followed by bilateral tension pneumothoraces. Autopsy demonstrated marked subcutaneous emphysema, including periorbital swelling. The tube had been removed before the autopsy, precluding assessment of its placement. This particular view demonstrates air bubbles within the subcutaneous fat. It is important that all tubes remain in the body for objective postmortem (autopsy) evaluation of their placement.

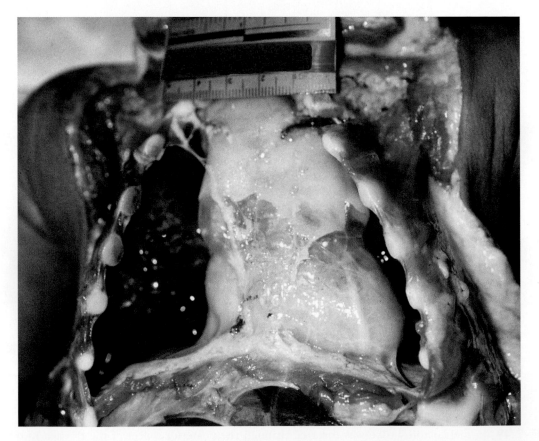

Figure 2.51 Soft-tissue emphysema. Anterior chest with air bubbles throughout the mediastinal soft tissues. This may be commonly observed with vigorous resuscitation and/or trauma. Palpation of these regions often reveals crepitus.

Figure 2.52 One must be careful while examining injuries altered by therapeutic intervention. This picture demonstrates a catheter placed into an injured blood vessel through a stab wound.

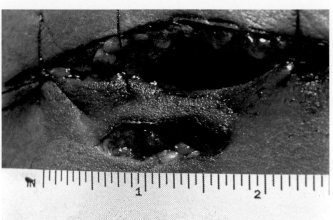

Figure 2.53 This demonstrates a stab wound adjacent to a sutured chest tube incision. This may make injury interpretation more challenging.

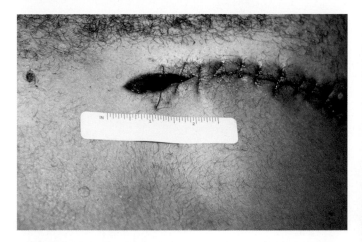

Figure 2.54 This demonstrates a stab wound that the clinicians converted along one side (edge) into a thoracotomy incision. If at all possible, this should never be done because it makes injury interpretation much more difficult.

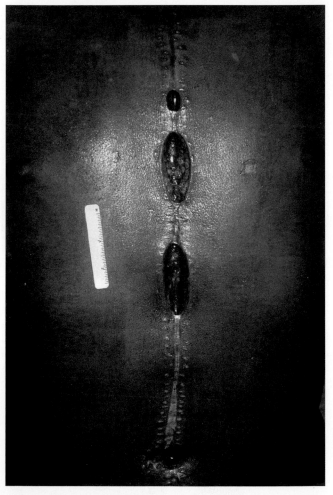

Figure 2.55 Healing infected incision. This individual died of septic complications of his initial trauma. Had it not been for this trauma, the infection that took his life would not have occurred. The manner of death in this case was ruled accidental.

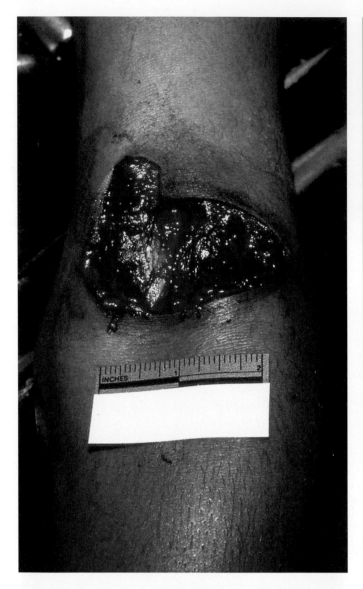

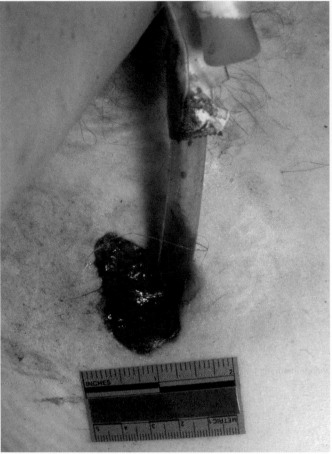

Figure 2.57 This chest tube was inserted through a previously existing perforation. Notice, however, that along the left margin of this perforation (from the 7 to 11 o'clock positions), there is a distinct abrasion. Further investigation established that the chest tube was inserted through a previously sustained entrance gunshot wound, thus explaining the abraded margin of this perforation.

Figure 2.56 This is a "cutdown site" used for vascular access by a hospital emergency department (ED) physician, created by a transverse incision within the antecubital fossa. This decedent had also sustained stab and incised wounds in other parts of their body. Again, this illustrates the importance of having a complete medical record and discussions with the treating ED physicians and/or trauma surgeons in order to properly differentiate between therapeutic interventions and injuries sustained before such therapeutic interventions.

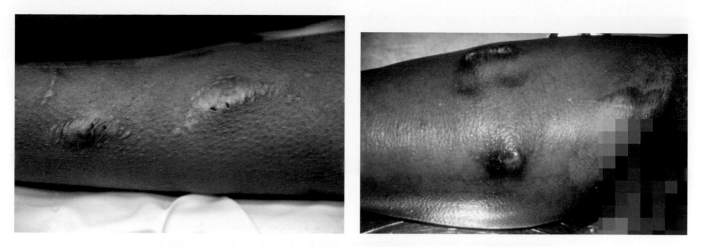

Figures 2.58 and 2.59 Arteriovenous hemodialysis grafts with healing needle puncture marks.

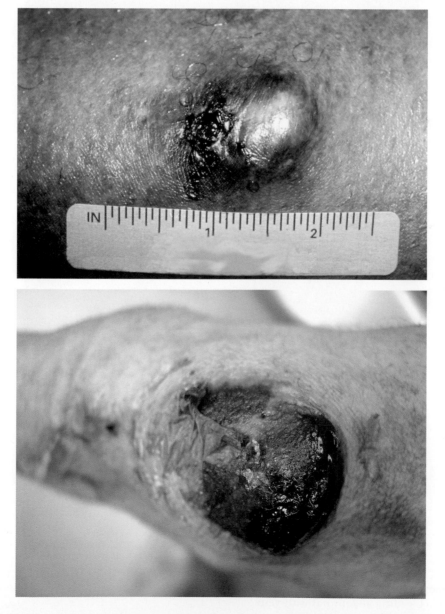

Figures 2.60 and 2.61 These individuals exsanguinated in their residences following ruptures of their infected arteriovenous dialysis grafts.

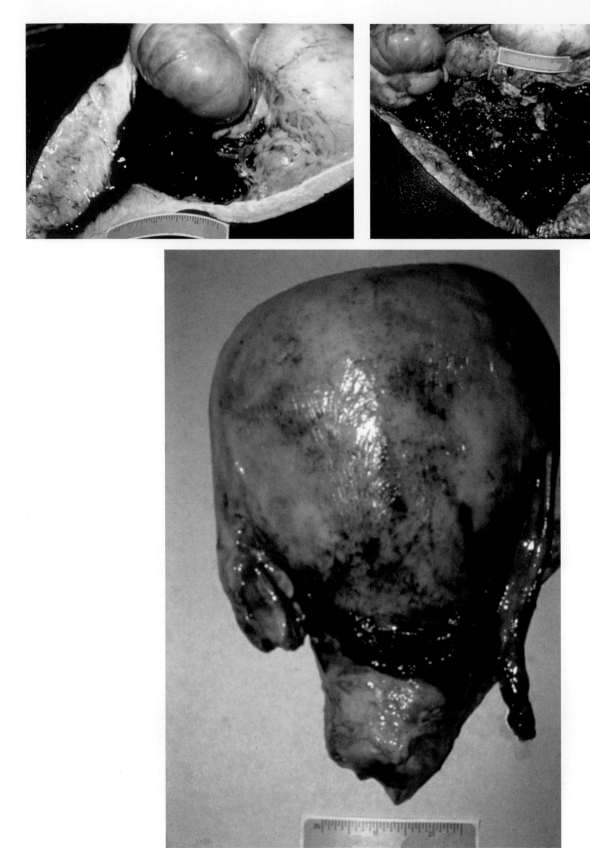

Figures 2.62–2.64 This woman underwent cesarean section for an otherwise unremarkable term pregnancy hours before going into hemorrhagic shock while in the recovery room. Autopsy disclosed a large hemoperitoneum with clotted blood extending from a bleeding abdominal wall vein.

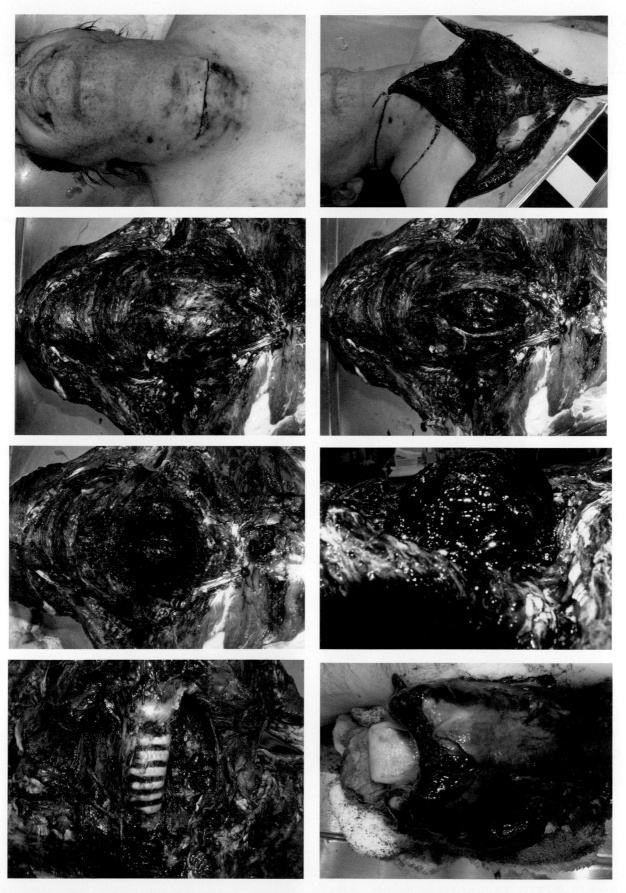

Figures 2.65–2.72 This individual died of hemorrhagic complications following thyroidectomy. A large accumulation of clotted blood collapsed his airway while he was sedated at home. He was found unresponsive lying on a sofa.

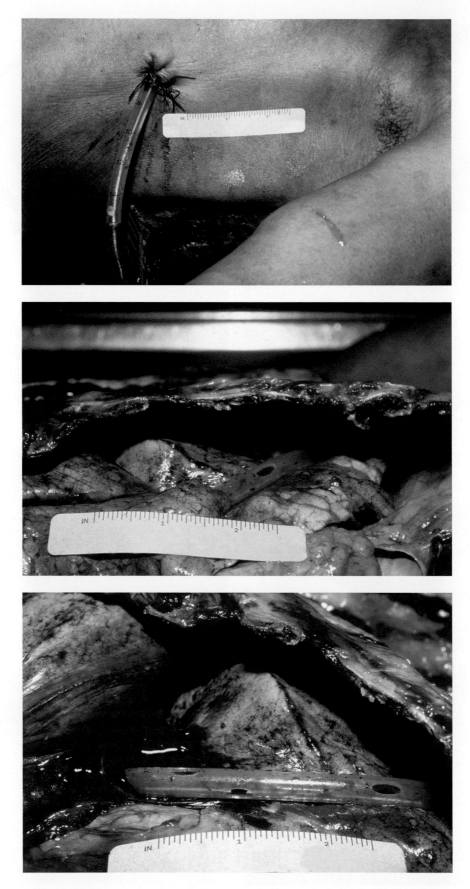

Figures 2.73–2.75 This patient was admitted in cardiac arrest following an acute asthma attack. Chest tube placement was inserted through the lung parenchyma during resuscitation. Approximately 150 mL of liquid blood was recovered from the left hemithorax, indicating that this injury was perimortem and iatrogenic.

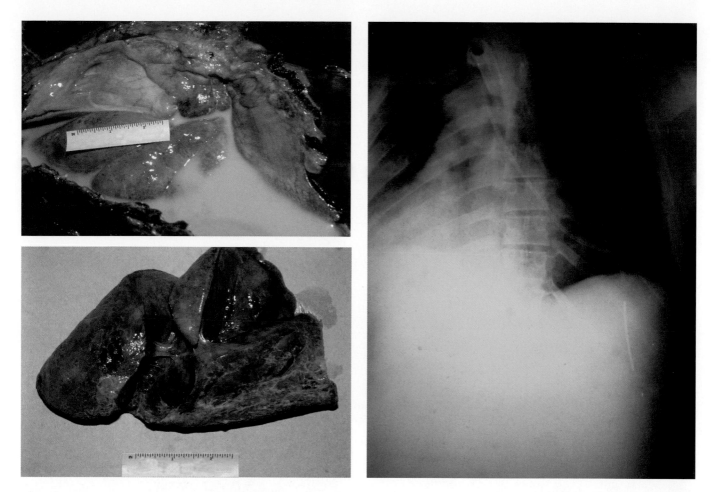

Figures 2.76–2.78 This individual underwent placement of a nasogastric tube that perforated the esophagus and entered the right thoracic cavity (hemithorax). The injury went unnoticed for many hours. The decedent was fed through the nasogastric tube, which is demonstrated by the accumulation of yellow fluid within the thoracic cavity. Autopsy revealed a fibrinous pleuritis and an early pneumonia.

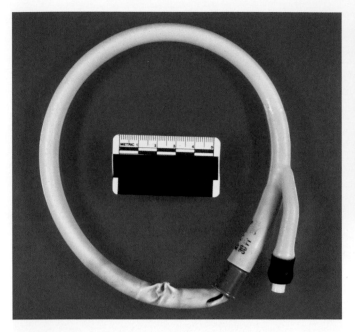

Figure 2.79 PEG feeding tube.

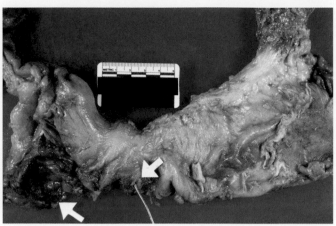

Figure 2.80 Panoramic view illustrating the anterior gastric wall, with a probe through the previous PEG site, also demarcated by an arrow, and the other arrow demonstrating greater omentum with fibrinous exudate. Similarly appearing exudate can also be seen on the anterior surface of the gastric body and fundus.

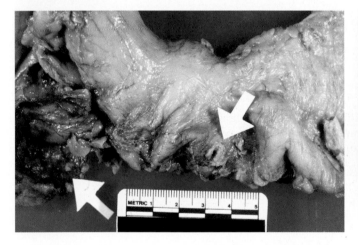

Figure 2.81 This is a close-up anterior view of the stomach, demonstrating the previous PEG site through the anterior gastric wall, as well fibrinous exudate on the surface of the greater omentum, with both features demarcated by arrows.

Figure 2.82 This depicts the parietal peritoneum with a gray, shaggy, fibrinous exudate.

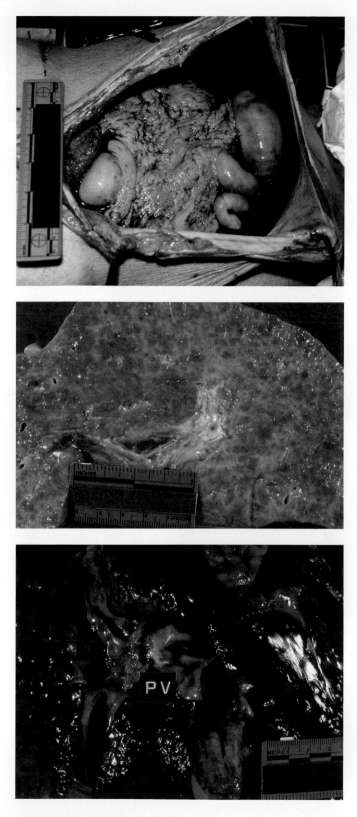

Figures 2.83–2.85 This was a middle-aged woman with primary biliary cirrhosis who underwent a transjugular intrahepatic portosystemic shunt (TIPS) for decompression of high portal venous pressure (portal hypertension). The picture depicts a large hemoperitoneum, with greater omentum, stomach, and intestines floating on top of a pool of blood. There was advanced end-stage cirrhosis, with confluent scar enveloping and entrapping regenerative parenchymal nodules. Liver diseases such as this are associated with an increased risk of hemorrhagic complications due to coagulopathy and portal hypertension. This fatal hemorrhage resulted from laceration of a portal vein branch occurring during stent placement.

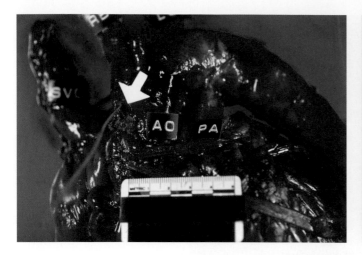

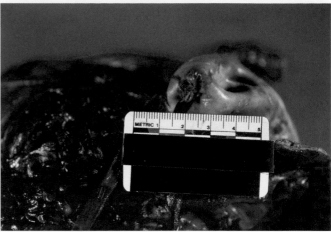

Figure 2.86 Note the probe inserted through the perforation site, which is also demonstrated with the arrow.

Figure 2.87 This image demonstrates the sutured cannu-
lation site as well as one of the bypass grafts.

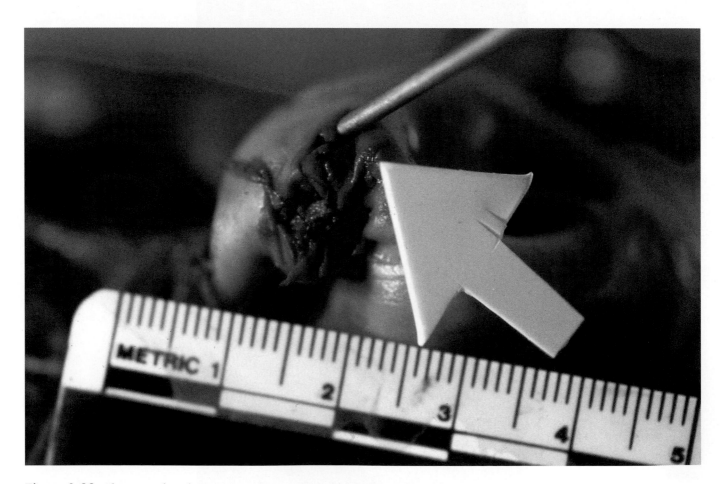

Figure 2.88 Close-up of perforation site demonstrated by probe and arrow.

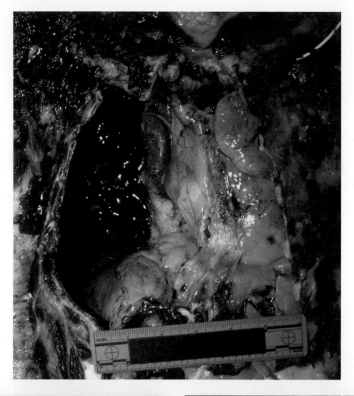

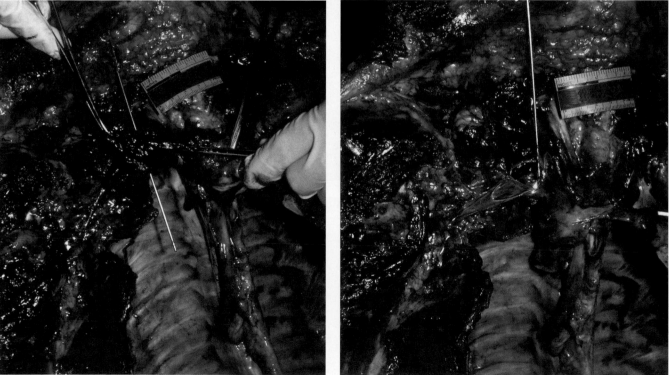

Figures 2.89–2.91 Right hemothorax due to perforation of right internal jugular vein, complicating catheter insertion. Note the probe demonstrating the perforation through the right internal jugular vein and the hemorrhage within the anterior overlying soft tissues.

Figures 2.92–2.94 This case involved complications of a transbronchial biopsy in an individual who was HIV-positive and was slightly thrombocytopenic (platelet count: ~75,000/μL). The procedure was followed by extensive pulmonary hemorrhage, which culminated in respiratory compromise and death. Figure 2.92 demonstrates a Swan–Ganz catheter within the pulmonary arterial system. Note Figure 2.94 is a close-up view with a probe through a perforation of one of the large branches of the right main pulmonary artery with the arrow head demarcating the tip of the probe.

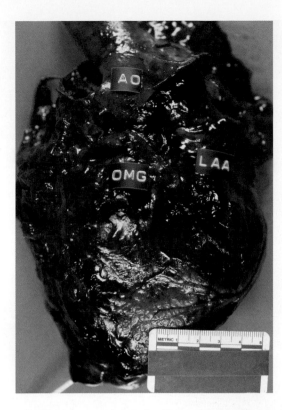

Figure 2.95 Heart with labels illustrating the aorta (AO), obtuse marginal graft (OMG), and left atrial appendage (LAA).

Figure 2.96 Close-up view of grafts.

Figure 2.97 This image demonstrates the relationship of OMG and native obtuse marginal vessel, as well as a stent protruding through the lacerated native obtuse marginal artery.

Figure 2.98 Close-up view of the junction between the OMG and the native obtuse marginal artery demonstrating the irregularity in the arterial wall.

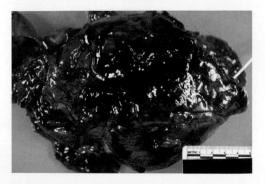

Figure 2.99 Posterior view of heart demonstrating confluent epicardial hemorrhage associated with this procedure.

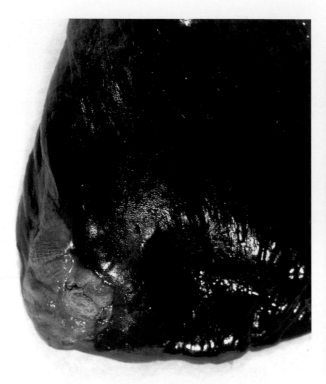

Figure 2.100 This depicts the lower lobe of the left lung with congestion and pneumonia. Note at the inferolateral aspect of the left lower lobe is a fragment of gauze that was inadvertently left behind during another operation months earlier. The gauze is adherent to the surface with overlying adhesions and adjacent purulent exudate.

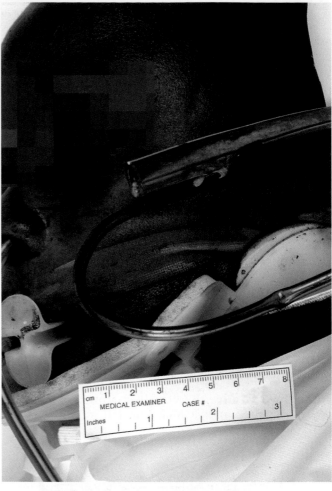

Figure 2.101 This individual was in a motor vehicle accident and sustained a skull fracture involving the cribriform plate. A nasogastric tube was inserted, which inadvertently penetrated the cranium. The tube was placed on intermittent suction. Aspirated brain matter is visible at the end of the tube.

Figure 2.102 This demonstrates a large gray-tan thrombus encasing a pacemaker lead extending from the heart.

Figure 2.103 In busy trauma centers, the body is sometimes received with multiple instruments used for resuscitative efforts. This photograph was taken after the body bag was opened at the morgue. It is always important to be careful of sharps that have been inadvertently left behind.

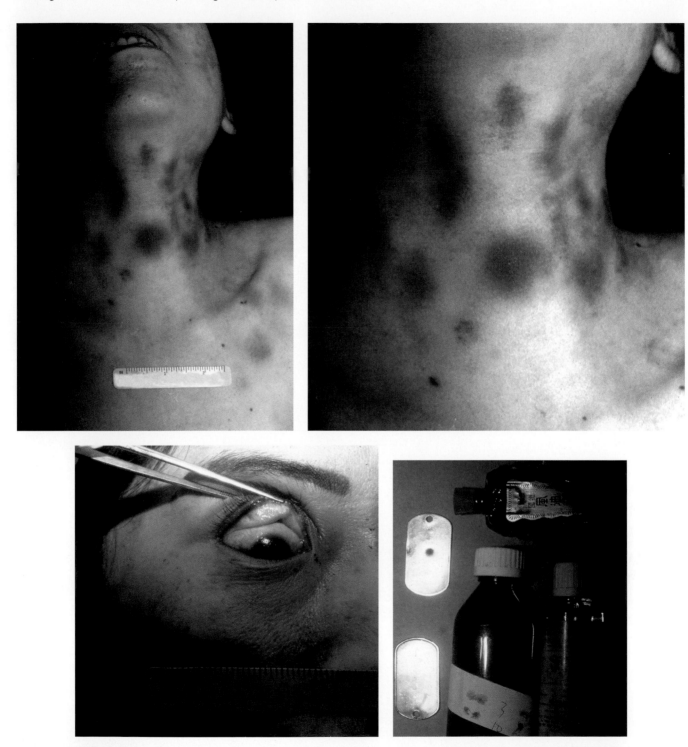

Figures 2.104–2.107 This Vietnamese woman died of Takayasu arteritis that was complicated by a ruptured aortic aneurysm. She was treated at home by her grandmother with Southeast Asian folklore remedies, including coining. These red to brown contusions, some with abrasions, were produced by another person rubbing her neck with metal dog tags and medicinal oils while praying. Note the unusual location of the coin marks at her neck. At first this was mistaken for manual strangulation. There were no internal neck injuries and no scleral or conjunctivae hemorrhages.

Substance Abuse and Poisoning

CHARLES A. CATANESE AND LAURA M. LABAY

3

Contents

The term "substance abuse" is most simply defined as the excessive use of one or numerous drugs. In general, most people typically have access to various types of drugs, including legitimately prescribed medications, and on average, will benefit from their appropriate use. However, the term "substance abuse" may be applied to a variety of situations or circumstances where these drugs or medications are misused. For example, one person may intentionally be abusing a multitude of substances including illicit drugs, prescribed medications, and over-the-counter remedies (i.e., supplements, herbals, diet aids, etc.). This is in contrast to another individual who may only be taking a single medication, but deliberately using it in a manner that is not consistent with normal therapeutic use. It stands to reason that when an individual begins to abuse one or more substances, and uses them in an uncontrolled manner without the appropriate oversight, they place themselves in a potentially harmful or lethal situation.

In a forensic or medicolegal setting it often becomes a matter of necessity to interpret drug findings and render an opinion regarding the toxicological, physiological, and pathological impact that the drugs may have had upon an individual. To this end, it is important to evaluate and consider a host of factors. These factors are not always straightforward or quantifiable, but nevertheless include the drug's inherent physical and chemical properties, the dosage of the drug used, the frequency of the drug intake, the route of drug administration, the concentration of drug and drug metabolite found, the person's tolerance level to the drug, and any medical conditions or disease states the person may have experienced.

It is important to recognize that for a particular drug to ultimately produce a toxic or lethal effect, it must be present in an individual at a sufficient concentration for a sufficient length of time. However, while references and other texts are available that help to classify drug concentrations as "therapeutic," "toxic," or "lethal," interpretation is often not so simple. For example, postmortem methadone concentrations are often challenging to interpret because the range of blood concentrations that may be detected in people enrolled in narcotic maintenance programs may overlap the blood concentrations found in overdose or lethal situations.

Also, some drugs, depending on their physical and chemical properties and their concentrations in the body, will exert their most toxic or lethal effects in an acute manner while others will take a longer length of time to act. In general, deaths associated with substance abuse may be related to acute or chronic complications. *Acute substance abuse* indicates that the death was related to direct toxic effects of the drug shortly after administration. A *delayed overdose* is an exception where the drug produces damage to the body over hours or days following acute intoxication with complications that may include coma, sepsis, brain swelling, and herniation. This process may evolve over days with the drug(s) metabolized from the body. The underlying process that sets off this sequence of events is the acute intoxication.

Depending on the type of drug and its half-life, there may be no or minimal amount of drug left in the blood or other tissues at the time of death. However, the possibility exists that the drug or its metabolite(s) may still be detected and identified in the urine. In these circumstances, it is important to take into account that urine is really a pooled specimen, collected in the bladder over a period of time, and that a quantitative result only represents the average drug–urine concentration over the period of time that the urine was produced. Therefore, this type of specimen does not accurately reflect the blood–drug concentration at any single point in time. Rather, a positive finding of a drug or drug metabolite in urine only indicates prior exposure to that particular drug, and in this regard, it is relevant to consider other information (e.g., case history, medical records, anatomical findings, etc.) as well.

If a decedent suffered trauma while intoxicated and developed an *epidural or subdural hemorrhage*, you would expect to find the drug present in these samples, even after many days. *Chronic sequelae* associated with substance abuse include complications of infections, including HIV disease, hepatitis, hepatic cirrhosis, and endocarditis. Injection of ground-up oral medications may lead to pulmonary failure with multiple foreign body granulomas and fibrosis demonstrated on histopathologic section. There are many other complications, including Wernicke—Korsakoff's encephalopathy, alcoholic cardiomyopathy, and hardening of the arteries due to cocaine use.

Intravenous drug abuse may present with many different features. If the drugs are injected acutely in the same vein during binges, they appear as multiple fresh needle marks in a row. These are called fresh track marks because they resemble a pattern of railroad ties being laid down one after another. It may be possible to detect the parent drug by excising the immediate area surrounding the injection site and submitting this section for toxicological analysis. If several injection sites are observed and a decision is made to submit more than one for testing, make certain to package the specimens in separate containers, identify the sites from which each were taken, and note their age and appearance. Alternatively, the syringe or other drug paraphernalia such as vials, pipes, or spoons, if available, may also be submitted for analysis. This is a good option if, for whatever reason, limited biological specimen exists. Once the nonbiological contents of the items are identified, directed toxicological analysis on the biological specimens could then proceed. If this is done, it is important that the items are packaged in individual containers, away from biological specimens, so that contamination does not occur.

Injecting drugs into blood vessels can lead to the introduction of many types of infections. Sharing of needles may cause transmission of the hepatitis virus or the human immunodeficiency virus. Various types of bacteria may also be introduced during injection, leading to vasculitis, cellulitis, pneumonia, and endocarditis. Acute intravenous fatalities, such as those caused when individuals inject themselves, are usually classified as

Accident. If one can demonstrate the drug was given to the individual in order to purposefully cause his or her death, the manner would be classified as *Homicide.* Also, if another individual injects the drug into the decedent's arm, the manner of death should be *Homicide.*

As the vein is chronically abused, it will scar and develop a chronic track mark. Chronic track marks appear as linear scars that traverse the path of underlying veins. Histological sections from these regions often show polarizable debris from impurities found in past-injected drugs. If a chronic intravenous drug abuser consistently rotates the injection sites from one vein to another, they will not develop chronic track marks.

Skin-popping refers to drugs, such as heroin, injected into the subcutaneous tissues. This usually indicates a long history of drug abuse with destruction of the previously accessible peripheral veins. This may appear as fresh needle marks usually at the surface of the thighs, or in other places without an underlying vein. These sites often get infected and lead to cellulites, abscess formation, and scarring.

Another route of drug administration includes inhalation. Inhalation (i.e., snorting) of drugs may lead to mucosal reddening from direct irritation. Crack pipes may become very hot during use and burn the drug abuser's mouth and lips. Sometimes histopathology sections of the lungs reveal numerous pigment-laden macrophages from constant inhalation of smoke and debris from inhaled burning drugs like crack. Chronic snorting of drugs may lead to a perforated nasal septum.

Keep in mind, it is not only the illicit drugs such as cocaine or heroin that may be inhaled; an individual may choose to crush and "snort" a tablet or pill as well. In some instances, residue may be observed in the nasal or oral cavity, and these areas may be swabbed and the parent drug identified through analytical testing. Individuals may also choose to inhale or "huff" commercial products such as gases, fuels, aerosols, solvents, or propellants as a means of abuse. This may be accomplished by breathing in the fumes from a rag that has been soaked in the material or by placing a bag containing the fumes over the nose and mouth. In some cases, the inhalation may directly take place from the item (i.e., aerosol can, glue bottle) as well. Users have died from hypoxia, pneumonia, cardiac failure, or aspiration of vomit. If the latter situation is relevant to the case, it is important to inform the toxicology lab of this, as most routine toxicology screens do not include these substances in the scope of their analysis. For these cases lung tissue or tracheal air, in addition to the routine biological samples, may be collected as well.

Transdermal drug delivery systems introduce medications into the general circulation through a slow diffusion process, and may be considered a desirable alternative to taking oral medications or using substances that require repeated injection. In addition, the transdermal systems, perhaps most importantly, help to minimize the extreme blood spikes and trough levels that may be experienced with orally administered medications. Instead, blood–drug concentrations are maintained at more consistent concentrations.

Examples of commonly encountered medications delivered through transdermal systems include nicotine, hormones (i.e., contraceptives), and the potent narcotic analgesic fentanyl. However, similar to any medication, these patch-style systems may be subject to abuse. For instance, a person may make the decision to apply a multiple number of patches to their body, or through manual or chemical means remove the drug from the drug reservoir or from the adhesive matrix. It is also not uncommon for a person to chew or even swallow them. In these cases remnants of patches may be observed in the oral cavity or the gastric content. Other signs of this type of abuse would be if a person presented with patches applied in a manner not consistent with normal therapeutic use. For these cases, document the number of patches found on the body, their locations, any writing or markings on the patches, and any other descriptive features. Make an attempt to ascertain whether all the patches represent a single acute application or whether some of the patches may be from remote use.

In these types of death situations where patch use is known or suspected (i.e., old adhesive markings are noted on the body), it is important to make certain that specimens are not collected in close proximity to a vein or artery that is in the immediate vicinity of a patch or patch marking. As a specific example, following the death of an individual wearing a fentanyl patch, some drug may still be present in the depot beneath the patch. If a blood specimen is collected from an area immediately beneath or near the location of the patch, the concentration of fentanyl may not accurately reflect the circulating concentration at or around the time of death.

Similar to the patch, suppositories represent another type of drug delivery system. Suppositories contain medicated material for insertion into a bodily passage or cavity such as the rectum. Once the suppository, typically a solid substance, is inserted, it will begin to dissolve over time and subsequently will deliver the medication into the body. Substance abuse using this route of administration is relatively rare.

Postmortem Redistribution

Besides only contending with the issue of contamination as caused by trauma, drugs and their metabolites may also be subject to postmortem redistribution.

Postmortem redistribution is the movement of drugs between tissues, organs, and bodily fluids after death. The rate and extent of this movement vary according to several factors, including the nature of the drug and the time interval between death and the postmortem collection time of specimens. Within the torso, the major organs constitute potential drug pools, and the gastrointestinal tract might contain considerable quantities of unabsorbed drug. Therefore, central blood is subject to redistribution from these local organs. In general, redistribution into central vessels is greater than redistribution into peripheral vessels and this is why it is preferred that final quantitative amounts are determined from a peripheral blood source. Therefore, while central blood pools are acceptable for screening purposes, it is always better to get a peripheral blood sample for quantitative confirmation work, if possible.

Embalmed Cases

Cases sometimes present after the body has been embalmed. In these situations, hair, fluid, and/or tissue can be retrieved from the body and submitted for toxicological analysis. During the embalming process a formaldehyde-based fluid (e.g., embalming fluid) is infused into the body through the vasculature. Determined concentrations, if any, will ultimately be dependent upon several variables. These variables include, but are not necessarily limited to, the quality of the embalming process, the location of the organs within the body at the time of embalming, and the length of time the embalming fluid has been in physical contact with any substance. Furthermore, it is known that the stability and recovery of numerous analytes in decomposing tissues can be variable. To this end, it is expected that the determined concentration of any substance may not be a true representation of what was present at or around the time of death. Perhaps the most valuable finding is the one that demonstrates past use and/or exposure to a substance that was previously unknown. In these situations, thorough investigative work may help to determine whether the person displayed the adverse signs and symptoms associated with the substance at some point prior to death. It is good practice to collect some of the embalming fluid along with any other compound (e.g., drying compound) that may have come into contact with the body, if available, as well. These materials may not have to undergo analysis in conjunction with the biological material, but, depending upon the analytical findings, it may be necessary to determine whether the target substance was introduced into the body during preparation for burial.

Drugs

Acute and Chronic Alcoholism

Death occurring from acute alcoholism is usually classified as *Natural*, although this may not always be the case. A young adult at a party trying to impress friends may attempt to guzzle a liter of whisky. This is more than enough alcohol at one time to kill most adults. In this case the manner of death would be *Accident*. Sometimes depressed people with an acute triggering event tell their family that they are going to "drink themselves to death." After several days of drinking large quantities of alcohol, they die. If you can establish the intent to do harm, the manner of death would be *Suicide*. If someone at a party drinks alcohol from a funnel and a hose, by pouring the alcohol themselves, and then dies, the manner of death would be *Accident*. If someone holds the hose and pours the alcohol for them, the manner of death should be *Homicide*.

An individual with a history of chronic alcoholism, including varying degrees of liver disease, intoxications, and withdrawal, is mostly certified as *Natural*. Chronic alcoholics who stop drinking abruptly may get the "shakes" and eventually experience seizures leading to death. Withdrawal of many other drugs without other underlying natural disease will not typically cause death.

It is very difficult to give an opinion about an individual's state of mind or behavior while they were drinking or using any drug for that matter. One has no way to know an individual's true thought processes unless their behavior was witnessed or somehow clearly documented. Chronic alcoholics, with a high degree of tolerance, may be able to achieve a high blood alcohol level and not show visible signs or symptoms consistent with intoxication. Some alcoholics become aggressive, loud, and agitated while others become subdued and complacent.

It is important to obtain blood samples with care in cases where there is suspected alcohol use and trauma played a role in the person's death. If one only obtains a blood sample from the pericardial sac or chest cavity, where other visceral lacerations may exist, contamination with gastric contents or other bodily fluids is a likely possibility. In turn, the measured blood alcohol level may be markedly increased as compared to the actual circulating blood concentration at and around the time of death.

As a more specific example, relating to alcohol, when death is a consequence of multiple traumatic injuries there is the possibility that significant damage to the internal organs occurred. These organs include, but are not necessarily limited to, the stomach, small intestine, and liver. If those organs, now damaged, contained unabsorbed alcohol, a blood specimen collected from the chest area may readily become contaminated. As a result, the concentration of alcohol determined may not accurately reflect the circulating concentration at and around the time of the fatal event. Instead, ideally, for postmortem alcohol analysis and to mitigate some of these issues, an alternative specimen type should be harvested. These specimen types would include a vitreous specimen, a urine specimen, and/or blood collected from a peripheral site, such as the femoral vein. This is because in those cases where the heart blood may have become contaminated due to events such as trauma, the alternative specimen can be used to help provide an interpretable alcohol concentration.

Alternative specimens, such as vitreous fluid, are vital to collect especially when alcohol is suspected or involved. It is important to recognize that alcohol may form postmortem, and analytical testing cannot make the distinction between this type of alcohol and alcohol that was present prior to death. Indeed an alcohol finding may represent a combination of these two circumstances. To prevent or minimize postmortem formation, once blood is collected it should be placed into an appropriate type of specimen collection container, one that contains preservatives that help to inhibit microbial growth. If the postmortem formation of alcohol is a concern, such as in a case where marked decomposition has occurred, a positive alcohol finding may be confirmed in the vitreous fluid, a specimen type that is more resistant to microbial growth.

Barbiturates

Barbiturates have been in clinical use since the early 1900s. Modification of the core molecule has produced several analogs with different durations of action, and it is by this that different barbiturates are categorized. The relationship between structure and activity is impacted through alteration of the aliphatic chain at the C_{5a} or C_{5b} position. The lengthening of this side chain increases the lipid solubility of the molecule and, as a consequence, the potency is increased, but the duration of action decreased. The four main categories are (a) ultra-short-acting, (b) short-acting, (c) intermediate-acting, and (d) long-acting. The ultra-short-acting barbiturates are used to induce surgical anesthesia, while the intermediate-action ones are used as sedative-hypnotics. Some barbiturates that are commonly detected include butalbital (used in the treatment of migraines), phenobarbital (used as

an anticonvulsant), and pentobarbital (used to relieve intracranial pressure following trauma). Because significant impairing effects have been associated with barbiturates, their use over the years has declined as safer alternatives (e.g., benzodiazepines) have become available.

Belladonna Alkaloids

Atropine
Atropine is an anticholinergic alkaloid derived from certain plants, including jimson weed (*Datura stramonium*) and deadly nightshade (*Atropa belladonna*). It is used in preanesthetic therapy to control airway secretions and as an antispasmodic to control gastrointestinal spasms. It is frequently used as an antidote in the treatment of poisoning by cholinesterase inhibitors. Toxic effects of atropine have considerable individual variation; however, at high doses, signs and symptoms include mydriasis, hot dry reddened skin, delirium, and hallucinations.

Atropine is also used in resuscitative attempts. In resuscitative failure, most of the administered drug remains confined to the intravascular injection pathway. Often the drug is still present in the postmortem blood collected from the heart sampled at autopsy.

Scopolamine
Scopolamine is an alkaloid derived from jimson weed (*Datura stramonium*) and henbane (*Hyoscyamus niger*). It is close in structure to atropine, differing in only the oxygen bridge on the scopine moiety. Scopolamine has many therapeutic applications, including use as a preanesthetic medication, treatment of Parkinsonism, gastrointestinal disorders, and prevention of motion sickness. Toxic effects of therapy include blurred vision, dryness of the throat, dilated pupils, somnolence, mydriasis, skin flushing, hallucinations, and confusion.

Benzodiazepines

Benzodiazepines are one of the most commonly prescribed drug classes. They are used as anxiolytics, antidepressants, and anticonvulsants, and as preoperative sedatives. Commonly detected benzodiazepines include alprazolam, lorazepam, clonazepam, and diazepam. Benzodiazepines undergo extensive hepatic metabolism, and metabolic routes include dealkylation, deamination, hydroxylation, and reduction. It is important to recognize that the metabolites may have central nervous system (CNS) depressant properties that affect potency and duration of action. Benzodiazepines are often found in combination with other drugs such as ethanol, antidepressants, opiates, and illicit drugs. Due to their high therapeutic index, death directly attributed to the exclusive use of a benzodiazepine is not commonly encountered. Instead, the more likely scenario when a benzodiazepine is identified is that the death is due to multiple drug intoxication.

From an analytical perspective, capturing all the benzodiazepines and their metabolites with one analytical test is challenging. This is due to the varied functional groups that are present and because blood concentrations, depending upon the benzodiazepine, may range across several orders of magnitude. Many laboratories have developed benzodiazepine panels or incorporated them into multidrug class screens. This targeted style of testing aids the case reviewer because the scope of analysis with limit of quantification (Reporting Limit) can readily be ascertained. Screening may also take place by immunoassay. With this, it is important to recognize that even though there is good cross-reactivity with many benzodiazepines, not all may be excluded by this style of testing.

Cocaine

Cocaine, a Schedule II controlled substance, is found in the leaves of a South American shrub called *Erythroxylon coca* and is one of the most potent of the naturally occurring CNS stimulants. It was first isolated in 1855 and has been used medicinally as a local anesthetic. However, because of its high potential for abuse the use of cocaine for clinical situations has become severely limited. When cocaine is taken for illicit reasons, it is taken either as the water-soluble hydrochloride salt by nasal insufflation ("snorting") or intravenous injection or as the free base ("crack") by smoking. Regardless of the chemical form or route of administration, once cocaine is administered it is rapidly absorbed and distributed throughout the body. Once inside the body, the dosage form of cocaine cannot be distinguished and analytical determinations are reported as the free base form.

Cocaine is rapidly biotransformed in the body to a few major metabolites and products, including benzoylecgonine, ecgonine methyl ester, ethylecgonine, and ecgonine. These metabolites are all pharmacologically inactive. Small amounts of an active metabolite, norcocaine, may also be produced. However, this product is rarely detected in blood. Cocaethylene is a pharmacologically active substance formed in the liver when cocaine and ethanol are co-ingested. The most predominant cocaine product detected in the majority of biological specimens is benzoylecgonine. Elimination on half-lives is approximately 4.5 hours for benzoylecgonine and approximately 0.8 hours for cocaine.

Effects displayed by an individual under the influence of cocaine may include dilated pupils, increased blood pressure, increased pulse rate, increased blood pressure, and sense of strength or invincibility. It is believed that cocaine is toxic to the cardiovascular system causing thrombosis, myocardial infarction, tachycardia, or fibrillation in cases of acute and chronic abuse.

Designer Drugs

Designer drugs or novel psychoactive substances (NPS) are synthetic analogs of controlled substances that have been purposefully designed to circumvent current drug laws. They have been marketed and sold as "research chemicals," "bath salts," or "plant food," and packages may be marked "not for human consumption." Analogs are created through the chemical alteration of the molecule, so even though the structure is different, the pharmacological effects associated with the starting drug is maintained or enhanced. This concept is not new in that chemical modification of parent drugs has occurred for decades. Historical examples include, but are not limited to, the amphetamine analog MDMA and the fentanyl analog α-methylfentanyl. Synthetic cathinones are drugs that have been developed from cathinone, a constituent of the plant *Catha edulis* or "khat," and the designer phenylethylamines and tryptamines encompass a large class of synthetic and naturally occurring compounds. Many of the phenylethylamine analogs are produced from phenylethylamine or amphetamine, while the tryptamine analogs are made to impact the serotonin system.

There is a paucity of data examining dosage, pharmacokinetic profiles, metabolism, and effects. Instead, toxicologists and clinicians have had to depend on the accuracy of self-reporting and case studies associating analytical results with witnessed events and actions. Often, toxicology testing is not even performed. The overall lack of controlled studies can make interpretation of analytical results challenging. Case studies, however, have demonstrated that these drugs can produce a myriad of symptoms that adversely impact the physical and mental health status of users. Some of these include hypertension, tachycardia, hyperthermia, agitation, aggressiveness, dizziness, confusion, hallucinations, and paranoia.

Fentanyl

Fentanyl is a synthetic opioid analgesic of high potency and short duration of action that predominately interacts with the μ-opioid receptor. These receptors are located along the spinal column, brain, and certain tissues. Its primary action of therapeutic value is as an analgesic and sedative. It is approximately 15–20 times more potent than heroin and 80–100 times more potent than morphine. Fentanyl may increase the patient's tolerance for pain and decrease the perception of suffering, although the presence of the pain itself may still be recognized. Because of the potency of the drug, concentrations encountered in serum and plasma are typically in the low nanogram per mL range.

Fentanyl may be provided by an intravenous line or through the use of a transdermal patch. The fentanyl transdermal delivery system releases fentanyl from the drug reservoir at a nearly constant amount per unit time. The concentration gradient existing between the saturated solution of drug in the reservoir and the lower concentration in the skin drives the drug release. Following application of a patch the skin beneath begins to absorb fentanyl so that a deposit of drug concentrates in the upper skin layers. Fentanyl then becomes available to the systemic circulation. Serum fentanyl levels gradually increase following the initial application of the patch and then level off between 12 and 24 hours. For the remainder of the 72-hour application period, fentanyl levels will remain relatively constant. For the event of several sequential 72-hour applications, fentanyl levels reach and maintain steady-state concentrations that are dependent on factors such as skin permeability and the body clearance rate of the individual. Drug abusers have been known to smoke or ingest patches as well as mixing the powdered form with heroin.

Signs associated with fentanyl toxicity include severe respiratory depression, seizures, hypotension, coma, and death. When collecting postmortem samples for toxicology testing, it is important to try and obtain blood samples at a site not in close proximity to an applied patch.

Flunitrazepam

Flunitrazepam is a drug that has been associated with drug-facilitated crimes. It is a benzodiazepine analog that has been used as a hypnotic and anesthetic induction agent. The drug undergoes extensive biotransformation, with 7-aminoflunitrazepam being the primary urinary metabolite. Signs and symptoms associated with use/exposure include ataxia, drowsiness, hypotension, respiratory depression, and coma. The drug is not approved for medical use in the United States, but is prescribed in other countries.

Gamma Hydroxybutyric Acid

Gamma hydroxybutyric acid (GHB) is a drug with sedative and amnesiac effects, and has been implicated in drug-facilitated crimes. It is important to recognize that GHB is an endogenous substance, so from an analytical perspective, it may be detected in case samples even without any exogenous use or exposure. The use of cut-off concentrations to differentiate exogenous from endogenous exposure in antemortem collections has been proposed. These cut-off concentrations in blood and urine are 2 mcg/mL and 10 mcg/mL, respectively. Another interpretive consideration that should be taken into account is the pharmacokinetic profile of the drug. Following a single use, the window of detection is approximately 8 hours in blood and approximately 12 hours in urine. The use of a gray top tube for postmortem cases is recommended, and citrate containing collection containers (light blue tubes) should be avoided, as reports demonstrate that GHB concentrations may increase in these tube types. Adverse effects from the abuse of GHB include severe drowsiness, hallucinations, confusion, convulsions, combative and self-injurious behavior, coma, and reported death. GHB concentrations in postmortem blood stored in containers without sodium fluoride preservative at room temperature have been reported to exceed several hundred mcg/mL.

Heroin

Heroin is a Schedule I controlled substance and a synthetic derivative of morphine. It is made by first extracting morphine from opium and then chemically treating the morphine with acetic anhydride, sodium chloride, and hydrochloric acid.

Once it is taken into the body, most frequently by injection, smoking, or inhalation, the heroin is rapidly deacetylated to 6-monoacetylmorphine (6-MAM), a product that is then hydrolyzed at somewhat of a slower rate to morphine. Unlike the heroin, which has little affinity for the opiate receptors in brain tissue, both 6-MAM and morphine are pharmacologically active. Because 6-MAM is a specific product of heroin, if it is found to be present in a biological specimen, it may be concluded that the individual either used or was exposed to heroin at some point prior to death. However, due in part to the short half-life of 6-MAM, morphine is most often the predominant species detected in biological specimens. Therefore, in cases where heroin is suspected to be the lethal agent and morphine is found in the blood, but 6-MAM is not, it may be of benefit to test an alternate specimen type such as urine or vitreous fluid for the presence of this heroin-specific marker as well.

The primary toxic manifestations of heroin use may last for approximately 4–6 hours and include the same effects most commonly associated with other opioids. Some of the more common effects include, but are not limited to, drowsiness, loss of coordination, decreased blood pressure, decreased pulse and respiration, mental clouding, sedation, and sweating. At sufficiently high levels, the user may slip into a coma and ultimately stop breathing.

LSD

LSD, a Schedule I semisynthetic controlled substance, is manufactured from the main precursor chemicals lysergic acid, lysergic acid amide, and ergotamine tartrate. LSD is normally taken by placing a "dot," laced with the material, on the tongue. The LSD is then dissolved by the saliva and readily absorbed through the mucous membranes. This method of ingestion allows for its effects to be rapidly felt. Other means of ingestion include mixing the LSD with liquids or adding it to sugar cubes. However, the drug cannot be taken into the body by smoking, as pyrolysis destroys the LSD.

LSD is generally classified as a hallucinogen or psychedelic drug, and may produce both auditory and visual illusions. Approximately 30–60 minutes after ingestion, the user will experience the initial effects and, in general, the effects may last for about 8–12 hours. Physiological effects are primarily sympathomimetic and may include mydriasis, hyperthermia, seizures, panic, and paranoid reactions. Flashback reactions, a brief recurrence of the LSD experience, are not uncommon in the experienced user, and may occur for weeks, months, or years after the last usage.

Death due to the pharmacological effects of LSD is rare, with most deaths occurring as a result of LSD-induced suicide and accidental trauma.

Marijuana

Marijuana, a Schedule I controlled substance, is a complex mixture of several products, obtained from various parts of the *Cannabis sativa* plant, and is the most widely used illicit substance in the United States and the rest of the world. There are more than 400 chemical substances found in marijuana. Sixty of these substances are called cannabinoids and are responsible for the psychoactive properties of the plant. The most relevant cannabinoid is tetrahydrocannabinol (THC) as it is the primary psychoactive ingredient in marijuana.

One of the most notable features of this drug is its long half-life with some metabolic components exceeding 50 hours. This is because the drug is highly lipid soluble and may undergo significant enterohepatic recirculation. In fact, the redistribution of THC from tissue to blood has been shown to be the rate-limiting step in its metabolism. In the body THC is metabolized to two major metabolites, 11-hydroxy-THC (11-OH-THC) and tetrahydoxycarboxylic acid (THCC). The former metabolite is pharmacologically active, while the latter is devoid of any pharmacological activity.

Marijuana is most frequently smoked, although it may be ingested as well. THC rapidly leaves the blood, even during a smoking period, and falls to below detectable levels within several hours. The most common physical effects are acceleration of heart rate, a moderate increase in blood pressure, a slight decrease in body temperature, reddening of the eyes, and dryness of the mouth. The psychological effects of marijuana use include a pleasant feeling of well-being and euphoria, distortion of time, reduced ability to concentrate and memorize, and impaired short-term memory. Individuals under the influence of marijuana may have difficulties in tracking movement and demonstrate an inability to appropriately respond to stimuli. In general, this condition may persist for hours after the feelings of intoxication have dissipated, leaving users with a false sense of security concerning their abilities to safely operate a motor vehicle or machinery.

Death strictly due to the pharmacological effects of marijuana is not well documented, with most deaths occurring as a result of accidental trauma.

Methamphetamine

Methamphetamine is a Schedule II controlled substance with a very high potential for addiction and abuse. There are two different chemical forms or isomers of methamphetamine, each producing effects that differ in scope and magnitude. The L-isomer of methamphetamine may be found in over-the-counter nasal inhalers and is used for its vasoconstrictive properties. Compared to D-methamphetamine it is a weak CNS stimulant. In contrast, the D-isomer may represent the licit and/or illicit forms of methamphetamine. In terms of legitimate or legal use methamphetamine may be prescribed for a limited number of medical conditions such as weight loss, narcolepsy, and attention deficit disorder. However, because other less addictive and less dangerous substances that do not quickly result in patient tolerance to the drug are also available, it is not that frequently prescribed.

Methamphetamine in the body undergoes demethylation to its primary active metabolite amphetamine; in most cases both methamphetamine and amphetamine will be detected. Analytical methods that differentiate the isomers of methamphetamine (and amphetamine) exist and may be employed if warranted.

People who abuse methamphetamine experience certain sequelae of such drug use. In general, the effects of methamphetamine can be broken down into three main stages. The first stage is the "high" where blood concentrations are at their greatest and people are feeling the stimulant effects of methamphetamine. The second stage is the "tweaking" period where blood levels are on the decline, and it is this period where people crave the drug and may behave in an aggressive and violent manner. Lastly, the third stage is the "crash" where people feel exhausted and drained. High doses of methamphetamine can elicit restlessness, confusion, hallucinations, circulatory collapse, and convulsions.

Methadone

Methadone is a Schedule II controlled substance that is often prescribed during the process of narcotic detoxification, narcotic maintenance, and treatment programs, and to control severe and chronic pain. As compared to morphine it produces less sedation and euphoria, but cessation of its use may result in withdrawal symptoms, not as severe as those seen with morphine, but longer in duration. Methadone works by decreasing the withdrawal symptoms felt by the narcotic abuser, and when a person attempts to reuse, the desired effects of the illicit drug are minimized.

In the body, methadone is metabolized to 2-ethylidene-1,5-dimethyl-3,3-diphenylpyrrolidine (EDDP) and 2-ethyl-5-methyl-3,3-diphenylpyrroline (EMDP). These metabolites do not possess any pharmacological activity and do not accumulate to an appreciable extent in plasma during therapy.

Methadone overdose is characterized by stupor, lethargy, pupillary constriction, hypotension, coma, respiratory collapse, and death.

MDMA

MDMA (3,4-methylenedioxymethamphetamine) is a synthetic sympathomimetic compound with mixed stimulant, psychotropic, and hallucinogenic activities. It was used briefly as an adjunct to psychotherapy, but because of widespread abuse it has now been reclassified as a Schedule I controlled substance. The synthesis of MDMA is both complex and time-consuming. As a direct result, the final product may contain a variety of impurities that may be toxic in their own right. Also, drug manufacturers may add an illicit substance or a stimulant in an attempt to enhance the effects of the MDMA. The drug is available in tablet and powder form, and it may be injected, inhaled, or ingested. Tablets of MDMA come in a litany of colors and shapes, and may be imprinted with a variety of images such as peace symbols, cartoon characters, butterflies, and angels.

In the body, MDMA is metabolized to many other compounds, but the main metabolite is a demethylated product called methylenedioxyamphetamine (MDA).

The effects of MDMA are related to the dose. A lower-level dose (approximately 50 mg) may result in feelings of enhanced creativity, while mid-level doses (approximately 100 mg) may make the user feel open to improved communication and empathy. The ability of the user to undergo self-exploration and analysis is achieved with the doses typically greater than 125 mg. In general, the psychological effects are much more pronounced than the physical effects. Abusers of the drug have been reported to experience long-lasting neurobehavioral disorders following cessation of its use. Symptoms of MDMA toxicity include visual hallucinations, confusion, hypotension, agitation, coma, and death.

Phencyclidine

Phencyclidine (PCP) is a Schedule II controlled substance that was developed and marketed in the 1950s for use as an intravenous anesthetic. However, it was discontinued for medicinal use in 1965 as patients frequently would become agitated, delusional, and irrational, and experience the distortion of sights and sounds. In the early 1960s PCP gained reputation as a drug that produced certain desired feelings such as detachment and dissociation, but also caused the user to sometimes experience unwanted reactions (i.e., bad trips).

At low doses, PCP may cause changes in body awareness and produce psychological effects of euphoria, an alteration of time and space, confusion, bizarre behavior, and panic. Physical effects produced by PCP include impaired motor skills, shallow breathing, sweating, blank staring, speech disturbance, and an inability to regulate body temperature. At high doses, PCP may result in hallucinations, seizure, coma, and death. Because PCP has sedative-like effects, interactions with other CNS depressants, such as alcohol and benzodiazepines, may also lead to a life-threatening situation. In general, chronic PCP users may repeatedly use the drug for days at a time and, during this period, go without food or sleep. There appears to be no relation between plasma levels of PCP and the degree of intoxication that a person may experience.

Oxycodone

Oxycodone is a Schedule II controlled semisynthetic narcotic analgesic derived from thebaine. It is used to control pain associated with such ailments as bursitis, injuries, simple fractures, and neuralgia, and is often found in combination with other drugs such as acetaminophen and aspirin. The addiction liability of oxycodone is about the same as for morphine.

Oxymorphone is a pharmacologically active metabolite of oxycodone that may be seen in blood in very low concentrations. Of interest is that oxymorphone may be prescribed as a parent drug and has a greater analgesic potency than morphine.

In overdose, oxycodone can produce stupor, coma, muscle flaccidity, severe respiratory depression, hypotension, and cardiac arrest. However, sustained-release preparations appear to produce adverse reactions, up to and including death, at lower-level concentrations, especially in combination with other CNS depressants, depending on use pattern and route of administration.

Synthetic Cannabinoids

Cannabis (marijuana) is one of the most widely used drugs in world. It contains more than 400 compounds including nitrogenous compounds, hydrocarbons, amino acids, sugars, and terpenes. When used at low doses, a combination of CNS depressant and stimulant effects are observed, but at higher does, the depressant effects are more pronounced. Delta-9 THC, the main psychoactive cannabis ingredient, interacts with two cannabinoid receptors, CB_1 and CB_2. These receptors have been targeted as a mechanism to treat a variety of symptoms associated with disease states.

Synthetic cannabinoid receptor agonists were developed in an attempt to provide therapeutic benefit while limiting the psychoactive effects. Even though hundreds of these compounds were synthesized they are often referred to by the names Spice or K2. They are dissolved and sprayed onto herbal material. Packages may be colorful in their appearance and marked, "not for human consumption." They were introduced in Europe in 2004, and wanting to curtail their use in the United States, they underwent emergency scheduling. One analytical challenge is that when one of the synthetic cannabinoids becomes scheduled, manufacturers simply substitute the illicit substance with another. It is therefore important to understand the analytical scope of any synthetic cannabinoid test. At times, if nonbiological material is available it may behoove the toxicology laboratory to have this material analyzed prior to testing the biological or, if the material has already been analyzed, to be made aware of the testing outcome.

Very little pharmacokinetic information is known about the synthetic cannabinoids, but some of the signs and symptoms associated with their use include CNS effects (agitation, confusion, psychosis), cardiovascular effects (arrhythmia, tachycardia), and gastrointestinal effects (nausea, vomiting). Some publications have attributed lethal outcome to the use of the synthetic cannabinoids.

Zolpidem

Zolpidem (Ambien®) is a sleep aid classified as a nonbenzodiazepine hypnotic of the imidazopyridine class that is prescribed for the short-term treatment of insomnia. The drug is available in 5 mg and 10 mg dosages for oral administration, and it is recommended that the drug be taken immediately before trying to go to sleep.

Some of the adverse effects associated with zolpidem use include dizziness, headache, and nausea. However, also associated with zolpidem use are somnambulism and anterograde amnesia. Somnambulism is a sleep disorder where the person engages in activities that are normally associated with wakefulness while he or she is asleep or in a sleep-like state, and anterograde amnesia is a loss of memory *subsequent* to a particular event. While these latter effects are considered rare, cases have been reported where people, after taking zolpidem, carried out certain complex tasks, but then had little or no memory about the events following awakening. Some of these tasks have included eating, shopping, cleaning the house, having a conversation, or driving a car.

Zolpidem undergoes extensive metabolism, and when urine is the only matrix available, the analysis of the zolpidem main metabolites (e.g., zolpidem phenyl-4-carboxylic acid and zolpidem 6-carboxylic acid) may be necessary.

Poisons

Arsenic

Arsenic is a metalloid that is present in all parts of the environment and, for example, may be found in the water, soil, and sediment. In broad terms there are two main forms of arsenic: organic arsenic and inorganic arsenic. Organic arsenic is present in food, with crustaceans and fish being some of the richest sources. These organic forms of arsenic (arsenobentaine and arsenocholine) are considered to be relatively nontoxic and will be rapidly excreted unchanged in the urine. Inorganic arsenic occurs in two oxidation states: a trivalent form arsenite and a pentavalent form arsenate, with the trivalent form being more toxic than the pentavalent form. This type of arsenic undergoes metabolism to monomethylarsonic acid (MMA) and dimethylarsenic acid (DMA). MMA and DMA are then excreted in the urine.

Arsenic inactivates up to 200 enzymes, most notably those involved in cellular energy pathways, and DNA replication and repair. Unbound arsenic also exerts its toxicity by generating reactive oxygen intermediates that cause lipid peroxidation and DNA damage. Inorganic arsenic binds thiol or sulfhydryl groups in tissue proteins of the liver, lungs, kidney, spleen, gastrointestinal mucosa, and keratin-rich tissues such as the skin, hair, and nails.

The lethal dose of arsenic in acute poisoning ranges from 100 to 300 mg. Severe acute arsenic intoxication produces several well-described symptoms. Bloody vomit and diarrhea may occur within 1–4 hours of ingestion. Gastrointestinal volume loss is compounded by profound capillary permeability produced by arsenic's interruption of cellular energy metabolism. Cerebral edema, microhemorrhage, encephalopathy, and seizures may also arise from loss of capillary integrity. QT_c prolongation and tachyarrhythmias may develop.

Subacute arsenic toxicity involves predominately the neurologic and cardiovascular systems. Within days to weeks after ingestion, many untreated or undiagnosed patients describe debilitating peripheral neuropathy, characterized by excruciating pain and severe motor weakness. Persistent QT_c prolongation and the accompanying risk of torsades de pointes, a specific type of cardiac arrhythmia, occur among patients with clinically significant body burdens of arsenic.

Chronic arsenic toxicity presents itself following months or years of exposure. Some hallmark features of this type of toxicity not described above include hyperpigmentation of the skin, hyperkeratosis of the hands and feet, and the appearance of Mee's lines in the fingernails.

It is important to note that death may occur in all of the above situations (i.e., acute, subacute, and chronic) if the person is exposed to a sufficiently high dose of arsenic.

Carbon Monoxide

Carbon monoxide (CO) is an odorless, colorless gas without taste that forms as the result of the incomplete combustion of carbon-containing material. Motor vehicles, appliances, and heaters that use carbon-based fuels are major sources of exposure. However, it is important to note that natural sources of carbon monoxide also exist. These sources include fire, gases emitted from mines, marine algae, and human metabolism. Carbon monoxide is endogenously produced when hemoglobin, the molecule responsible for oxygen transport, and other heme-containing substances are degraded or broken down. Because of this, endogenous levels of carbon monoxide, analytically measured as carboxyhemoglobin, are typically less than 1%. It is important to note that carbon monoxide levels within the body may vary depending on several other factors as well. For example, since cigarette smoke contains carbon monoxide, a smoker may exhibit carboxyhemoglobin levels as high as 8% saturation.

A person becomes exposed to carbon monoxide via inhalation with the ultimate biological saturation level dependent on several factors, including carbon monoxide concentration, duration of exposure, and the activity level of the individual. Carbon monoxide poisoning produces hypoxia by two main mechanisms of action. First, carbon monoxide binds to hemoglobin with an affinity that is greater than 200 times that of oxygen, and therefore by occupying the oxygen-binding sites of hemoglobin, carbon monoxide directly decreases the oxygen-carrying capacity of blood. Second, when carbon monoxide binds to hemoglobin the hemoglobin undergoes a change in its configuration so that oxygen release from the hemoglobin is hindered. Early signs of carbon monoxide poisoning include headache, nausea, and vomiting. As the carbon monoxide poisoning progresses, the person may experience impaired mental function, an inability to concentrate, and personality changes. Finally the individual may develop seizures, coma, and death. Classic pathological signs that are most often associated with carbon monoxide poisoning, although rarely observed, include cherry red skin and retinal hemorrhages.

Cyanide

Cyanide is a potent, rapidly acting lethal poison and death may occur within minutes following its ingestion. Common sources of cyanide include industrial manufacturing by-products, plants, fruit pits, chemicals, and combustion products of certain plastics. Because of the latter, cyanide may play a role in the hypoxic events from fires. Some of the population is able to detect its presence by an odor of bitter almonds.

Cyanide exerts its effects by disrupting electron transport at the cytochrome c oxidase step and this in turn adversely impacts the production of ATP. This break in the oxidative phosphorylation process stops the Krebs cycle and this ultimately causes a metabolic acidosis as both pyruvic and lactic acids begin to accumulate.

The signs and symptoms of toxicity are dependent on several factors. These factors include, but are not necessarily limited to, the form of the cyanide (e.g., gas versus solid), the route of exposure (e.g., inhalation versus ingestion), and the duration and extent of exposure. The minimum lethal dose in an adult has been estimated to be 100 mg for hydrocyanic acid and 200 mg for potassium cyanide.

Cyanide produces a range of symptoms, including dizziness, weakness, motor impairment, and mental impairment. These symptoms may progress toward slowed respiration, lactic acidosis, seizures, coma, and death.

It is important to recognize that blood concentrations of cyanide can increase or decrease during storage depending on the length of time, the temperature, and the presence of cyanogenic bacteria.

Ethylene Glycol

Ethylene glycol is a nonvolatile liquid that is a common ingredient of automotive products such as antifreeze, de-icers, and coolants. It may also be found in some preservatives and as a glycerin substitute. Pure ethylene glycol is colorless, odorless, and tastes sweet.

Following ingestion ethylene glycol is rapidly absorbed and manifestations of toxicity may be noted within approximately 30 minutes. Ethylene glycol is metabolized in the liver to several toxic metabolites, including glycolaldehyde, glycolic acid, glyoxylic acid, and oxalic acid, and it is these metabolites that then may elicit CNS, cardiopulmonary, and renal dysfunction as well as produce severe metabolic acidosis. The magnitude of toxicity depends on dose and the onset and success of treatment, which includes giving ethanol and fomepizole.

The effects of ethylene glycol exposure are typically described in three main stages. In the first stage (0.5–12 hours postingestion), neurological symptoms are manifested including signs consistent with ethanol intoxication. Coma, convulsions, and possibly death may result in this stage. The second stage (12–24 hours postingestion) is often characterized by cardiopulmonary disturbances including tachycardia, tachypnea, and hypertension. In severe ingestions, congestive heart failure, pulmonary edema, and circulatory collapse may be seen. The end stage of ethylene glycol toxicity is renal failure (24–72 hours postingestion). Autopsy typically reveals oxalate crystals concentrated in the kidneys, which is seen under the microscope more readily when polarized. The presence of these crystals is not pathognomic for ethylene glycol poisoning.

Hydrogen Sulfide

Hydrogen sulfide is a colorless, flammable gas that is highly toxic. It is a natural gas that can be produced by decaying organic matter or as a by-product of various industrial processes, including petroleum refining and mining. Hydrogen sulfide is insidious in that even though the gas has a distinctive rotten-egg odor that may be detectable at concentrations as low as 0.5 ppb, olfactory fatigue, depending on concentration and length of exposure, may also occur. At room temperature hydrogen sulfide is a gas and, since it is heavier than oxygen, it tends to accumulate in poorly ventilated low-lying areas. Inhalation is the major route of exposure, and its mechanism of action is such that it causes disruption of the mitochondrial electron transport system. Scene responders must be careful not to get exposed to concentrated gas that might be present in sewers, chemical plants, or suicide scenes where chemicals were mixed together. If there is any question about scene safety, it should be cleared for safe entry by appropriate personnel such as hazmat.

Situations involving hydrogen sulfide gas exposures are frequently encountered in the practice of forensic toxicology, and the interpretation of analytical findings is directly dependent on selecting the appropriate marker of exposure. In the body hydrogen sulfide is rapidly metabolized to its major oxidation product thiosulfate and it is mostly for this reason that this metabolite has often been used as a biomarker in the evaluation of nonfatal and fatal hydrogen sulfide exposure cases. Also, even though sulfide may also be used as an indicator of exposure, the detection of sulfide is difficult, especially in nonfatal cases, since it undergoes rapid metabolism in the body. Another potential complexity involving the interpretation of a postmortem sulfide level is that sulfide may be formed during the decomposition process.

Although postmortem cases usually involve suspected occupational exposures, suicides have been reported where household cleaning products (containing sulfur and an acid) were purposefully mixed together to create hydrogen sulfide gas.

Methanol

Methanol is a type of alcohol that is an extremely versatile type of substance, and in this regard may be found as a component in industrial solvents, fuels, and antifreeze preparations and as a denaturant for ethanol. Methanol may be introduced into the body through multiple routes of administration, including inhalation and ingestion. Once in the body methanol is first metabolized to formaldehyde and then to formic acid. Interestingly, even though formaldehyde is considered a toxic substance, it has on average a half-life of only several minutes, and it is the formic acid that ultimately produces the hallmark features of methanol toxicity, including metabolic acidosis and the loss of visual acuity. Methanol poisoning may be treated by the administration of ethanol, since both methanol and ethanol share a common metabolic pathway. In essence, the ethanol competes for binding to the alcohol dehydrogenase enzyme and indirectly limits the formation of formic acid. Acute methanol exposure may produce severe signs and symptoms of toxicity, including nausea, abdominal pain, and lethargy. In some cases, the poisoning will progress so that the person experiences an anion gap metabolic acidosis leading to coma, seizure, and respiratory collapse. It is important to recognize that methanol may be a component found in embalming fluids and, because of this, tissues or other samples that have come into contact with this type of material may test positive for the presence of methanol.

Mustard Gas

Mustard gas (H, HD, and HT) is a chemical warfare agent that was introduced in World War I. It is an oily brown to yellow liquid that has a mustard to garlic odor. It is a blistering agent or vesicant that can persist in the environment for an extended period of time (days to months) following its use. Like some other gases (e.g., carbon monoxide and hydrogen sulfide) its density is greater than that of air and, as a consequence, tends to accumulate in low-lying areas. The physical damage, depending on concentration and duration of exposure, can be severe. The skin, eyes, and respiratory tract are especially sensitive. Some signs and symptoms associated with exposure include redness, itching, and blistering of the skin; irritation, burning, and tearing of the eyes; and cough and shortness of breath. Mustard gas also causes the decreased formation of blood cells and can cause aplastic anemia or pancytopenia. If inhaled, death may occur from pneumonitis within several days.

Pollonium

The illness and subsequent death of Alexander Litvinenko with pollonium in 2006 brought attention to the use of radioactive material as a poisoning agent. Pollonium (Po-210) is a naturally occurring radioactive material that is found in low concentrations within the environment, but it may also be manufactured. Its half-life is 138 days. The substance emits alpha particles and is 5000 times more radioactive than radium. Because alpha particles lose most of their energy on impact, they cannot penetrate through surfaces such as human skin. Instead, Po-210 must be taken into the body for it to produce damage. Routes of administration can be ingestion, inhalation, or through broken skin. People who are handling Po-210-contaminated bio-fluids are also at risk. Signs and symptoms of exposure are related to the amount of exposure, but include nausea, malaise, fatigue, hair loss, hematopoietic syndrome, loss of fluids, and electrolyte disturbance. Death, especially without medical intervention, is a likely outcome.

Poison Hemlock

Poison hemlock (*Conium maculatum*) is a biennial member of the carrot family that grows wild throughout the United States, especially along roadsides. Socrates is thought to have died from ingestion of poison hemlock. The toxicity of poison hemlock is from several simple piperidine alkaloids, including coniine, gamma-coniceine, conhydrine, N-methylconiine, and pseudoconhydrine. Coniine and gamma-coniceine are thought to have the most significant contribution to the toxic affects, which are similar to nicotine poisoning.

Thallium

Thallium is a metal that was once used in rodenticides, insecticides, and depilatories, and was banned for residential use in the 1970s. Today it is used in the semiconductor industry and may be found in switches and electronic devices. Thallium is readily absorbed from the gastrointestinal tract and may be detected in most of the body's tissues and fluids, including blood, brain, liver, kidney, spleen, bone, hair, and urine. The half-life of thallium in the blood is approximately 2–4 days with one of the hallmark symptoms of this type of poisoning, alopecia or loss of hair, occurring after about 1–3 weeks. Symptoms of acute exposure include severe gastrointestinal distress, tingling of the hands and feet, paralysis, and respiratory failure. In people being chronically exposed additional signs and symptoms include paralysis, hepatic and renal issues, and respiratory failure.

Ricin

Ricin is a highly lethal protein toxin produced in seeds from the castor oil plant, *Ricinus communis*. In a purified concentrated form, several grains the size of table salt may be fatal within several days from complication including hypoxia, hypotension, and seizure. In an unconcentrated form, as little as five seeds or beans may be fatal in an adult following ingestion.

Sarin

Sarin is a colorless, odorless organophosphorus compound and a nerve agent that is in a volatile liquid form. It is an agent of organic esters of phosphoric acid that can easily be transformed into a gas form. It causes cholinergic syndromes due to irreversible binding to acetylcholinesterase. Deaths may be fatal within minutes primarily due to acute respiratory failure caused by bronchorrhea and bronchospasm.

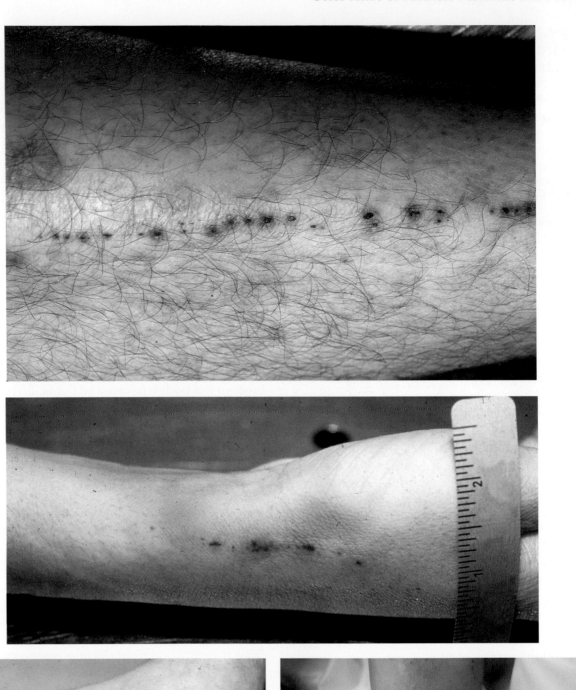

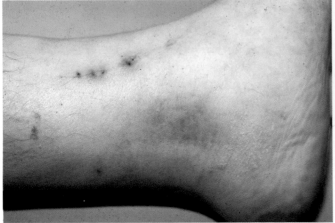
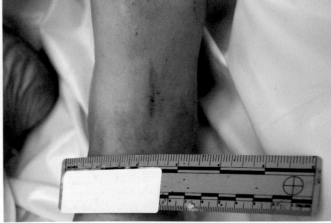

Figures 3.1–3.4 "Acute track marks." Multiple fresh needle mark injection sites that traverse the path of underlying veins. Incision of these regions will often reveal underlying hemorrhage. Toxicological testing of underlying injection site tissue may reveal the parent compounds such as heroine.

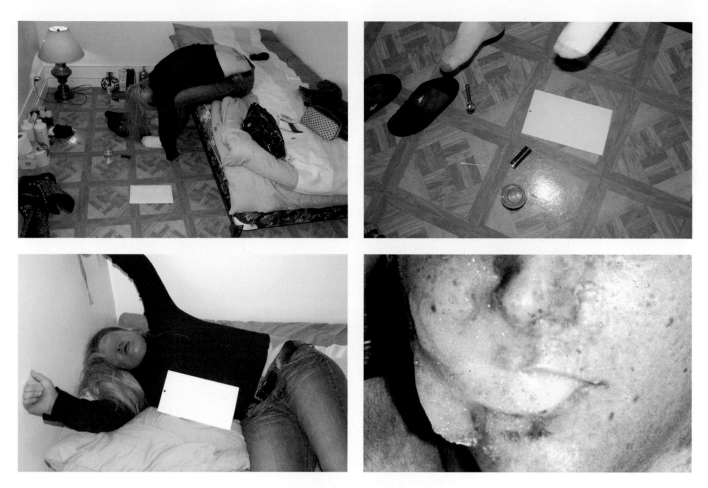

Figures 3.5–3.8 This individual died acutely after injecting heroin into the back of her right hand. She was found frozen in rigor mortis while seated on the bed with her head down. Note the significant lividity to her arms and face. There were sclera hemorrhages, due to gravity causing marked lividity, which in the absence of a proper scene investigation could be misinterpreted as being caused by neck compression.

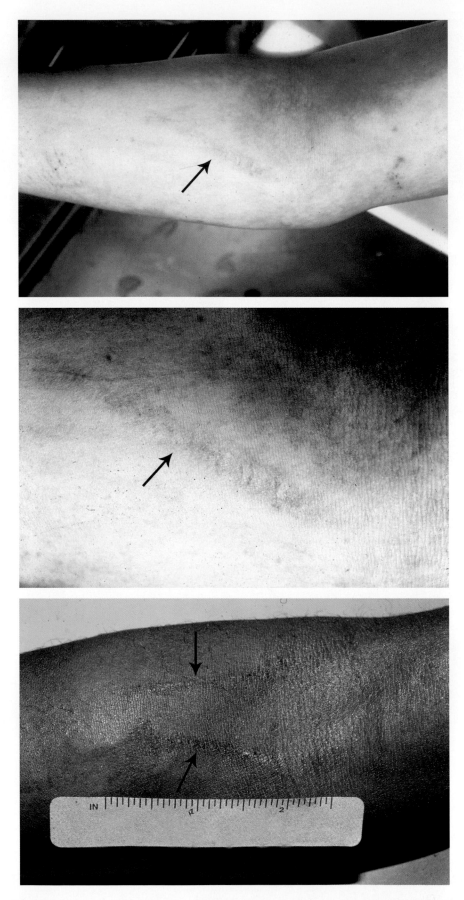

Figures 3.9–3.11 "Chronic track marks." Linear scars that traverse the path of underlying veins. Microscopic sections may demonstrate inorganic debris in subadjacent soft tissues.

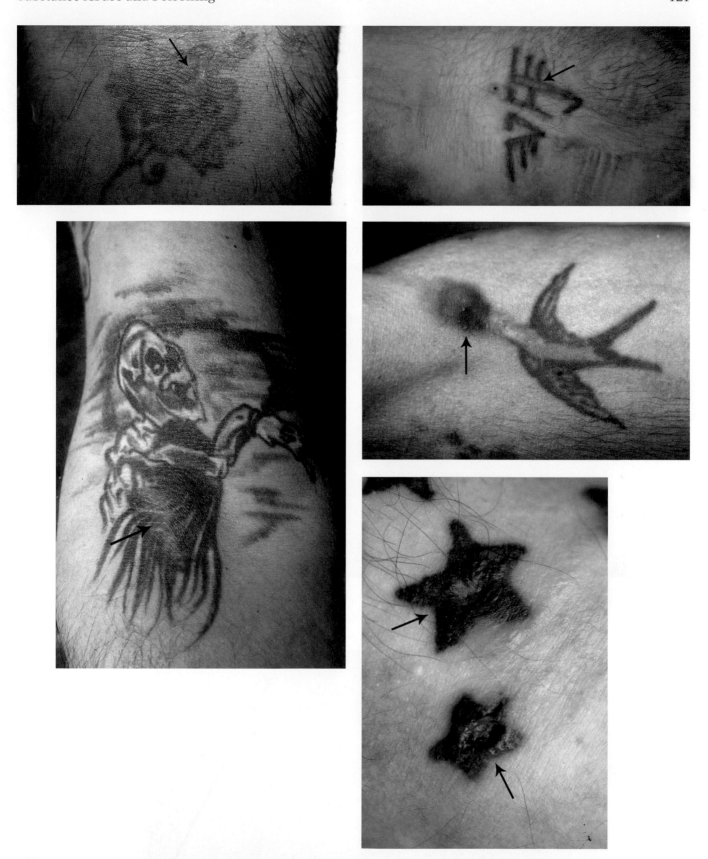

Figures 3.12–3.16 Tattoos are sometimes used to disguise intravenous drug abuse. The following are examples of track marks in tattoos. Note the fresh injection site at the tip of the bird beak and the healing injection sites at the stars as well as other chronic linear track marks.

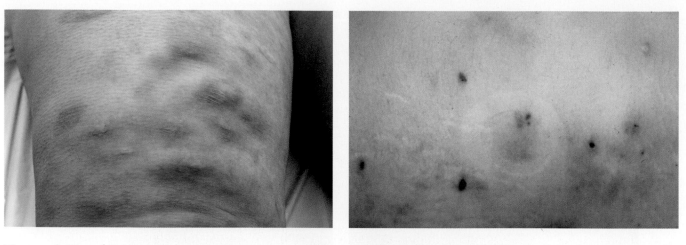

Figures 3.17 and 3.18 Fresh "skin popping" lesions. When the drug abuser exhausts peripheral vein access, they may start injecting drugs subcutaneously.

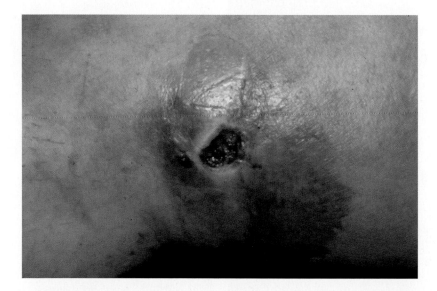

Figure 3.19 Recent healing-infected "skin popping" lesion with adjacent cellulites. It is common for these lesions to become infected due to the nonsterile nature of the injection.

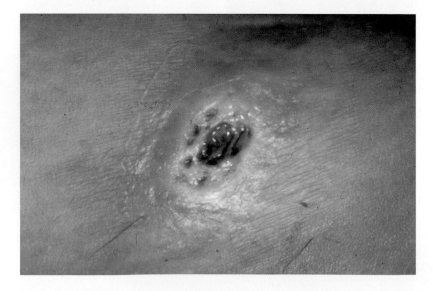

Figure 3.20 Recent healing-infected "skin popping" lesion.

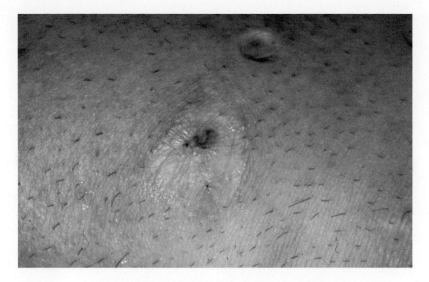

Figure 3.21 Healed and almost completely healed skin popping lesions. Note the lower wound has almost complete replacement by scar except for the central healing defect.

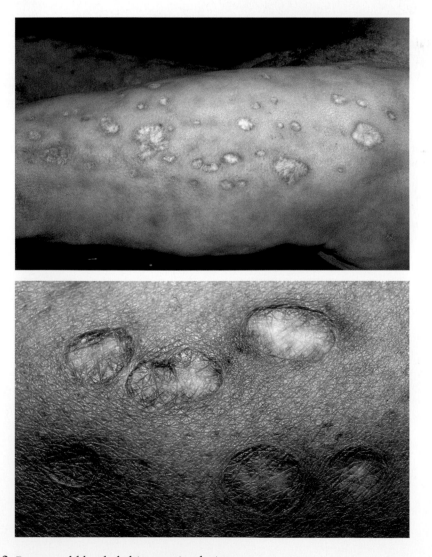

Figures 3.22 and 3.23 Remote old healed skin popping lesions.

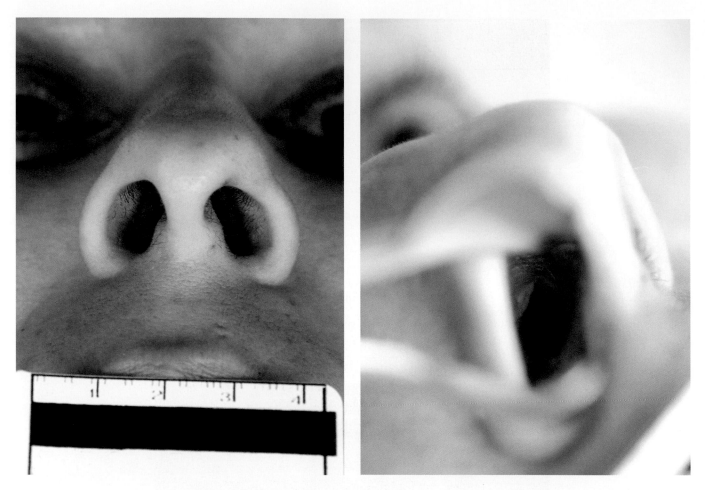

Figures 3.24 and 3.25 This individual died of acute cocaine intoxication. He had a history of using cocaine chronically on and off for years. Note the perforated nasal septum associated with chronic cocaine abuse due to vessel constriction and decreased blood flow.

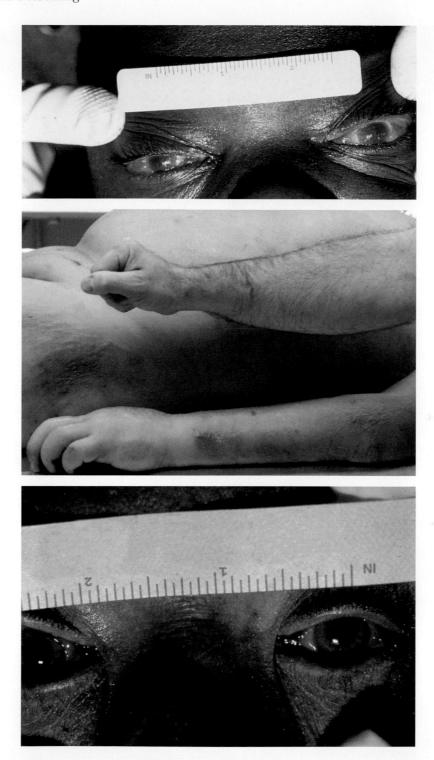

Figures 3.26–3.28 Examples of jaundice due to hepatic failure due to hepatic cirrhosis due to chronic alcoholism, and viral hepatitis due to chronic intravenous drug abuse. Note the yellow discoloration in the sclera and skin. Figure 3.27 demonstrates a comparison to a nonjaundice individual. Also note the patchy areas of ecchymosis due to coagulopathy associated with the liver disease.

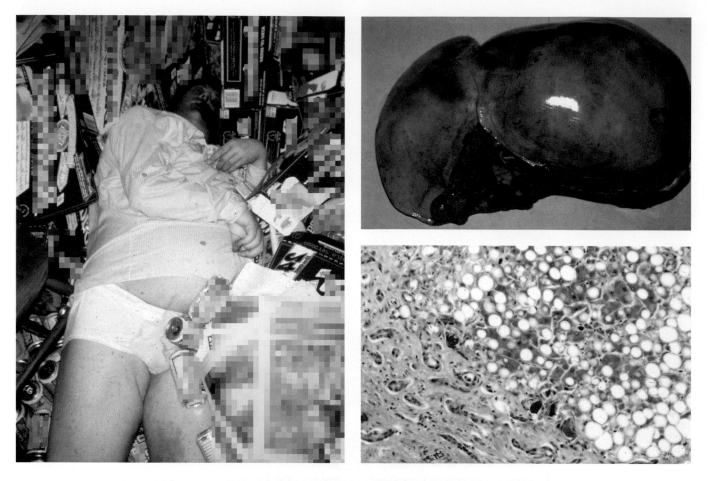

Figures 3.29–3.31 Marked hepatic steatosis due to acute alcoholism.

Figure 3.32 This image demonstrates cut portions of liver. Normal liver is brown. The yellow section demonstrates marked steatosis or fatty liver. The green section demonstrates micronodular cirrhosis due to chronic alcoholism with inspissated bile. The bile imparts this green discoloration.

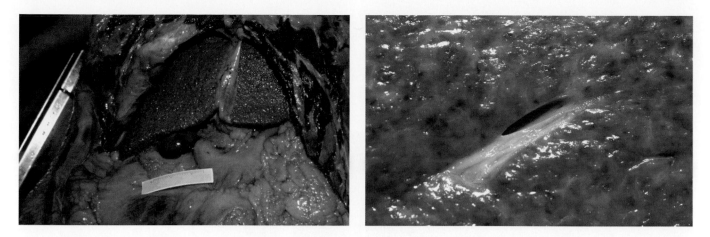

Figures 3.33 and 3.34 Micronodular hepatic cirrhosis with steatosis due to chronic alcoholism.

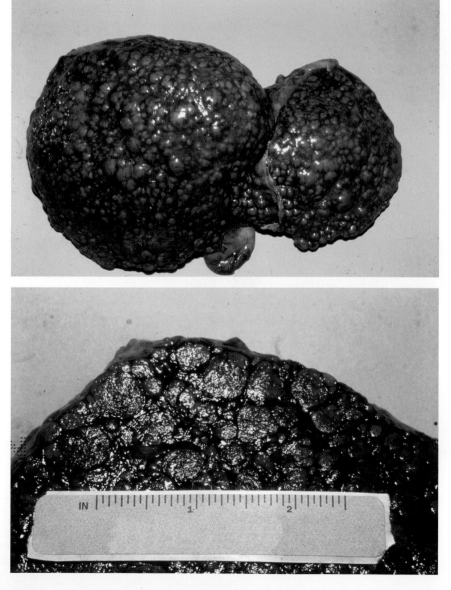

Figures 3.35 and 3.36 Macronodular hepatic cirrhosis due to hepatitis B infection due to chronic intravenous drug abuse.

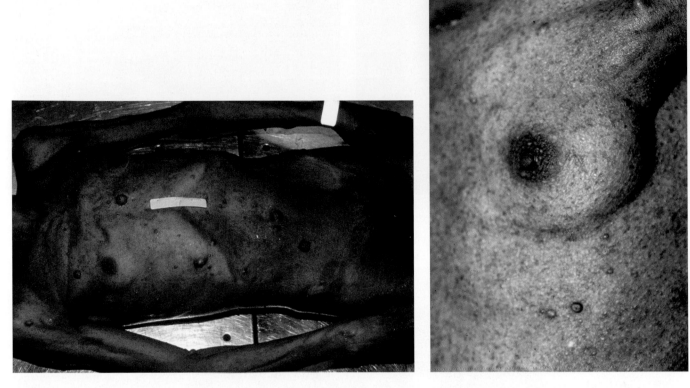

Figures 3.37 and 3.38 Chronic alcoholic with hepatic cirrhosis and gynecomastia. This individual also had neurofibromatosis, which is demonstrated by the multiple subcutaneous nodules.

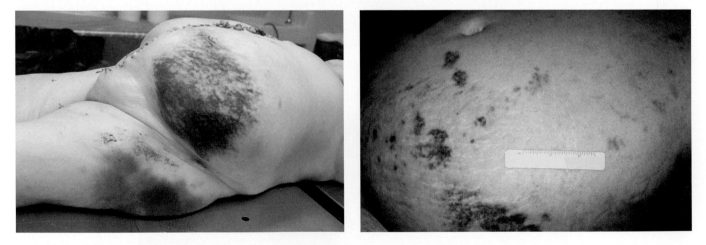

Figures 3.39 and 3.40 Chronic alcoholic with hepatic cirrhosis and coagulopathy. Note the multiple areas of ecchymosis and contusion caused by minimal blunt force trauma.

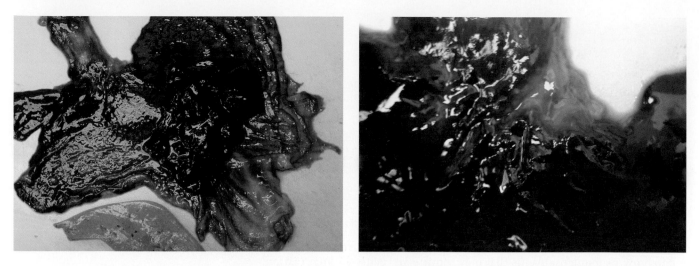

Figures 3.41 and 3.42 Gastrointestinal hemorrhage due to Mallory–Weiss tears in a chronic alcoholic. Note the laceration of the gastro-esophageal junction leading to death from gastrointestinal hemorrhage following multiple episodes of vomiting.

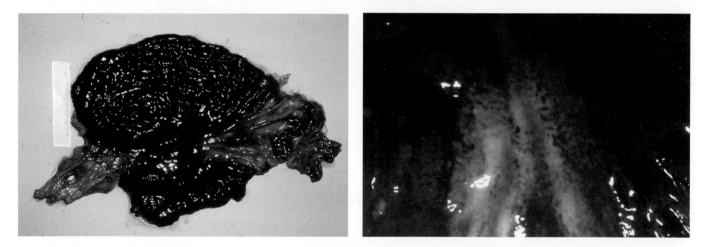

Figures 3.43 and 3.44 Acute gastritis associated with chronic alcoholism. Note the red discoloration of the mucosa.

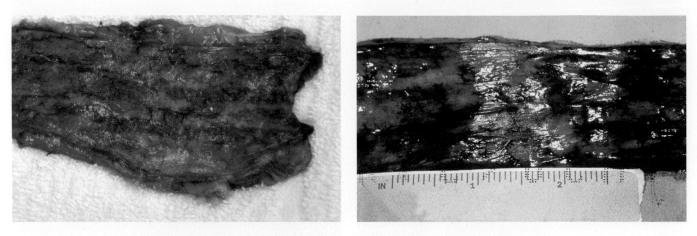

Figure 3.45 and 3.46 Esophageal varices due to hepatic cirrhosis and increased portal hypertension. Note the dialated red to brown submucosal veins that may rupture and cause exsanguination.

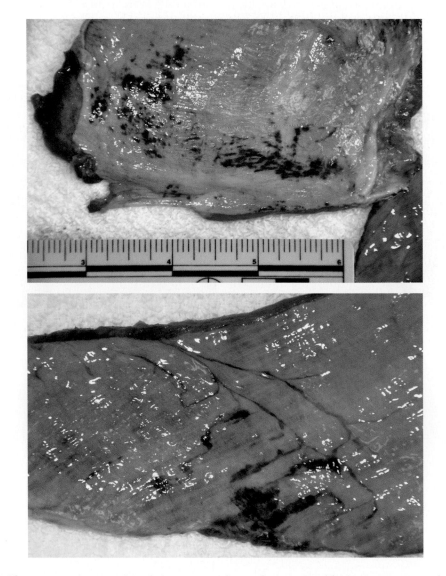

Figures 3.47 and 3.48 Varices associated with hepatic cirrhosis due to portal hypertension may be found on the undersurface of the diaphragm. These demonstrate ruptured diaphragmatic varices with hemoperitoneum. In such cases the source of bleeding may be difficult to ascertain.

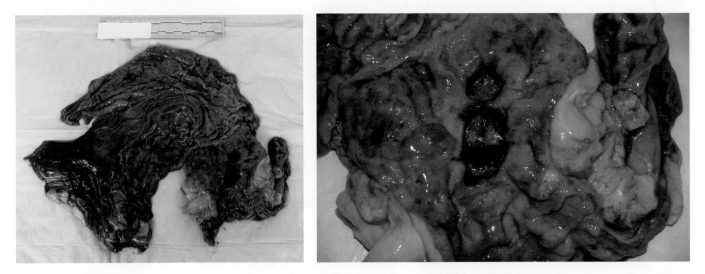

Figures 3.49 and 3.50 Bleeding peptic ulcers in a chronic alcoholic with gastrointestinal hemorrhage and hepatic cirrhosis.

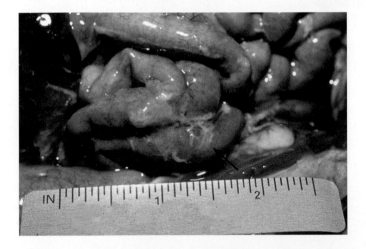

Figure 3.51 Acute peritonitis in a chronic alcoholic. Note the purulent exudate at the intestinal surface.

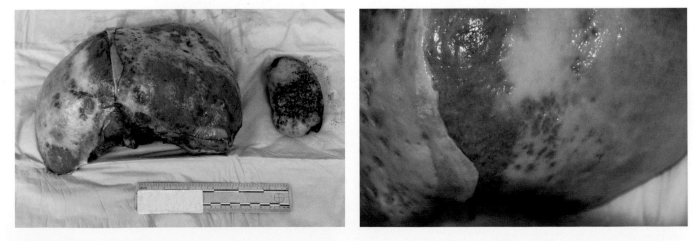

Figures 3.52 and 3.53 Hyaloserositis. Old healed peritonitis with fibrosis at the surface of the liver and spleen in a chronic alcoholic.

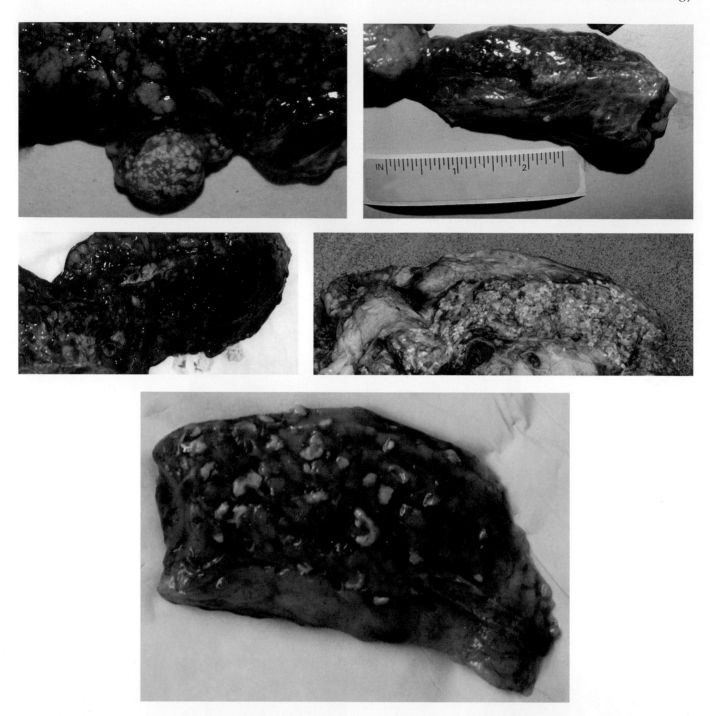

Figures 3.54–3.58 Acute pancreatitis due to chronic alcoholism. Note the white flecks due to fat necrosis and areas of hemorrhage.

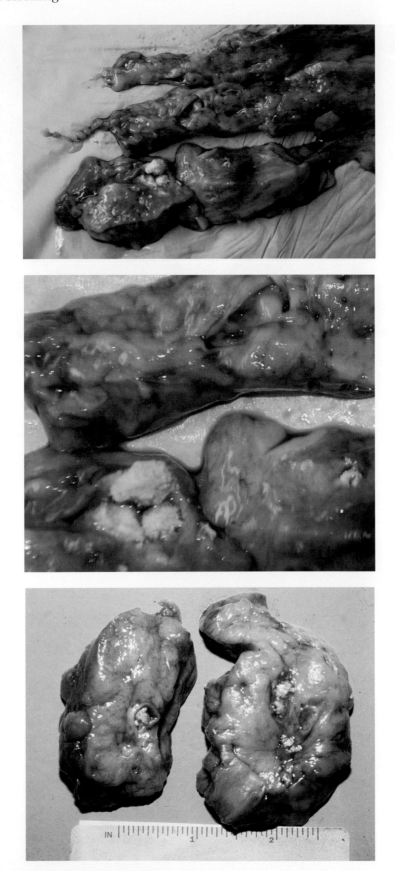

Figures 3.59–3.61 Chronic pancreatitis due to chronic alcoholism with ductal concretions. Note the loss of lobulated parenchyma with extensive fibrosis in Figures 3.59 and 3.60. In Figure 3.61, note the fatty metamorphosis or atrophy of the pancreas.

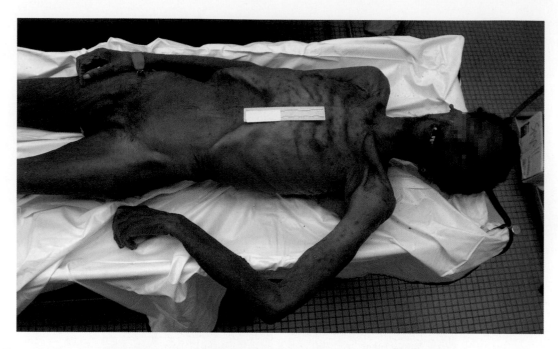

Figure 3.62 Cachexia with patchy alopecia and multiple areas of skin discoloration due to acquired immunodeficiency syndrome (AIDS) from chronic intravenous drug abuse.

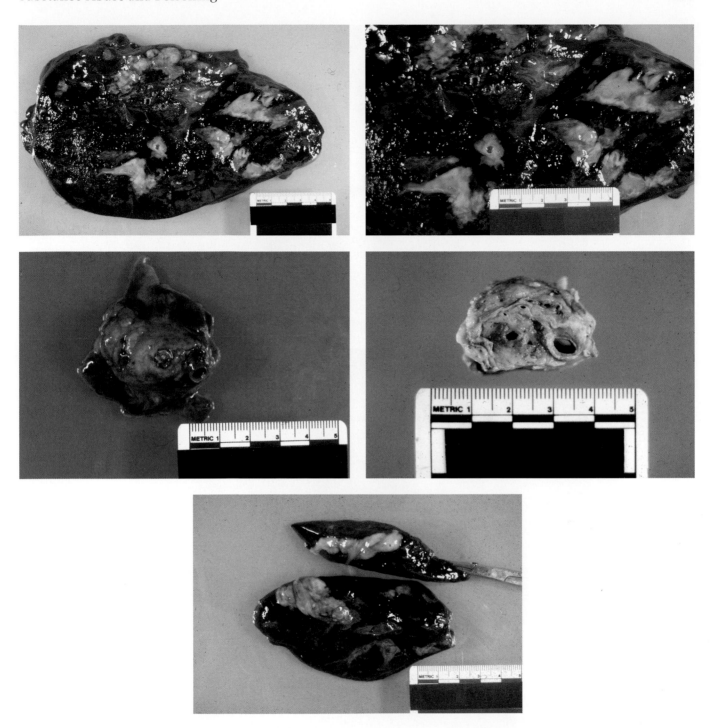

Figures 3.63–3.67 Pyogenic liver abscesses. This decedent had a history of chronic alcoholism with chronic pancre-atitis and recent abdominal pain of unknown etiology. This photo depicts multiple geographic, creamy yellow-white collections of purulent material within the liver parenchyma that microscopically proved to be dense collections of neutrophils, karyorrhectic nuclear debris, and masses of faintly basophilic, fine filamentous bacteria. Samples of the abscesses were submitted to the microbiology laboratory but the best that they could do was anaerobic Gram-negative rods. Candidates included *Bacteroides*, *Prevotella*, and *Fusobacterium*. Actinomyces would have been a consideration but they are Gram positive. Pyogenic liver abscesses, while relatively rare, are known complications of chronic alcoholism and pancreatitis.

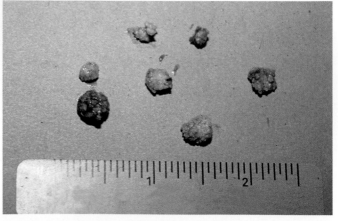

Figures 3.68–3.71 Suicidal overdoses demonstrating intact and fragmented granular pieces of partially digested pills. Note the containers with the granular white flecks at the bottom demonstrating pill fragments.

Figures 3.72–3.74 Suicidal overdose due to pill ingestion. Note the multiple white fragments of medication (Figure 3.72), partially digested pills (Figure 3.73), and the thick paste from a partially digested aggregate of multiple pills (Figure 3.74).

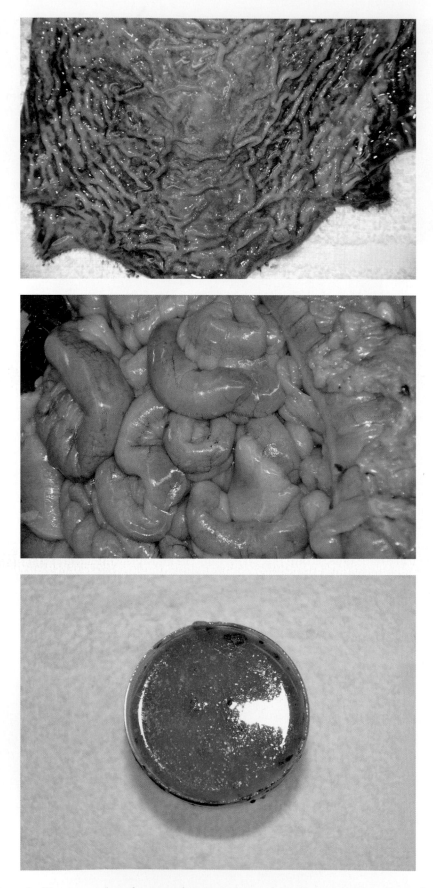

Figure 3.75–3.77 Note the blue green discoloration due to pigments from the coating on the surface of multiple ingested pills.

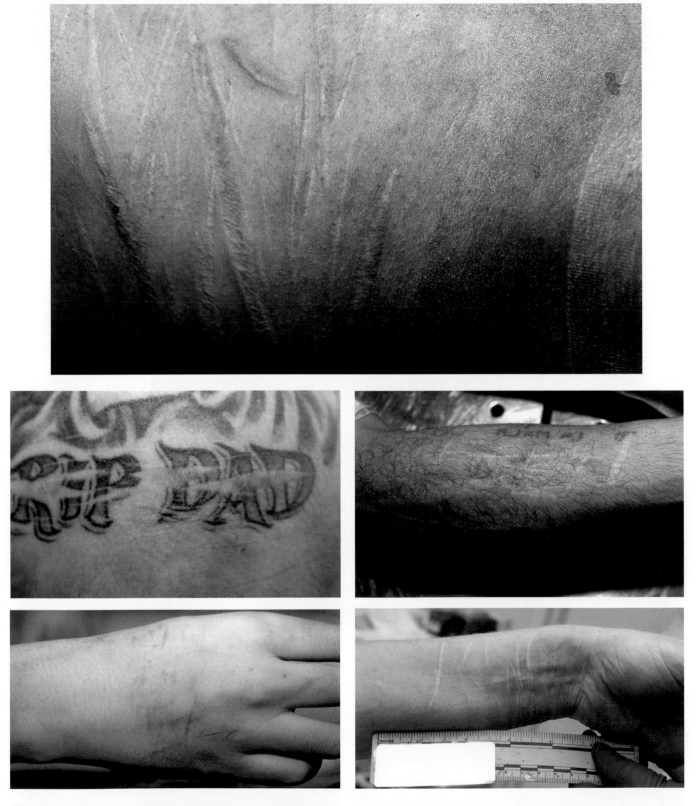

Figures 3.78–3.82 Note the multiple scars demonstrating destructive behavior associated with drug abuse, mental illness, and suicide.

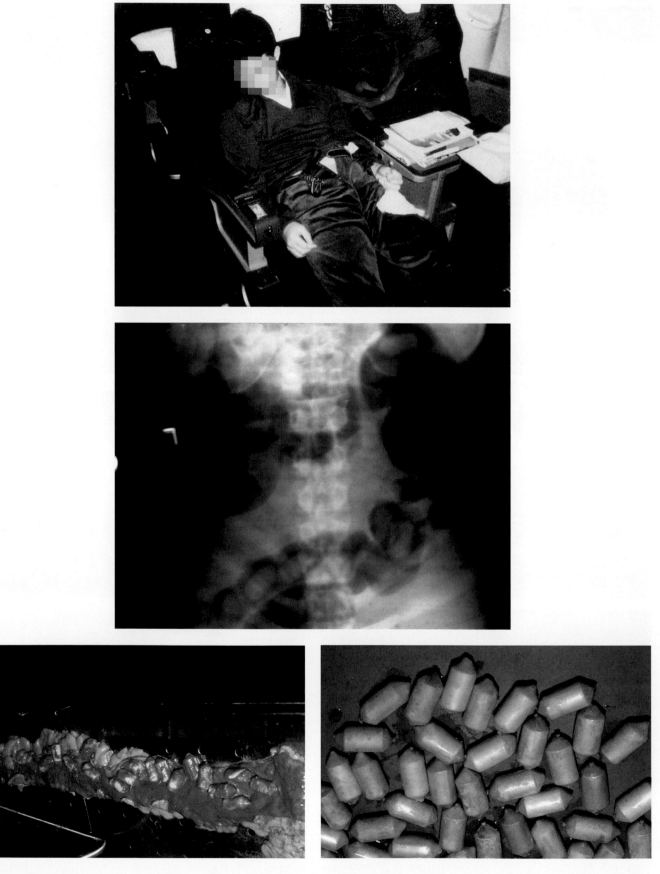

Figures 3.83–3.86 Acting as a "mule," this person ingested multiple packets of drugs to smuggle them into the country. One of the packets ruptured and the individual died of a drug overdose before the plane landed. Note the typical x-ray findings demonstrating these packets within the GI tract.

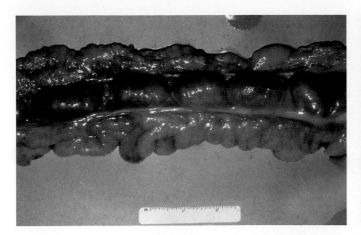
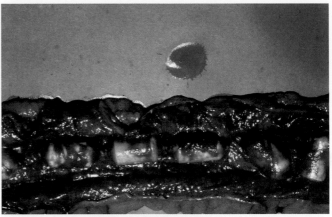
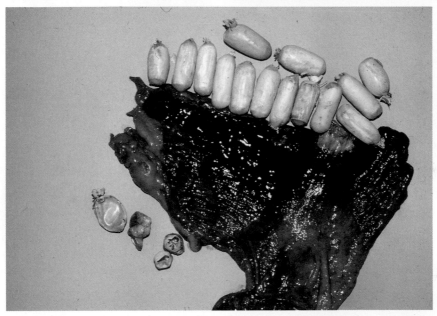

Figures 3.87–3.89 Packets of drugs discovered at autopsy in individuals who died in hotels next to an airport. Note the broken packets demonstrated at the bottom of Figure 3.89.

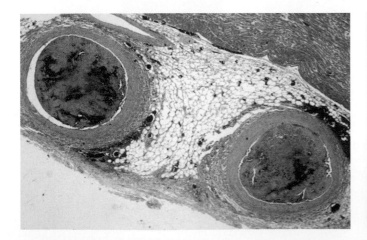
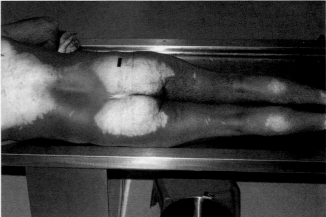

Figure 3.90 Epicardial vessels with slight atherosclerosis and occluding thrombosis associated with acute cocaine intoxication.

Figure 3.91 Carbon monoxide poisoning with cherry red lividity. Cherry red lividity usually becomes apparent in light-skinned individuals when carbon monoxide levels reach 30%–35%. His level was 68%.

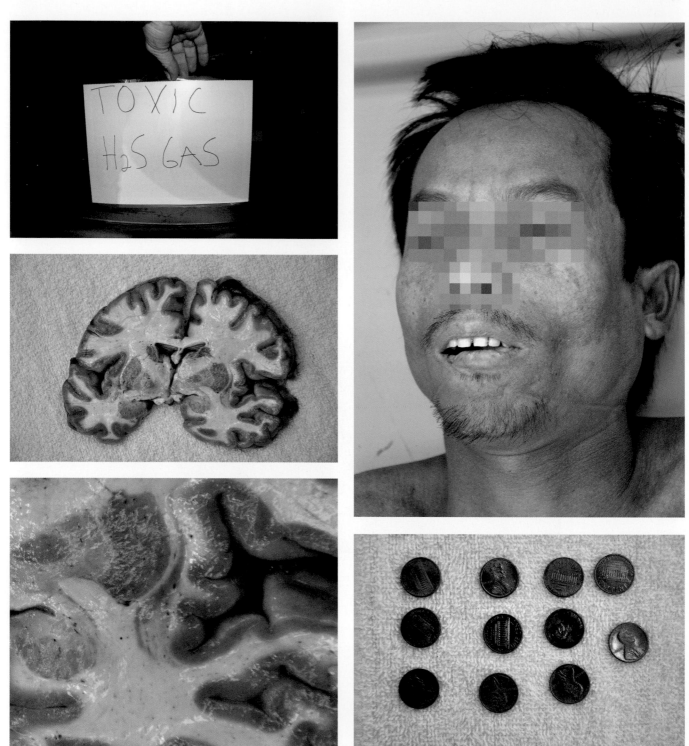

Figures 3.92–3.96 Hydrogen sulfide gas poisoning in a suicide case where an individual mixed various cleaning solvents within his closed locked car and placed a warning note in the window to protect our rescue workers. Hazmat team was called and the environment was deemed safe before medical investigations and scene evaluation ensued. Note the green discoloration of the skin and brain with oxidation of coins.

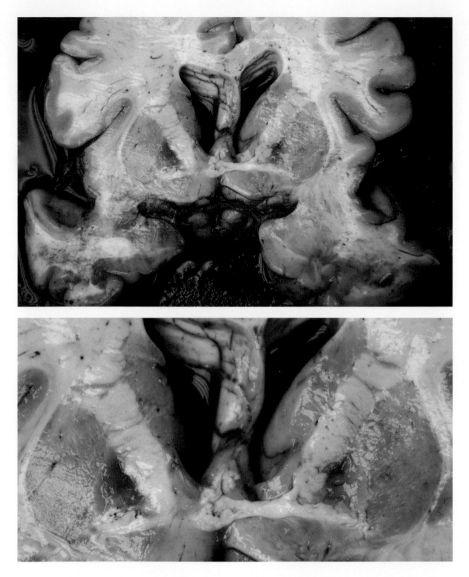

Figures 3.97 and 3.98 Necrosis of globus pallidus. This may be seen in an individual who survives after poisoning or intoxication from carbon monoxide, methanol, cocaine, opiates, and cyanide.

Postmortem Change and Time of Death

4

CHARLES A. CATANESE, BRUCE LEVY,
AND GERARD CATANESE

Contents

Introduction

In most jurisdictions the time of death is legally defined as the time that the person is declared or recognized to be dead. Thus, a decomposed body or skeletonized remains, clearly deceased for significant periods of time, may have an official time of death that is days, weeks, months, or even years after the actual death occurred. However, being able to estimate the actual time of death (or the postmortem interval) can be critically important in criminal investigations, civil litigation, or settlement of the deceased's estate.

It is important to realize interpreting postmortem change is not an exact science, as some TV shows lead you to believe. The concept of a "window of death," approximation of when the actual death occurred, was developed to help answer these questions. This window can be initially bracketed by the time that the person was last known to be alive and the time he or she was declared dead. Forensic science can then apply a variety of observations and tests in an attempt to narrow that window as much as is scientifically and medically possible. Accurate interpretation of postmortem change is crucial in helping to establish the actual time of death.

Postmortem changes can be subdivided into several categories. These categories include early moderate and advanced postmortem changes during which autolysis and putrefaction are ongoing. Each has characteristics that can overlap with advancing time and are variable depending on environmental conditions and the physiologic state of the body at the time of death. The activity of insects and animals will also create artifacts that can lead to misinterpretation of the postmortem interval. Interpreting postmortem changes is not an exact science, and without a witness, one can only estimate a time period in which the death was most likely to have occurred.

Early Postmortem Changes

Generally considered to occur or evolve within the initial 24 hours after death, these consist of algor mortis, livor mortis, and rigor mortis.

Algor Mortis

Algor mortis is the cooling of the body after death. After death the body will gradually cool until it equilibrates with the ambient temperature. Under standard climate-controlled conditions, with average humidity and a room temperature of about 72°F, the body generally loses about 2°F per hour for the first 12 hours and then approximately 1°F per hour for the next 12–18 hours. If the ambient temperature is greater than the body temperature, algor mortis occurs in reverse and the body temperature rises until it reaches the ambient temperature.

The above calculations apply only at or near room temperature and will become variable as the ambient temperature changes. As a general rule, the rate of temperature change in a body is proportional to the difference between the temperature of the body and its environment. In other words, if the ambient temperature is below 72°F, the rate of heat loss will be increased from the numbers above. The reverse would be true for temperatures greater than 72°F. Moving air will cool faster than still air, and wet bodies will cool faster than dry bodies. Bodies found in stagnant water, flowing water, or those found buried in the ground will cool at different rates from those in the air and from each other. When the body and environment are at the same temperature, they have reached steady state and estimates of time of death based on temperature are limited to a minimum period of time.

Many other variables can influence algor mortis. In general, an elevated body temperature at the time of death will give the appearance of a shorter postmortem interval based on a measurement of the body temperature. A lower body temperature will have the reverse effect. Things that affect body temperature include infection, strokes, seizures, thyroid disease, and many other natural diseases. Whether or not the person was involved in strenuous physical activity prior to death (such as a violent struggle) will increase body temperature. Many other factors, including the age of the person, his or her overall health, and many drugs or medications, can also have an effect on the calculation of postmortem interval based on this and other observations.

It is important to make certain there is consistency in how the body temperature is obtained. First, these calculations are based on a core body temperature, meaning either taking a rectal temperature or, more ideally, introducing a thermometer into the abdominal cavity beneath the liver to measure core temperature. Temperature readings on the surface of the body, including axillary, oral, or ear temperature, are unacceptable for determining a postmortem interval. The thermometer must be kept in place long enough for the body temperature to equilibrate.

Livor Mortis

Livor mortis is the settling of blood under the effects of gravity after death. It can first be appreciated as early as 20 minutes after death in very light-skinned individuals. The color of the livor will deepen to a purple color over the first 8–12 hours after death. During this period the livor is typically blanching, meaning that pressure on an area of livor will cause the color to briefly leave the area, resulting in a pale mark. After about 12 hours the livor will become fixed and no longer blanch under pressure. As with algor mortis, temperature will influence the rate

at which livor becomes fixed, with increased temperatures shortening the time for livor to become fixed and decreased temperatures lengthening the fixation time. In some cases, livor mortis advances to cause small visible hemorrhages in the skin known as Tardieu spots, which should be distinguished from petechiae.

The medical condition of the person and the cause of the death can also create changes in livor mortis. People who are anemic (low blood count) or sustain an injury resulting in significant loss of blood might have very faint or even absent livor mortis. It can also be difficult to appreciate livor in dark-skinned individuals. Also physiologic conditions such as congestive heart failure can lead to earlier formation due to significant decreased circulation in conjunction with gravity.

When evaluating livor mortis, it is important to note its location, intensity, whether it is blanching or fixed, and whether it is appropriate for the position of the body. If livor is inappropriate for position, you can conclude that the person was moved at some point after the onset of livor. You can also evaluate livor for its color. For example, people who die as a result of carbon monoxide or cyanide poisoning will have a bright "cherry red" color to their livor mortis. People who die in a cold environment might also have a similar red color to their livor. Death due to hydrogen sulfide poisoning may be associated with slight green lividity.

Rigor Mortis

Rigor mortis is the stiffening of the body after death. It is the result of a physiochemical process within the muscles of the body that does not cause actual contraction of the muscles but rather the muscles retains the position they were in before. Muscles need a constant supply of ATP to stay relaxed, and after death, metabolism ceases, ATP stores are depleted, and the muscle remains in a fixed state. Under standard conditions, rigor will first be appreciated within 30 minutes to 2 hours after death. It will progress to a maximum intensity over the first 12 hours and remain at a maximum until about 24 hours after death. It will then "pass" from the body between 24 and 36 hours after death, after which the body will remain flaccid.

As with algor mortis and livor mortis, many variables will affect the rate of development and passing of rigor mortis. In general, increased environmental or body temperatures will speed the rate of development and passing of rigor mortis. Lower environmental or body temperatures will have the reverse effect. Also, the physiologic state of the body can affect the rate of formation such as strenuous activity, prior to death, where ATP stores are depleted, for instance, static epilepticus. People at the extremes of age (children and the elderly) will have different rates of appreciation of rigor mortis due to the decreased muscle mass in these age groups.

When evaluating rigor mortis, it is important to note its location and intensity and whether it is appropriate for the position of the body. Rigor mortis may be described as slight, moderate, and full. Slight rigor mortis may occur in the early phases of formation or during the late phases of passing through. Rigor mortis can be mechanically broken by pulling the muscle apart. Before rigor mortis becomes fully formed, it may be broken and then continue to form in another position. In accurately assessing rigor mortis one must take into account the individual's muscle mass. Full rigor mortis in a muscular person will be harder to break than full rigor mortis in a thin nonmuscular person. If rigor is inappropriate for position, you can conclude that the person was moved at some point after the onset of rigor.

Decomposition

As time advances, decomposition gradually increases. This category includes autolysis, putrefaction, and mummification. While they can be seen in isolation, careful observation will typically reveal features of all simultaneously.

Putrefaction

Decomposition occurs predominately due to the actions of bacteria and may include other microorganisms. The bacteria typically break down the body from the inside out, causing many of the changes we associate with a person who has been deceased for a longer period of time. However, when there is penetrating trauma that breaks the surface of the body, bacteria from the environment can gain access and hasten putrefaction. These changes include darkening and slipping of the skin, the production of a foul-smelling gas, with bloating of the body and marbling of blood vessels. A dark-colored bloody-appearing purge fluid will come from the nose and mouth and should not be confused with blood related to trauma.

This process is extremely environmentally dependent. As with the early postmortem changes, warmer temperatures accelerate this process and cooler temperatures slow it down, with many of the same factors playing a role. A body placed in a dark dumpster in the hot summer sun for half a day can reach a state of putrefaction equivalent to a body left at room temperature for several days or one in the winter cold for greater than a week. In the case of fire fatalities, charring and smoke will preserve the body and decelerate this process. A frozen body that has thawed will putrefy at a markedly accelerated rate due to spaces left by frozen ice crystals.

Mummification

After death, dehydration will occur as water seeps out and evaporates. One should note that organ weights gradually decrease as the postmortem interval increases and will not reflect their actual weight during life in cases in moderate to advanced decomposition. Mummification occurs in a dry environment, typically such dry outside environments as a desert, or in heated indoor environments during the winter months when the relative humidity is low. Initially, there is a darkening and hardening of the skin. This will progress to produce flaking of the skin surface that can give extremities the appearance of a log, thus the term "tree barking." As with putrefaction, the skin will begin to disintegrate and eventually the skin and soft tissues are also lost.

Skeletonization

Both putrefaction and mummification eventually lead to skeletonization of the body. The loss of soft tissue progresses at a variable rate, depending on the environmental conditions and access of the body to a variety of animals and insects. The face and ends of the extremities are the first areas where bone is exposed, and the pelvic soft tissues are the last to be lost. While this process is usually measured in months, work performed at the Anthropologic Research Facility at the University of Tennessee in Knoxville has demonstrated that complete skeletonization of a person can occur within days under appropriate conditions.

Autolysis

Autolysis associated with decomposition occurs after cell death and is due to the actions of digestive and catalytic enzymes released from cells in the body. This term, "self-destruction," is advanced in certain organs, especially the intestinal tract and pancreas, due to their rich enzyme content. This is important to note because autolysis can mimic certain disease processes at the time of gross examination. Maceration of stillborns who were dead inside a uterus for days is a type of autolysis associated with moist sterile environments, appearing as a red discoloration with skin slippage, and is not to be confused with trauma or disease. Gastromalacia is associated with decomposition and is characterized by the stomach mucosa turning red and the loss of rugal folds. This may be misinterpreted for gastritis.

Adipocere

Adipocere is a process that is rarely seen outside of exhumation cases. It is a chemical change that occurs in the fatty tissues of the body exposed to wet conditions. Adipocere takes many months to develop, and once it forms, it is extremely persistent, stopping the typical loss of soft tissue and skeletonization of the body.

Other Factors in Evaluating Postmortem Interval

When a deceased body has been exposed to insect or animal activity, we can make observations that might assist in the determination of the postmortem interval. Maggots (the larval stage of blowflies) can be collected from the body and examined by an entomologist. You need to collect two sets of specimens. One set should be kept alive, while the other set is killed. The entomologist will determine the exact species of fly from the matured living specimens and the likely time of death from the killed specimens. In persons who have been deceased for a prolonged period of time (months to years), an evaluation of the type and age of plants growing up through the body might also provide useful information.

Examination of the stomach and intestinal contents can also provide clues to help us in the determination of time of death. Our bodies digest food at a fairly predictable rate, depending on the quantity and types of foods consumed. Higher caloric content foods, such as fats, are digested slower than less complex foods. Larger meals remain in the stomach for a longer period of time. The rate of stomach emptying can be accelerated or slowed by natural disease, drugs, alcohol, or emotional stress. The description of the quantity, type, and condition of food in the stomach is part of the routine autopsy. This can be combined with information about that person's recent consumption of food obtained during the investigation to estimate the time from the eating of that meal until the time of death. Even without information about the last meal consumed, the stomach contents might provide clues as to when death occurred based on the types of food in the stomach. It should also be noted that brain death prior to body death may significantly delay gastric emptying time.

Finally, markers found at the scene of death might provide the best information regarding the date or time of death of the individual. Observations regarding uncollected mail or newspapers, information from the telephone company about the last time the phone was used, dated sales receipts, or a noted change in habitual behavior might assist with determining the date of death. The clothing the person is wearing or the status of lighting in the home might provide clues regarding the time of the day or night that death occurred.

In conclusion, determining the postmortem interval can be challenging. Start with a broad window of death (last-known-alive to found-dead). Then use as many of the above elements as are available to attempt to narrow that window as much as possible. It is important to remember that there is variability of these observations and calculations, so keep an open mind and be willing to reevaluate your opinion based on new information as it becomes available.

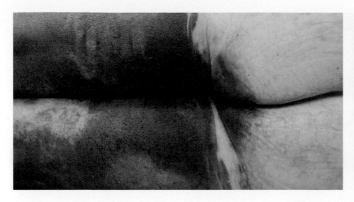
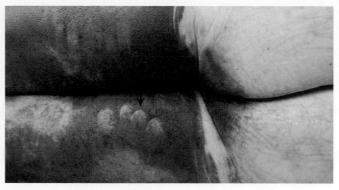

Figures 4.1 and 4.2 Blanching lividity. Note the finger marks caused by pressing the blood away from the skin surface at the posteromedial aspect of the right thigh. It is also good practice to document the amount of pressure necessary to cause blanching, such as slight, moderate, and marked.

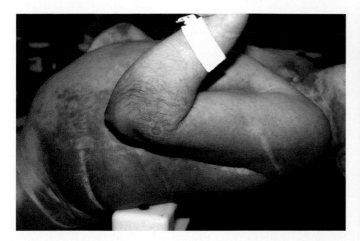
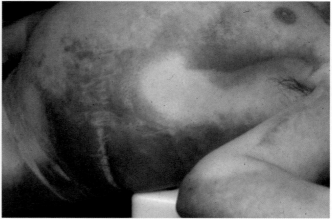

Figures 4.3 and 4.4 Fixed lividity at the left lateral and posterior torso. Note the absence of lividity under the arm due to the original position the body was found. The body was discovered lying on its left side. The body was stored on its back in a cold refrigerator for many hours prior to being autopsied and the lividity did not redistribute.

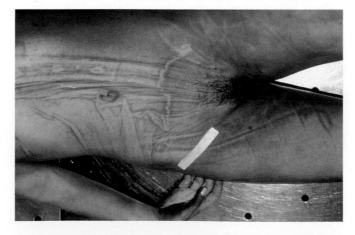

Figure 4.5 This individual was placed in the morgue on her back the day before examination. Note the fixed anterior lividity partial sparing over with pressure points caused by laying on a wrinkled bed spread. Also note the early putrefactive consisting of slight green discoloration of the lower right abdomen.

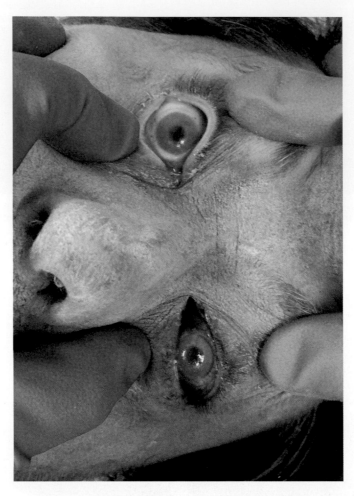

Figure 4.6 Note the red injected appearance of the left eye due to fixed lividity in this individual that was found lying on his left side. Note that the funeral home makeup partially obscures the lividity on the left side of the face. It is always important to clean the surface of the body during external examinations; such makeup can hide injuries as well.

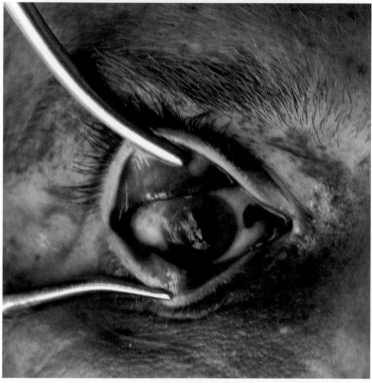

Figures 4.7 and 4.8 Postmortem eye hemorrhages due to the body initially lying in a prone position with anterior partially fixed lividity. Note the inconsistent rigor mortis indicating the body had been moved. These hemorrhages would not happen to a body lying in a supine position. That is another reason why it is always important to make certain that the body is transported and stored under refrigeration while in a supine position. Refer to Figures 10.74–10.76.

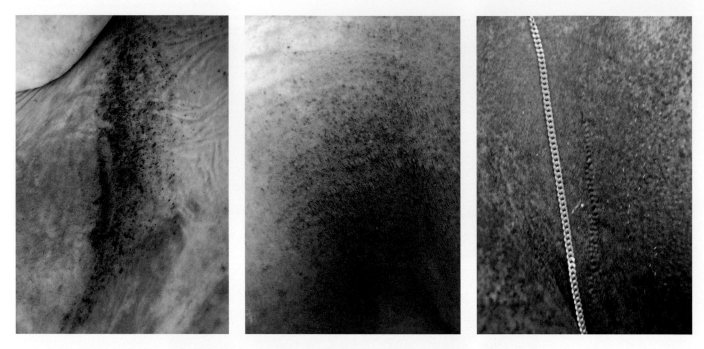

Figures 4.9–4.11 Marked fixed lividity with dark purple spots known as "tardieu spots." Also note the vague chain pattern. It is not unusual for objects such as this to leave postmortem imprints.

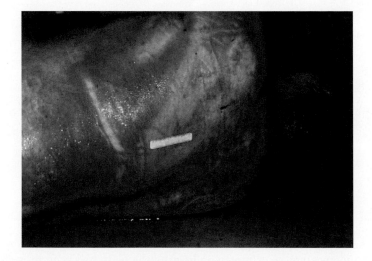

Figure 4.12 In carbon monoxide poisoning, the color of the livor mortis is more of a bright red color instead of the typical red/purple color. This color change can also be seen in cases of cyanide poisoning or in bodies that are stored in cold environments. Note the color differences are very subtle and it may not be possible to make a determination from visual inspection alone. It may become more obvious during the autopsy process, where blood is observed to have a brighter, shinier characteristic over internal structures such as adipose tissue.

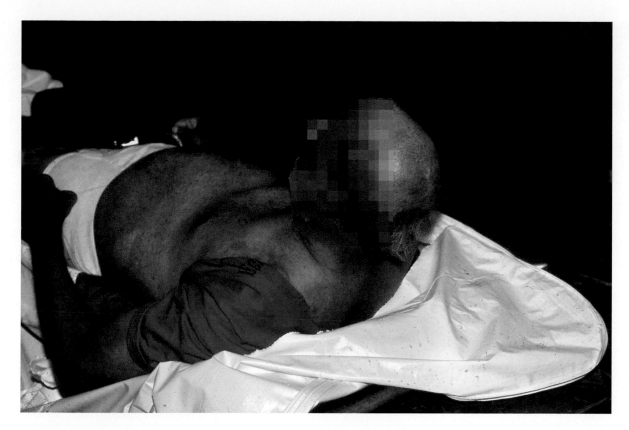

Figure 4.13 The decedent was found lying on his back with his head elevated under several pillows. He was in full rigor mortis at the scene and maintained this position through his arrival into the morgue and later flattened out. This position may be associated with disease processes such as alkalizing spondylosis.

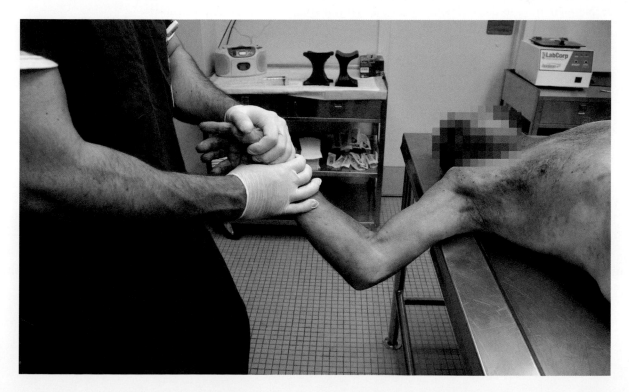

Figure 4.14 Full rigor mortis. Note the morgue technician pulling tightly on this decedent's arm that is stuck in a bent position.

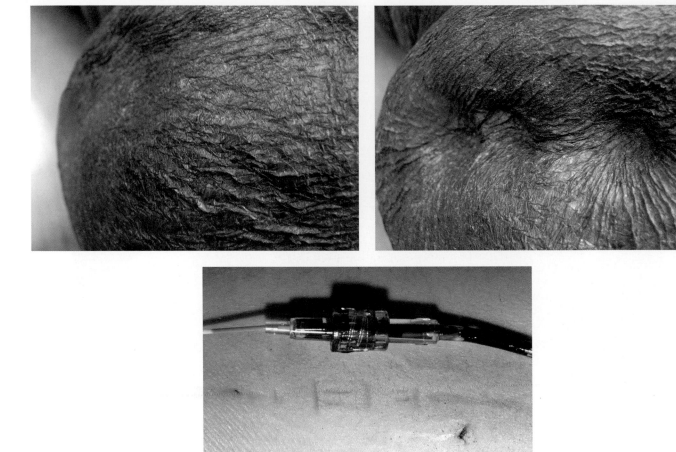

Figures 4.15–4.17 "Congealing of fat." Adipose tissue at very cold temperatures may demonstrate increased viscosity. This may be mistaken for poor skin elasticity due to dehydration. Dehydration may or may not be present with congealing of fat. Note Figure 4.16 has retained indentations following pressure exerted by fingers.

Figure 4.18 Refrigeration overnight with the decedent lying on this piece of rope demonstrates the absence of lividity over pressure points with congealing of fat demonstrating the rope imprint.

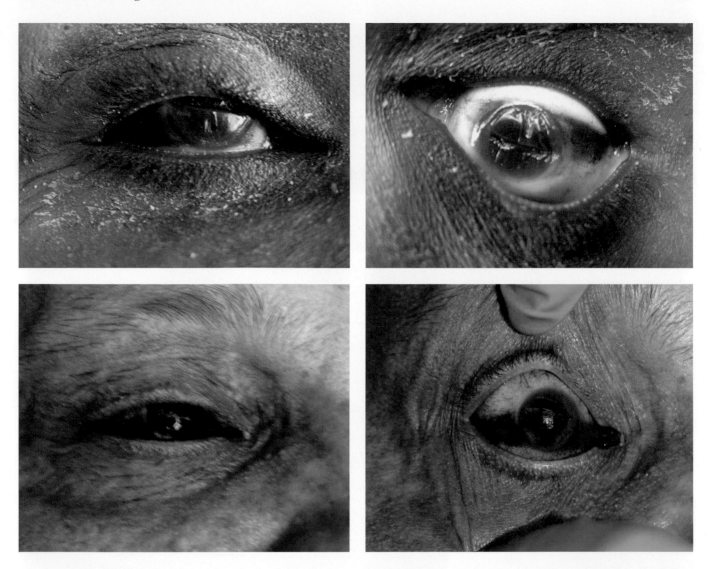

Figures 4.19–4.22 These are examples of "tache noire," which means "black line," a dark discoloration of a portion of sclera caused by drying from exposure to air. This is usually brown to red and formation may take minutes or longer depending on the humidity and other environmental factors. This postmortem change may be misinterpreted as hemorrhage associated with strangulation.

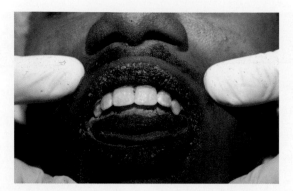

Figure 4.23 This is drying of the lips and tongue with dark discoloration due to postmortem change. This is mummification associated with mucosal exposure to air. This may be misinterpreted as an antemortem finding resulting from ingestion of caustic substances. This individual committed suicide by hanging, which caused his tongue to stick out and become dry and dark.

Figures 4.24 and 4.25 Postmortem drying with dark discoloration of the scrotum and shaft of the penis. This may also be mistaken for an antemortem injury such as an abrasion or contusion. If there is doubt, one may make an incision to document underlying hemorrhage.

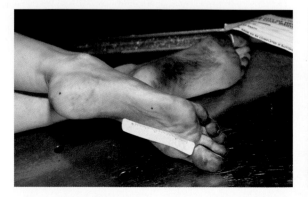

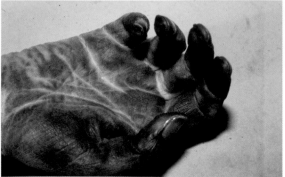

Figures 4.26 and 4.27 This is early mummification with drying of the hands and feet. Note the firm, dark discoloration of the fingers with wrinkling from dehydration. Portions of the body with larger surface areas with less underlying tissue mass will mummify more rapidly.

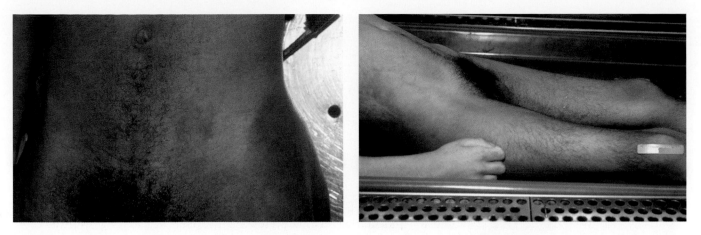

Figures 4.28 and 4.29 Early putrefactive change with green-brown discoloration of the lower abdomen. The first place for this to occur is typically the lower left abdomen above the cecal region, where bacteria from fecal material is closest to the abdominal wall.

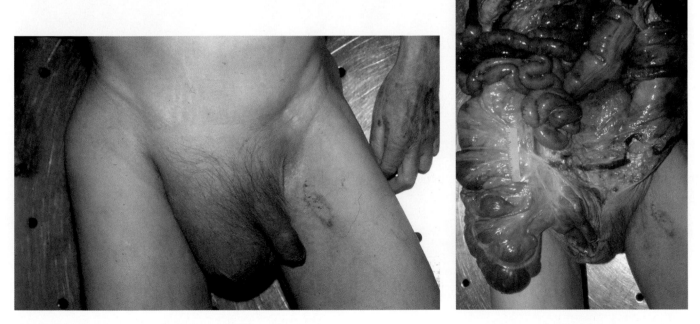

Figures 4.30 and 4.31 This large hernia demonstrates early decomposition with slight green discoloration of the scrotum due to a portion of the large intestine extending into the scrotal sac.

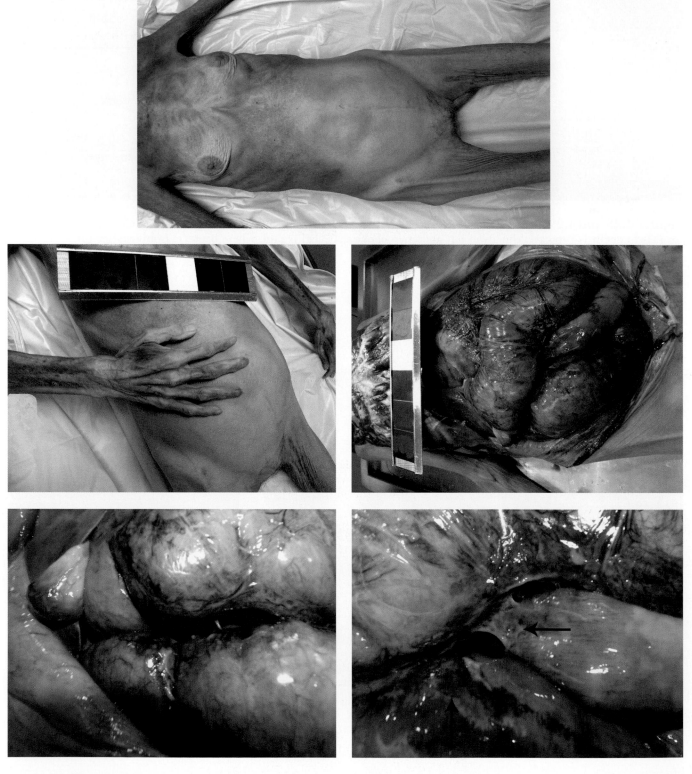

Figures 4.32–4.36 Disproportionate advancing putrefactive change of the abdomen due to acute peritonitis. Note the green discoloration of the abdomen and the absence of green discoloration elsewhere. The presence of infection with bacteria caused this regionally accelerated process. Note the purulent exudate at the intestine surface with areas of red discoloration.

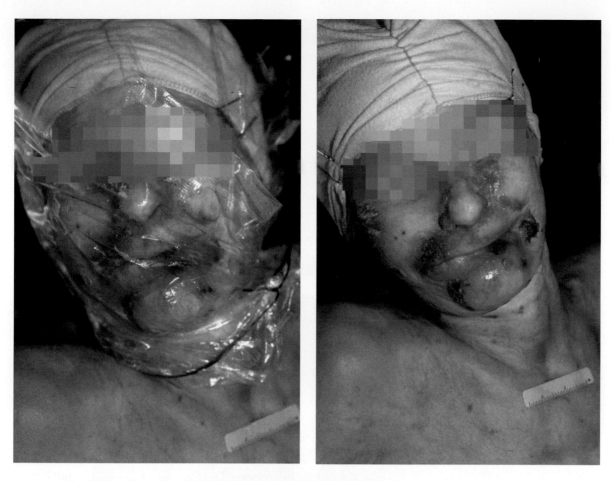

Figures 4.37 and 4.38 This individual committed suicide by ingesting excess prescription medication and placed a loose plastic bag over their head. The moisture collecting at the face covered by plastic during breathing helped to create an environment where mold and mildew could form at the chin and face.

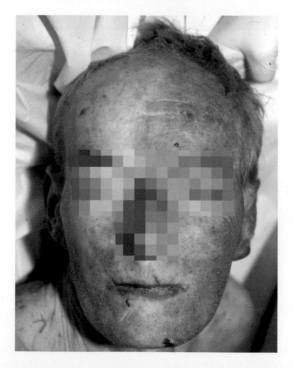

Figure 4.39 Postmortem hot water burns of the face in this individual who was found partially submerged in warm water of a bathtub. He suffered a cardiac event while taking a shower. It requires less heat to cause thermal damage to a dead body than to a living body.

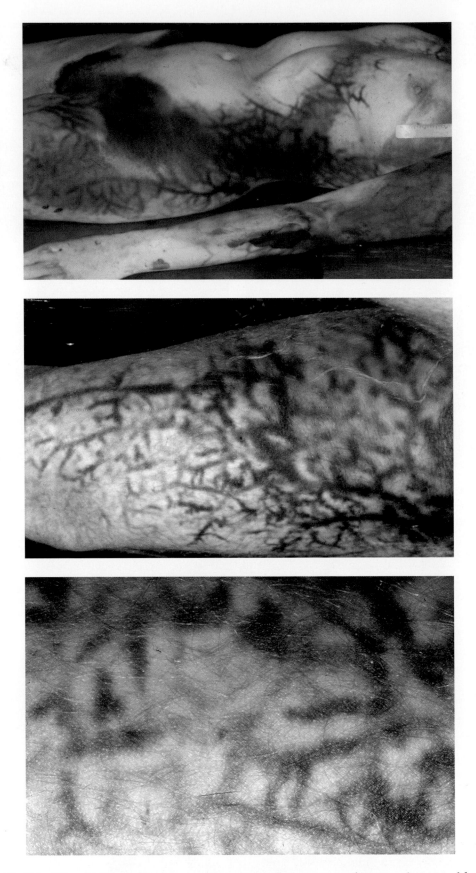

Figures 4.40–4.42 "Marbling." This early presentation of putrefaction is predominantly caused by bacteria tracking through the superficial blood vessels and causing pigment changes in blood and vessel walls as microorganisms digest the body.

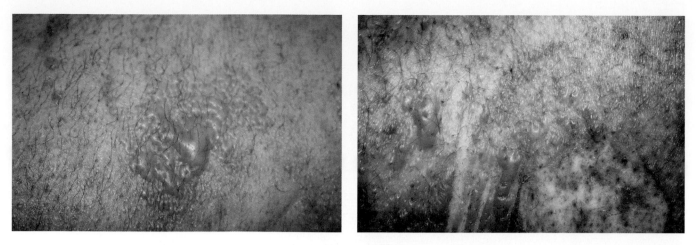

Figures 4.43 and 4.44 Early putrefactive change with yellow-clear fluid-filled blister formation. The rupture of these blisters would appear as skin slippage.

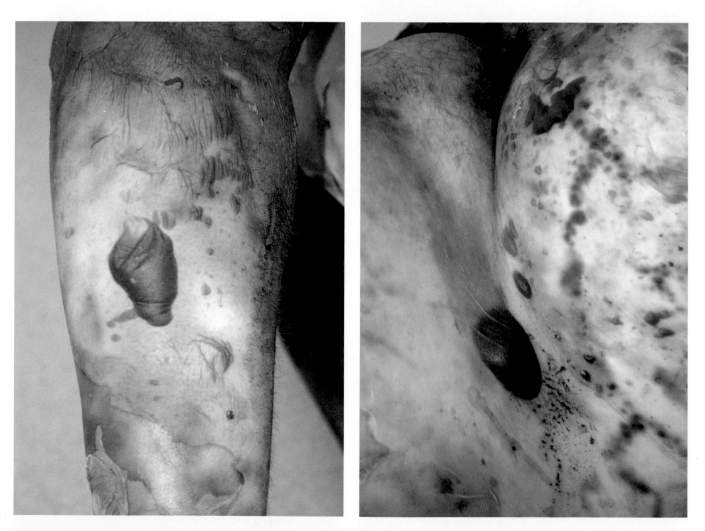

Figures 4.45 and 4.46 Early to moderate putrefactive change with green-brown fluid-filled blisters. Such blisters may be mistaken for second-degree thermal burns or aggressive antemortem bacterial skin infections. These blisters are caused by breakdown of cell junctions between the epidermis and dermis with fluid seepage from the underlying tissues.

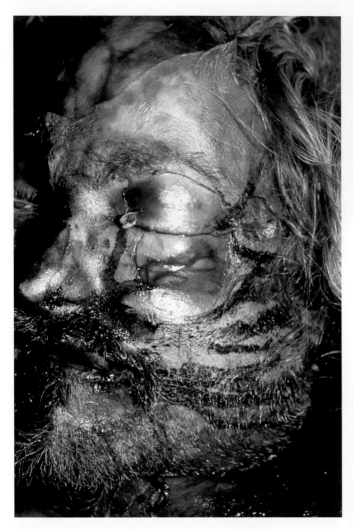

Figure 4.47 Putrefaction with "purging." Note the red to brown fluid gurgling from the mouth and nose. This can sometimes be mistaken for an upper gastrointestinal hemorrhage.

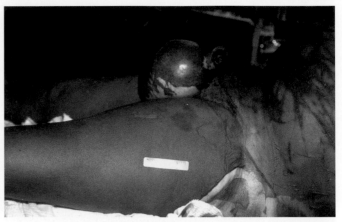

Figure 4.48 Putrefactive change with bloating and expansion of the scrotum due to gas accumulation.

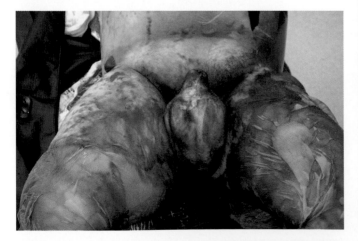

Figure 4.49 Green-brown-red discoloration with fluid-filled blister formation and skin slippage; scrotal enlargement from gas formation due to metabolism of proliferating microorganisms.

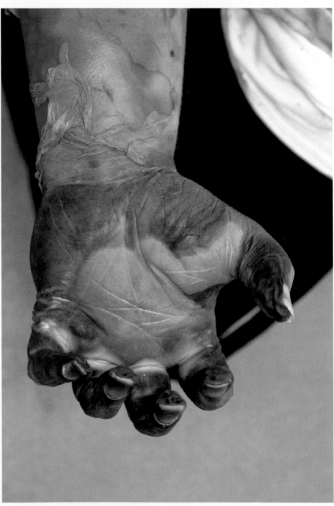

Figure 4.50 There is mummification of the fingertips with an expanded gas-filled blister and green to brown putrefied fluid in its inferior aspect.

Figure 4.51 This decomposing individual died of natural causes while sitting in a warm tub. Note the bloating from putrefactive gases causing the body to float near the surface. People who drown in bathtubs are incapacitated by disease, injury, or intoxication. Sometimes homicide victims are placed in bathtubs to wash evidence off the body. Bodies found in larger areas of water will typically float to the surface as intestinal putrefactive gases increase, causing the rear end to bob up and down with waves similar to an appearance of a tire.

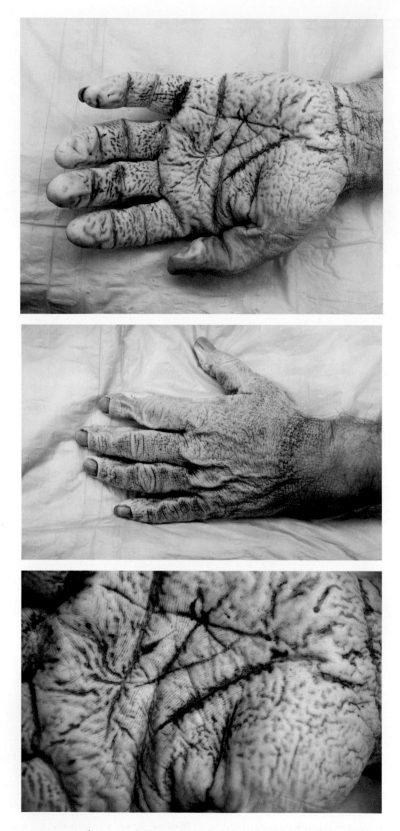

Figures 4.52–4.54 Water immersion skin, washerwoman's hands, or pruning of the fingers due to immersion in water.

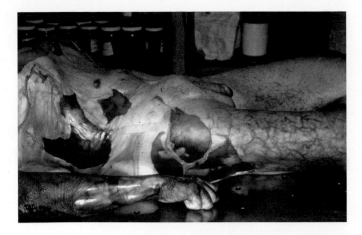

Figure 4.55 Marbling and skin slippage, early to moderate putrefaction.

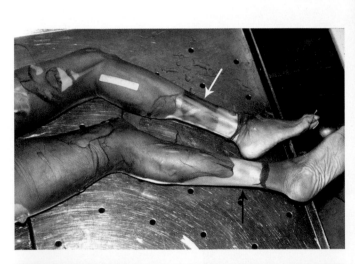

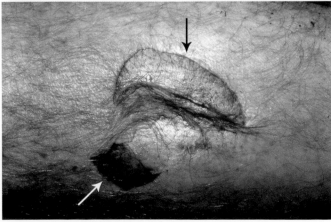

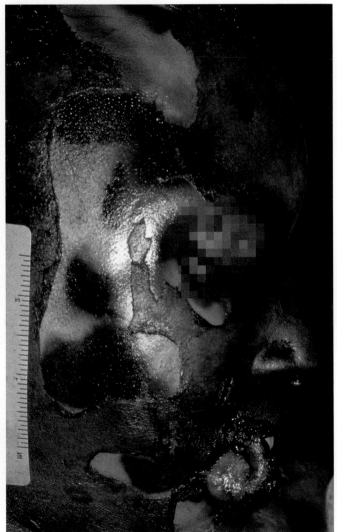

Figures 4.56 and 4.57 These images demonstrate skin slippage that occurred at different times. Note the regions of underlying dermis that are dry and dark indicating older regions of skin slippage (white arrow). Also note the other adjacent regions that are moist, pale, and less dark indicating shorter duration of underlying dermis exposure to air (black arrow). This darker discoloration is due to more drying and longer exposure to the air.

Figure 4.58 Decomposing homicide victim with multiple decomposing blunt impact injuries. The combination of postmortem change with injuries may make interpretation challenging. Note the red to brown abraded contusions at the individual's face and head with skin slippage and darker discoloration.

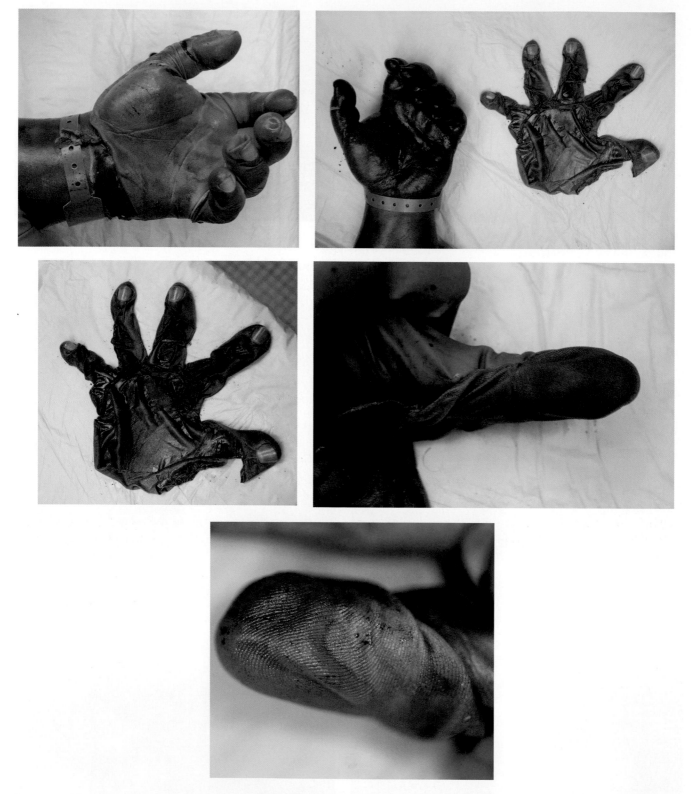

Figures 4.59–4.63 This demonstrates a way to get fingerprints from a decomposing body with significant skin slippage. The skin of the hand can be removed and worn like a glove.

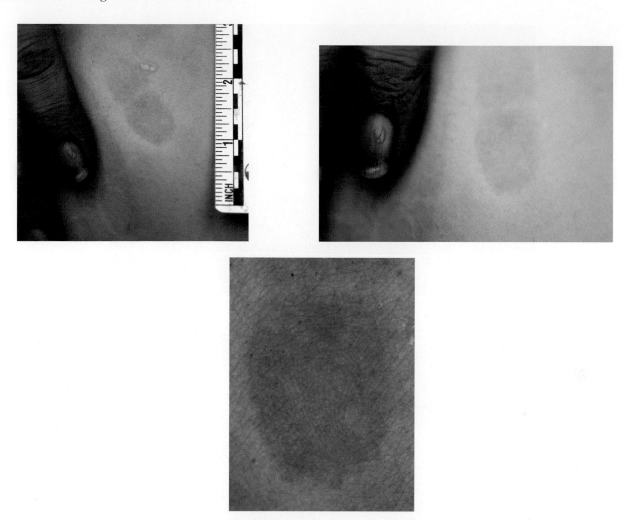

Figures 4.64–4.66 This is an unusual case where fingerprints were actually visible on the decedents body without processing. Note the fingerprint impressions on the skin. Note the whirling ridges from the fingerprint pattern shown in Figure 4.66.

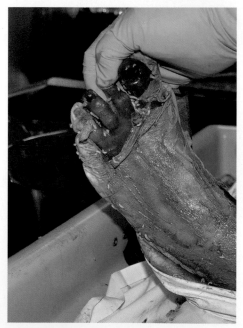

Figure 4.67 Note the webbed toes, which helped achieve positive identification, on this individual with significant decomposition. This occurs one in 2000–2500 live births.

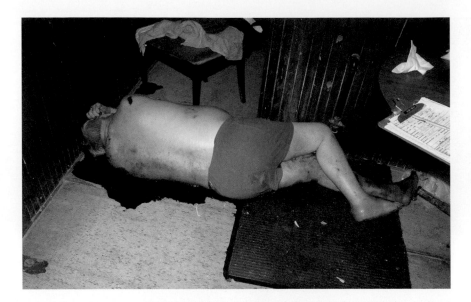

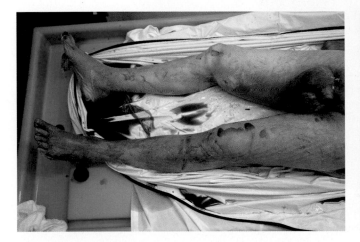

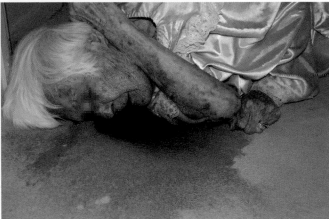

Figures 4.68–4.70 These individuals were found lying on their sides with a mild to moderate degree of putrefaction. Note the puddle of purge fluid underneath his upper trunk and head. Also note the greater decomposition with green discoloration in the regions of dependent lividity where the body contacted the warm floor. Purge fluid such as this is often misinterpreted as blood resulting from traumatic injury.

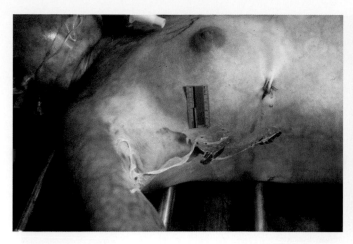

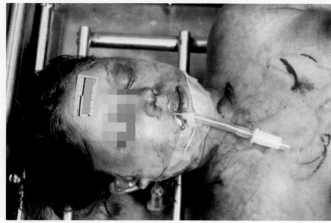

Figures 4.71 and 4.72 Accelerated putrefaction due to bacterial sepsis at the time of death. This picture depicts the left side of the patient's body with extensive skin slippage as well as green discoloration within the left infraclavicular area. Additionally, an endotracheal tube can be seen protruding from the mouth and taped to the side of her face. Such a depiction might lead one to conclude that overzealous paramedics had worked on a decedent who was decomposing. Marbling is also visible on the lateral and anterior aspects of the left arm. What this case really illustrates is the rapidity with which bacteria, already present within the bloodstream at the time of death, can disseminate and propagate throughout the blood system, leading to accelerated postmortem putrefactive change.

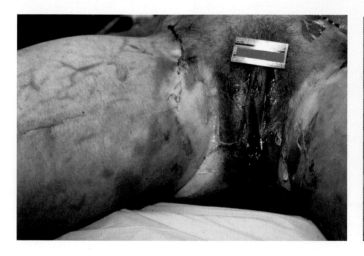

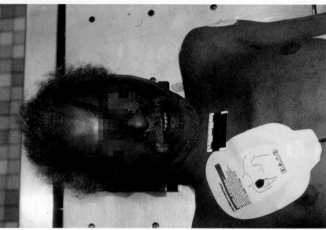

Figure 4.73 This is the same case demonstrating skin slippage and exudation of hemolytic fluid from the external genital region.

Figure 4.74 This is another case, depicting a decedent with dark red-brown discoloration due to postmortem putrefactive change that was accelerated by the probably bacteremic state at the time of death.

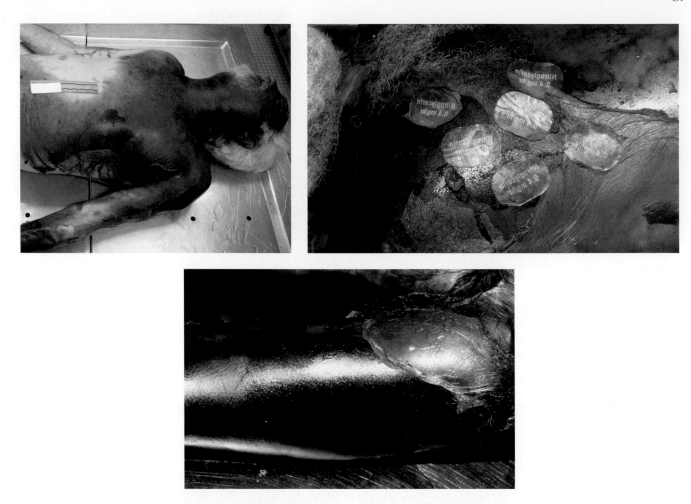

Figures 4.75–4.77 Skin slippage with confluent red to brown discoloration, moderate putrefaction. Note the top image shows multiple nitroglycerin patches in an individual with known significant heart disease.

Figure 4.78 Moderate to marked putrefaction with dark brown discoloration and early mummification. Note the maggots at the surface of the body.

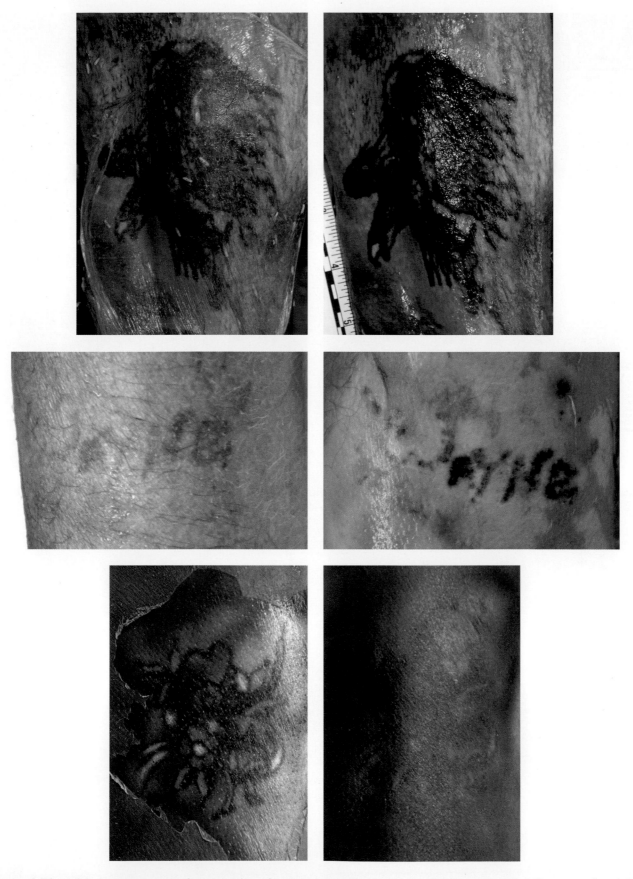

Figures 4.79–4.84 Moderate putrefaction. Identification may sometimes be challenging with advancing decomposition. These tattoos were initially difficult to see due to putrefactive change. Cleaning of this surface area with removal of the superficial layers of skin made visualization easier.

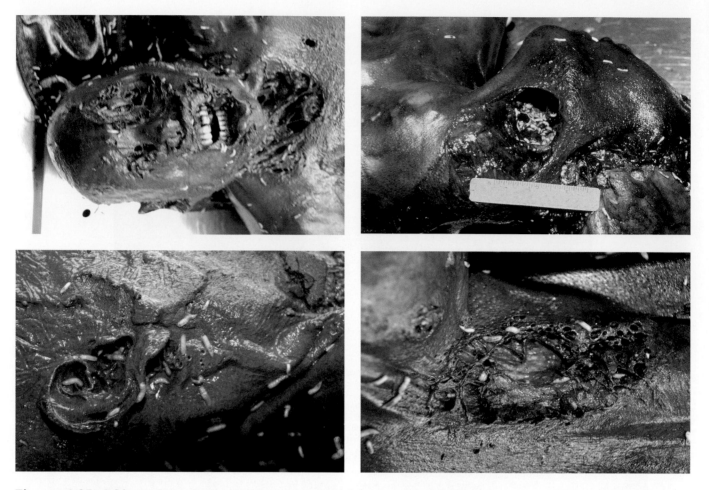

Figures 4.85–4.88 Marked putrefactive change with dark brown discoloration, and maggot feeding. Note the small circular perforations caused by maggots tunneling through skin and soft tissue.

Figures 4.89–4.91 Mummified fetuses retrieved from dried-out formaldehyde containers found within an abandoned building that once housed a doctor's office that closed over 30 years earlier.

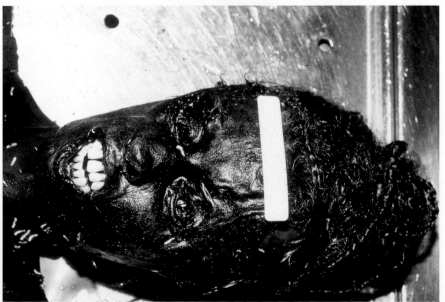

Figures 4.92 and 4.93 Advanced decomposition with mummification of the entire body. Note the dry dark leathery appearance of the skin.

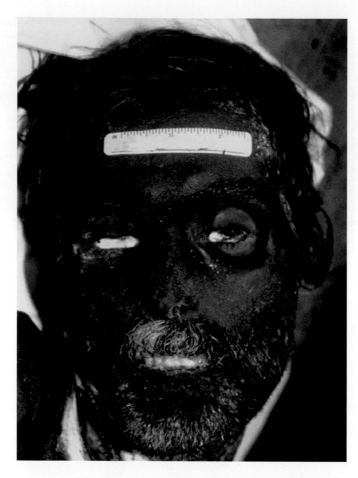

Figure 4.94 This person has advanced into the middle phases of mummification. The skin not only darkens but also becomes dry and hard. Deposition of fly eggs around the facial orifices and eyes are also seen.

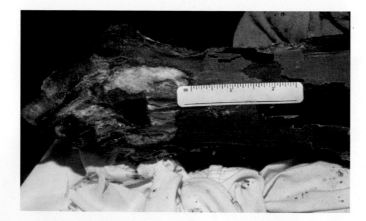

Figure 4.95 As part of the advancing process of mummification, the forearm of this body shows darkening, drying, and flaking of the skin. This gives the surface the appearance of the bark of a tree. This "tree barking" is typically seen late in the mummification process.

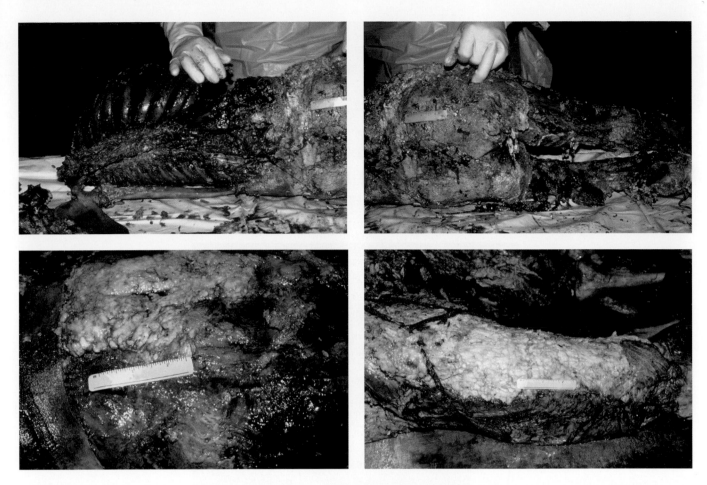

Figures 4.96–4.99 Adipocere is a decomposition process seen with immersions or damp, warm environments. The neutral fats are converted to oleic, palmitic, and stearic acids. Note the white/tan-colored adipocere, which has a waxy feel. In some areas you can see a light sheen of oil on the surface. Once formed, adipocere is resistant to further decomposition.

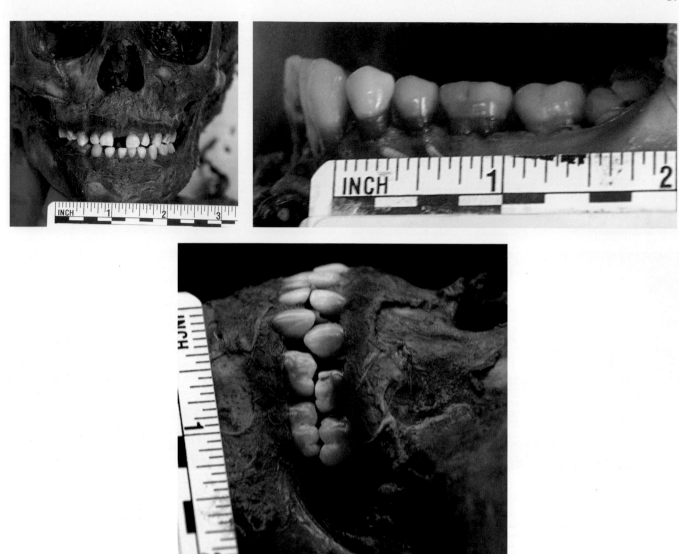

Figures 4.100–4.102 Note the red discoloration of the teeth due to hemoglobin diffusion associated with advanced decomposition. Comparison to an old photograph of the decedent showed the same gap between the upper central incisors.

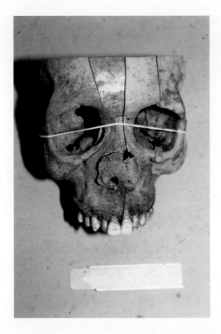

Figure 4.103 Skull found tucked under the bottom of a stairwell in the basement of a Brownstone in Brooklyn, New York. Note the dried skin at the nose. There was resin and perforation of the cribiform plate. This was the historical remains of an Egyptian mummy skull that was most likely used in religious ceremonies. There were also comingled chicken bone, feathers, and wax.

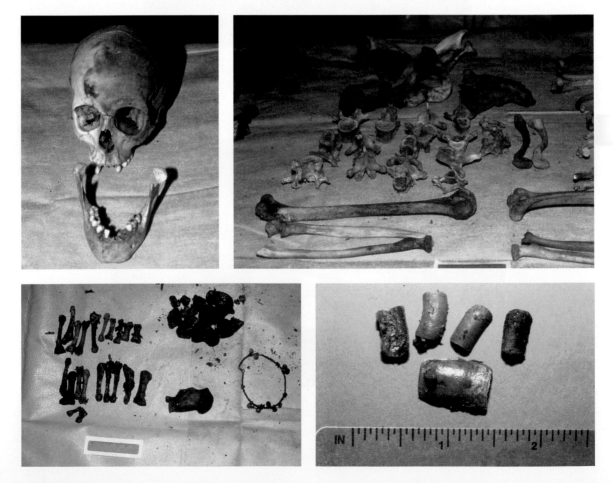

Figures 4.104–4.107 Advanced decomposition with skeletonization from a body dumped in a wooded area approximately 1 year earlier. The last image demonstrates five toenails from inside a shoe.

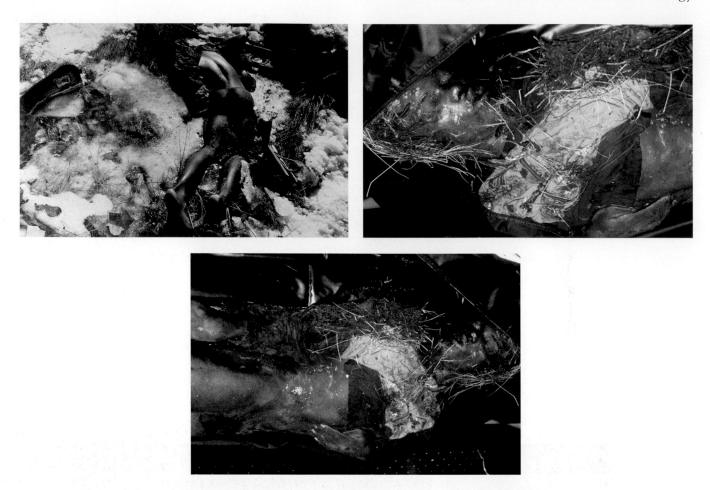

Figures 4.108–4.110 This frozen individual was murdered approximately 1 month prior to being found. His body was in a slight state of putrefaction due to the preservation by the freezing cold winter temperature. Once the body thawed out for autopsy, putrefaction advanced at a markedly accelerated rate.

Figure 4.111 Photograph taken at the time of autopsy. Note the advancing putrefaction with skin slippage. Also note the scalp laceration.

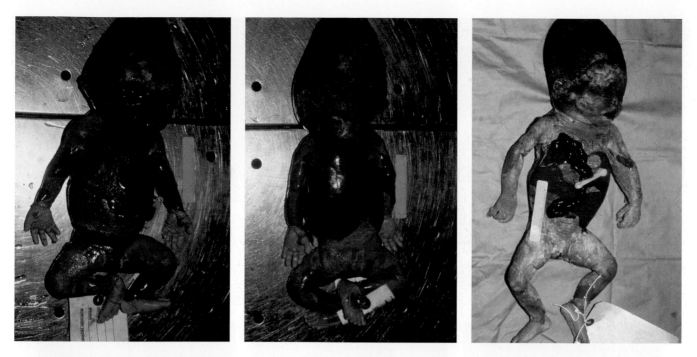

Figures 4.112–4.114 Macerated stillborns with red to brown discoloration. This type of decomposition is autolysis. The womb is normally a sterile environment and there should not be putrefaction unless there is an infection such as chorioamnionitis.

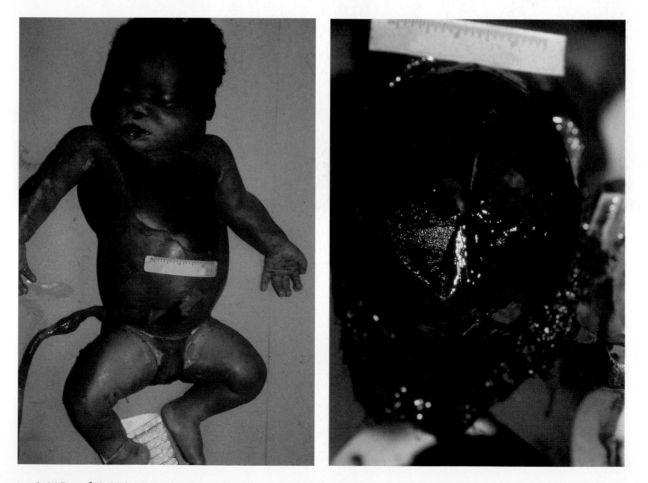

Figures 4.115 and 4.116 This child was discovered in the back of a garbage truck after being crushed by the trash compactor. The child was comingled with rotting food. Note the green discoloration of the skin due to putrefaction. Note the skull fracture with hemorrhage and dark discoloration due to putrefaction.

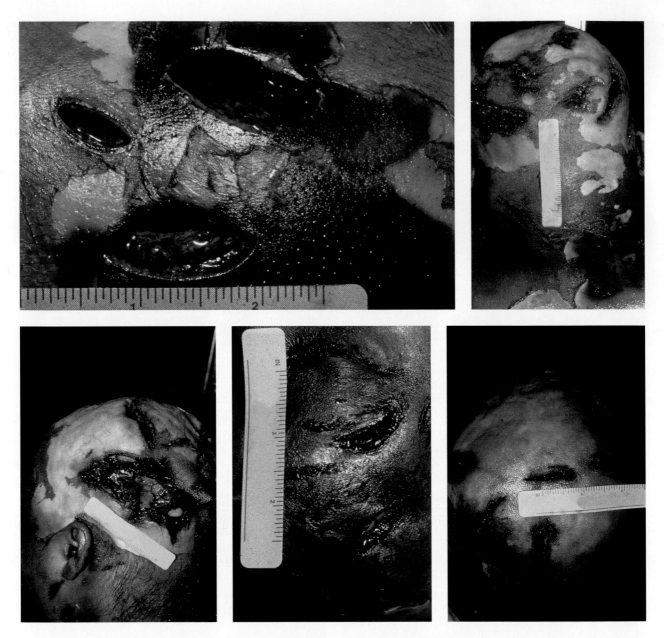

Figures 4.117–4.121 These slides show antemortem injuries that have been obscured by postmortem change. These individuals had multiple stab wounds and lacerations. Note the wound margins are dark and irregular due to drying. This may make wound interpretation challenging and, at some point, not possible. Also, animals and insects will often more readily feed from injured areas with exposed soft tissue and blood, further obscuring these findings.

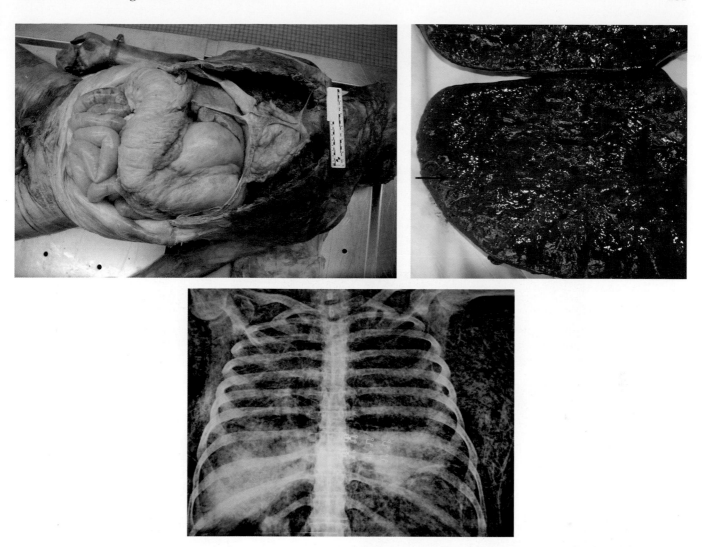

Figures 4.122–4.124 Bloating with numerous gas-filled cavities due to collections of gas associated with microbial metabolism due to putrefaction. Note the feathery appearance of the soft tissue on the x-ray due to gas accumulation.

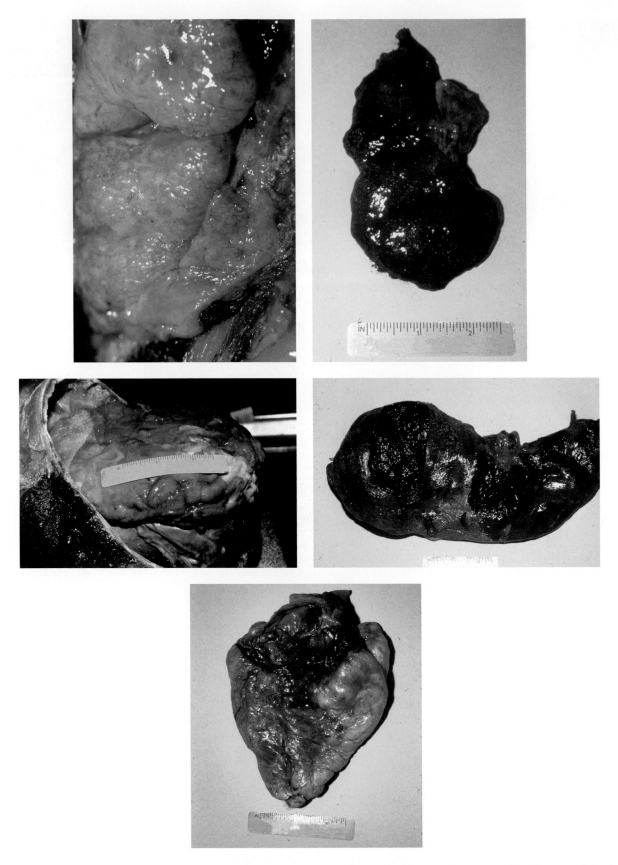

Figures 4.125–4.129 These are examples of moderate putrefactive changes of internal organs with softening, dehydration, shrinkage, and partial loss of architecture. In Figure 4.125 note the crepitant adipose tissue due to expanding cavities of gas from proliferating microorganism metabolism. Also note in Figure 4.127 the gray discoloration of the brain with partial loss of architecture. As central nervous system putrefaction advances, the brain will develop into a liquid, oatmeal-like consistency with few or more recognizable structures. Figure 4.128 shows putrefying liver, and Figure 4.129 shows putrefying heart.

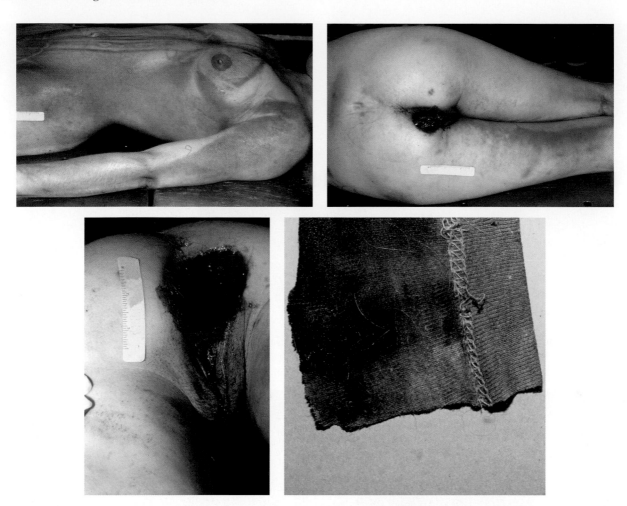

Figures 4.130–4.133 Note the fixed anterior lividity. The decedent was lying prone on a bed with a wrinkled comforter. Postmortem dog feeding occurred around the anus. Autopsy revealed the absence of large portions of intestines. Note the torn clothing has dog hairs and blood staining. This case was first suspicious for homicidal violence. Large amounts of blood had drained from the body to the bedding that was further spread about by the dog.

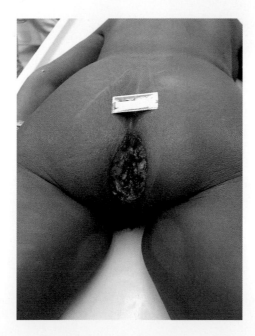

Figure 4.134 This is another example of postmortem dog feeding that often initially involves the face, genitals, anus, and areas of wounds.

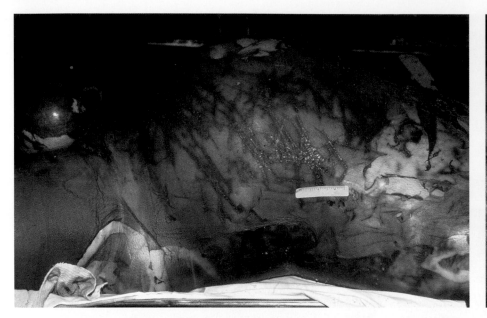
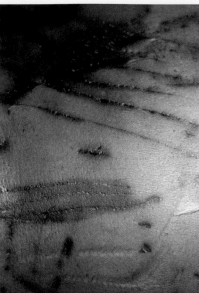

Figures 4.135 and 4.136 Postmortem animal feeding with dog claw abrasions.

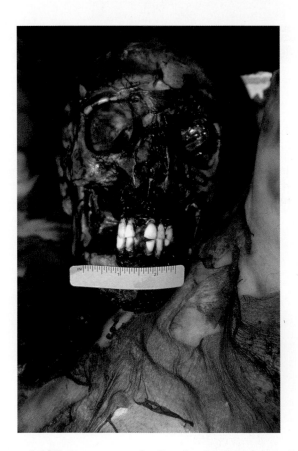

Figure 4.138 Postmortem anemic superficial linear abrasions from a body retrieved from the Hudson River. This region of the body was noted to be scraping against a rocky surface just prior to retrieval from the water.

Figure 4.137 Postmortem feeding by the decedent's dog.

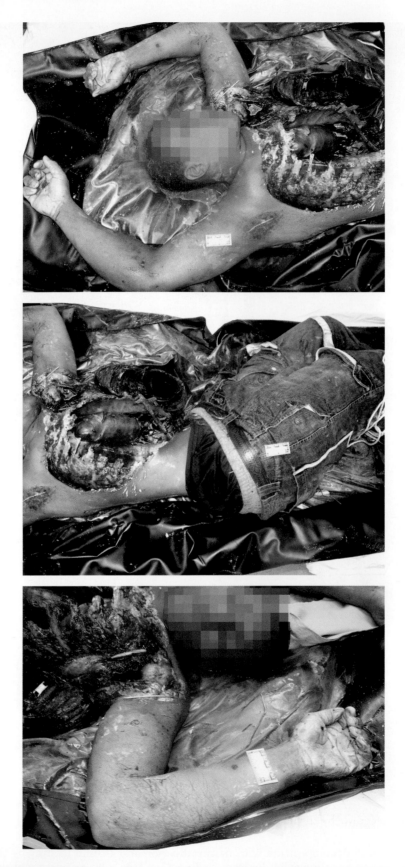

Figures 4.139–4.141 Larger carnivore activity is common in rural and suburban areas. In many cases, there may be activity from several different animals in the same environment. In this case, the damage appears to mostly be from the canine family (likely wild) with evidence of tearing of the skin and ribs. There is no obvious vital reaction, indicating the damage occurred postmortem. In these cases one must consider whether the postmortem activity has obscured injuries sustained during life.

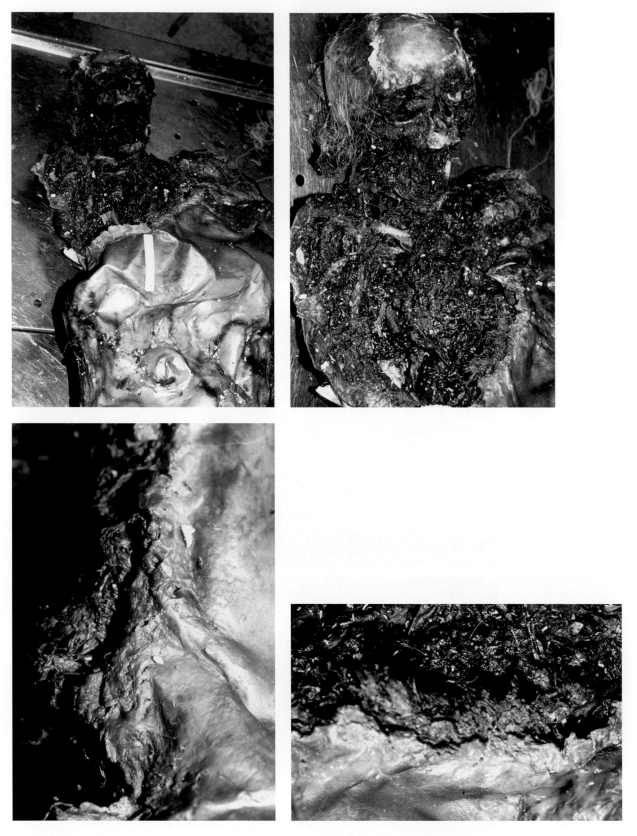

Figures 4.142–4.145 Advanced decomposition with mummification and animal feeding by the decedent's cats. Note the margin with claw marks and a scalloped border from feeding. One arm, a larger portion of the chest, and most of the internal organs were absent.

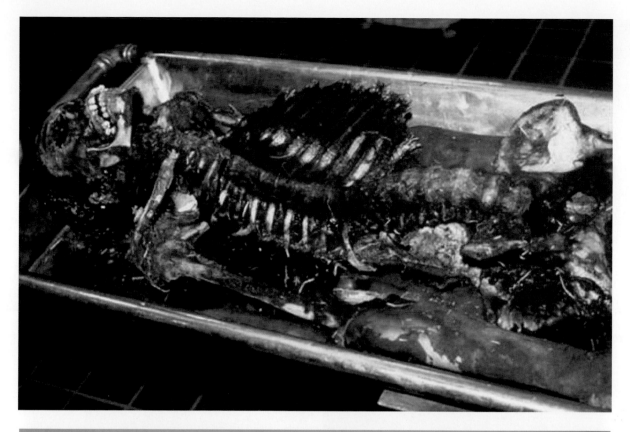

Figures 4.146 and 4.147 In this case the carnivore activity was caused by domestic pigs.

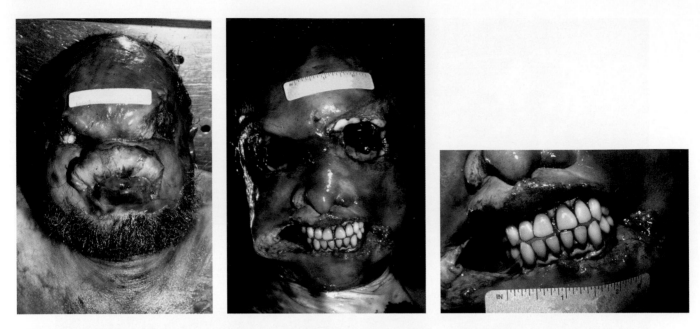

Figures 4.148–4.150 Postmortem feeding from fish and crustaceans found on these bodies retrieved from the ocean.

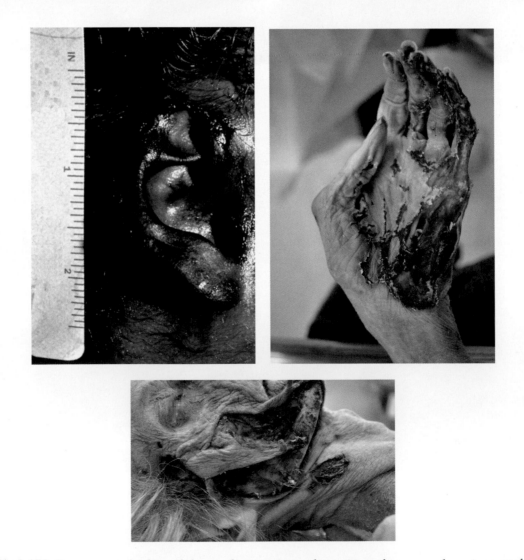

Figures 4.151–4.153 Postmortem feeding of the ear due to mice and rats. Note the mouse droppings on the anemic soft tissue defects.

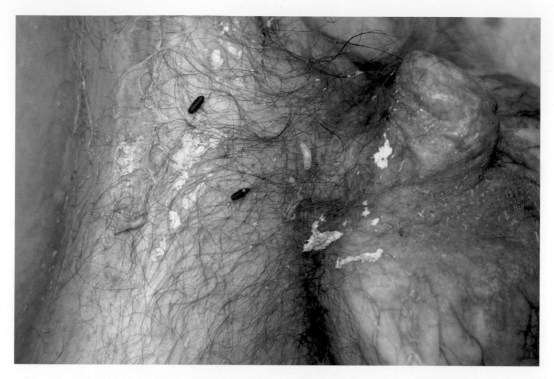

Figure 4.154 Note the varying stages of blowfly development. Eggs have an appearance similar to grated cheese or saw-dust. When the eggs hatch, maggots develop and are shown in this picture in varying sizes as small, white, and wormlike. The dark brown pupa cases are also apparent from hatching flies. This entire cycle is accelerated in hotter temperatures.

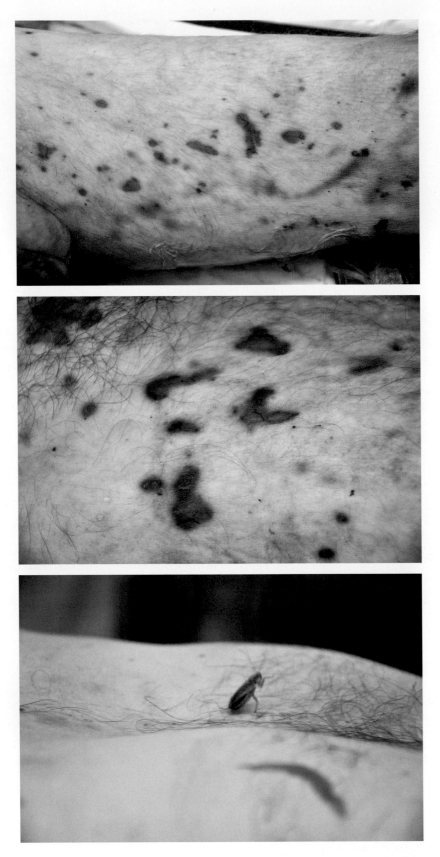

Figures 4.155–4.157 Note the irregular, angulated, superficial, yellow anemic erosions due to postmortem insect feeding by cockroaches.

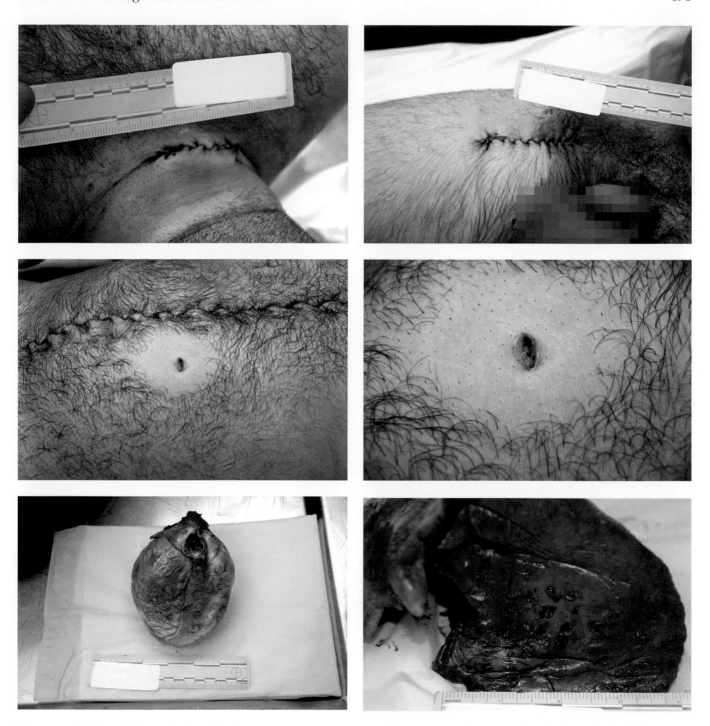

Figures 4.158–4.163 Embalmed body. Figures 4.158 and 4.159 show sutured incisions made by funeral directors to gain access for blood removal with addition of embalming fluid. Figures 4.160 and 4.161 show multiple "trocar" puncture marks through the body surface and organs. A trocar is a metal rod used to infuse embalming fluid. These may be misinterpreted as injuries.

Pediatric Forensic Pathology

5

MICHAEL J. CAPLAN, CHARLES A. CATANESE,
ALEX K. WILLIAMSON, AND ZHONGXUE HUA

Contents

Pediatric forensic pathology, a subspecialty of forensic pathology, is concerned with investigating the sudden, unexpected, and/or violent deaths of fetuses, neonates, infants, toddlers, children, and, in most jurisdictions, adolescents up to and including the age of 18 years. Evaluating potential forensic issues across such a spectrum of age requires a commanding knowledge of normal growth and maturation, as well as a thoughtful consideration of the unique anatomy and physiology that characterizes each stage of development. Unfortunately, very few forensic pathologists are specifically trained in pediatric pathology, and the number of hospital-based pediatric pathologists who engage in medicolegal death investigation is equally small, especially in the United States. The consequences of incompetent pediatric medicolegal death investigation can be devastating for multiple members of a community. It is, for example, as important to correctly identify and process a child homicide as it is to exonerate an innocent caretaker who is wrongfully suspected of child harm. Forensic investigations in the pediatric population are thankfully infrequent, but when they arise, they can present intellectually challenging, and at times emotionally taxing, scenarios.

The fetal period is characterized by, among other features, an intrauterine existence and dependence upon a placenta for respiration. The neonatal period, defined as the first 28 days of extrauterine life, marks the beginning of terrestrial life with dependence on lungs for respiration. Encompassing the transition between fetus and neonate is the perinatal period, which includes the time immediately before and after birth. Most fetal and neonatal deaths are related to natural pathologies affecting mother, placenta, and/or baby, and are therefore commonly—and appropriately—investigated by hospital-based perinatal pathologists. However, in certain circumstances, such as those involving accidental or nonaccidental maternal trauma or maternal substance abuse, a fetal demise or neonatal death will be evaluated by a forensic pathologist. Or, considering that a person's risk of being murdered is greatest on the first day of life, the rare but tragic discovery of a baby

in a Dumpster, for example, represents one of the most difficult death investigations confronting a forensic pathologist, as it usually necessitates differentiating an abandoned stillborn fetus from a murdered live-born neonate. In order to properly evaluate perinatal deaths such as these, postmortem artifacts must be correctly recognized and interpreted, organ maturation must be assessed as reliably as possible, and natural pathology must be considered.

Another challenging task confronting forensic pathologists involves determining the cause and manner of death when an infant, who was previously in good health, is found dead by a caretaker minutes or hours after being put to sleep. Although congenital anomalies and complications of low birth weight represent the most common causes of death in the first year of life, sudden unexplained infant death (SUID) is the leading cause of death from 1 to 12 months of age, with a peak incidence around 3 months of life. SUID is defined as the sudden death of an infant that remains unexplained after investigating the circumstances of death, performing a complete postmortem examination, and reviewing the decedent's medical history. Many of these deaths were previously described by the term sudden infant death syndrome (SIDS). Since the debut of SIDS as a cause of death in 1969, the term has served two important functions: it helped remove stigmatism from caretakers who lost an infant to unknown causes, and it identified a vexing problem for epidemiology and science to solve. Even though the etiology of some infant deaths remains a mystery today, the term SIDS is practically meaningless. Death is always due to at least one anatomic and/or physiologic derangement (whether presently identifiable or not), and, as any pathologist involved with investigating infant death knows all too well, there is no one constellation of specific findings in SUID cases that warrants their classification as a syndrome.

One of the biggest advances in understanding how infants can die in their sleep occurred in the 1980s, when the Back to Sleep Campaign (now the Safe to Sleep campaign) raised awareness about infant sleeping position. It is now recognized that a substantial proportion of SUID cases are in fact due to asphyxia, particularly through smothering mechanisms. Prone infant sleeping position, an infant's sleeping on a sofa or other furniture, the use of soft bedding materials including pillows and blankets, the covering of an infant's mouth by bedding materials, and an infant's sharing a sleeping space with an adult (e.g., co-sleeping, bed-sharing) are each recognized risk factors for infant asphyxia while sleeping. Careful scene investigations, including doll re-enactments to illustrate the position in which an infant was put to sleep and subsequently found unresponsive, frequently reveal potentially dangerous infant sleep environments.

Exciting research over the past few decades and continuing today complements the emphasis appropriately placed on safe infant sleep environments. Unraveling developmental pathways and biochemistry in the infant brain has provided valuable insights into why some sleeping infants are more susceptible to asphyxia in the first months of life. Furthermore, the discovery of and evolving capability to detect cardiac channelopathies in recent years exemplify the progress being made in elucidating molecular causes of sudden death in infants and older individuals as well. These and related advances in medical research highlight the important roles forensic pathologists play in accurately determining cause and manner of death and in collecting and preserving appropriate specimens so that such progress continues. It must be remembered, however, that the combination of diligent scene investigation, competent autopsy performance including traditional and emerging ancillary tests, and thoughtful review of a medical history is what allows a substantial number of sudden infant deaths to be appropriately classified. For those infants in which a convincing explanation of death remains elusive after disease, infection, and mechanical or toxicologic injury have been excluded, use of the term SUID is justified and encouraged.

Beyond infancy, throughout adolescence, and into adulthood, most deaths are caused by accidental trauma, with suicidal and homicidal injuries emerging as important causes of death in older pediatric populations. And regardless of age, the forensic pathologist must always remain vigilant for the possibility of child abuse, perpetrated by either intention or negligence. Although the medicolegal investigation of violent deaths is similarly conducted in the pediatric and adult populations, it must be appreciated that forces act on and manifest in younger bodies differently than they do in older bodies. For example, the pediatric abdomen, with its smaller body surface-to-volume ratio, larger proportion of cavity volume occupied by vital organs,

and relatively immature viscera, is more vulnerable than is an adult abdomen to a given amount of applied blunt force.

Additionally, when assessing pediatric injuries, the forensic pathologist must be mindful of the way in which underlying disease can mimic or influence the severity of an injury. Viral gastroenteritis, for example, can induce a hemorrhagic diathesis in some children, and the resulting mucosal bleeding may emulate traumatic bleeding from an orifice. A child with severe vitamin D deficiency, as another example, may sustain one or more fractures that appear inconsistent with the amount of applied force or which simply would not arise in normally mineralized bone. In such cases, failure to recognize the presence or contribution of underlying disease can lead to misinterpretation of pathologic findings, and such mistakes may have disastrous medicolegal implications.

Also, many children who in the past would have died from congenital disease or malignancy are now alive because of impressive surgical and medical advancements. When some children unfortunately succumb to these diseases in spite of appropriate intervention, it is often the responsibility of the forensic pathologist to determine whether the intervention may have caused or altered the manner of death. As an example, a young adult may succumb to complications of hepatic cirrhosis years after successfully undergoing a Fontan procedure for the treatment of complex congenital heart disease. Although heart disease is the underlying cause of death, recognizing that liver cirrhosis potentially represents a complication of the Fontan procedure may allow the death to be more appropriately classified as a therapeutic complication. Such a classification, although not implying culpability, provides important epidemiologic information that may help improve management of other patients who have undergone the procedure.

Interpreting injuries is another area that can be extremely challenging. Perhaps one of the most illustrative examples of this concept that children are not just small adults is the assessment of nonaccidental or inflicted head trauma in infants and very young children. An understanding of this type of injury would not be possible without being thoroughly acquainted with the unique anatomic features of the pediatric head, which may be summarized as follows: (1) the elasticity of the infant's scalp, such that it could potentially sustain a serious blunt impact without necessarily manifesting the impact in the form of a subgaleal contusion (although this school of thought admittedly remains controversial and lacks consensus among forensic pathologists and experts in pediatric head injury); (2)

the thin, pliable, unilaminar quality of the skull that renders it less susceptible to fracture but also allows it to transmit forces to the underlying brain more readily; (3) the broad, shallow skull base in infants, which facilitates rotational movement of the brain and lowers the threshold for diffuse brain (axonal) injury; (4) the incompletely myelinated infant brain, with a white-matter water content substantially higher than that of an adult, imparting a consistency of unset gelatin and making the brain more vulnerable to shearing forces; and (5) the top-heavy calvaria and the weak, underdeveloped neck muscles that fail to effectively dampen the oscillations that are initiated when rotational movement of the brain begins. It is the interface of pediatric and forensic pathology that allows the most complete and comprehensive understanding of these concepts to be achieved; however, very few individuals actually have such expertise in both fields. As a result, forensic pathologists may benefit significantly by relying on pediatric pathologists, neuropathologists, and neuro or pediatric radiologists when they are evaluating difficult, complex, or problematic deaths in the pediatric population.

Traumatic brain injury (TBI) is the leading cause of death and disability in children. It is estimated that 2000 children die in the United States annually from abuse and neglect. Guthkelch and Caffey described shaken baby syndrome (SBS) four decades ago, and the original concept of SBS has been evolved and/or expanded to shaken impact syndrome (SIS) and a more recently abusive head trauma (AHT) by the American Academy of Pediatrics. Additional terms offered by forensic neuropathologists and child abuse experts include nonaccidental injury (NAI), nonaccidental head injury (NAHI), and inflicted TBI. Regardless of the specific term that is employed, inflicted TBI is commonly characterized by the triad of subdural hemorrhage, retinal hemorrhage, and anoxic encephalopathy. SBS/SIS/AHT is commonly characterized by a triad—subdural hemorrhage, retinal hemorrhage, and anoxic encephalopathy. The SBS/SIS/AHT hypothesis described the physical disruption of dural bridging veins, retinal vessels, and axons within the central nervous system. However, when the triad is separated into isolated components, each component could result from abusive (inflicted) trauma, accidental trauma, or specific natural disease processes. A valid diagnosis of SBS/SIS/AHT therefore requires the rigorous exclusion of accidental trauma (and including birth trauma) and natural disease mimics (such as primary coagulopathy, cerebral venous thrombosis, and other rare genetic diseases).

The neuropathology of SBS/SIS/AHT is dominated for frequently by features of hypoxic-ischemic encephalopathy (HIE), in the form of vascular axonal injury (VAI), than traumatic encephalopathy (traumatic diffuse axonal injury [dTAI]). The SBS/SIS/AHT hypothesis described a *significant force* (equivalent to that sustained in a motor vehicle accident or a several-story fall) that triggered *immediate neurological symptoms*. Although uncommon, lethal short falls and delayed clinical deterioration are well-documented phenomena in forensic pathology and neuropathology. The assessment of the timing (the aging) of the head trauma should be made with extreme caution, and a layer-wise examination (of the scalp, skull, dura leptomeninges, and brain) is critical for a complete study. Additionally, a posterior neck dissection for potential soft tissue, bony (vertebral), ligamentous, spinal cord, and spinal nerve trauma should always be performed.

The subject of diffuse brain (axonal) injury in the pediatric age group, specifically in infants and young children, is one that continues to generate a considerable amount of controversy. While such controversy is desirable in the sense that it stimulates ongoing research and data-gathering, thus advancing the overall body of knowledge in this area, it also has the potential to polarize triers of fact when multiple divergent opinions are being proffered by experts in forensic pathology and pediatric neurotrauma. While we must admit that much remains incompletely understood, this segment will attempt to summarize what is presently known regarding the topic of diffuse traumatic pediatric brain injury and which avenues we must pursue in order to educate ourselves so that we can handle these very difficult cases more effectively.

One important factor to consider is that the relevance of the pathologic findings observed in cases of nonaccidental (inflicted) head trauma is dependent on the degree to which such findings can be integrated into the context of the clinical case history and circumstances surrounding the injury-producing event. Consistently challenging the forensic pathologist's efforts to correlate the anamnestic information with the autopsy findings is the fact that the majority of such accounts are either partially or entirely untruthful. It must be acknowledged that the clinical information is potentially impeachable, and that the injuries may be discordant with the event as it is presented. Clearly, this is an overriding theme in forensic pathology, and therefore it is especially [critical] for the forensic pathologist to consider all reasonable possibilities before making a determination as to whether a particular pattern of injuries is or is not consistent with the explanation offered as to how they occurred.

In cases of inflicted pediatric head trauma, there are a few predictably recurrent themes in the accounts that are provided, which are laid out as follows: (1) there is a history of minor trauma, such as a fall from a couch onto a padded or carpeted floor, or from a changing table or car seat onto some similar surface; (2) the infant or young child, shortly after being observed in a "normal state of health and/or activity" (referred to as the "functional interval"), is discovered in a state of profound neurologic dysfunction (i.e., lethargic, somnolent, or frankly comatose), frequently accompanied by abnormal or absent respirations, vomiting, and seizure activity—all signs of profound brainstem derangement; or (3) the infant or child is found dead. It is precisely because these infants present as moribund ("gravely ill") that it often becomes difficult or impossible to reconstruct the sequence of events that gave rise to the injury and the clinical picture that is presented.

Diffuse axonal injury (DAI) is the term that has been chosen to designate the most extreme (severe) end of the spectrum of diffuse TBI and is defined most broadly as injury that is imparted to the head when forces of acceleration or deceleration cause the head to move rotationally about its axis or along the cervicomedullary junction. It has been shown that while the head can tolerate translational motion reasonably well, it is much more vulnerable to forces that initiate rotational movement because this type of movement is most deleterious to axons. While admittedly controversial, this overview chooses to maintain that such forces may be created by either one (1) of two (2) potential mechanisms, namely: (1) impact by a moving object striking the resting but movable head, by the moving head striking a fixed object, or occasionally, by a moving head striking or being struck by a moving object, such as the case in a high-speed motor vehicle collision; or (2) a nonimpact inertial movement (i.e., shaking).

The precise neuropathophysiologic process that characterizes DAI is only partially understood but is believed to be initiated by small breaches or tears within the walls of axons; once this occurs, variable influxes of proteases and calcium ion (Ca^{2+}) into the axon proper disrupt the integrity of the axon, a process referred to as secondary axotomy. The injured axon subsequently swells and assumes a "beaded," rounded, or spherical configuration, giving rise to the term axonal "swellings" or "spheroids."

In adults—who have adult-sized axons—the neuropathologic demonstration of DAI is relatively easy. The classically described findings of DAI in adults consist of punctate to streaklike hemorrhages (contusions) that predominate within neuroanatomical regions of predilection, namely, the parasagittal white matter, the corpus callosum, and the superior cerebellar peduncles (which are located within the dorsolateral quadrants of the rostral pons). Microscopic (histopathologic) examination of these grossly demonstrable hemorrhages with standard hematoxylin and eosin (H&E)-stained sections reveals round to oval swellings of the axons. Typically, they require approximately 18–24 hours following the time of the primary brain injury to manifest themselves. Methods to enhance their sensitivity have been pursued, mainly with silver (Bielschowsky) stains, which have had moderate success.

The problem is that the above-outlined "classic" findings of DAI in adults are rarely if ever encountered in the pediatric brain. The forensic pathologist almost never observes punctate hemorrhages within the vulnerable neuroanatomical regions on gross examination. Furthermore, axonal swellings are exceedingly difficult to demonstrate with routine H&E and even with Bielschowsky silver stains by virtue of the relatively diminutive caliber of infants' and young children's axons. For this reason, other findings that are readily demonstrable on gross examination of the pediatric brain, optic nerves, and eyes—namely, subdural hemorrhages, subarachnoid hemorrhages, brain swelling, and retinal and optic nerve sheath hemorrhages—have been traditionally employed as surrogate "markers" of DAI in these settings.

With the discovery of the beta-amyloid precursor protein (βAPP) in the mid-1990s, it became theoretically feasible for the first time to demonstrate traumatic DAI directly in the pediatric brain. βAPP immunohistochemical staining has since become a widely used technique in forensic neuropathology; but, as with all new techniques, new problems and issues have arisen. βAPP is a transmembrane protein, synthesized by a gene on chromosome 21, whose exact function is unknown. It is produced within neurons and is transported along the axon in a standard anterograde fashion, but because it is synthesized in such small amounts within the neuron, it does not achieve a concentration that allows it to be demonstrated by immunohistochemical methods. However, when axons are injured, the normal anterograde transport of βAPP becomes interrupted while it continues to be produced within the neuronal cell body; this results in an accumulation of βAPP proximal to the site of injury and in a concentration sufficient to be detectable by immunostaining. Furthermore, the superior sensitivity of βAPP immunoexpression allows it to be visualized within a few hours after injury—substantially earlier than the 18–24 hours' postinjury latency period that is imposed by H&E stains. It is important that the forensic pathologist be cognizant of the fact that the accumulation of βAPP proximal to the site of axonal injury and its immunoexpression *is not etiologically specific*—that is, it may occur in settings of both traumatic and nontraumatic axonal injury. For this reason, βAPP immunoexpression should not be construed as synonymous with dTAI, and this remains a consistent caveat regarding the evaluation of βAPP immunostaining.

As familiarity with βAPP immunoexpression has increased, it has come to be appreciated that different categories or patterns of DAI may be demonstrated:

1. *dTAI:* Scattered individual or grouped βAPP-immunoreactive axonal swellings (typically along the long axis of the axon) that are widely distributed within the cerebral hemispheric white matter, corpus callosum, and rostral brainstem (superior cerebellar peduncles).
2. *Multifocal traumatic axonal injury (mTAI):* Features indistinguishable from dTAI except for absence of βAPP-immunoreactive axonal swellings within the brainstem (i.e., supratentorial).
3. *VAI:* A "zig-zag" or wavy pattern of βAPP-immunoreactive axonal swellings configured as aggregates or clusters whose immunostaining is unrelated to the course of the axon (a well-demarcated or "punched-out" area of staining within a long white matter tract, in contrast to TAI), and occurring secondary to vascular compromise (hypoperfusion) with resultant global hypoxic-ischemic injury; it has a vascular distribution and involves both gray and white matter.
4. *Metabolic axonal injury (MAI):* Scattered βAPP-immunoreactivity related to a cause other than trauma or vascular compromise (i.e., hypoglycemia).
5. *Penumbral axonal injury (PAI):* βAPP-immunoreactivity adjacent or in proximity to focal lesions (i.e., cerebral infarct, laceration, or abscess).

One of the potential hazards of interpreting βAPP immunoexpression is that each type is not necessarily exclusive; that is, multiple patterns of axonal injury may be present not only in the same case but also within the same microscopic section! This phenomenon of overlapping patterns of βAPP immunoreactivity has become probably the most problematic aspect of its evaluation and interpretation in cases of pediatric head injury. Just as we know that primary brain injury, which occurs at the time of its infliction (i.e., immediately), may be complicated by the secondary processes of posttraumatic brain swelling, raised intracranial pressure, intracranial hematomas, global hypoxic-ischemic injury, and herniation, if sufficient time permits them to evolve, the identification and differentiation of such processes can be extraordinary challenging for the forensic pathologist or neuropathologist. Stated alternatively, the presence of VAI may partially or completely mask the recognition of TAI. An additional consideration to keep in mind is that the absence of βAPP immunoexpression does not

exclude the possibility that TBI (and specifically, dTAI) has occurred for the following reasons: (1) the survival interval may have been too short to allow for the detection of the βAPP-immunoreactive axons (i.e., <2–3 hours postinjury); and (2) even in cases where the survival interval equals or exceeds 2–3 hours, it is conceivable that brain swelling may have impaired cerebral perfusion to a degree that sufficient amounts of βAPP to enable its immunodetection may not have accumulated.

One recent study of βAPP immunoreactivity highlights particularly well some of the difficulties that arise in attempting to use βAPP immunoexpression as an ancillary diagnostic tool in forensic neuropathology. In this study published in 2011 in the *Journal of Forensic Sciences*, using data acquired from the State of Maryland Office of the Chief Medical Examiner in 1999, the authors identified a total of 153 deaths occurring in infants and children under 3 years of age, which included 18 homicides, of which 7 were caused by inflicted blunt head trauma. These 7 cases were combined with 7 age-matched control cases (not involving TBI) and with 10 cases of sudden unexplained death in infancy (SUDI) or SIDS. The objective of the study was to examine the independent diagnostic utility of βAPP immunostaining in the determination of cause and manner of infant and young pediatric deaths. Stated slightly differently, these investigators tested the ability of βAPP expression to differentiate traumatic from nontraumatic head brain injury as part of their working hypothesis that traumatic and nontraumatic brain injury could be distinguished by the pattern of axonal damage. The results may be summarized as follows: five of the seven cases of inflicted blunt head trauma were correctly identified on the basis of βAPP immunostaining patterns by three reviewers who were blinded to the case histories and autopsy findings (for a sensitivity of 71.4%). Conversely, 2 of the 17 cases not associated with inflicted blunt head injury demonstrated multifocal βAPP immunoexpression (for a specificity of 88.2%). Specifically, these two cases—one, a co-sleeping with adult parents in an adult bed; the other, a near-drowning—were accompanied by prolonged postresuscitation survival periods of 12–21 hours, respectively. The authors concluded the following: (1) that infants and young children who do not sustain traumatic head injury but who are successfully resuscitated and persist for a considerable or prolonged period of time on ventilator support may exhibit widespread βAPP immunoexpression that could potentially be misinterpreted as dTAI; for this reason, βAPP immunoexpression should never be employed as the sole criterion or decisive factor for making the determination of TBI; and (2) that the absence of βAPP immunoexpression may be a useful pertinent negative finding in infants and young children with intermediate postinjury survival times, sufficiently long to allow for the detection of βAPP-immunoreactive axons but not be obscured or confounded by global hypoxic-ischemic injury.

Despite cumulative experience and ongoing research, uncertainty persists regarding the precise mechanism of inflicted TBI in infants and young children; and all too frequently it is not possible to ascertain precisely how a particular injury was sustained (i.e., mechanism). While βAPP immunostaining is a useful diagnostic tool in the neuropathologic evaluation of inflicted TBI (as it is disproportionately observed in this setting), it must be remembered that similar patterns of βAPP immunoreactivity may be produced by pure nontraumatic hypoxic-ischemic brain injury. Therefore, both the pattern and location of βAPP immunostaining must be interpreted within the context of the entire case. Suffice it to say that understanding the pathophysiology of inflicted pediatric brain injury is extremely challenging; and as with all matters in forensic pathology, the pathologist must integrate the scene investigation (circumstances of death), medical records, autopsy findings, and ancillary studies in order to attain the most complete understanding of a particular case.

Another challenging area of forensic pediatric investigation may involve suspicion of sexual abuse. There may not be any visible trauma associated with child abuse. When trauma does exist it may manifest like any other injury. It may be challenging at times to interpret penetration injuries to the anus or vagina. The anus may appear dilated as a normal progression of decomposition due to loss of muscle tone. Great care must be taken not to misinterpret such findings for abuse. There are accidental causes of genital trauma, which include sports-related injuries, including falls from bicycles. A history with a specific time frame and circumstances should always be established concerning any previous injuries. When lacerations are present they need to be explained and a careful history should be obtained including all medical procedures documenting whether the injuries were there before medical examination or were a result of a medical procedure. Injuries that lack significant hemorrhage may be postmortem or perimortem. Another area of concern presents with interpretation challenges involving female genitals with respect to the hymen. The hymen is a relatively avascular membrane, without nerve innervations, that partially or fully covers (imperforate that is rare) the external vaginal opening. Trauma to the hymen alone may be associated with little or no bleeding due to the relative avascular nature. The spectrum of normal appearance is represented in the below diagram, which includes the spectrum of being completely open or closed at birth.

Less than half of women report bleeding while losing their virginity, which when it does occur, may involve deeper adjacent soft tissue injury. It has been well documented that sexual intercourse may not be associated with any trauma at all during virginity loss. The hymen normally may appear pink and may even have some red discoloration. As girls enter puberty, hormonal changes cause the hymen and surrounding tissues to become much more elastic, giving an ability to stretch significantly more before tearing. Prepubescent girls would usually have visible trauma with much less force as compared with postpubescent girls. Women of childbearing age are much less likely to have vaginal injury associated with sexual assault as compared with children or the elderly. The presence or absence of a hymen may not be an accurate indicator of virginity loss and, in some cases, sexual assault. The force and size of an object used during penetration will dictate much more accurately the possibility of visible trauma. If available, colposcopy is a useful tool in evaluating such injuries as microtears may be difficult to see. Another point is that trauma is more likely to occur in association with penetration involving an unwilling partner. If multiple past traumatic episodes occurred, there may be healing with fibrosis and dilatation. Positive venereal disease cultures indicate abuse unless a connection can be made to transmission during vaginal delivery.

As the above examples illustrate, the competent practice of pediatric forensic pathology—which spans intrauterine fetal life into young adulthood—affords many challenges. Such challenges are best approached through (1) appreciating the subject's complexities, (2) constantly acquiring and maintaining proficiency in relevant pediatric pathology disciplines, and, perhaps most importantly, (3) knowing when to seek assistance from related specialists.

References

Dolinak D, Matshes E. *Medicolegal Neuropathology: A Color Atlas*. Boca Raton, FL: CRC Press; 2002.

Dolinak D, Reichard R. An overview of inflicted head injury in infants and young children, with a review of β-amyloid precursor protein immunohistochemistry. *Arch Pathol Lab Med* 2006;130:712–717.

Geddes JF, Whitwell HL. Inflicted head injury in infants. *For Sci Int* 2004;146:83–88.

Johnson MW, Stoll L, Rubio A, et al. Axonal injury in young pediatric head trauma: A comparison study of β-amyloid precursor protein (βAPP) immunohistochemical staining in traumatic and nontraumatic deaths. *J Forensic Sci* 2011;56:1198–1205.

Reichard RR, White CL, Hladic CL, Dolinak D. Beta-amyloid precursor protein staining of nonaccidental central nervous system injury in pediatric autopsies. *J Neurotrauma* 2003;20:347–355.

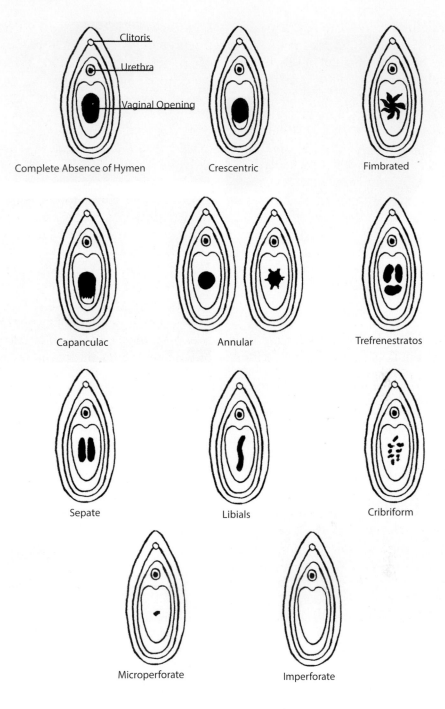

Complete Absence of Hymen

Clitoris

Urethra

Vaginal Opening

Crescentric

Fimbrated

Capanculac

Annular

Trefrenestratos

Sepate

Libials

Cribriform

Microperforate

Imperforate

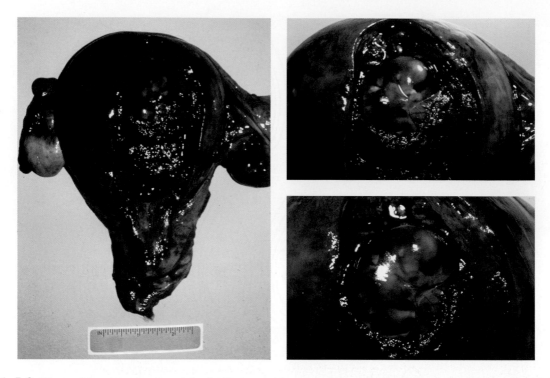

Figures 5.1–5.3 First trimester pregnancy, including gravid uterus (Figure 5.1) with a fetus enclosed within an intact amniotic sac and placenta (Figures 5.2 and 5.3).

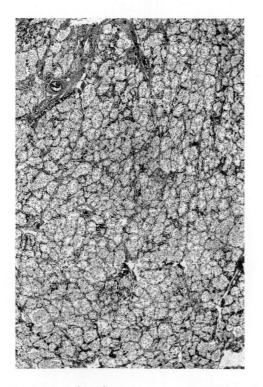

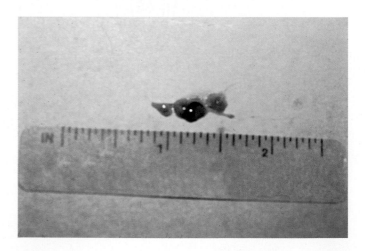

Figure 5.5 Early first trimester pregnancy.

Figure 5.4 Brown fat, the common type of fat in fetuses. Fetal, neonatal, and pediatric tissues are different than those in adults.

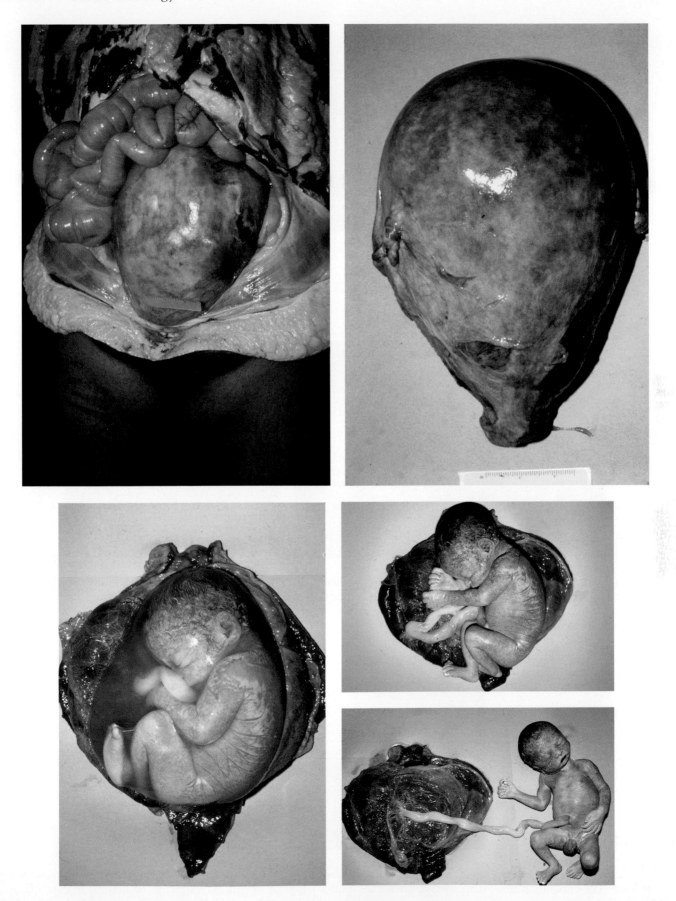

Figures 5.6–5.10 Late second trimester pregnancy, including gravid uterus (Figures 5.6 and 5.7) with placenta and an intact amniotic sac surrounding the fetus (Figure 5.8). Fetus and placenta connected by umbilical cord (Figures 5.9 and 5.10).

Figures 5.11–5.14 Second trimester stillborn with omphalocele (a type of abdominal wall defect), illegally aborted following administration of drugs given by a nonmedical practitioner. Note the x-ray and the sunken lungs at the bottom of the water container indicate no breaths were taken. The fetal lungs sink in water (Figure 5.13), and an x-ray shows no radiolucent air in the lungs (Figure 5.14).

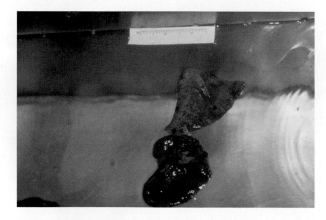

Figure 5.15 These lungs (from a different case) float in water, supporting a live birth with neonatal inspiration of air (breathing). The "floatation test" (i.e., assessing whether fetal lungs float or sink in water) can be helpful in determining stillbirth versus live birth, but the test must be interpreted with caution. For example, postmortem bacterial gas production can enable lungs from a stillborn fetus to float in water. While the utero-placental unit is usually a sterile environment, bacteria may be introduced in cases of chorioamnionitis, for example.

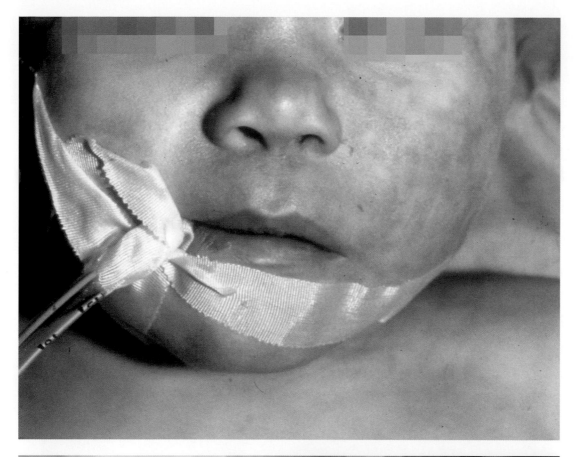

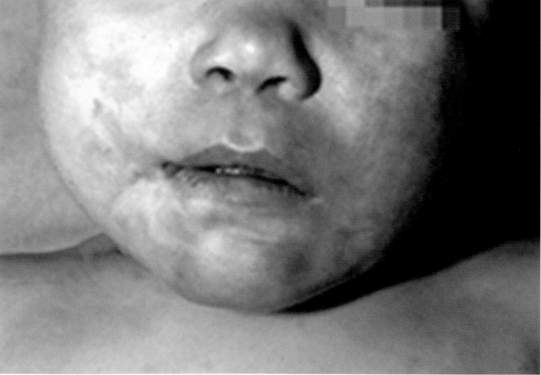

Figures 5.16 and 5.17 This child was brought to the emergency room and vigorously resuscitated. Note the marks and discoloration on the face as a result of endotracheal intubation and application of tape. It is important to document such findings at autopsy, but they should not be misinterpreted to have been caused by smothering, for example. It is very important for clinicians to leave all interventions on or in the body so that their placement and effects can be accurately interpreted at autopsy.

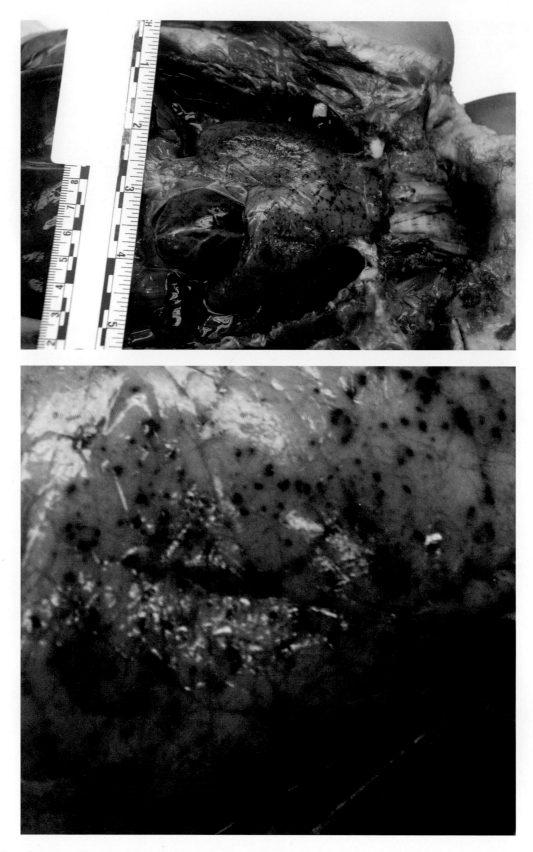

Figures 5.18 and 5.19 Sudden infant death syndrome (SIDS), which is a diagnosis of exclusion in a baby under 1 year of age. This usually occurs between 2 and 4 months. Thymic petechiae as demonstrated are a nonspecific finding, commonly seen in SIDS. Diagnosis of exclusion means all other causes of death and unsafe conditions, including unsafe sleep practice, has been ruled out. Unsafe sleep practices include co-sleeping, sleeping on soft bedding, and sleeping in a prone position. The "Back to Sleep" program, where the child is placed to sleep in a supine position, has reduced the occurrence of sudden unexpected infant death (SUID).

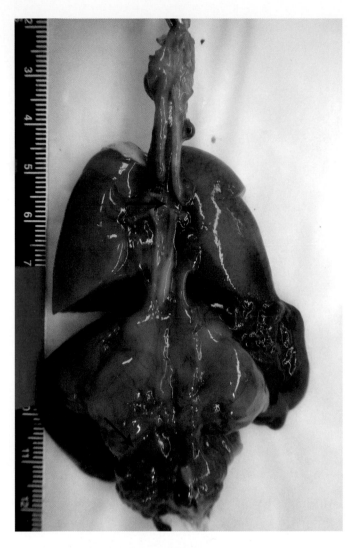

Figure 5.20 Congenital anomalies are the leading cause of death in infancy. This *en bloc* resection from larynx (top) to rectum (bottom), viewed from the back, shows a tracheoesophageal fistula (upper arrow) and multicystic renal dysplasia (lower arrow), two components of the VATER association. The best way to evaluate and document organ system malformations in fetuses and infants is with the *en bloc* evisceration method.

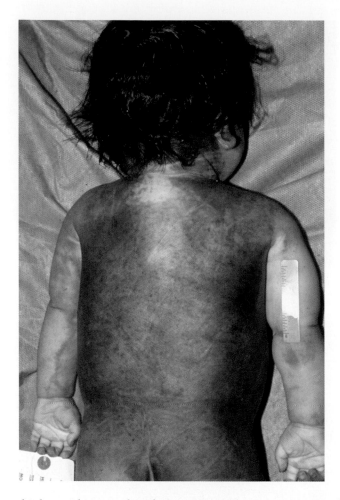

Figure 5.21 Posterior lividity, which may be mistaken for injuries such as contusions related to child abuse.

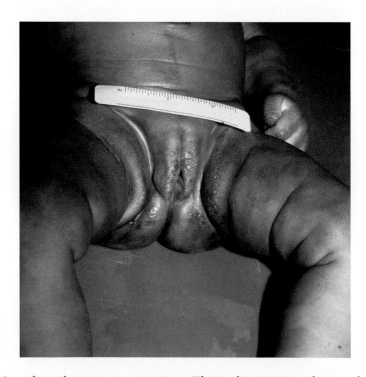

Figure 5.22 Diaper rash. Note the red cutaneous eruptions. This indicates some degree of neglect.

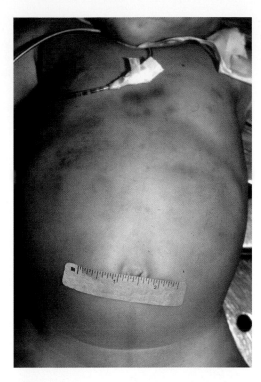

Figure 5.23 Child abuse case with resuscitative effects, including perimortem sternal contusions due to chest compressions. Note other small contusions on the right lower chest and upper abdomen. These were inflicted while the child was grabbed and flung about violently during the assault.

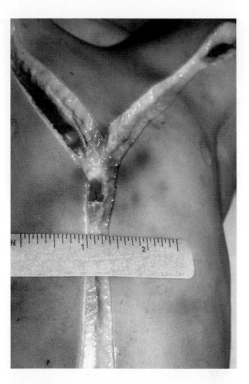

Figure 5.24 The same case showing perimortem subcutaneous contusions in the middle chest secondary to resuscitation. Note the other segment of the autopsy Y-shaped incision is devoid of hemorrhage.

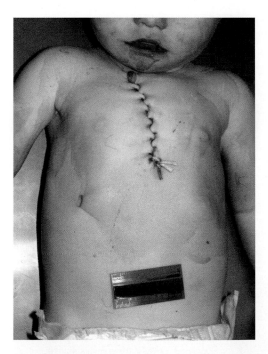

Figure 5.25 This case involved an infant who was found unresponsive in her crib. The case was referred to the medical examiner's office for autopsy. However, this sutured midline incision was noticed during external examination. Further inquires revealed that the emergency department (ED) physician had authorized postmortem procurement of the infant's heart for heart valves. When this was discovered, the organ procurement agency was contacted, who released the heart to the medical examiner's office. The heart was found to have an anomalous origin of the left coronary artery from the right sinus of Valsalva, a rare yet documented cause of sudden death in adults and infants. The issue of organ procurement remains a controversial and, at times, problematic one for the forensic pathologist. For example, consistently reliable methods for evaluating the coronary ostia have not been established in many tissue procurement agencies.

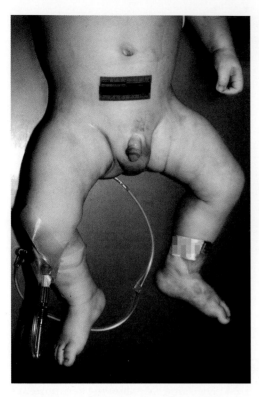

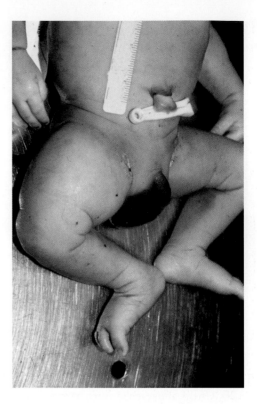

Figure 5.26 View of lower trunk, external genitalia, and lower extremities depicting a right-sided intraosseous (tibia) catheter. This a common mode of resuscitation in infants with extremely small, often collapsed blood vessels.

Figure 5.27 Hemorrhage with swelling of the thigh due to a misplaced femoral line.

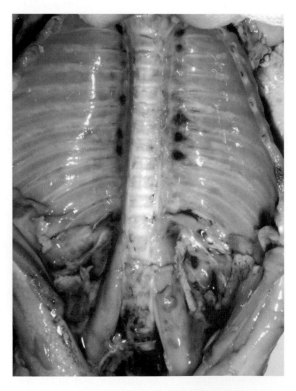

Figure 5.28 Antemortem or perimortem rib fractures are identified by the presence of hemorrhage in the adjacent soft tissue. These posterior thoracic rib fractures were sustained during cardiopulmonary resuscitation (CPR) of a neonate, which involves anterior-posterior chest compression. Posterior rib fractures can arise from either therapeutic or abusive chest compressions. They have also been noted to occur during organ donation. Clinical history and/or scene investigation are vital to understanding the circumstances under which such injuries are sustained.

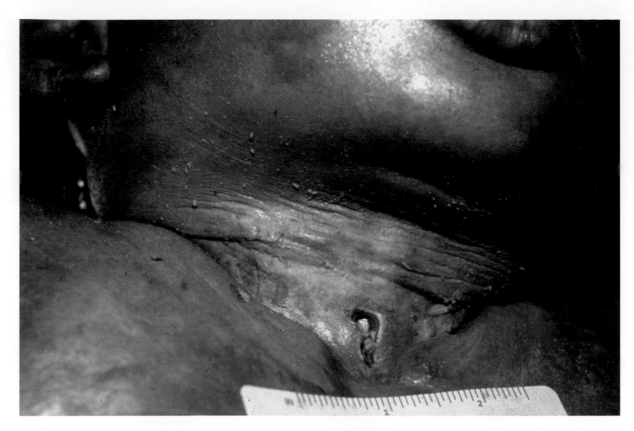

Figure 5.29 Healing but infected tracheotomy incision.

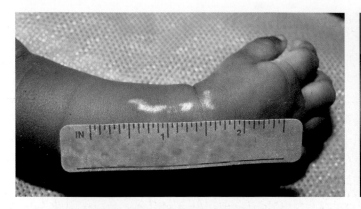 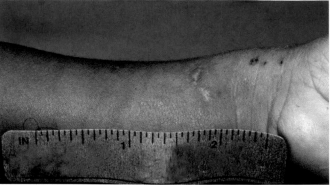

Figures 5.30 and 5.31 Scars to each wrist due to past cardiovascular access lines. Note Figure 5.31 has fresh needle puncture marks as well. Therapeutic procedures should not be mistaken for injuries.

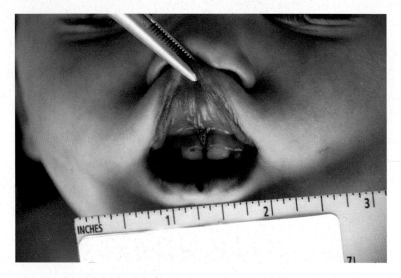

Figure 5.32 Small tear of the upper frenulum due to vigorous resuscitative efforts by an untrained person. Note the small bruise on the left cheek, which occurred several days earlier due to a fall. The resuscitative efforts were captured on a department store video camera in this child that became lifeless following a seizure.

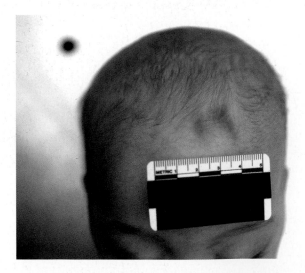

Figure 5.33 This case involved an infant who suffered an asphyxial death. He was found with his head compressed (wedged) between an adult bed and a wall. He was pulseless, apneic, and asystolic, and despite resuscitative efforts, he could not be revived.

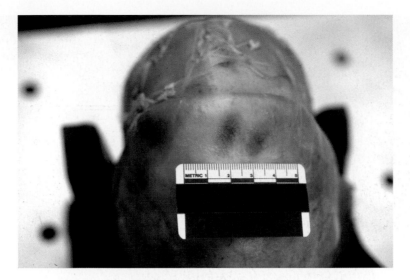

Figure 5.34 Same case, this time depicting the frontal and temporal regions of the scalp with two ill-defined contusions within the frontal subgaleal tissue, corroborates application of force at this site due to wedging.

Figure 5.35 This view shows the relationship between the mattress and the wall. The mattress was separated from the wall by at least several inches, which allowed the infant to descend into the space and become compressed.

Figure 5.36 This picture is a view looking down toward the floor where the infant (position marked by blanket) was found lying wedged between the wall and the mattress.

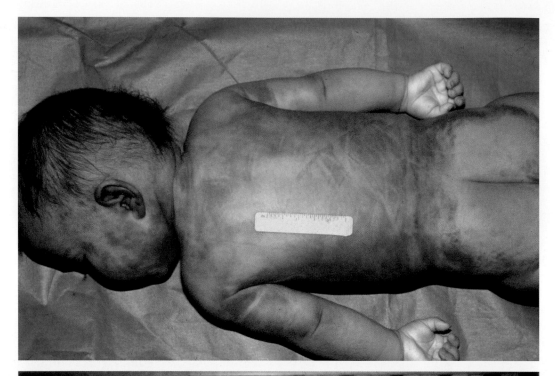

Figures 5.37 and 5.38 This child was brought to the emergency department (ED) by parents who did not speak English well. The child was reportedly found dead in his crib. Note the posterior patchy red lividity. There is also a faint area of dark discoloration on the left buttock ("Mongolian spot"). Subsequent scene investigation by the medical examiner's office and police department revealed that the child had actually died from positional asphyxia, having slipped down and wedged between the crib's mattress and frame. There were no marks on the child's body at autopsy. The mattress was from another crib and was slightly smaller than the frame. The doll demonstrates the position in which the dead infant was found. Such doll reenactments are a very important component of SUID scene investigations.

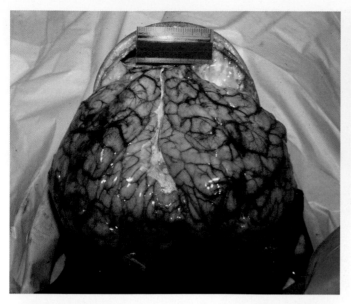

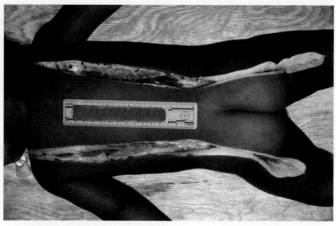

Figure 5.39 This image demonstrates brain swelling with flattening of gyri and obliteration of sulci due to hypoxic-ischemic brain injury. This 7-month-old female infant was found unresponsive in a seat that had fallen to the floor from an adult bed, resulting in her chin being tightly apposed to her chest, satisfying the criteria for positional asphyxia. She survived for several days and was ultimately declared brain dead. No other injuries were identified at autopsy.

Figure 5.40 This 9-month-old child with a history of asthma was found unresponsive in her crib. Autopsy demonstrated multiple mucous plugs within the medium-sized airways, along with other characteristic pathologic features of asthma. No injuries were found. Death was certified as complications of bronchial asthma, which, although rare at this age, is a recognized cause of sudden death. In order to verify the absence of injury, incisions into the subcutis of the trunk and extremities are made at autopsy, especially in dark-skinned individuals in whom bruises cannot be easily recognized on the body. In this case, there are no subcutaneous contusions.

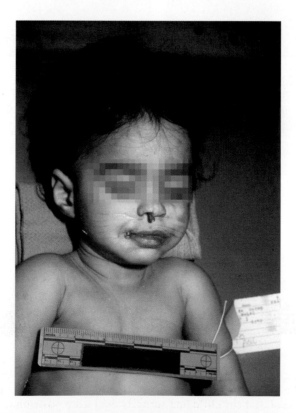

Figure 5.41 This previously healthy female infant was found by her mother submerged in a bathtub. The mother had allegedly left the infant and her 18-month-old brother unattended in an empty bathtub, and the mother postulated that the brother must have turned on the faucets when she was away. When attempting to reconstruct the scene, police discovered that the brother was unable to turn on the faucets by himself. Although the cause of death in this case was certified as drowning and the manner homicide, the mother was released on probation.

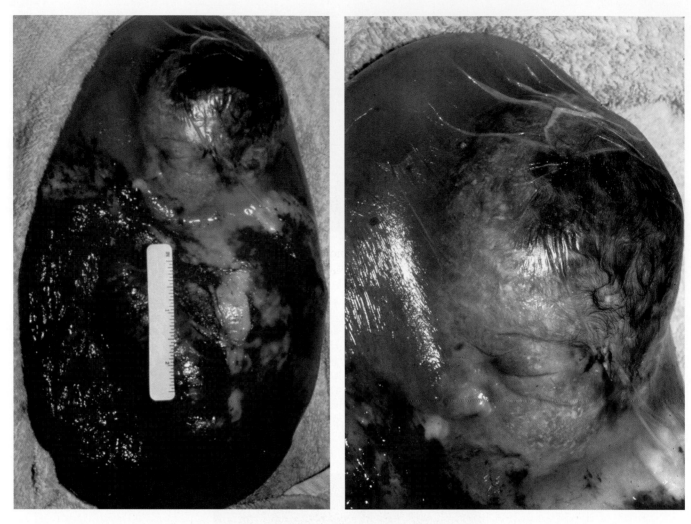

Figures 5.42 and 5.43 This normally developed fetus and placenta were spontaneously delivered by a young mother who did not have the requisite medical knowledge to know that membranes have to be ruptured following delivery so that the baby can breathe. Mom reported fetal movement in the amniotic sac for a period of time following delivery. The baby died of asphyxia and the manner of death was certified as natural.

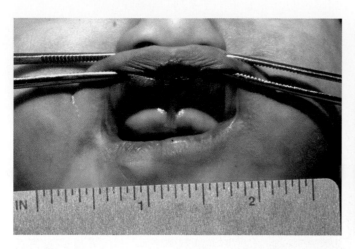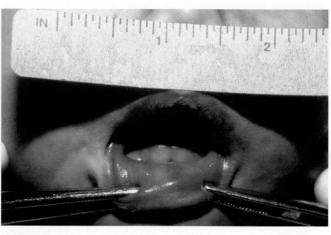

Figures 5.44 and 5.45 In infants, it is important to examine the face around the nose and mouth and the oral cavity, including the frenulum, to rule out trauma such as smothering. Both of these cases show no injuries.

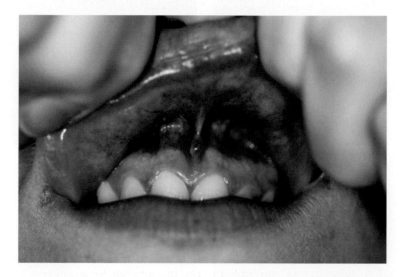

Figure 5.46 Healed frenulum laceration. This individual had fallen in the past and accidently struck his face on a kitchen cabinet.

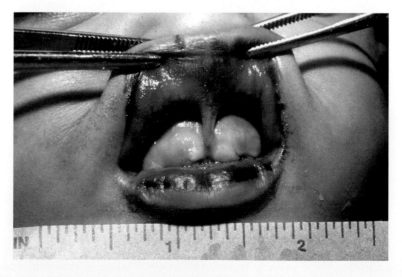

Figure 5.47 Intact frenulum with postmortem drying of the lips. The latter finding is a postmortem change and should not suggest child abuse.

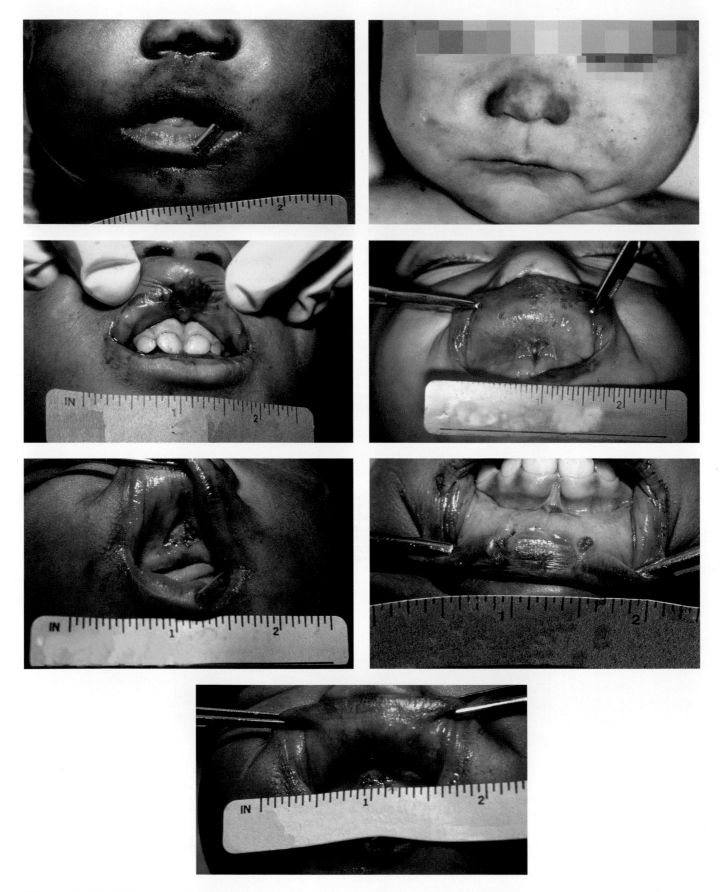

Figures 5.48–5.54 These children show variable trauma to the face, including abrasions and contusions on the skin, as well as lacerations in the lips and frenula. All are from cases of homicidal smothering. It is important to realize that a homicidal smothering may occur without leaving marks on the body as well.

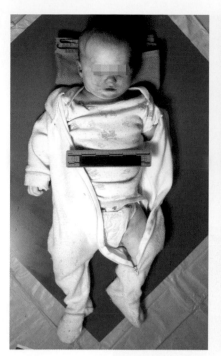

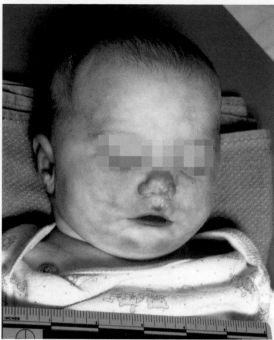

Figures 5.55 and 5.56 These images show a several-month-old infant who was found unresponsive in her crib. She had no known previous illness. If possible, it is always important to photograph infants as they are found, which allows for more accurate reconstruction of the terminal events (e.g., sleeping position, stains of blood-tinged fluid on clothing). These photos demonstrate clear fluid emanating from the left nostril, with a faintly frothy quality, probably indicative of pulmonary edema, which is a common and nonspecific finding in SUID cases, particularly following resuscitative efforts. Vigorous resuscitation efforts, which include chest compressions, contribute to the formation of edema fluid, which is often blood-tinged due to rupture of small capillaries in the lungs. Oftentimes, the blood-tinged fluid is misinterpreted by scene investigation personnel as being suspicious of foul play. It is important for pathologists and EMS personnel to educate people with nonmedical backgrounds regarding the distinction between blood-tinged edema fluid and actual blood.

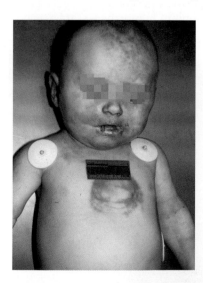

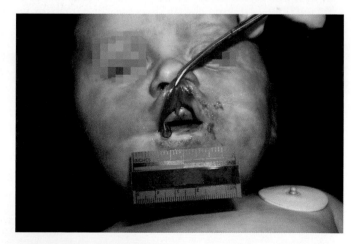

Figure 5.58 Same case. An intact upper frenulum with dried blood-tinged secretion around the left side of the mouth and no trauma.

Figure 5.57 This case involved the sudden death of an otherwise healthy infant. The confluent burns/abrasions on his anterior chest reflect application of defibrillator paddles during resuscitation. Additional therapeutic interventions can be seen, including an endotracheal tube and ECG pads. The blotchy red discoloration of the forehead and face (left side slightly greater than right side) might be interpreted as livor mortis, but it is important to realize that vigorous resuscitative efforts may also alter the patterns of vascular congestion.

Figure 5.59 This infant was found unresponsive in his crib and could not be resuscitated. Maternal history was significant only for group B streptococcal infection. This picture depicts prominent petechiae on the anterior surface of the thymus. Petechiae involving the thymus, visceral pleura, and epicardial surfaces are common findings in SUID, including deaths that have been ascribed to SIDS (up to ~85% of SIDS fatalities). The precise mechanism underlying the formation of petechiae remains elusive, but is believed to be related to the negative intrathoracic pressure created by terminal gasping in infants. However, it is well known that petechiae are not in any way specific or pathognomonic for SUID, and they may be found in deaths due to many other causes, including definable natural disease conditions, accidental injuries, and inflicted injuries (homicides). In this case, the petechiae, which appear as pinpoint hemorrhages, are particularly striking.

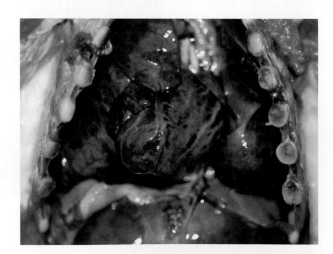

Figure 5.60 This is a view of the thoracic contents of an infant who was found unresponsive in a supine position while bed sharing with his mother. She called 911 and paramedics arrived to find him apneic and pulseless. He could not be resuscitated. Pertinent history included prematurity, maternal group B streptococcal infection, and a recent upper respiratory infection. The only significant findings at autopsy were a moderately cellular mononuclear leptomeningeal exudate, consistent with a viral meningoencephalitis. However, there was no significant brain swelling. This fatality occurred in the early to mid-1990s and the death was ascribed to SIDS. If a similar case were encountered today, the cause of death should be SUID, "bed sharing in an adult bed" should be listed as a risk factor in part two of the cause of death statement, and the manner of death should be undetermined. This picture depicts prominent petechiae on the anterior epicardial surface of the heart.

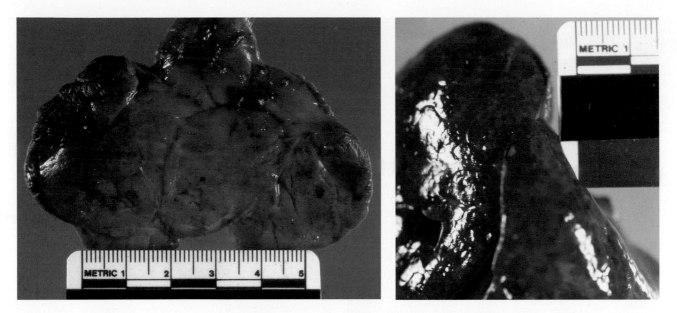

Figures 5.61 and 5.62 This case involved an infant who was born prematurely at 35 weeks gestation and was found prone in a bassinet with his face between a "covered" adult-sized pillow and the corner of the bassinet. The findings of this case were not sufficient to render a diagnosis of mechanical asphyxia, but asphyxia was of sufficient concern to denote the cause of death as SUID and the manner undetermined. This picture shows sparse, inconspicuous petechiae on the visceral pleura and thymus, which were the only gross findings at autopsy.

Figure 5.63 This view of the mediastinal surface of the left lung demonstrates confluent subpleural hemorrhages within the lower lobe, likely an artifact of vigorous CPR. Note the way that the hemorrhages conform to anatomic boundaries, similar to what is observed in aspiration of blood.

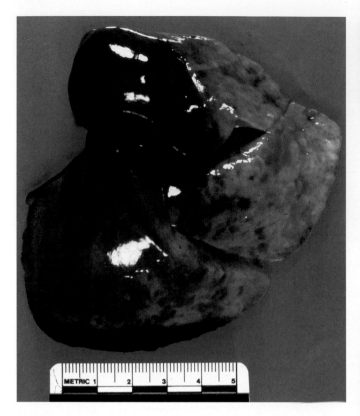

Figure 5.64 Same case demonstrating the costal surface of the lung, with blotchy subpleural hemorrhages, some slightly larger than petechiae. Note also the confluent congestion within the posterior aspects of the lung, most likely a result of postmortem hypostasis, or settling of blood due to gravity.

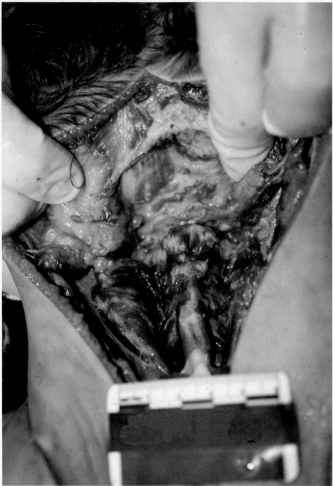

Figure 5.65 This was a case involving the enigmatic death of a 2-year old child who was previously healthy. She had finished a course of amoxicillin for otitis media 3 days prior to her death. On the day before her death, she apparently fell off a "teeter-totter" and struck her head on the ground, which was a muddy, grassy surface, but she never lost consciousness and experienced no mental status changes. She could not be aroused from an afternoon nap and could not be resuscitated following Pediatric Life Support protocol. The gross autopsy findings were unrevealing, including absence of scalp, skull, and brain injuries. The only findings in addition to thymic, epicardial, and visceral pleural petechiae was fibromuscular hyperplasia of the AV nodal artery, which was discovered by an expert cardiac pathologist who consulted on the case. This picture depicts a posterior neck dissection, demonstrating soft tissues and skeletal muscles that are free of injury. In this case anterior neck dissection was negative for injuries as well.

Figure 5.66 Same case, depicting prominent epicardial petechiae on the anterior surface of the heart. This case illustrates that the findings of intrathoracic petechiae are not confined to infants but can also be seen in young children.

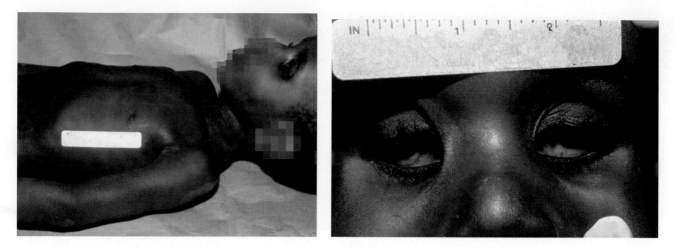

Figures 5.67 and 5.68 This child died of complications of dehydration following a prolonged viral gastroenteritis. The sunken eyes reflect fluid deficit.

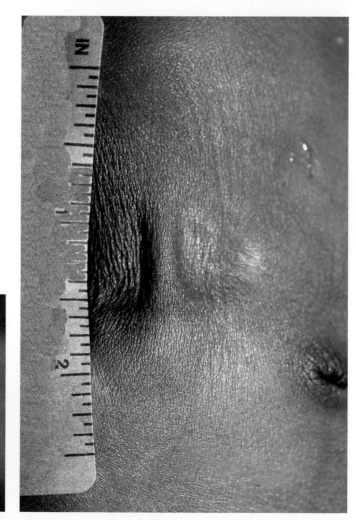

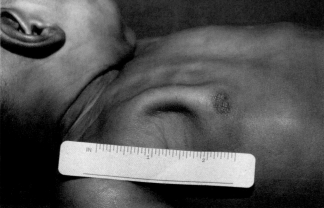

Figures 5.69 and 5.70 Artifactual poor skin elasticity (turgor) is demonstrated in these infants that were refrigerated in the morgue overnight. These infants were shown not to be dehydrated by vitreous analyte determination and ante-mortem hospital chemistry testing. The poor skin elasticity in these cases is due to the congealing of fat as a result of postmortem refrigeration.

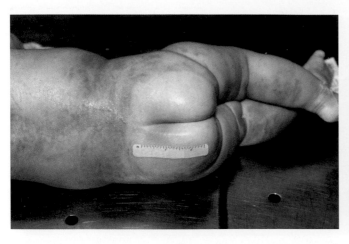

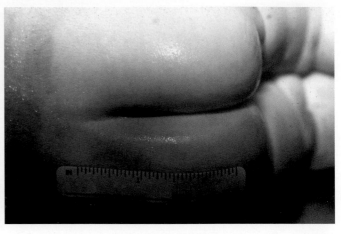

Figures 5.71 and 5.72 Mongolian spot. This birthmark associated with the gluteal fold can be mistaken for a contusion. The two entities can be distinguished by making an incision through the lesion; the presence or absence of subcutaneous blood indicates a contusion or a birthmark, respectively. Rarely, a contusion can be adjacent to or superimposed upon a Mongolian spot.

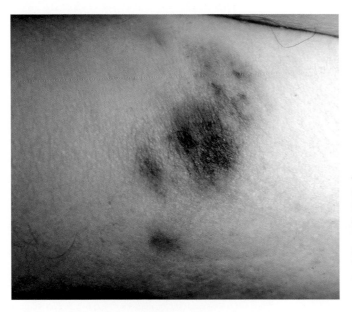

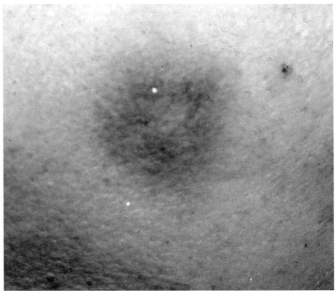

Figure 5.73 Dating contusions is not reliable, but recent contusions tend to be more red-purple.

Figure 5.74 Dating contusions is not reliable, but older contusions tend to be more brown to yellow or green.

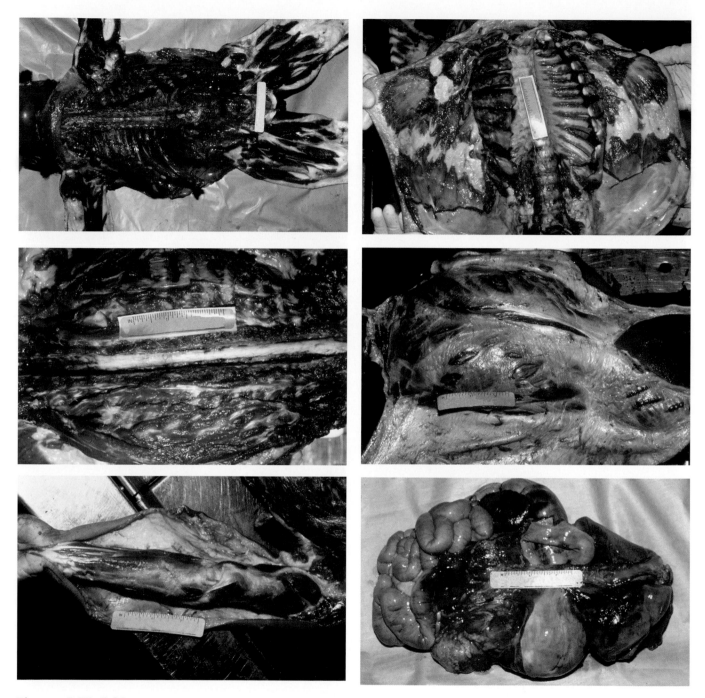

Figures 5.75–5.80 A competent autopsy in suspected child abuse cases includes incising the posterior neck, torso, and extremities so that the underlying soft tissues can be carefully examined for hemorrhages. In some children, and particularly in those with darker skin, deep injuries may not be visible on the body's surface. Additionally, the parietal pleura should be stripped so that each rib can be individually examined and removed, if needed.

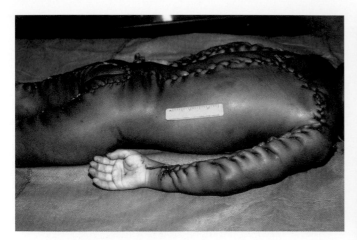

Figure 5.81 Following autopsy, all incisions are carefully closed and the body is released to the funeral home. Customary open casket viewings do not show evidence of any autopsy incisions.

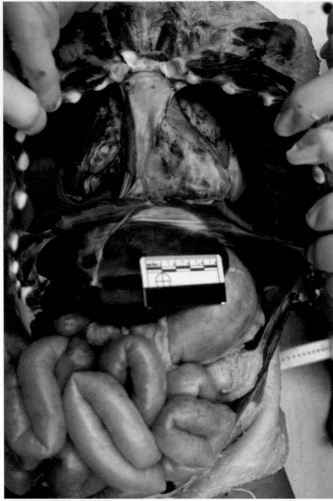

Figure 5.82 This 2-year-old child was brought to the ED by his mother's boyfriend after being found unresponsive. The only external injury was a small faint contusion to the child's forehead. Autopsy revealed a fracture of the lumbar spine with a transected descending thoracic aorta, hemothoraces, and an old healed fracture of one clavicle.

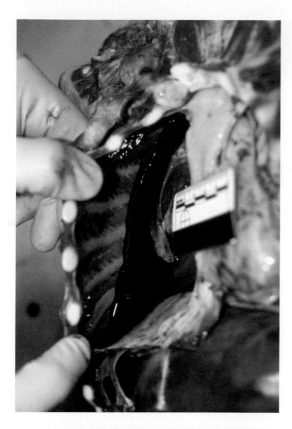

Figure 5.83 Same case. Right hemothorax due to aortic transection.

Figure 5.84 Same case. Approximately 165 cc of blood was present in the chest. In a case such as this, death is probably due to more than one mechanism, including blood loss, spinal cord injury, and sympathetic nervous system dysfunction.

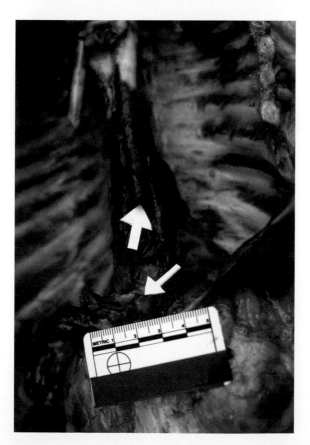

Figure 5.85 Same case. Free ends of transected descending thoracic aorta, marked with arrows.

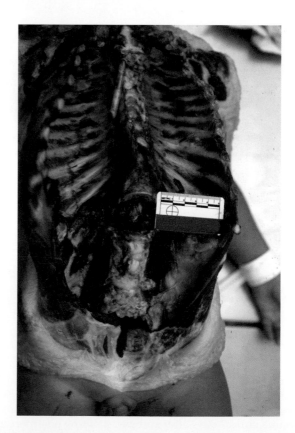

Figure 5.86 Same case. Fracture in lumbar vertebral body, which resembles a "hinge."

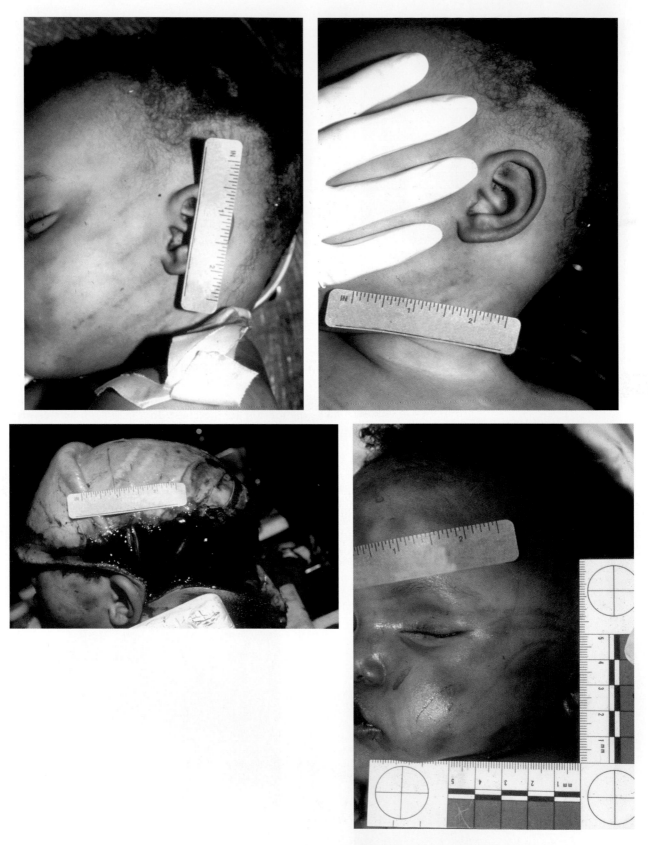

Figures 5.87–5.90 This child died from multiple blunt force injuries. The pattern of parallel contusions on the left face (Figure 5.87) is consistent with a hand imprint (Figure 5.88). External examination does not disclose extensive scalp hemorrhage over the left skull, which is only revealed following incision and reflection of the scalp (Figure 5.89). A picture of the same child 2 days after autopsy, showing postmortem enhancement of the facial contusions. Additional examination of a body after performing an autopsy can reveal or clarify subtle findings.

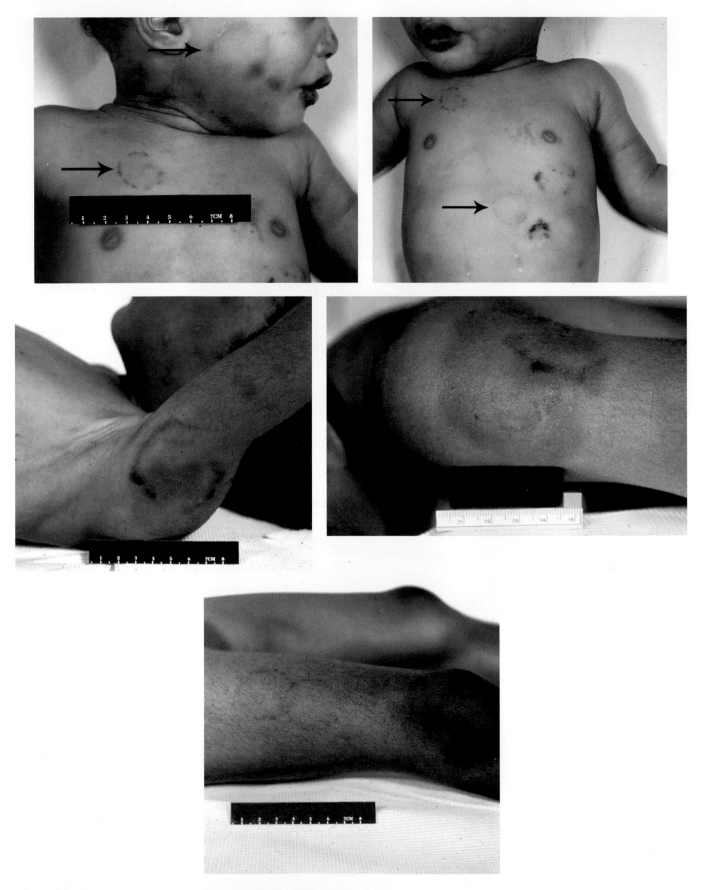

Figures 5.91–5.95 Multiple examples of recent human bite marks. Note the circular pattern and the red mark in the center of the bite mark in Figure 5.93 indicating a greater force.

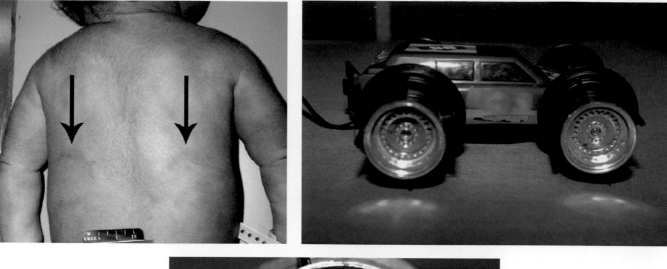

Figures 5.96–5.98 Bruises to this child's back were initially interpreted as bite marks by hospital personnel; further evaluation with scene investigation and interviews revealed these marks to be caused by toy truck tires.

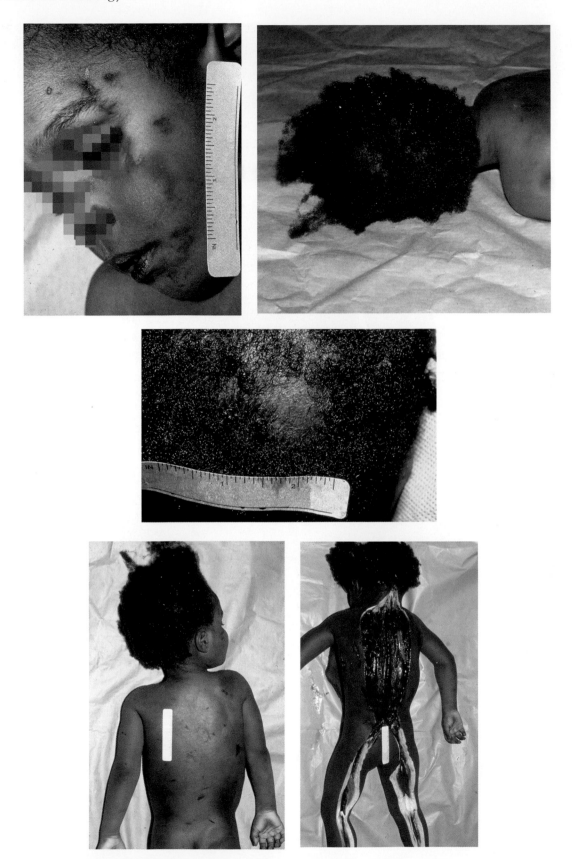

Figures 5.99–5.103 This child sustained multiple blunt force injuries to his head, back, and extremities. The child's hair was traumatically pulled from his scalp (Figures 5.100 and 5.101). Note the multiple, angulated, red to brown, abraded contusions on the child's back (Figure 5.102), the pattern of which is consistent with striking with a belt buckle. Incision into the back's skin and subcutis reveals extensive hemorrhage (Figure 5.103), which was not as apparent on external examination. In contrast, note the clean yellow appearance of the lower extremities' subcutaneous tissue (Figure 5.103).

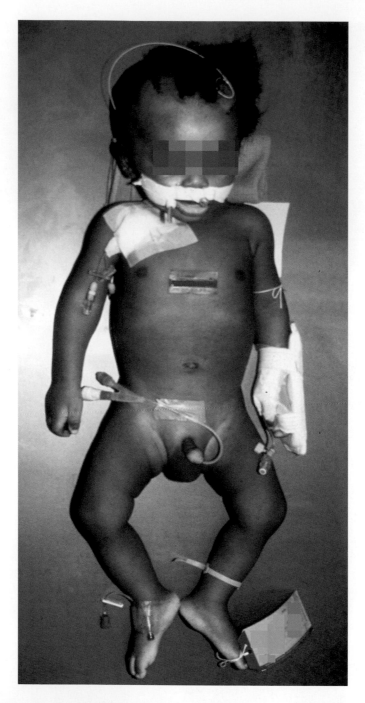

Figure 5.104 Multiple therapeutic interventions present at autopsy. Documenting such interventions is important to help prevent misinterpretation of therapeutic intervention as injury.

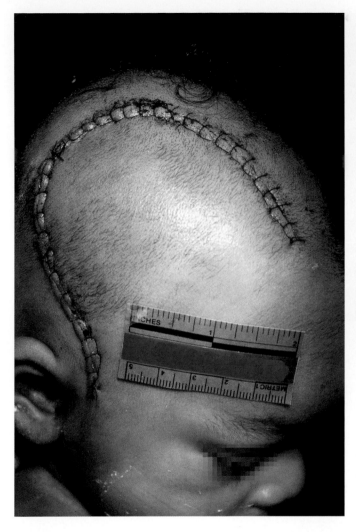

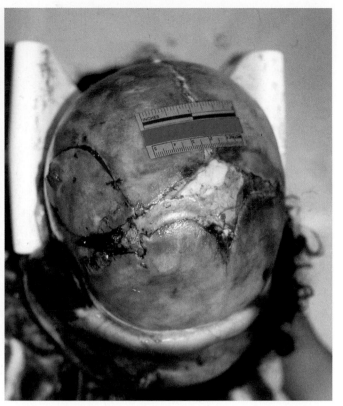

Figure 5.106 Same case. This superior view of the calvarium illustrates marked widening (diastasis) of the coronal suture and anterior fontanelle secondary to brain edema.

Figure 5.105 Same case. This sutured right-sided scalp incision is consistent with a recent craniotomy performed for evacuation of a right-sided subdural hematoma.

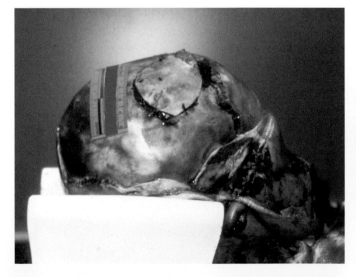

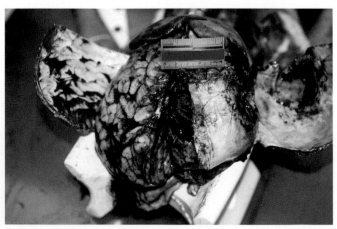

Figure 5.108 Same case. Residual right-sided subdural hemorrhage and marked brain edema, the latter best appreciated on the left side by flattening of gyri and effacement of intervening sulci. The inner left surface of the dura is also bloodstained.

Figure 5.107 Same case. Right side of face and skull, including craniotomy site. Marked diastasis of the coronal suture is also present.

Figure 5.109 Formaldehyde-fixed piece of dura mater from an approximately 4-month-old infant with a history of tetralogy of Fallot who was found unresponsive by his mother's boyfriend. The boyfriend claimed that the infant had fallen approximately 3 ft. from a couch onto a carpeted floor. Such explanations are often incompatible with the spectrum of injuries observed at autopsy. In this case, the adherent, thin-layered, clotted subdural blood indicates a duration of approximately 3–4 days following the injury, which correlates with the survival period of this infant after being found unresponsive.

Figure 5.110 Same case. Formaldehyde-fixed, markedly friable, fragmented brain of the infant. The friability of the brain is attributable to marked hypoxic-ischemic injury, and is therefore a nonspecific finding, as hypoxic-ischemic brain injury can result from various natural and traumatic processes.

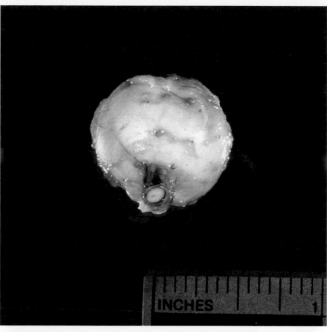

Figure 5.111 Same case. Cross section of the optic nerve located on the same side as the subdural hematoma, which had been evacuated. The infant never regained consciousness and was declared brain dead approximately 3 days following the surgery. Optic nerve sheath hemorrhage, which is correlated with retinal hemorrhage, is not specific for inflicted injury, as it may be seen in conditions of sepsis, hemorrhagic diathesis, and other rare natural conditions.

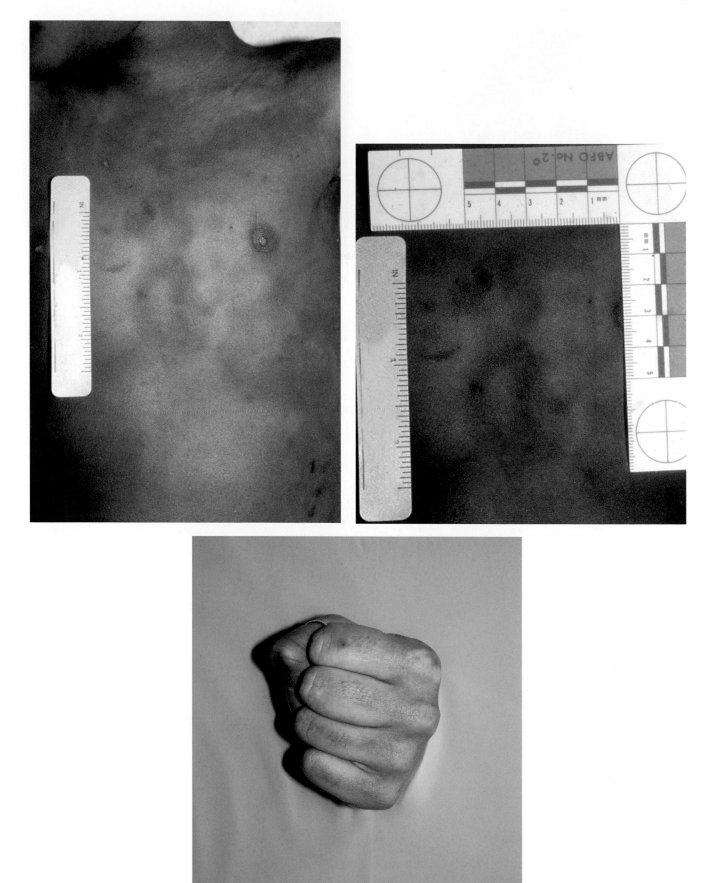

Figures 5.112–5.114 Vague pattern of contusions on anterior torso (Figures 5.112 and 5.113), as well as an abrasion and vague contusions on the fist (Figure 5.114). This physically abused child died of multiple blunt impact injuries and was discovered dead at the scene in full rigor. No resuscitation was performed.

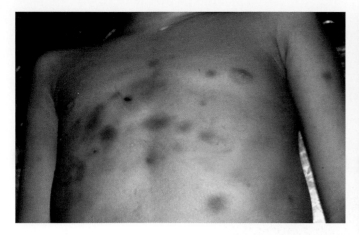

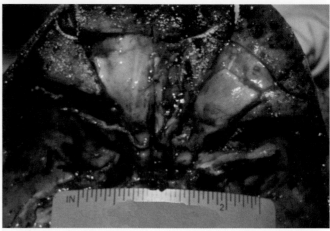

Figure 5.115 Antemortem contusions on middle and lower anterior torso due to abusive trauma, in conjunction with perimortem contusions overlying the sternum related to resuscitation.

Figure 5.116 To retrieve eyes for examination at autopsy, the anterior cranial fossa (orbital plate) is incised to expose the orbit, optic nerves, and associated soft tissues.

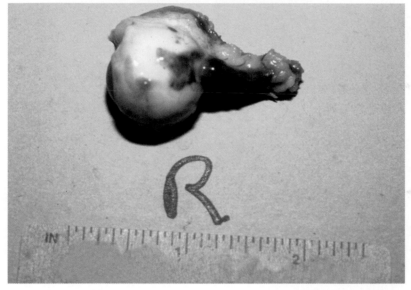

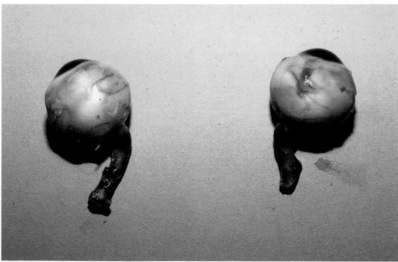

Figures 5.117 and 5.118 Eyes of child who died from violent shaking, showing hemorrhages in the optic nerves and focally in the sclera. Microscopic examination also revealed retinal hemorrhages. There was no evidence of natural disease, such as coagulopathic syndromes or connective tissue disorders, which could account for the hemorrhages.

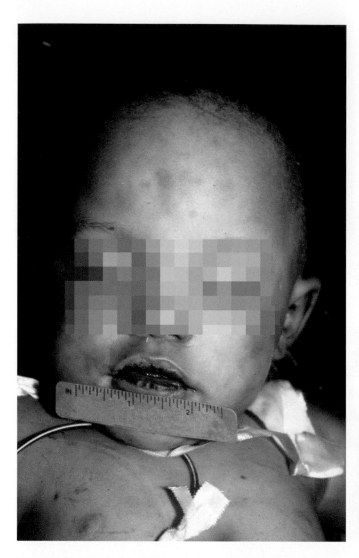

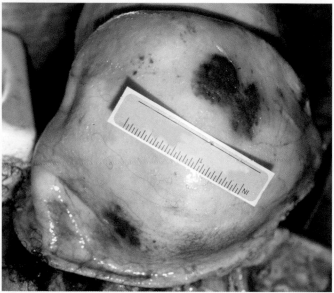

Figures 5.119 and 5.120 Vague contusions on the forehead of a physically abused child (Figure 5.119). Reflection of the scalp reveals prominent soft tissue (subgaleal) hemorrhage (Figure 5.120). It is important to correlate external and internal findings at autopsy.

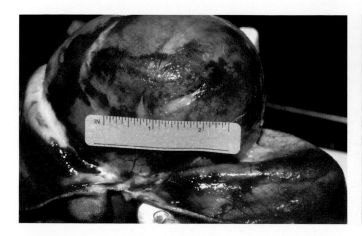

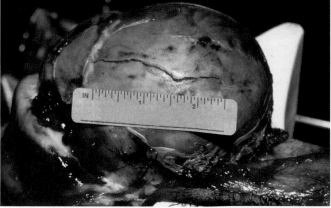

Figures 5.121 and 5.122 Child abuse case. Reflected scalp shows hemorrhage, and the underlying skull shows a linear fracture, together corroborating blunt force trauma to the area.

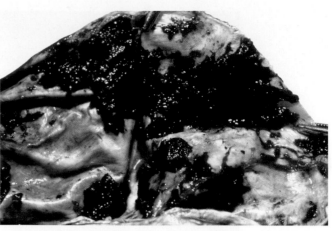

Figure 5.131 Inside view of calvarium showing recent subdural hemorrhage associated with left vertex dura (overlying the left cerebral hemisphere). There is also separation of the dura from the left temporal-parietal-occipital skull adjacent to sites of skull fracture.

Figure 5.132 Piece of formaldehyde-fixed dura mater saved for additional neuropathologic evaluation, showing adherent black-brown subdural blood clot.

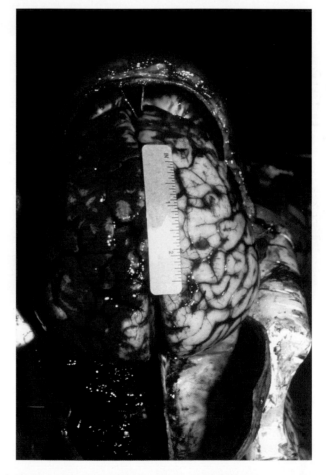

Figure 5.133 Formaldehyde-fixed segment of spinal cord removed with the dura mater showing subdural hemorrhage. It is important to remove the spinal cord as carefully as possible in order to avoid potentially troublesome artifacts.

Figure 5.134 Calvarium reflected backward for removal of the brain at autopsy. The dura mater, adherent to the inner aspect of the skull (endocalvarial surface), shows a large, left-sided, adherent subdural blood clot (bottom left of image). There is also diffuse cerebral edema, manifested by flattening of the gyral configuration and obliteration of the intervening sulci. The reddish discoloration over the left cerebral hemisphere represents patchy subarachnoid hemorrhage. Subarachnoid and subdural hemorrhages together often reflect blunt force trauma to the head.

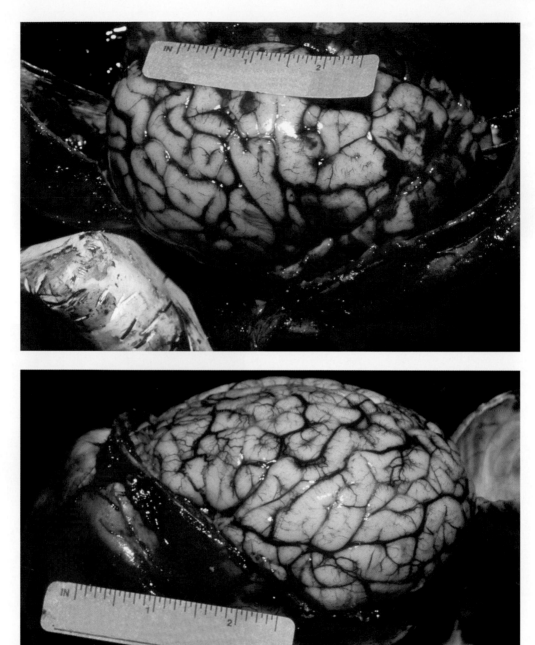

Figures 5.135 and 5.136 Close-up views of brain edema, with flattening of gyri and obliteration of intervening sulci in a child who survived several days following homicidal blunt force trauma.

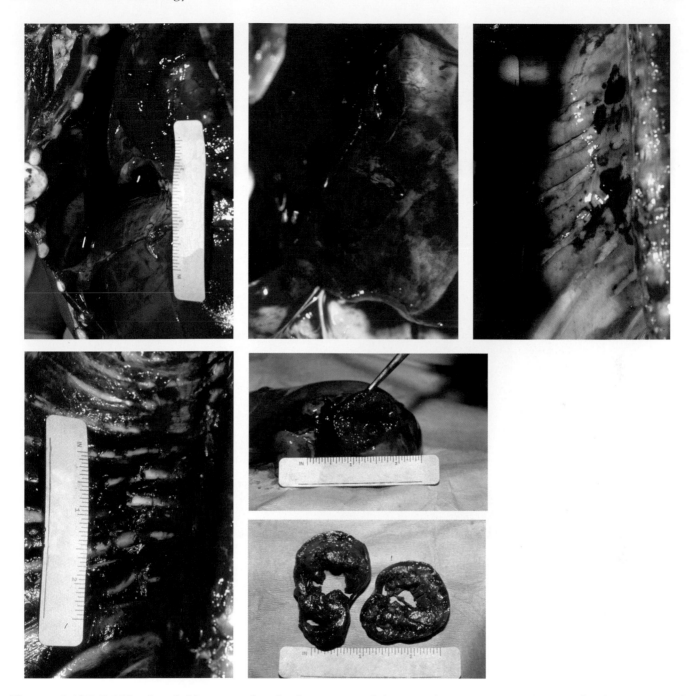

Figures 5.137–5.142 This child sustained multiple posterior rib fractures (Figures 5.139 and 5.140) after being stomped on by an adult while lying face-down on the floor. The fractured rib segments penetrated the posterior right lung, producing extensive pulmonary and intrathoracic hemorrhage (Figures 5.137 and 5.138). There were also large lacerations in the posterior aspects of the liver (Figure 5.141) and heart (Figure 5.142).

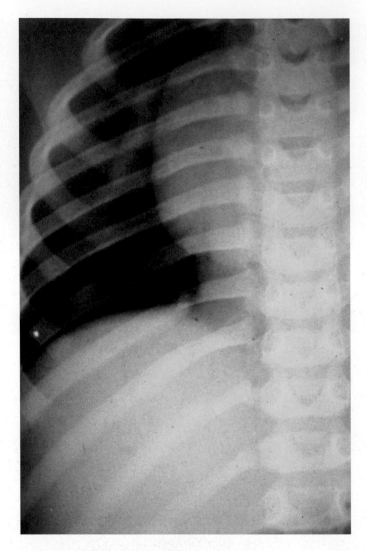

Figure 5.143 X-ray showing multiple recent rib fractures.

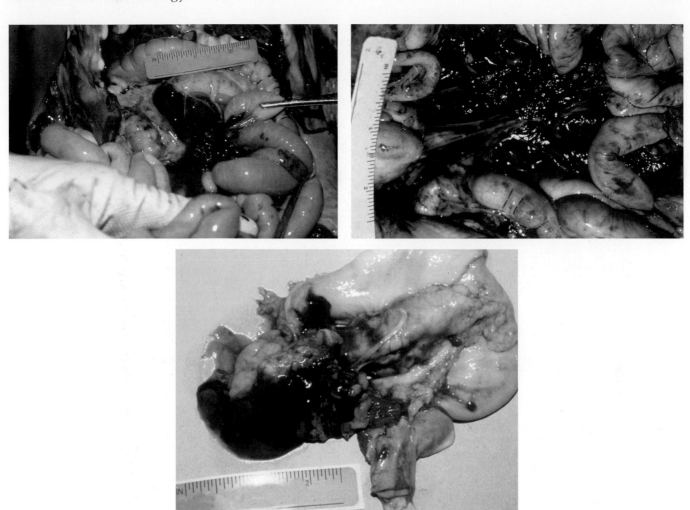

Figures 5.144–5.146 These images demonstrate multiple lacerations involving the mesentery (Figure 5.144), meso-colon (Figure 5.145), and peripancreatic soft tissues (Figure 5.146) following blunt abdominal impacts associated with homicidal violence.

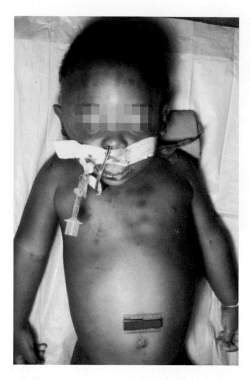

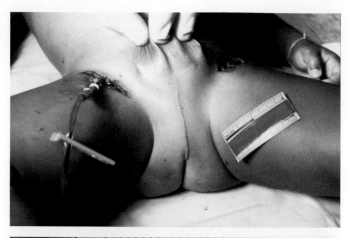

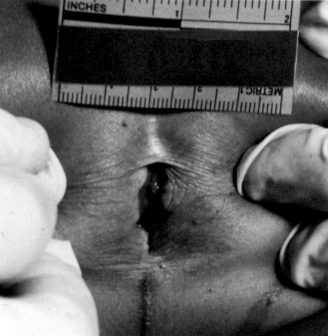

Figure 5.147 This 2-year-old child was found unresponsive in a bathtub. There are patchy contusions on the forehead and anterior chest. An autopsy revealed confluent subgaleal contusions, essentially spanning from ear to ear, along with brain swelling, although the skull was intact. Death was attributed to blunt impact injuries to the head with brain edema. A component of drowning could not be ruled out in this case. The chest contusions were probably secondary to resuscitative efforts. Differentiating between the effects of therapy and antecedent injuries can be problematic, however, and the two processes may coexist. Of note, the defendant in this case was convicted of second-degree murder.

Figures 5.149 and 5.150 Perineum (Figure 5.149) and anus (Figure 5.150) of a child. No injuries are evident. In all cases of potential child abuse, it is good practice to photographically document relevant normal as well as all abnormal findings. When examination of the external pelvis suggests the possibility of injury, or absence of injury is not clear, the authors recommend *en bloc* removal and subsequent dissection of the pelvic and perineal structures.

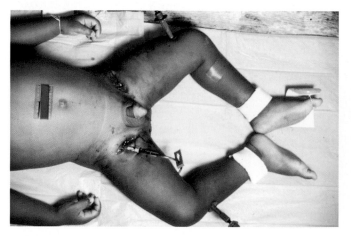

Figure 5.148 Lower trunk and extremities of a child, with multiple therapeutic interventions including transverse cut-down sites in the groins (for vascular access), bilateral intraosseous catheters, and a right groin catheter.

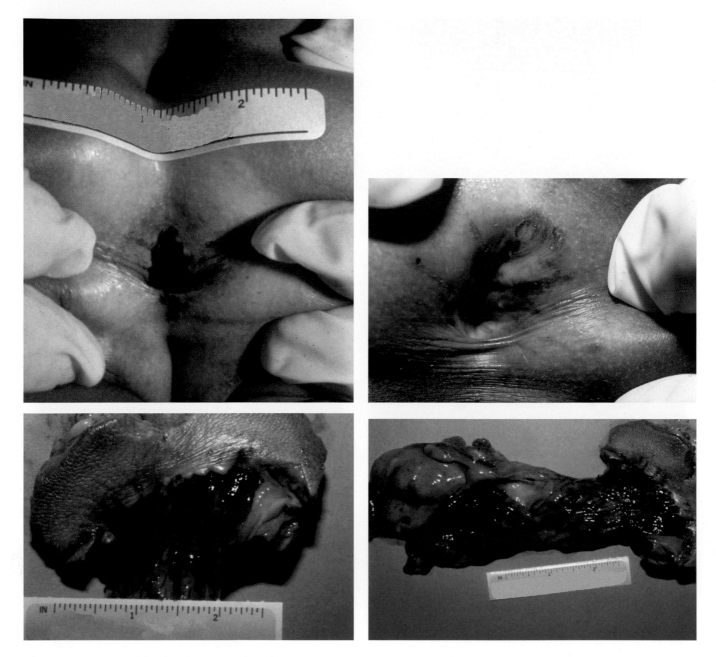

Figures 5.151–5.154 These images demonstrate sexual abuse in a young child. Note the abrasions and lacerations around the anus (Figures 5.151 and 5.152). Examination of *en bloc* resection of the anus and rectum (Figures 5.153 and 5.154) reveals internal lacerations near the anal junction (Figures 5.153 and 5.154) and mucosal hemorrhages in the rectum (Figure 5.154).

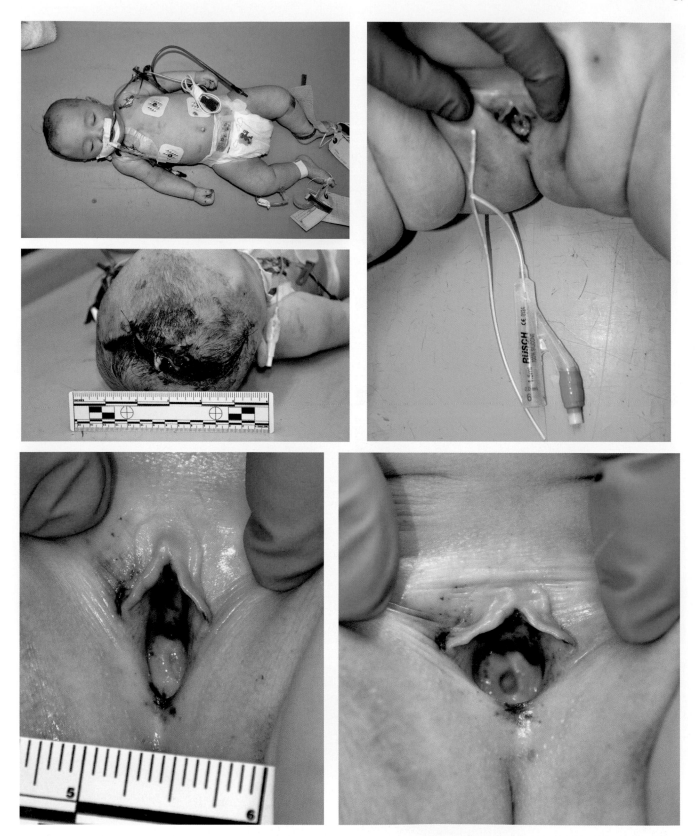

Figures 5.155–5.159 This child was ejected from a car seat during a motor vehicle collision where he sustained a skull fracture and a scalp laceration. The child was vigorously resuscitated and the new intern had a difficult time placing the urethral catheter, causing the contusions and abrasions as seen in Figures 5.158 and 5.159. This was initially interpreted by the medical examiner as possible child abuse.

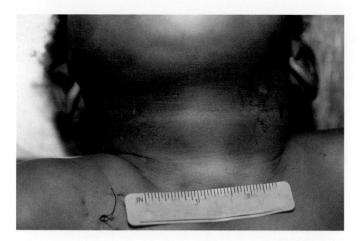

Figure 5.160 Superficial, healing, criss-crossed, linear abrasions due to rubbing of Velcro jacket patches on each side of this child's neck. This suggests rough handling. This child was later killed by multiple blunt impact injuries during an assault. Note the suture and fresh needle marks on the right chest from a removed subclavian line.

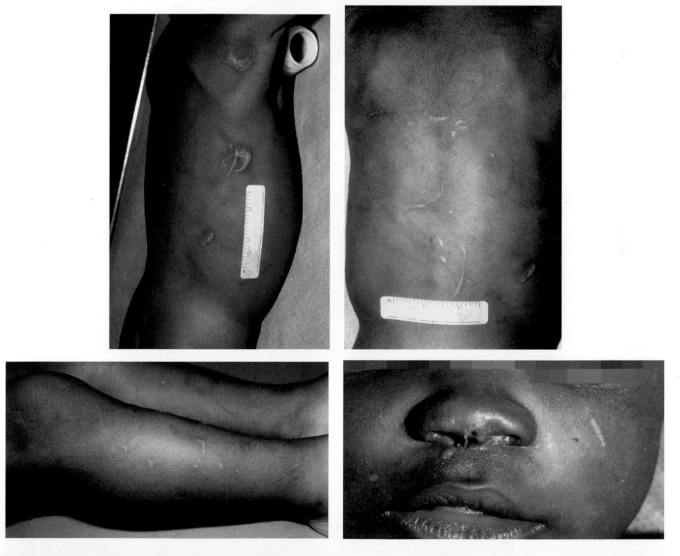

Figures 5.161–5.164 Multiple scars, many of which were due to recurrent child abuse. When evaluating old injuries it is important to take into context the child's age and developmental status. A child who can run and jump will occasionally fall and sustain (accidental) blunt impact injuries. Sometimes it may be difficult, if not impossible, to formulate the nature of old injuries without history or witnesses. Figures 5.161 and 5.162 are associated with abuse, while Figures 5.163 and 5.164 represent healed scars from accidental injuries. Note the healing injury on the nose secondary to therapeutic nasogastric tube placement.

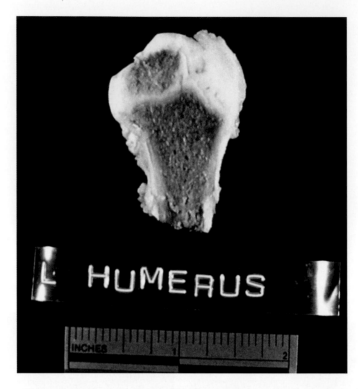

Figure 5.165 Coronal section of a humerus. Long bones are often removed and macroscopically, radiographically, and microscopically examined in potential cases of child abuse. Small fractures, including the transmetaphyseal or "bucket-handle" fracture (which commonly results from application of shearing force to the bone), are sometimes only detectable with such detailed examination methods.

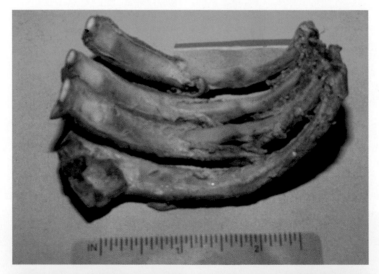

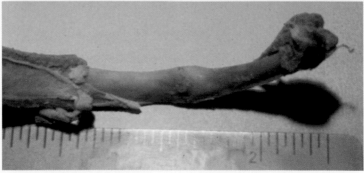

Figures 5.166 and 5.167 Old healed rib fractures from a case of recurrent child abuse.

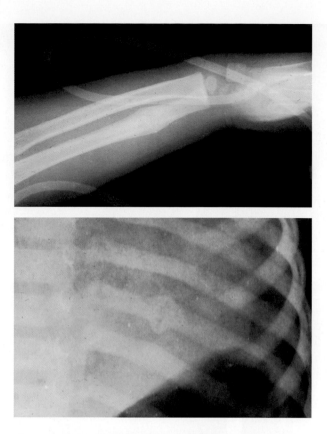

Figures 5.168 and 5.169 X-rays demonstrating healing fractures.

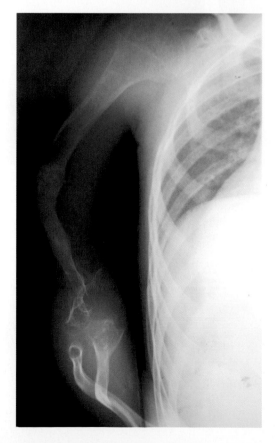

Figure 5.170 Osteogenesis imperfecta, with multiple long bone fractures in various stages of healing. In patients with metabolic bone diseases such as osteogenesis imperfecta or vitamin D deficiency, fractures can occur following minimal application of force and may not reflect intentionally inflicted trauma.

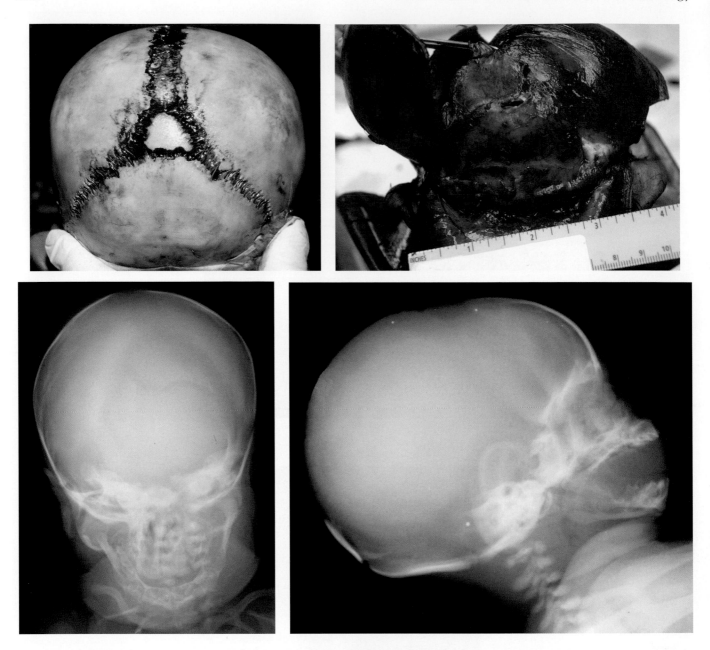

Figures 5.171–5.174 A Wormian bone (gross examination, Figures 5.171 and 5.172; x-ray, Figures 5.173 and 5.174) represents an anatomic variant in which a small bone is located within a suture or fontanelle. They should not be mistaken as evidence of fracture. In these particular cases where the bone is inter-parietal-occipital, it is also referred to as an Inca bone.

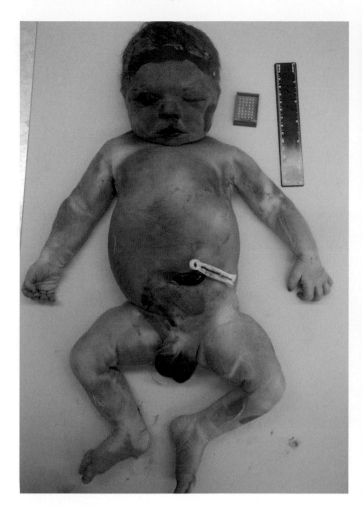 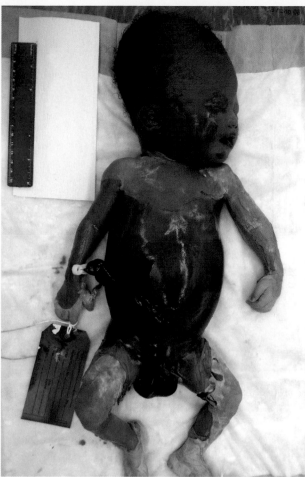

Figures 5.175 and 5.176 Maceration refers to intrauterine postmortem decomposition following fetal demise. Early changes include focal skin slippage, drying of thin mucosal membranes (lips, scrotum), and red discoloration of the umbilical cord, whereas later changes include extensive skin slippage, red discoloration of body, and softening of tissues and joints. Maceration can be used to corroborate intrauterine fetal death and estimate an interval between demise and delivery.

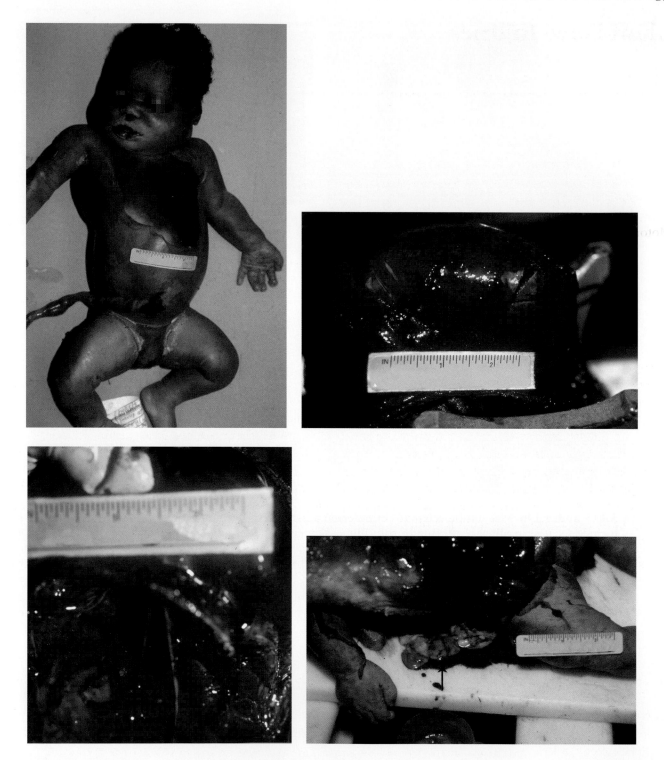

Figures 5.177–5.180 This decedent was retrieved from the back of a garbage truck partially tied within a torn plastic bag following compression by a trash compactor. Note the confluent hemorrhage to the scalp and the largely empty cranial vault. This child was mildly to moderately decomposed with bloating and separation of tissue planes. The brain material was squeezed from the cranium through the neck following compression of the head by the compactor. When the initial Y-shaped autopsy incision was made to the skin of the trunk, brain material leaked from the chest region (arrow). The child's body was found mixed with decomposing food material. Note the green discoloration from putrefaction (see Figures 4.115 and 4.116 in the Decomposition chapter) in contrast to maceration alone. Children born via vaginal delivery often have scalp hemorrhages, and it was not possible to characterize the skull fractures as antemortem.

Blunt-Force Injuries

6

CHARLES A. CATANESE

Contents

Introduction

These are injuries produced when the body is struck with, or strikes, a blunt object. A blunt surface produces injuries by scraping, tearing, shearing, crushing, or ripping. This is in contrast to a sharp force injury, which cuts and separates the tissue as it penetrates. The extent of injury resulting from trauma is a balance between the amounts of force applied, the surface area over which the force is applied, and the duration the force is applied. In general, the greater the force, smaller the area, and shorter the duration, the greater the injury will be. Taking into account that force = mass × acceleration and acceleration = velocity ÷ time, if time decreases and velocity remains constant, acceleration increases. If acceleration increases and the mass remains constant, force increases. So decreased time means increased force and increased damage. The sharper or smaller the surface area, the less force is required to separate the tissue planes and penetrate the body. Blunt objects have a relatively large surface area in contrast to sharp objects, where the cutting edge has a relatively small surface area. It takes much less force to penetrate the skin with an ice pick than with the end of a baseball bat. Examples of blunt objects are fists, shoes, pipes, bricks, bats, hammers, roadways, sidewalks, cars, trains, airplanes, walls, etc. Classifications of blunt-force injuries to skin include *abrasions, contusions*, and *lacerations*. These may occur separately but are often present at the same time. As an example, an injury may be described as an abraded contusion with central laceration. *Fractures* are breaks in the bone as a result of blunt force. *Avulsions* are splits in the soft tissue or soft tissue planes with or without a laceration as a result of shearing forces.

Abrasions

Abrasions are scrapes. They are produced as the body contacts a surface and rubs across it with sufficient force. The distance of travel can be very short, such as falling and scraping your knee, or very long, like being dragged under a car. It is often possible to determine the direction of impact. Layers of skin are scraped away and bead up at the margin where the contact to the wound last occurred. Fragments of skin beading up at the inferior wound margin indicate a downward impact. Antemortem abrasions, those that occur during life, are typically red to brown and will eventually form a scab with dried blood. Postmortem abrasions are yellow in non-lividity-dependent areas. In general, one needs a beating heart with blood pressure to produce hemorrhage and a red to brown discoloration. A postmortem scrape in a lividity-dependent region will appear red and may be difficult to differentiate from an antemortem injury.

This is important in certain cases. Interpretation differences regarding timing of the injury can lead to different conclusions. For example, some may argue that an injury occurred during resuscitative efforts in the hospital, or the body was dropped from the stretcher in the morgue. Some other arguments may include: he was dead already when the second car hit him, the other perpetrator shot the body after he was dead, the child had no injuries before entering the hospital, etc.

Abrasions may also change character with increasing time. For example, initial examination of a body retrieved from water may reveal no or much less obvious injuries due to the moisture from the water at the skin's surface. As the body is stored in the morgue overnight and allowed to dry, the abrasions will darken and may become much more apparent.

Contusions

Contusions are bruises. These are produced following an impact where the soft tissues and blood vessels, underneath or within the skin, are torn and produce hemorrhage. Grabbing an arm tightly can produce bruising with minimal impact and greater crushing force. One needs a beating heart and blood pressure to produce a contusion. A postmortem impact may accumulate blood due to lividity in a gravity-dependent area. This type of postmortem artifact may be difficult to differentiate from an antemortem injury.

One must exercise great care when dating contusions at the time of autopsy with gross findings alone. One must account for skin color, whether the contusion is deep or superficial, the presence of hematoma, etc. Bruises go through various color changes with advancing time as the body reacts to repair the injury. This depends on the size of the injury, the physiologic state of the individual, including immune response and coagulation system function, the vascular efficiency adjacent to the damaged tissue, etc. Color changes range from light blue-red to dark purple then green to yellow-brown as time progresses. Inaccurate interpretations by dating contusions based only upon a visual gross examination of skin color changes may create problems in court. If one sees a variability with color ranges demonstrating some bruises as red-purple and others as yellow-brown, it is reasonable to say that some injuries are older than others. It is much more accurate to use histopathology to date the injuries using established time ranges for advancing inflammation, granulation tissue formation, hemosiderin-laden macrophages, and eventual healing with fibrosis. Random sections of injuries should be taken including the wound margins. The first several hours reveal hemorrhage-with no inflammation. Estimation of injury dating should be given in time ranges due the variable nature of all of these parameters.

Bruises can also change appearance as the postmortem time interval increases. A contusion will become more obvious as blood settles away from the skin surrounding the contusion. The surrounding tissue will become paler and the contusion will be more prominent, as in a supine body with anterior contusions in full livor mortis. Bleeding associated with a contusion does not settle away from the impact site as lividity forms because it is spread throughout the soft tissues and cannot flow away within blood vessels. Another example is that during vigorous emergency room resuscitation, the head and upper trunk may become congested. If a contusion is in the congested region, it will be less obvious. As lividity settles to the back of the head, contusions to the face may become more prominent. Clinicians may sometimes miss these subtle contusions that may become very obvious the next day during autopsy.

It is also important to realize that deep contusions may not be visible at all externally and may be visualized only after incisions are made. Clinicians should realize this and create a medical record that is as accurate as possible. If one documents that no bruises are present to regions of the body, yet they are found on autopsy, this may potentially cause more questions in court and raise possibilities about other suspicions and reasonable doubt. Accurate, concise, truthful, objective documentation is always best. The autopsy remains the most accurate way to demonstrate these findings.

Lacerations

Lacerations are tears of soft tissues including skin, internal organs, or vessels as a result of an impact, overstretching, or crushing-type forces. These injuries are characterized by irregular margins, often with an abrasion and underlying soft tissue bridging caused by fibrous strands and small blood vessels. If the laceration is large and gaping, tissue bridging may not be present due to the strands' being pulled apart. Skin lacerations tend to occur more often over hard surfaces, such as the scalp, knees, elbows, etc. The direction of the impact can be determined by the presence of soft tissue undermining. The underlying soft tissue adjacent to the laceration may form a pocket of separation extending in the direction of impact. With respect to standard anatomic planes, a downward impact will produce undermining at the inferior aspect of the laceration. These directions should be described in the autopsy report with reference to standard anatomic planes.

Motor Vehicle Injuries

Motor vehicles include any motorized means of carrying or transporting someone. These include trucks, buses, cars, motorcycles, mopeds, snow mobiles, etc. It is always important to be as accurate as possible, including the *type of vehicle* on the death certification for vital records. The type of vehicle is obviously important when evaluating injuries.

It is important to recognize various patterns that might help *differentiate drivers from passengers*. In high-speed collisions with unrestrained occupants, people may be ejected from the vehicle. If criminal or civil charges are filed, the living driver may indicate that the dead passenger was driving, regardless of the truth.

One should look for steering wheel impact marks to the chest, seatbelt-related abraded contusions, and pattern injuries associated with impacts to the windshield, dashboard, or vehicle roof. *Front and back windshields* are often made of laminated glass and fracture with elongated curves or splinters. *Side windows* are often made of tempered glass and fracture into small cubes. Seatbelt-patterned injuries or side impact dicing pattern injuries to the right or left side of the head will help formulate opinions about an individual's seating position. Dicing injuries to the left side of the head of an individual found next to a car with a broken left side window is evidence that he or she was the driver. One could also collect DNA samples from these regions and compare it with ejected occupants. Those not wearing seatbelts are much more likely to be ejected from the vehicle, especially in a rollover accident. Those who are ejected may impact other objects such as a tree or pole, or may sustain crush injuries due to the vehicle's rolling over them.

Pedestrian clothing and impact sites to the body can reveal many clues with evidence about the circumstances of a collision. Questions one should ask include: Was the pedestrian standing, squatting, or lying in the street? Was the individual run over or run under by the vehicle? Was more than one vehicle involved? Impact sites may reveal different front grill or tire pattern injuries. With standing pedestrian impacts, one should measure the distance between the leg impact site and the bottom of the heel. The shoe height including the heel size could be added in estimating the pedestrian leg height at the time of the incident. It may be necessary to incise this region of impact to the leg to visualize this hemorrhagic site better, which is also associated with formation of a pocket of crushed tissue. It is good practice to include the measuring ruler in the picture. This may give insight into whether the vehicle was braking before the impact occurred because as this happens the front end of a car will go downward. Fractures may occur more readily to weight-bearing legs. Fracture patterns may be difficult to interpret when the bone is splintered into many pieces. Generally speaking, as a force passes through a bone, the fracture pattern extends in an outward direction, away from the impact site, similar to a skull fracture from an entrance gunshot wound producing internal beveling. With posterior standing pedestrian impact, one might find stretch marks at the inguinal region opposite the impact site. This is caused by hyperextension of the hip and leg in an anterior direction.

Slow-moving vehicles tend to run over people. Fast-moving vehicles tend to run under people, meaning after being struck, the victim is tossed onto and over the hood. Other characteristic pattern-type injuries include flaps of skin torn away as a tire passes over a body. The clothing worn by the individuals struck by the vehicles may yield significant evidence such as paint fragments. The car may have fragments of blood and hair that can be used for DNA analysis in cases of hit-and-run incidents. This can be useful when there are multiple pedestrians and cars involved in collisions. Pedestrian collisions may involve children, who are sometimes impulsive, careless, and may run out into oncoming traffic. Elderly, sick, or intoxicated individuals may not be quick enough to get out of the way of a car, or an individual with psychopathology, such as a homeless person, may think it is not dangerous to cross a busy freeway in the dark.

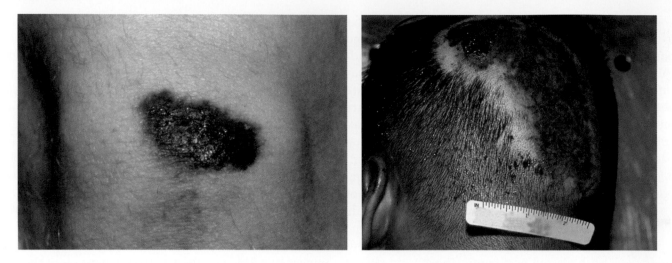

Figures 6.1 and 6.2 Recent antemortem abrasions with red discoloration indicating hemorrhage.

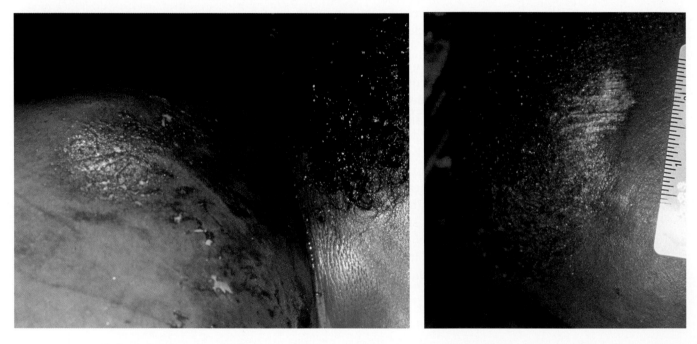

Figures 6.3 and 6.4 Recent deep antemortem abrasions with red discoloration indicating hemorrhage, as opposed to Figure 6.125 with large yellow anemic postmortem abrasion without red discoloration, indicating no hemorrhage.

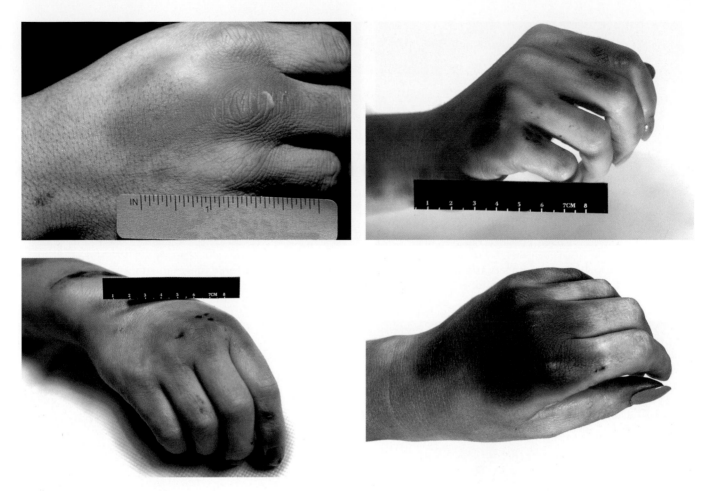

Figures 6.5–6.8 Recent contusion of the hands associated with a fight. These are defensive wounds by history but may have been caused by any blunt force trauma. Note the first figure with laceration caused by an impact with a tooth.

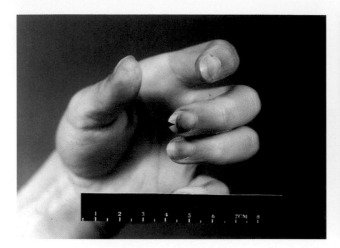 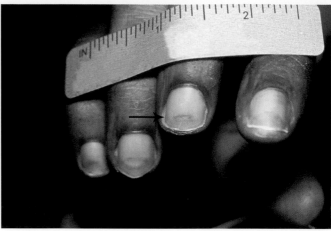

Figure 6.9 and 6.10 Broken fingernails with contusions of the nail beds. Blunt force injury during struggle with grabbing and bending of the nails backward.

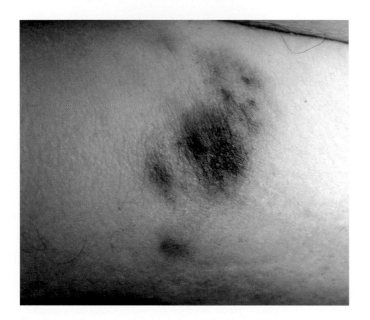 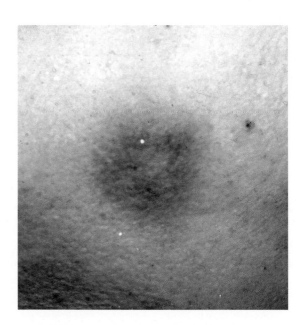

Figure 6.11 Recent purple contusion of arm.   **Figure 6.12** Older yellow/brown contusion.

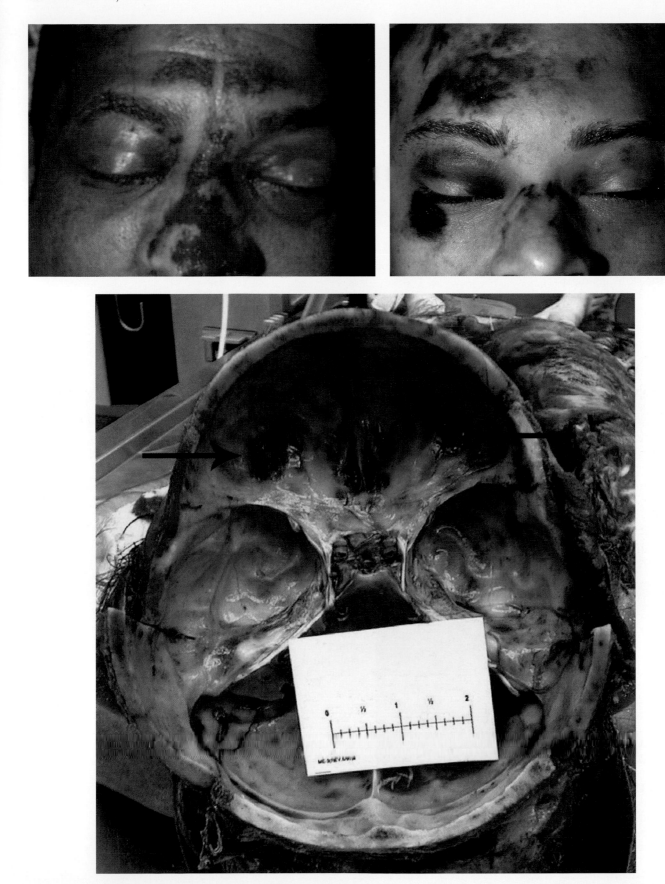

Figure 6.13–6.15 Multiple abrasions and contusions of face. Note the bilateral periorbital ecchymosis associated with fracture of the anterior cranial fossa. This is also known as "raccoon eyes." A similar injury is Battle's sign, hemorrhage behind the ear, also a sign of basilar skull fractures. Figure 6.15 demonstrates a basilar skull fracture.

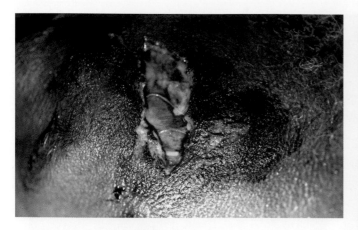

Figure 6.16 Recent laceration with adjacent abrasion. Note the irregular margin at the point of skin separation due to the skin ripping apart.

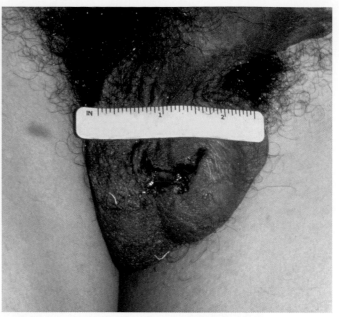

Figure 6.17 Recent laceration of scrotum.

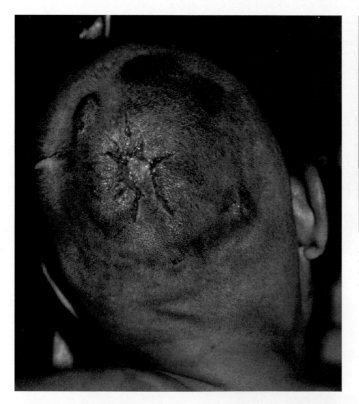

Figure 6.18 Large recent abraded contusion at the back of the head with a stellate laceration. This individual was intoxicated at a party on a rooftop. He was taking a group photograph and, while backing up, accidentally fell three stories to the pavement below. He had a comminuted skull fracture.

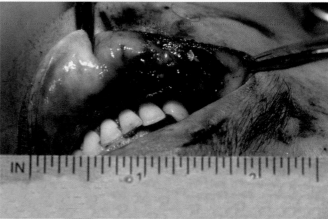

Figure 6.19 These are multiple recent lacerations and contusions at the inner aspect of the mouth following multiple blunt impacts to this individual's face with a fist.

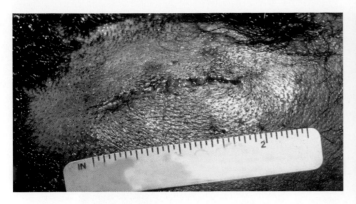

Figure 6.20 This is a postmortem anemic laceration in an individual who was stabbed to death in an apartment and later thrown out of a window.

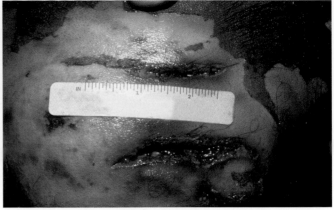

Figure 6.21 This decomposing body has skin slippage with separation of scalp hair. Note the scalp lacerations with slight to moderate decomposition.

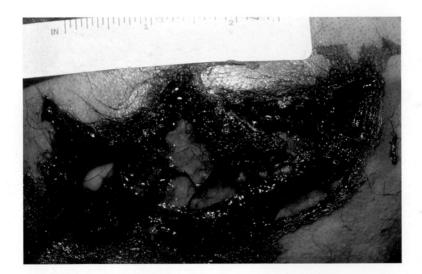

Figure 6.22 This individual died of multiple homicidal blunt and sharp force injuries. These are scalp lacerations in an individual with moderate decomposition. Note the extensive drying of the wound margins with clotted blood and fragments of hair. Also note the separation of the scalp from the skull with subadjacent fractures.

Figure 6.23 This individual was struck by a train. Note the soft tissue avulsion underneath the intact thick skin.

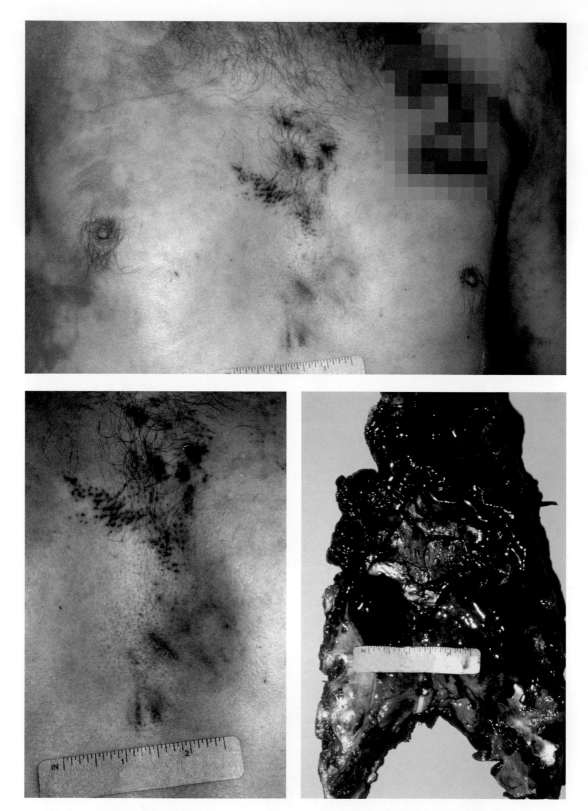

Figures 6.24–6.26 Note the recent abraded contusion to the middle aspect of the chest. This individual had multiple layers of clothing and was reportedly stomped on by an individual with heavy boots following assaults with other weapons. The abraded contusion to the middle aspect of his chest forms a vague outline of a boot. The multiple layers of clothing prevented a more discernible defined boot pattern. The individual also had a fractured sternum as shown in Figure 6.26 depicting the undersurface of the sternum with fractures surrounded by hemorrhage. This portion of the chest plate was removed during normal autopsy procedure. This individual also had a cardiac contusion.

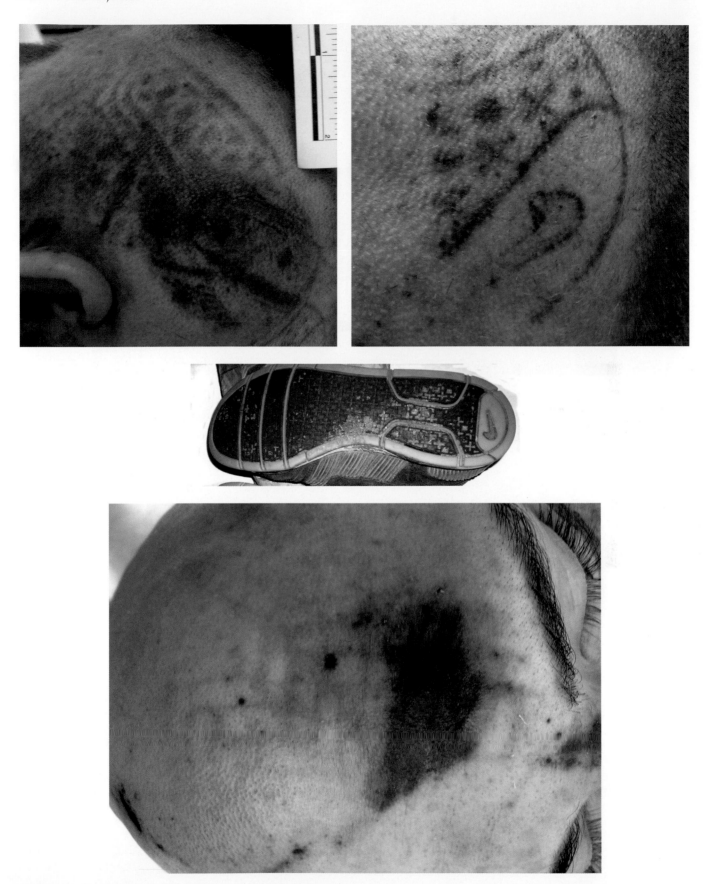

Figures 6.27–6.30 Pattern injuries associated with impacts from the bottom of a shoe while being stomped and kicked.

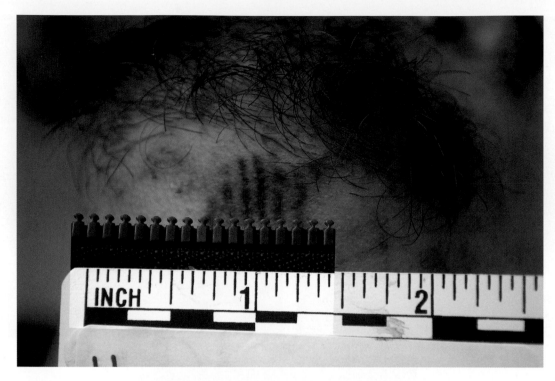

Figure 6.31 A composite of two photographs, showing an abraded contusion zipper pattern on the decedent's forehead, and the zipper from the decedent's jacket. This was associated with motor vehicle impact and airbag deployment.

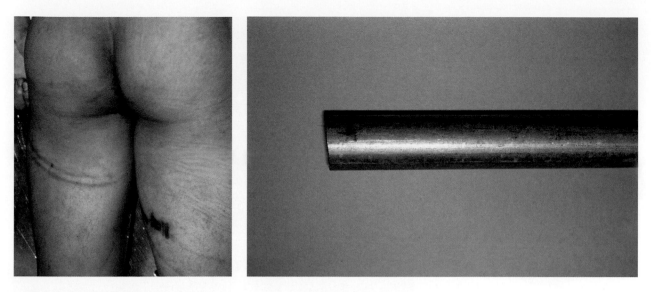

Figures 6.32 and 6.33 This individual was assaulted with fists and a metal pipe/rod. Note the parallel linear contusions at the superior aspect of the middle left thigh. Depression of the soft tissues contacting the rod causes stretching at each margin with blood vessel injury and parallel linear bruises.

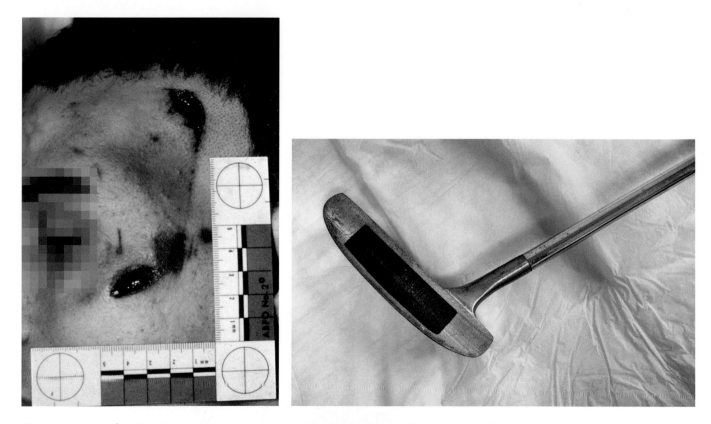

Figure 6.34 and 6.35 This individual was struck multiple times with a putter golf club. Note the pattern injury at the forehead and face with the shaft of the club extending at the inferior aspect.

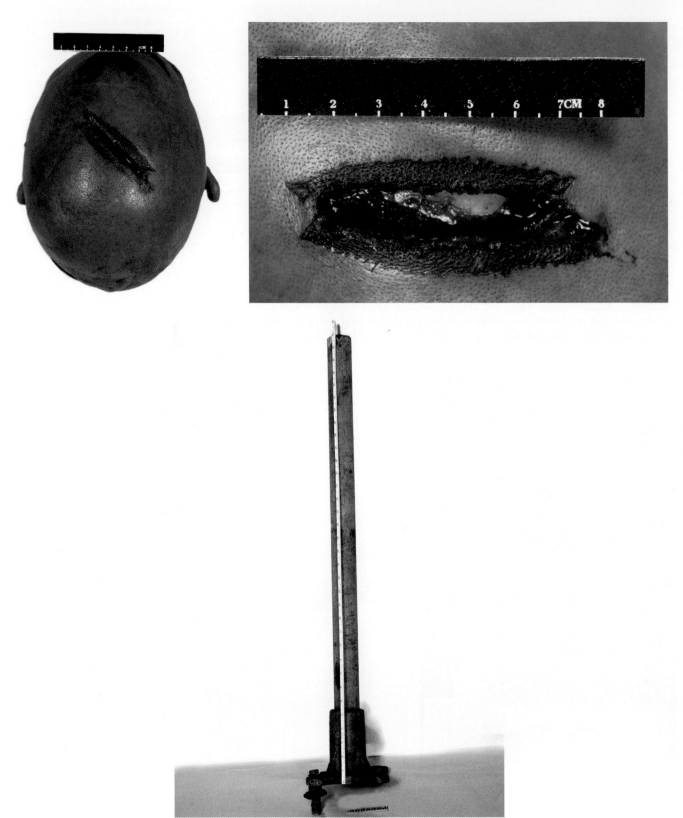

Figures 6.36–6.38 This individual was struck with great force by a heavy metal rod (Figure 6.38) causing underlying laceration and abraded margins.

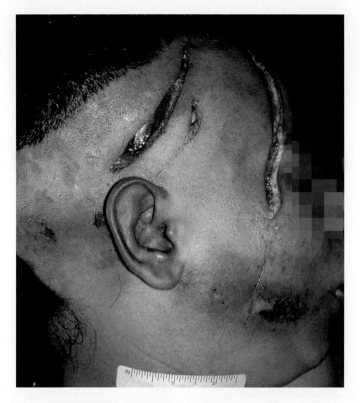

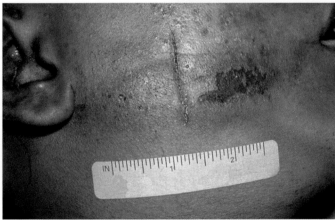
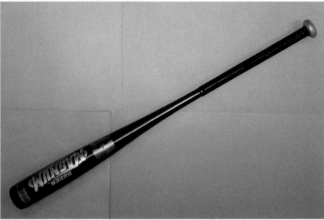

Figures 6.39–6.41 This individual was assaulted by multiple people with bottles and a baseball bat. These abraded contusions at his face and head are characteristic of a baseball bat impact. Note the oval-shaped contusion with sparing of the central aspect with overlying abrasion. Also note the abraded central region.

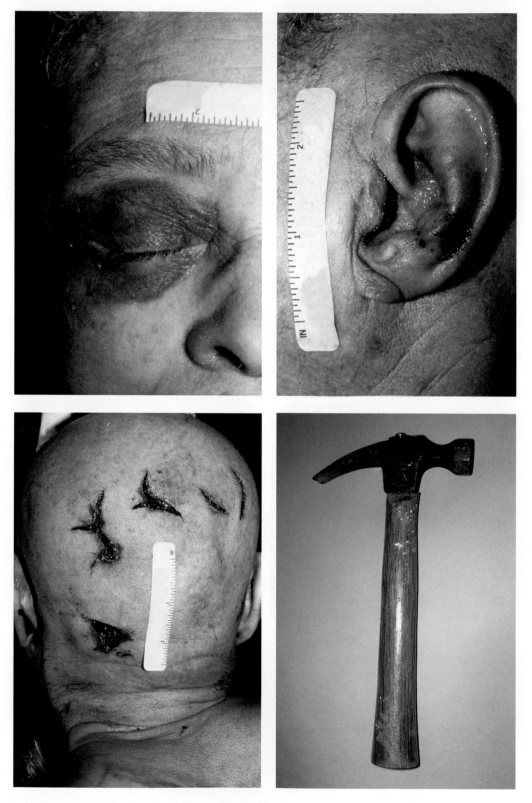

Figures 6.42–6.45 This elderly woman lived with her sister who had Alzheimer's disease. The decedent had a history of an unsteady gait associated with Parkinson's disease and remote stroke. She was found in her apartment with several impact injuries to her scalp. It was initially thought by investigators that she had fallen several times and possibly suffered a heart attack. Further examination of her scalp revealed more lacerations and impacts that were initially not observed at the scene due to poor lighting and dried blood matted in her scalp hair. These scalp lacerations were produced by being struck with a hammer head. Further evaluation of the scene revealed a hammer underneath her bed. Note the orbital contusion to her left eye, which is a recessed area of her face and not usually associated with a fall while striking a flat surface.

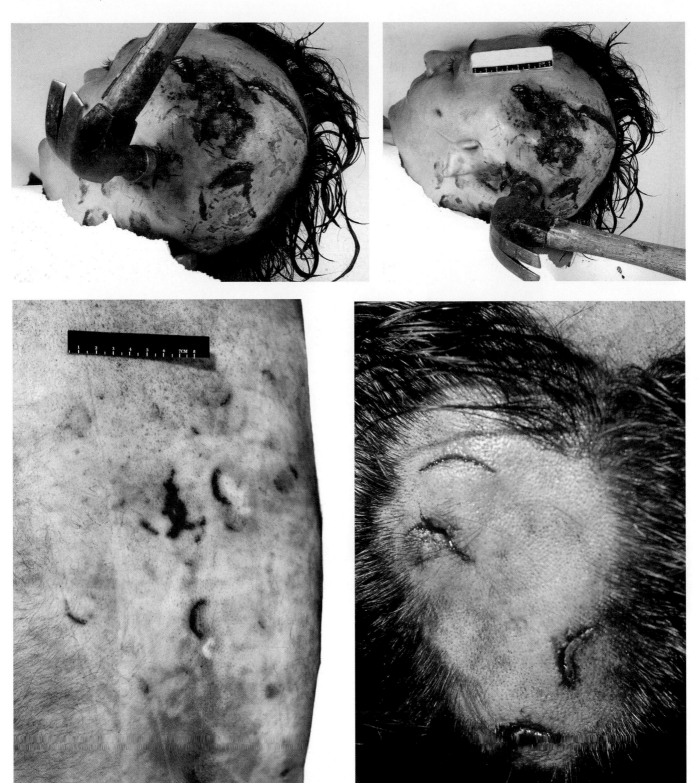

Figures 6.46–6.49 Other examples of injuries associated with the hammer strike. The above images show the hammer that was found on top of the individual's body. It would be considered bad practice to bring a suspect's hammer, not found at the scene, into the morgue for comparison to injuries due to possible risk of evidence contamination.

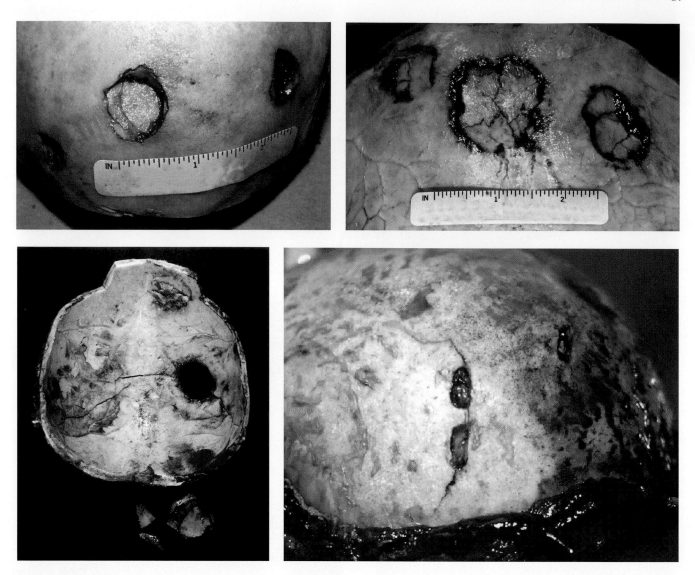

Figures 6.50–6.53 Depressed skull fractures due to multiple impacts with the head and claw of a hammer. Standard household hammer heads have a diameter of 3/4 to 1 inch, and the injuries on the skull tend to reflect this.

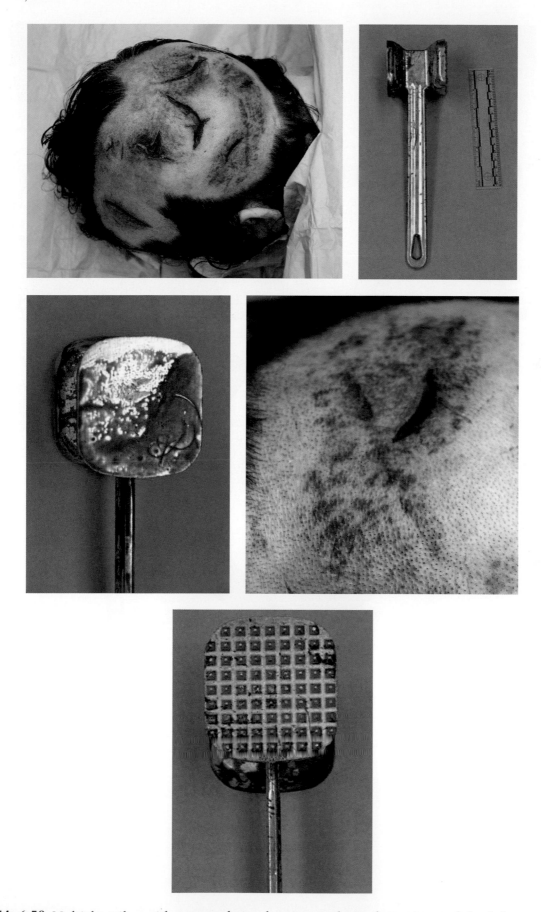

Figures 6.54–6.58 Multiple strikes with meat tenderizer hammer producing lacerations and abraded contusion pattern consistent with this hammer.

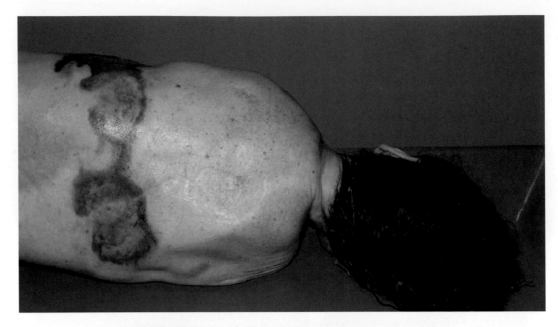

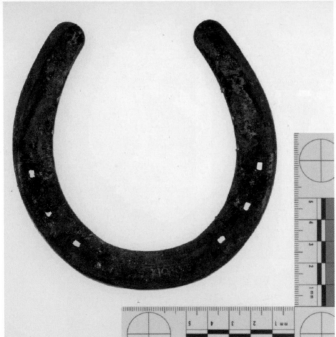

Figures 6.59 and 6.60 Horse stomping with pattern abrasion from horseshoes.

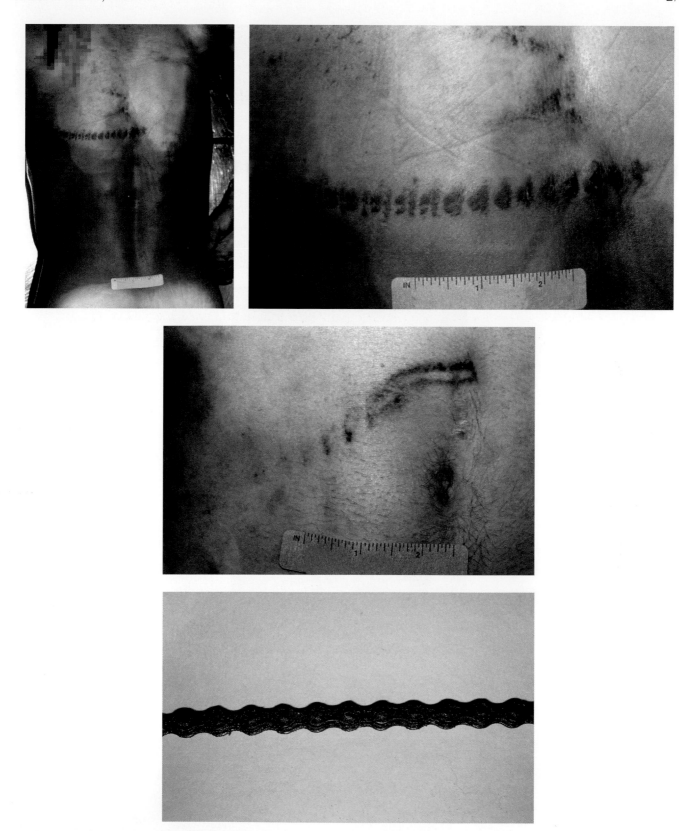

Figures 6.61–6.64 This individual was assaulted by multiple people including one with a bicycle chain. These injuries are characteristic for bicycle chain impacts.

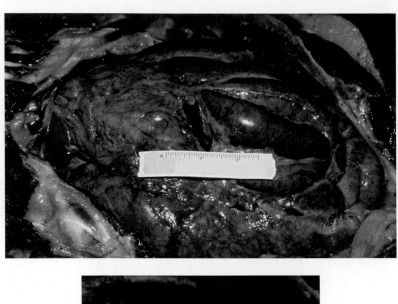

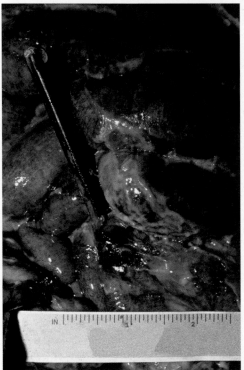

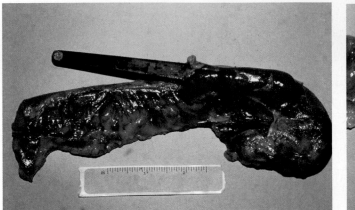

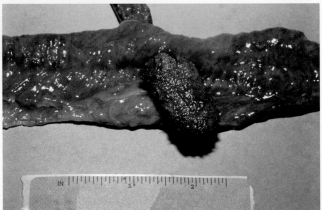

Figures 6.65–6.68 This psych patient had a history of swallowing miscellaneous objects (pica). The blunt side of this toothbrush, in conjunction with peristalsis, eroded through the intestinal wall. This person died of peritonitis with septic complications.

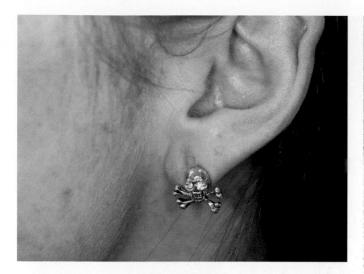

Figure 6.69 Pierced ear lobe with sociopathic pirate earring.

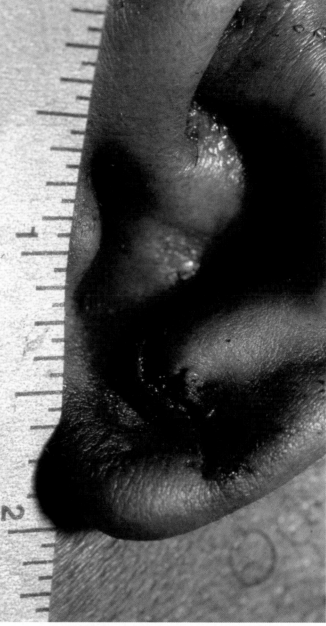

Figure 6.70 This is a homicide case where the individual had her earring torn from her ear lobe during the assault.

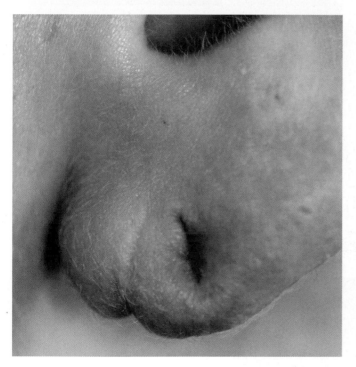

Figure 6.71 Note the slit elongation of the piercing site from wearing very heavy earrings. Also note the healed linear scar to the left due to a traumatic tearing of the earring from the ear lobe with complete separation and nonplastic surgical repair.

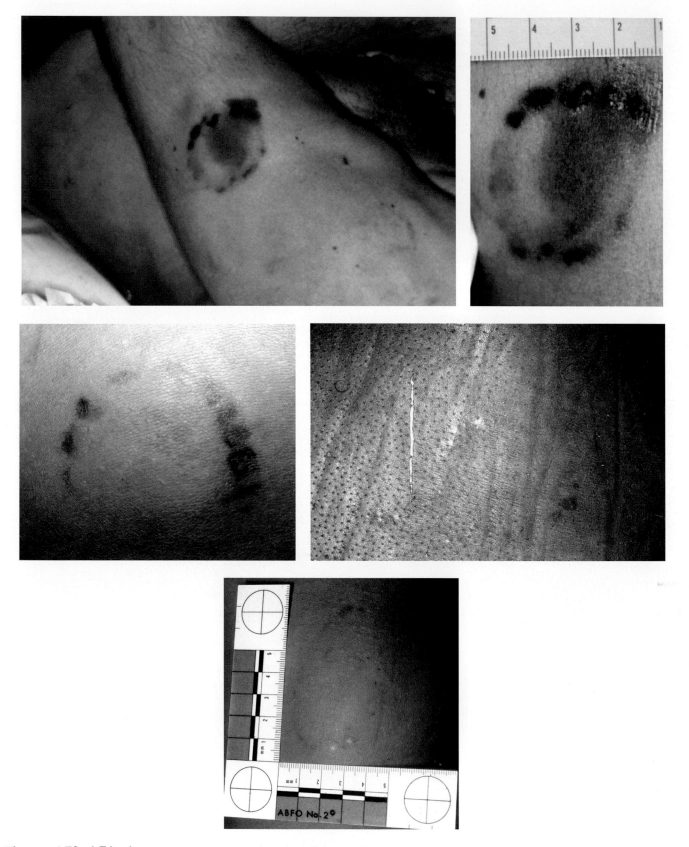

Figures 6.72–6.76 These are various examples of recent bite marks with different placement of the mouth while exerting pressure and different degrees of force applied. Note some patterns are very vague and others are extremely prominent. The typical example of a bite mark reveals a circular pattern with a central region of contusion. It is good practice to consult a forensic dentist as soon as possible whenever a bite mark is suspected. The injury should not be cleaned until swabs are taken to detect oral DNA left behind from the perpetrator. As time goes on with drying and decomposition, the injury may yield less valuable information for dental comparison and DNA analysis.

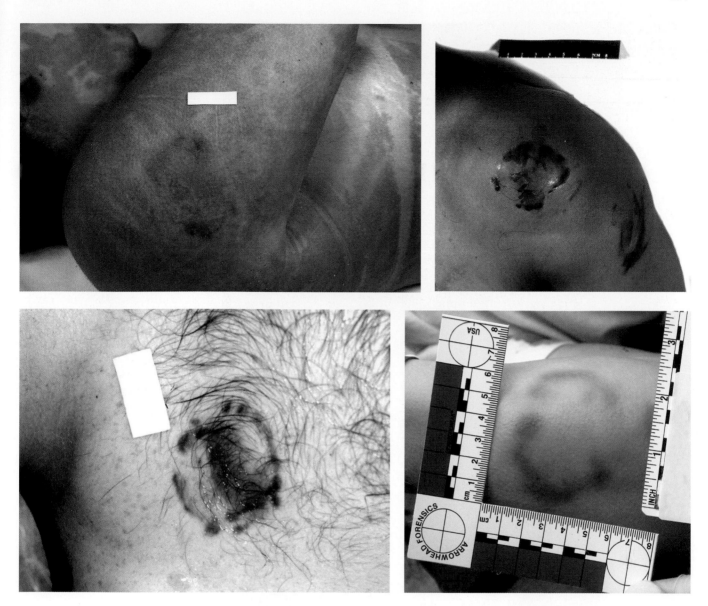

Figures 6.77–6.80 Other examples of recent human bites with varying degrees of potential comparability to suspect's teeth.

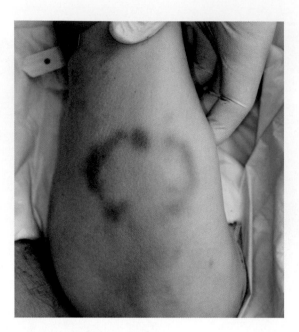

Figure 6.81 Human bite mark.

Figure 6.82 Therapeutic mark left by EKG patch. This mark left by an EKG patch was initially misinterpreted as a bite mark.

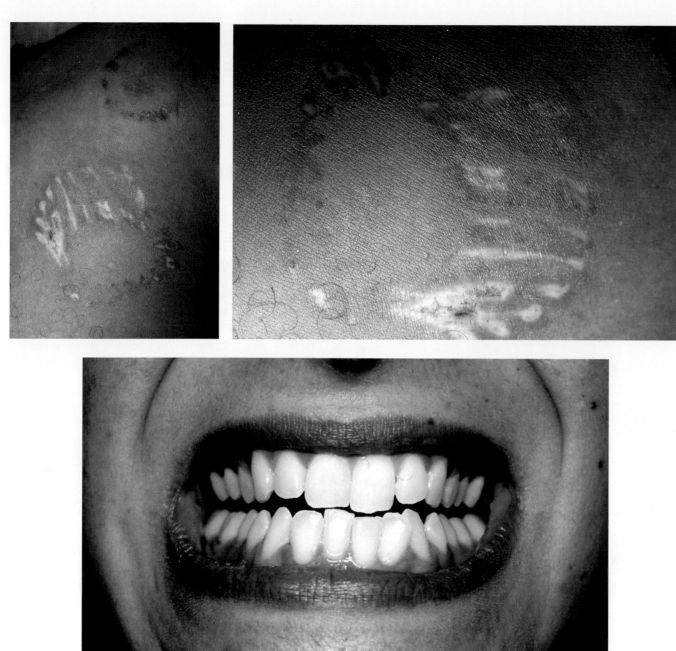

Figures 6.83–6.85 Image 6.83 demonstrates both a recent and healed bite mark. The old bite mark is largely healed with hypopigmented white to gray scar from teeth being dragging across the skin surface.

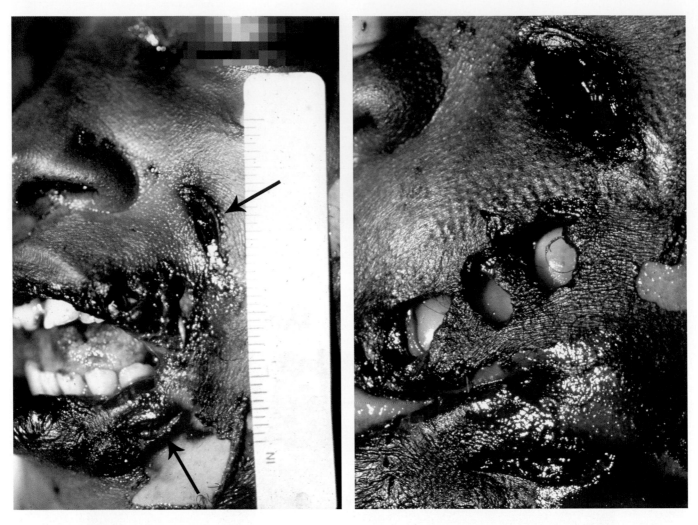

Figures 6.86 and 6.87 This individual and her roommate were found in her apartment with multiple blunt and sharp force injuries. Note the roughly semicircular lacerations on the superior and inferior aspects of the cheek with the deeper lacerations of the lip revealing exposed underlying teeth. There was a large cylindrical storefront padlock within a tube sock found at the scene. There were multiple other pattern injuries to the decedent's body consistent with these roughly circular impacts.

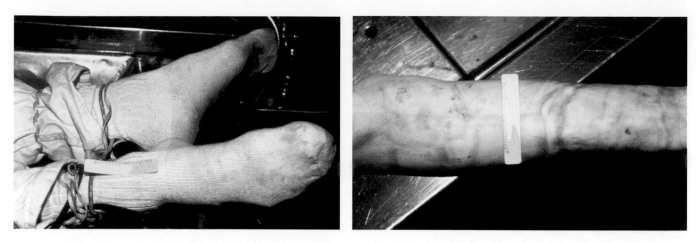

Figures 6.88 and 6.89 Note the furrow indentations associated with extremities bound by rope and cord prior to being stabbed to death.

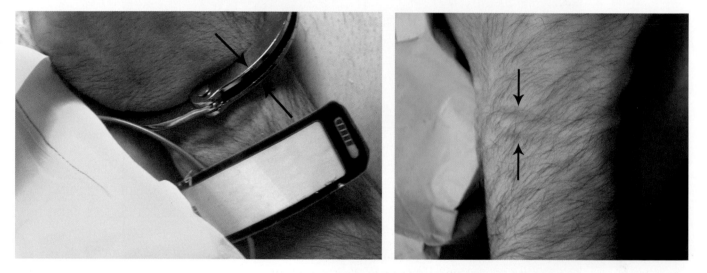

Figures 6.90 and 6.91 Marks left by handcuffs. Note the parallel linear marks consist of a portion of the handcuff indicated by the arrow (in Figure 6.91).

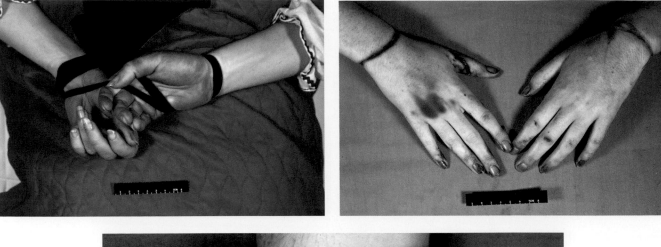

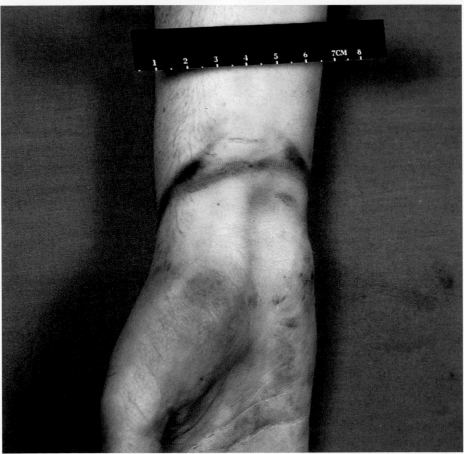

Figures 6.92–6.94 These individuals were abducted and assaulted over a period of time with their hands bound behind their backs. Note the furrow pattern with red/brown vital reaction of these abrasions and contusions, which were associated with struggle. Note the abrasions and contusions to the knuckles and fingers.

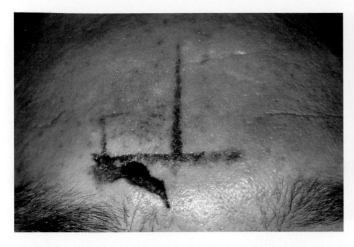

Figure 6.95 This individual suffered a witnessed fall from a fatal cardiac event while standing. While falling to the ground he sustained this pattern injury by striking his head on a radiator.

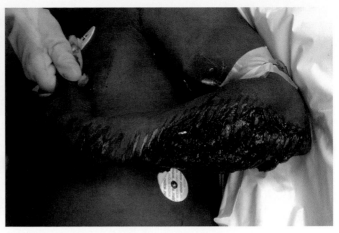

Figure 6.96 This individual suffered a fatal cardiac event while riding on an escalator. He was found lying at the bottom of the escalator. Note the pattern injury to his arm from the continued rubbing of escalator treads.

Figure 6.97 This individual was ejected from a motor vehicle and impacted a fence at a high rate of speed, leaving a pattern injury from the top of the fence post contacting his chest.

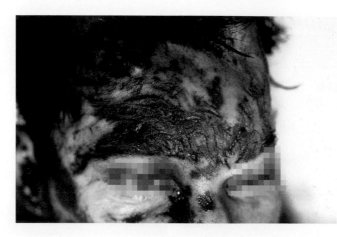

Figure 6.98 This individual was an unrestrained passenger in a motor vehicle during a head-on collision. His face went through the front windshield. He sustained multiple curvilinear lacerations and sharp force injuries from broken glass and impact with the car roof. This type of pattern is consistent with a front windshield impact.

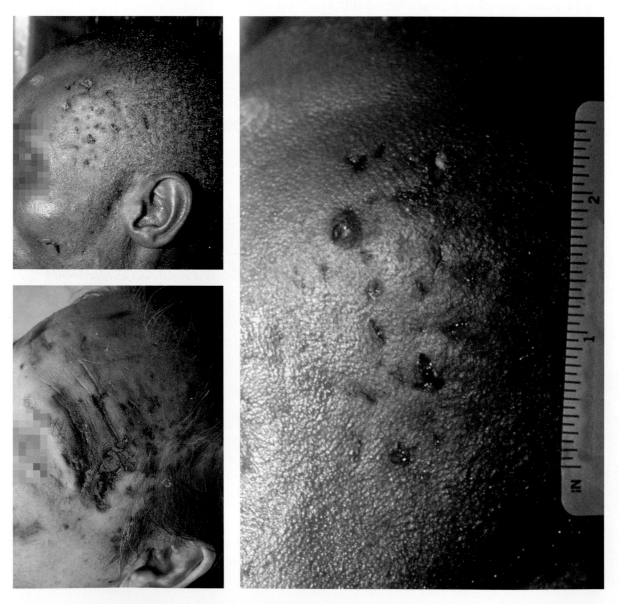

Figures 6.99–6.101 Note the dicing type injuries to the scalp with cubed fragments of glass imbedded in some of these injuries. This type of injury is consistent with an impact and fracture of tempered glass, which is present in many side windows. These individuals were passengers with left door window head impact.

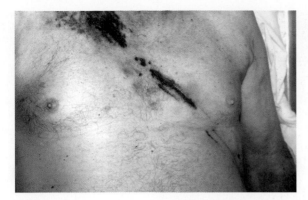

Figure 6.102 This individual was the passenger in a front seat collision. Note the abraded contusion from his seatbelt.

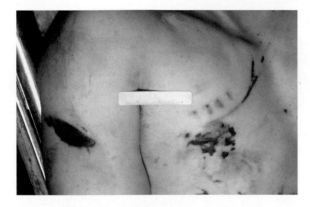

Figure 6.104 Note the abraded contusion at the chest and arm of this individual from a steering wheel impact. He was the driver of this car in a multiple fatality vehicular accident.

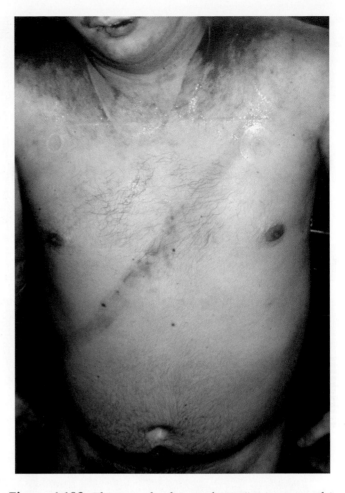

Figure 6.103 This was the driver of a car in a motor vehicle accident. Note the abraded contusion from the seat belt.

Figure 6.105 This demonstrates a transection of the aorta in the proximal descending region just distal to the ductus ligatosum. This is a common location of laceration.

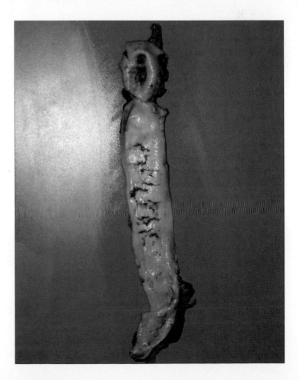

Figure 6.106 Aortic tears from submarining in a motor vehicle accident.

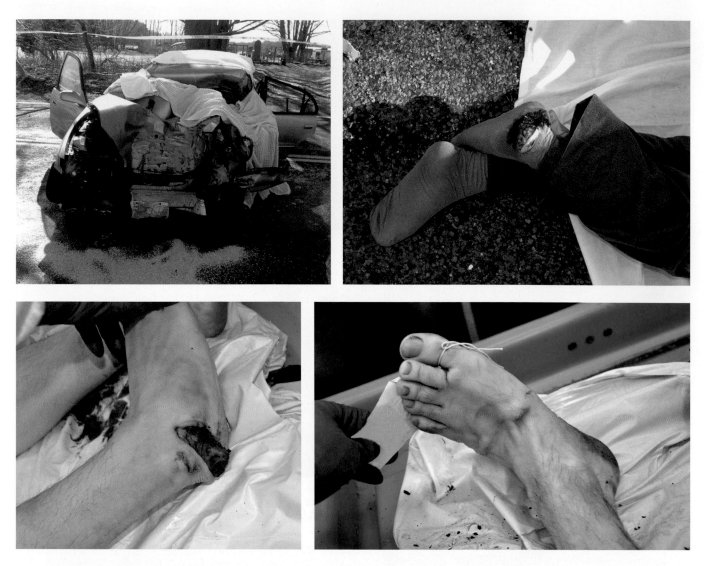

Figures 6.107–6.110 These front-seated individuals broke their foot and ankle due to high speed front end motor vehicle impact associated with forward seat movement. Rarely the presence of shoe sole patterns may be observed on the accelerator or brake pedals, indicating what the driver was doing at the time of the impact.

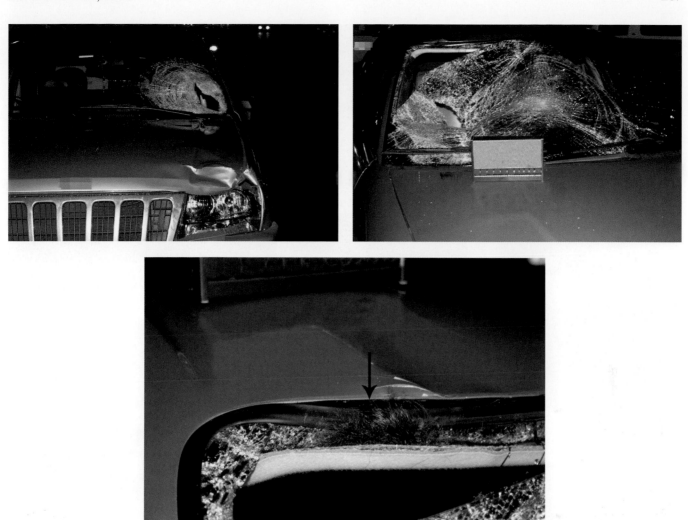

Figures 6.111–6.113 These pictures of a car show an impact from a pedestrian who was struck and run under. Note the fragment of scalp with scalp hair imbedded in the top part of the windshield and adjacent car roof. The driver of this car initially fled the scene.

Figure 6.114 This scene photograph demonstrates an individual who was struck at a high rate of speed and struck the pavement headfirst with great force. Note the exposed comminuted skull fracture with brain material.

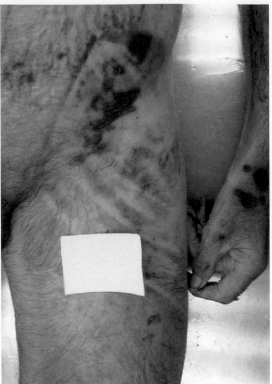

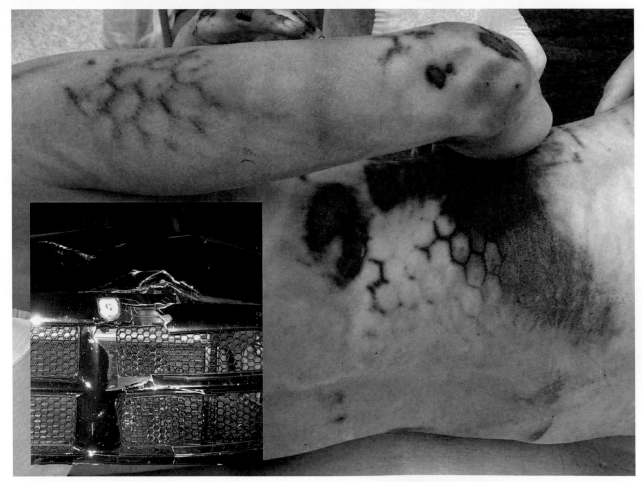

Figures 6.115–6.117 Pedestrians struck by cars with grill pattern injuries.

Figures 6.118–6.120 Motor vehicle accident with decapitation associated with cell phone use in a truck lane.

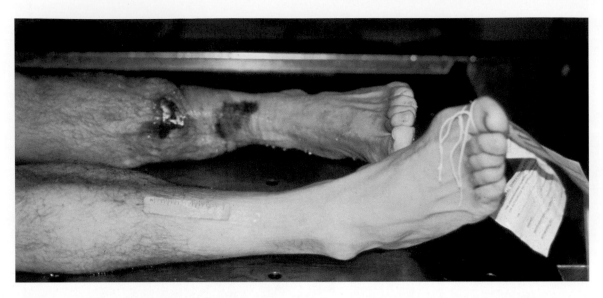

Figure 6.121 This is another pedestrian who was struck by a car. Note the tibia fracture at the weight-bearing left leg.

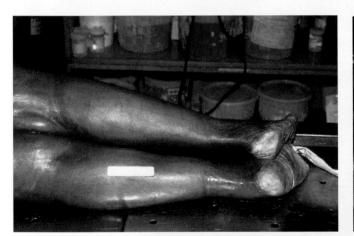 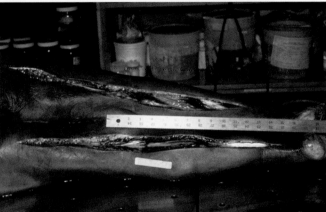

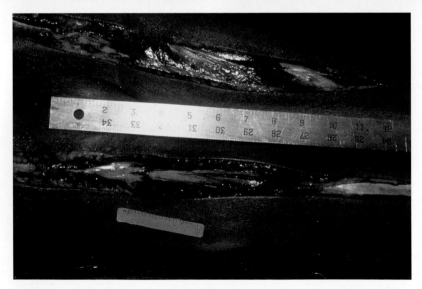

Figures 6.122–6.124 This individual was a pedestrian who was struck from behind by a car. Due to her dark skin, the contusions are not obvious from external examination alone. Incision of the posterior aspects of her leg reveals hemorrhage due to the bumper impact. It is good practice to photograph these impact sites with a ruler to demonstrate the distance from the decedent's heels. This can be matched to a particular car and to whether the driver applied brakes or not before striking this pedestrian. The front of the motor vehicle will go downward when the braking occurs.

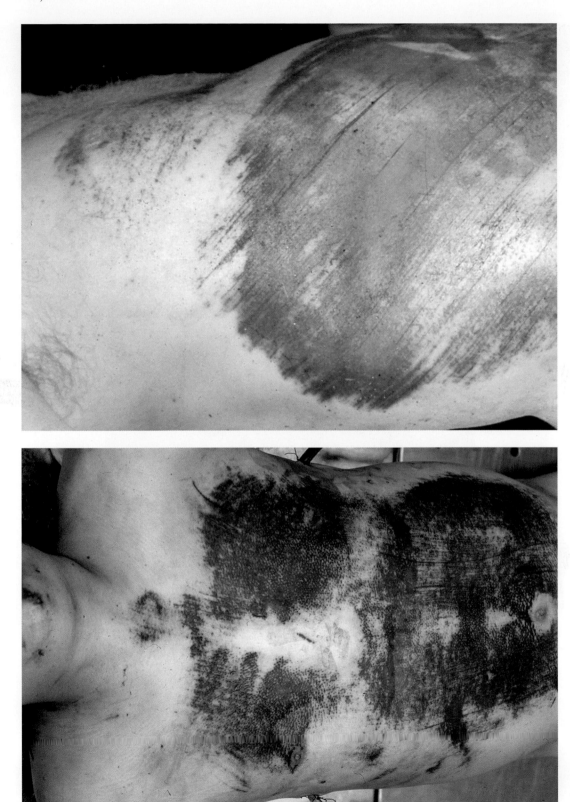

Figures 6.125 and 6.126 These individuals were both struck by cars and dragged across the pavement. The yellow, anemic abrasions occurred after the first impact where the decedent sustained extensive central nervous system injury and a transected aorta. He was thrown into another lane of traffic and dragged by another car. The anemic nature of this injury and yellow discoloration suggest decreased blood perfusion. The other injury shows red to brown discoloration, which is significant for vital reaction in an individual who had an intact beating heart with blood pressure.

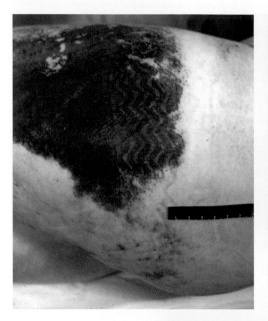
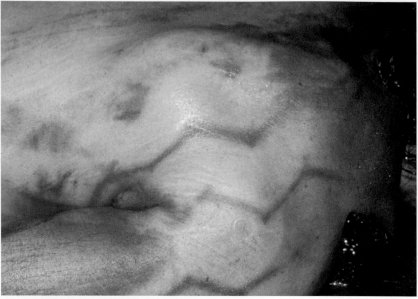

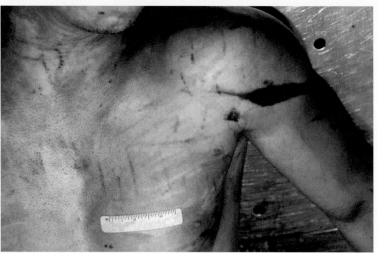

Figures 6.127–6.129 These are multiple examples of tire imprints from people who were run over by a motor vehicle. In one case the individual was thrown into another lane of traffic after being struck. The second motor vehicle driver denied hitting the individual, but the tire pattern was a match and there was forensic evidence found on the undersurface of his motor vehicle.

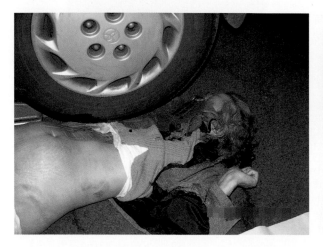
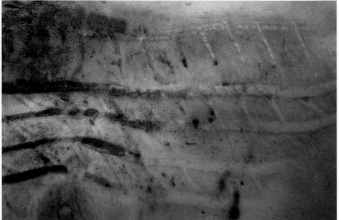

Figures 6.130 and 6.131 Individual trapped under a car with tire imprint to chest. Note several pressure blisters between the tire tread pattern.

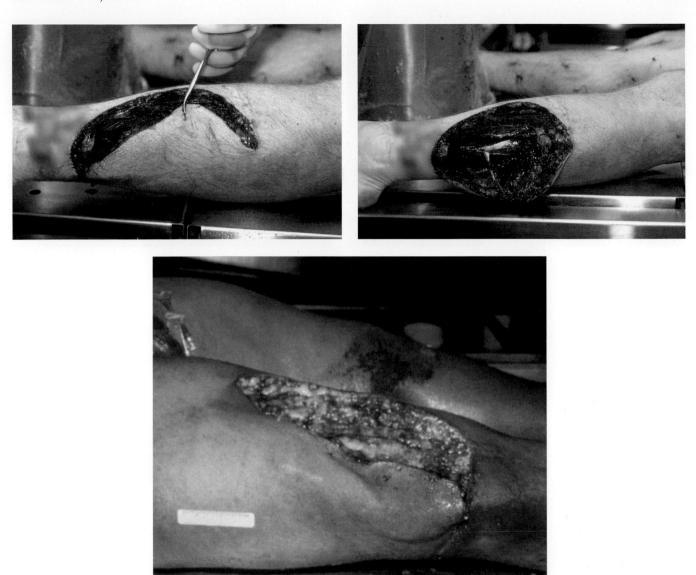

Figures 6.132–6.134 These individuals were run over by motor vehicles while lying on the ground. Note the flap of skin being torn away from the leg as the tire rolled across the skin.

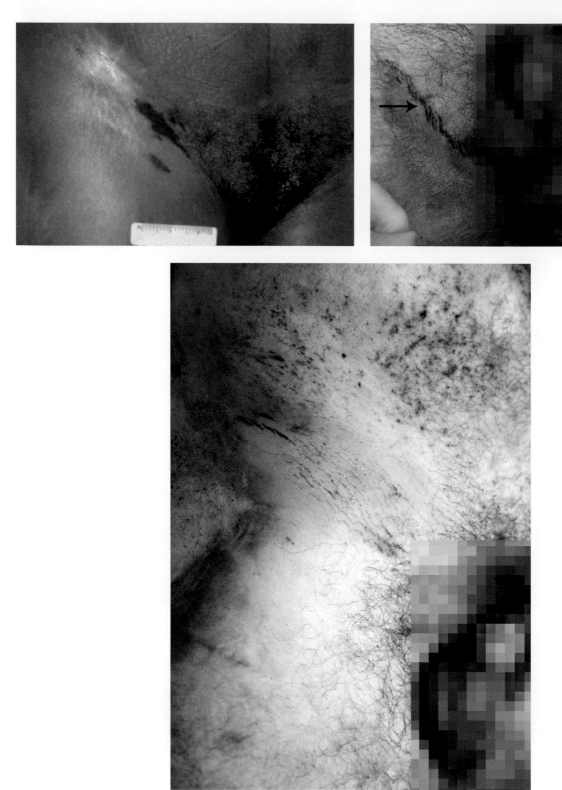

Figure 6.135–6.137 These individuals were struck from behind by a car. Note the inguinal stretch marks caused by hyperextension of the hips and legs at the time of impact.

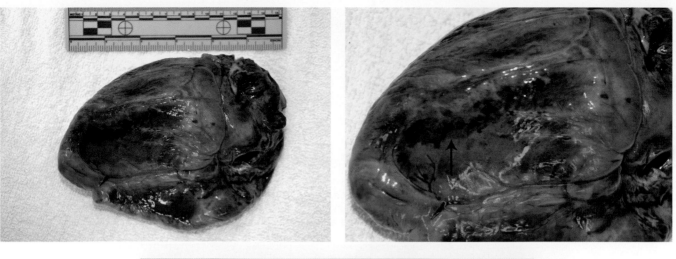

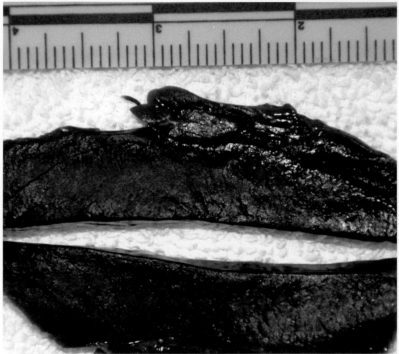

Figures 6.138–6.140 This individual sustained multiple blunt force injuries in a motor vehicle collision but did not have a lethal volume of blood loss. Note the cardiac contusion, which resulted in death by fatal arrhythmia.

Figures 6.141 and 6.144 This individual was struck by a car on an overpass and thrown over the rail into oncoming traffic of an expressway. He was struck by multiple cars. Note the extensive trauma, far exceeding what one would typically see in a single motor vehicle impact.

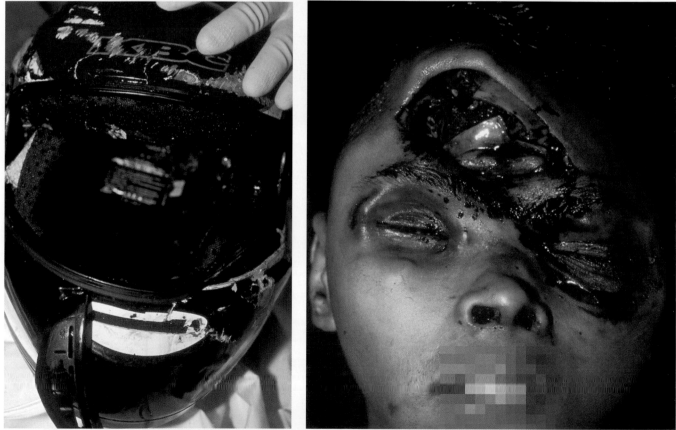

Figure 6.145–6.147 This broken motorcycle helmet shows blood clot and brain material from an individual who fractured his skull after striking a pole. This demonstrates the dangerous nature of motorcycle collisions even with high-quality protective gear.

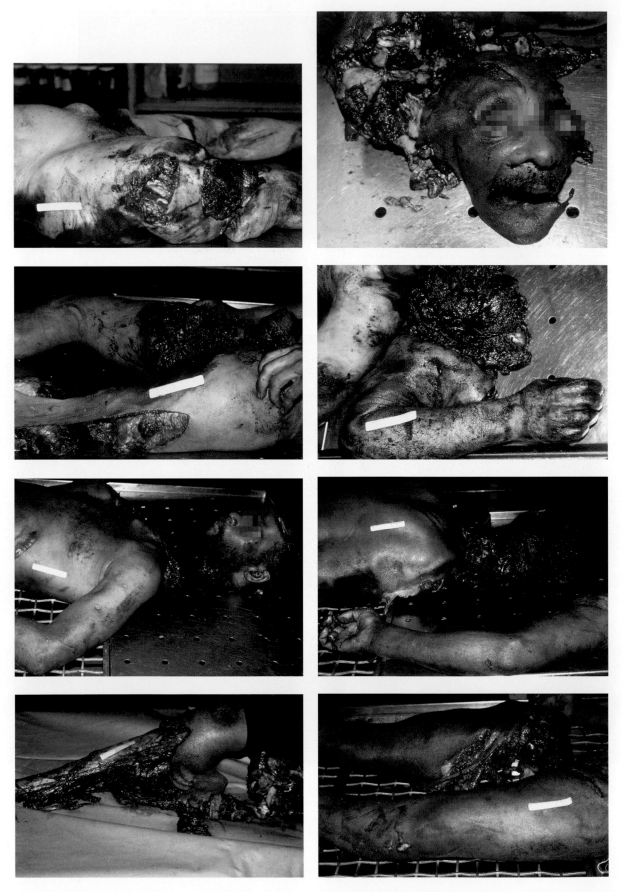

Figures 6.148–6.155 These figures demonstrate various subway fatalities where individuals were run over by trains. Note the separated body portions with extensive crush injury and axle grease from the train wheels.

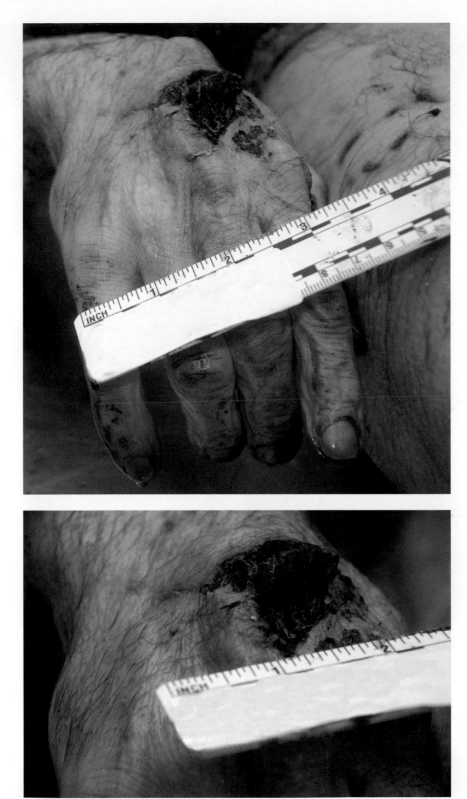

Figures 6.156 and 6.157 This shows a hand fracture of a pilot involved in a fatal airplane collision. This is caused by grabbing and bracing oneself with the steering mechanism at the time of impact. This represents a control surface injury.

Figure 6.158 This individual fell from the top of her steps and sustained multiple blunt impact injuries including a femur fracture and a skull fracture. Note the slipper at the top steps.

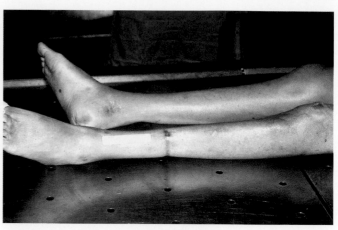

Figure 6.159 This individual has a femur fracture. Note that the fractured leg is shorter and the foot is laterally rotated.

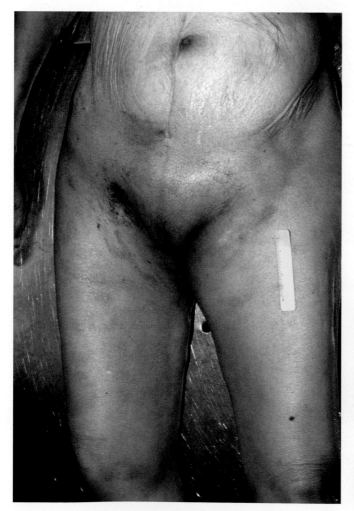

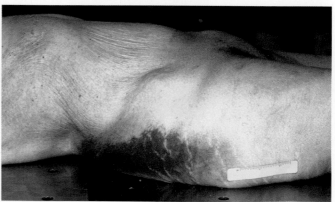

Figures 6.160 and 6.161 People with significant osteoporosis may fracture bones with little force. These two pictures demonstrate large areas of contusion and ecchymosis following a femur fracture secondary to a standing height fall.

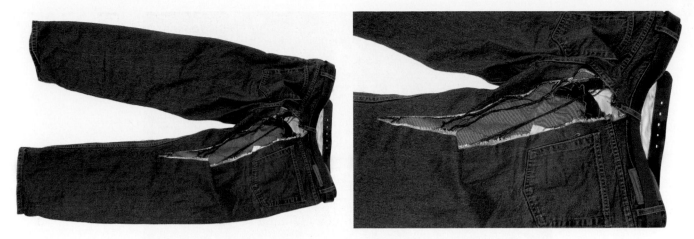

Figures 6.162 and 6.163 Individuals falling great distances may have their clothes torn due to the impact with the ground. This may sometimes be mistaken for an assault.

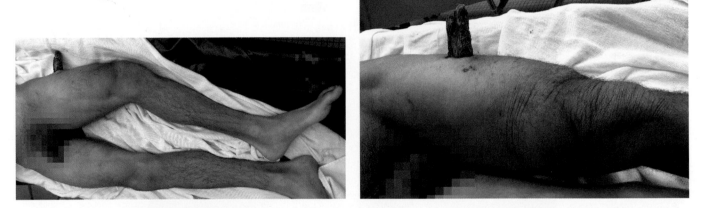

Figures 6.164 and 6.165 This decedent jumped from a great height and fractured his right femur. Note the fractured bone protruding from the thigh. Also note the shortening of the right leg with lateral rotation.

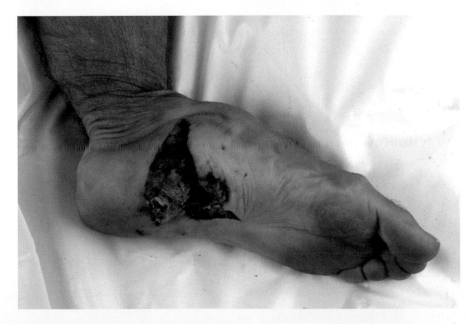

Figure 6.166 The decedent fell from a great height and landed on his feet. The fractured tibia was forced through the bottom of the foot upon impact.

Figures 6.167 and 6.168 Angulated irregular abrasions of back due to striking a gravel bed with great force.

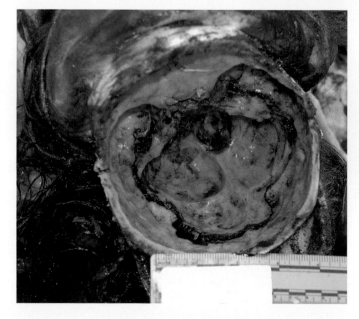

Figure 6.169 Ring fracture. This usually occurs following a fall with initial impact to the feet or buttocks.

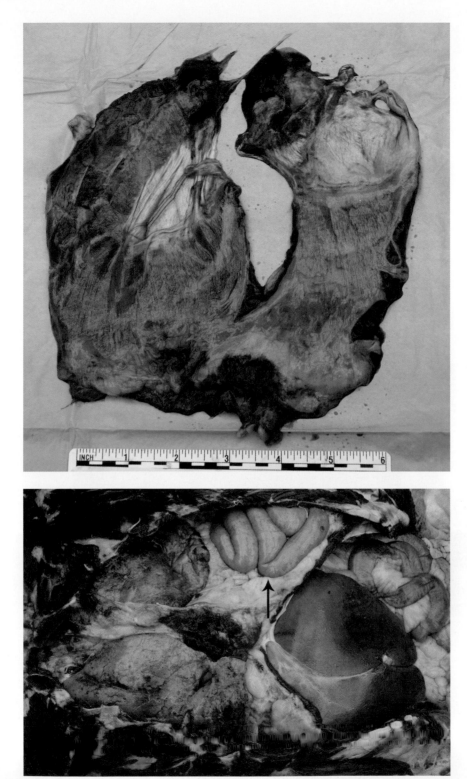

Figures 6.170 and 6.171 This motor vehicle fatality sustained a lacerated diaphragm and was found to have a large portion of his intestines within his left thoracic cavity.

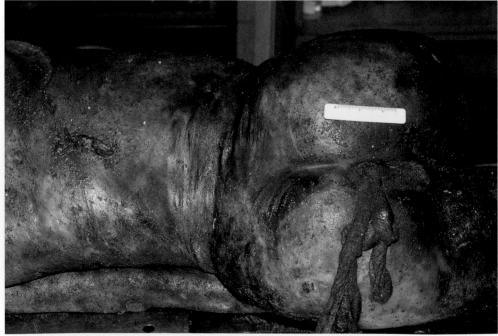

Figures 6.172 and 6.173 This individual was placed in a Dumpster and left to decompose. The trash compactor in the truck was engaged before the body was observed. Note the garbage truck shovel laceration to the back. Also note the intestines forced from the anus following compactor compression.

Figures 6.174–6.177 This individual was shot in the head, processed through a trash compactor, and left to decompose. Note the flattening of the body with extensive blunt force injury and fragmentation.

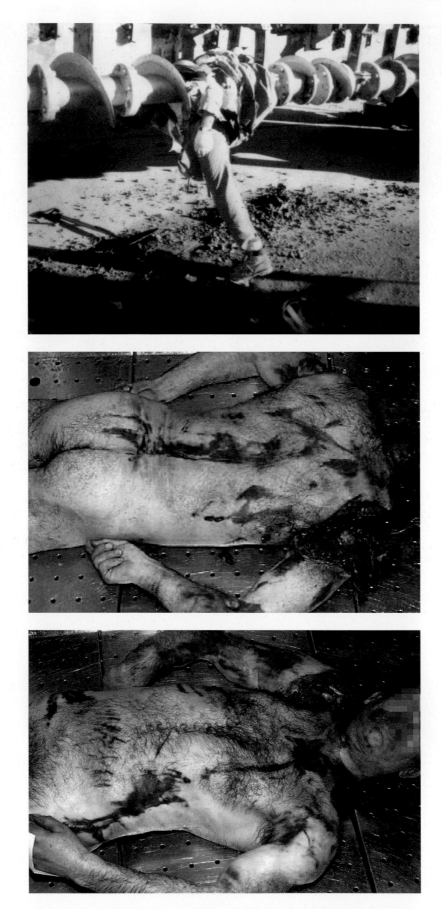

Figures 6.178–6.180 This individual slipped into a terrain leveler and sustained multiple abrasions, with blunt and sharp force injuries including extensive fractures and internal lacerations.

Figure 6.181 This individual had a severe blunt impact to his face, which caused the atlanto-occipital ligaments to stretch and dislocate. This resulted in brainstem and upper cervical spinal cord injury resulting in asystole and apnea.

Figure 6.182 This picture of the base of the brain shows a medullary pontine laceration with extensive subarachnoid hemorrhage.

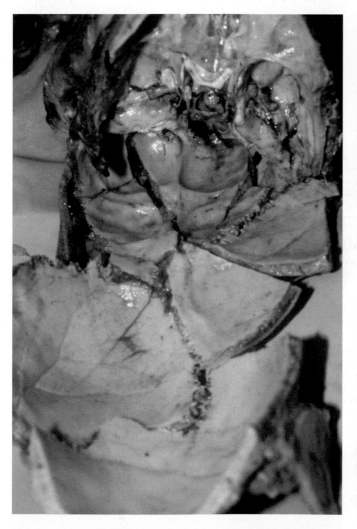

Figure 6.183 Comminuted skull fracture where the bone is broken into separate pieces.

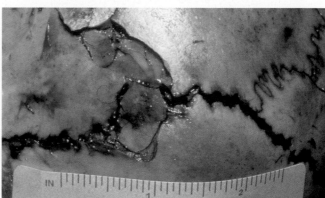

Figure 6.184 Diastatic skull fracture showing the fracture site passes through a cranial suture.

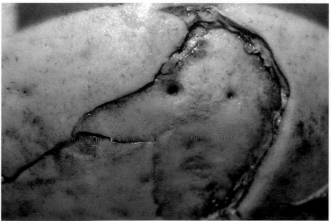

Figure 6.185 Healing skull fracture.

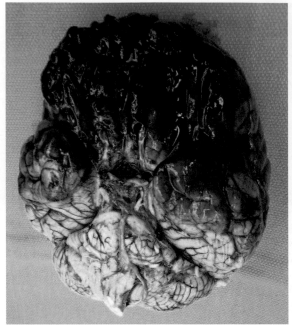

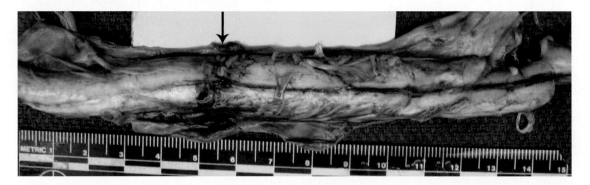

Figure 6.188 Temporal lobe with multiple splinter-type hemorrhages demonstrating typical cerebrocortical contusions.

Figure 6.186 Frontal and temporal contusional hematomas associated with a falling impact to the back of the head in an individual with liver disease.

Figure 6.187 Spinal cord with a region of purple discoloration and softening demonstrating a spinal cord contusion.

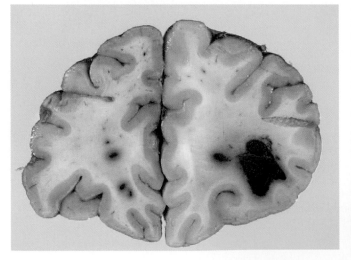

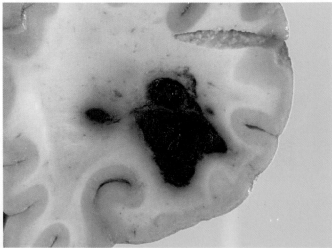

Figures 6.189 and 6.190 These images demonstrate gliding cortical contusions, which typically occur near the white and gray matter junction following blunt force head trauma.

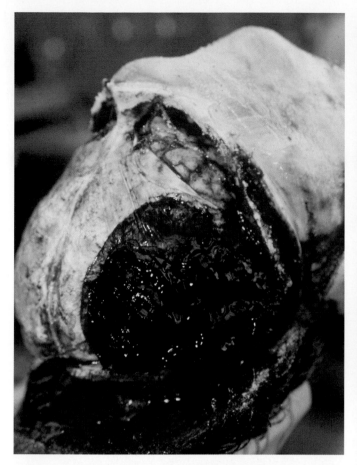

Figure 6.191 Epidural hemorrhage in an individual with a temporal bone fracture and middle meningeal artery laceration. Note the clotted blood at the surface of the dura mater.

Figure 6.192 Epidural hemorrhage.

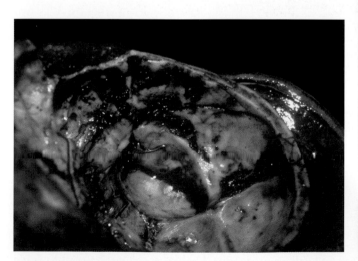

Figures 6.193 and 6.194 This shows the dura mater stripped from the inner aspect of the calvarium. Note the clotted adherent epidural hemorrhage within the temporal region of the skull.

Figure 6.195 Acute subdural hemorrhage.

Figure 6.196 Subdural hemorrhage that is slightly older with clotted adherent blood.

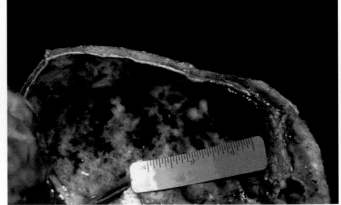

Figures 6.197 and 6.198 This demonstrates an older, clotted, red, adherent, subdural hemorrhage with portions of rust discoloration and membrane formation.

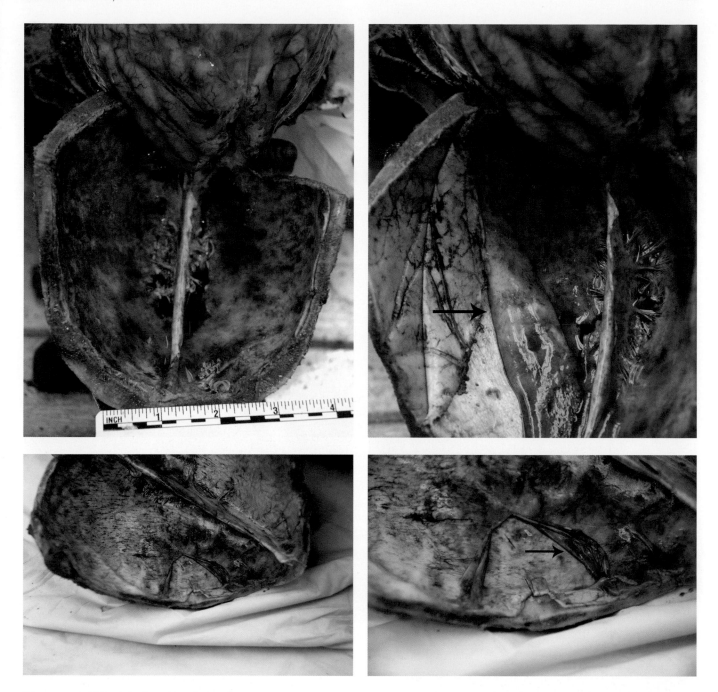

Figures 6.199–6.202 Old subdural membrane. Note the softer rust-colored membrane that is peeled away from the dural surface.

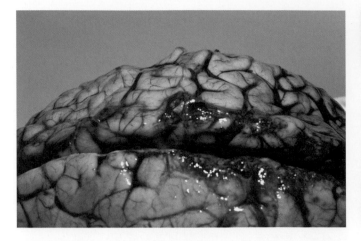

Figure 6.203 This cerebral cortex demonstrates an irregular flattened surface caused by a chronic subdural hematoma. In contrast, a chronic epidural hematoma generally leaves a flattened and less irregular cerebral cortex deformation.

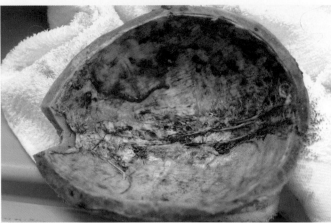

Figure 6.204 Old subdural hemorrhage with clear to rust-colored membrane formation. Note the membrane separation with beading up away from the midline caused by scraping a scalpel blade along the subdural surface.

Figures 6.205 and 6.206 Large antemortem subdural hemorrhage altered by excessive heat due to fire.

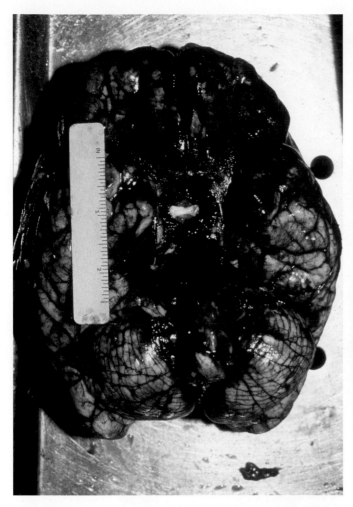

Figure 6.208 This demonstrates a large subarachnoid hemorrhage in an individual who died several days following a traumatic head injury.

Figure 6.207 This brain demonstrates multifocal subarachnoid hemorrhage with subarachnoid hematoma at the base of the brain. This hemorrhage occurred following a blunt impact to the face, causing hyperextension and rotation of the head with laceration of the right vertebral artery.

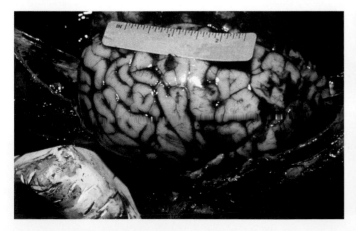

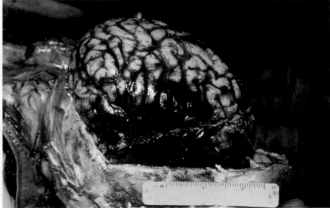

Figures 6.209 and 6.210 These brains are diffusely swollen with flattened gyral configuration and sulci obliteration. These individuals lived from several hours to several days after the initial insult.

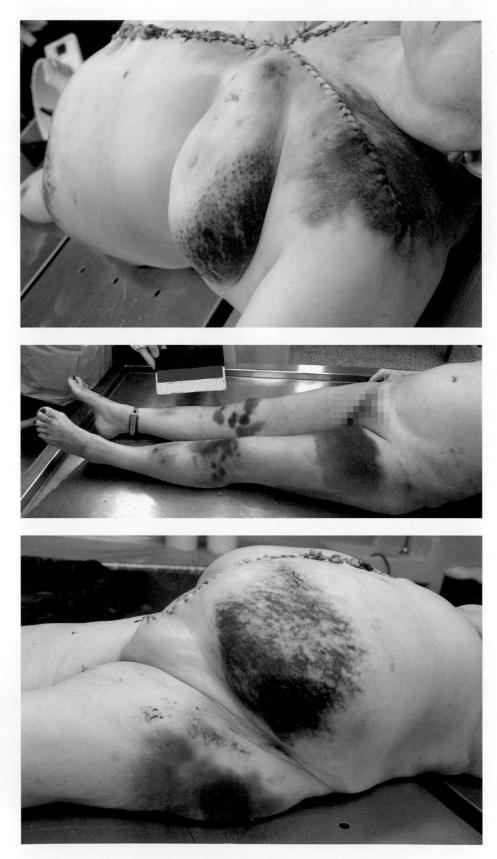

Figures 6.211–6.213 Note the large areas of contusion with ecchymosis following minimal trauma in these individuals with chronic alcoholism, hepatic cirrhosis, and coagulopathy.

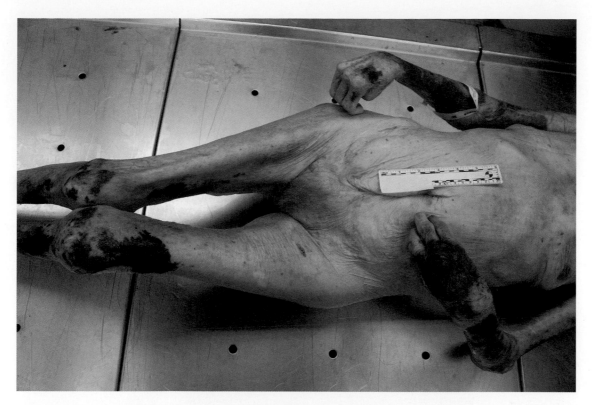

Figure 6.214 *Senile* purpura or ecchymosis may be caused by minimal trauma due to extreme skin and connective tissue fragility in elderly patients. Careful evaluation should still be performed to assess possible elder abuse. Note the superficial lacerations of the left hand caused by catheter tape removal. Some areas of ecchymosis occurred in association with fresh needle marks from therapy. The bruising to the legs was not associated with therapy.

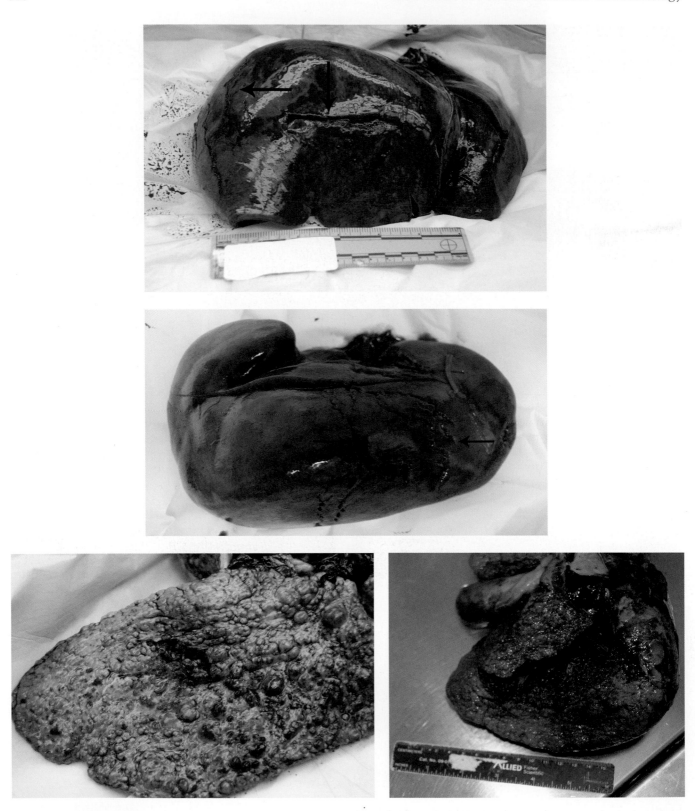

Figures 6.215–6.218 Laceration of liver and kidneys due to blunt force trauma. Note the last two livers have hepatic cirrhosis. Hepatic cirrhosis is less commonly associated with laceration due to the increased fibrosis. A normal liver is the most common organ in the peritoneal cavity to lacerate in association with blunt force trauma.

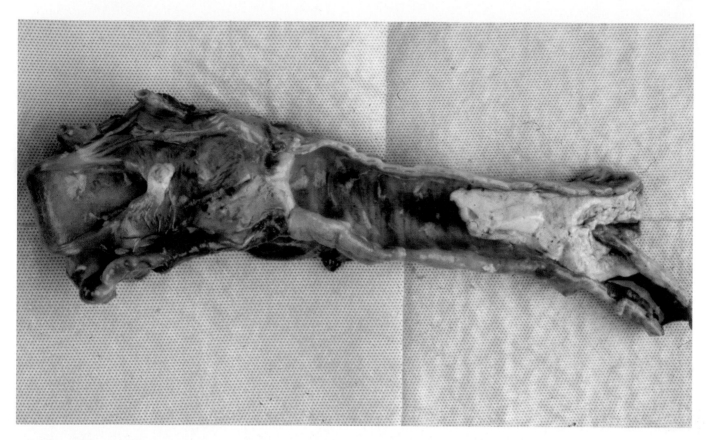

Figure 6.219 This opened airway demonstrates a large piece of aspirated brain in an individual who was resuscitated following extensive blunt force head trauma with comminuted skull fracture and communicating lacerations extending into the oral cavity. When Emergency Services arrived, the decedent was found in agonal respirations.

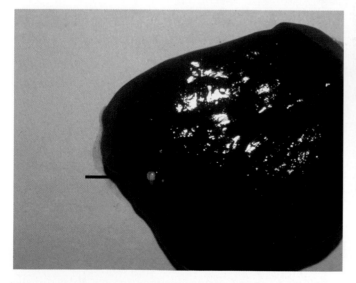

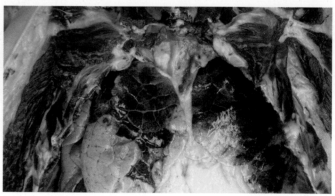

Figure 6.221 Note the patchy red to purple discoloration indicating aspiration of blood in an individual with a gunshot wound to the head, lacerations extending to the oral pharynx, and residual respiratory effort before death.

Figure 6.220 This cut section of lung demonstrates a small white to gray fragment in the parenchyma on the lower lateral aspect. Microscopic examination of this revealed intravascular embolic cerebellar tissue. This individual sustained a comminuted skull fracture with multiple central nervous system lacerations. He was vigorously resuscitated several times over the course of several hours. Brain tissue embolized through damaged blood vessels at the base of the brain.

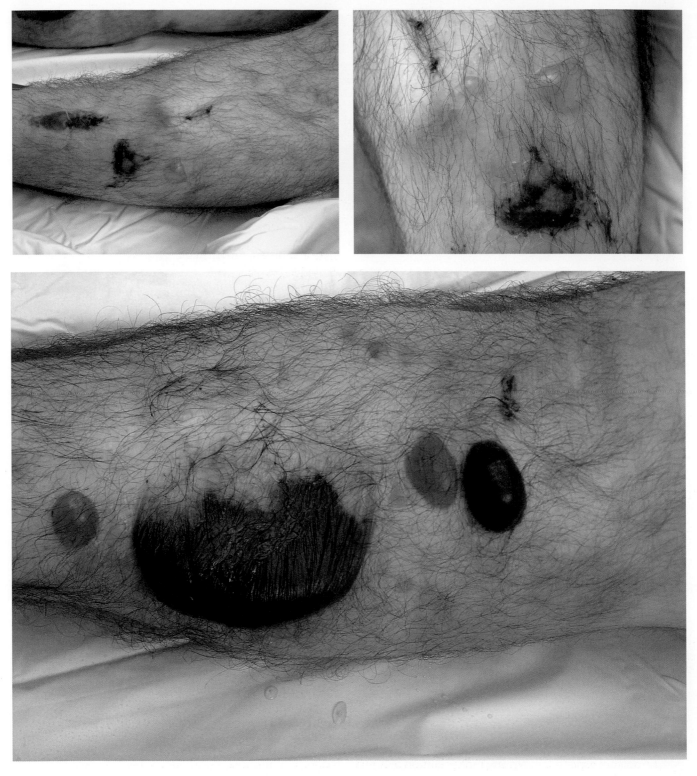

Figures 6.222–6.224 This is another pedestrian who was struck by a car and survived approximately 2 days in the hospital. Note the tibial fracture with adjacent abrasions and broken skin. There is also blister formation confined to this region associated with sepsis following infection associated with this trauma.

Sharp-Force Injuries

CHARLES A. CATANESE

7

Contents

Introduction

Sharp-force injuries are defined as injuries produced by an instrument with a thin edge or point. Examples of these instruments include a knife, razor, box cutter, scalpel, sharp-edged piece of metal, broken glass bottle, broken glass window, scissor, ice pick, fork, propeller, screw driver, saw blade, axe, machete, arrow, nail, pickaxe, spiked fence post, meat cleaver, and so on. This is in contrast to a blunt-force injury, where contact with the body is by a nonsharp object such as a baseball bat or the floor. Included in sharp-force injuries are stab and incised wounds.

A *stab wound* is typically made by a knife blade and is defined as having a greater depth of penetration than surface dimension. An *incised wound* is a slicing-type injury where the surface dimension is greater than the depth of penetration.

Accurate, concise, and organized wound documentation is important, as with all other injuries. Each injury should have a documented location on the body, including a description of adjacent abrasions or contusions, wound dimensions, depth of penetration, and direction of penetration into the body. All injured structures should be documented, including the amount of hemorrhage both in the wound track and within body cavities. In cases where there are multiple injuries, it is acceptable to group them with ranges. It is good practice to take overall photographs of the body before and after cleaning, as well as close-up photographs of each wound.

Important aspects concerning interpretation of injury involve pattern recognition. Familiarization with this will allow opinion formulation concerning correlation of a particular instrument to a particular wound. One example where this would come in handy involved the arrest of several suspects with different concealed weapons. The police may approach you to render an opinion about what type of weapon produced injuries so they can focus their early investigation. In one actual case, each suspect had a different instrument in their pocket, including a flat-edged pocket knife, a box cutter, a screwdriver, and a slightly bent serrated table knife. The injuries to the decedent's body consisted of slit-like perforations with multiple, adjacent, parallel linear abrasions. This pattern injury is consistent with a serrated knife. Many of the images in this chapter are designed to help with pattern recognition.

Location and Direction of Injury

This should be given with reference to a particular body position, usually standard anatomic planes. Each wound should be documented by location on the body's surface, and measured from vertical and horizontal planes of reference. An example of this would be from below the top of the head or above the feet, to the right or left of the midline, and in a front–back direction. Standard anatomic planes are demonstrated with the body in an upright position with the head tilted slightly upward, the legs together, the arms at the sides, and palms facing forward. The head is superior and the feet inferior; medial is toward the midline and lateral away from the midline. The anterior or front of the body includes the face, chest, and the palms. The posterior part of the body includes the back, buttocks, and so on. The direction of the wound into or through the body should be given with reference to three planes when possible: front–back, right–left, and up–down. This is important because it allows one to correlate the injuries to possible assault descriptions and help discredit or substantiate statements.

Wound Dimension

This should be documented separately for each sharp-force injury, unless there are many that can be grouped together and described in ranges. Example: There are twenty 1-inch to 2-inch by up to 1/4-inch, stab wounds within a 5-inch to 7-inch region on the middle aspect of the right chest, which is centered 13 inches below the top of the head and 4 inches to the right of the midline.

It is good practice to document the injury as it exists on the body and then again when in a relaxed state. The important aspect is to document the wound dimension in ranges that most closely reflect the actual dimensions of the knife blade or instrument. A stab wound can be put into a relaxed state by pressing the surrounding skin toward the wound and releasing the surrounding tension, or by placing tape over the perforation site to approximate the margins. It is also acceptable to cut a square around the surrounding skin to release the tension. The skin and underlying tissues are elastic, with different degrees of tension. This can make the surface dimension of the wound length and width slightly variable depending on the location and orientation of the body. It should also be noted that inflicted injuries may be cut into a greater dimension if after penetration the sharp end of the blade is forced sideways through the soft tissue. Cut marks through bone and cartilage often reflect accurate weapon dimension with tool marks and should be retained in formaldehyde for possible future comparison. It should also be noted that soft tissue will change dimension during fixation.

This same concept applies for depth of penetration as well. Dimensions should be given in a range to account for some changes when examined on the autopsy table compared with the body position when the injuries were inflicted. Variables that may change this parameter while the assault is taking place include deep breaths or exhalations, flexion, extension, rotation, the force used to inflict the injury, the location on the body including underlying bone or soft tissue, and so on. If someone is stabbed strongly in the abdomen when relaxed, the blade may penetrate deeper than the length of the knife blade.

Adjacent Abrasions and Contusions

These may indicate body contact from the knife handle, lower part of the knife blade, or the knife hilt. This is important information in formulating an opinion as to how much force was needed to produce the injury. If the knife blade penetrates a bone and there are hilt marks adjacent to the perforation site, one can extrapolate that the knife must have been stuck into the body with greater force than a blade that only penetrated half the length of a blade. If the knife blade perforated a thick bone, it would take great force.

Injured Organs or Structures

This information helps to allow interpretation of how functional one might be after an assault. The number and extent of internal injuries give insight into the nature of the assault and perpetrator.

For instance, "I stabbed him in the neck and he continued to chase me so I stabbed him again in the chest and abdomen." If the neck wound transected the spinal cord, you know the statement may be false because the victim would no longer have voluntary movement to part of the body, as with a tendon or peripheral nerve being cut. Also, depending on the structures damaged, the rate of blood loss may be quite variable. This would help estimate how fast the individual would lose blood, and what the individual might be capable of doing after the injury, and for how long. Questions like this may come up in trial. A transected aorta would incapacitate someone more rapidly than a transected brachial (arm) artery, which would be more rapid than a transected cephalic (superficial) vein. Someone with a stab wound to the heart will often lose consciousness within minutes but until then still be capable of running away, defending themselves, or continuing an assault, particularly if the heart does not go into a lethal arrhythmia. It is possible for someone to get stabbed in the heart, run a couple of blocks, and shoot several people before dying.

Figure 7.1 Stab wound consisting of a flat slit-like perforation with minimal surrounding skin tension.

Figure 7.2 Stab wound with moderate surrounding skin tension. Note the separation of the wound margins.

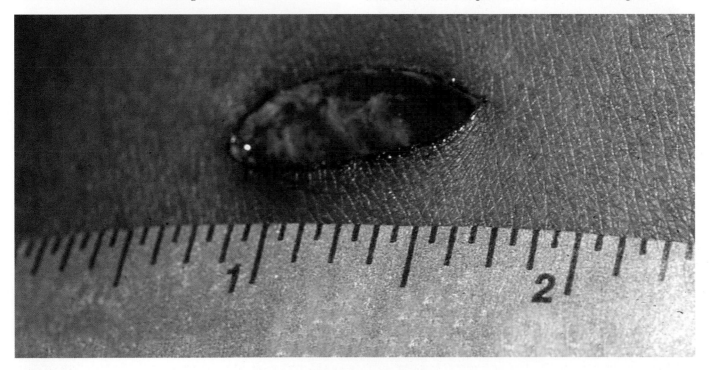

Figure 7.3 Gaping stab wound consisting of an oval-shaped perforation caused by significant surrounding skin tension.

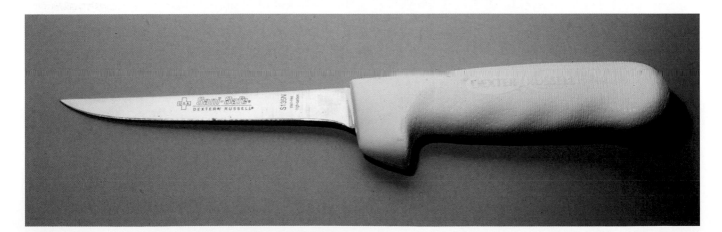

Figure 7.4 A nonserrated knife blade similar to the one used to inflict these wounds. It is important to take the surrounding skin tension into account when estimating the size and type of weapon used. It is possible for a serrated knife to produce similar injuries.

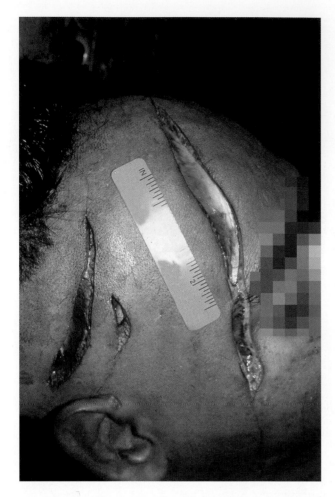

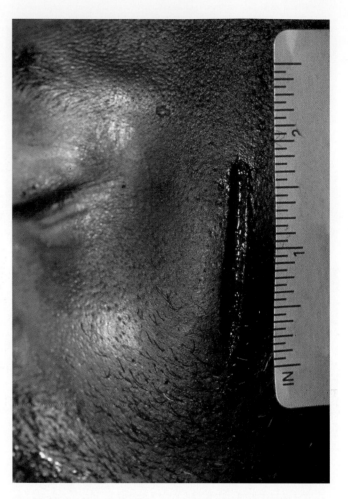

Figure 7.5 Incised wounds produced by a broken bottle.

Figure 7.6 Incised wound to the face produced by a knife in a gang member accused of snitching who is killed later by multiple stab wounds. Cuts between the ear and the mouth sometimes indicate a retaliation toward someone who informed the authorities.

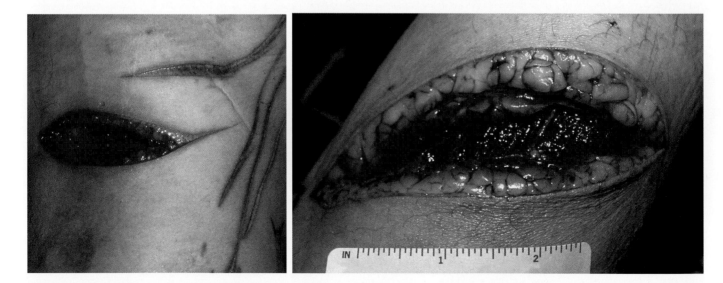

Figures 7.7 and 7.8 Incised wounds produced by a box cutter.

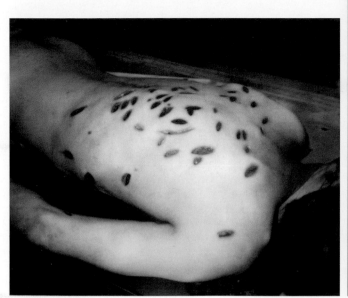

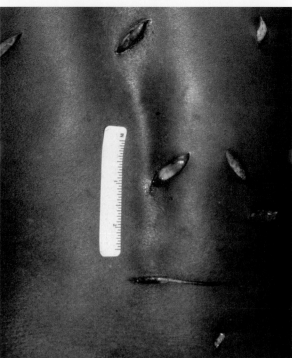

Figures 7.9 and 7.10 These are multiple stab wounds to the back. Note the varying dimensions and gaping nature due to the varying degrees of skin tension from underlying tissue planes in different locations.

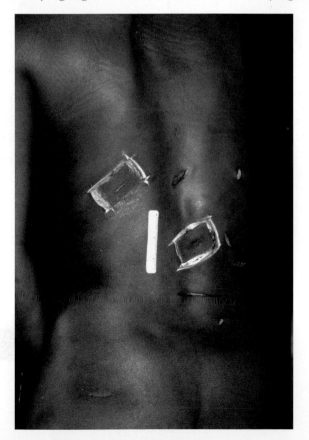

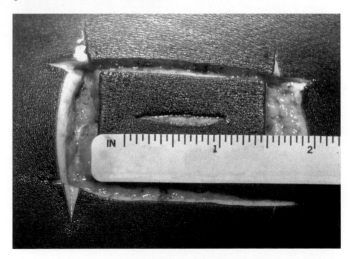

Figure 7.12 This is a close-up of one of the wounds that were cut into a relaxed state and measured. Note the sharp end on the left aspect and the blunt end on the right aspect.

Figure 7.11 Several of these wounds were chosen based on estimation that they were more reflective of the actual knife blade size. These wounds were then cut into a relaxed state and remeasured to help estimate the actual size of the knife blade.

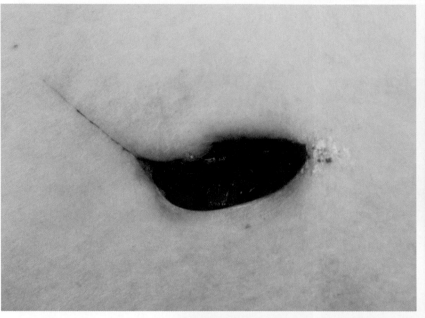

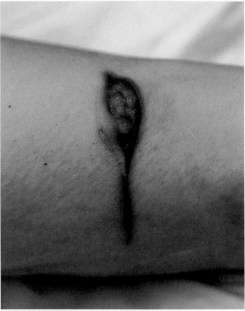

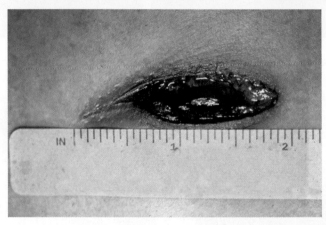

Figures 7.13–7.15 Stab wounds to body with slight drying of the margins and a "linear extension" from one end due to the sharp part of the knife blade or point being dragged through the wound and across the body surface, which may change the dimension of the injury.

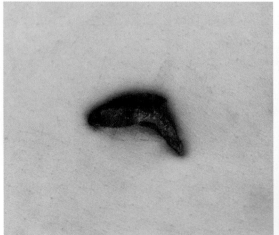

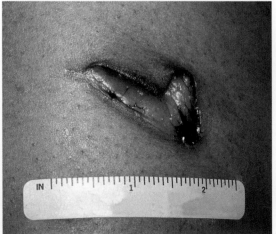

Figures 7.16 and 7.17 These two images demonstrate a "swallow-tail" type injury where the knife was inserted into the body in one direction, turned, and then removed in another direction, producing two angulated cuts. This type of injury may be produced by the movement of the perpetrator, victim, or both.

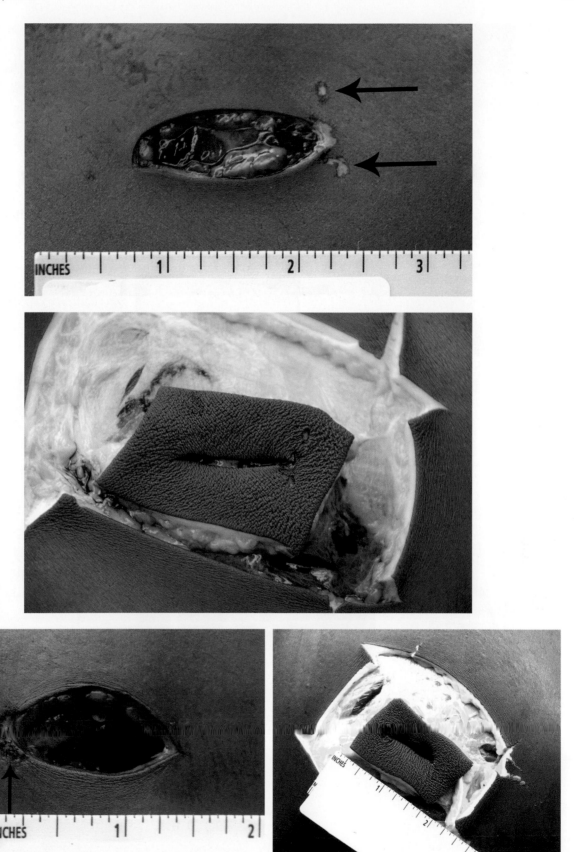

Figures 7.18–7.21 These stab wounds demonstrate adjacent abrasions from the hilt of the knife contacting the skin with great force.

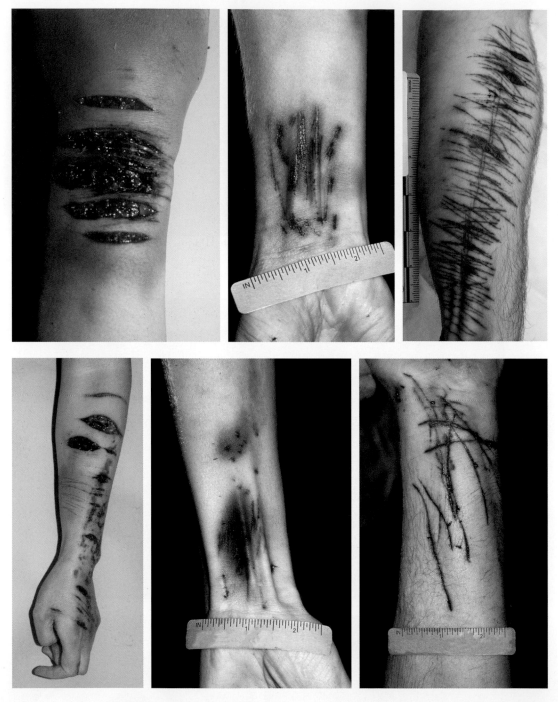

Figures 7.22–7.27 Multiple self-inflected linear abrasions and incised wounds to the arms and wrists demonstrating hesitation marks in individuals who committed suicide with other lethal injuries. The red discoloration indicates vital reaction.

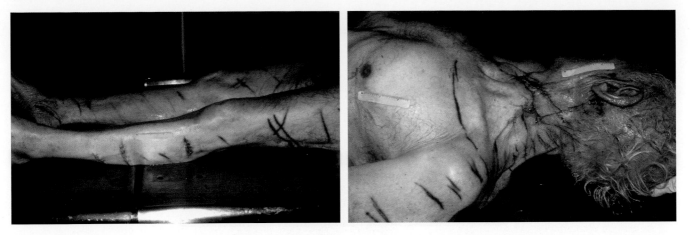

Figures 7.28 and 7.29 Multiple linear incised wounds in an individual who lived for several hours. He died of a heart attack associated with the stress and blood loss from the self-inflicted injuries. The manner of death in this case was classified as suicide. The cause of death was listed as both multiple incised wounds and heart disease.

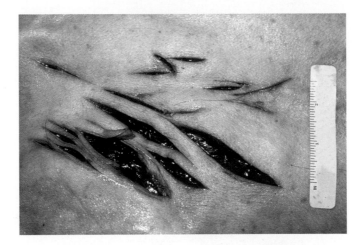

Figure 7.30 Multiple self-inflicted sharp-force injuries including stab and incised wounds. Note the tightly clustered orientation of these injuries, which is common in suicides.

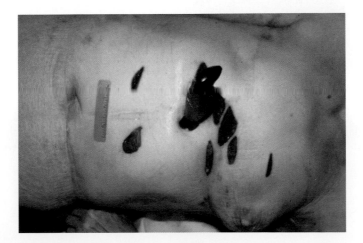

Figure 7.31 Multiple self-inflicted stab wounds. This individual was found with her hands surrounding the knife handle in a moderate state of rigor mortis.

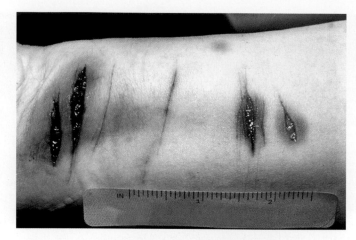

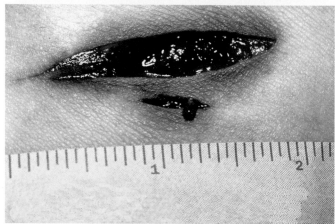

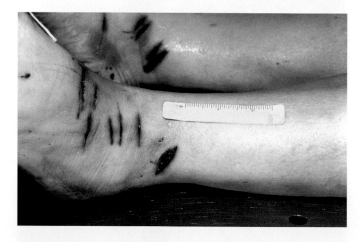

Figures 7.32–7.34 This individual died from blunt-force trauma after jumping from a window. She was found with multiple, clustered linear abrasions, incised wounds, and stab wounds to the wrists, arms, and ankles. The decedent first attempted suicide by ingesting large quantities of acetaminophen, then inflicted the above sharp-force injuries. Note the erythema around the wounds indicating vital reaction. There was blood noted all over the apartment. The individual later jumped out a window and died from blunt-impact injuries. The above are hesitation wounds.

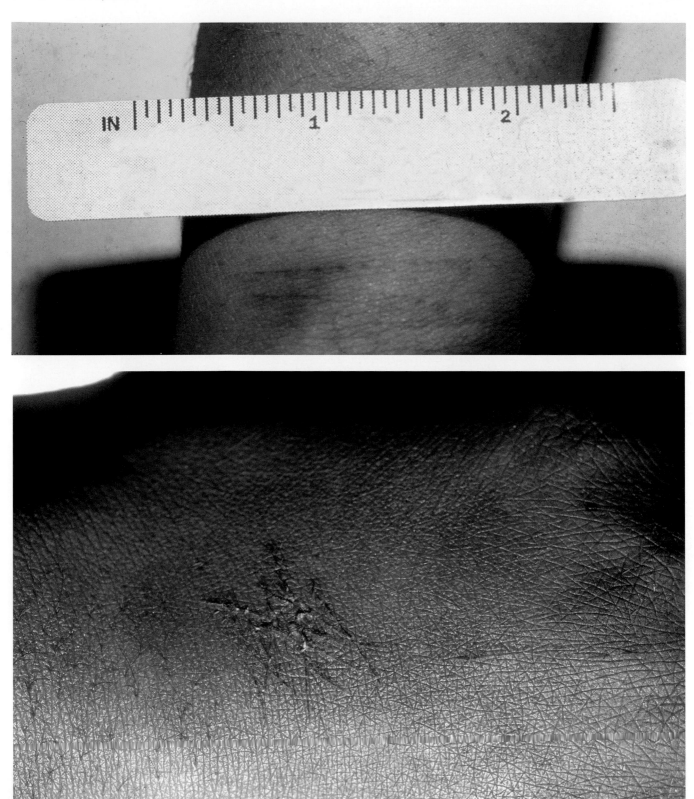

Figures 7.35 and 7.36 Superficial linear abrasions caused by dragging a knife blade across the wrist and hand prior to committing suicide by hanging.

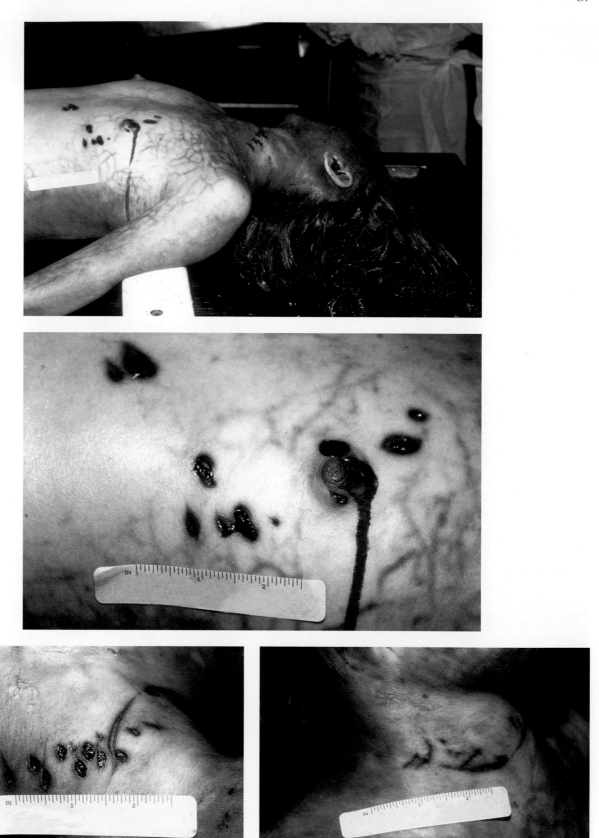

Figures 7.37–7.40 Multiple clustered self-inflicted incised and stab wounds located on each side of the neck and chest in an individual who committed suicide. Most of these stab wounds were very superficial in depth of penetration and may be described as hesitation marks. Three of these stab wounds to the chest entered the thoracic cavity and penetrated the heart and lung, causing death. Note the slight degree of decomposition with wound margin drying.

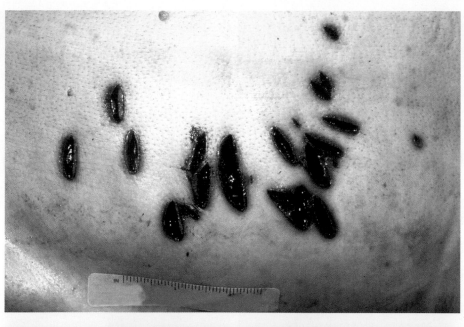

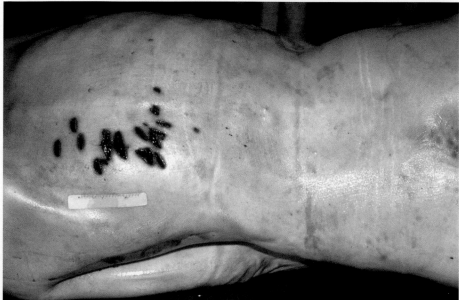

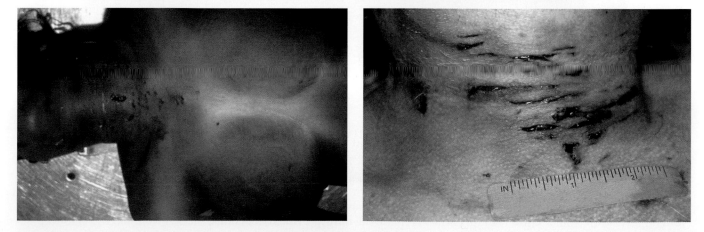

Figures 7.41–7.44 Multiple clustered homicidal stab wounds in individuals who were also bound during a sexual assault. Note the location of the multiple clustered stab wounds to the middle aspect of the individual's back, making it virtually impossible for them to have been self-inflicted.

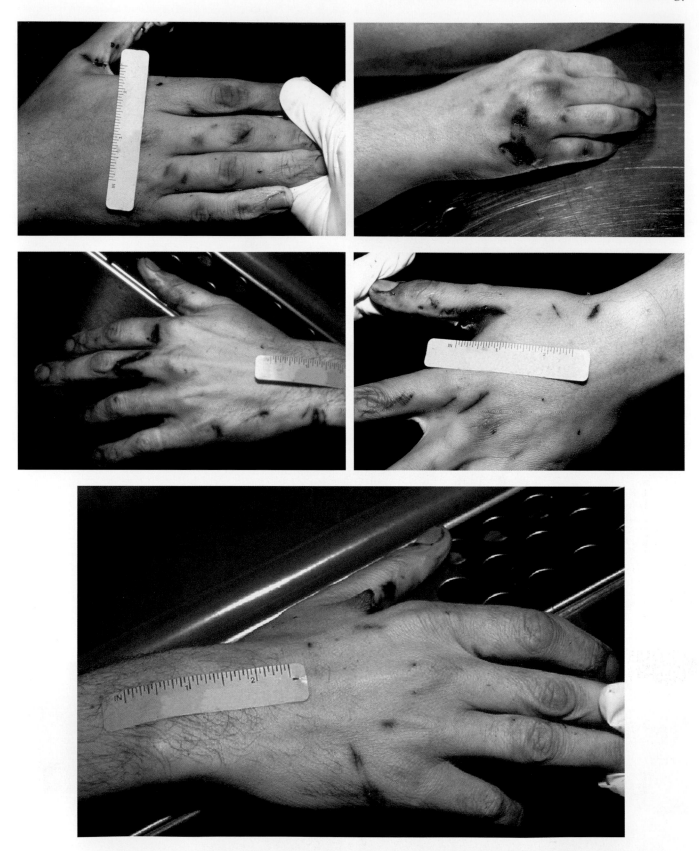

Figures 7.45–7.49 These are multiple examples of defensive-type wounds from individuals who were attempting to ward off an assault from a knife-wielding attacker. Note the multiple linear abrasions, incised wounds, and stab wounds to the hands. Several of these injuries show cut marks between the thumb and fingers due to the individual attempting to grab the knife blade.

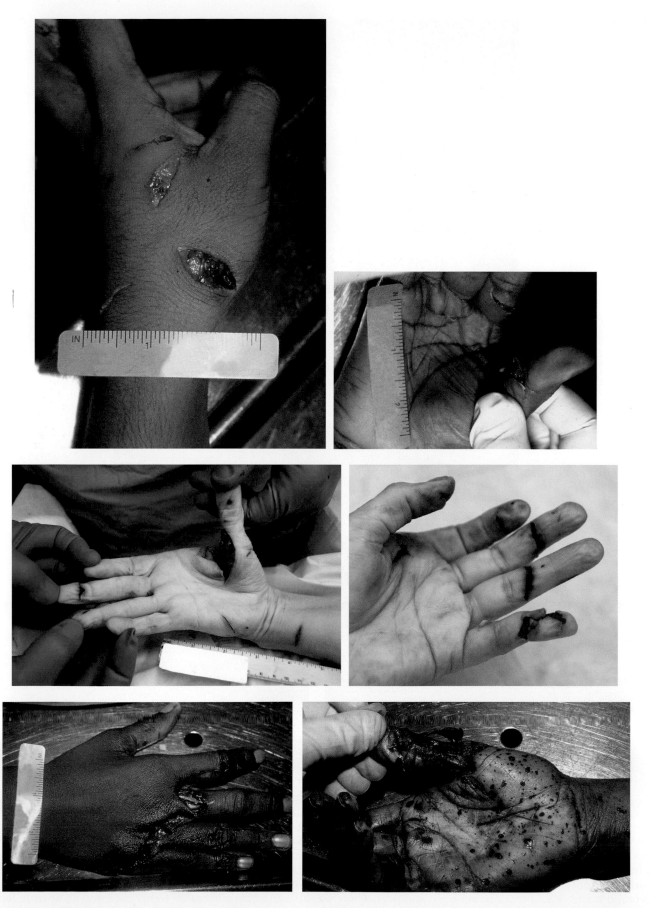

Figures 7.50–7.55 Other examples of wounds consistent with being inflicted while an individual was fending off an attack.

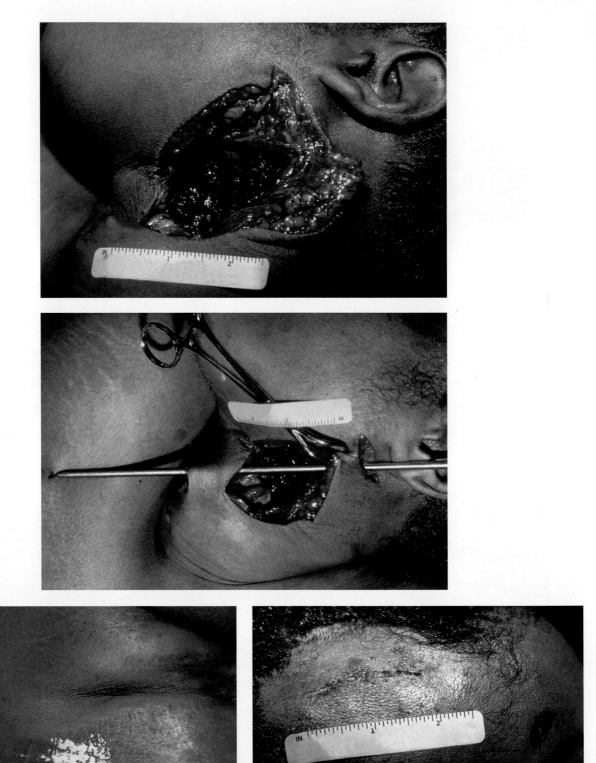

Figures 7.56–7.59 This individual was stabbed in the neck and then thrown from a window. The perpetrator described the injuries as being self-inflicted by the decedent who cut herself and then jumped out a window. The window ledge and outside wall were smeared with blood, which was easily visible from below and led the police directly to the apartment. During autopsy, approximation of the margins revealed a stab wound just below the left ear from a knife blade that exited through her neck and stuck in her right shoulder. There was also an anemic abrasion to her back and an anemic laceration to the scalp, indicating the decedent had lost much of her blood volume and did not have a beating heart with blood pressure enough to produce hemorrhage from the injuries sustained when striking the ground.

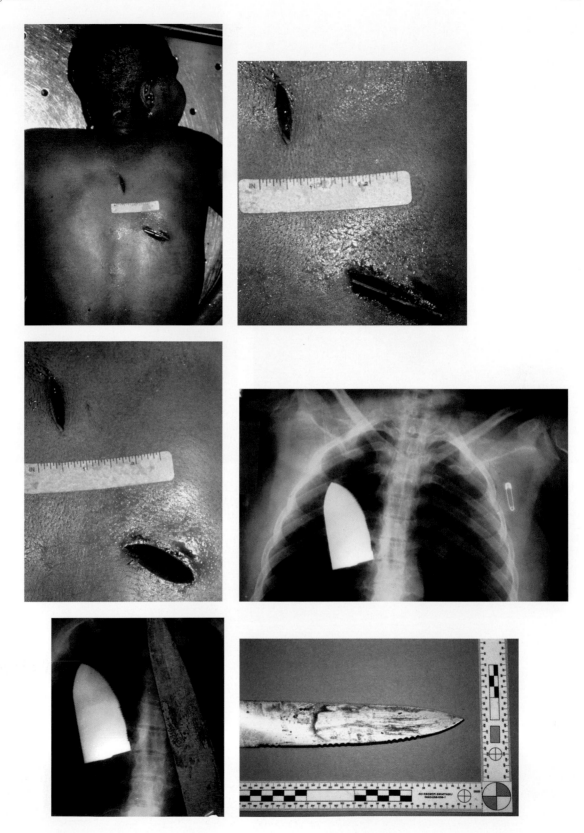

Figures 7.60–7.65 Note the two stab wounds to the left back and the broken knife blade extending from one of the wound tracks. Note the close-up view of the back demonstrating the knife within the wound track and then with the knife removed. Note the change in the wound dimension after the knife was removed. This demonstrates the elastic nature of skin and the possible challenges of correlating a weapon to a particular wound dimension. Also note the x-ray that demonstrates the knife blade within the body. Note the dimension of the actual knife blade compared to the dimension of the blade image on the x-ray. This is due to the angle in which the x-rays contacted the knife blade in the thoracic cavity.

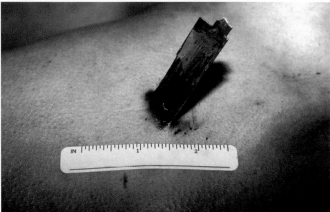

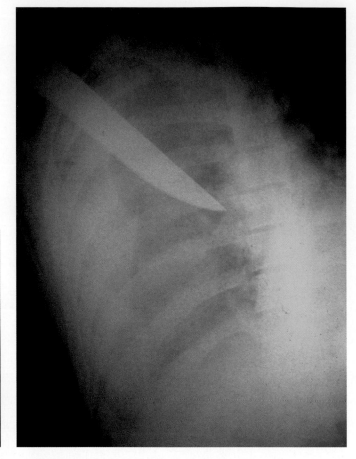

Figures 7.66 and 7.67 Broken knife blade left in body during a homicidal assault. This knife was stuck into this individual with great force and the blade got wedged in a bone. When the perpetrator attempted to remove it, the handle broke off and the knife blade was left behind.

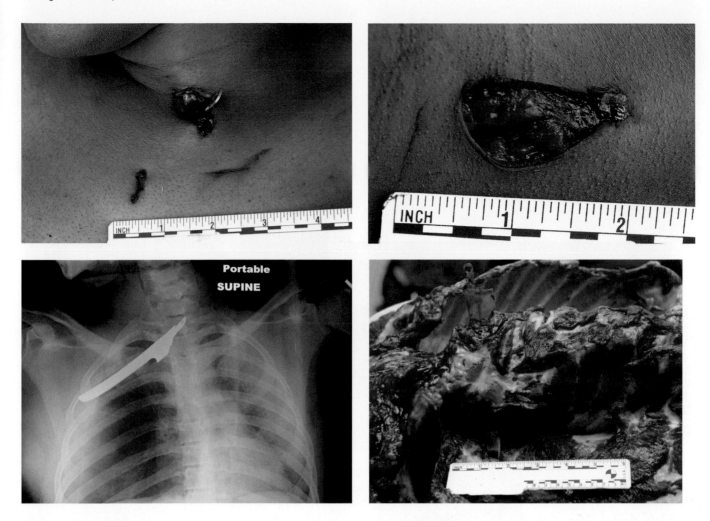

Figures 7.68–7.71 This individual was stabbed in the neck with great force causing the blade to be stuck in her scapula, which resulted in the handle being separated from the knife blade. Note the hilt mark in Figure 7.69, which consists of a dark abrasion at the right wound margin. This knife blade perforated the entire thoracic cavity including the left scapula, indicating great force was used during this assault.

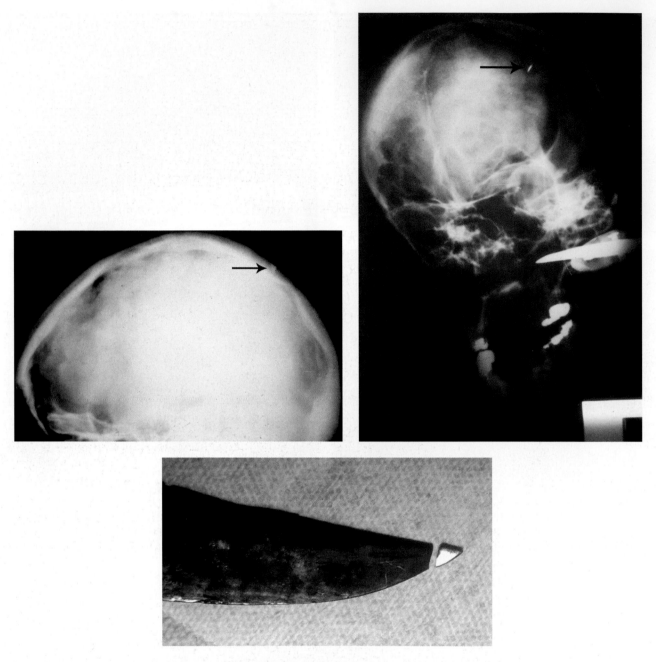

Figures 7.72–7.74 This individual was stabbed over 75 times by a scorned lover. The tip of the knife blade broke off in this individual's skull during this violent assault. Note the small radiodense fragment depicted in these skull x-rays. This reinforces the notion that it is good practice to x-ray all sharp-force homicidal violence cases. A fragmented portion of knife blade can later be matched to a suspect's knife.

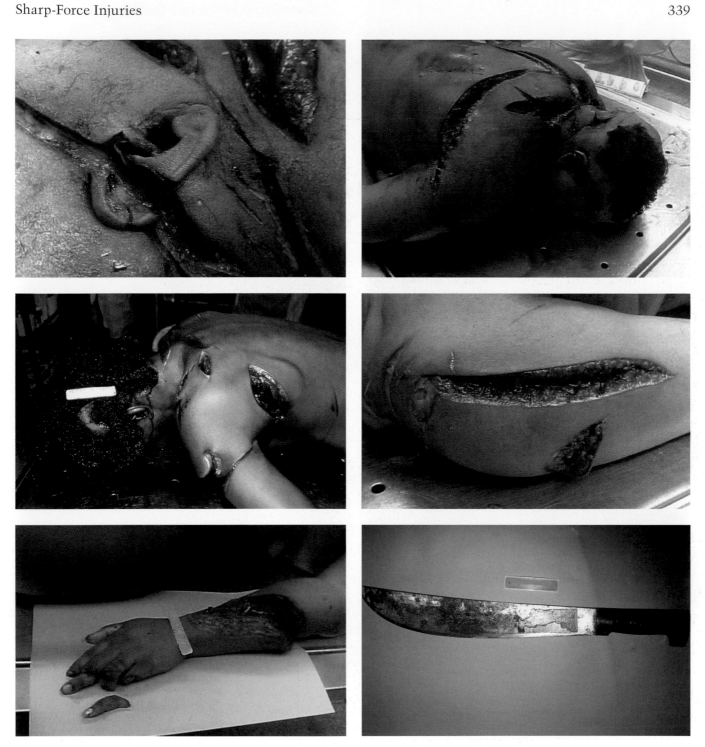

Figures 7.75–7.80 These individuals were struck multiple times with machetes. Note the long gaping hack marks, several of which cut into and through bone. Most often this degree of violent rage indicates the victim and the perpetrator had a relationship.

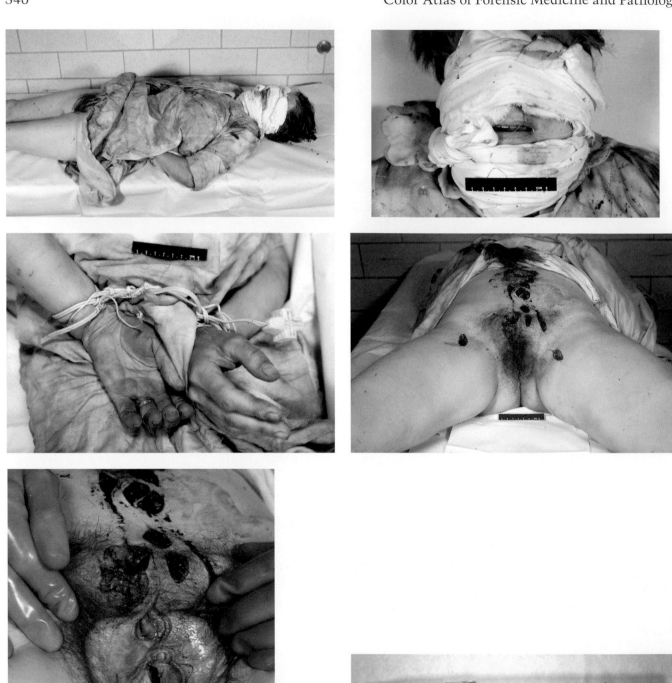

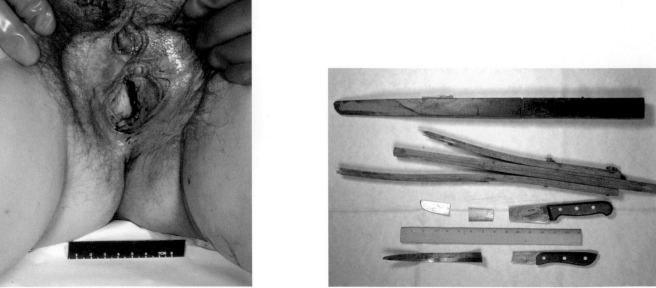

Figures 7.81–7.86 Paraphilia; abduction with ligature binding and multiple sharp-force injuries with the instruments in Figure 7.86 including vaginal mutilation. These injuries span the spectrum of antemortem–perimortem–postmortem with varying degrees of hemorrhage to being completely anemic. This is consistent with necrophilia. Paraphilia (see Chapter 10)

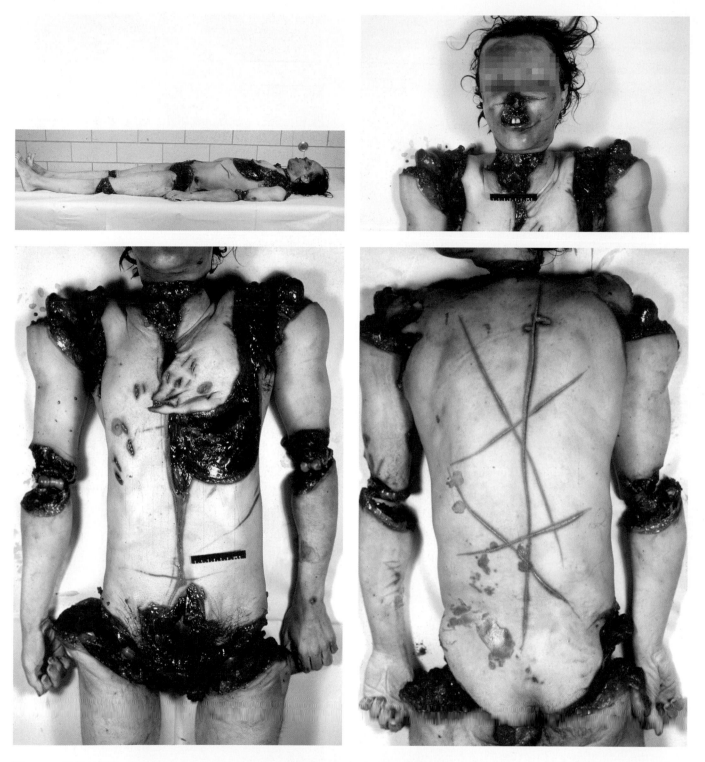

Figures 7.87–7.90 Paraphilia; postmortem mutilation with destruction of breasts, genitals, and face consistent with necrophilia. Destruction of the face indicates depersonalization.

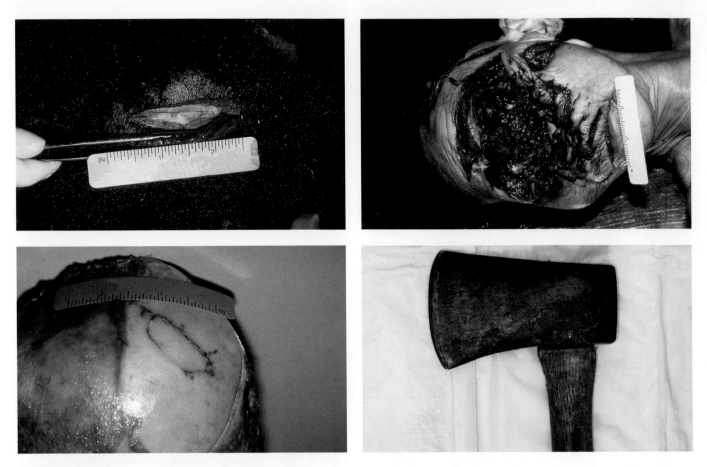

Figures 7.91–7.94 Chopping-type sharp-force injuries produced by an axe. Figure 7.92 shows an individual who had her eyes chopped out by another person with a long history of psychosis. These types of assaults are not common. He reportedly did this because she kept staring at him.

Figures 7.95–7.99 This individual was chased up several flights of stairs in an apartment complex and was cut multiple times with a box cutter. Note the blood splatter pattern on the steps. Also note that the individual was almost decapitated. This was reportedly over a dispute concerning gang-related drug dealing territory.

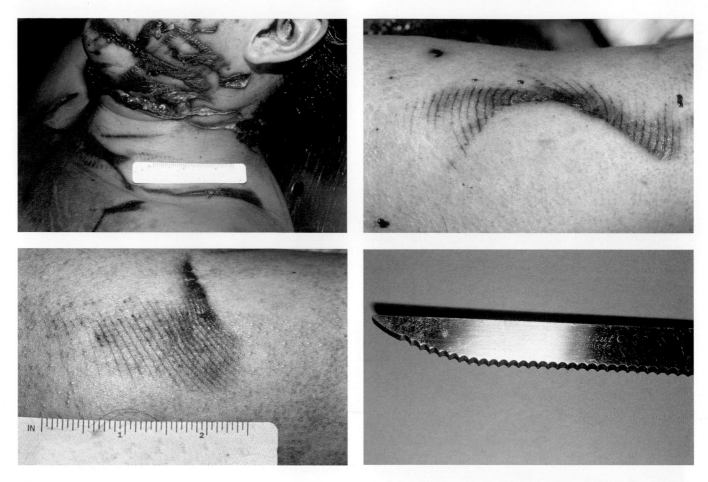

Figures 7.100–7.103 This individual had multiple stab wounds with adjacent abrasions consisting of multiple, superficial, linear parallel lines. This is a typical pattern found during a serrated knife attack. The absence of these marks does not preclude the use of a serrated knife. If a serrated knife is stuck directly into a body and not dragged across the surface, there will be no parallel linear abrasions.

Figures 7.104–7.107 This individual was stabbed multiple times with a Ginsu-type knife. His dwelling was then set on fire and he sustained extensive thermal burns with charring of the skin. Note the costal cartilages with tool markings forming an imprint of the knife blade. Figure 7.107 demonstrates a similar knife to the one used in the attack.

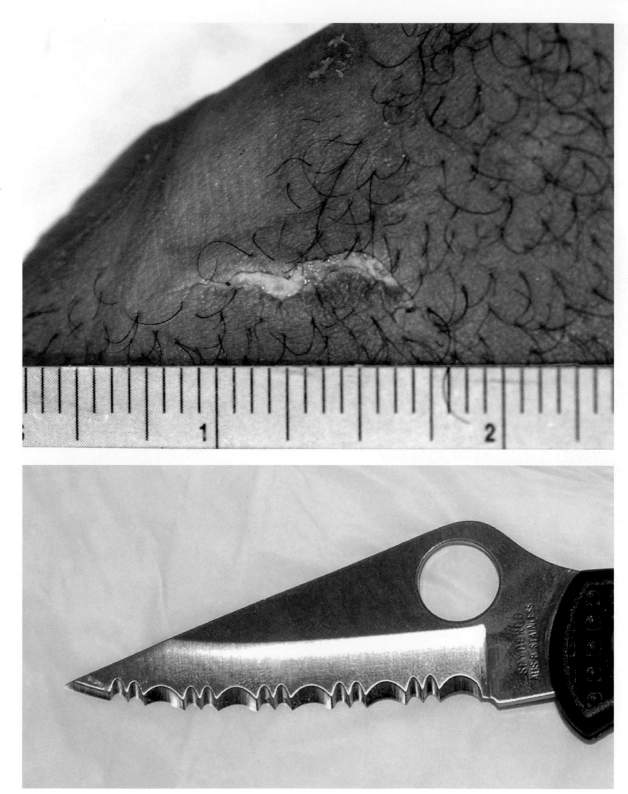

Figures 7.108 and 7.109 Note this irregular incised wound with curved sharp margins produced by a knife similar to the one depicted above.

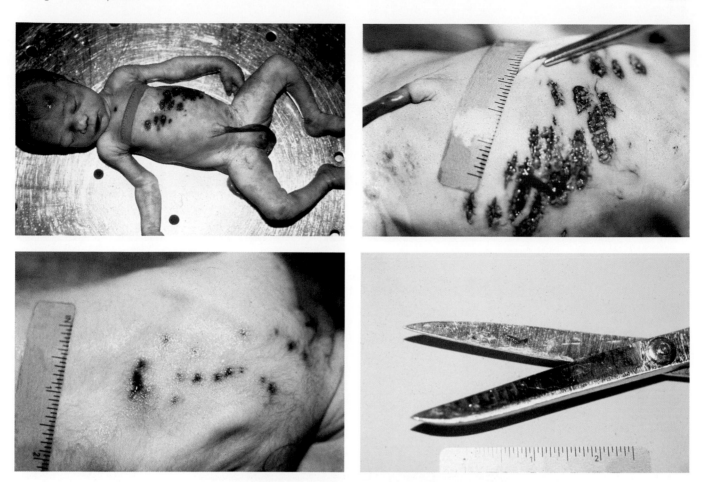

Figures 7.110–7.113 This infant was stabbed multiple times with a pair of scissors. Note the entrance defects to the anterior trunk have a slightly widened angulated character consistent with being inflicted by a pair of scissors. The posterior trunk demonstrates the pointed end of the scissor perforating the entire body and exiting the back.

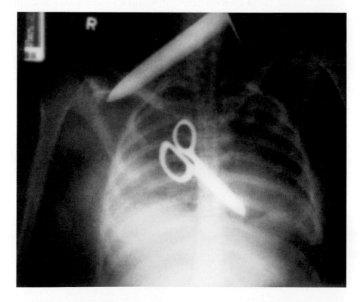

Figure 7.114 This image shows an x-ray of an adult who was stabbed with a pair of scissors, which were left in the wound.

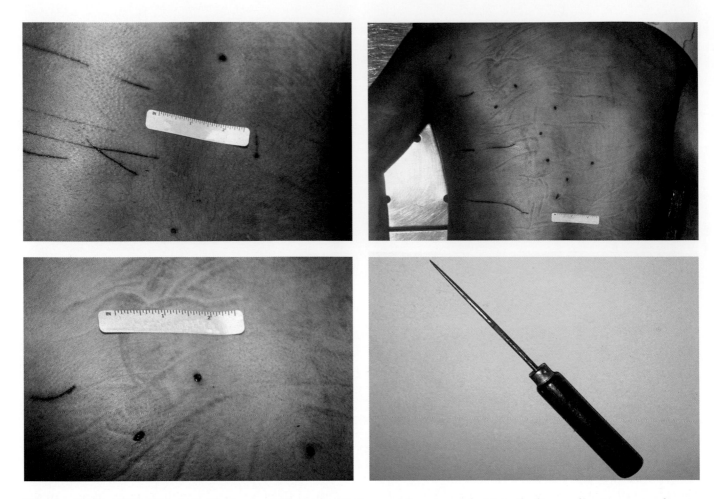

Figures 7.115–7.118 This individual was stabbed over 75 times with an ice pick. Note the linear abrasions extending in different angles across the back as the tip of the ice pick was dragged across the skin's surface. The small dimension of these perforation wounds would take more time to lose enough blood to cause shock compared to a typical knife blade. Generally speaking, the larger the wound, the faster the blood flow. There was evidence of a violent struggle over a long period of time in this case.

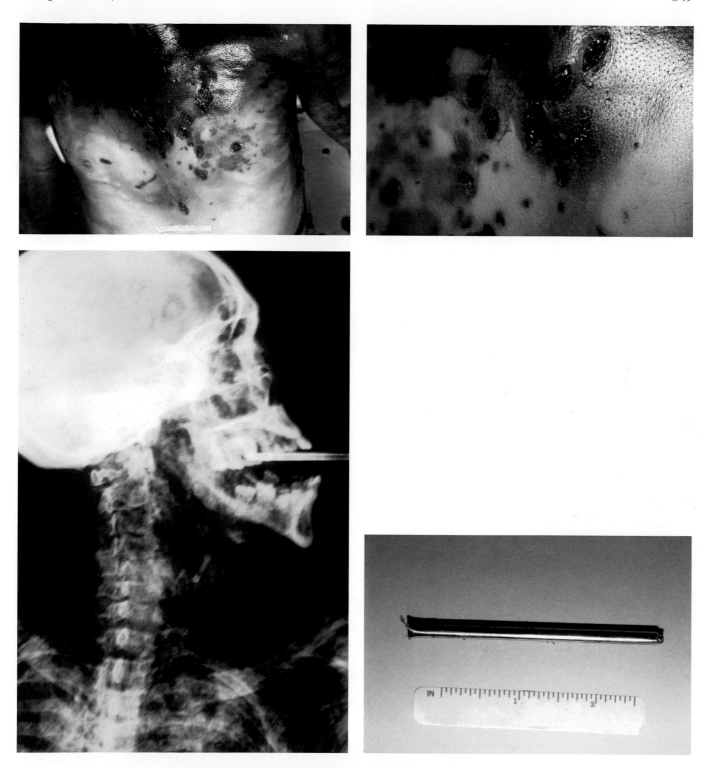

Figures 7.119–7.122 This individual was found within a crack house, in a mild to moderate state of decomposition. He sustained multiple stab wounds and puncture-type wounds to his body. The puncture-type injuries were produced by broken pieces of antenna previously used as crack pipes. One of these antennas was jammed down his throat. He also sustained multiple blunt-impact injuries with rib fractures and other broken bones from being stomped. Note the drying and the slight distortion of the wound margins due to decomposition and the typical x-ray pattern revealing gas between the soft tissue planes.

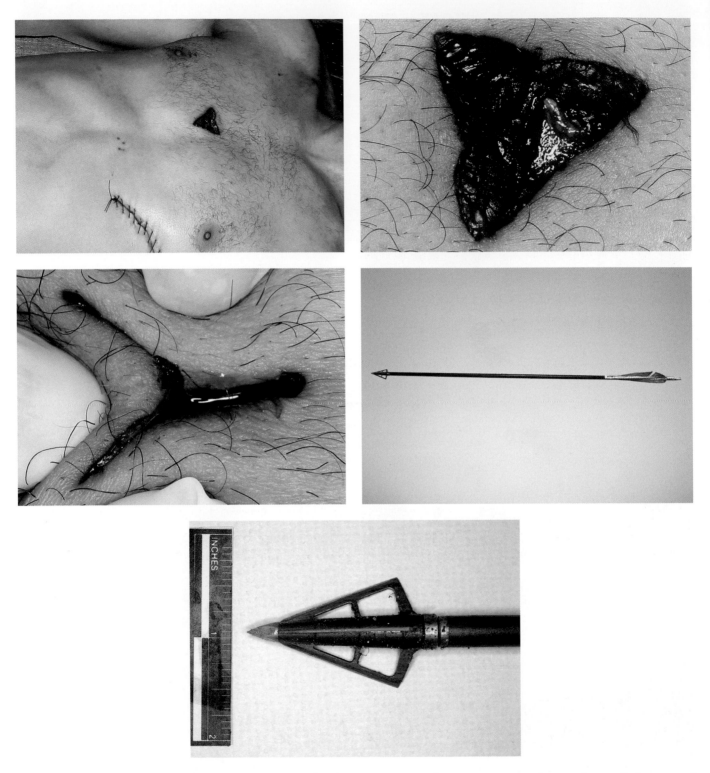

Figures 7.123–7.127 This individual was shot with a hunting arrow. The entrance wound is to the medial aspect of the right chest, and the exit wound was to the right back. Note the comparison of the injury to the arrowhead when the margins are approximated.

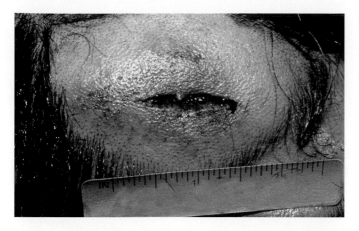

Figure 7.128 This individual was struck with a bottle that produced a minimal abrasion with a greater underlying contusion and a central laceration. Note the slightly irregular margins at the laceration site due to this blunt impact. The surrounding scalp hair was shaved to demonstrate the injury in greater detail. The presence of the scalp hair at the time this injury was inflicted also served to cushion the impact site.

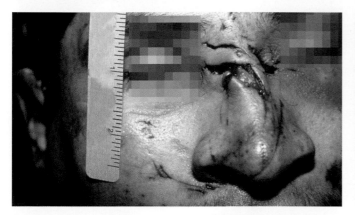

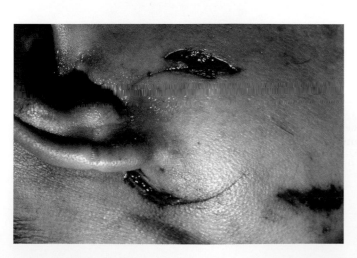

Figures 7.129–7.132 This is the same individual who was then cut multiple times with the sharp broken end of the glass bottle, producing a partial transection to the carotid artery and exsanguination.

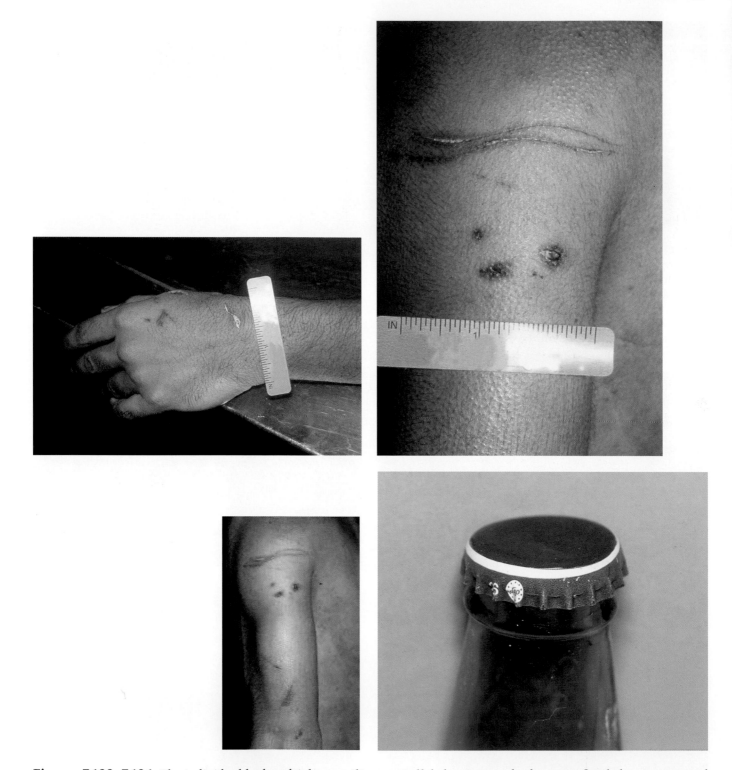

Figures 7.133–7.136 The individual had multiple, curvilinear parallel abrasions and other superficial abrasions caused by a bottle top and broken glass scraping across the body surface during the assault. This initial argument began over which rival baseball team was better.

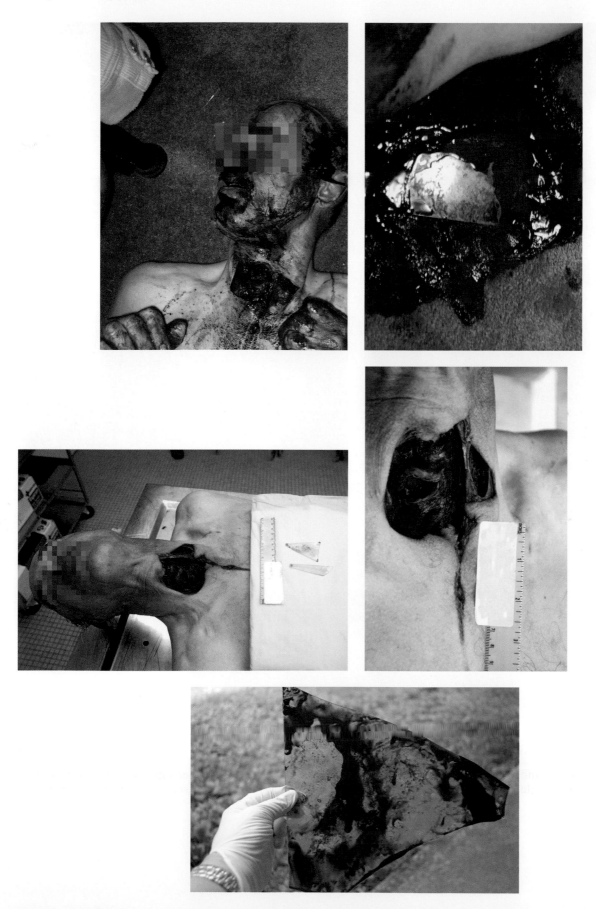

Figures 7.137–7.141 Suicide by multiple sharp-force injuries with broken glass from an empty picture frame. It is unknown what picture was originally in the frame.

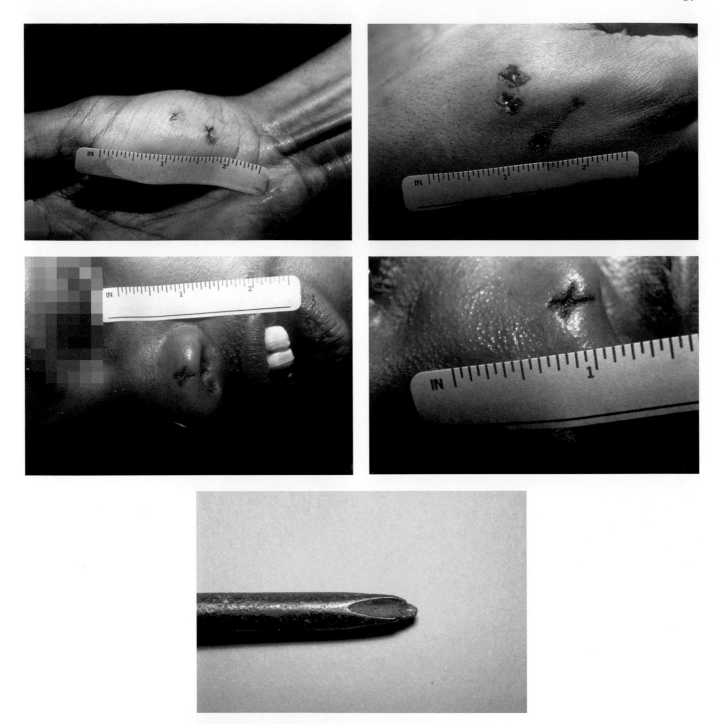

Figures 7.142–7.146 These are multiple examples of puncture wounds caused by a Phillips head screwdriver, demonstrating the range of presentation of this type of injury.

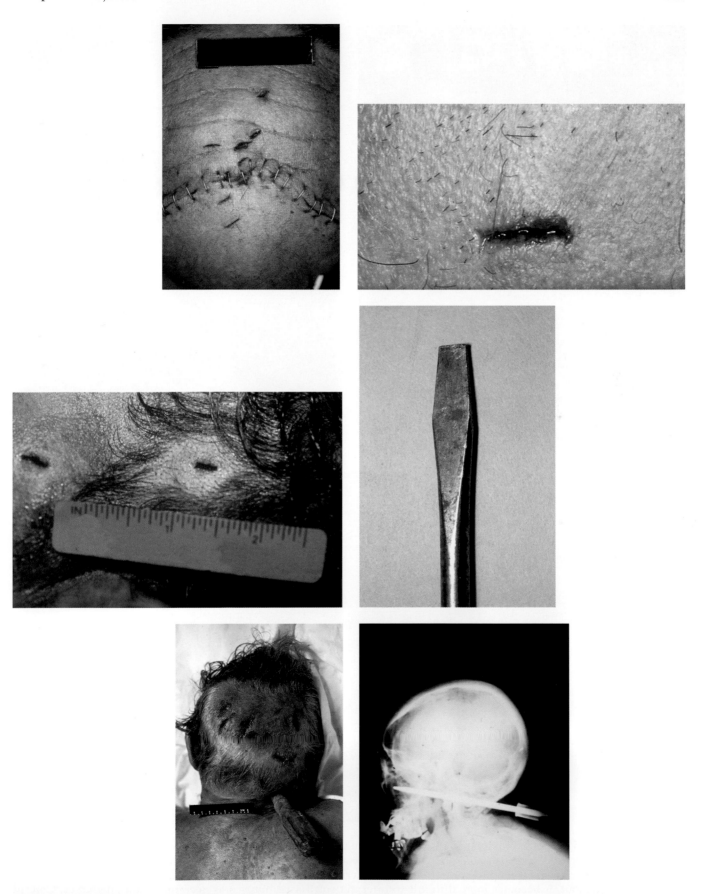

Figures 7.147–7.152 These are multiple examples of flat-head screwdriver puncture wounds. Note the slightly abraded margin caused when the tip of the screwdriver stretched and abraded the skin. In Figures 7.151 and 7.152, there are other abraded lacerations caused by being struck with the handle side of the screwdriver.

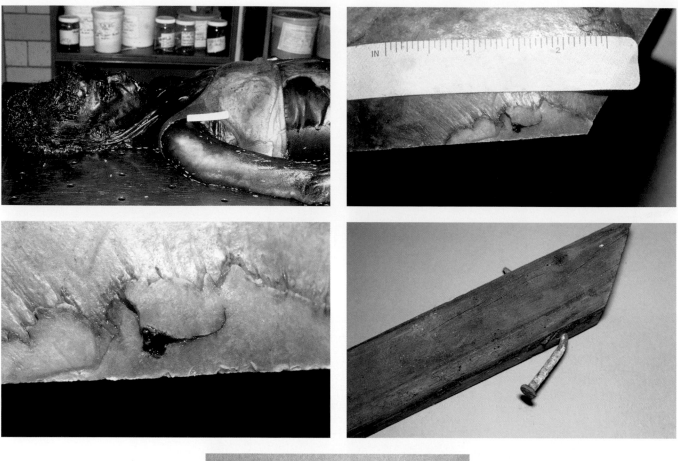

Figures 7.153–7.157 This approximately 30-year-old woman was found naked from the waist down in a construction yard. She had moderate decompositional changes with insect and animal feeding. She had multiple defects to her scalp and face with numerous maggots tracking through the underlying soft tissue. The soft tissues in this region were darkly discolored throughout. It becomes more difficult to interpret soft tissue injuries as decomposition progresses. Careful examination of the underlying bone, in such cases, may often yield valuable information. Note the approximately 1/4" linear skull fracture with a 1/16" roughly square indentation at the superior right temporal bone. Further examination of the scene revealed a bloodstained board with a nail, on the opposite side of the construction site.

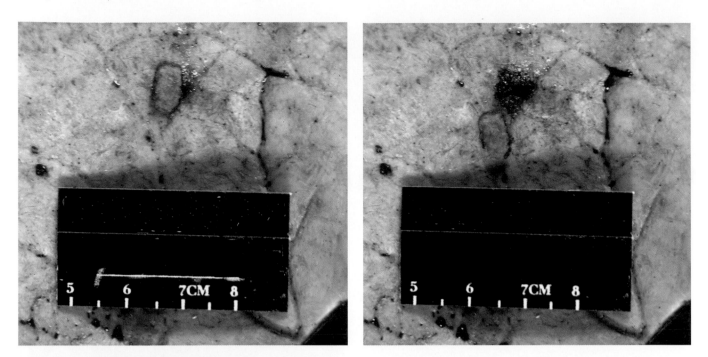

Figures 7.158 and 7.159 The inner aspect of the skull showing internal beveling and flexes of bone into the cranial vault.

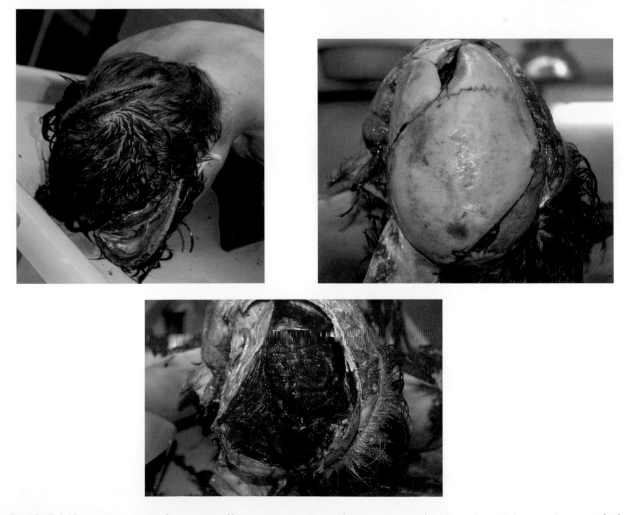

Figures 7.160–7.162 Antemortem boat propeller injuries. Note the presence of subarachnoid hemorrhage and the parallel slicing-type injuries.

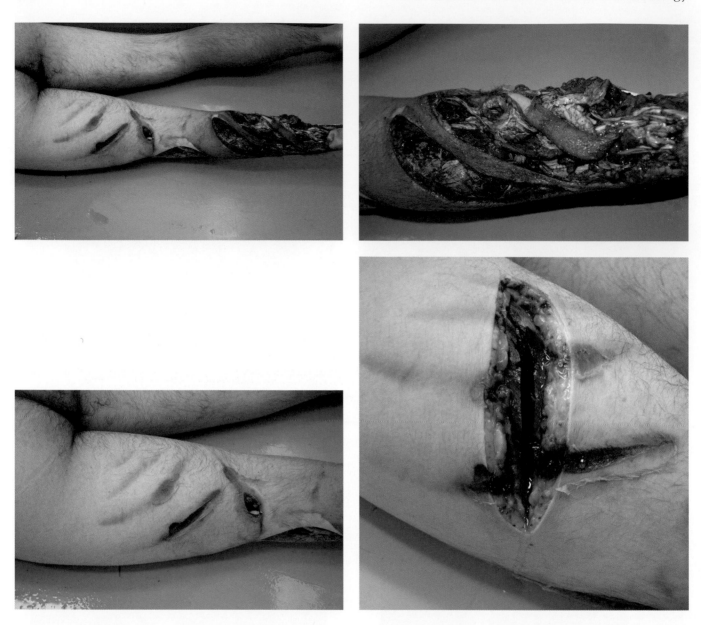

Figures 7.163–7.166 Injuries produced by a boat propeller. Note the hemorrhage at the autopsy incision demonstrating the individual was alive when these injuries occurred. Note the range of injury presentation including superficial abrasion to deep slicing-type wounds with extensive soft tissue damage.

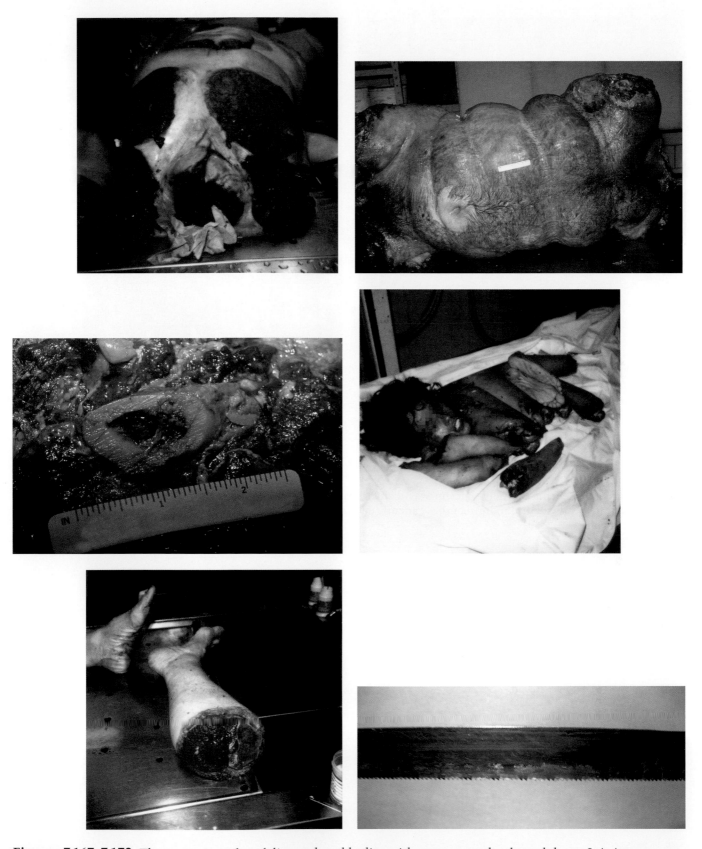

Figures 7.167–7.172 These are examples of dismembered bodies with saw cut marks through bone. It is important to save these portions of bone for possible later tool mark comparison with saw blades used during the dismemberment. Note Figure 7.167, where sexual mutilation was performed with the breasts cut from the body. Also note Figure 7.170 of this young individual who was cut into multiple pieces and scattered about a rooftop. These bodies were dismembered by a similar saw to the one depicted. Dismemberment due to disarticulation of joints usually indicates the perpetrator had a knowledge of anatomy from hunting or medical practice.

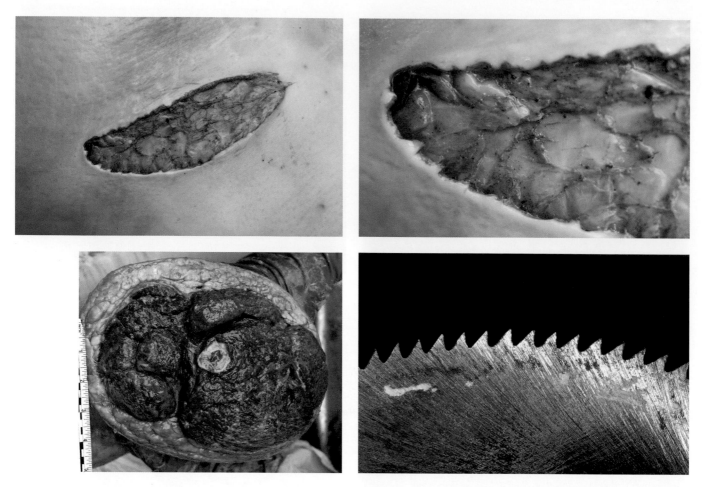

Figures 7.173–7.176 This homicide victim was dismembered after strangulation using a circular saw. Note the saw tooth pattern shown at the skin margin of these anemic defects to the trunk indicating infliction after death. A saw blade similar to this one was used.

Figure 7.177–7.182 This individual committed suicide by self inflicted sharp force injuries. Note the knife and all of the blood are confined to the bathroom, which further substantiates the wounds to be self-inflicted. Given the extensive blood loss if such trauma was inflicted by another individual it would be unusual not to see blood elsewhere in the house, as demonstrated in Figure 7.182.

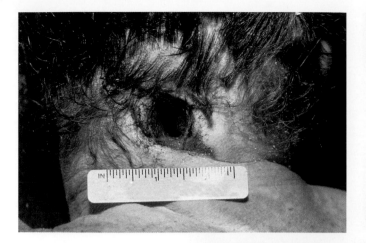

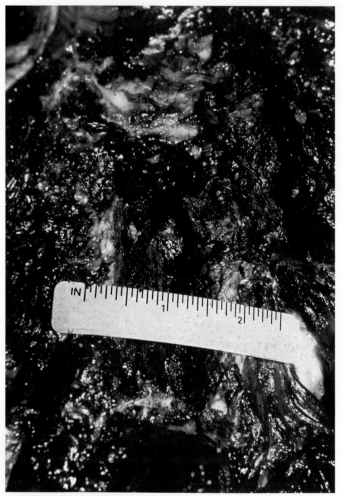

Figures 7.183–7.185 This individual was killed by being struck in the back of the neck with a pickaxe. Note the abraded margin and the perforation matching the roughly squared dimension of the pickaxe. This dispute was reportedly over not receiving back pay after complete work.

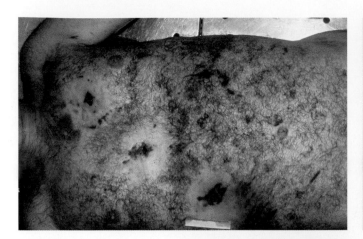
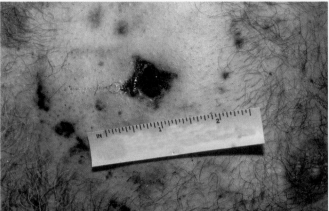

Figures 7.186–7.188 This individual committed suicide by jumping out of a window and landed on top of a spiked metal fence similar to the one shown in Figure 7.188. The hair surrounding these injuries was shaved to demonstrate the nature of the wound in greater detail. Note the pointed circular perforation site leading into a square abrasion, which was perfectly consistent with the fence spike that penetrated his chest.

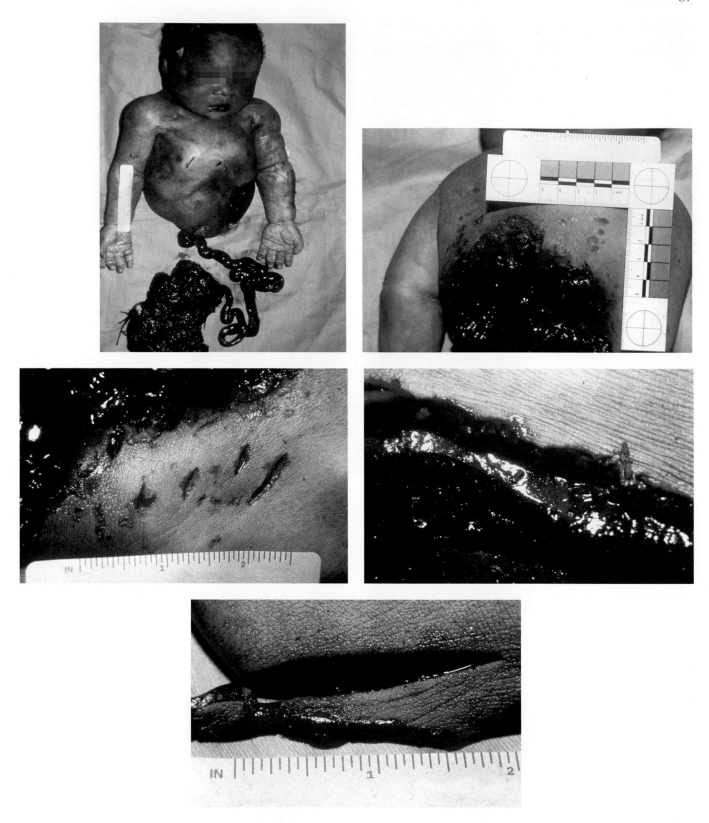

Figures 7.189–7.193 This infant was found partially eaten by dogs in a building courtyard. Note the irregular nature of the wounds to the back (Figures 7.190–7.192) demonstrating scalloped borders produced by teeth and claws. Other injuries to the child's body were inconsistent with animal feeding and more likely produced by a sharp instrument such as a knife. Note the sharp wound margins in Figure 7.193. Dogs may eat decomposing bodies when they are left to starve or they may kill living individuals, more often without eating them. It has been the author's experience that it is rare for a domesticated dog to eat an individual unless it is coaxed into it by exposing the hungry dog to initiate feeding activity. The dog should always be examined, including the gastrointestinal contents. In one such case neatly cut strips of soft tissue were found within the dog's stomach, which were fed to the dog by the perpetrator to initiate more feeding activity.

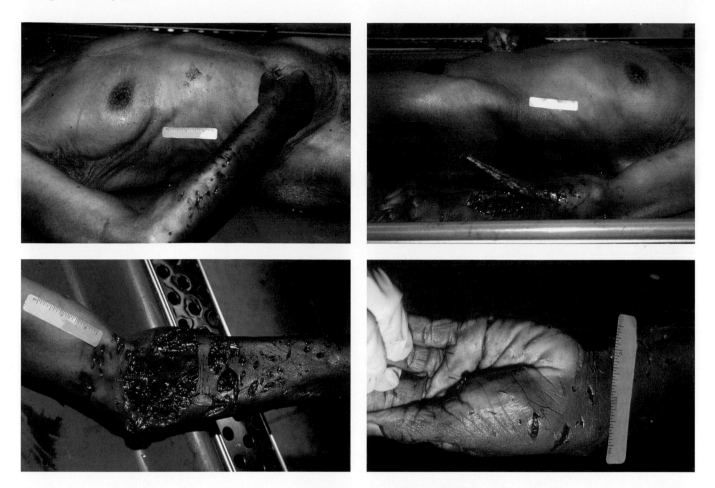

Figures 7.194–7.197 These are multiple puncture marks and lacerations with extensive soft tissue hemorrhage due to an antemortem dog attack by a pit bull. This individual died as a result of blood loss.

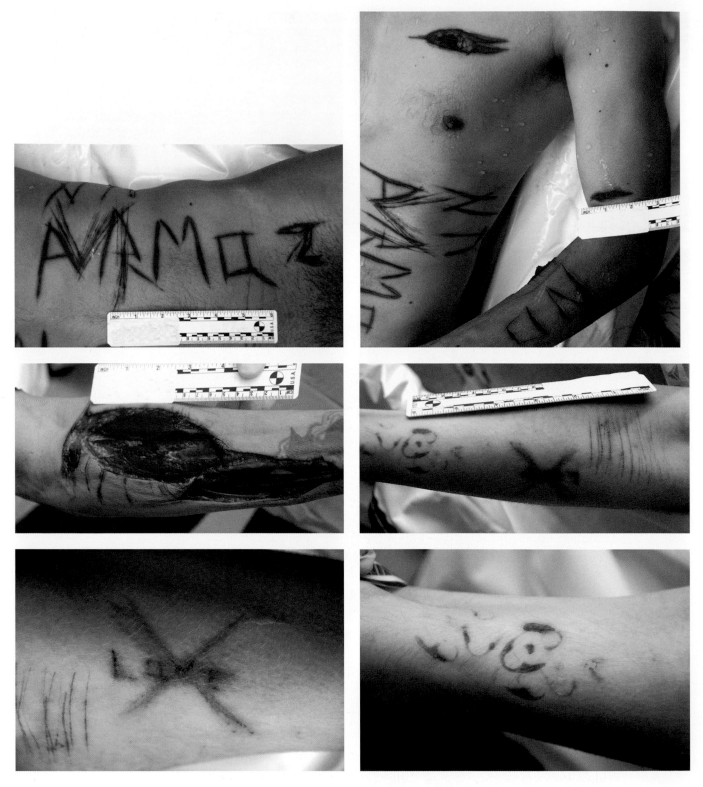

Figures 7.198–7.203 All six images are different examples of individuals who committed suicide after carving messages into their body. Self-mutilation may not always be associated with suicidal intent. This individual died of blood loss due to multiple sharp-force injuries. This individual burned himself multiple times with the top of a lighter.

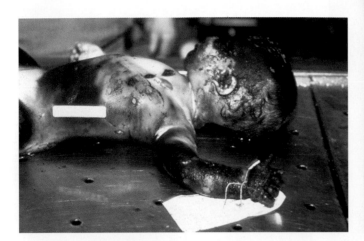
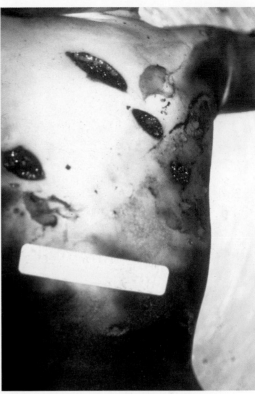

Figures 7.204–7.205 This perpetrator killed his family by inflicting multiple stab wounds and then setting their house on fire. Note the relationship between environmental factors such as heat, and the change in wound characteristics. This is demonstrated to a greater degree in the following figures.

Figures 7.206 and 7.207 This individual was stabbed multiple times and his apartment was set on fire to conceal evidence of the crime. Note the charring of the skin with the sharply margined defect, which was from a stab wound. Internal examination revealed extensive hemorrhage throughout and surrounding the wound track. Sometimes the surface interpretation of such injuries can be challenging. Thermal damage may cause cracking of the skin, which may be misinterpreted as antemortem sharp or blunt force injuries.

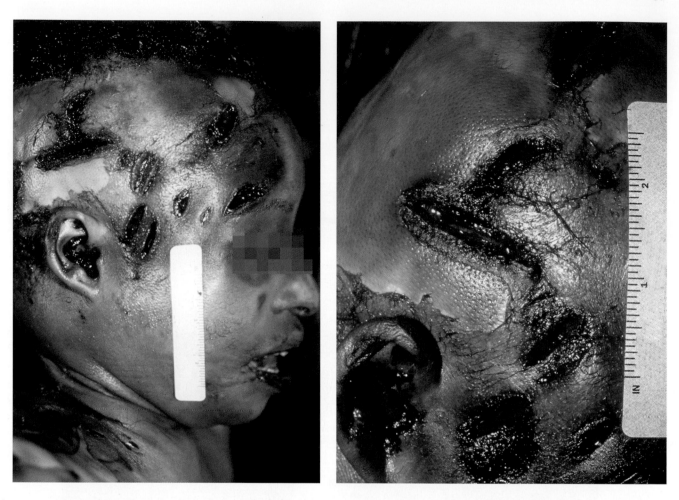

Figures 7.208 and 7.209 This individual sustained multiple blunt- and sharp-force injuries due to homicidal violence. She was found many hours after the assault during a hot summer month. Note the putrefactive changes with skin slippage and green to brown discoloration. Also note the wound margins are dry and dark. Some of these wounds could obviously be classified as lacerations or stab wounds and others could not be classified due to distortion by decomposition.

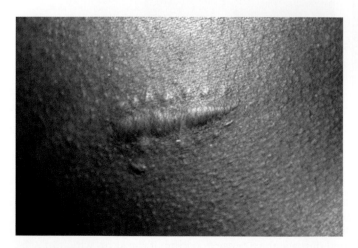

Figure 7.210 Healed stab wound inflicted in an assault.

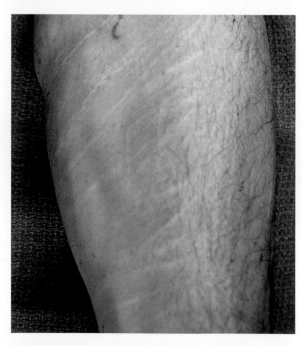

Figure 7.211 Past suicide attempt with multiple healed self-inflicted sharp-force injuries.

Gunshot Wounds

CHARLES A. CATANESE AND THOMAS GILSON

8

Contents

Introduction

The evaluation of gunshot wounds is an area of importance in forensic medicine. Analysis of gunshot wounds should involve:

Differentiation of wounds of entrance from exit
Range of fire estimation for entrance wounds
Determination of trajectory through the body
Recovery of evidence (e.g., ballistics)

Whenever possible, clothing worn by a gunshot wound victim should also be examined.

Entrance and Exit Differentiation

Entrance Gunshot Wounds

Most entrance wounds appear as circular perforations with a collar or margin of abrasion. The margin of abrasion is produced by stretching with eventual tearing of the adjacent skin surface as the bullet enters the body. It is the most reliable feature in identifying entrance gunshot wounds. Exit gunshot wounds lack this feature, as the undersurface of the skin is stretched outward when a bullet exits the body. The margin of abrasion may provide useful preliminary information regarding trajectory of a bullet through the body. When the bullet enters the body perpendicular to the surface, the margin of abrasion is symmetric. As the bullet enters the body on an angle, the margin will be elongated on the side where the bullet first contacts the skin. The trajectory is confirmed by subsequent internal examination. It should be noted, however, that exit wounds may have adjacent abrasions due to shoring, which is discussed later.

Exit Gunshot Wounds

These types of wounds typically appear as slit-like or irregular perforations without margins of abrasion. An exception to this is a shored or supported exit, which occurs when a bullet exits from the body where the skin is firmly supported such as occurs as a bullet exits when an individual is leaning against a wall, lying on the sidewalk, or even wearing tight-fitting clothing. These wounds generally have a more rounded appearance and may have superficial, usually more irregular, abrasion around the defect.

Atypical Gunshot Wounds

These are entrance wounds characterized by a more irregular appearance. They have irregular or obscure margins of abrasion. The skin adjacent to the entrance wound typically shows irregular abrasions or lacerations due to loss of ballistic stability and the deformed bullet striking the body other than the front end first. Sometimes these perforations may appear as irregular tears. Ricochet bullets, or bullets that pass through intermediate targets, often produce atypical entrance wounds. Sometimes the jacket and the slug may separate and produce two separate irregular entrance wounds. Bullets may strike surfaces such as concrete and fragment into pieces, causing multiple irregular defects from impacts of both twisted metal and rock fragments. Fragments from upholstery, chrome, plastic, and so on may be found on the wound surface or even within the wound track. This atypical appearance may also be seen in certain areas of the body where the skin is thicker (palms and soles) or the skin contour is irregular (face). Atypical wounds may be difficult to interpret, particularly in perforating gunshot wounds where the bullet passes through soft tissue only. Fracture characteristics of bone (especially flat bones such as the skull) and lead fragmentation patterns on x-ray may help establish the direction of fire.

Range of Fire Estimation

In estimating the range of fire, an attempt is made to determine the distance from the end of the barrel of the gun to an entrance wound at the time the weapon is discharged. This is most reliably estimated by observing the wound and trying to re-create an observed gunpowder residue pattern by test-firing the weapon. Because the weapon is often not available, estimates based on the physical characteristics of the wound are frequently employed.

An understanding of ammunition aids in understanding range of fire estimation. The ammunition placed into a firearm is a cartridge. A cartridge consists of a bullet, which rests atop and inside a casing containing gunpowder. A primer located at the base of the cartridge ignites the powder. The primer is itself ignited by the mechanical action of the hammer of the firearm, when the hammer strikes the base of the cartridge. The bullet is the portion of the cartridge that exits the barrel. It is propelled by the burning gunpowder and associated expanding gases. In general, there is some residual gunpowder that does not burn. In addition to the bullet, burned and unburned gunpowder exits the barrel when a weapon is discharged. This forms the basis of range of fire estimation.

Range of fire can be divided into three major categories. These include *close range*, *intermediate range*, and *distant range*. As noted, range of fire is best estimated by the use of test firings employing the known weapon with similar ammunition. Lacking these ideal conditions, estimates can be made on the basic wound characteristics as described next. Even when test firings can be performed it is worth remembering that the wounding characteristics of skin are not identical to gunpowder residue deposition on a test-firing cloth.

Close Range of Fire

This is characterized by the presence of *soot* on the adjacent skin surface or within the wound track. Soot is burned gunpowder residue with a dark powdery appearance. It is critical to remember that soot can be wiped from the body's surface, so gunshot wounds need to be examined prior to any washing, whenever possible. The presence of soot indicates the end of the barrel of the gun was held within approximately 6–8 inches from the body's surface. Different guns may have different ranges. The closer the end of the barrel to the body, the denser the soot deposition. As this distance increases, the soot deposition becomes sparser. Soot may be present with stippling (see intermediate range of fire), but this is more accurately still considered close range of fire. When the end of the barrel is very close to the body, there may also be searing of the adjacent skin from burning gunpowder and flame that extends from the end of the barrel. Soot can be filtered away through intermediate targets such as clothing, car doors, walls, and in such cases no soot will be observed on the skin surface while the gun was discharged within a close range. This pattern of soot deposition becomes more dispersed as the distance becomes greater.

Within the close-range-of-fire category are contact gunshot wounds where the end of the barrel touches the body. These may be further subdivided into *tight contact* and *loose contact*. Some classify wounds where the barrel is very close to the body as *near contact*. The term "close contact" is redundant, potentially confusing, and best avoided. It is important to examine the body before cleaning because soot can be wiped away, unlike stippling.

Tight Contact Gunshot Wounds

These are produced when the barrel of the gun is held tightly against the body's surface. Most of the soot will be deposited within the wound track and may not be apparent until internal autopsy examination. Small amounts of soot may be present at the wound margins. Depending on the body region, type of gun, type of ammunition, and force with which the gun is pressed against the body, the wound may appear different. There are often abrasions adjacent to the gunshot wound associated with the muzzle of the gun rubbing against the body's surface as the gun is discharged. These may take the form of a semicircular rim or a complete imprint pattern of the entire muzzle. When the gun is held tightly to the body, particularly over a bony surface such as the skull, sternum, or iliac crest, there may be multiple radiating linear lacerations. These lacerations may be small or large and are more commonly associated with larger-caliber bullets. Approximation of the laceration margins reveals a central circular perforation typical of an entrance wound with abraded margins. Observation of the muscle under a tight contact wound may reveal a pink/red discoloration owing to the introduction of combustion products into the wound track, such as nitrites and especially carbon monoxide binding with myoglobin.

Loose Contact and Near Contact

When a gun is held less tightly against the body, soot may escape more readily to the skin's surface. If the gun is discharged at an angle to the body's surface, the pattern of soot dispersion will extend over a greater surface area in the direction of fire. A partial muzzle imprint may be observed. In near contact wounds, the soot is deposited in a dense, relatively small area around the entrance and searing of the skin may be observed as noted above.

Intermediate Range of Fire

This range of fire is characterized by the presence of *stippling* defects around the entrance wound. These are small (approximately 1/16 inch), red to brown, punctuate abrasions or erosions of the skin's surface. Stippling indicates the end of the barrel of the gun was held up to approximately 18–24 inches away from the body's surface. These defects are produced primarily by fragments of unburned or burning gunpowder that exit the barrel with the bullet. These fragments strike the body with greater force than soot and produce permanent defects. Such defects cannot be wiped away from the body's surface. The appearance of stippling may vary depending on the type of gunpowder used in the cartridge (e.g., ball, disk, or flake).

The term *stippling* applies to the defects in the body's surface. This pattern will become more dispersed as the distance from the weapon to the body's surface increases. Like soot, stippling can be dampened or completely filtered by clothing or other intermediate targets. Powder residue found on intermediate targets at this range of fire is characterized by small, separate, gunpowder fragments.

Soot or stippling defects may be present on an outstretched hand but not surrounding the entrance wound. For this reason, close examination of the upper extremities in gunshot wound cases may be helpful. Range of fire is estimated in the same way and the distance between the weapon and the entrance wound can be approximated by factoring in the distance from the wound to the upper-extremity findings.

Occasional "pseudostippling" may be seen around an entrance wound. This phenomenon is generally seen when a bullet passes through an intermediate target and fragments of the intermediate target strike the skin's surface, causing abrasions around the entrance wound. As noted, such entrance defects tend to be irregular and the adjacent stippling defects exhibit wider size variation than true stippling, where the abrading gunpowder tends to produce skin defects of relatively uniform size.

Distant Range of Fire

This range of fire is characterized by the absence of gunpowder residue around an entrance gunshot wound without an intermediate target between the end of the barrel and the wound. This indicates the end of the barrel of the gun was held more than approximately 18–24 inches away from the body's surface. Some experts prefer to call this *indeterminate range*, especially when the possibility of an intermediate target cannot be excluded.

Trajectory Determination

The path a bullet takes through the body may have substantial medicolegal significance. In some cases, the trajectory can be easily determined by careful dissection. In other cases, with multiple gunshot wounds, full delineation of wound tracks may be harder to accomplish as a result of extensive internal injury with overlapping wound tracks while the decedent was a shot in a different position. Surgical intervention may also obscure wound tracks in part. It is also worth mentioning that a wound sustained while an individual is in a fetal position may look out of alignment with the body lying supine on the autopsy table. Superficial wounds can pose difficulties in trajectory determination as entry and exit wounds may not be easily identified. These include graze and tangential gunshot wounds.

Graze-Type Gunshot Wounds

These are produced when the bullet contacts the skin superficially at a very narrow angle, producing an elongated superficial oval abrasion. One may determine the direction of fire by a semicircular margin of abrasion on the initial side of skin contact and a more irregular margin on the opposite side.

Tangential Gunshot Wounds

These are produced when the bullet strikes the skin superficially at a narrow angle and creates lacerations of the underlying subcutaneous tissue and overlying skin. Direction of fire may be established by the presence of a semicircular margin of abrasion on the entrance side. Also, the laceration of the skin overlying the wound track produces tears with skin tag formation. These tags will extend outward on angles. The tips of these tags, at their most medial aspects (e.g., within the wound track), point toward the side from where the bullet entered the body.

Gunshot Wounds in Bone

Gunshot injuries of bone may be helpful in trajectory determination, especially in the skull and, less frequently, other flat bones. When a bullet passes through the skull, it creates a cone-shaped beveled defect. The entry point has crisp margins and the exit point is larger and represents the wider portion of the cone. Bullets entering the skull produce internal beveling, and those exiting the skull produce external beveling. A tangential bullet strike of the skull may cause the bullet to fragment and result in complex beveling if a portion enters the cranial cavity and a portion shears off and remains outside the surface. In such cases, the bony defect created may exhibit internal and external beveling. Such defects are referred to as "keyhole" defects, as their appearance may resemble a keyhole. As bullets pass through other bones, there is often an outward splintering at the exit side.

High-Velocity Gunshot Wounds

Trajectory delineation in high-velocity gunshot wounds is similar to low-velocity injury; however, the extent of injury is far more significant and exit wounds are often dramatically large. Hunting ammunition used at high velocity will fragment more in the body than low-velocity bullets, creating a characteristic x-ray picture called a "lead snowstorm."

Evidence Recovery

Bullets retained in the body must be recovered at autopsy. Rifled firearms leave characteristic markings on bullets that can be used for identification of a firearm by comparison with projectiles known to have been fired from that weapon. Care must be taken during dissection to avoid or minimize the creation of any additional marks on the bullet that might obscure the rifling marks. This also applies to identifying marks inscribed on the bullet after recovery. These identifying marks should be inscribed on the base of the bullet and not on the sides. Older bullets should be recovered at the time of autopsy. These may be enclosed in fibrous capsules at the site of lodgment and often have a dull gray appearance as a result of oxidation. Rifling marks may still be present and useful for ballistic comparison.

Shotgun Wounds

Because of differences in construction and ammunition, shotguns merit special consideration. Shotguns can be used to fire a single projectile (slug) or several pellets (shot). Shot size can vary (buckshot versus birdshot). Slugs behave essentially as single projectiles. The shotgun cartridge (or shell) contains some additional components (e.g., wadding, filler material) that might produce injuries that can be used in range of fire estimation. Soot and stippling remain useful in close- and intermediate-range determinations. The wounds produced by shotgun shells containing shot look different from conventional bullet wounds. Soot, stippling, wadding, and other components can be used for range of fire estimation, but the behavior of the pellet cluster over distance provides additional information regarding range of fire. When the shot exits the barrel, it travels initially as a tightly grouped cluster. Striking the skin, the tight cluster produces a round defect. The grouping opens up over distance with the first noticeable change in wound appearance occurring at about 3 feet. A single defect is still observed but the margins now take on a scalloped appearance. With further distance and more pellet dispersal, wounds now consist of a central defect with scattered satellite defects surrounding them. These satellite defects increase in number with greater distance, until the central defect is lost entirely. The dispersal pattern of pellets is not predictable once an intermediate surface intervenes. It is not possible to evaluate these wounds for range estimations, and for similar reasons, estimates of range of fire by x-ray examination are unreliable. As with other firearms, test firings are the most reliable means for range of fire approximations.

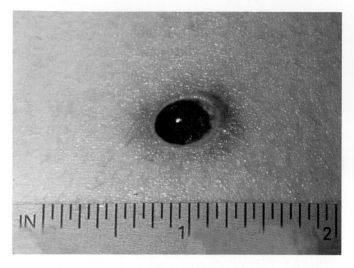

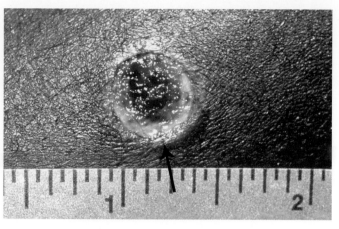

Figure 8.1 Distant entrance gunshot wound. This bullet struck the body nose end first roughly perpendicular to the surface. Note the thin and roughly symmetric margin of abrasion surrounding the slightly oval perforation.

Figure 8.2 Distant entrance gunshot wound in a darker-skinned individual. Note the slightly asymmetric margin of abrasion, which is greatest at its inferior aspect. This indicates the bullet struck the body nose first, and at a slight upward and left-to-right trajectory relative to the body.

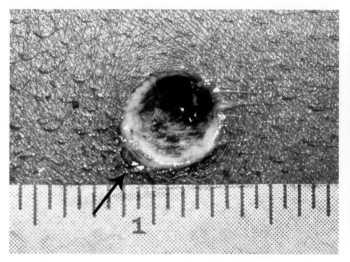

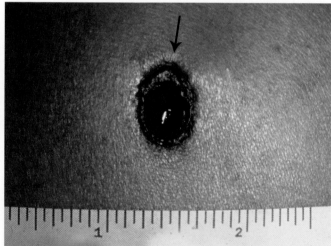

Figure 8.3 Distant entrance gunshot wound with slightly asymmetric margin of abrasion, which is greatest at its right inferior aspect. This usually indicates the bullet struck the body nose first, almost perpendicular and at a slightly upward and right-to-left trajectory relative to the body.

Figure 8.4 Distant entrance gunshot wound with slightly asymmetric margin of abrasion greatest on its superior and left aspect. This usually indicates that the bullet struck the body nose first, almost perpendicular and at a slightly downward, left-to-right trajectory relative to the body.

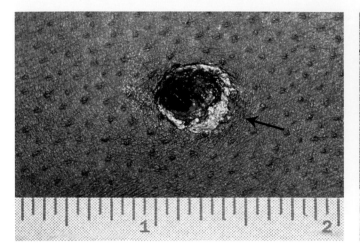

Figure 8.5 Distant entrance gunshot wound with slightly irregular, widened, margin of abrasion, which is greatest at the left lateral aspect relative to the body. This indicates the bullet struck the body from a slightly inferior and left-to-right trajectory. The slightly irregular nature of the margin of abrasion may sometimes be seen as the bullet perforates clothing first.

Figure 8.6 Distant entrance gunshot wound that is slightly stretched into an oval shape due to skin tension. Note the slightly asymmetric margin of abrasion, which is greatest at the 9 o'clock through 12 o'clock position, indicating the bullet struck the body with a slightly downward and right-to-left trajectory relative to the body.

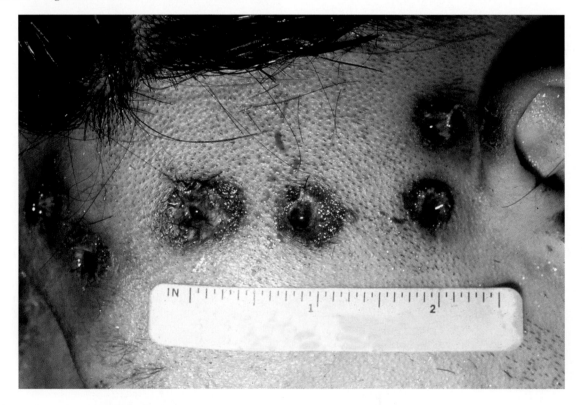

Figure 8.7 There are six separate clustered entrance gunshot wounds to this individual's head. Note the abrasion to the posterior ear helix caused by a bullet. Shaving the hair is recommended for external examination of such gunshot wounds.

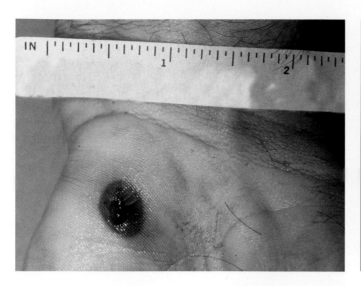

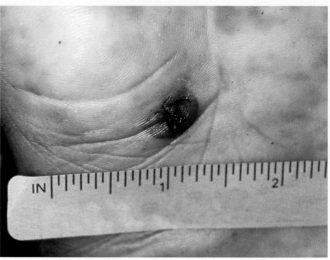

Figure 8.8 Distant entrance gunshot wound to the palm of the hand through thick skin.

Figure 8.9 Indeterminate entrance gunshot wound through the thick skin of the sole of the foot. This bullet first perforated the bottom of a shoe and a sock before entering the body.

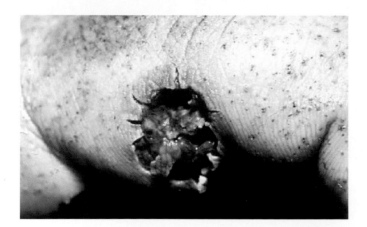

Figure 8.10 Entrance gunshot wound with surrounding stippling defects indicating intermediate range of fire. This gunshot wound to the thick skin of the palm of the hand reveals typical small radiating lacerations without prominent margin of abrasion. These characteristics are typical for gunshot wounds of the palms of the hand and soles of the feet.

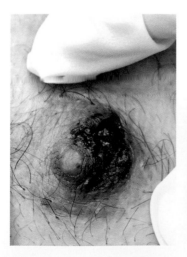

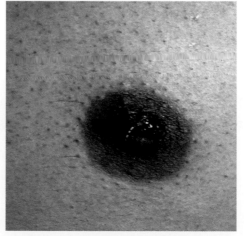

Figures 8.11 and 8.12 Gunshot wounds to the areolae that may appear more atypical and smaller due to looser underlying connective tissue and more delicate skin.

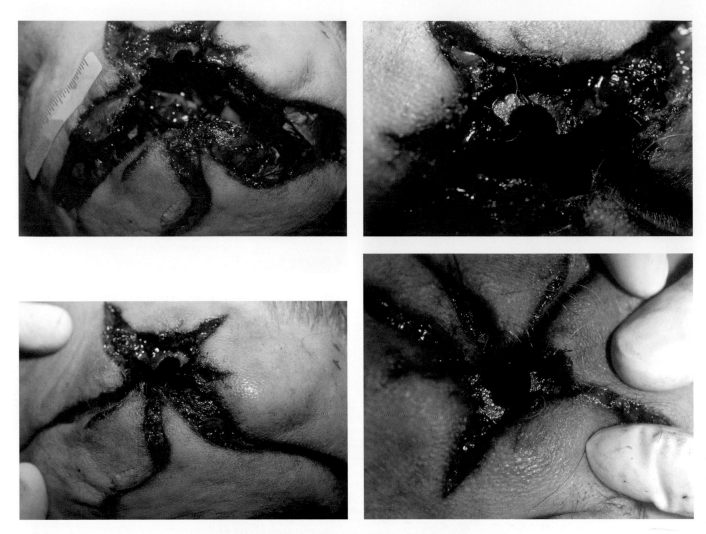

Figures 8.13–8.16 These images represent the same contact gunshot wound with varying degrees of tension to the wound's surface in order to approximate the margins. Note that with approximation of the margins (lower images) the wound forms a roughly circular perforation with margin of abrasion typical of an entrance gunshot wound. Also note the copious amounts of soot within the wound track and on the underlying bone surface. Such large radiating linear lacerations are usually associated with higher-caliber guns, and tight contact of the gun muzzle on the body surface with underlying bone close to the skin. The expanding gases from burning gunpowder forced into the wound track cause such lacerations. Larger lacerations are typically in older individuals, where skin is less elastic.

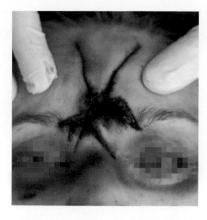

Figure 8.17 Contact gunshot wound with margins approximated.

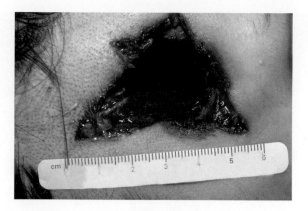

Figure 8.18 Contact gunshot wound to the scalp with radiating lacerations and soot deposition within the wound track and at the wound margins. These lacerations are caused by burning gunpowder with expanding gases forced into the wound track and causing the overlying skin to lacerate.

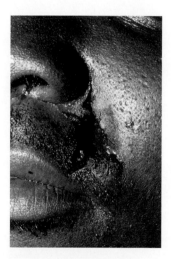

Figure 8.19 Contact gunshot wound to the face. Note the stellate lacerations radiating from the perforation site with soot deposition.

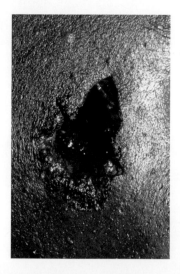

Figure 8.20 A close view of the GSW (gunshot wound) shown in Figure 8.19 with a different orientation.

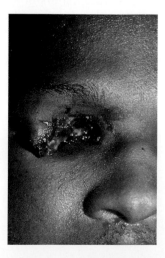

Figure 8.21 Contact gunshot wound to the eye. Note the lacerations of the eyelid and eye globe with soot deposition at the adjacent skin and within the wound track.

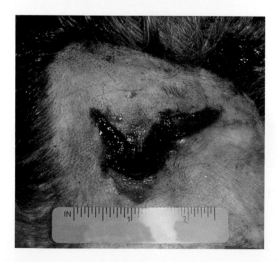

Figure 8.22 Contact gunshot wound to the right temporal region. Note the larger lacerations extending from the perforation site with adjacent soot deposition.

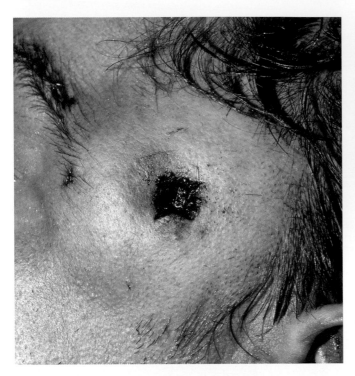

Figure 8.23 Contact gunshot wound to the temple. Note the small radiating lacerations from the perforation site. Note the presence of soot within the wound track and adjacent skin.

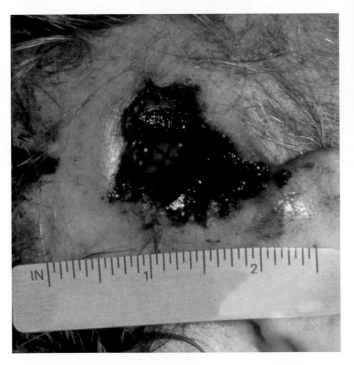

Figure 8.26 Contact gunshot wound to the scalp. Note the small radiating lacerations with soot deposition.

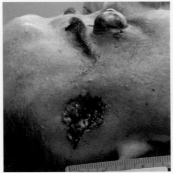
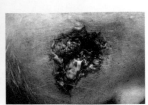

Figures 8.24 and 8.25 Note this tight contact gunshot wound to the right temporal region with lacerated borders and soot deposition. This .357 Magnum caused a comminuted skull fracture with head deformity and the eye protruding from the socket.

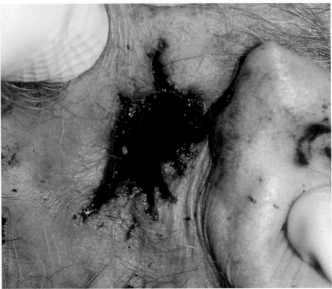

Figure 8.27 This is the same gunshot wound as shown in the previous image. Note the same wound from Figure 8.26 after cleaning, with small amounts of soot still present. The tension surrounding the wound is relieved by pressing the surrounding skin inward toward the perforation. This will approximate the wound margins and reveal a roughly circular perforation with margin of abrasion characteristic for an entrance GSW. Note that even after cleaning, small amounts of soot is still present at the wound margins. Further cleaning might eliminate this gunpowder residue as well. In many cases, such as this one, it was essential to first photograph the body before cleaning.

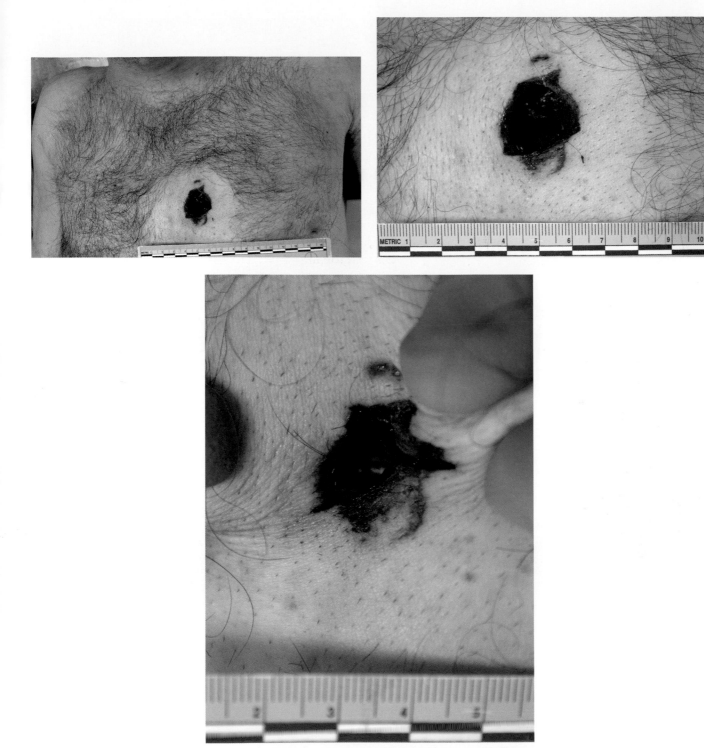

Figures 8.28–8.30 This tight contact gunshot wound to the middle of the chest directly overlying the sternum produced an injury similar in nature to a gunshot wound to the scalp because of bone directly underlying the skin. Note the muzzle imprint, soot deposition at the margins, and lacerations. Figure 8.30 shows the approximation of the margins, demonstrating a roughly circular perforation.

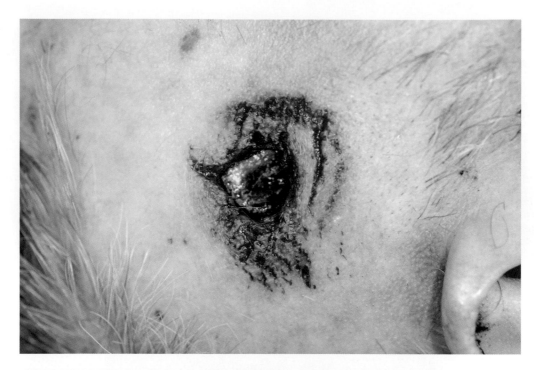

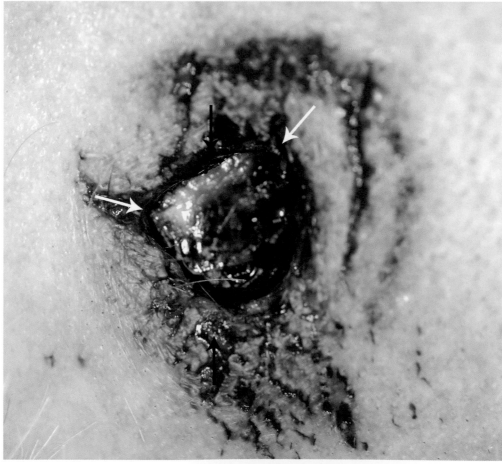

Figures 8.31 and 8.32 Contact gunshot wound with stretch marks surrounding the perforation site consisting of superficial red tears at the skin surface. There is a minimal amount of soot at the adjacent skin, margin, and deep within the wound track. The black arrows demonstrate small areas of soot deposition on the surface. Note at the lower aspect of this perforation there is more of a circular pattern consistent with an entrance wound and at the superior aspect there are tears on each side (white arrows) causing wider separation and giving a slightly squared-off appearance. If the wound margins were approximated at the top, the wound would take on more of a circular appearance.

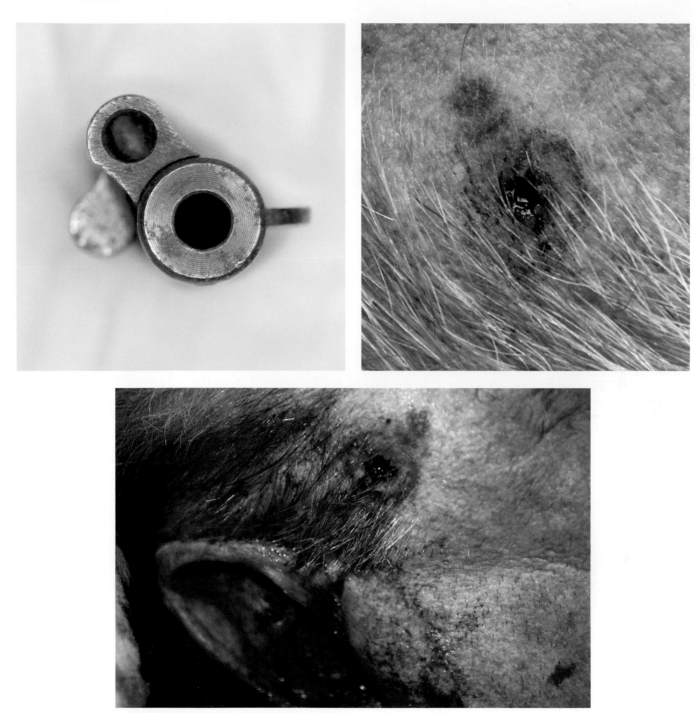

Figures 8.33–8.35 Contact wound with muzzle imprint. It is very important to be very careful, when cleaning the wound for photographs, not to remove gunpowder residue soot.

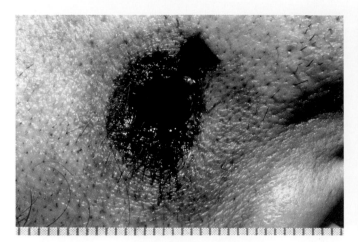

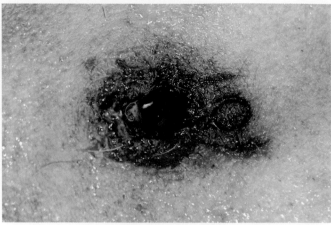

Figure 8.36 Contact entrance gunshot wound to the temple. Note the abraded imprint of the eyepiece portion of the gun at the superior aspect. The perforation site has a margin of abrasion. There is no obvious soot on the surface of the adjacent skin, but there are copious amounts of soot within the wound track. Note the pink to red discoloration, surrounding the perforation, due to nitrates and carbon monoxide released from burning gunpowder. These components may sometimes cause this discoloration when reacting with the underlying muscle. In this case it is more obvious due to the decedent's light skin color.

Figure 8.37 Contact gunshot wound with muzzle imprint.

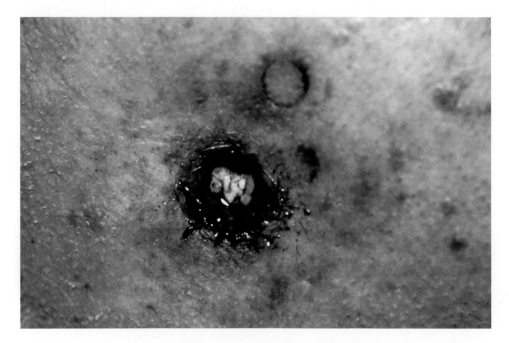

Figure 8.38 Contact gunshot wound. Note the adjacent abrasion to the perforation site due to contact with a revolver ejector rod when the gun was discharged. There are also small amounts of soot visible at the wound margins and more within the wound track.

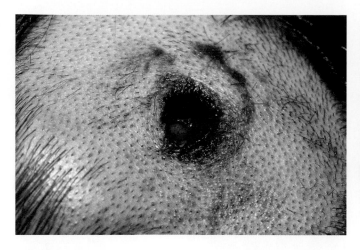

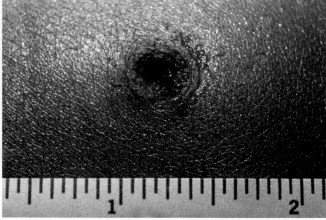

Figure 8.39 Contact gunshot wound to the scalp with an abrasion at the superior left aspect due to the gun muzzle. There is visible soot within the wound track. Sometimes it may be difficult to visualize the presence of gunpowder residue on thick dark scalp hair.

Figure 8.40 Contact gunshot wound. Note the soot at the margin of the perforation site. Note the surrounding abrasion from a partial muzzle imprint.

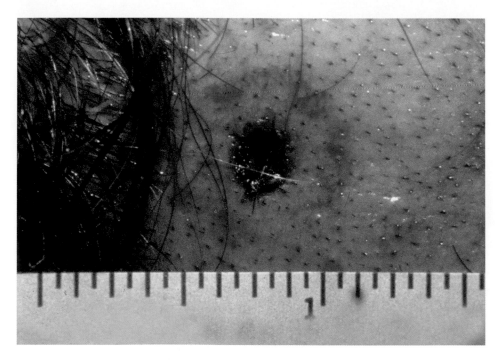

Figure 8.41 Contact gunshot wound to the right temporal scalp. Note the soot deposition surrounding the margin and the red discoloration of the adjacent skin.

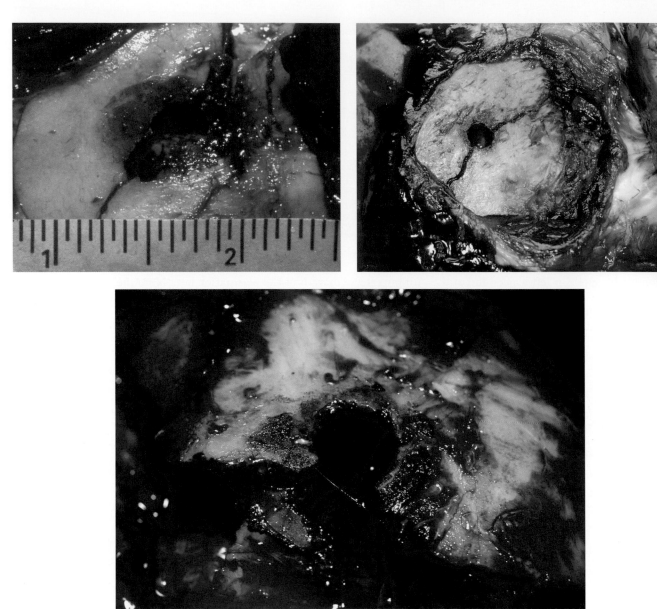

Figures 8.42–8.44 Underlying soot deposition within the wound track and on the outer surface of the skull. This is typically seen with a tight contact gunshot wound where soot is forced into the wound track. In such cases there may be minimal soot at the skin surface.

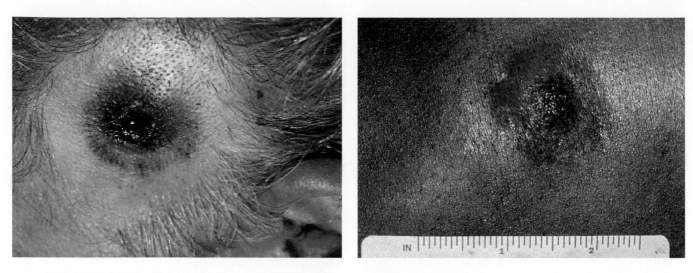

Figures 8.45 and 8.46 Close-range gunshot wounds with soot deposition.

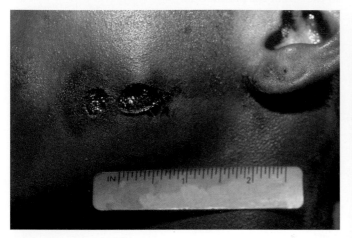

Figure 8.47 Note the entrance wound is to the left where soot is visible at the adjacent skin.

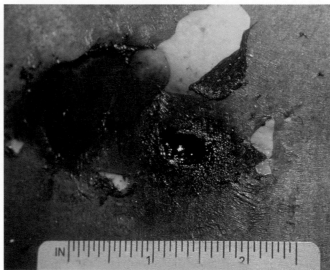

Figure 8.48 Close-range gunshot wound to a body with early decompositional changes. Note the soot deposition surrounding the perforation site. These early putrefactive changes consist of skin slippage and discoloration.

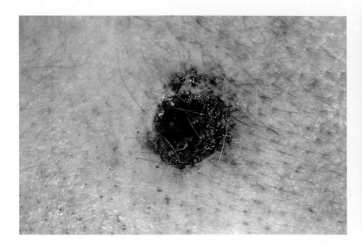

Figure 8.49 Loose contact with more soot extending to the right side of the perforation.

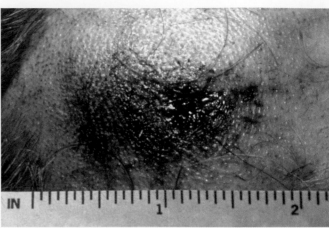

Figure 8.50 Loose contact with the muzzle more tightly applied at the right aspect. Note the greater soot deposition to the left of the perforation.

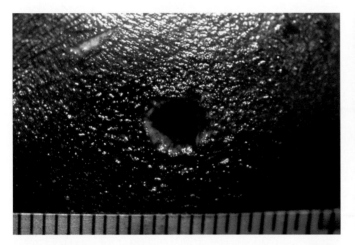

Figure 8.51 Close range gunshot wound in a very dark-skinned individual. Note the gunpowder residue surrounding the entrance gunshot wound.

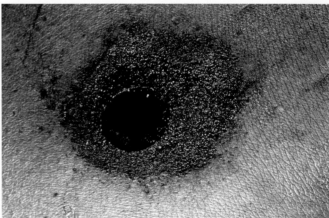

Figure 8.52 Close-range gunshot wound with a muzzle flare burn and soot encircling the perforation site.

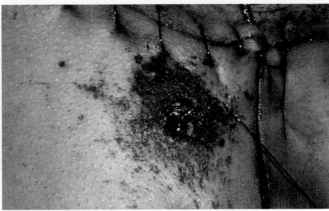

Figure 8.53 Close-range gunshot wound with sparse soot deposition surrounding the perforation site with adjacent superficial skin erosions due to muzzle flare.

Figure 8.54 Close-range gunshot wound with soot deposition, superficial skin erosions from muzzle flare, and tightly compact stippling-type defects.

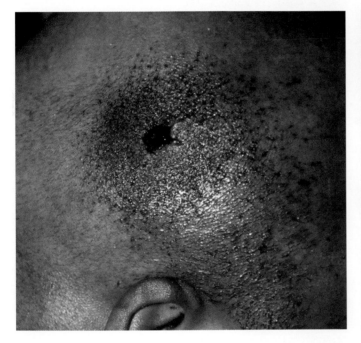

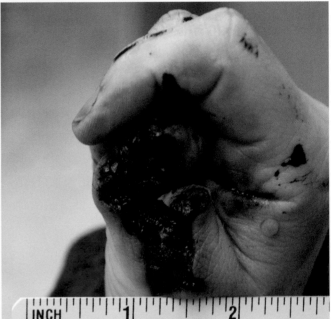

Figure 8.55 Close-range gunshot wound to the scalp with sparse soot deposition, adjacent burning of the scalp due to muzzle flare, and closely packed stippling defects.

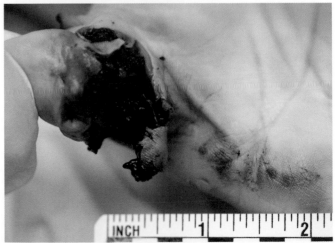

Figures 8.56 and 8.57 Tangential contact gunshot wound to hand with soot deposition. The gun was discharged during a fight with struggle to gain control of the gun.

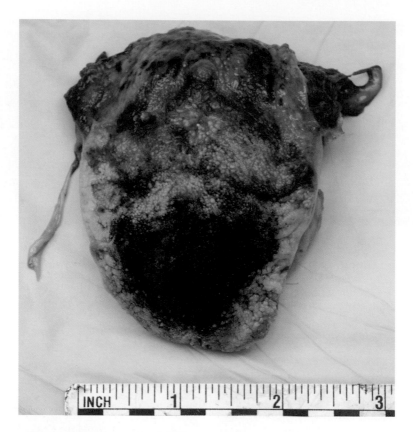

Figure 8.58 Note the soot deposition from a suicidal interoral gunshot wound on this autopsy-removed tongue.

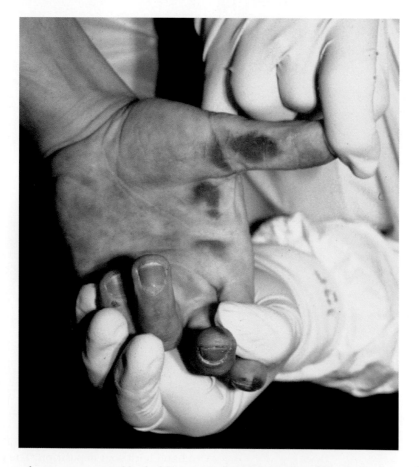

Figure 8.59 This pattern of soot was caused by holding a revolving cylinder while discharging the weapon.

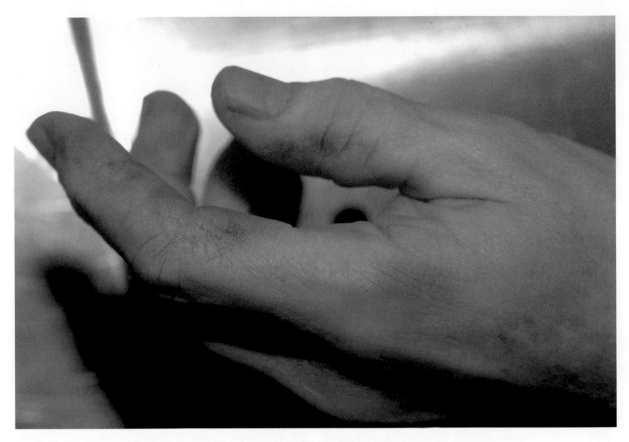

Figure 8.60 Gunpowder residue at the fingers due to firing a handgun. This individual died from a self-inflicted gunshot wound to the head. The amount of gunpowder residue following discharge of a firearm may be quite variable and sometimes not very obvious.

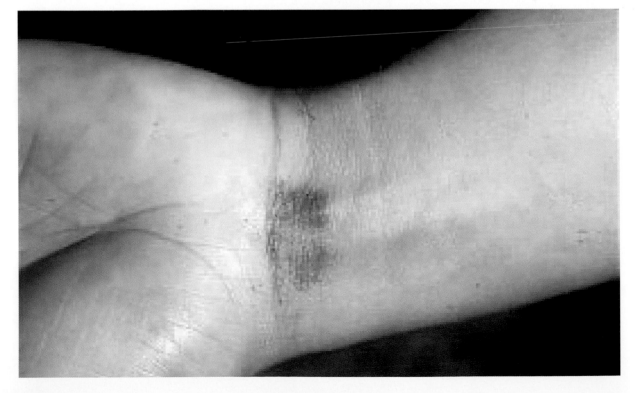

Figure 8.61 Soot may also be deposited as it exits from the muzzle of the gun or from cylinder gap in revolver-type handguns.

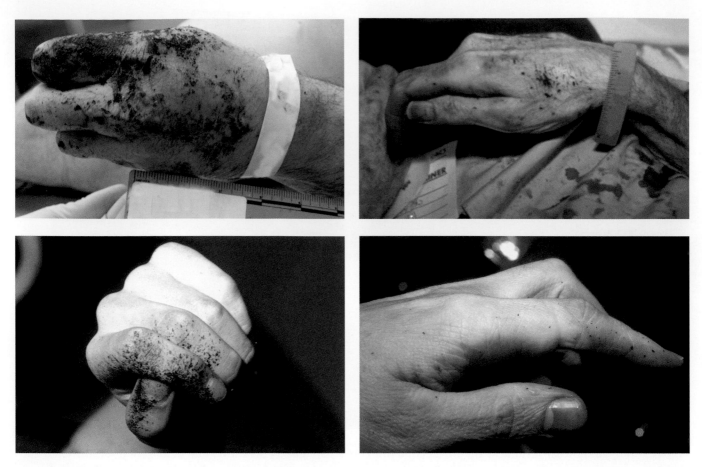

Figures 8.62–8.65 Note the "blowback" blood spatter pattern on the hands of these individuals who died from self-inflicted gunshot wounds to the head. Note that in Figure 8.62 the spatter pattern is partially obscured by subsequent contact deposit of blood. Also note in Figure 8.65 the extent of spatter may be minimal.

Figures 8.66–8.68 All of these articles of clothing demonstrate close-range gunshot perforations with soot deposition. It is always important to inspect the decedent's clothing. Multiple layers of heavy clothing may filter gunpowder residue from the body surface. It is also important to distinguish bullet wipe from soot deposition. Bullet wipe is a small encircling gray discoloration around the perforation site of the clothing due to lubricants and residue from within the barrel of the gun that adhere to the bullet surface as it passes through the barrel. Unlike soot, bullet wipe is not useful in range of fire estimations.

Figure 8.69 Clothing with soot indicating close range of fire. The individual wearing the hat had long curly black hair and there was no appreciable soot noted at the scalp.

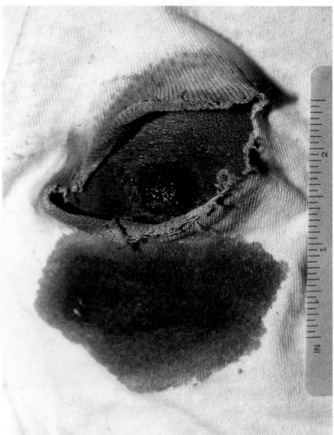

Figures 8.70 and 8.71 Note the large tear in the clothing from this contact wound and the minimal amount of adjacent external hemorrhage. This is an antemortem injury with over a liter of blood observed in the thoracic cavity during autopsy.

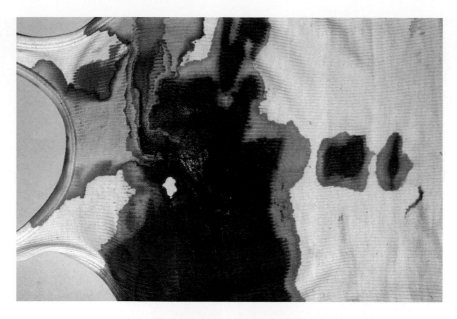

Figure 8.72 This entrance gunshot defect is surrounded by dark clotted blood. The dark discoloration of blood, particularly on dark clothing, may make it difficult to observe soot. This is a distant gunshot wound.

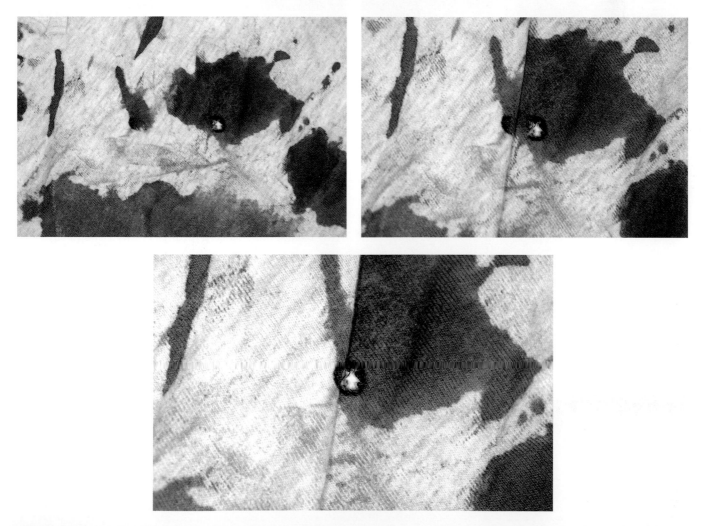

Figures 8.73–8.75 Bullet wipe. This individual had his shirt tucked in with folded cloth. Note the dark discoloration around the perforation site with the right aspect separated several inches from the site of bullet entry. By refolding the shirt and approximating the margins we can simulate how the individual actually wore his shirt.

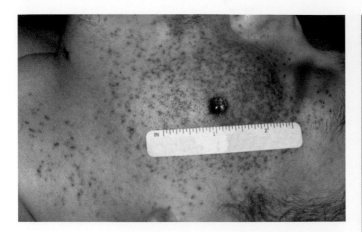

Figure 8.76 Intermediate range of fire. Tightly packed stippling defects surrounding this entrance gunshot wound to the cheek. There is no apparent soot deposition.

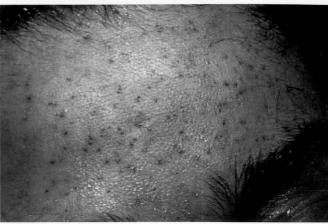

Figure 8.77 Multiple stippling defects to this individual's forehead indicating intermediate range of fire.

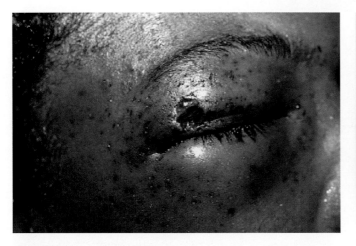

Figure 8.78 Intermediate range of fire with stippling defects. Stippling defects represent abrasions that, unlike soot, cannot be wiped away.

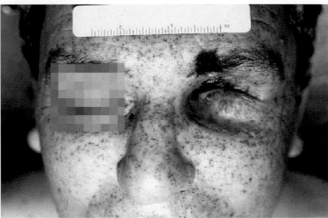

Figure 8.79 Intermediate-range entrance gunshot wound to the eyebrow with stippling defects across the face. Note the irregular nature of the wound due to the location of the gunshot wound through the eyebrow ridge with the underlying frontal bone closely subadjacent to the skin surface.

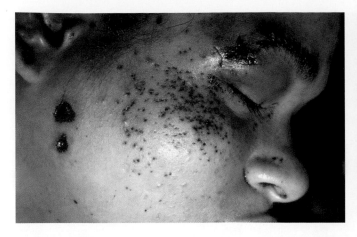

Figure 8.80 Intermediate range of fire.

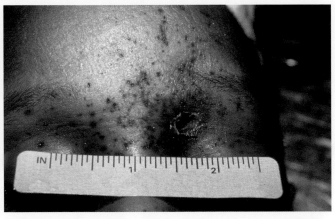

Figure 8.82 Entrance gunshot wound with stippling defects indicating intermediate range of fire.

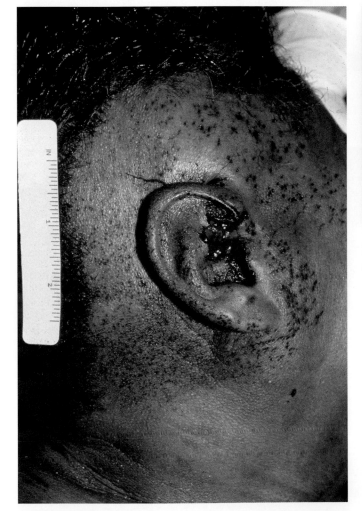

Figure 8.81 Intermediate-range entrance gunshot wound with stippling defects. The scalp is partially shaved. Note the decreased number of defects in the shaved area as a result of hair dampening the effect. This weapon was a sawed-off 30/30 hunting rifle that was reportedly discharged approximately 15″ away from the decedent's head. In this case the exit wound was much larger than the entrance.

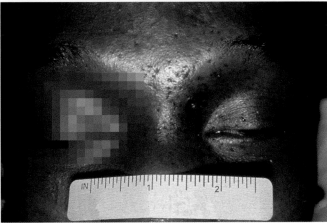

Figure 8.83 Intermediate-range gunshot wound with stippling in a dark-skinned individual.

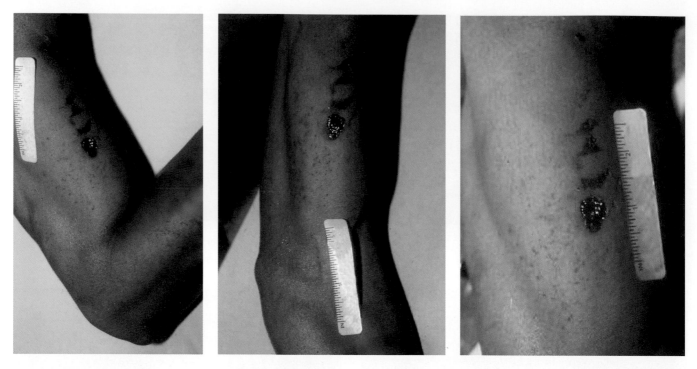

Figures 8.84–8.86 Intermediate-range gunshot wound. Note the sparse stippling defects along the bicep and forearm with sparing of the antecubital fossa region. This indicates the decedent had his arm bent when he was shot.

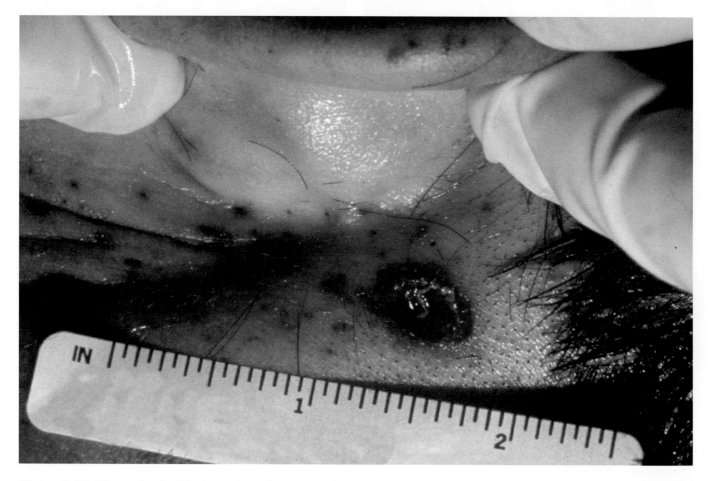

Figure 8.87 This individual had stippling defects involving the posterior portion of his lateral outer ear and temporal scalp. Note the sparing of the posterior medial ear.

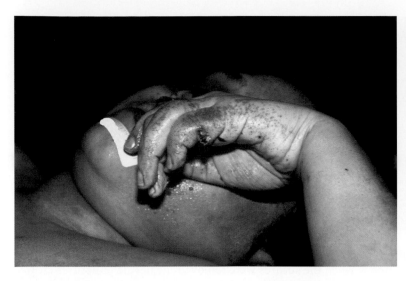
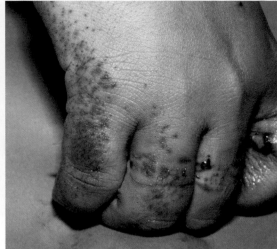

Figures 8.88 and 8.89 Stippling defects with soot deposition on the side of an outstretched hand, indicating intermediate to close range of fire.

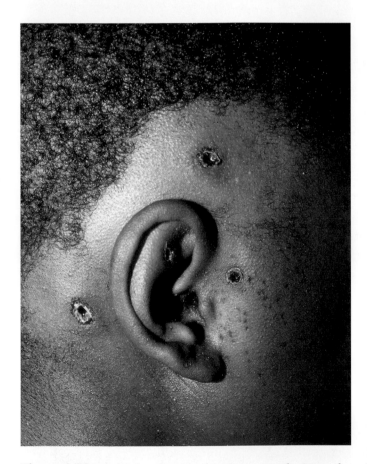
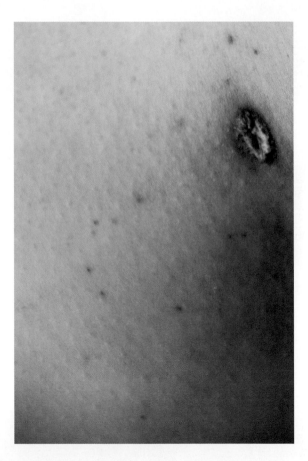

Figure 8.90 Multiple entrance gunshot wounds. Note the sparse stippling defects indicating intermediate range of fire at the skin anterior to the ear. The further away a gun is discharged from the body, the more spread out the stippling defects become.

Figure 8.91 Intermediate range of fire. Note the sparse vague stippling defect surrounding the bullet perforation site, indicating the range of fire to be near the outermost range.

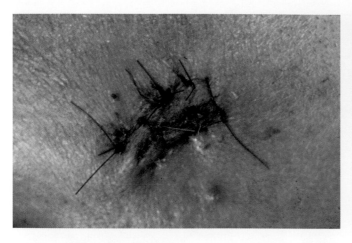
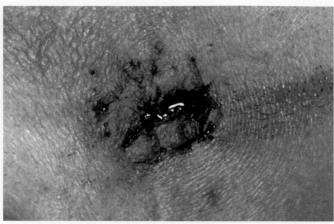

Figures 8.92 and 8.93 Pseudostippling. This individual survived in the hospital for a short time after getting shot in the head. Note the wounds were sutured closed. At autopsy when the sutures were removed the needle punctures created red defects that may be misinterpreted as stippling.

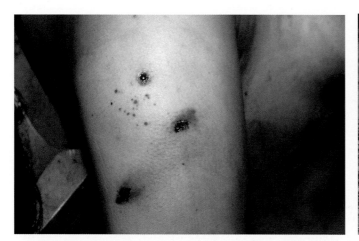
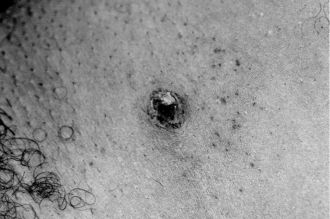

Figures 8.94 and 8.95 A few sparse stippling defects indicating intermediate range of fire. Note the contusion surrounding the perforating gunshot wound at the arm. This dark discoloration should not be confused with gunpowder residue.

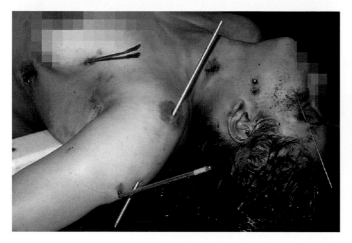
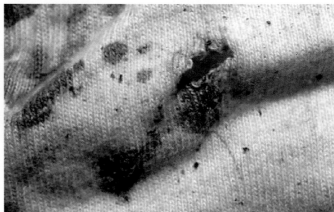

Figure 8.96 Note the multiple gunshot wounds to this individual in varying directions. She was shot multiple times while jumping in different directions, in an attempt to run away. Note the contusion to her left shoulder and the stippling defects to her face. It is important to realize that the direction of fire may vary greatly during one assault.

Figure 8.97 Gunshot wound perforation of clothing with multiple gunpowder residue flecks on the surrounding surface. The underlying entrance gunshot wound still revealed a sparse stippling pattern consistent with intermediate range of fire.

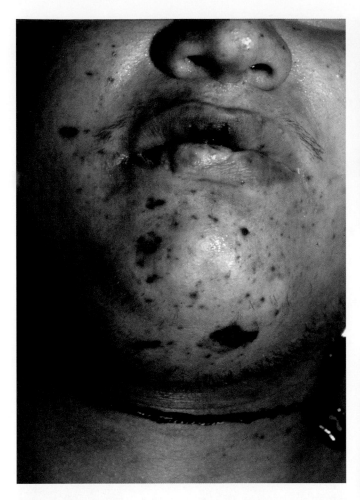

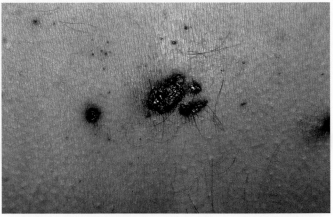

Figure 8.99 Distant gunshot wound with pseudostippling. Note the large size variation in the abrasions adjacent to the gunshot wound. True stippling defects are more uniform in size.

Figure 8.98 Distant gunshot wound with pseudostippling to this individual's face caused by fragmented debris as the bullet passed through a car window.

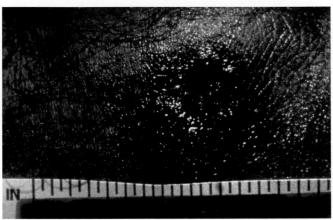

Figure 8.101 Distant entrance gunshot wound with surrounding clotted blood. In this case histopathology of the adjacent skin failed to demonstrate dark particles consistent with gunpowder residue. It may be challenging to visualize soot when it is mixed with dried blood. Dried clotted blood has a more shiny character than gunpowder residue, which has a more dull appearance. It may be challenging to interpret range of fire when both dried blood and soot are present simultaneously. If there is any question concerning the presence of soot, the author recommends microscopic examination to help clarify this point.

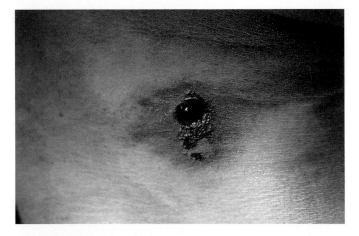

Figure 8.100 Atypical distant entrance gunshot wound with surrounding contusion.

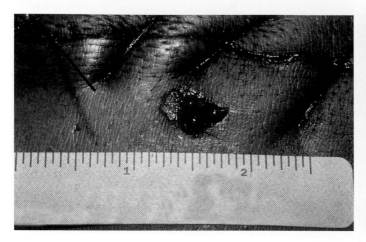

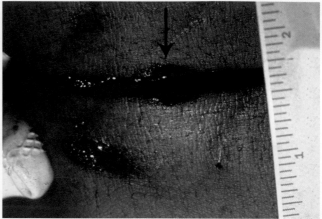

Figures 8.102 and 8.103 Thoracotomy incision through entrance gunshot wound. One should never cut through the wound during resuscitative efforts. No one would argue the importance of saving the individual's life. Cutting next to the wound will not affect the chances for survival. Cutting through the wound may make wound interpretation very difficult and hinder criminal proceedings. Note one gunshot wound was cut through and hidden in the suture line. The defect becomes more obvious with suture removal.

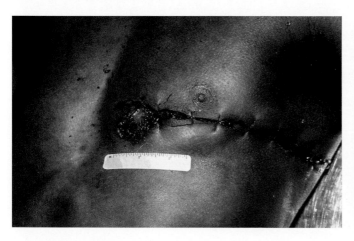

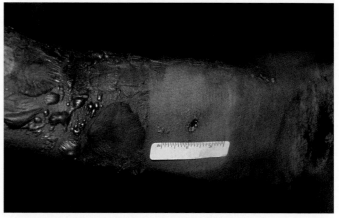

Figure 8.104 Note the large gunshot wound at the medial aspect of this thoracotomy incision.

Figure 8.105 This is a gunshot wound that is several days old. This person died of septic complications. Note the adjacent wound infection distal to the GSW site consisting of swelling and blister formation from gangrene.

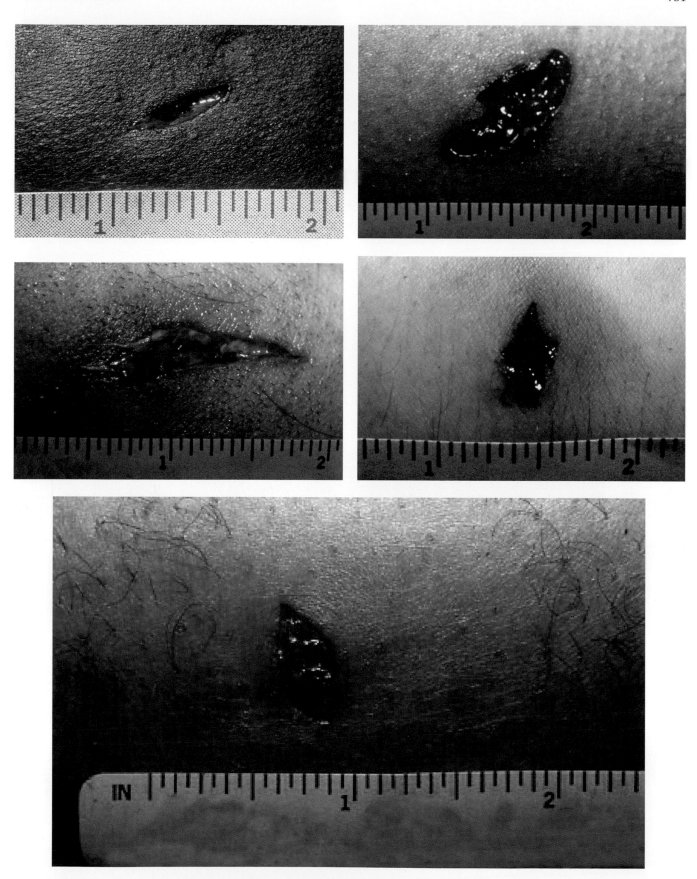

Figures 8.106–8.110 Exit gunshot wounds. Note the typical often irregular slit-like defects without margins of abrasion. The appearance is generally more irregular and less round than the entrance wound. On occasion it may appear rounded as well.

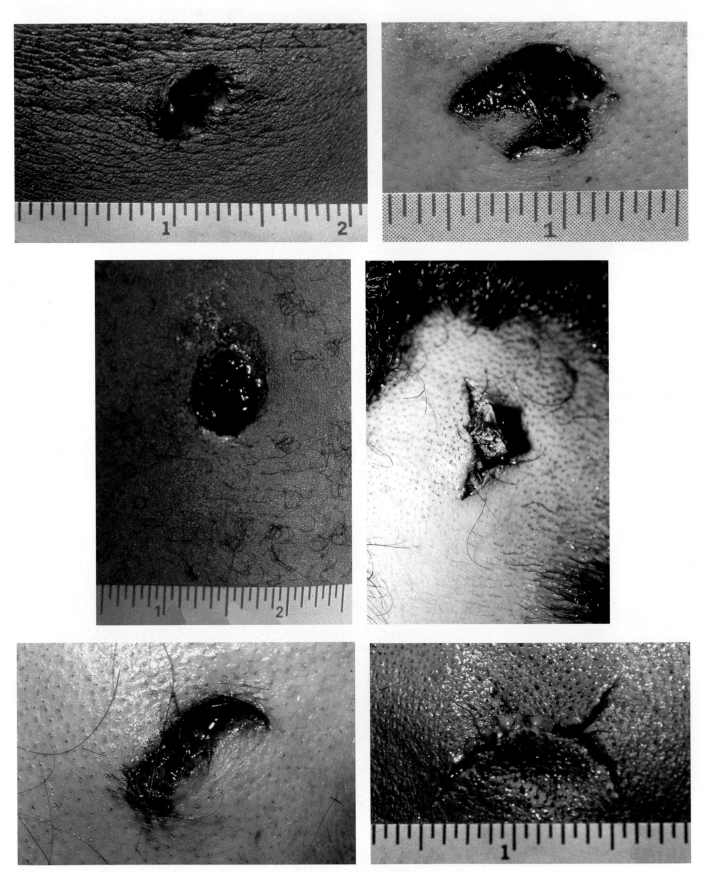

Figures 8.111–8.116 Exit gunshot wounds. Note Figure 8.114 has a piece of fractured bone extending from the perforation, which was dragged outward as the bullet exited the body.

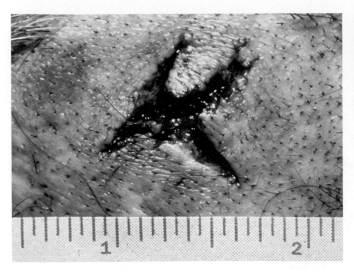

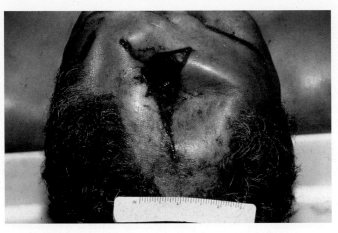

Figure 8.117 Exit wound with lacerated margins.

Figure 8.118 Exit wound from a sawed-off 30/30 hunting rifle, which was much larger than the entrance wound.

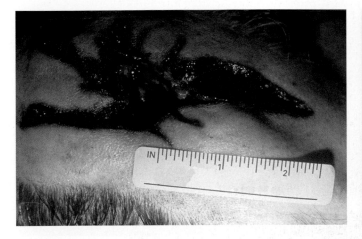

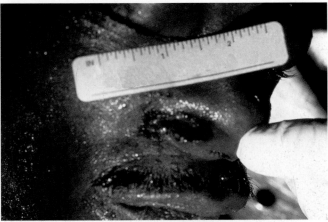

Figure 8.119 Exit wound from a handgun. It is not typical to get such a large laceration from a medium-caliber bullet that already perforated the skull.

Figure 8.120 Exit gunshot wound through the right nares.

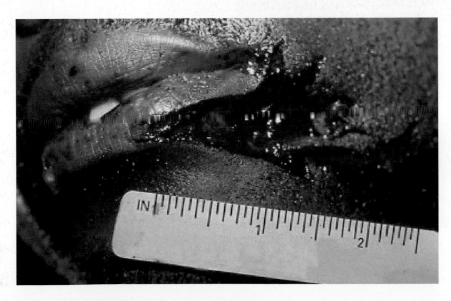

Figure 8.121 Exit gunshot wound to the lower face caused by a bullet that was markedly deformed by striking underlying bone before exiting.

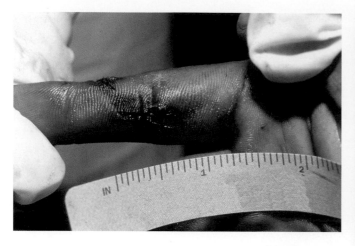

Figure 8.122 Exit gunshot wound through the finger.

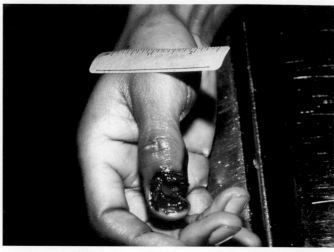

Figure 8.124 Exit gunshot wound through the thumb nail bed.

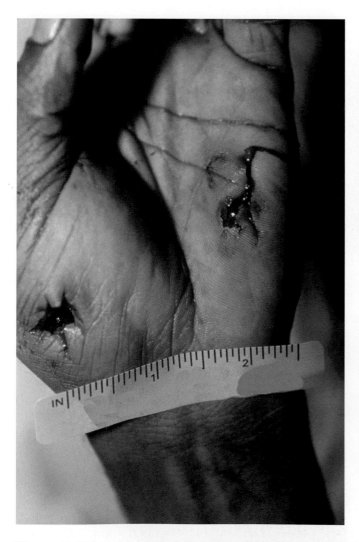

Figure 8.123 Exit gunshot wounds through the palm hand.

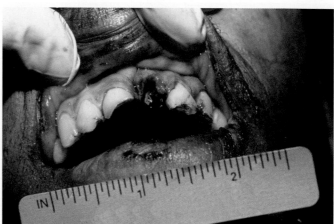

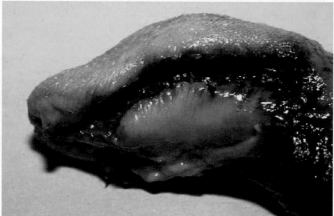

Figures 8.125 and 8.126 This individual was shot in the lower back while leaning forward. The bullet perforated the structures of the thoracic cavity, neck, and produced a grazing-type gunshot wound to the tongue. The bullet then knocked out the individual's front tooth before exiting the body from the open mouth.

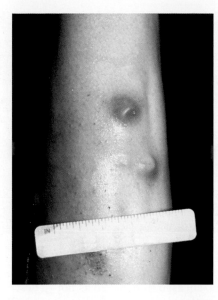

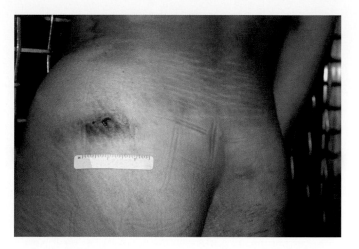

Figure 8.128 A bullet was retrieved just beneath the surface of the skin within this area of contusion.

Figure 8.127 Note these bulges emanating from underneath the skin's surface. These are bullets that did not have enough kinetic energy to exit the body.

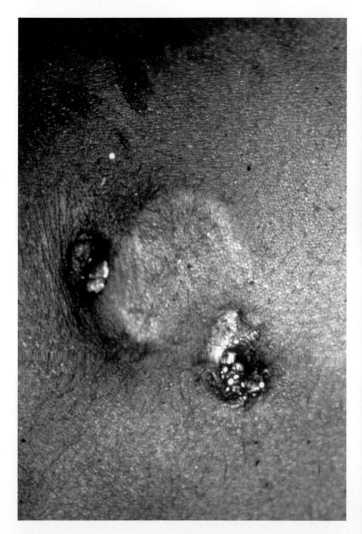

Figure 8.129 There is a large deformed gray metal slug just underneath the surface of the skin, which is partially visible underneath the broken skin.

Figure 8.130 Bullet retrieved from skull fracture directly underneath the skin's surface.

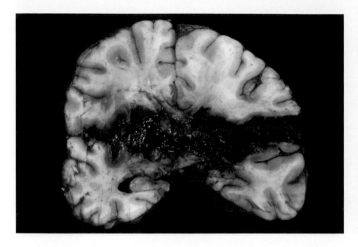

Figure 8.131 This image demonstrates a hemorrhagic pulpified wound track through the cerebral hemispheres caused by a medium-caliber handgun bullet.

Figure 8.132 This bullet was retrieved within this portion of thoracic vertebra. It is important to carefully remove such bullets, encased in bone, so as not to destroy ballistic markings on the sides of the bullet. Lead bullets within joint cavities may be dissolved by synovial fluid leading to lead poisoning.

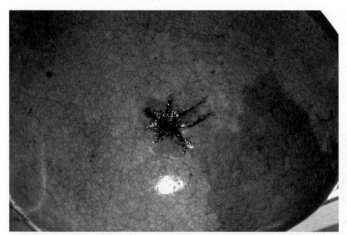

Figures 8.133 and 8.134 These figures demonstrate a wound track through the liver, caused by a medium-caliber handgun.

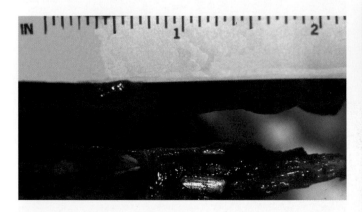

Figure 8.135 This individual had been shot several weeks earlier with a .22-caliber handgun. One of his ribs fractured while removing the breastplate during autopsy and a bullet was retrieved from within the medullary cavity.

Figure 8.136 This figure demonstrates wound track through the aorta with adjacent surrounding hemorrhage. This wound was caused by a medium-caliber weapon.

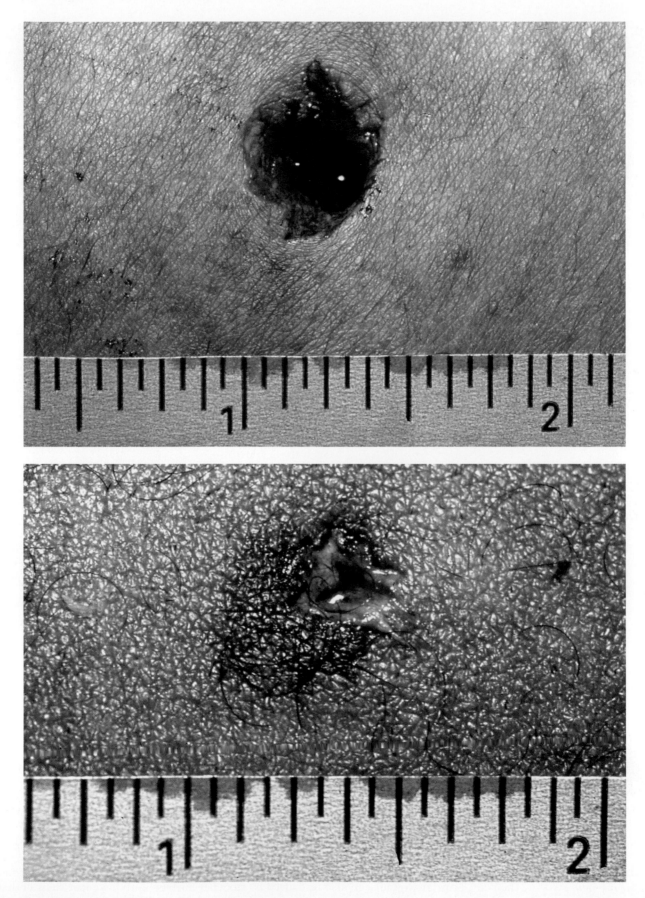

Figures 8.137 and 8.138 Shored exits. These wounds were produced by bullets exiting the body where the skin's surface is supported (e.g., by a firm surface or tight clothing).

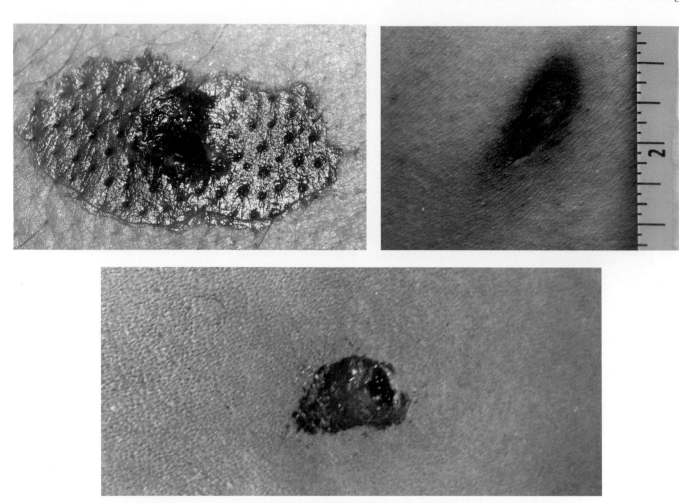

Figures 8.139–8.141 Shored exit wounds.

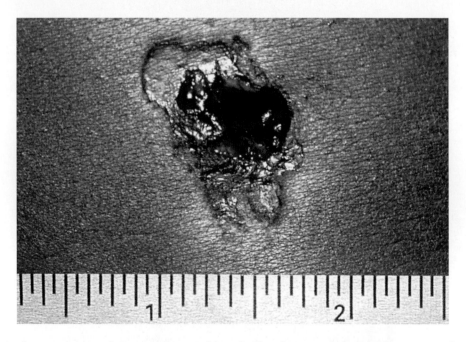

Figure 8.142 Atypical entrance gunshot wound caused by a bullet that was deformed by passing through an intermediate target before striking the body. Similar wounds can also be caused by ricochet bullets. Both have lost their ballistic stability, or are often deformed, and may strike the body sideways or even backward. This will create an atypical abrasion and perforation, when compared to a bullet striking a body nose first. Note the large irregular abrasion caused by the deformed edges of the bullet striking the skin surface.

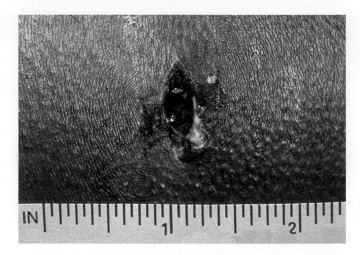

Figure 8.143 Irregular exit gunshot wound with adjacent abrasion due to its location on the body through a region of folded skin.

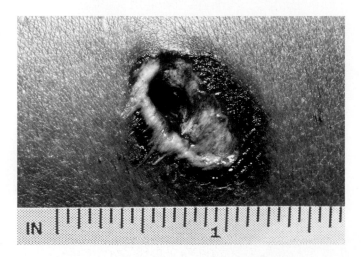

Figure 8.144 This distant entrance gunshot wound has slightly oval shape with an irregular margin of abrasion that is greatest at its inferior right aspect. This wound was produced by a ricochet bullet that first struck a brick wall. Part of the bullet had an irregular scratched surface. Also this bullet most likely struck the body sideways. This bullet entered the abdominal wall and perforated the iliac artery, causing death. It did not strike any bones in the body or hard surfaces while entering the body that would account for the bullet becoming deformed. This collaborated the perpetrator's story that he was not shooting anywhere near the bystander.

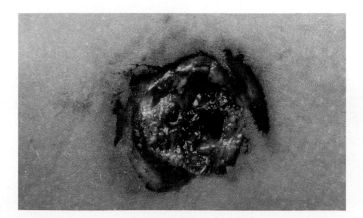

Figure 8.145 Atypical gunshot wound. This is a reentry GSW produced from a bullet that was markedly deformed from striking a bone in another part of the body. Note the irregular nature of the perforation with the irregular adjacent abrasions.

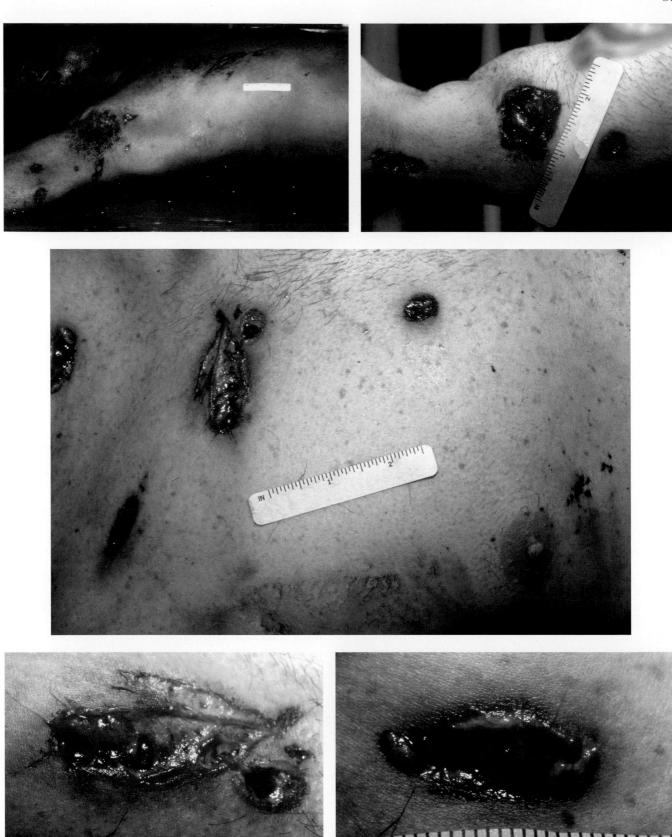

Figures 8.146–8.150 Atypical gunshot wounds from deformed and fragmented bullets that passed through an intermediate target, such as a car door and window, before entering and exiting the body. Note the markedly irregular nature of these injuries.

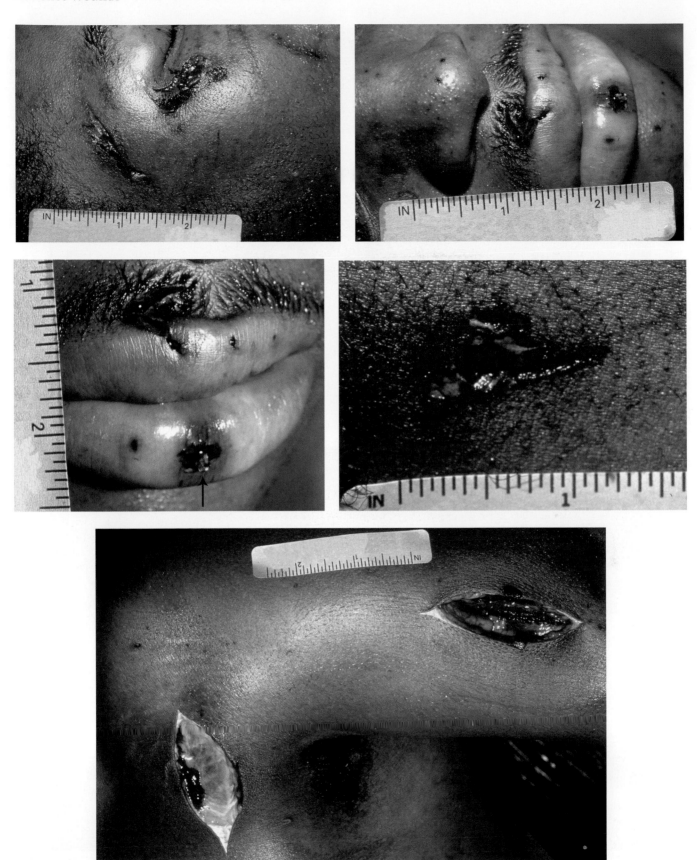

Figures 8.151–8.155 Multiple atypical entrance gunshot wounds produced by fragmented pieces of lead caused by .22-caliber nonjacketed bullets that struck concrete and fragmented before striking an individual who was lying on the sidewalk. Note the irregular nature of these injuries with superficial fragmented pieces of lead observed in several of the wound tracks.

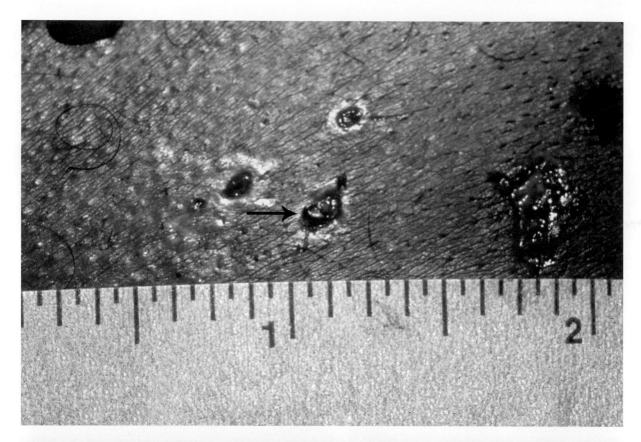

Figures 8.156 and 8.157 These are several atypical injuries produced by fragmented nonjacketed lead bullets. The individual survived in the hospital for days. Note the healing margins and fragments of lead being pushed from the underlying soft tissue.

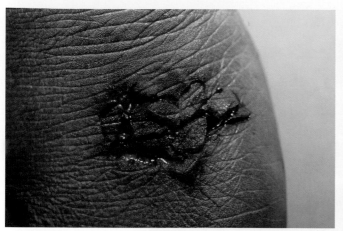 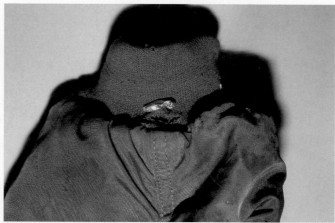

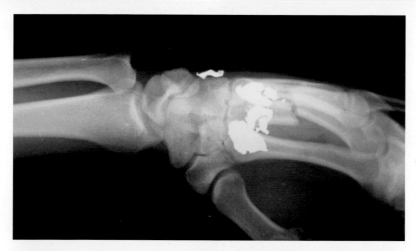

Figures 8.158–8.161 This child was shot multiple times. One of the bullets struck another object, fragmented, and produced this atypical entrance wound to his wrist. There were fragments of bullets retrieved from the decedent's jacket corresponding to this location. X-ray shows multiple fragments of deformed metal retrieved just underneath the skin surface adjacent to the bones of the hand. This last image shows all the bullet fragments retrieved from this individual's hand and wrist. There were no other wounds to this region of the body.

Figure 8.162 This ricochet bullet was retrieved within the abdomen of an individual with a perforated iliac artery. This bullet perforated the individual's shirt and did not strike bone while passing through the body. This bullet corresponds to the entrance wound demonstrated in Figure 8.145.

 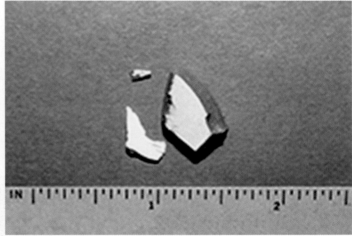

Figures 8.163 and 8.164 This bullet struck the ground, fragmented portions of tile, and became markedly deformed before ricocheting upward and striking the body of an individual already lying on the ground. The resulting gunshot wound was markedly atypical, producing irregular injuries to the body surface.

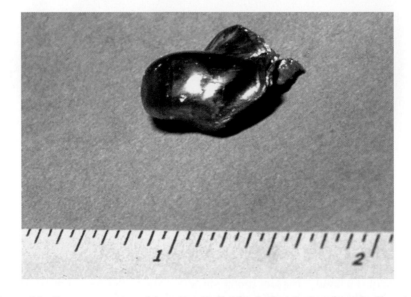

Figure 8.165 This deformed bullet was retrieved from an individual after it ricocheted off an intermediate target.

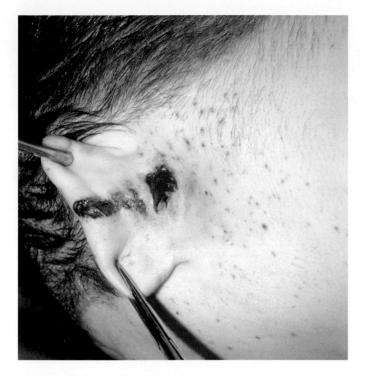

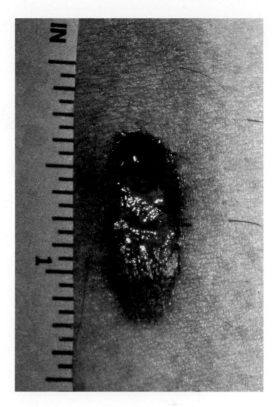

Figure 8.166 Intermediate entrance gunshot wound with stippling. Note the irregular natural of the wound due to the location on the body. The bullet entered between the posterior ear and the fold of skin at the scalp. Note the elongated abrasion at the posterior ear due to the bullet grazing the skin before entering the body.

Figure 8.167 Distant entrance gunshot wound with an asymmetric margin of abrasion. This indicates that the bullet grazed the body at an upward trajectory before perforating the skin.

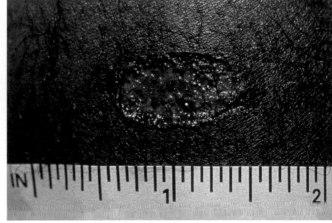

Figures 8.168 and 8.169 Graze gunshot wounds. The first picture to the left is more atypical.

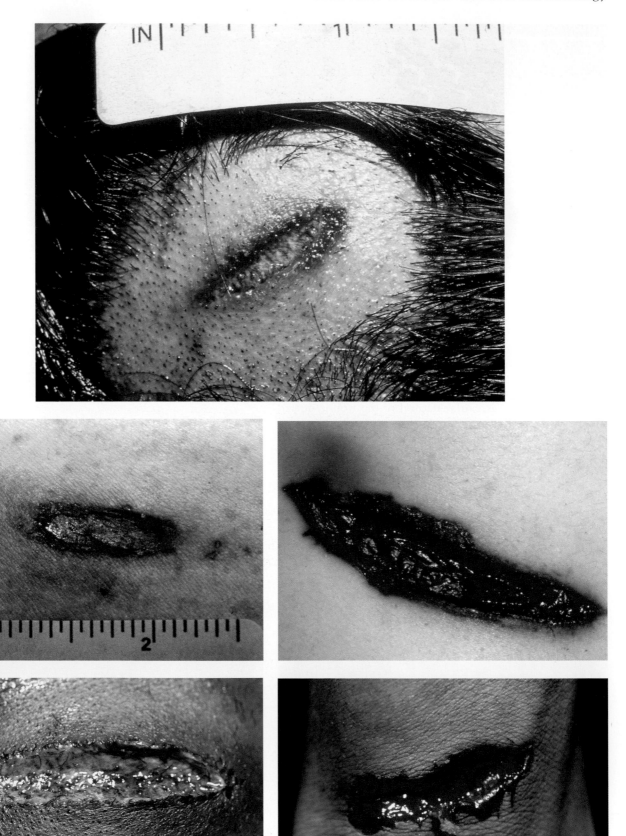

Figures 8.170–8.174 Graze gunshot wounds.

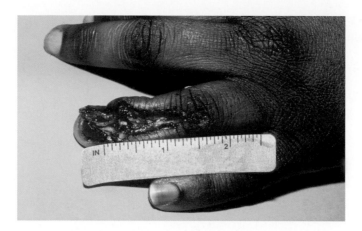

Figure 8.175 Tangential gunshot wound with a trajectory from the middle to distal aspect of the finger. Note the semi-circular entrance defect on the right side of this wound overlying the proximal middle phalange.

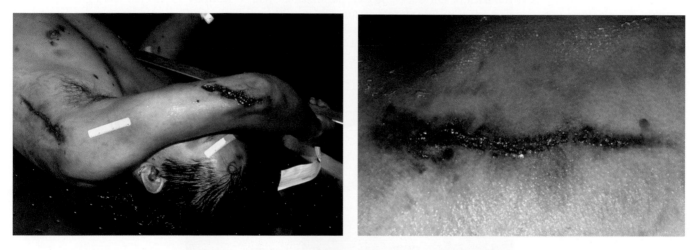

Figures 8.176 and 8.177 Tangential gunshot wounds to the arm and trunk. Note the skin tag formation at the wound margin produced as the bullet perforated underneath the skins surface.

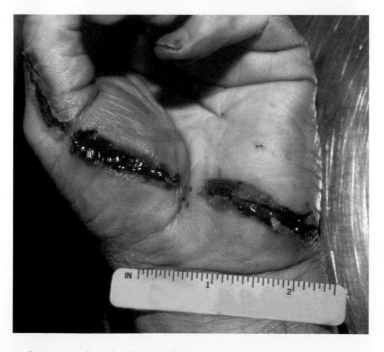

Figure 8.178 Tangential gunshot wound with skin tag formation. The direction of fire is from left to right.

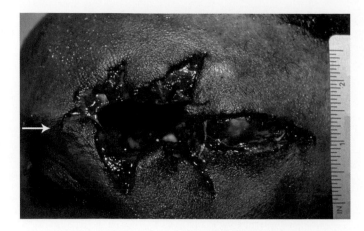

Figure 8.179 Distant tangential gunshot wound. Tangential gunshot wounds are produced when the bullet strikes the body at a narrow angle, producing skin tag formation. Usually the bullet exits the body, leaving an open wound through the skin's surface, connecting the path of entrance and exit perforations. These wounds are deeper than graze gunshot wounds. This wound is associated with bullet fragmentation and partial exit. This may occur when the bullet strikes the body at a surface directly adjacent to underlying bone. This is an example with bullet fragmentation, partial exit, and underlying keyhole deformity of the skull. Note the entrance side of this wound is at the anterior aspect. There is a semicircular margin of abrasion leading into this laceration. The direction of fire is from the decedent's front to back, as indicated by the arrow.

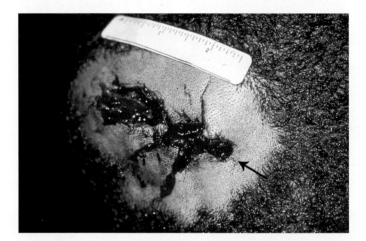

Figure 8.180 Tangential gunshot wound of the scalp. The direction of fire is from right to left. Note the skin tag formation pointing away from the semicircular entrance site. The direction of fire is indicated by the arrow.

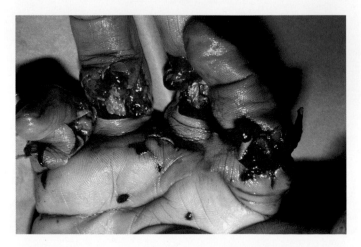

Figure 8.181 Note the tangential gunshot wound through the palmar surfaces of the fingers.

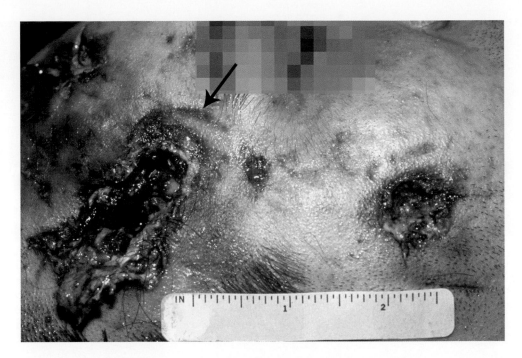

Figure 8.182 Tangential gunshot wound to the forehead. Part of this bullet entered the cranium and a portion of the bullet exited the body. There was an underlying keyhole deformity to the skull. The arrow indicates direction of fire.

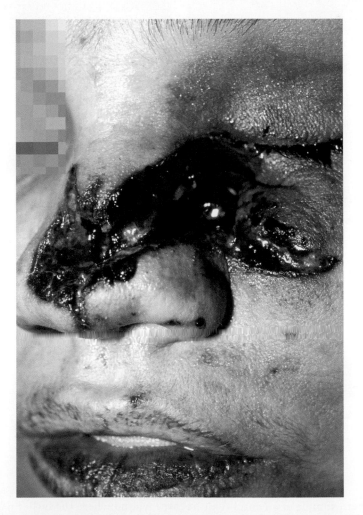

Figure 8.183 After this bullet perforated the fingers (Figure 8.181), it produced a tangential gunshot wound to the nose before entering the body at the face.

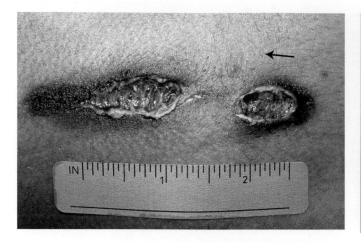

Figure 8.184 This demonstrates an entrance and exit gunshot wound that passed superficially beneath the skin surface. The direction of fire is indicated by the arrow. Note the perforation on the right side has a more uniform oval shape with a more symmetric margin of abrasion. The exit component to this wound is more irregular.

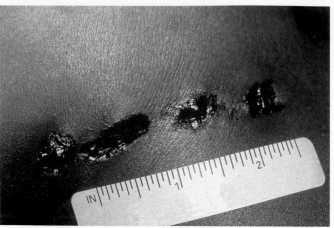

Figure 8.185 This gunshot wound produced multiple tears and perforations to the surface of the skin as the bullet passed close to the underlying surface. Such injuries often occur in regions of the body where skin folded on itself like the inguinal, gluteal, and axillary regions.

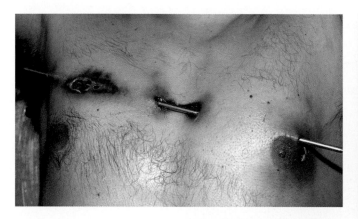

Figure 8.186 This single gunshot wound passed through the superficial soft tissues of the chest, producing multiple perforations and tears to the surface. Note the irregular nature of the torn skin and irregular abrasions at the exit reentry site.

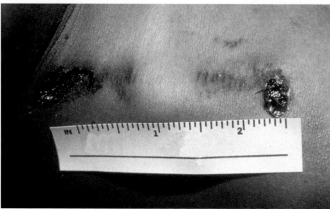

Figure 8.187 This is an entrance and exit gunshot wound where the bullet passed very close to the undersurface of the skin, causing stretching and darker drying of the skin surface between the two perforations.

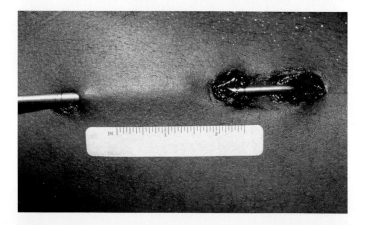

Figure 8.188 This is another example of an entry–exit–reentry wound where the bullet passed close to the underlying skin surface. Note the larger irregular abrasions connecting the exit and reentry sites. Also note the dark discoloration due to drying.

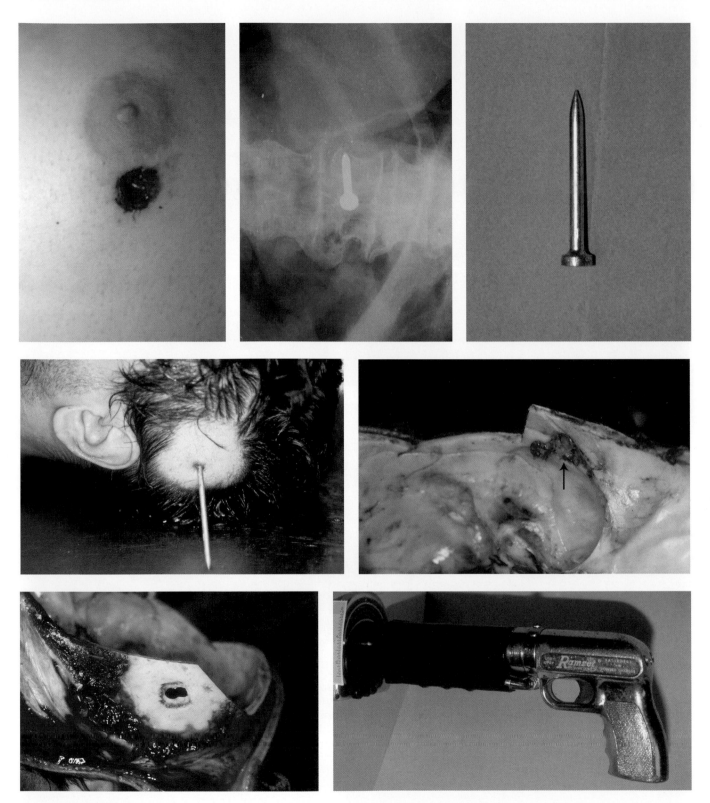

Figures 8.189–8.195 These images show different examples of nail gun wounds. Both of these cases were suicides. Both nail guns used were similar to the one depicted above, which used gunpowder-loaded cartridges. Both entrance wounds consisted of circular perforations with symmetric margins of abrasion indistinguishable from typical entrance gunshot wounds. Note the orange plastic ejected into the entrance perforation of the temporal skull, which is used in some nail guns to hold and steady the nail prior to discharge.

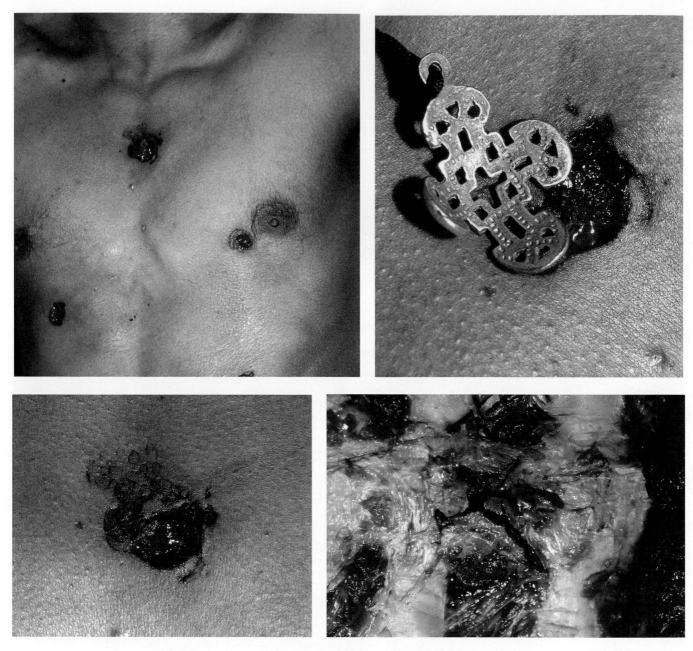

Figures 8.196–8.199 This individual was shot multiple times. Note the exit gunshot wound to the superior aspect of his middle chest. The individual was wearing a medallion on a string, which was struck by the bullet as it exited the body, producing an imprint on the skin surface. The chest surface was most likely pressing against another object when the bullet exited. The photograph illustrating the medallion actually demonstrates it facing the wrong way. The medallion should be oriented with the inward curvature facing the chest. This was at first erroneously thought to be an entrance gunshot wound. Among other points arguing this to be an exit wound was the sternum fracture with bone splinters pointing in an outward anterior direction.

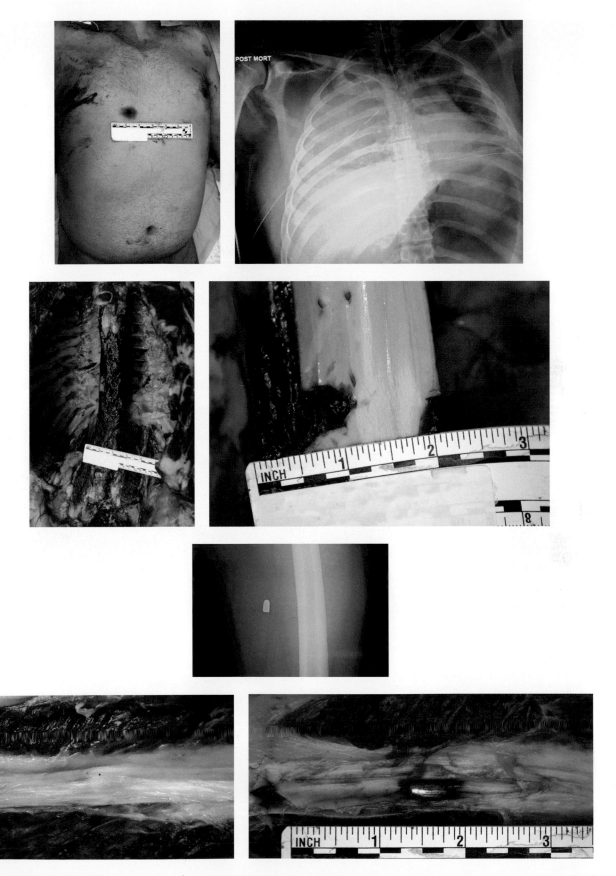

Figures 8.200–8.206 This individual was shot in the chest. Initial x-ray revealed no bullet to be found in the trunk. Autopsy examination revealed a perforating wound to the aorta where the bullet ricocheted off vertebrae back into the aortic lumen and then embolized to the left femoral artery.

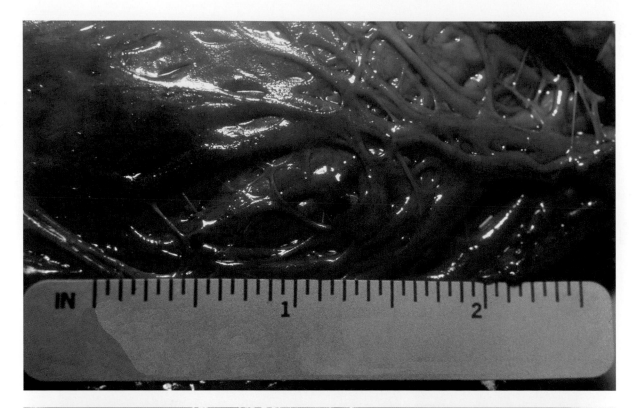

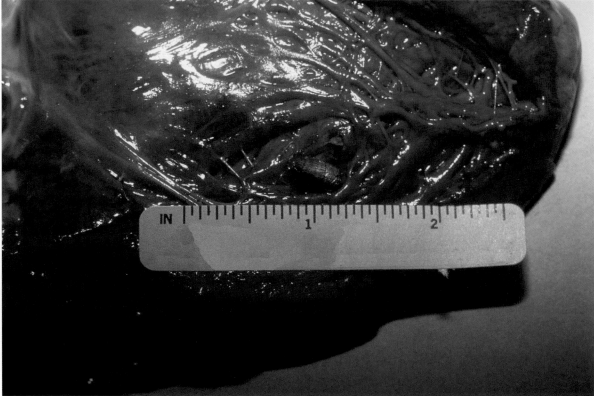

Figures 8.207 and 8.208 This individual was shot multiple times and survived in the hospital for approximately 2 weeks. One of the bullets entered the lung parenchyma and embolized to the heart where it got wedged in papillary muscles of the left ventricle. He developed a bronchopneumonia and his lung wound reopened causing hemorrhage and death.

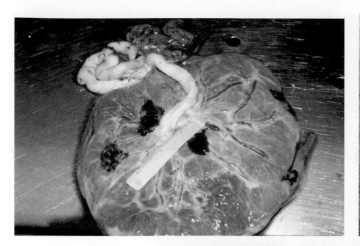
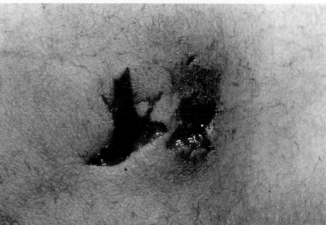
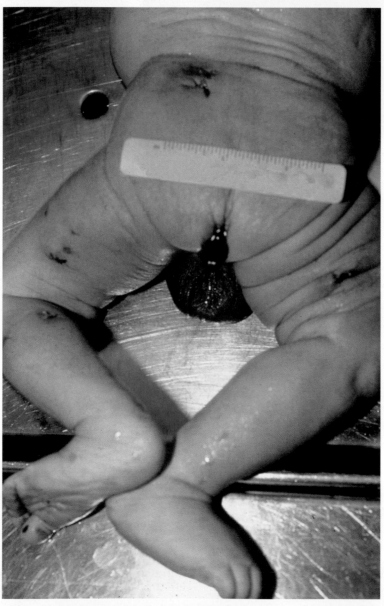

Figures 8.209–8.211 An otherwise healthy, full-term pregnant woman was shot multiple times in the abdomen. There were multiple perforating GSWs to her fetus. The gunshot wounds to the fetus were atypical due to the intermediate targets including the mother, uteroplacental unit, and amniotic fluid. All the fetal wounds appeared as irregular lacerations with irregular abrasions. Direction of fire could not be determined.

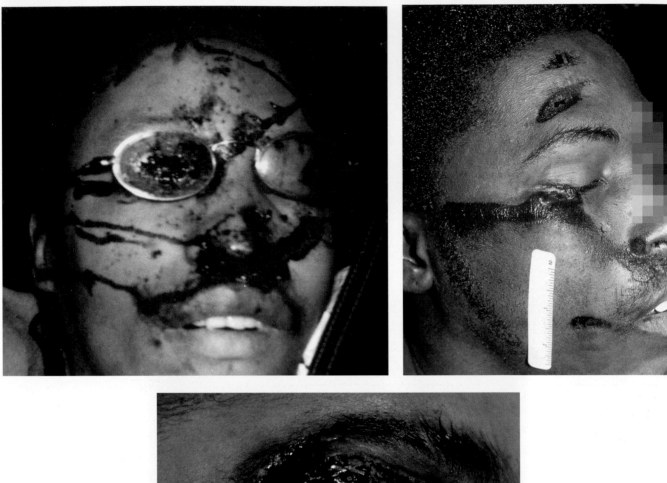

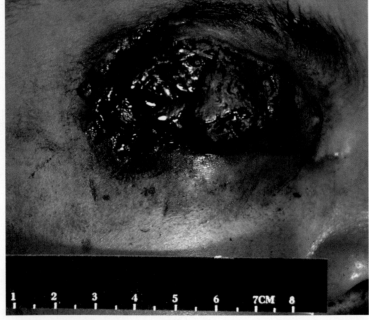

Figures 8.212–8.214 This individual was shot in the face while wearing eyeglasses. Note the irregular nature of the entrance gunshot wound just beneath the eye and the elongated abrasion extending across the cheek to the decedent's ear, corresponding to the eyeglass frame. Another case where a glass fragmentation caused other adjacent orbital lacerations.

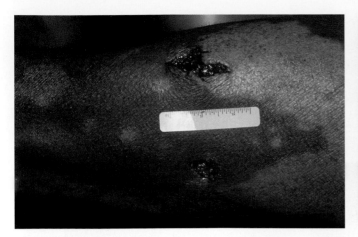

Figures 8.215 and 8.216 This individual was shot multiple times and had psoriatic skin disease. Note the irregular nature of this entrance gunshot wound through one of the plaques. The skin had small radiating lacerations and decreased abrasion similar to what is sometimes seen with gunshot wounds through thick skin found on the palms of the hands or soles of the feet.

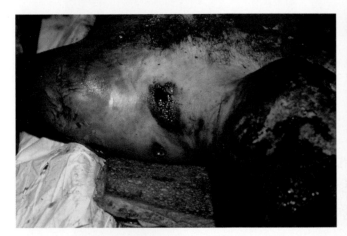

Figures 8.217 and 8.218 These are gunshot wounds to an individual who was set on fire to destroy evidence after being shot while in his residence. His carbon monoxide blood level was negligible. Note the change in character of these injuries due to thermal effect. These thermal burns are postmortem.

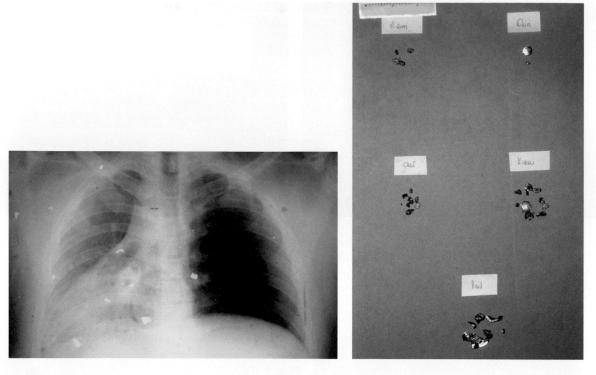

Figures 8.219 and 8.220 This individual was shot multiple times where the bullet struck bones and fragmented into multiple pieces. It is important to keep track of which bullets are associated with which gunshot wounds. There may be several different shooters and only one of the bullet wounds lethal. Linking the lethal bullet to a particular shooter may have different legal implications.

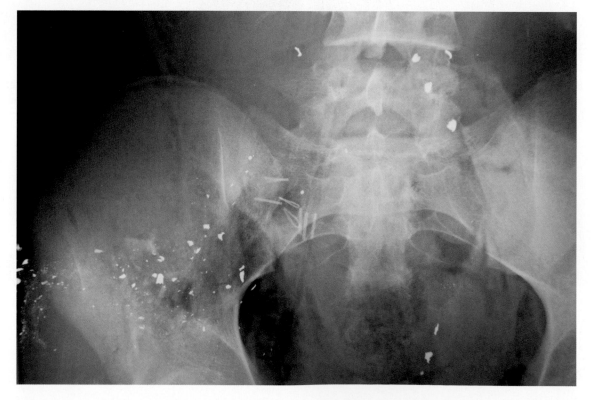

Figure 8.221 This individual was shot in the abdomen with a hunting rifle. Note the snowstorm effect of bullet lead fragmentation depicted on this x-ray.

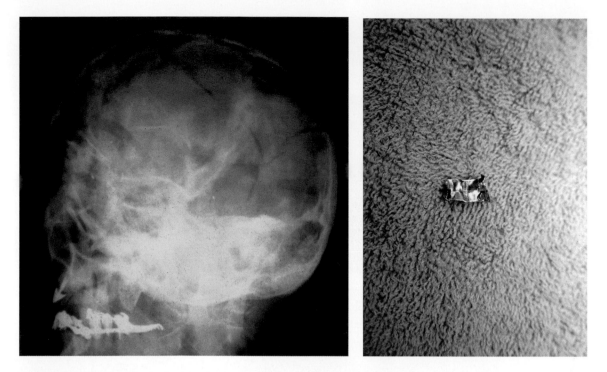

Figures 8.222 and 8.223 This individual was shot with an aluminum jacketed bullet. This fragment of aluminum was retrieved within the wound track. Aluminum, being a relatively less dense metal, may not be apparent on x-ray, particularly when it is lying over a dense thick bone.

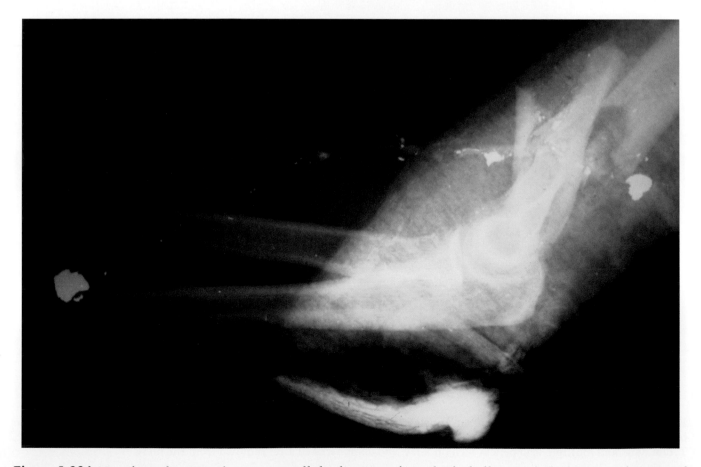

Figure 8.224 Note from this x-ray that one can tell the direction of travel. The bullet struck the humerus, fragmented into pieces, and then left a trail of metal fragments as it passed through the soft tissues before coming to rest.

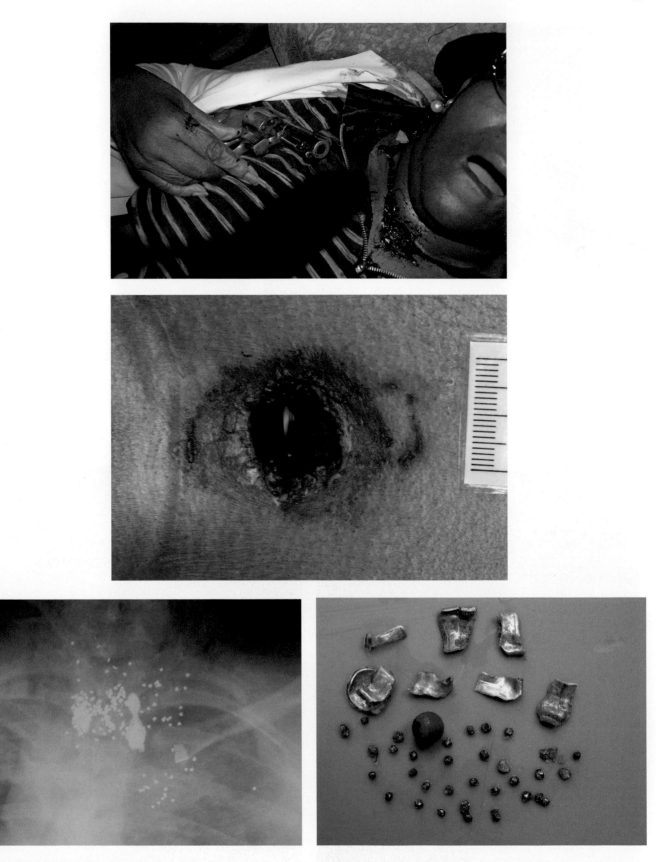

Figures 8.225–8.228 This is a contact gunshot wound to the chest with visible muzzle imprint abrasion. Note the blue-tipped Teflon plug Glaser safety ammunition visible within the revolver chamber. Note the yellow metal jacket, Teflon plug, and multiple lead pellets seen on x-ray, and demonstrated after removal from the body.

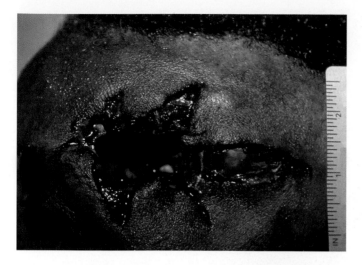

Figure 8.229 Tangential distant gunshot wound produced by Mag-safe ammunition.

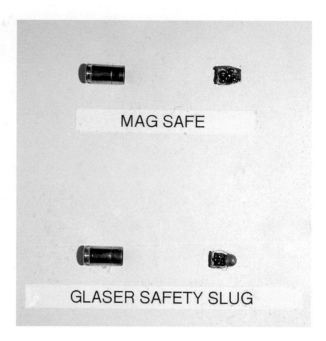

Figure 8.232 This diagram shows a comparison of the components of a Mag-safe ammunition and Glaser safety slug.

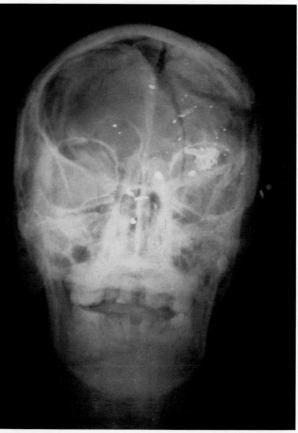

Figures 8.230 and 8.231 This x-ray is taken from an individual shot with Mag-safe ammunition. Note the metal jacket, gray to blue epoxy fragments, and gray metal pellets.

Figure 8.233 This demonstrates a bullet retrieved from an individual who was shot approximately one day prior to autopsy. Note the shiny surface of the bullet signifying no significant oxidation.

Figure 8.234 This demonstrates a bullet retrieved from an individual who was shot over a year before. This bullet remained in his body until it was retrieved during autopsy after somebody else shot and killed him. Note the dull oxidized surface on this old bullet.

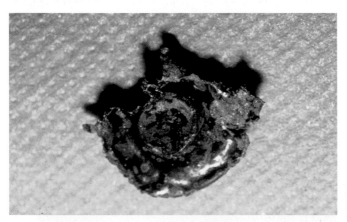

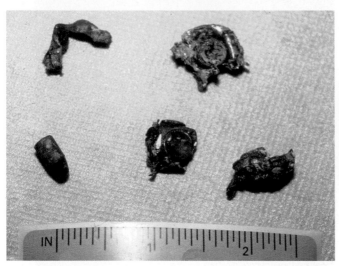

Figures 8.235 and 8.236 These are multiple weathered fragments of bullet retrieved from underneath and within a body of a partially skeletonized individual who was shot and thrown down a well shaft several years earlier. Note the irregular weathering marks on the surface of the bullet due to erosion.

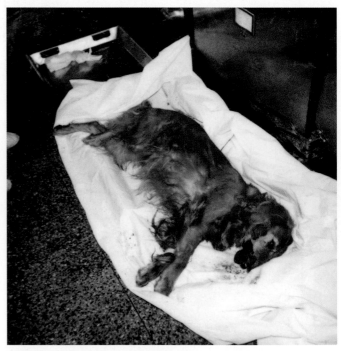

Figure 8.237 The homicide victim who owned this dog died of multiple perforating gunshot wounds. This dog sustained penetrating gunshot wounds during the attack. The dog was autopsied to retrieve ballistic evidence.

Figure 8.238 This is a recent gunshot wound to an individual who was shot through the subcutaneous and fatty tissues of the gluteal region and thigh. Note the curvature of the wound track. This demonstrates how a wound track may change when the body is laid on a flat autopsy table. One must keep this in mind when formulating bullet trajectories with reference to standard anatomic planes. This information may later be used as a reference to help explain possible body positions during the actual shooting. Interpreting wound track directions can become complicated when there are multiple gunshot wounds in close proximity, particularly when the individual was shot while curled up in a fetal position and then later examined spread out on a flat autopsy table. Directions should be stated with reference to standard anatomic planes.

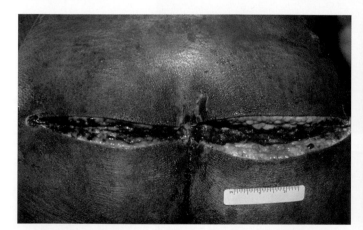
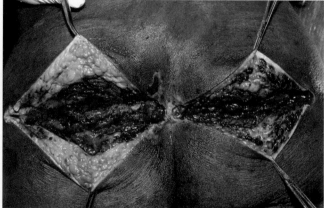

Figures 8.239 and 8.240 This is a healing wound track through the subcutaneous and fatty tissues of the gluteal region. Note the dull granular nature due to healing and the presence of granulation tissue.

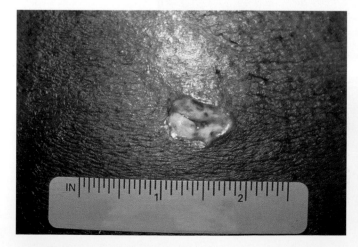
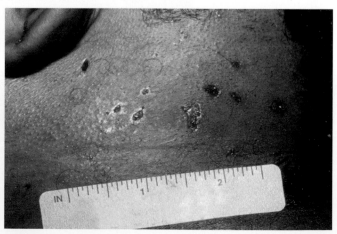

Figure 8.241 This is a healing gunshot wound that is approximately a week old.

Figure 8.242 Atypical healing gunshot wounds with fragmented pieces of lead.

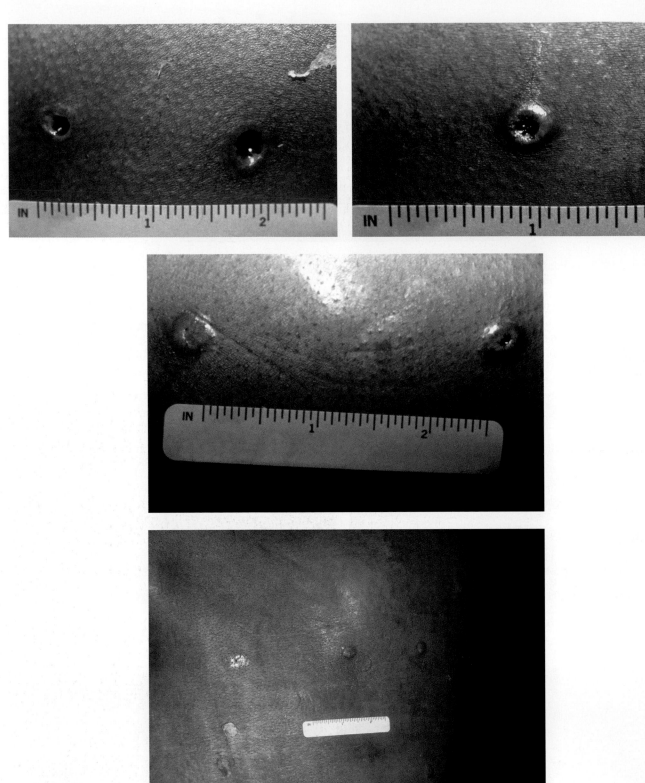

Figures 8.243–8.246 Varying stages of healing gunshot wounds, the most recent being Figure 8.243 and the oldest being Figure 8.246. As wound healing progresses, closing occurs due to secondary intention.

Figures 8.247–8.250 This case involves a suicidal tight contact intraoral .44-caliber rifle wound with extensive fractures and lacerations to the head. This individual was standing when the gun was discharged. Note the gaping injury at the top of the head with the empty cranial vault. The brain was ejected upward almost entirely intact, and landed at the decedent's feet.

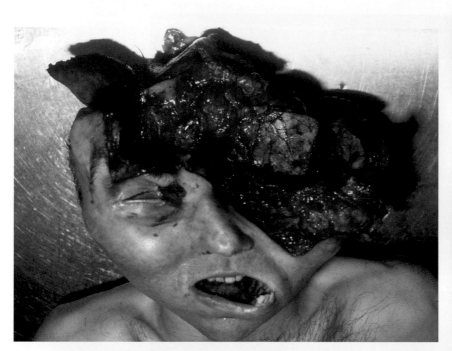

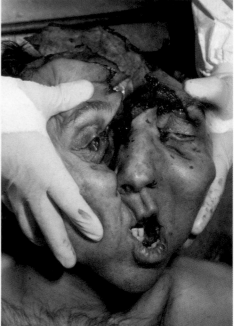

Figures 8.251–8.253 This individual died from a self-inflicted contact 16-gauge buckshot shotgun wound to his forehead. This individual's cerebral hemispheres were ejected from the cranium almost completely intact. The cerebral hemispheres were discovered behind the body. Note reconstruction of this wound produces an obvious circular perforation with soot at the individual's forehead. Initially at the scene investigation it was thought to have been an intraoral shotgun wound. Many of the intraoral shotgun wounds are associated with stretching and lacerations of the lips and mouth region.

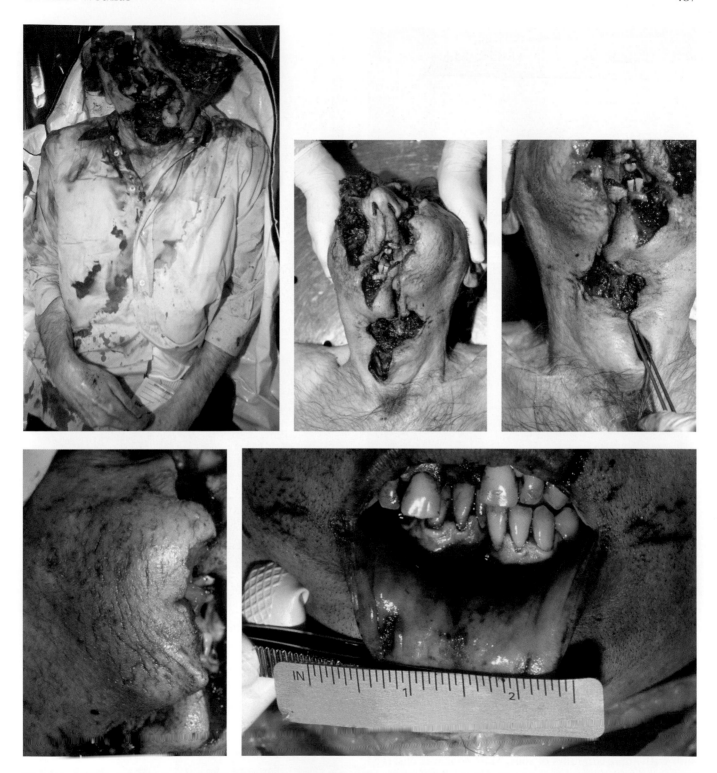

Figures 8.254–8.258 This individual died of a self-inflicted, contact, 12-gauge shotgun wound to the superior aspect of his neck, underneath his chin. Note approximation of the wound margins produces a roughly circular perforation with soot. There were extensive lacerations to the face and head. Note the extensive stretch marks on the decedent's face. Note the blood spatter pattern and gunpowder residue on the individual's hand.

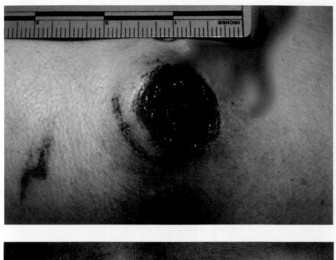

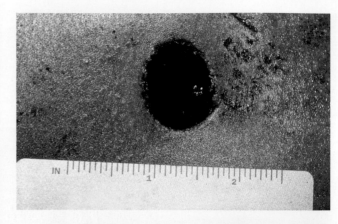

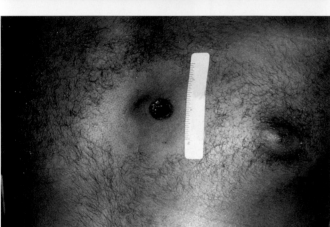

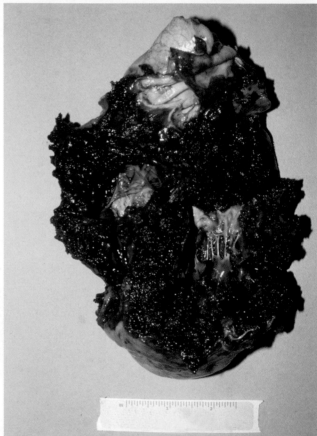

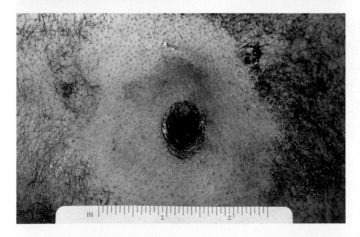

Figures 8.259–8.261 These are contact shotgun wounds to the chest. Note the roughly symmetric margin of abrasion with small amounts of soot. More soot was observed within the wound track. Note in Figure 8.236 there is another encircling abraded ring corresponding to where the muzzle contacted the body when the gun was discharged. Note in Figures 8.237–8.238 there is an encircling vague pink discoloration from carbon monoxide and nitrites in the burning gunpowder that reacted with the underlying muscle and blood, producing this red discoloration.

Figures 8.262–8.264 This is another example of a shotgun slug wound. Note the extensive fragmentation and laceration to the heart. The last image shows the deformed lead shotgun slug with wadding retrieved from the wound track.

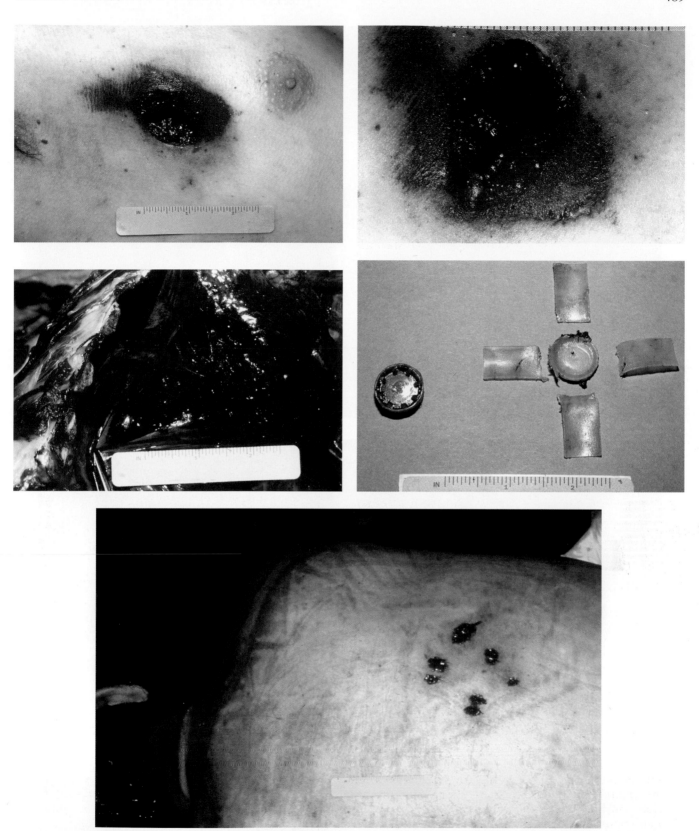

Figures 8.265–8.269 This is a .12-gauge shotgun wound through clothing showing few stippling defects and a larger abrasion adjacent to the entrance defect. The power piston was retrieved within the wound track. Note the abrasions adjacent to the entrance wound due to power piston impact. There was extensive fragmentation of the lung. Note the multiple exit buckshot pellet wounds to the decedent's back.

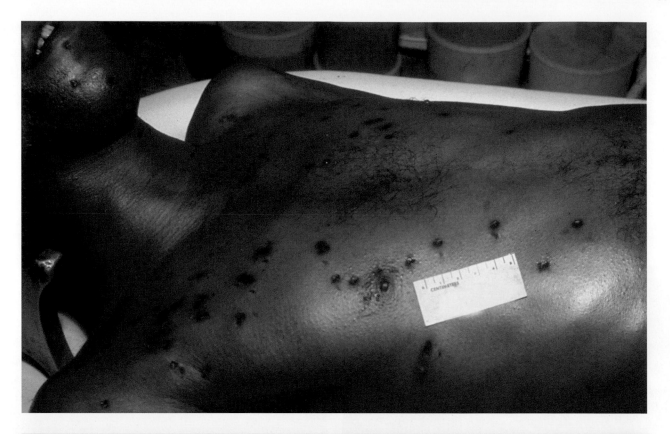

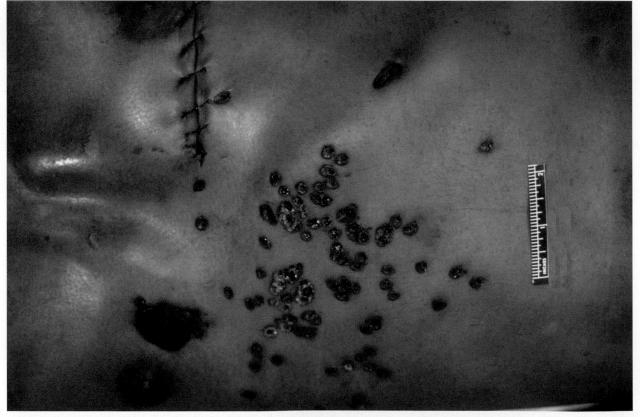

Figures 8.270 and 8.271 Distant birdshot shotgun wounds.

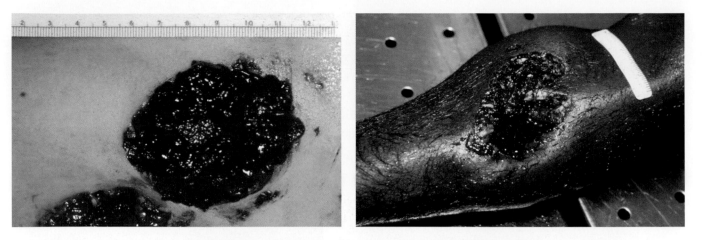

Figures 8.272 and 8.273 These birdshot shotgun wounds are estimated at a range of approximately 3–4 feet.

Figure 8.274 Birdshot with power piston-type cup from a shotgun shell.

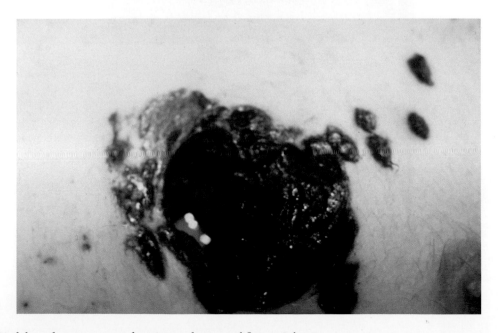

Figure 8.275 Birdshot shotgun wound estimated range of fire 4–5 feet.

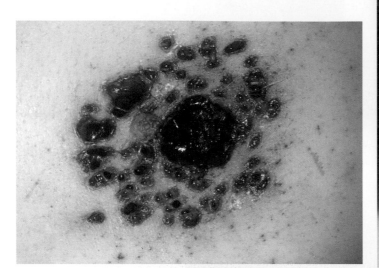

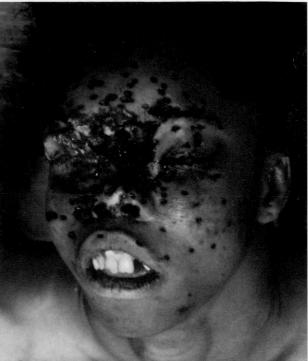

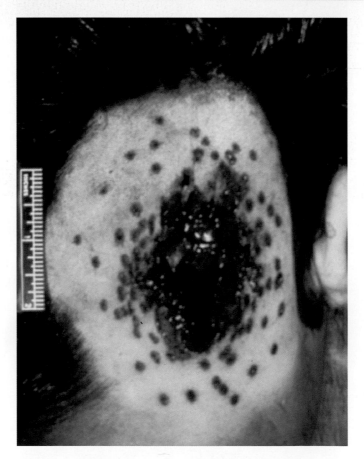

Figures 8.276–8.278 Birdshot shotgun wound estimated range of fire 6–8 feet.

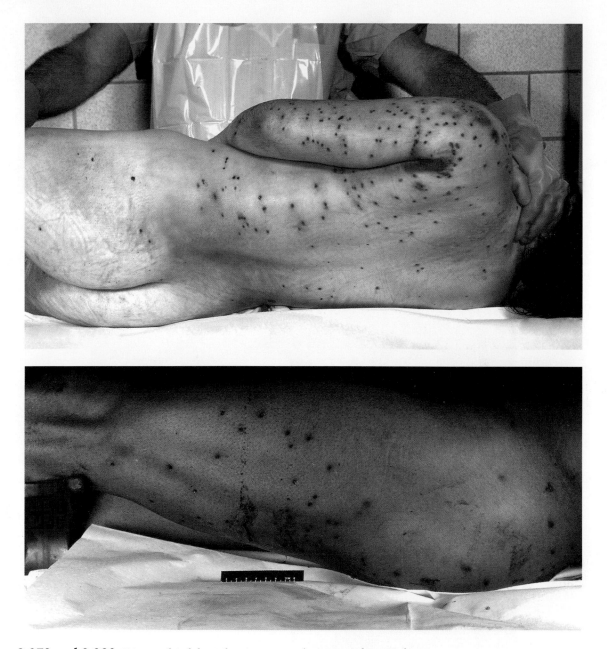

Figures 8.279 and 8.280 Distant birdshot shotgun wounds greater than 10 feet.

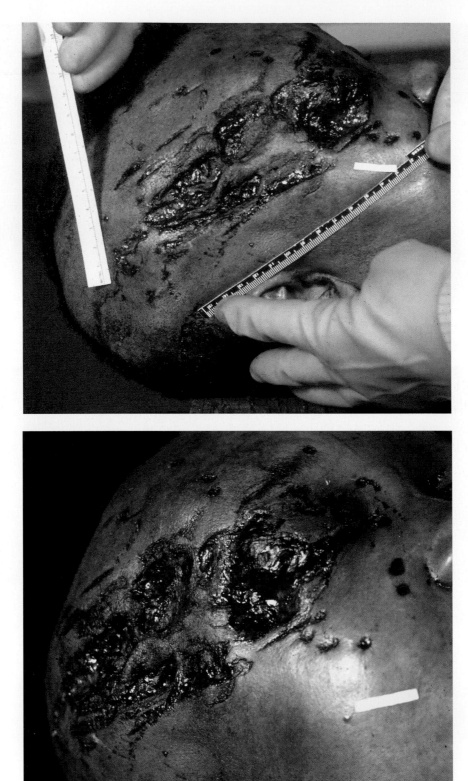

Figures 8.281 and 8.282 Partially tangential birdshot shotgun wound to the head.

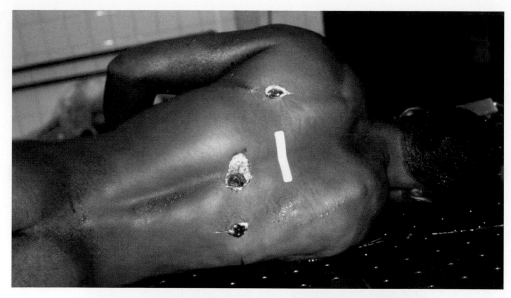

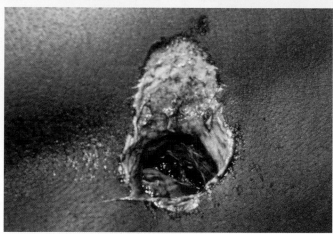

Figures 8.283 and 8.284 This individual was shot multiple times with shotgun slugs. Note the large circular perforations with margins of abrasions typical for entrance handgun wounds. Note the elongated margin of abrasion at the middle wound indicating the slug struck the body on an angle, traveling in a left to right direction.

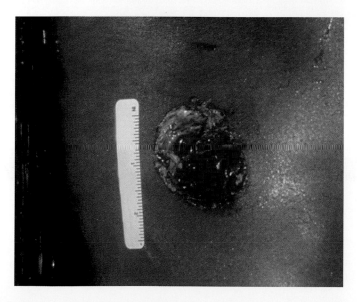

Figure 8.285 Entrance shotgun wound with an estimated range of fire of 3–4 feet based on the scalloped appearance of the wound margins.

Figure 8.286 Mini-14 Ruger rifle.

Figure 8.287 Flash suppressor.

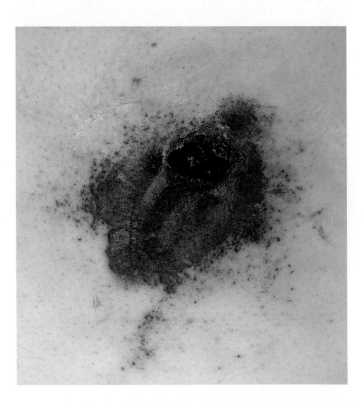

Figure 8.288 Contact Ruger mini-14 gunshot wound with a .223 bullet. Note the flash suppressor burns with soot deposition.

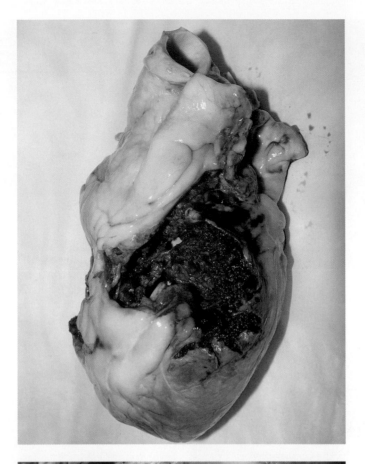

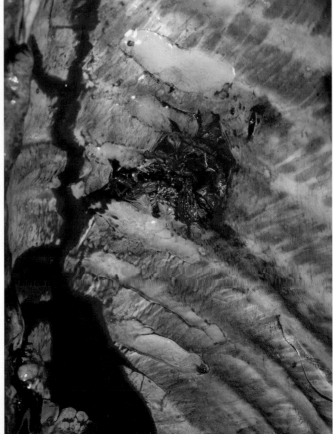

Figures 8.289 and 8.290 Internal injuries caused by a .223-caliber high-velocity military bullet.

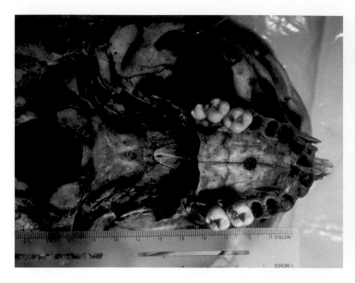

Figure 8.291 Entrance gunshot wound to the roof of the mouth in the skeletonized remains of this individual with a history of depression. The remains were found with a handgun.

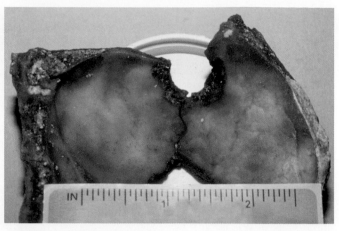

Figure 8.292 This is the inner aspect of a fractured portion of skull with a roughly circular perforation and internal beveling visible at the inner aspect of the skull, indicating this to be an entrance gunshot wound.

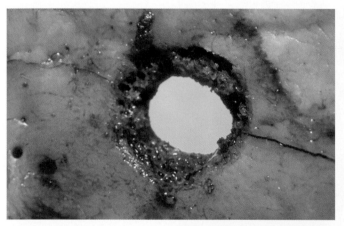

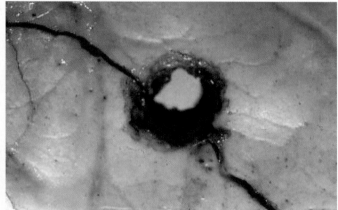

Figures 8.293 and 8.294 Entrance gunshot wounds to the head demonstrating internal beveling of the inner skull.

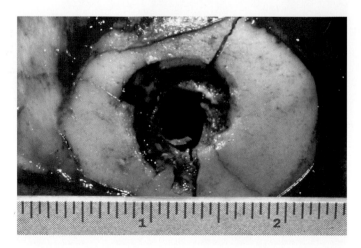

Figure 8.295 Exit gunshot wound through the skull. This image demonstrates the surface of the skull with external beveling typical for an exit GSW.

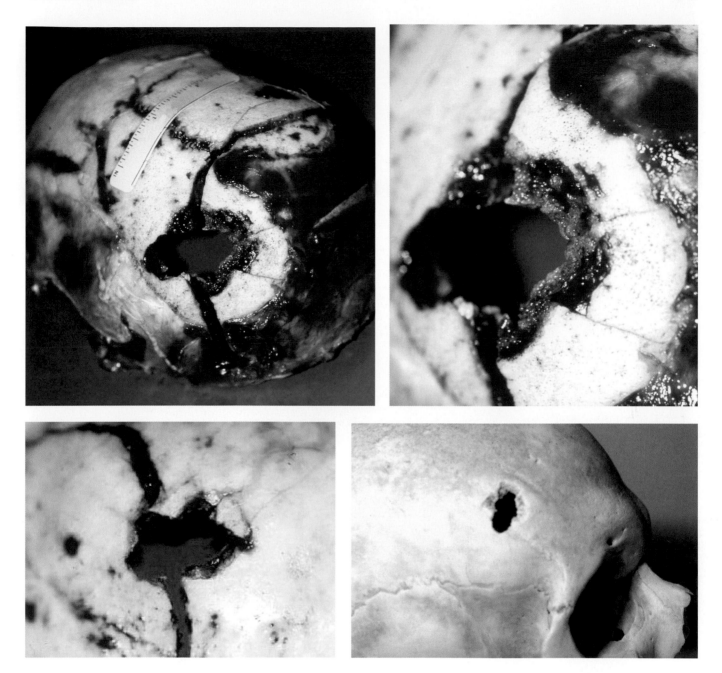

Figures 8.296–8.299 These defects on the external surface of these skulls were produced by an tangential entrance gunshot wound. This demonstrates a keyhole deformity with both internal and external beveling. The bullet typically strikes the bone tangentially, producing internal beveling on the entrance side. Then it will often fragment and partially exit the body. The exit side will have external beveling.

Burns

9

CHARLES A. CATANESE AND GERARD CATANESE

Contents

Introduction

Burns may occur following exposure to heat (thermal burns), electricity, chemicals, or radiation.

First-degree burns are the most superficial and involve the epidermis. They appear as a red discoloration of the skin. An example of this would be sunburn without blister formation. *Second-degree burns* have deeper penetration of injury involving the epidermis and dermis, causing blister formation. An example of this may occur when one touches a hot pot on a stove and pulls the hand away quickly. *Third-degree burns* are full thickness, involving the epidermis, dermis, and subcutaneous layer, and appear as collapsed blisters with skin sloughing and red-to-brown discoloration. *Fourth-degree burns* have even deeper penetration of damage, often with charring and exposed underlying tissue, including bone. The bones may be fractured from intense heat, and the internal organs may have a firm, discolored, and shrunken appearance.

Burns following exposure to heat are *thermal burns,* which may occur following contact with hot liquid or fire. Children may be scalded while left unattended in a bathtub. They may inadvertently hit the hot water knob to increase hot water flow. They may jump into a bathtub full of very hot water, scalding their feet. One must exercise great care in evaluating these cases as they may be a result of abuse or neglect. A child with both feet scalded with scarring around a shoe pattern is more likely the result of abuse or neglect. A child who is waiting to take a bath will not usually have shoes on and will most likely step one foot into the tub at a time. The burns will be on one foot but not usually both. Both feet scalded at once may indicate dunking into hot water as punishment.

If an individual dies and is placed in a tub full of hot water after death, the body will develop thermal injury more readily than if a living body was placed in the same water. A living body can counteract heat injury by vasodilation and circulating the heat to the body's core away from the surface, thus providing some protection to the surface. A dead body left in warm water will quickly develop postmortem thermal burns that appear as skin slippage and progress decomposition due to elevated temperature that also present with skin slippage and blister formation. An individual may sustain full-thickness burns to much greater than half of his or her body and still be conscious without immediate death. Death may occur later due to electrolyte imbalances or infection.

Also, mortality increases with age. Second- to third-degree thermal burns to half the body's surface would much more likely kill a senior citizen than a child. Second-degree burns are more painful than third- or fourth-degree burns due to less damage to nerve endings.

Antemortem burns may be characterized by fluid-filled-blister formation. To have fluid-filled blisters in a nondecomposing body in a nongravity-dependent area not adjacent to an area with more extensive burns with contracted tissue, one needs a blood pressure and a beating heart. Antemortem blisters also typically have a red base with surrounding erythema. This concept remains controversial in some jurisdictions. Also, a dead body from a house fire, which is exposed to intense heat, will decompose at a much slower rate than a dead body not exposed to smoke and intense heat. Smoke and heat serve as preservatives. Low heat will accelerate the putrefaction process. Radiant heat in a dry environment will cause tissue to become firm due to dehydration and coagulation of the soft tissues; hair is often still present but may be discolored by smoke. How this process advances depends on the amount of heat and humidity and the duration of exposure. Also, intense heat may produce postmortem artifacts that may be misinterpreted as antemortem injury, such as an epidural hemorrhage. Epidural hemorrhage may be postmortem and is caused by heat-related contracture of the dura mater, forcing blood from adjacent vessels into the epidural space. Subdural hemorrhages do not occur in this manner and are antemortem injuries.

Thermal burns sustained by fire may be accompanied by smoke inhalation. In general, most fatalities from house fires are caused by smoke inhalation. Decedents dying directly in house fires usually have mostly postmortem burns. Fire fatalities that occur outside in an open space often do not have significant smoke inhalation because the smoke rises rapidly and is not inhaled. In the case of a flash fire, inhaled super-heated gases damage the upper airways, including the laryngeal mucosa, causing death from reflexive closure of the airway at the level of the vocal cords with asphyxia and eventual fatal arrhythmia. The effects of smoke inhalation are often reflected by the amount of carbon monoxide present in the blood. This depends on the nature of the burning material. There are often other poisonous substances in smoke associated with house fires that may not be routinely tested for in toxicological analysis.

There are often other significant poisons associated with burning materials that can rapidly contribute to death, such as hydrogen cyanide. A fire victim does not need a lethal level of carbon monoxide to die of smoke inhalation. Carbon monoxide is produced from incomplete combustion of organic fuels. Carbon monoxide is a colorless, odorless gas that reversibly binds the hemoglobin molecule approximately 200 times greater than oxygen, resulting in hypoxia and possible death. Levels of carbon monoxide that exceed 50% saturation are considered life-threatening, but may cause death with levels less than 26% saturation. Carbon monoxide levels of greater than 80% are possible. These levels need to be correlated with the physiologic disease state of the individual's body, including heart disease, for example. Someone with marked coronary-artery atherosclerosis would often require much less carbon monoxide exposure to produce death than a young healthy individual with slight atherosclerosis. Cigarette smokers may reach carbon monoxide levels of 10%. Carbon monoxide levels of 15%–30% are associated with dizziness, nausea, and headache. Cherry-red lividity first becomes apparent at levels of 30%–35%. The half-life for carboxyhemoglobin elimination in a resting adult at sea level is generally 4–5 hours. This may be reduced to 80 minutes following administration of pure oxygen, and may be further reduced to 24 minutes by using oxygen at 3 atmospheres of pressure. Primary elimination of unchanged carbon monoxide occurs by pulmonary excretion. Also, if there is more than one fatality without obvious cause, one should consider carbon monoxide poisoning.

Electrical burns may be due to low- or high-voltage exposure. The electrical current may be direct or alternating in nature. Alternating current is more likely to cause a fatal cardiac arrhythmia than direct current. High voltage is generally defined as greater than 1000 volts for alternating current and greater than 1500 volts for direct current. High-voltage burns are usually associated with extensive obvious injury. Low voltage is generally defined as being less than 1000 volts for alternating current and less than 1500 volts for direct current. Low-voltage burns may present with no visible marks to the body's surface at all. The degree of injury depends on many factors, including the duration of exposure and the amount of heat generated.

Electrical burns may also occur as a result of a lightning strike. Lightning bolts occur with an enormous short-term release of electricity, often producing minimal injuries. Lightning strikes may also produce a fern-like red pattern on the skin's surface. Patterns similar to this may be observed in high-voltage electrocution. These types of electrical discharges present with different autopsy findings. The mechanism of death is usually arrhythmia and more likely to occur if the current passes directly through the heart. Death may also occur due to asphyxia if there is interference with the central nervous system's respiratory centers or paralysis of the chest muscles. To complete an electrical circuit one needs an entrance and exit point for electricity to pass through the body. An otherwise healthy individual may be found lying barefoot and on a damp floor next to a power tool with a frayed electrical cord. This is why adequate scene investigation is crucial. It is also important to keep the electrical device as evidence to be tested, and to prevent any other fatalities. There may or may not be burns to the body's surface at autopsy.

Chemical burns are due to exposures to caustic substances. These burns most often involve injury to the skin or mucosa, leaving red discoloration or sloughing of the superficial layers. More extensive injuries may involve damage to the underlying tissue, including bone. This depends on the strength and nature of the caustic substance, which include acids, bases, and other chemicals that can damage the body. Individuals may die acutely following chemical burns from many different mechanisms including hemorrhage, infection, or dehydration, or they may die many years following such injuries. For instance, if an individual attempts to commit suicide by ingesting lye 20 years earlier and later develops esophageal cancer as a result of these burns, the manner of death would be suicide. Children may accidently drink caustic substances, leading to gastrointestinal perforation that may lead to adhesion and gastrointestinal obstruction many years later. In this case, the manner of death would be accidental. It is always very important to find out the initial event that starts the ball rolling in the sequence of events that eventually leads to an individual's demise.

Radiation is defined as energy distributed as waves or particles across the electromagnetic spectrum. This includes electric, radio, radar, microwaves, infrared, visible light (lasers), ultraviolet light, x-rays, gamma rays, and cosmic radiation. Waves are characterized as having long wavelengths and low frequencies, whereas particles have short wavelengths and high frequencies. The types of biological effects vary greatly depending on the type of radiation, duration of exposure, and intermediate barriers. Acute exposure to skin may range from erythema to overt necrosis with eventual epidermal atrophy and dermal fibrosis. Biological effects include cataracts, burns to the retina and skin, necrosis, fibrosis, and cancer. Generally speaking, proliferating cells are affected more substantially with acute exposure as indicated by damage to the gastrointestinal and hematopoietic systems with increased risks of infection, nausea, vomiting, diarrhea, and hemorrhage. Damage to DNA may eventually lead to many different forms of cancer.

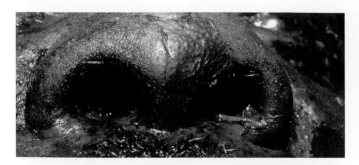

Figure 9.1 Soot within the nares and in the lower airway, indicating smoke inhalation.

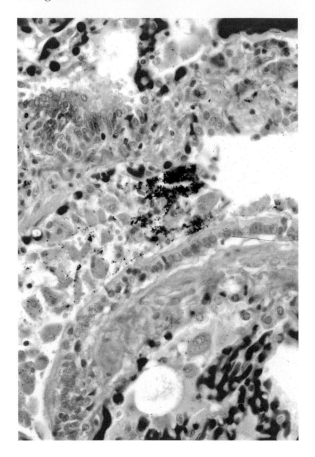

Figure 9.3 Microscopic view of lung with soot deposition in the distal bronchi.

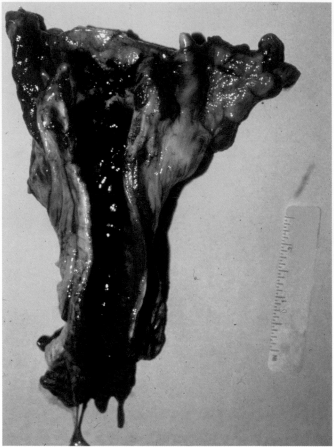

Figure 9.2 Smoke inhalation with soot deposition on the airway mucosa of the larynx and trachea.

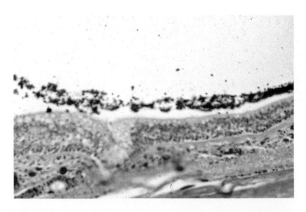

Figure 9.4 Microscopic view of airway with soot deposition on the surface of respiratory epithelium.

Figure 9.5 Note the soot extending down into the bronchial distribution.

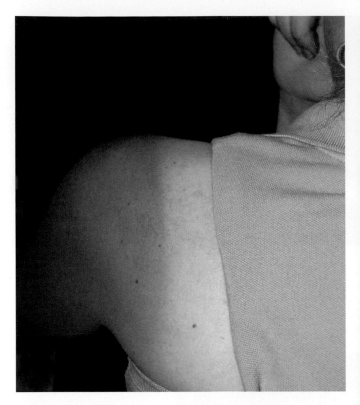

Figure 9.6 First-degree burn characterized by red discoloration with injury limited to the superficial layers of the skin including the epidermis; for example, a sunburn.

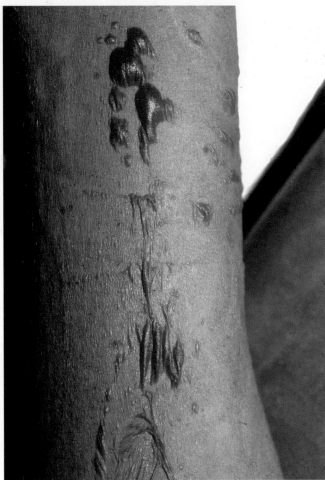

Figure 9.7 Second-degree thermal burns characterized by fluid-filled blister formation. Second-degree burns include damage to both the epidermis and the dermis. Second-degree burns are often more painful than third-degree burns due to less destruction of nerve endings.

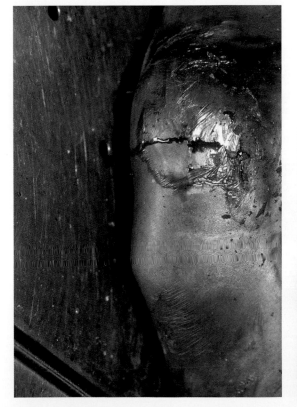

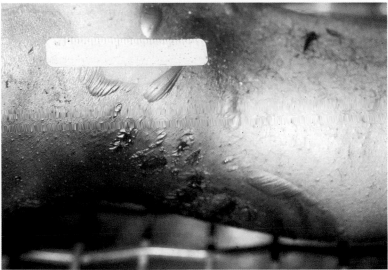

Figures 9.8 and 9.9 Second- to third-degree thermal burns with some areas of black charring due to forth-degree burns. There is debate in the literature about distinguishing antemortem from postmortem burns. Many believe blister formation in a nongravity-dependent area with a red border indicates vital reaction and antemortem occurrence.

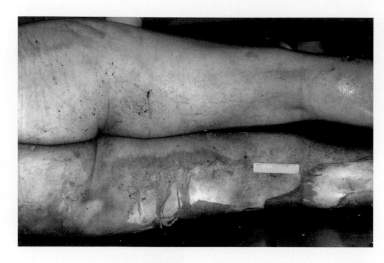

Figure 9.10 First- to third-degree thermal burns involving the posterior aspect of the left thigh and gluteal region. The right leg is without thermal burns. First-degree thermal burns in this picture are characterized by the red discoloration without blister formation or skin slippage. Note the areas of collapsed blister formation, which are consistent with a postmortem burn. Sometimes it is difficult to interpret antemortem burns if continued heat causes fluid-filled blisters to collapse and fluid to evaporate. Most fire fatalities succumb from smoke inhalation before extensive burns occur.

Figure 9.11 Second- to third-degree thermal burn with skin slippage and collapsed blister formation.

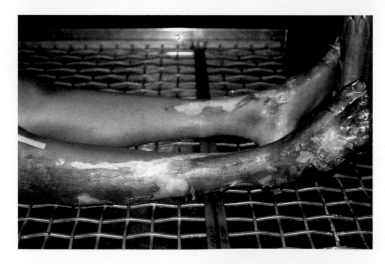

Figure 9.12 Full-thickness or third-degree burns in an individual who lived hours after being shot in the head and having their residence set on fire to destroy evidence. Full thickness refers to involvement of the epidermis, dermis, and subcutaneous layers. These are often less painful than second-degree burns due to more damage of nerve endings.

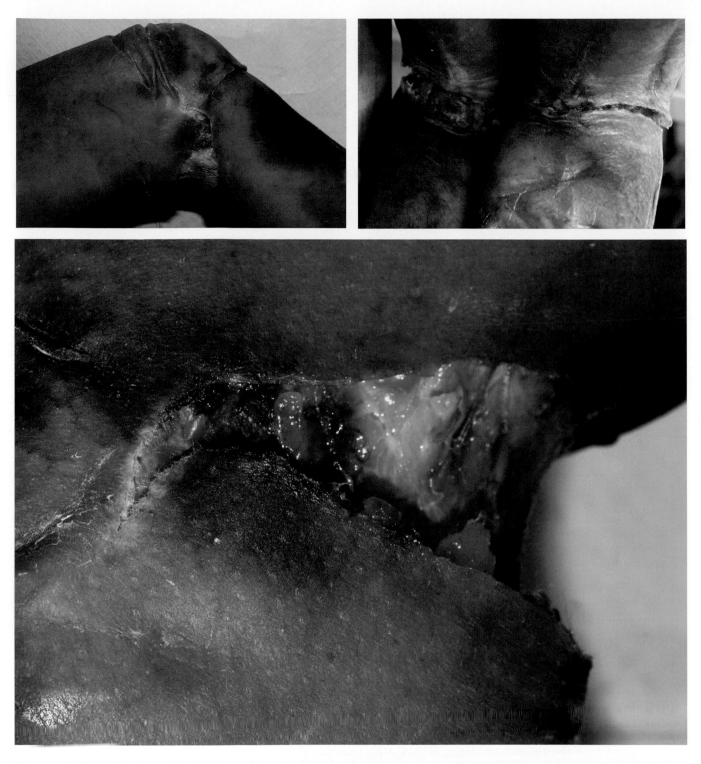

Figures 9.13–9.15 This individual committed suicide by running her car inside a closed garage. She had the heater turned up to full, the gas tank was empty, and she had not been seen for several days. Her body showed significant mummification with putrefaction and radiant heat damage. Note these postmortem anemic lacerations in the popliteal regions created when the body was moved to the autopsy table. Drying of skin is associated with decreased elasticity with greater tendency to lacerate instead of stretch. Also note the pale pink discoloration of the muscle due to prolonged exposure to low heat. This individual's carboxyhemoglobin level was only 17%, and death was attributed to asphyxia from exhaust inhalation with decreased oxygen as well.

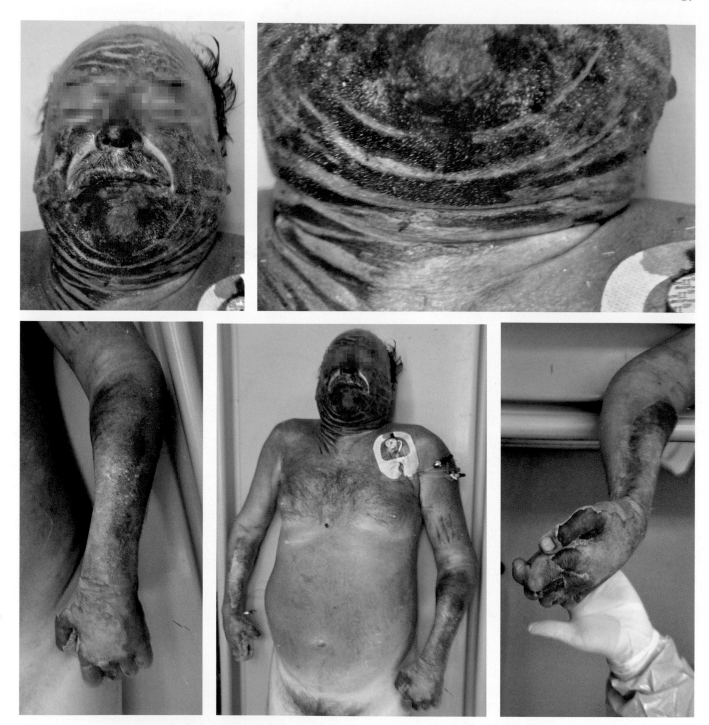

Figures 9.16–9.20 First- to third-degree thermal burns. This individual died as a result of a flash fire when his acetylene tank exploded. Note the uninvolved creases of skin on his face caused by recoiling due to the explosion. Note the sparing of the skin at the trunk and upper arms due to protection by his short-sleeve shirt. He had swelling and hyperemia of the upper airway, leading to obstruction and eventual fatal arrhythmia.

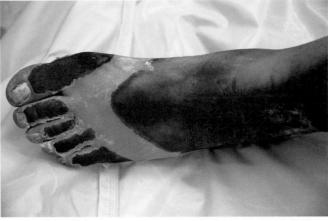

Figure 9.21 Note the sparing of thermal injury at the bottom of the decedent's foot due to protection by a shoe.

Figure 9.22 This is self-immolation of an individual who was wearing sandals. Note the lack of thermal injury in the region protected by the shoe strap.

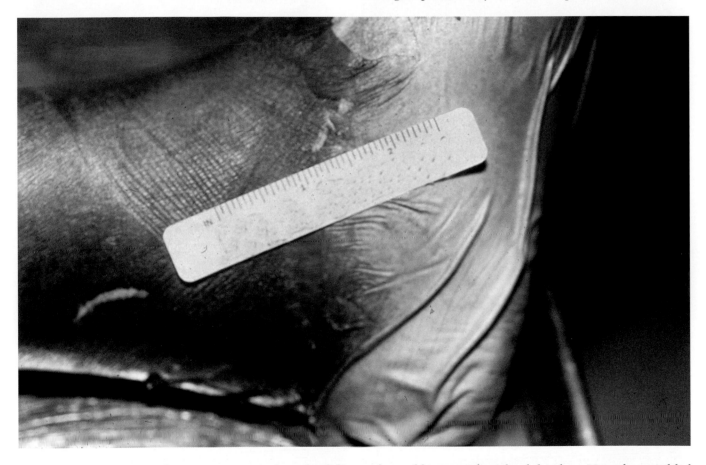

Figure 9.23 This image demonstrates second- to third-degree thermal burns to the sole of this foot. Note the wrinkled thick skin demonstrating skin slippage.

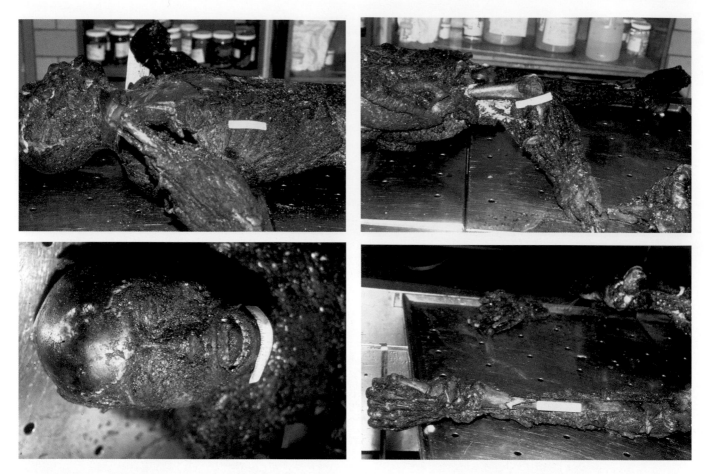

Figures 9.24–9.27 Fourth-degree thermal burns with extensive charring, and exposed muscle and bone. Note the post-mortem skeletal fractures due to extensive heat. Also note the pugilistic stance of the body with arms raised.

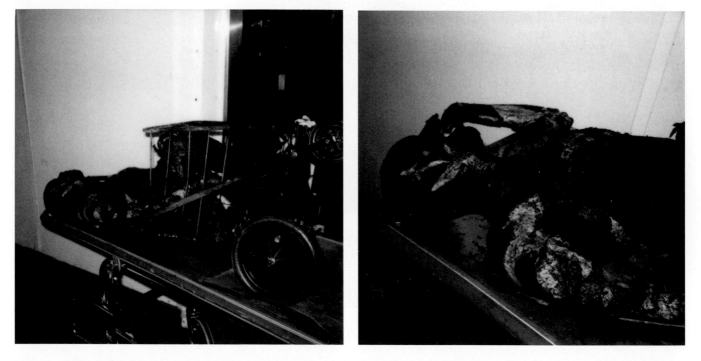

Figures 9.28 and 9.29 This individual was wheeled out of a building in a shopping cart and set on fire. Note the post-mortem cracking of the skin due to heat exposure. This is indicated by the exposed yellow subcutaneous tissue with no hemorrhage. There were extensive fourth-degree thermal burns to the entire body.

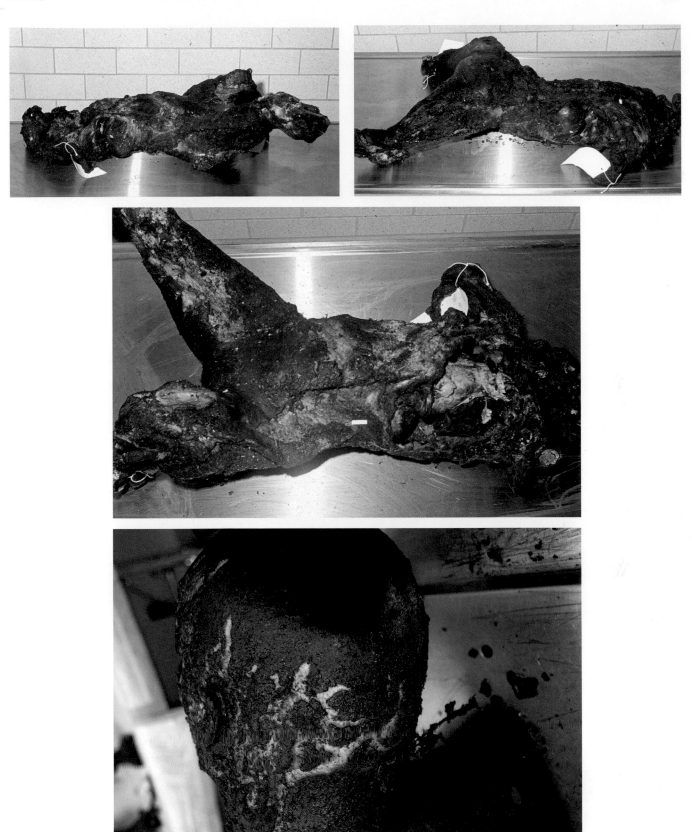

Figures 9.30–9.33 Postmortem fourth-degree burns. The organs of the trunk were remarkably well protected considering the amount of thermal injury to the surface.

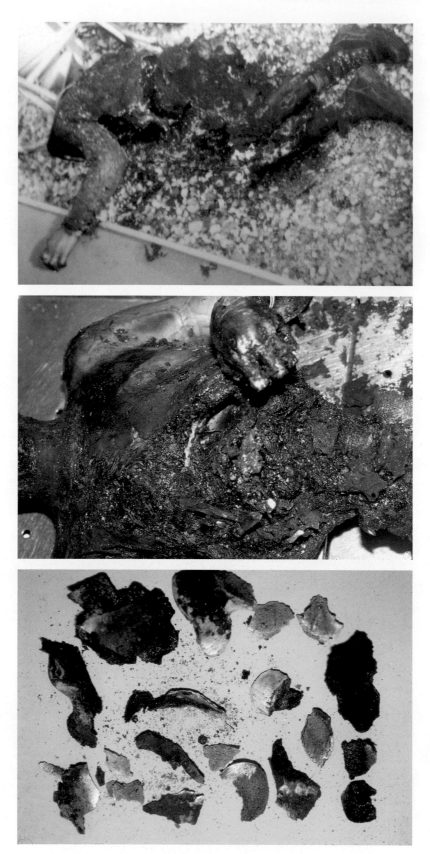

Figures 9.34–9.36 Extensive third- to fourth-degree thermal burns with partial skeletal fragmentation due to the wick effect. The wick effect refers to a self-perpetuating, low-intensity flame following ignition of certain materials contacting the body, where the skin is cracked from heat and the underlying fatty tissue is rendered into oil, which is absorbed into the charred clothing producing a wick. This low-level heat can produce extensive destruction to a body over hours. This process in the past has been referred to erroneously as spontaneous human combustion.

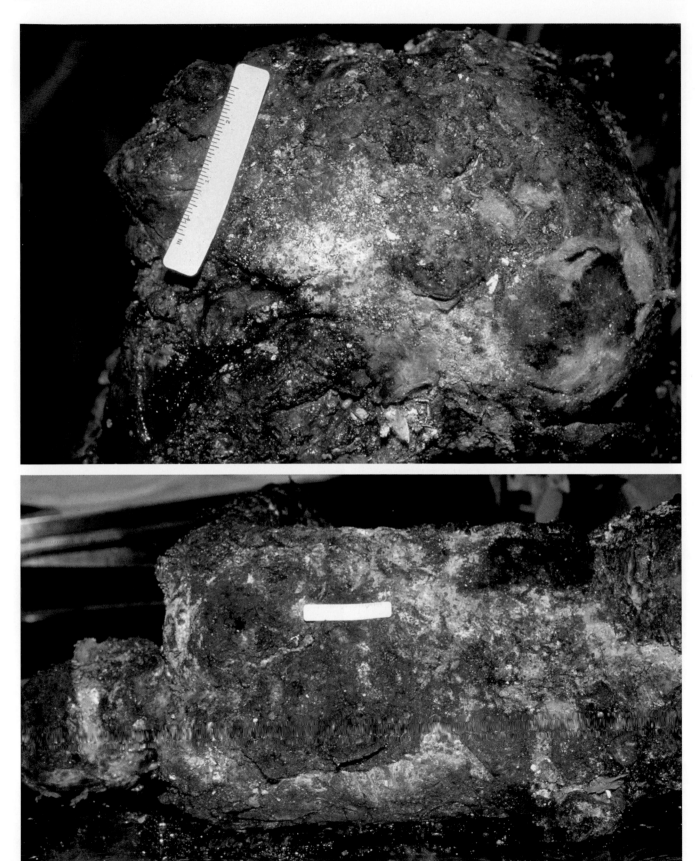

Figures 9.37 and 9.38 This is a rare finding of putrefactive change following extensive thermal injury. The decedent was involved in a fatal fire and the body was not discovered for several days after being soaked in water following fire extinguishing. Note the microorganisms and mold growing on the body surface shown by the gray-white discoloration. Putrefactive changes were markedly inhibited due to the effects of exposure to smoke and heat.

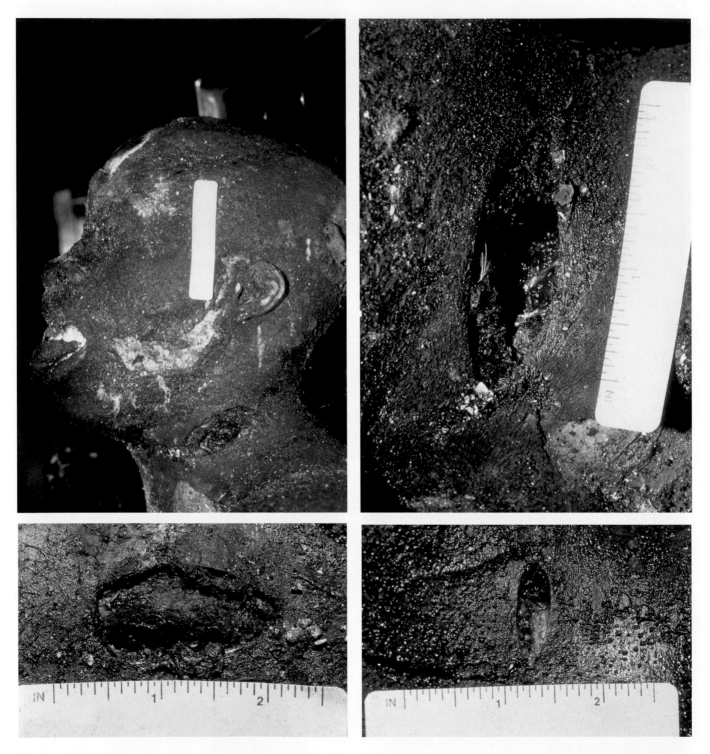

Figures 9.39–9.42 These are all examples of homicides where apartments or houses were set on fire to destroy evidence. Figures 9.39–9.41 are examples of antemortem stab wounds that have been altered by postmortem thermal burns. Note that the margins are relatively sharp and do not appear as though the skin has cracked secondary to heat exposure. Upon internal examination, these injuries become much more apparent with hemorrhage and blood accumulation. Note in Figure 9.38 there are areas of cracked skin with exposed yellow subcutaneous tissue without hemorrhage, which is indicative of postmortem thermal injuries. Note the wound at the upper aspect of the lateral left neck with hemorrhage due to an antemortem stab wound.

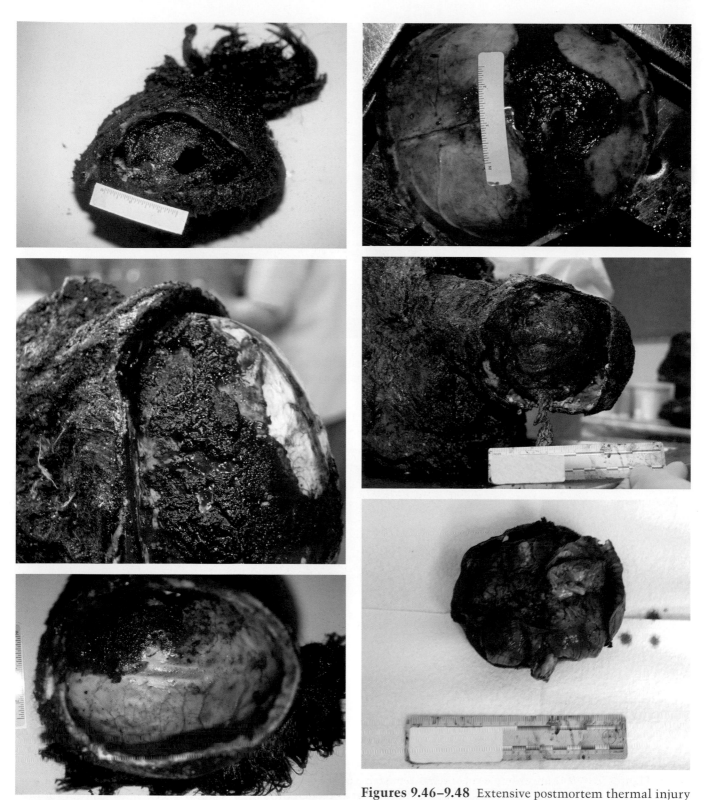

Figures 9.43–9.45 These figures demonstrate postmortem epidural hemorrhage. These can sometimes be misinterpreted as antemortem blunt-force trauma. With exposure to flames, the brain and dura mater contract, and blood is forced from the small vessels at the inner aspect of the skull and through the dural sinuses, producing epidural blood accumulation that will coagulate with heat.

Figures 9.46–9.48 Extensive postmortem thermal injury with brain shrinkage. Note the largest dimension of this entire adult brain is approximately 5 inches.

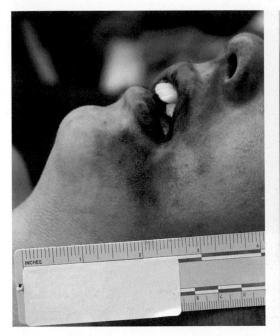
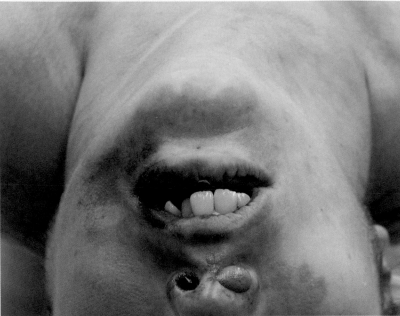

Figures 9.49 and 9.50 This individual died of an overdose and was found with dry vomitus of her face. Note the red discoloration caused by gastric acids producing burns around her mouth. This initially aroused suspicion of smothering with a pillow.

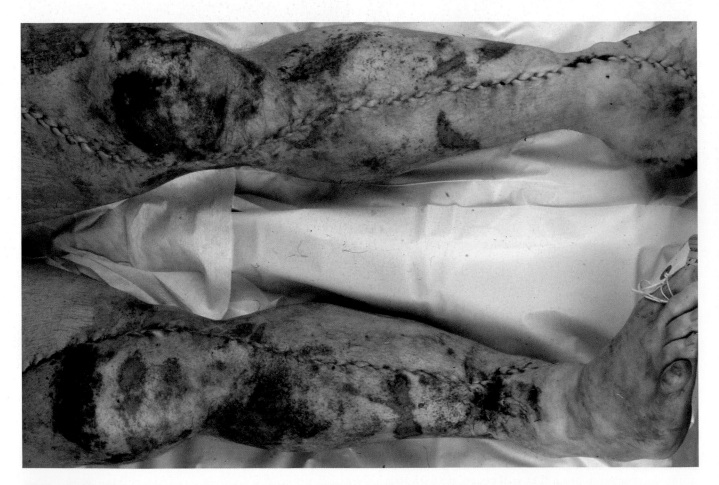

Figure 9.51 Chemical skin burns due to spilling sulfuric acid. The sutured linear incisions are due to organ donation with retrieval of bone and soft tissues.

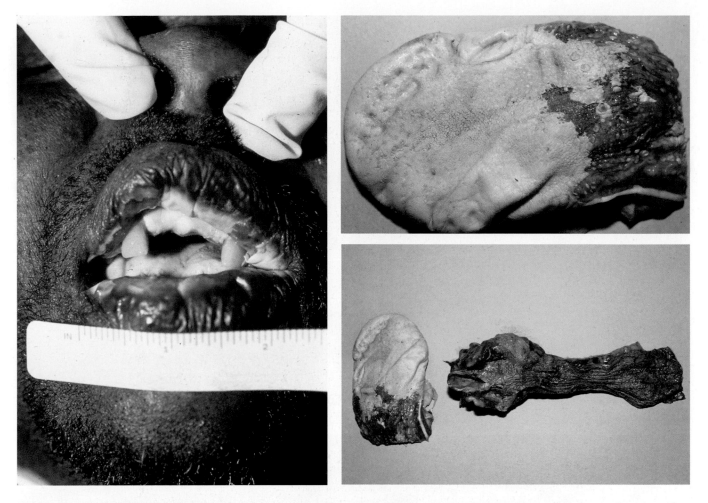

Figures 9.52–9.54 This individual drank a mixture of lye, kerosene, and other caustic chemicals. Note the white discoloration from chemical burns at the lips, mouth, tongue, and esophagus.

Figure 9.55 Note the red to brown discoloration in the abdominal cavity following gastric perforation and leakage of the caustic chemicals into the peritoneal cavity.

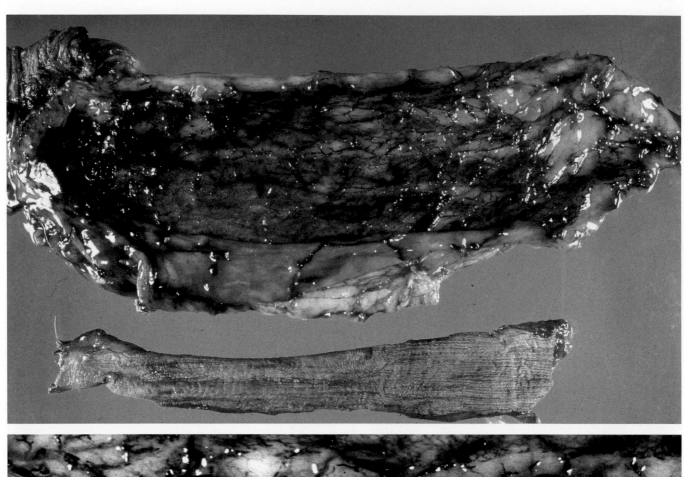

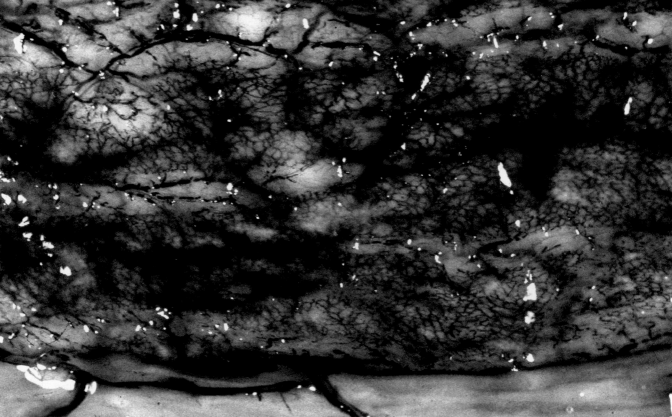

Figures 9.56 and 9.57 Chemical burns with disintegration of the stomach associated with drinking of a caustic liquid. Note the gray discoloration and chemical burns to the esophagus.

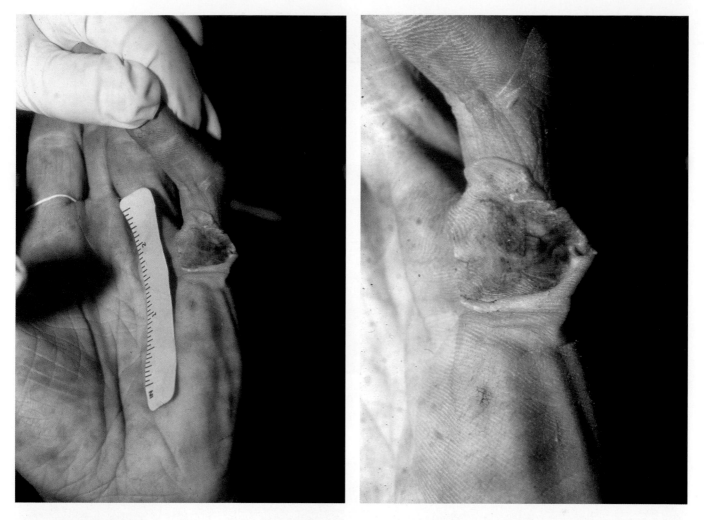

Figures 9.58 and 9.59 Electrical burn on this individual's hand who reached into a ceiling and grabbed onto a live wire. He was standing on an aluminum ladder wearing shorts. His leg contacting the ladder completed the circuit through his heart, producing a fatal arrhythmia.

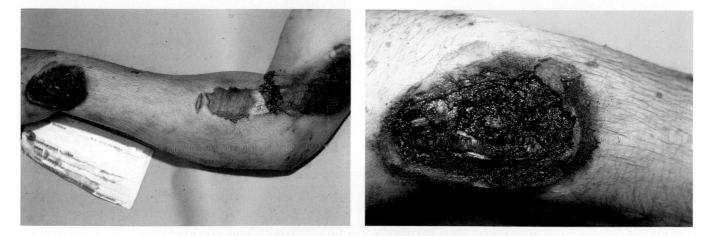

Figures 9.60 and 9.61 This individual fell from a subway platform onto the third rail and sustained these electrical burns.

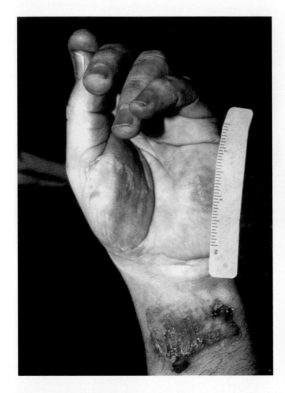

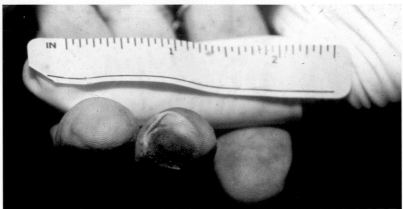

Figures 9.62 and 9.63 These are examples of second- to third-degree electrical burns caused by inadvertently contacting live wires at construction sites. These individuals died as a result of a fatal cardiac arrhythmia. The decedents fell to the ground lifeless within about 15–20 seconds after contact.

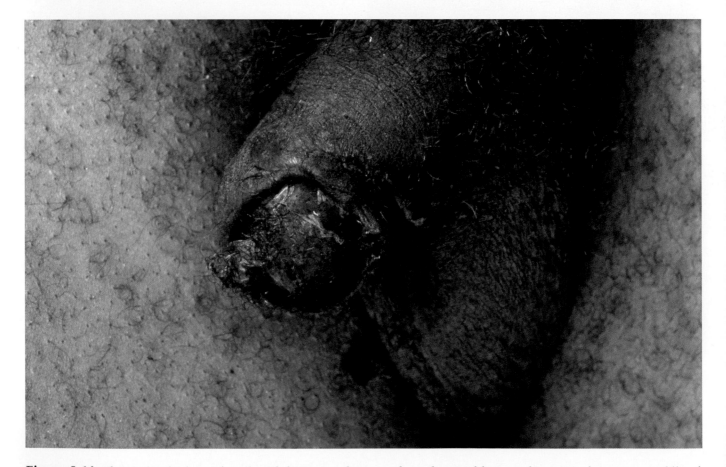

Figure 9.64 This individual was found with his pants down, and an electrical burn to his penis, lying in a puddle of urine, next to the third rail in a subway station. He was also intoxicated.

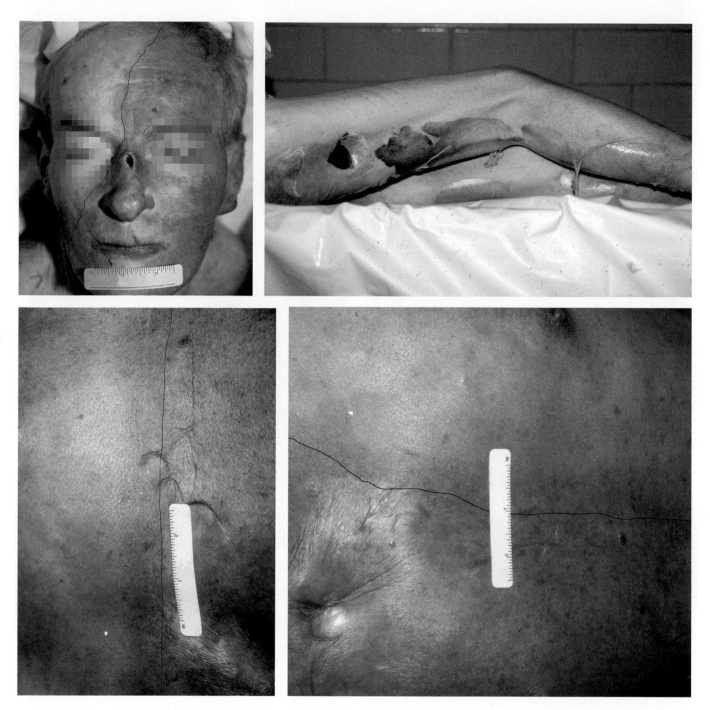

Figures 9.65–9.68 These individuals died of heart disease while taking a bath. These are examples of second- to third-degree postmortem burns due to being submerged in warm to hot water. Postmortem burns occur more readily with less heat than antemortem burns. Note the pictures demonstrate red discoloration with skin slippage and a sharply demarcated border defining the submerged and unsubmerged areas. To help the viewer distinguish between these regions we placed a line adjacent to this demarcation. Individuals who drown in bathtubs have some contributing factor dictating why they could not keep their head above the water. They may be neurologically compromised or intoxicated. People with seizures may accidentally drown.

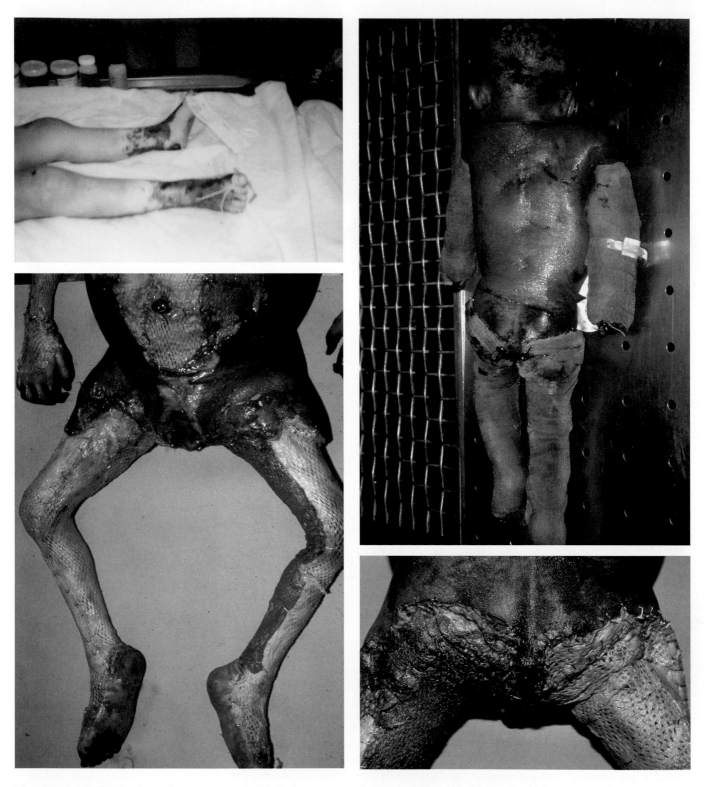

Figures 9.69–9.72 These demonstrate child abuse cases with homicidal scalding. Figure 9.72 demonstrates second- to third-degree burns to both feet and ankles from repeatedly being dunked in hot water. Figures 9.73–9.75 show skin grafting with therapeutic intervention in a child with fourth-degree burns who was left sitting in scalding water.

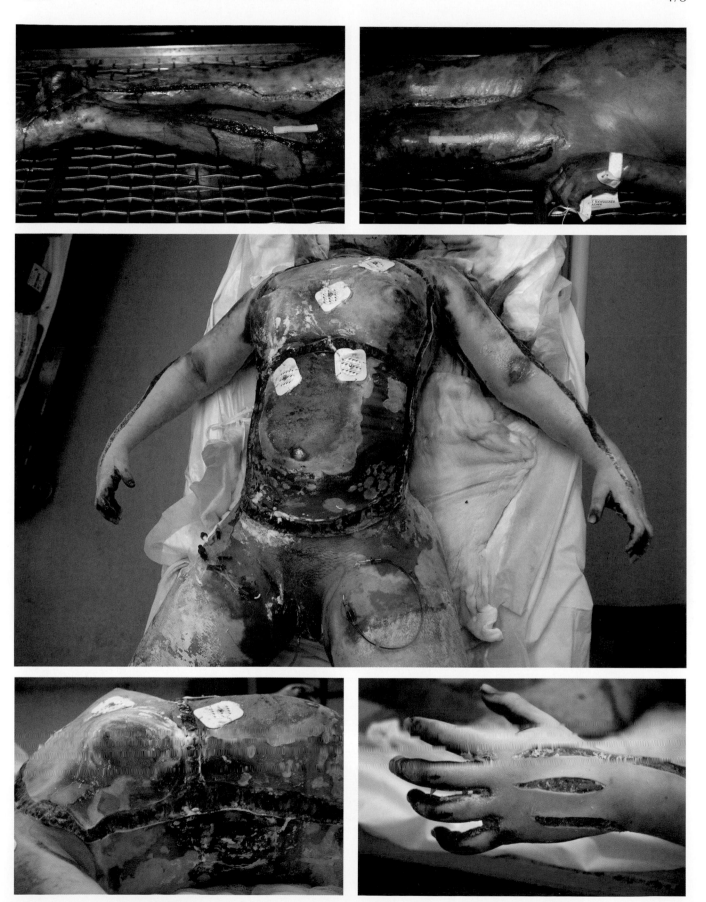

Figures 9.73–9.77 These are fasciotomy incisions made by physicians for medical therapy to relieve pressure in extremities.

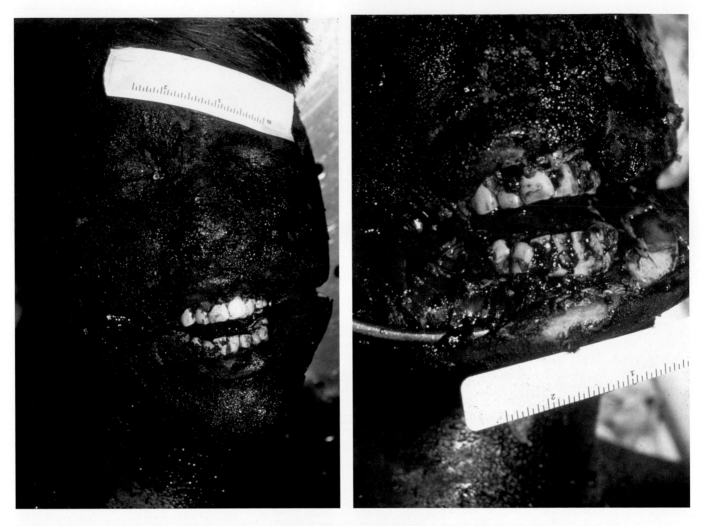

Figures 9.78 and 9.79 Identifications may be very challenging in fire fatalities. These cases may require dental analysis for identification. Incisions may be made in the face to access the teeth.

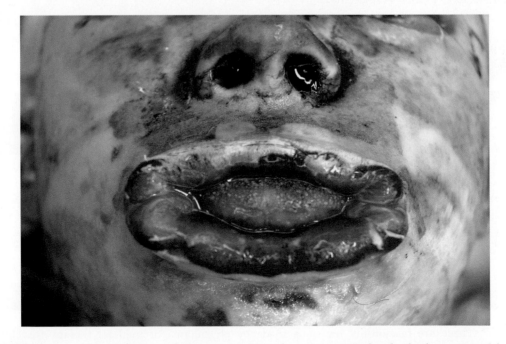

Figure 9.80 Swelling of the tongue due to inhaling super-heated gases in an individual who survived for one day.

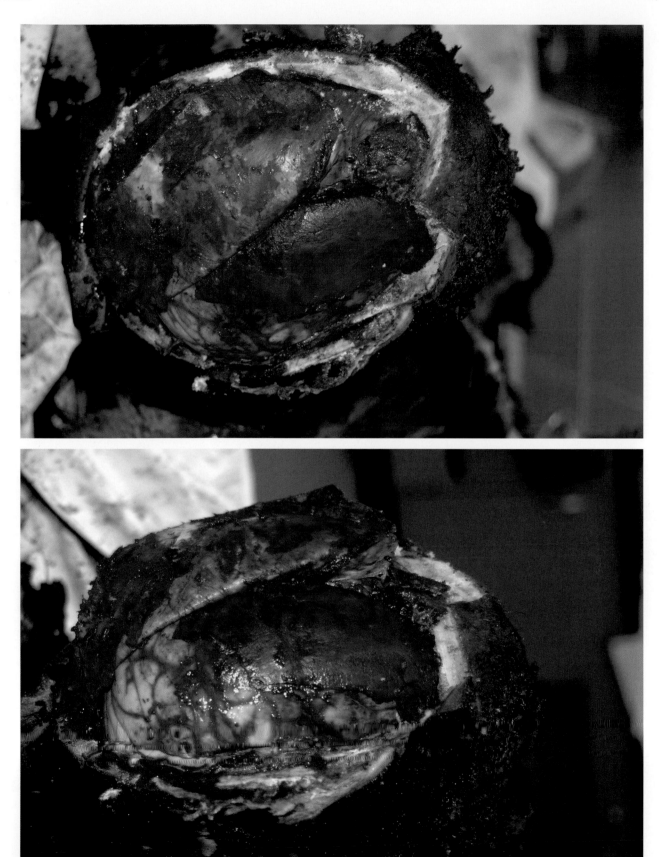

Figures 9.81 and 9.82 This individual crashed their airplane and sustained extensive blunt-force trauma. The above demonstrates an antemortem subdural hematoma altered by extensive postmortem thermal injuries.

Asphyxia

CHARLES A. CATANESE

10

This is a general term used to describe decreased oxygen uptake or use, together with decreased carbon dioxide elimination.

Airway obstruction may occur by smothering, neck compression, foreign body aspiration, excess secretions or swelling of the airway, etc. *Smothering* is defined as external occlusion of the mouth and/or nose, which prevents air exchange. Children may *aspirate foreign bodies* such as peanuts, hotdogs, popcorn, watch batteries, coins, etc., due to their impulsive nature. Adults who aspirate food are usually neurologically compromised (Alzheimer, Parkinson, brain infections, malignancies, etc.) or intoxicated. Airway obstruction due to *excess mucus or swelling*, as with asthma, anaphylaxis, or epiglottitis, may produce asphyxia. Also, various body positions may produce airway obstruction or the inability to expand one's chest *(positional asphyxia)* as with occupants of motor vehicles trapped after collisions or intoxicated people passing out and sliding into awkward positions that prevent air exchange.

Autopsy findings associated with *smothering* may be very subtle or nonexistent. Findings may include abrasions around the nose and/or mouth that *cannot* be explained by other means (e.g., resuscitative efforts). Great force is applied to the mouth and lips, which may cause tears to the frenulum of the lip, the mucous membrane that connects the inside of the lip to the corresponding gum. Smothering may occur with the use of hands or by placing an object over a face, such as a pillow.

Depending on the degree of force applied and the structures compressed, there may or may not be petechiae present on the skin of the face, mucous membranes, or in the eyes. Arguably, the greater the disparity in size and strength between the perpetrator and the victim (e.g., adult assaulting a young child), the less likely there will be a demonstrable injury such as petechiae and hemorrhages due to constant more overpowering force with little ability to effectively defend with struggle. It is important that in cases of suspected smothering, experienced police interrogators and medical investigators perform the interviews. In cases where autopsy findings are very subtle, well-documented descriptions of the circumstances with specific details are extremely important.

Chemicals can produce asphyxia. *Inert gases* such as methane or carbon dioxide will displace oxygen from the air and produce asphyxia by depletion or replacement of oxygen. Various *poisons* such as carbon monoxide or cyanide interfere with oxygen uptake and utilization, respectively.

Chest compression can produce asphyxia by *preventing air flow* into the lungs.

Neck compression, as with *hanging and strangulation*, can also produce asphyxia by obstruction of various neck structures, including the airway, venous circulation, and arterial circulation.

Interpretation of autopsy findings with respect to *hanging vs. strangulation* can be challenging. Each subheading below will describe the presenting classic and most common features of each, and then elaborate on less common features. It is important to realize that there is overlap between how the two present; depending on how the act is carried out, they may appear very similar. In establishing the manner of death, one should consider all aspects of the case including the past medical history (i.e., depression, end stage cancer, etc.), scene investigation, and autopsy findings.

Hanging refers to ligature compression of the neck mitigated by the gravitational forces of the hanging head, causing partial or complete obstruction of the neck structures, including blood vessels and the airway.

In a typical nonjudicial suicidal hanging an individual places a ligature with a slip knot encircling the superior aspect of his or her neck. He or she secures the other end of the rope to a fixed support and allows the entire or partial body weight to pull downward, occluding the neck structures until loss of consciousness and death. In this case there should be furrow pattern that matches the overlying ligature, which forms an inverted "V" mark or indentation, extending upward at the superior aspect of the neck and head. With the entire body weight pulling downward, all of the neck structures (i.e., arterial, venous, and airway) are usually occluded at the same time and one would not expect to find petechiae in the face or eyes. There are typically no hemorrhages or fractures of the neck structures or other injuries to the body indicating a struggle. The cervical vertebrae are rarely fractured in suicidal hangings. When the body hangs for longer periods of time, the furrow indentation becomes more prominent. Individuals cut down shortly after this act may have little or no furrow mark. This depends on the type of ligature used. A wide, soft ligature will leave less of a mark than a narrow, more resistant ligature. If the body is left to hang for days, decomposition with stretching may eventually lead to the head being pulled away from the body.

In the case of a judicial hanging, the body is dropped from a height to produce sufficient force to fracture the upper cervical vertebrae, resulting in spinal cord injury with cardiac and respiratory satiation.

An individual hanging in a sitting or lying position may have partial occlusion of the neck structures before loss of consciousness ensues. In situations where the body is adjacent to another structure, the individual may partially pull his or her body up and down, causing varying degrees of pressure–release before loss of consciousness. This will produce a similar effect to what is seen in strangulation. In these circumstances, the up-and-down motion of pressure release will obstruct different neck structures at different intervals. Venous circulation requires the least amount of pressure for occlusion, as compared to the arterial system and the airway. When venous circulation is obstructed and arterial circulation is not, the higher pressure arterial blood beats through the capillary beds, rupturing small blood vessels and producing petechiae. As this process continues, the hemorrhage size increases and may become confluent. These are most obvious within the sclera and conjunctivae. These movements may also produce hemorrhages or fractures to the neck structures, including the airway cartilages and hyoid bone. These findings are more characteristic for strangulation, but may be seen in hangings.

Though unusual, people have been known to tie their hands behind their backs during the process of hanging themselves. The individual may have tried to complete this act several times in the past but the will to survive overpowered the will to end life. The tied hands are usually loosely tangled and not tightly tied. This will give the individual enough time to prevent himself from stopping the process. There are usually no other signs of a struggle or defensive-type injuries.

With a free hanging and total body weight suspension, an otherwise healthy individual, using a slip knot, would be expected to lose consciousness within 15–20 seconds and suffer irreversible brain damage within 4–6 minutes.

Hanging is usually suicidal, but may be accidental or homicidal.

Strangulation may be by ligature or manual. A *ligature* is something flexible that can encircle the neck, like a cord, belt, or piece of clothing. *Manual* strangulation refers to the use of one's hands leading to compression and blockage of the neck structures.

Manual strangulation is usually characterized by multiple irregular, angulated, abraded contusions around the neck. The marks may be curvilinear, corresponding to fingernail marks. These external marks can be somewhat variable and can range from a few to many.

Ligature strangulation is usually characterized by a horizontal furrow or mark pattern around the neck. The extent of these injuries depends on the type of ligature, how broad and soft it is, the amount of struggle, etc.

The act of strangulation is often a very physically dominating, often non-premeditated, way of killing somebody. This act takes time and comes with the risk of injury to all those involved. The individual strangled is usually smaller and of weaker strength. Often a sexual component to the assault exists and a rape kit should be performed in all cases of suspected strangulation. Petechiae are usually present in the face and eyes. There are usually hemorrhages in the strap muscles of the neck, and there may be fractures of the laryngeal cartilages and/or hyoid bone. These fractures are more common in older victims because the cartilages are more calcified, brittle, and less elastic. Older people may also have osteoporosis. Younger victims or children tend to have more flexible upper airways that often will stretch or collapse rather than fracture. Depending on how great the struggle, the amount of force used, and the type of neck compression, there may or may not be petechiae and/or hemorrhages above the ligature or region of neck compression. The presence of petechiae formation is more likely when there is a pressure–release component associated with a struggle or if less variable force is applied and if the ligature is wide with a large surface area. The presence of petechiae is less common when the force is very strong, consistent, and applied with a small surface area ligature. The latter example is more similar in nature to a hanging. Victims of strangulation often have defensive-type injuries, including other abrasions and contusions to their bodies.

It is possible to ligature strangle yourself; it is not possible to manually strangle yourself. If one is able to apply enough force to lose consciousness manually, revival occurs after the pressure is released. Continued force is necessary for death to ensue.

Someone murdered by ligature strangulation may die within a similar time frame as someone hanged; however, the time frame is usually longer. If there are multiple petechiae with hemorrhages and fractures of the neck structures, whether ligature or manual, the time frame may be much longer. This latter example usually indicates pressure–release, pressure–release, over several minutes until loss of consciousness, and then continued pressure for several more minutes until death occurs. If an individual is released shortly following loss of consciousness, revival may follow.

Proper autopsy technique dictates that the *brain and visceral organs be removed prior to a layered neck dissection* being performed. Photographs of the neck dissection in layers are recommended.

Drowning occurs when water is inhaled, filling up the alveolar spaces and preventing gas exchange. Other definitions may include deaths that occur while submerged in a liquid. The manner of death will vary depending on how the individual came to be in the water. If the event is not witnessed, the manner often remains undetermined because it is unknown whether the individual was pushed, jumped, or slipped into the water. Also, with decomposition it may be impossible to tell whether the person died of drowning. Water in the lungs, or pulmonary edema and water within the paranasal sinus, is often present but neither is specific for only cases of drowning. These findings may also be found in cases with natural disease, including congestive heart failure with pulmonary edema. The degree of pulmonary edema may vary in a fraction of the cases due to the heart beating after respirations cease. As the heart beats, before eventual asystole, some of the fluid in the lungs will be absorbed and there may be little or no edema at the time of death. An adult may drown in a big pool or ocean but not in a small pool or bathtub unless *neurologically compromised or intoxicated*. Homicide victims are sometimes placed in a water-filled *bathtub* to wash away evidence. The story given may be, "I found him in the tub, and he must have drowned." Common sense would dictate that an individual does not need to move very much to get his head above the water.

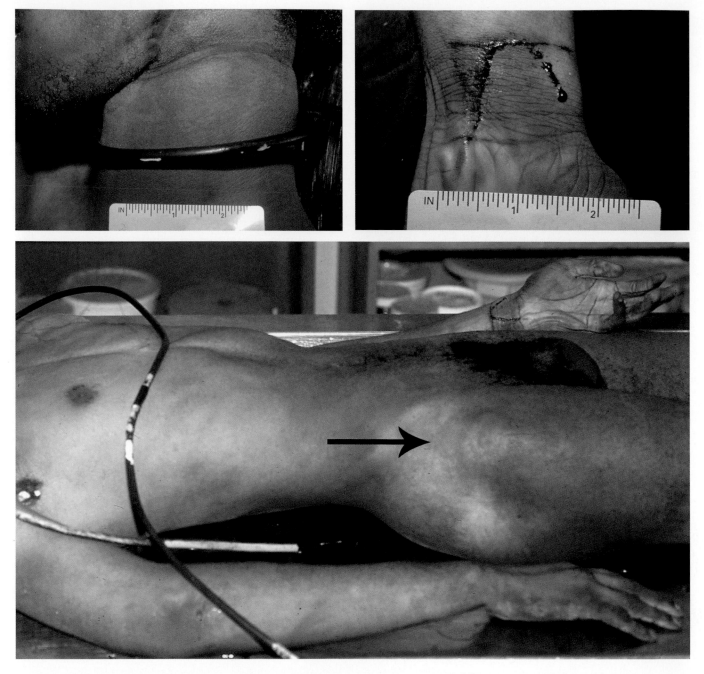

Figures 10.1–10.3 Suicidal hanging. Note the black cord that matches the underlying furrow pattern at the superior aspect of the neck with upward extension on the left side of the face. Also note the individual's lividity becomes more apparent and is fixed at the level of the upper thigh extending down to the feet. This fixed lividity pattern is appropriate for an individual that remained in an upright position for many hours after death. If his lividity was fixed posteriorly and not inferior, this would indicate prior scene alteration. There were hesitation marks at the wrist with blood seeping downward due to gravity.

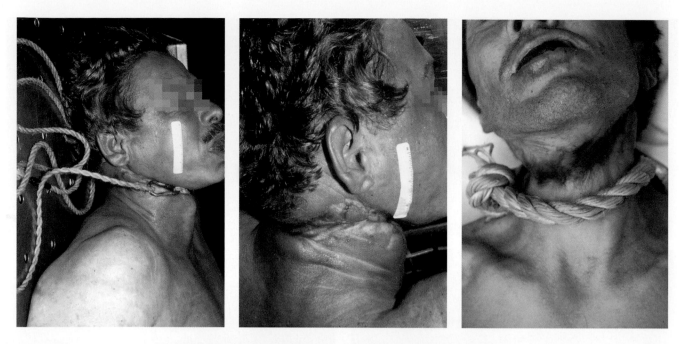

Figures 10.4–10.6 Suicidal hanging with matching rope and furrow pattern in circling superior aspect of the neck, forming a slight inverted "V" pattern behind the right ear.

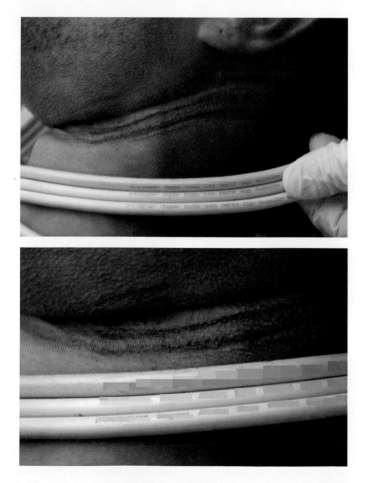

Figures 10.7 and 10.8 Suicidal hanging with computer cord.

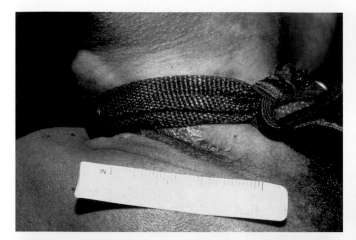

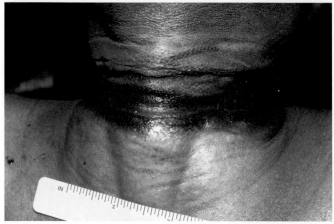

Figures 10.9 and 10.10 Suicidal hanging with nylon bag strap.

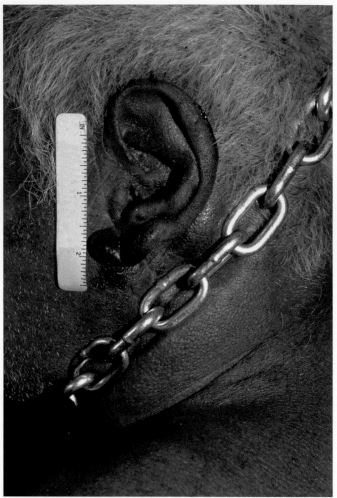

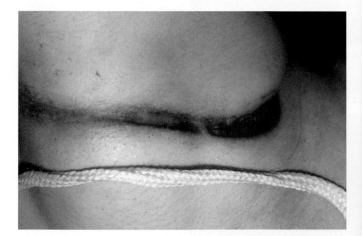

Figure 10.11 Accidental hanging in an individual with Alzheimer dementia who enjoyed whirling around in circles while sitting on a desk chair. They were left unattended for a short period of time by chronic care nursing staff, and got tangled in the cord from a window blind. This furrow pattern matches a blind cord as a ligature.

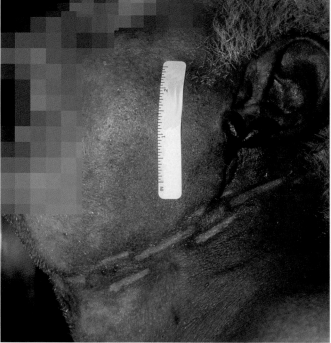

Figures 10.12 and 10.13 Suicidal hanging with chain.

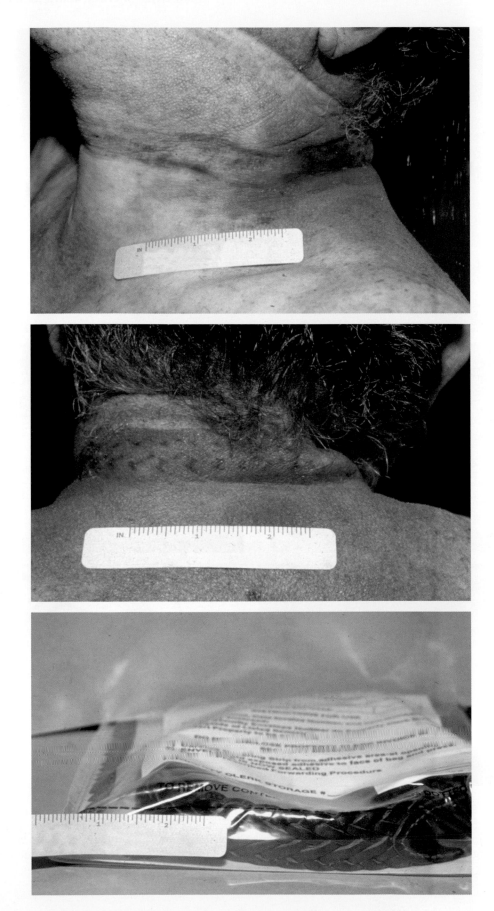

Figures 10.14–10.16 Suicidal hanging by braided belt. Note the matching skin pattern.

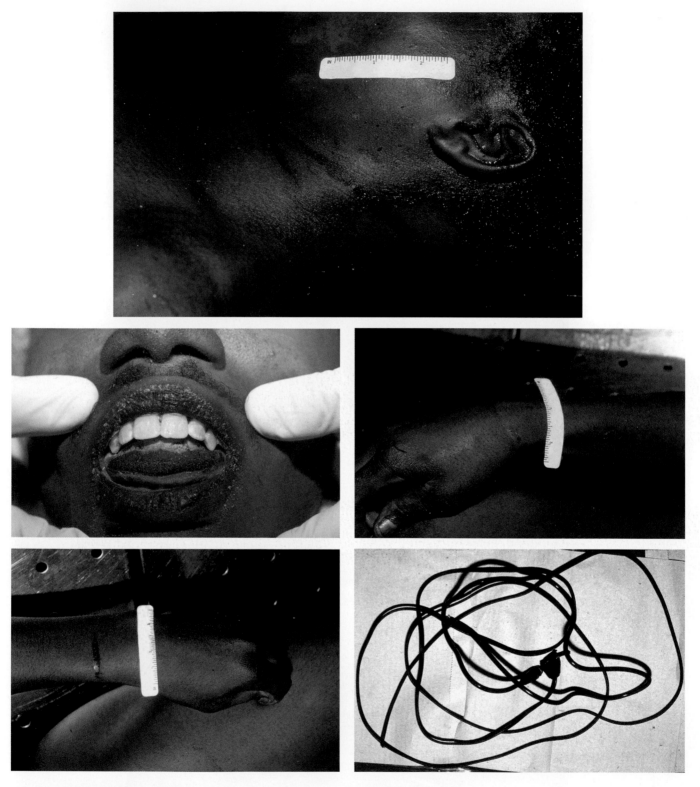

Figures 10.17–10.21 Suicidal hanging with earphone cord. This individual also took part of the cord and loosely wrapped his hands behind his back so he would not be able to reach up and prevent the hanging from being successful. It is not very unusual for people to hang themselves and loosely tie their hands in this fashion. Note the force of the ligature caused the tongue to protrude from his mouth. Also note the dark postmortem drying of the mucosa exposed to air.

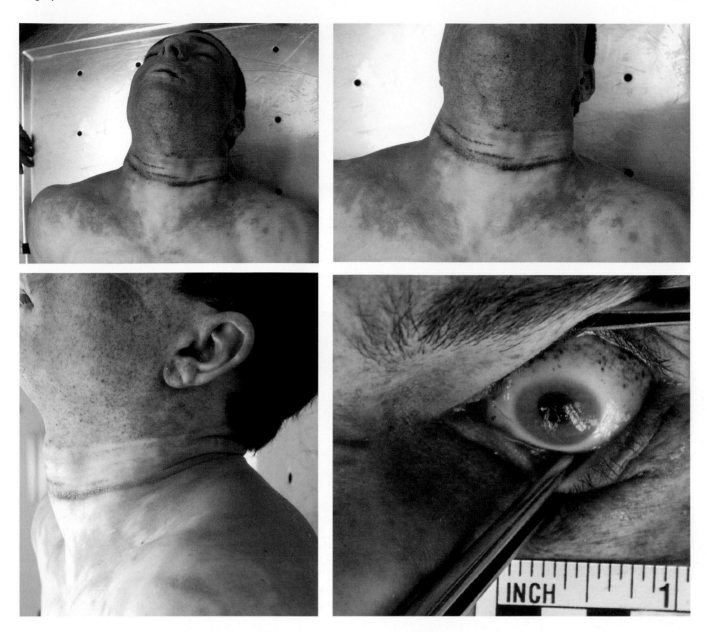

Figures 10.22–10.25 Suicidal hanging demonstrating marked congestion with petechial hemorrhages to the upper neck and head, above the ligature site. This individual had his feet contacting the floor. This indicates before losing consciousness he had periods of release by standing.

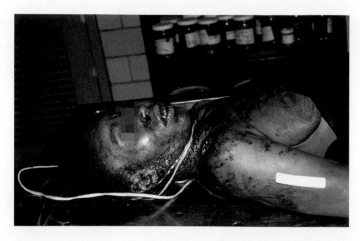

Figure 10.26 Homicidal ligature strangulation in a prostitute who had large amounts of cocaine and heroin in her system. Her fingers were also noted to be crushed by a pair of pliers during the assault.

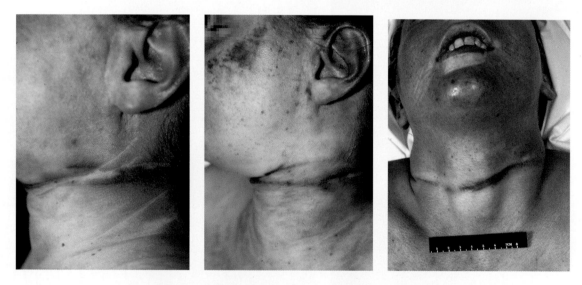

Figures 10.27–10.29 Homicidal ligature strangulation with horizontal cord marks surrounding the neck. Note the other injuries to the decedent's face in the second image, including abrasions. Both of these victims were also sexually assaulted.

Figure 10.30 This is a suicidal ligature strangulation in an individual with a long-standing history of depression who was found in a locked secured apartment with a suicide note. Note the cord is tied tightly around his neck. There is also a moderate state of putrefactive change with skin slippage, bloating, and purging.

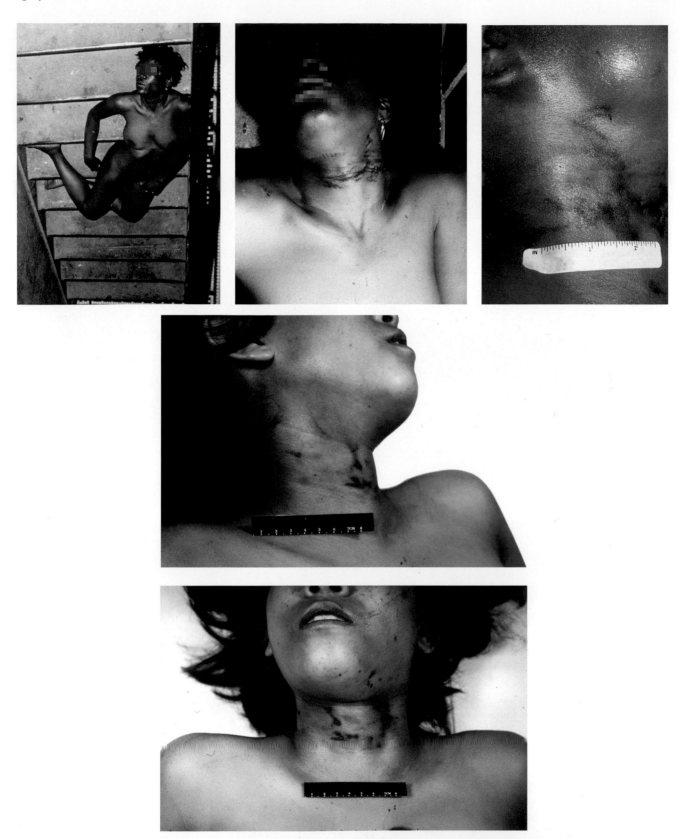

Figures 10.31–10.35 Manual strangulation. Note the multiple irregular abraded contusions at the neck. There were multiple areas of strap muscle hemorrhage and a fractured hyoid bone. In Figures 10.31–10.33 she was sexually assaulted in an apartment and left in a stairwell. Her clothing was discovered on the side of the building, after being thrown from a window. Each victim had multiple petechiae with areas of hemorrhage in the sclera and conjunctivae of each eye. The constellation of these findings is typical for a homicidal manual strangulation.

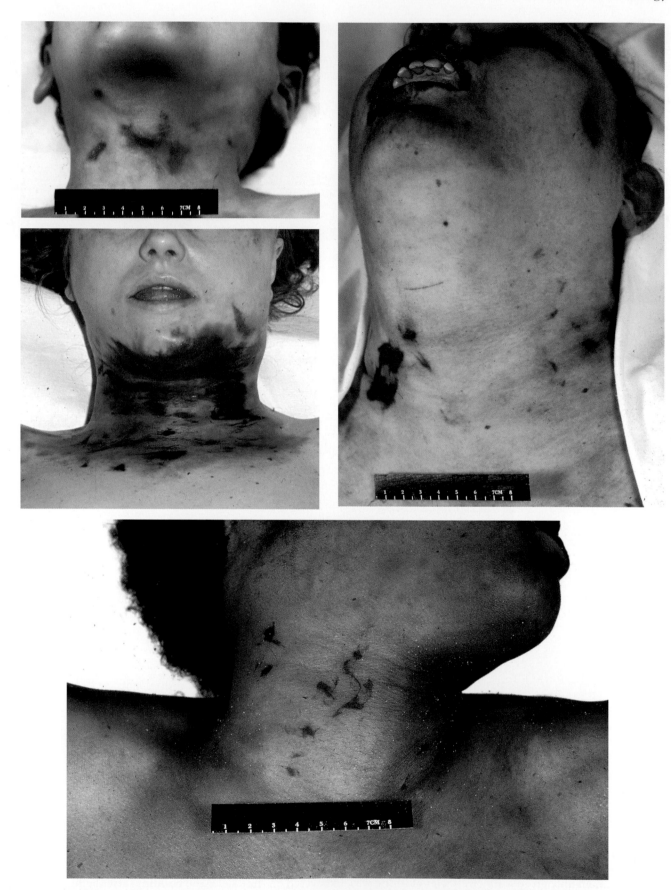

Figures 10.36–10.39 Manual strangulation. Each one of these individuals was sexually assaulted. It is important to perform rape kits on all strangulation homicides. Note the range of abrasions with darker drying and contusions. Also note the thin abrasions consistent with fingernail marks.

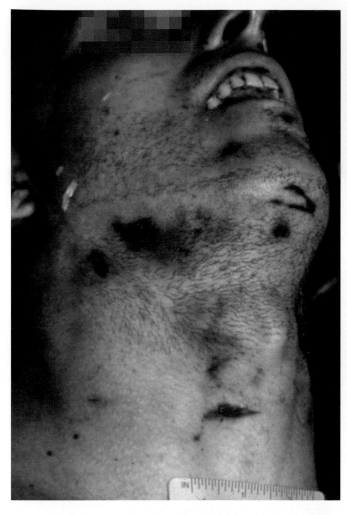

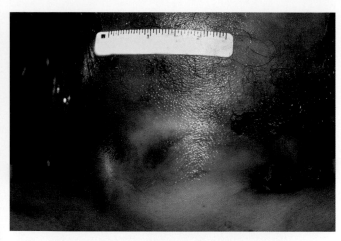

Figure 10.41 Manual strangulation. There is early decomposition with skin slippage. There are vague abrasions and superficial contusions at the neck. As decomposition progresses, it may become more difficult to interpret these findings.

Figure 10.40 Manual strangulation. Note the abraded contusions to the anterior neck.

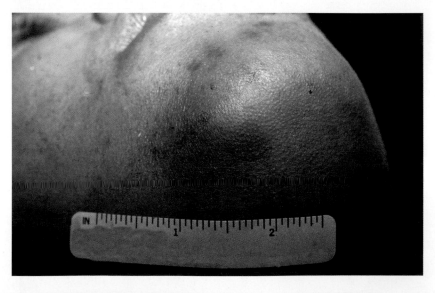

Figure 10.42 This individual was punched in the face and then yoked from behind during a sexual assault. There were no visible external injuries to the neck. There was a contusion at the border of the right chin. Careful internal examination after the brain and visceral organs had been removed revealed areas of hemorrhage within the anterior strap muscles and posterior paraspinal muscles. There were also petechiae with hemorrhage of the sclera and conjunctivae. This individual was found face down and the eye hemorrhages were initially thought by some to be associated with postmortem lividity. The perpetrator was caught after bragging about the assault.

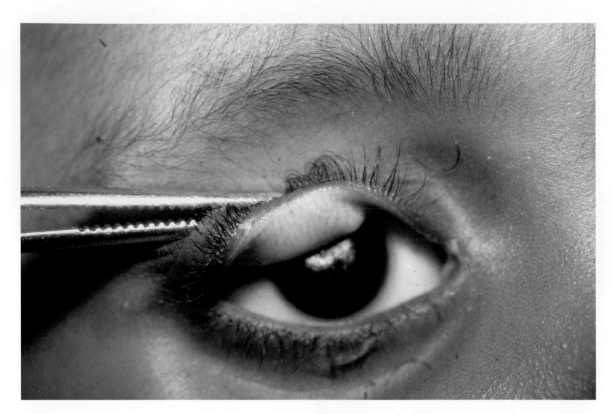

Figure 10.43 This image demonstrates an eye from a person who hanged himself. Note there are no petechiae or scleral/ conjunctival hemorrhages. The decedent's weight pulling down on the ligature produced a significant enough force to obstruct the entire blood supply to the head. Therefore, there was no pressure release mechanism, leading to capillary rupture and hemorrhage. The absence of scleral or conjunctivae hemorrhages is more typical in hanging fatalities.

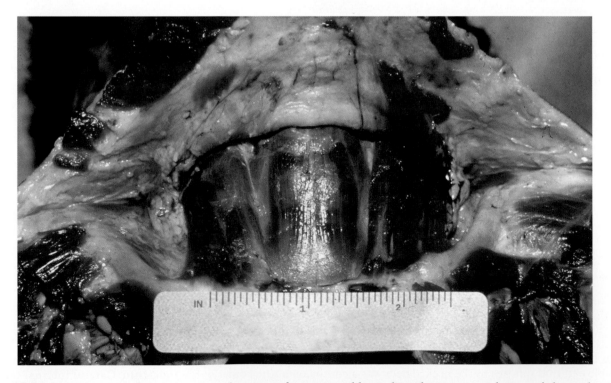

Figure 10.44 Anterior neck dissection after the visceral organs and brain have been removed. Part of the undersurface of the platysma muscle is visible at the top of this image adjacent to the yellow subcutaneous tissue of the neck. The anterior strap muscles are visible directly above the label and are free of antemortem injury. There were no hemorrhages or fractures of the remaining neck structures. The absence of injuries is common in hanging fatalities.

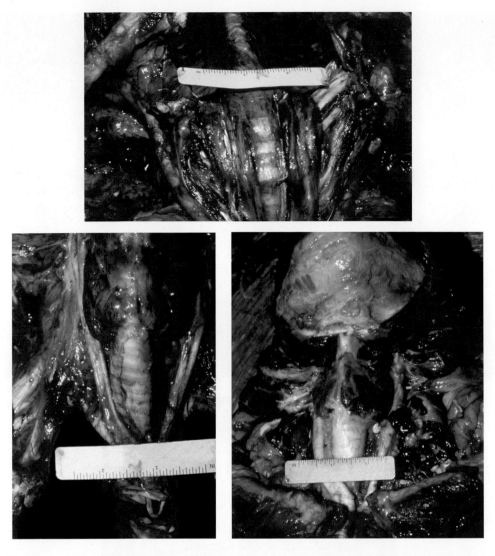

Figures 10.45–10.47 These figures demonstrate anterior neck dissections with no hemorrhages. The absence of hemorrhage is typical for most hangings.

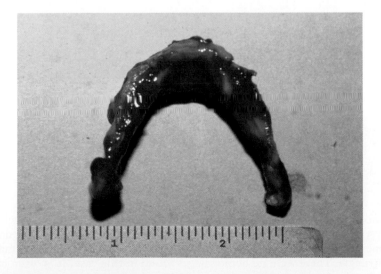

Figure 10.48 This demonstrates a normal hyoid bone with no fractures or contusions.

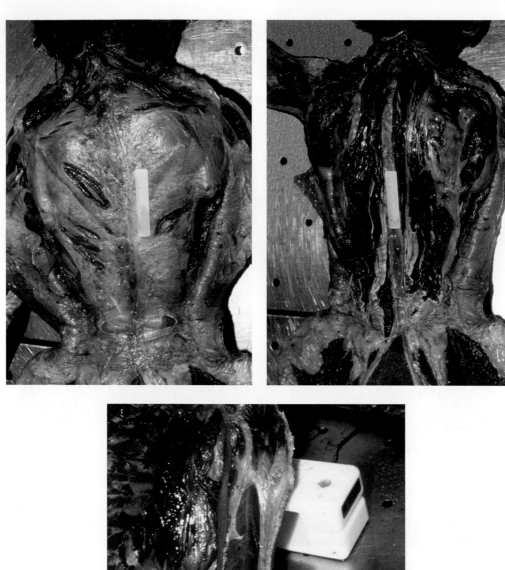

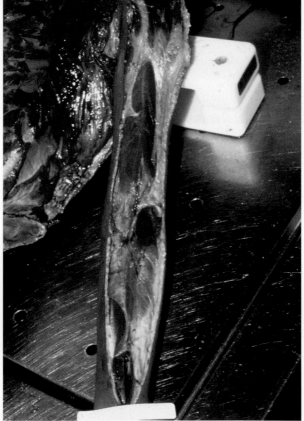

Figures 10.49–10.51 Some cases may require further evaluation, including a posterior neck and back dissection. This case involved a 12-year-old African American child that was strangled. Dissection should be done in a layer-by-layer fashion until the surface of bone is exposed. It is important to dissect the arms as well, which may demonstrate contusions from being held during a struggle. There were no hemorrhages found in this case. It is often more difficult to externally visualize contusions in darker-skinned individuals.

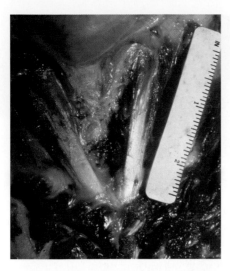

Figure 10.52 Strangulation. Hemorrhage of the medial left sternocleidomastoid muscle.

Figure 10.53 Strangulation. Note the large hemorrhage to the anterior neck structures including the left sterno-hyoid muscle.

Figure 10.54 Strangulation. Note the hemorrhage in the anterior neck structures.

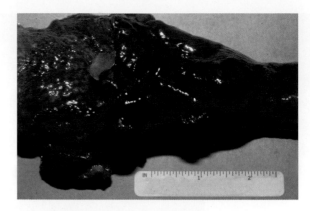

Figure 10.55 Strangulation. Note the hemorrhage overlying the left superior horn of the thyroid cartilage. The underlying cartilage was fractured.

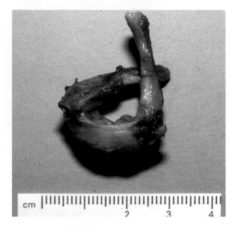

Figure 10.56 Note the fractures of this hyoid bone with vague hemorrhages in a decedent with slight to moderate decomposition. Fractures of the hyoid bone are often found in association with homicidal strangulation. The presence of a hyoid bone fracture does not indicate the case must be a strangulation, and the absence of fractures to the hyoid bone does not indicate the decedent was not strangled. Fractures can occur as a result of a blunt impact as well.

Figure 10.57 Strangulation. Posterior neck dissection with hemorrhage to the superior aspect of the semispinalis capitis muscle.

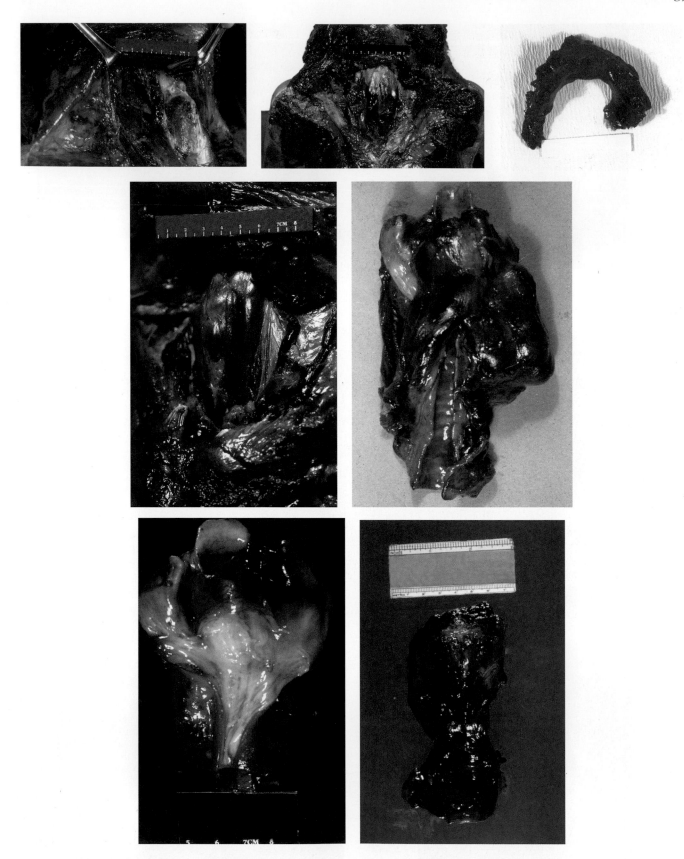

Figures 10.58–10.64 Cases of homicidal strangulation demonstrating multiple areas of red contusion caused by blunt-force trauma producing blood vessel injury with hemorrhage due to squeezing and/or blunt impacts. Note the fractured hyoid bone demonstrated in Figure 10.60; it more typically occurs in older individuals due to increased calcification.

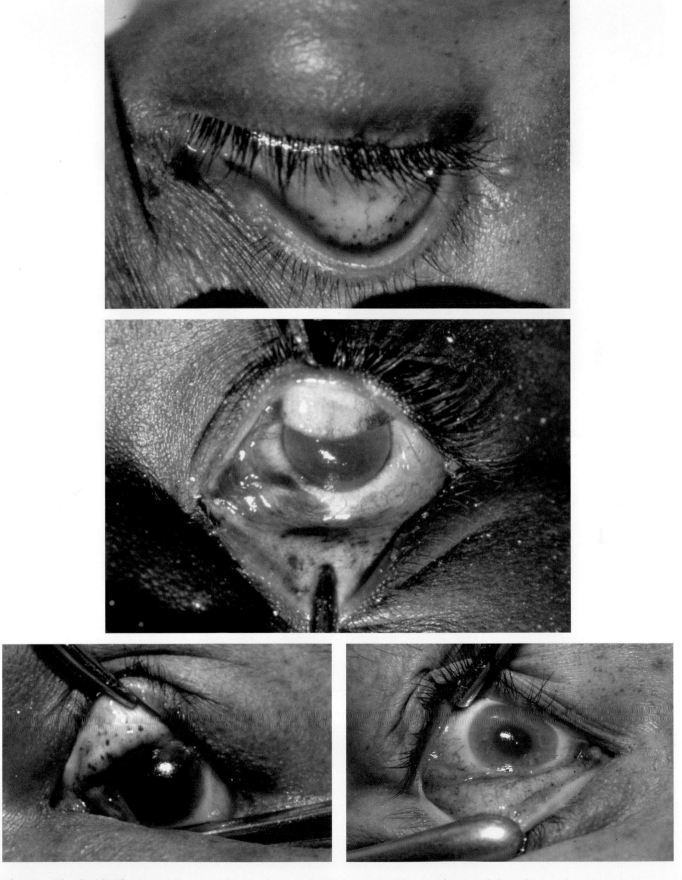

Figures 10.65–10.68 Cases of strangulation demonstrating petechial hemorrhages of the sclera and conjunctivae.

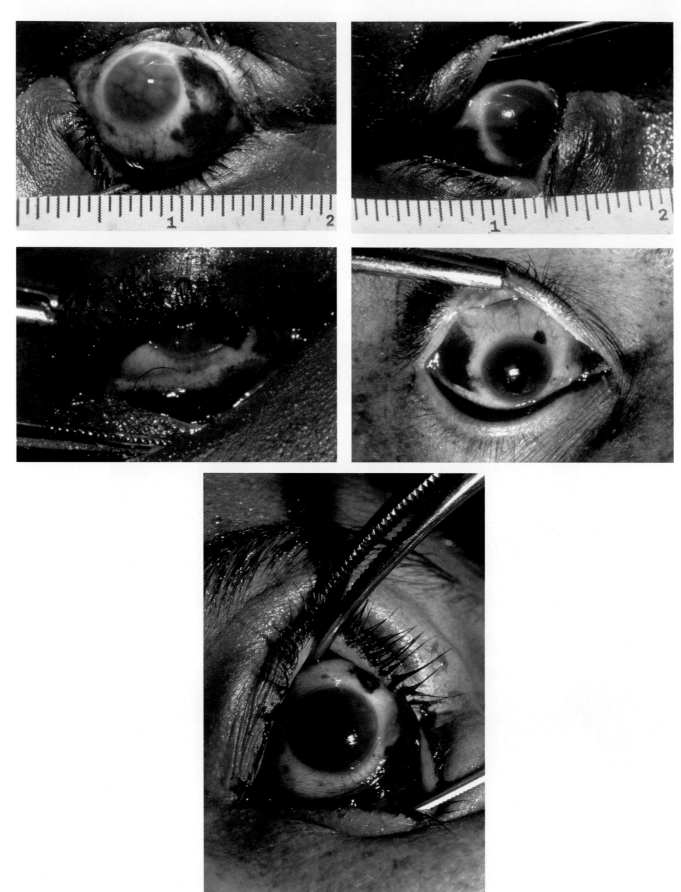

Figures 10.69–10.73 These demonstrate a range of scleral and conjunctival hemorrhages. As varied degrees of neck pressure continue after petechiae formation, hemorrhages progressively become larger and more confluent until death occurs.

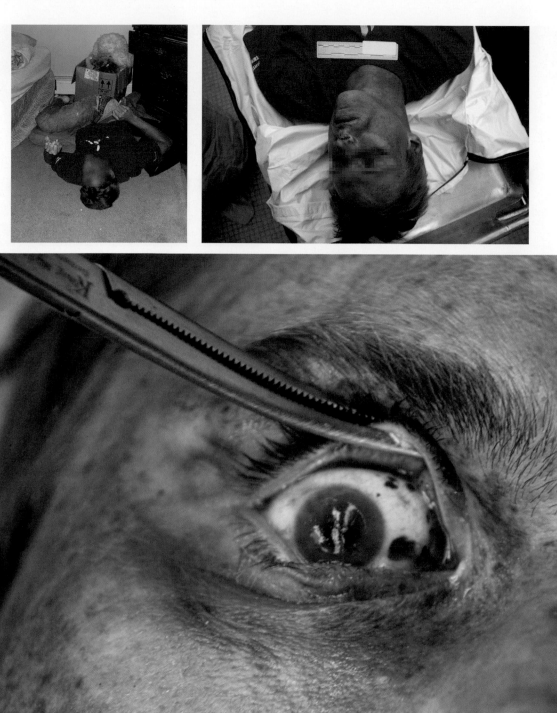

Figures 10.74–10.76 This individual was found in this position at initial scene investigation. He was obviously moved from a face-down position on top of the bed. Note the marked anterior lividity in Figure 10.74 as compared to less lividity in Figure 10.75 after he was placed on his back for a while and partial redistribution of blood occurred, depending on gravity. Note the areas of hemorrhage within the eyes and face associated with gravity-dependent settling of blood. This should not be associated with asphyxial deaths such as strangulation. Refer to Figures 10.65–10.73.

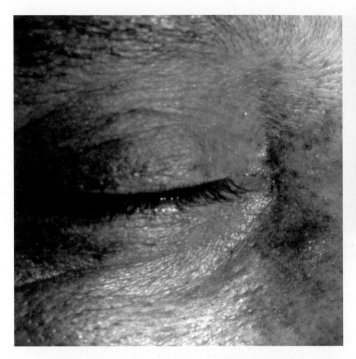

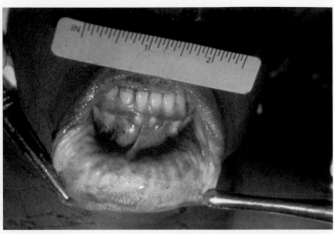

Figure 10.78 Strangulation. Petechial hemorrhages within the mucosal surface of the mouth. Petechiae are more obvious on paler surfaces of the body such as the sclera and conjunctiva. They are often present in other areas but may not be visible.

Figure 10.77 Petechial hemorrhages of the face in an individual who died of asphyxia associated with chest compression.

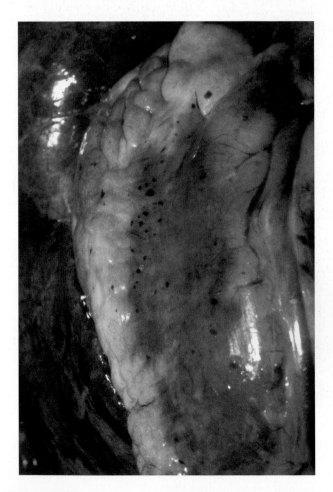

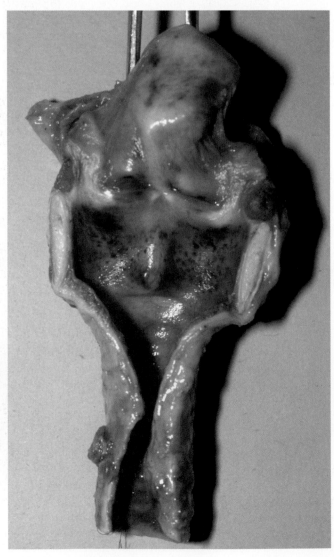

Figure 10.79 Petechial hemorrhages on the surface of the heart associated with asphyxia due to chest compression.

Figure 10.80 Strangulation. Petechial hemorrhages within the mucosa of the tracheal and laryngeal cartilage.

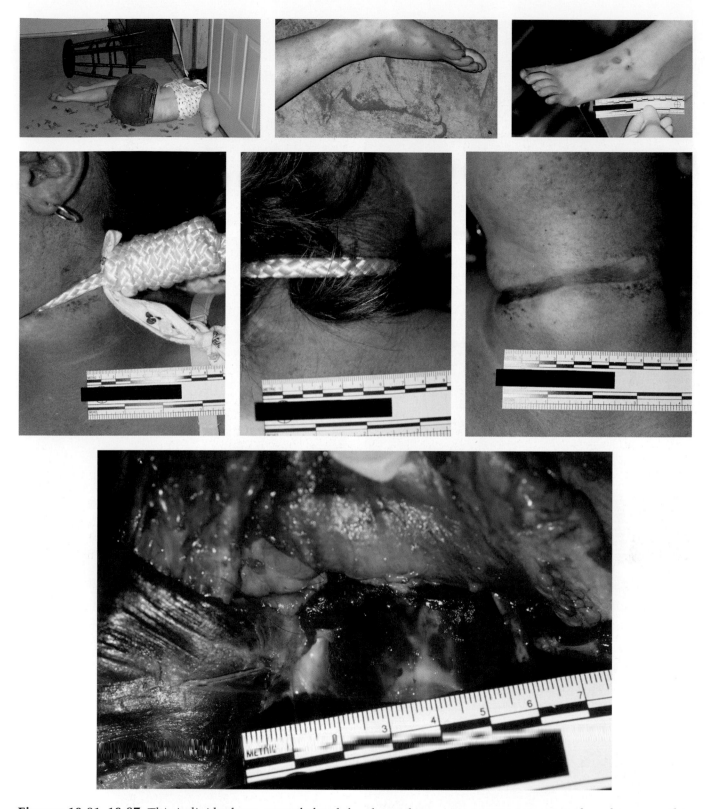

Figures 10.81–10.87 This individual was strangled and then hanged in an attempt to stage a suicide and cover up this crime. Note the injuries to the decedent's feet during a struggle and the haphazard scuff marks to the floor surrounding the body. Also note the decedent's hair and clothing stuck under the noose. There are also injuries with hemorrhage to the neck structures. These findings are inconsistent with a suicidal hanging.

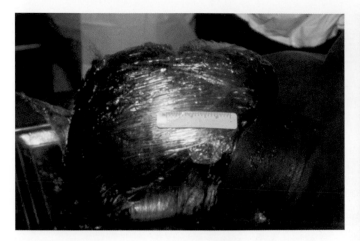

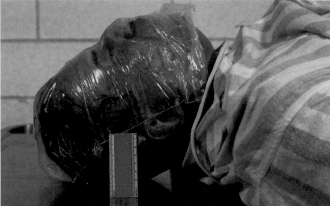

Figures 10.88 This individual was abducted, bound, and had multiple superficial stab wounds associated with a sexual assault. Her head was wrapped in multiple layers of plastic, which covered her mouth and nose.

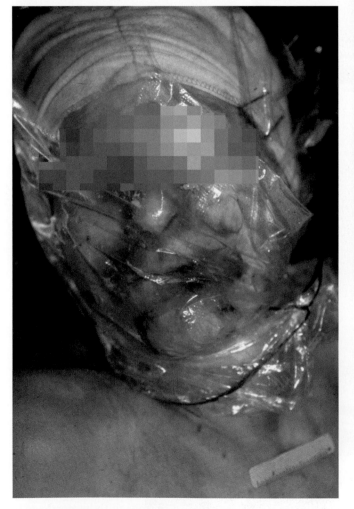

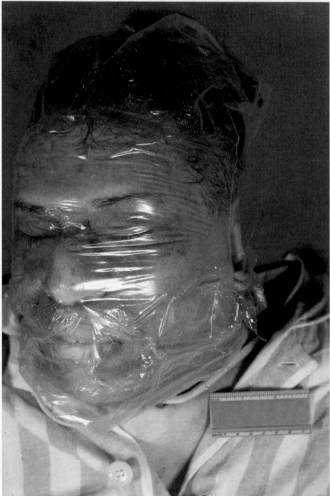

Figures 10.90 and 10.91 Suicidal asphyxia due to plastic bag tied over head.

Figure 10.89 This individual committed suicide by taking multiple pills and tying a plastic bag tightly over her head. Note the yellow to brown discoloration from mold and mildew forming on her face due to the moist environment from terminal breathing. It is the author's experience that it is better to pend these cases for toxicology.

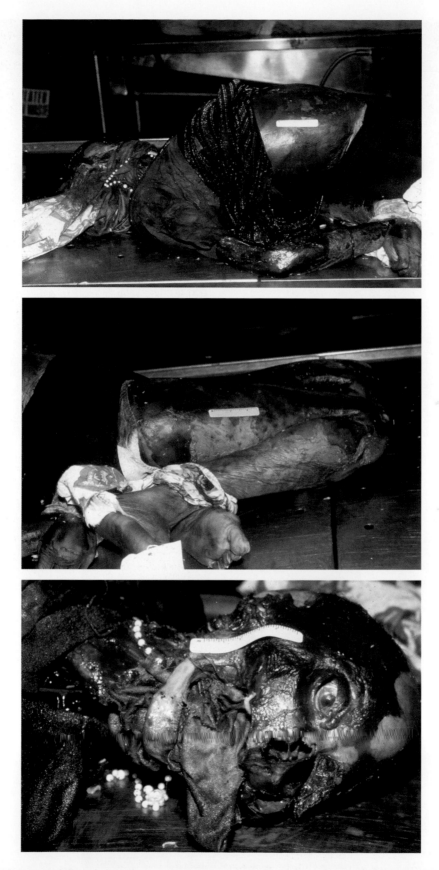

Figures 10.92–10.94 Homicidal asphyxia due to airway obstruction. This individual was found in a moderate to marked state of decomposition within her apartment. She was reportedly dealing drugs and was found tied up with a piece of cloth stuck down her mouth and throat.

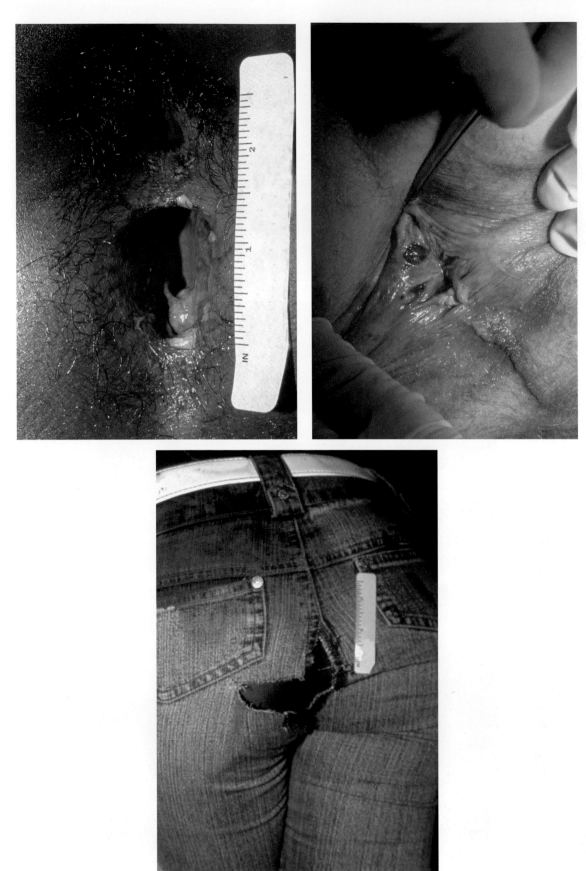

Figures 10.95–10.97 Anal trauma with abrasions and lacerations due to sexual assault during strangulation. One should always assume strangulation victims are sexually assaulted. A rape kit should always be performed in these cases.

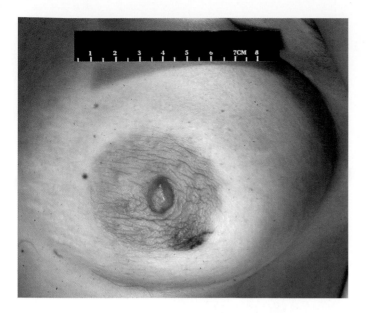

Figure 10.98 Abraded contusion to the areola.

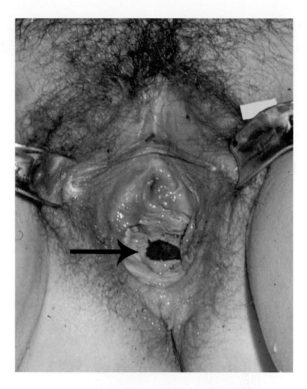

Figure 10.101 Paraphilia; anemic lacerations of the posterior vagina with fecal material present. This postmortem mutilation is consistent with necrophilia.

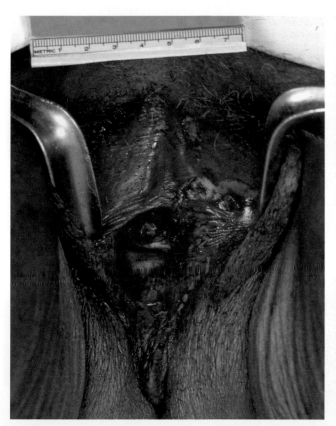

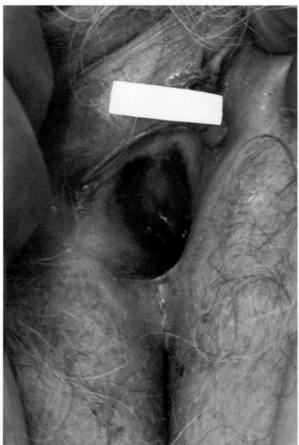

Figures 10.99 and 10.100 Paraphilia; sexual assault strangulation homicides with abrasions, contusions, and lacerations to the vaginal region, indicating forced abusive sexual contact.

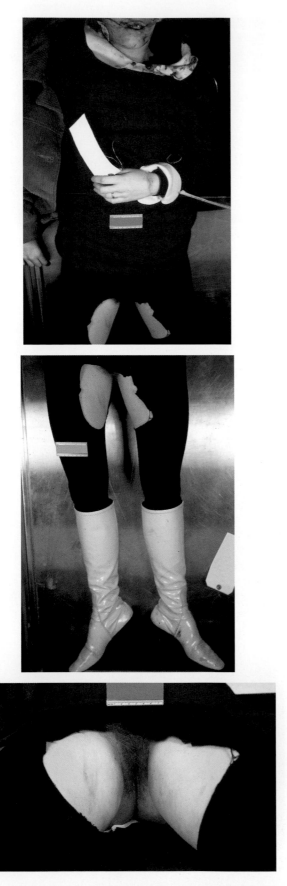

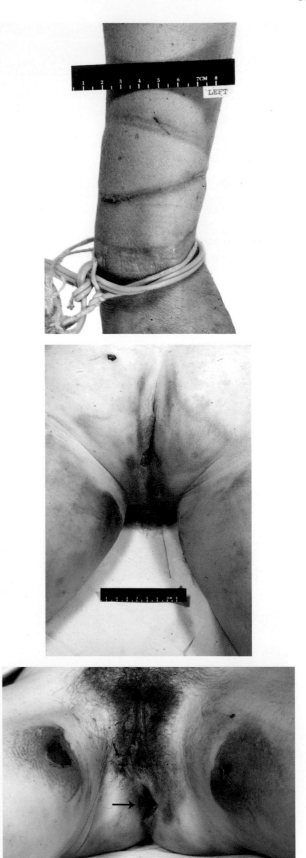

Figures 10.102–10.104 Homicidal strangulation with sexual assault. Note the ligature binding of the extremities during the assault.

Figures 10.105–10.107 An individual who was raped multiple times over a long period. Note the lacerations with hemorrhage to the anal region and the abrasion, braided contusions to the thighs from rubbing.

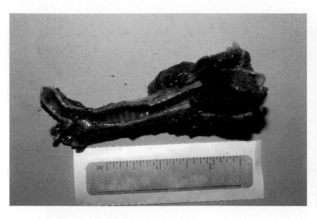 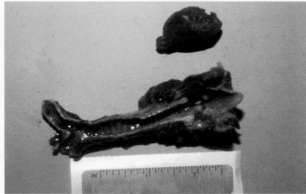

Figures 10.108 and 10.109 This is an airway from a 2-1/2-year-old that was fed a hot dog by her older sibling. The large size of the hot dog piece caused it to get wedged in her throat leading to asphyxia. Children are susceptible to such events because they are impulsive and may gulp food.

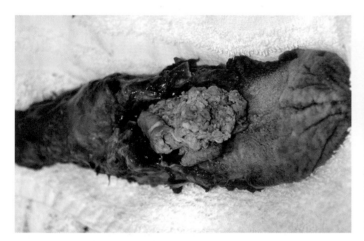 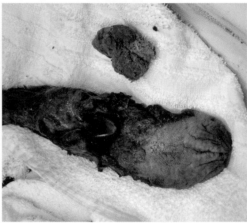

Figures 10.110 and 10.111 This adult airway was obstructed by a piece of chewed meat. This typically happens in somebody who is intoxicated or neurologically compromised.

Figures 10.112 and 10.113 This individual had a pencil in his mouth when he collapsed at work. The pencil was inhaled and wedged in the right main stem bronchus.

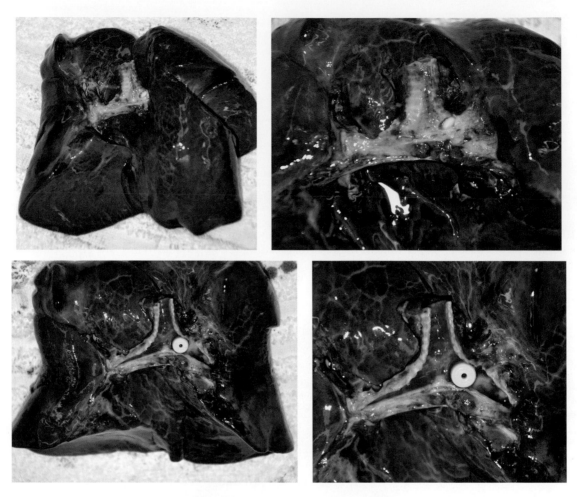

Figures 10.114–10.117 This picture demonstrates lungs of a child who inhaled a yellow bead, which obstructed his right main stem bronchus. This bead was radiolucent and not visible on x-ray.

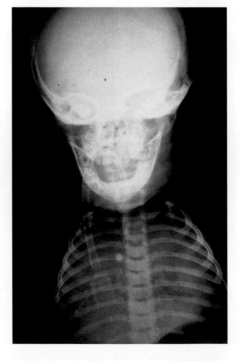

Figure 10.118 In a similar case, this child was found to have a pebble wedged within her right main stem bronchus evident on this radiograph.

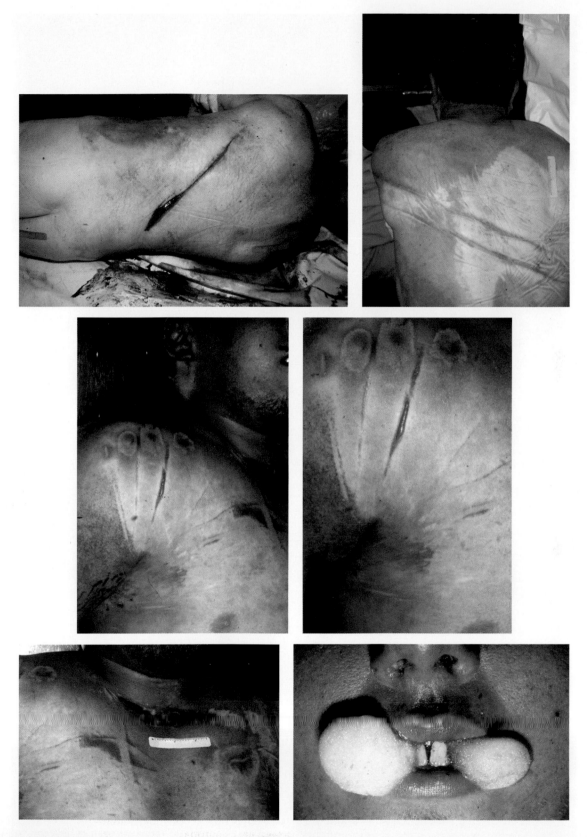

Figures 10.119–10.124 These individuals were trapped in machines, which caused chest compression and inability to breathe. One of these individuals was stuck in a box-folding machine, another trapped under a car, and another stuck under a single-person elevator lift. Note the imprint of the individual's hand while he was struggling to escape with the blister formation between these finger imprints. Also note the pulmonary edema demonstrated by froth coming out of the mouth. This individual also had numerous petechial hemorrhages of the upper trunk, face, eyes, and visceral organs including the heart.

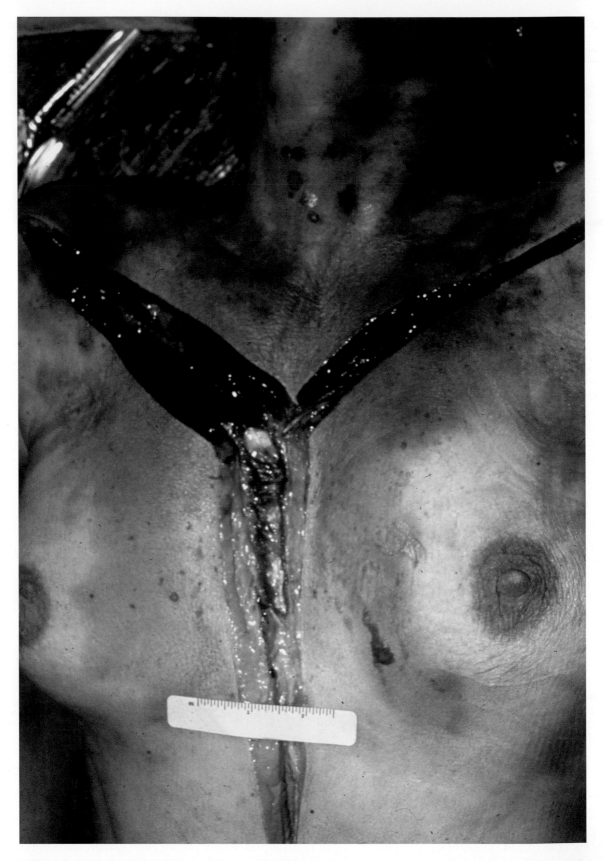

Figure 10.125 Homicidal asphyxia due to compression of chest and neck. Note the extensive hemorrhage at the superior chest visible at the superior aspect of the Y-shaped incision during autopsy. The lower aspect of this incision is yellow, anemic, and postmortem. This individual was punched, strangled, and then the perpetrator sat on her chest during the assault.

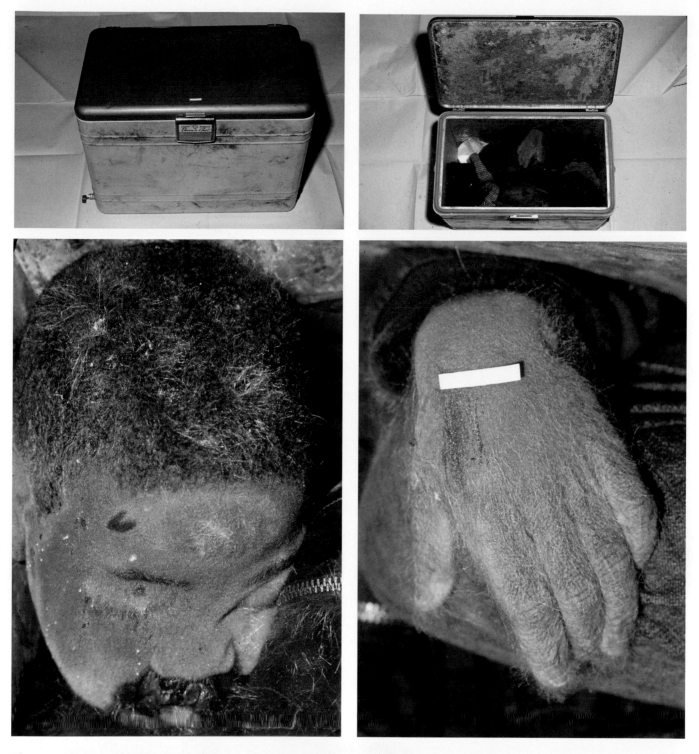

Figures 10.126–10.129 This child was found several days after disappearing while playing hide and seek. Note the decomposition with the mold on the body surface. This old-fashioned cooler had a locking mechanism that prevented the child from escaping after the lid closed.

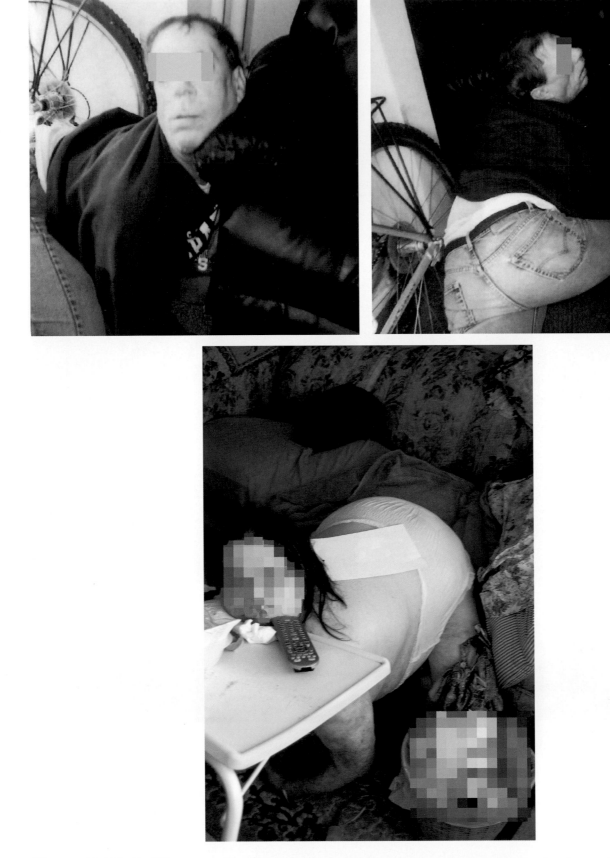

Figures 10.130–10.132 Positional asphyxia. These individuals were markedly intoxicated and passed out in a position, which prevented them from breathing and obstructed blood circulation.

Histology

11

CHARLES A. CATANESE, GERARD A. CATANESE,
AMY RAPKIEWICZ, AND JENNIFER ROMAN

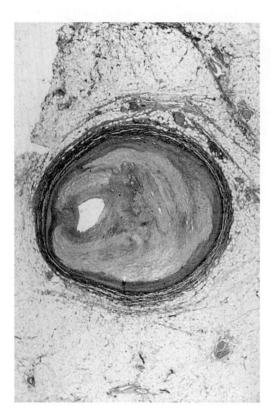

Figure 11.1 Marked coronary atherosclerosis in an epicardial vessel from a 29-year-old woman who just gave birth to a healthy baby. This is extremely unusual in a woman of childbearing age. She had an undocumented hypercholesterolemia.

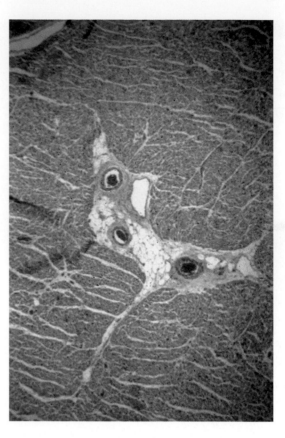

Figure 11.2 Low-power magnified view of small coronary arteries with thrombosis.

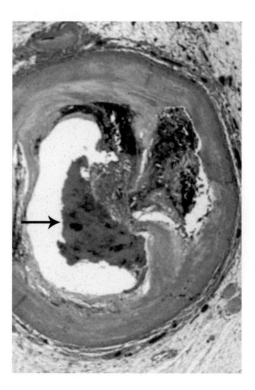

Figure 11.3 Coronary artery with a ruptured atherosclerotic plaque and thrombus formation. Note the aggregates of platelets and blood cells extending into the lumen from the plague rupture site.

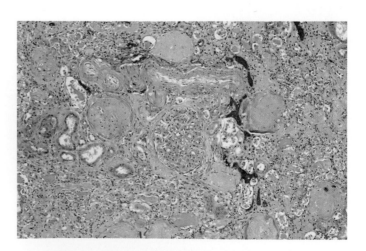

Figure 11.4 This is a microscopic section of kidney showing fibrosis, arteriolosclerosis, and nephrosclerosis due to hypertensive cardiovascular disease.

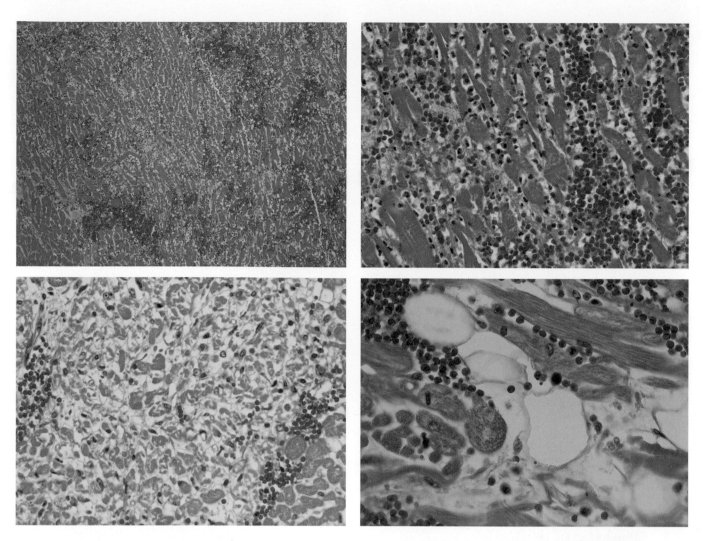

Figures 11.5–11.8 Acute myocardial infarction showing hemorrhage, interstitial edema, myocyte vacuolation with early acute inflammation. Acute myocardial infarctions may present with rapid death due to fatal arrhythmia from myocardial irritability. In this circumstance there will be no gross or microscopic changes.

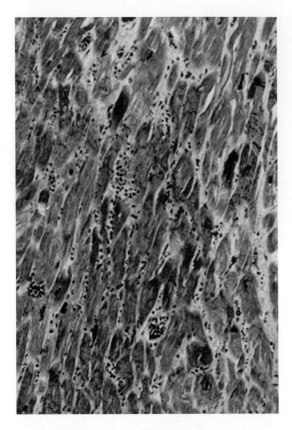

Figure 11.9 This acute myocardial infarction demonstrates coagulative necrosis with contraction bands. There is also polymorphonuclear cell infiltrates.

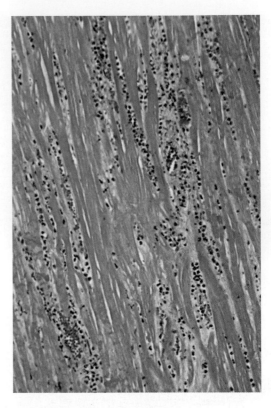

Figure 11.10 This microscopic section of heart muscle reveals an acute myocardial infarction with hemorrhage, polymorphonuclear cell infiltrates, and myocardial necrosis.

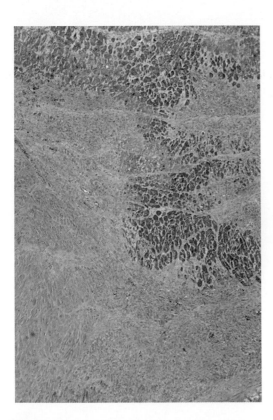

Figure 11.11 This histopathologic section of myocardium reveals an old infarction with fibrosis.

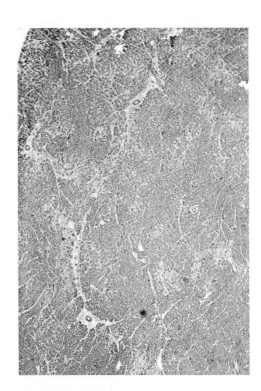

Figure 11.12 This low-power view of heart muscle reveals patchy areas of fibrosis consisting of healed hypoperfusion infarctions secondary to a remote trauma with severe shock. Also note the perivascular fibrosis.

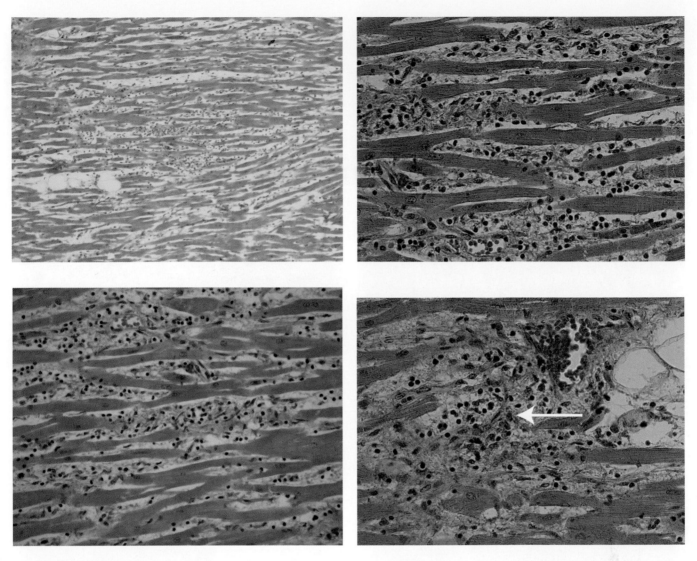

Figures 11.13–11.16 Myocarditis of probably viral etiology, H&E, high power. Active myocarditis requires an inflammatory infiltrate with myonecrosis (arrow) as per the modified Dallas criteria. Most cases of viral myocarditis are thought to be autoimmune in origin. Many forensic pathologists believe fatal arrhythmia can occur without the presence of necrosis.

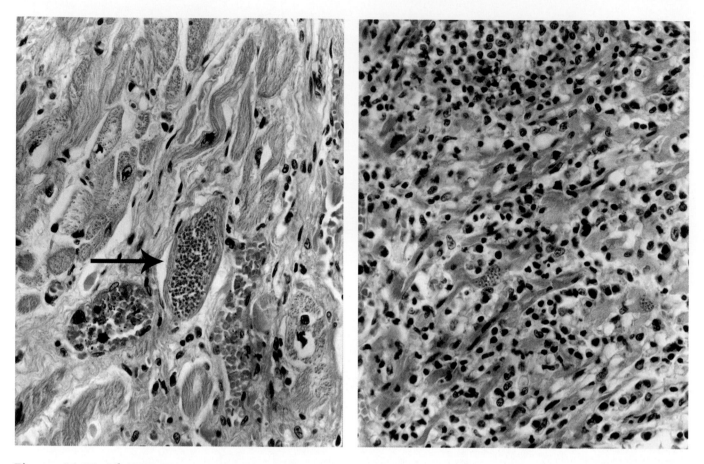

Figures 11.17 and 11.18 These microscopic myocardial views demonstrate Chagas disease. Note the extensive chronic inflammation and the large size of the cyst (arrow). This is caused by a tropical parasite, a protozoan. It is spread mostly by insects known as kissing bugs (*Triatominae*).

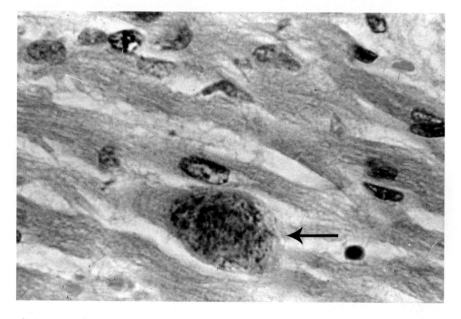

Figure 11.19 Myocarditis secondary to toxoplasmosis (arrow) in an individual with acquired immunodeficiency syndrome. Note the small size and lack of inflammation.

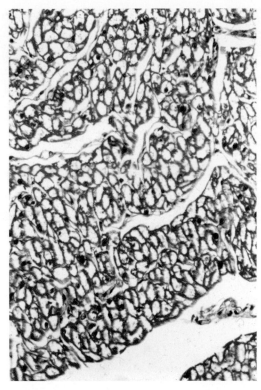

Figure 11.20 Microscopic view of myocardium in an individual who died of Pompe disease. Note the many artifactual empty vacuoles following processing leading to glycogen loss.

Figure 11.21 This candidal myocarditis was found in an individual with acquired immunodeficiency syndrome.

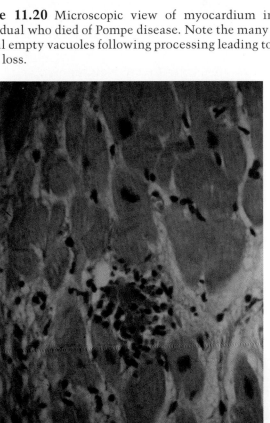

Figure 11.22 Focal myocarditis of probably viral etiology demonstrates myocardial necrosis with inflammation made up predominately of lymphocytes.

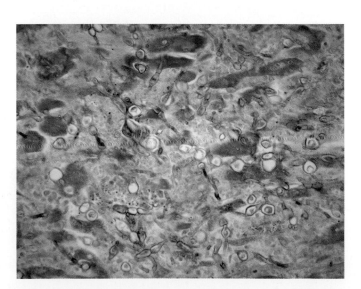

Figure 11.23 Aspergillosis myocarditis from an immunocompromised individual who underwent a recent bone marrow transplant.

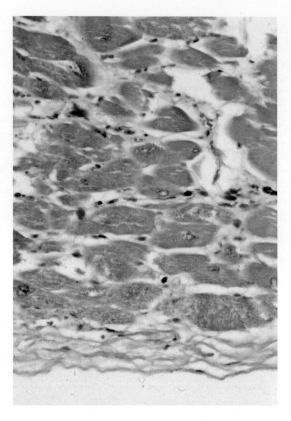

Figure 11.24 Microscopic section of heart showing iron deposition from secondary hemochromatosis associated with blood transfusions for treatment of beta-thalassemia major.

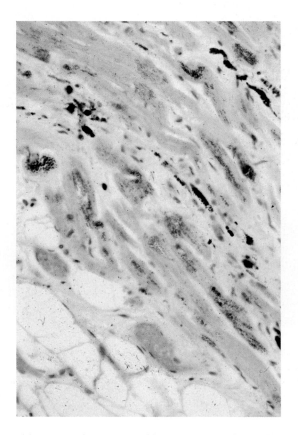

Figure 11.25 Microscopic section of heart with Prussian blue staining of iron deposits in the heart of the same individual with secondary hemochromatosis.

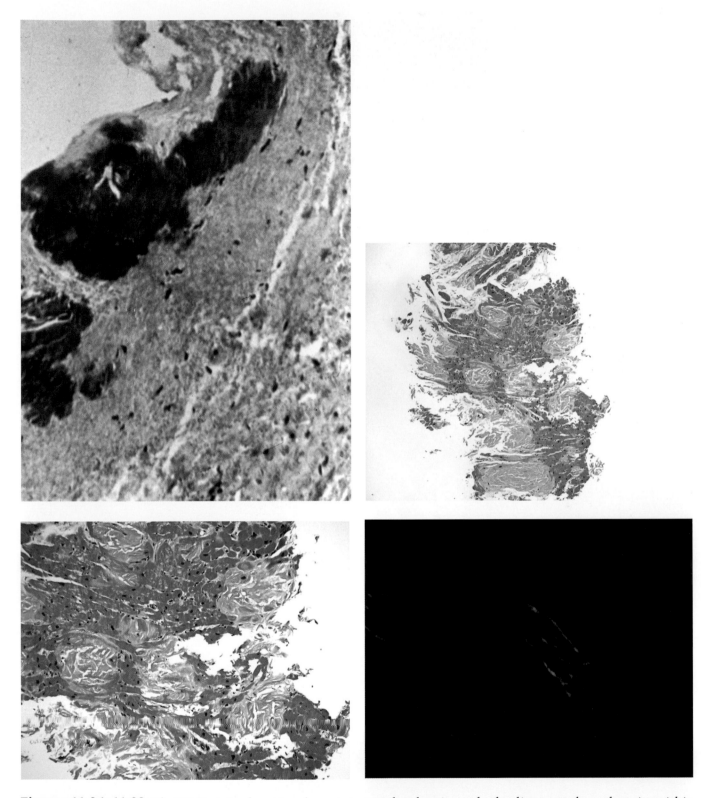

Figures 11.26–11.29 The H&E-stained section shows interstitial and perivascular hyaline amorphous deposits within the myocardium. Under polarized light, slides stained with Congo red show green birefringence. One of the most common types of amyloid seen in the heart at autopsy is transthyretin. Other types are amyloid light chain and amyloid A protein. Amyloid can be typed using mass spectroscopy.

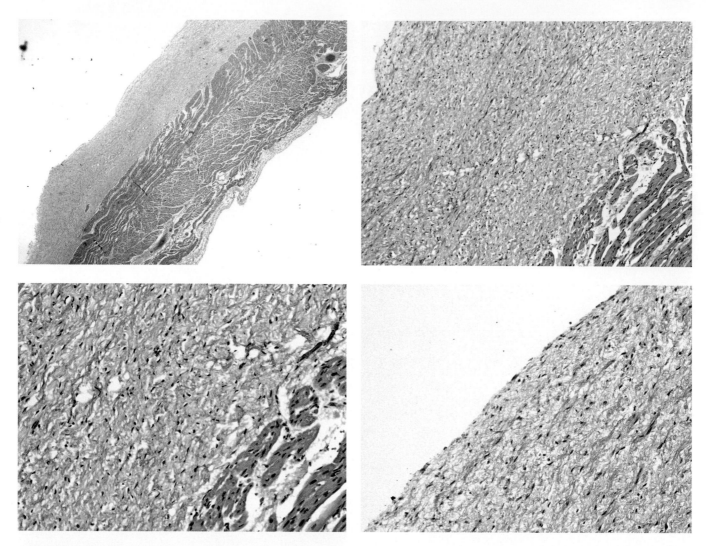

Figures 11.30–11.33 Endocardial fibroelastosis (at 2× [Figure 11.30], 10× [Figure 11.31], and 20× [Figure 11.32]; Figure 11.33 shows the endocardial surface at 20×) is a rare disorder usually occurring in children less than 2 years of age. It may present as a restrictive cardiomyopathy and is X linked or autosomal recessive.

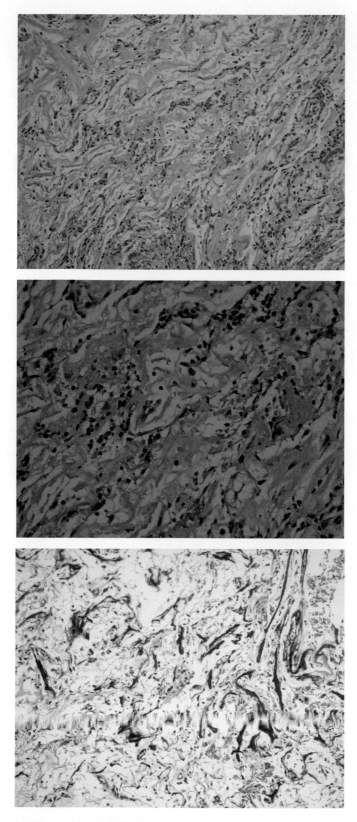

Figures 11.34–11.36 Cardiac myxoma, medium power, H&E. Typically atrial, cardiac myxomas are gelatinous and myxoid neoplasms are composed of ovoid to stellate "myxoma" cells with a perivascular distribution (Figure 11.34). Degenerative changes are common, including hemorrhage, fibrosis, hyalinization, ossification, or calcification, (Figure 11.35). Gamna-Gandy bodies (elastic fiber degeneration with calcification) can be found in some (Figure 11.36).

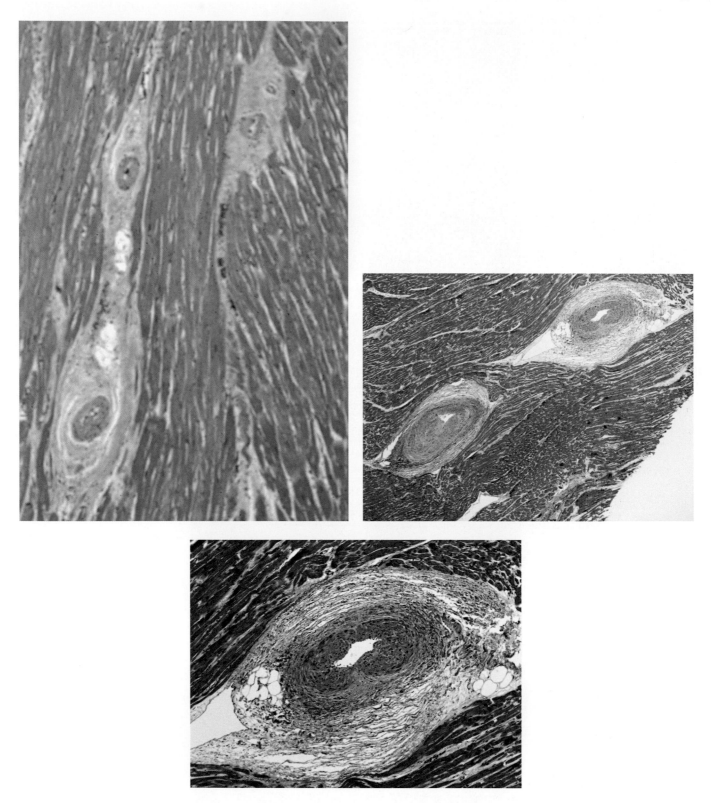

Figures 11.37–11.39 These microscopic images of myocardium reveal significant perivascular fibrosis and small vessel disease in a patient who had a long history of hypertensive cardiovascular disease and diabetes mellitus. Small vessel disease may be sometimes difficult to diagnose clinically. In such cases coronary artery bypass is ineffective. This can result in sudden cardiac death through the same mechanism as marked coronary artery disease within epicardial vessels.

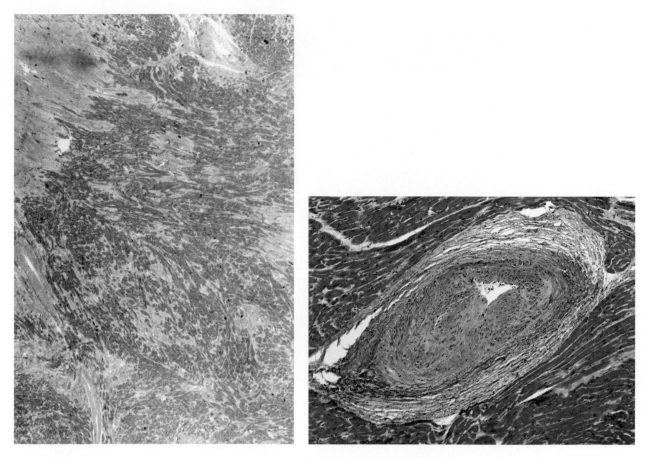

Figures 11.40 and 11.41 Hypertrophic cardiomyopathy with myocyte fiber disarray and fibrosis. Hypertrophic cardiomyopathy is also associated with fibromuscular dysplasia, causing marked narrowing of small coronary artery branches.

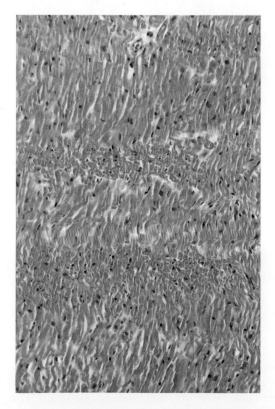

Figure 11.42 Hypertrophic cardiomyopathy with myocyte fiber bundle disorganization.

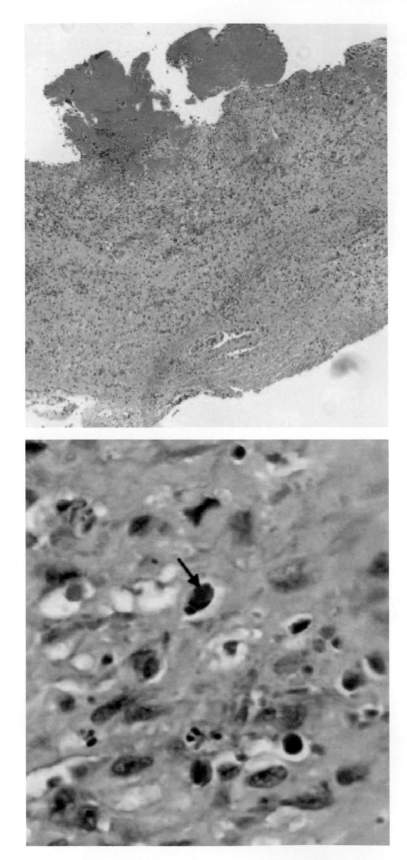

Figures 11.43 and 11.44 Libman–Sacks endocarditis is a type of verrucous endocarditis that occurs in patients with systemic lupus erythematosus. Fibrin-rich vegetations are on valves and most commonly involve the mitral valve. The valvular leaflet is thickened and shows a mixed lymphoplasmacytic infiltrate. LE cells can be found and are neutrophils that have engulfed the nuclei of other cells. Hematoxylin bodies are also seen. The vegetations can embolize.

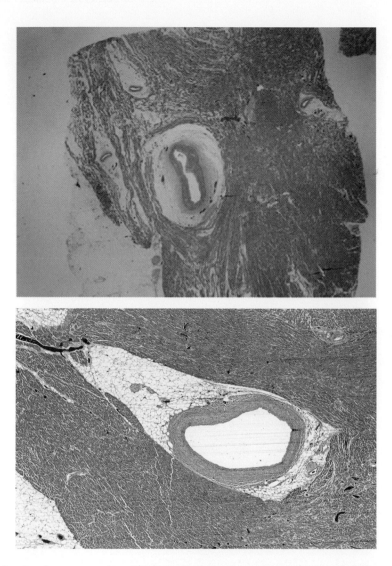

Figures 11.45 and 11.46 This low-power histopathologic view demonstrates myocardial tunneling or bridging where the left anterior descending coronary artery dipped deeply into the left ventricle wall. Although usually considered a benign condition, it can result in myocardial ischemia and death. Since the coronary arteries supply blood to the heart during diastole, compression of this vessel during systole usually will not create significant blood flow obstruction. An exception to this can occur during strenuous exertion with increased oxygen demand and rapid left ventricular contraction which has, on occasions, been shown to have an exclusive effect leading to ischemia, myocardial irritability, and arrhythmia.

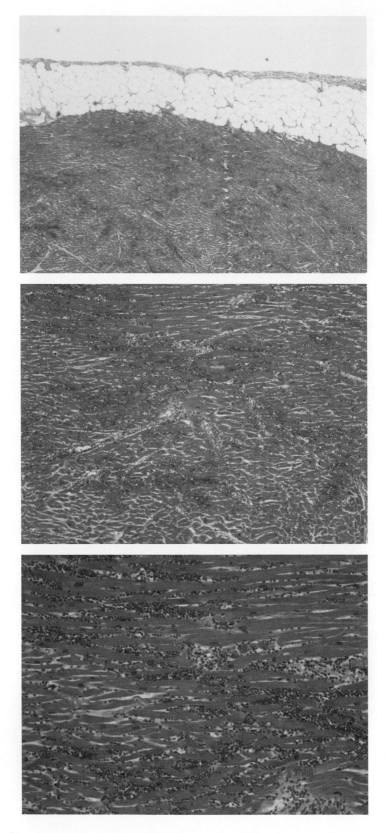

Figures 11.47–11.49 Cardiac contusion. Low- to high-power magnification showing hemorrhage in the myocardium of an individual who was in a motor vehicle collision and impacted his chest on the steering wheel. He was noted to be lifeless at the scene. All other causes of death were ruled out. The mechanism of this death was fatal arrhythmia due to commotio cordis.

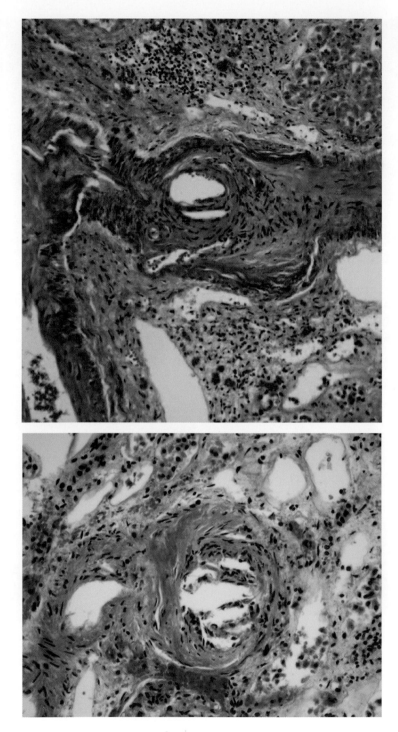

Figures 11.30 and 11.31 Atheroembolism occurs when atheromatous plaques fragment and embolize cellular and cholesterol debris. This can occur following trauma or surgical manipulation of the plaque. The occluded vessel will show cholesterol cleft and multinucleated giant cells.

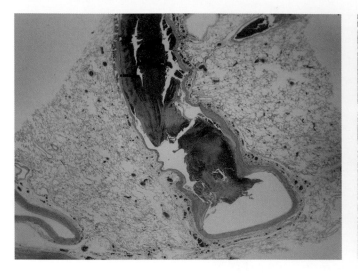

Figure 11.52 Pulmonary artery thrombosis; lines of Zahn. In a vascular system with low-pressure flow, in the setting of thrombosis, platelets and fibrin can layer with red blood cells, producing a parallel light–dark pattern known as lines of Zahn.

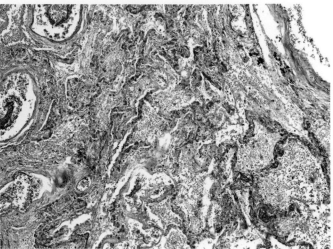

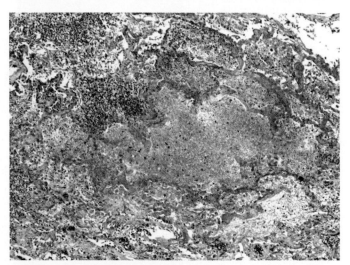

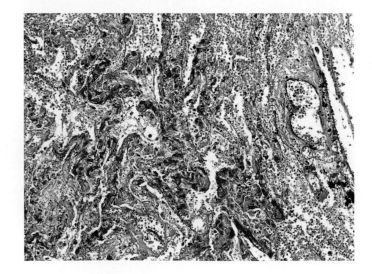

Figures 11.53–11.55 Pulmonary infarcts are red and firm grossly. Microscopically (at 10× [Figures 11.53 and 11.54], and at 20× [Figure 11.55]) there is hemorrhage with necrosis. They are not common due to the dual circulation of the lung tissue.

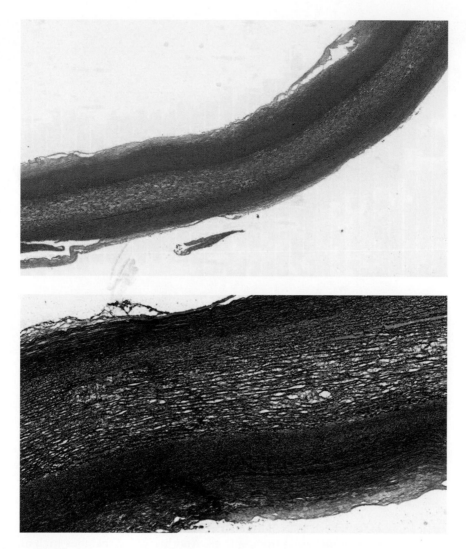

Figures 11.56 and 11.57 Cystic medial degeneration of the aorta with dissection. In cystic medial necrosis or degeneration, the tunica media of elastic arteries such as the aorta show loss of smooth muscle fibers and fragmentation of the elastic fibers with a cystic-like appearance, best seen on elastin stains. Fibrosis can also be present. Although characteristic in Marfan syndrome, these changes are nonspecific and degenerative. This process is seen to varying degrees in patients with systemic hypertension and annuloaortic ectasia and is a risk factor for aortic dissection.

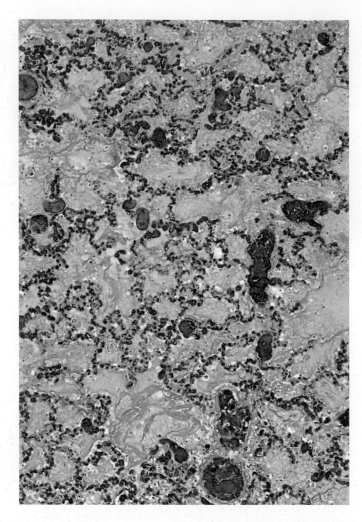

Figure 11.58 Microscopic view of lung with acute pulmonary edema. This is associated with many different types of heart diseases and some drug toxicities including from opiates. Another cause includes high-altitude sickness. Some degree of pulmonary congestion and edema are common findings at autopsy and associated with the terminal phases of death.

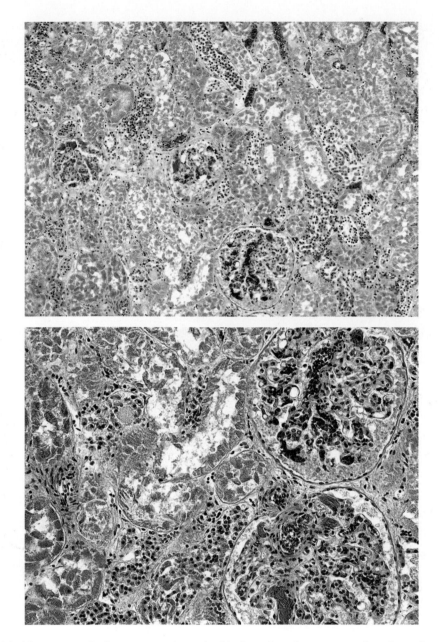

Figures 11.59 and 11.60 Acute tubular necrosis (ATN) of kidney (10× [Figure 11.59] and 20× [Figure 11.60]). ATN can be difficult to distinguish from postmortem autolysis as the proximal convoluted tubules are affected in both conditions. ATN can be a result of ischemia or nephrotoxic agents.

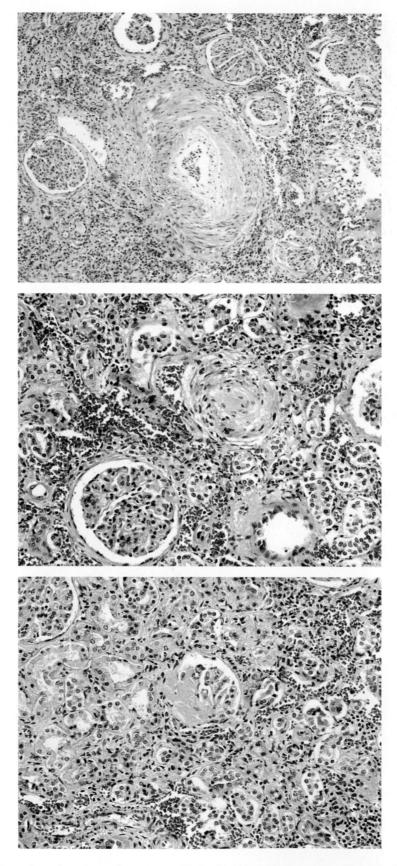

Figures 11.61–11.63 Note the sclerotic and artery wall thickening. Also associated with this is thrombotic micro-angiopathy with thrombi inside capillaries and arterioles, endothelial injury, and fibrinoid necrosis of the arterioles. Figures 11.61, malignant ATN at 10×, and Figures 11.62 and 11.63, malignant ATN 20×.

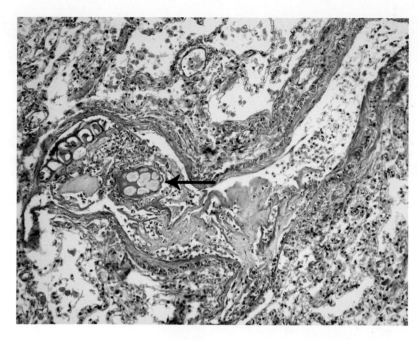

Figure 11.64 Food embolism of the lung vasculature. A variety of mechanisms are possible for this type of "food" material to be introduced into the pulmonary arterial system such as peripheral venous injection, atrioesophageal fistula, or enterovascular fistula into the systemic venous nonportal circulation, possibly related to a diverticula or diverticulitis, or arteriovenous fistula introduction possibly related to dialysis.

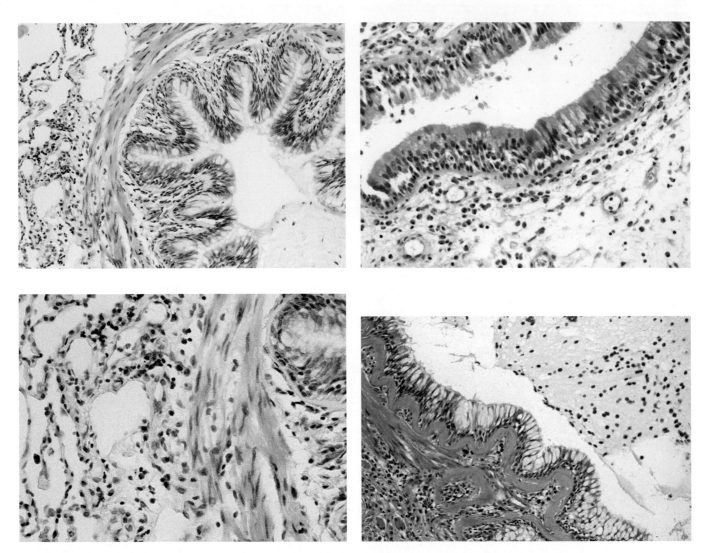

Figures 11.65–11.68 Asthma (H&E, medium power). In the respiratory epithelium, the goblet cells and submucosal glands will be increased, with increase in the basement membrane thickness. The lamina propria will contain excess numbers of eosinophils with edema. The bronchiolar smooth muscle may be hypertrophic. There may be large mucous plugs within the airway with numerous eosinophils. In acute asthma the lungs are hyperaerated and expand to overlie the pericardial sac. Upon removal of the lung, they appear markedly hyperaerated. If these lungs were placed on a water bath, they would float almost entirely on the surface. Cut section through the parenchyma reveals thick copious mucoid secretions within the bronchial distribution.

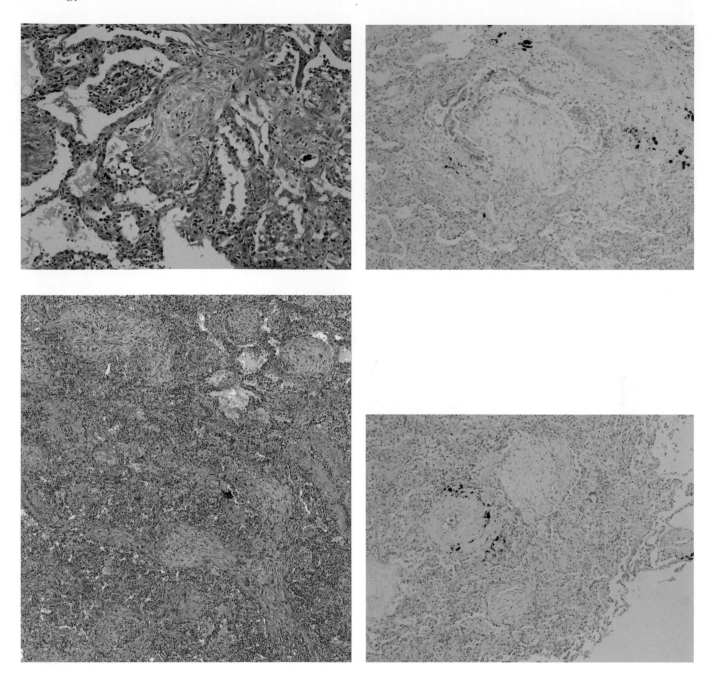

Figures 11.69–11.72 Cryptogenic organizing pneumonia, previously known as bronchiolitis obliterans organizing pneumonia or BOOP, is a disease of the distal airspace that can be due to multiple etiologies. This process is usually subacute with peripheral opacities on CT scan. The alveolar ducts and possibly bronchioles will be filled with loose fibro-myxoid plugs, sometimes in a "butterfly" pattern

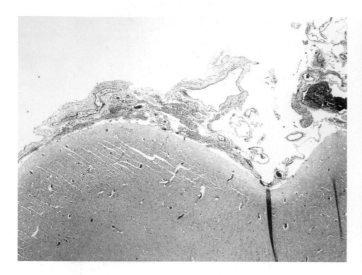

Figure 11.73 Meningitis 2×.

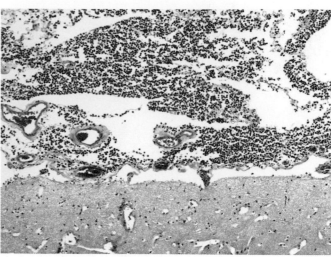

Figure 11.75 Meningitis 10×.

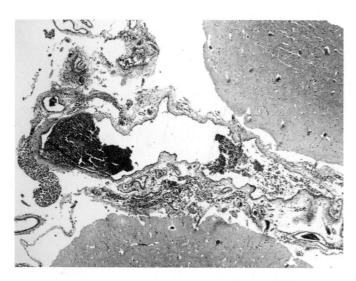

Figure 11.74 Meningitis 4×.

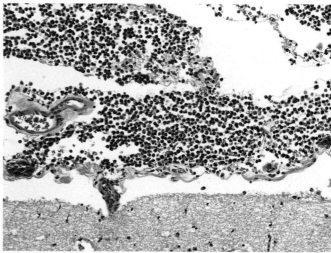

Figure 11.76 Meningitis with neutrophils 20×.

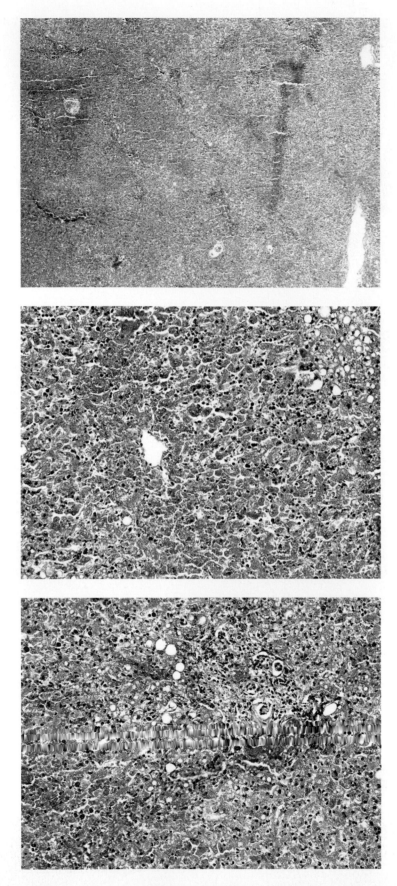

Figures 11.77–11.79 Acute inflammation of portal tracts that may be associated with cholangitis. Figure 11.77, centrilobular necrosis at 4×, Figure 11.78, acute inflammation with loss of hepatocyte nuclei 20×, and Figure 11.79, acute inflammation of portal tracts 20×.

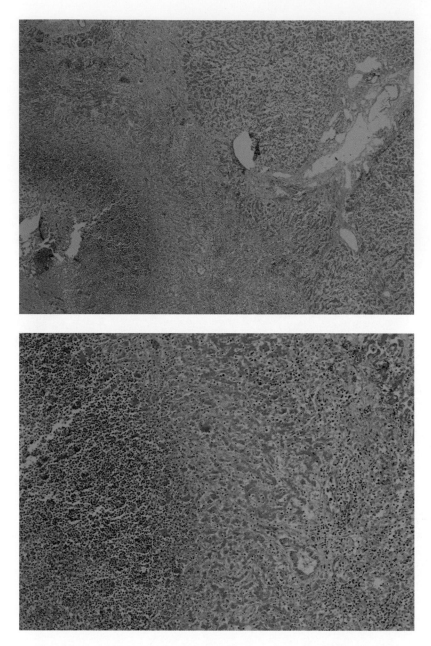

Figures 11.80 and 11.81 Liver abscess, low and medium power, H&E. On the left side of each image, the dense collection of neutrophils destroys the liver, leaving collapse of the hepatocytes at the periphery. Liver abscess can occur as a result of infection with pyogenic bacteria (both aerobic and anaerobic), fungal with *Candida* species being most common, amoebic, *Actinomyces*, ascariasis, or *Nocardia*. Many arise as a result of cholangitic spread. This type of visceral abscess can occur adjacent to a neoplasm.

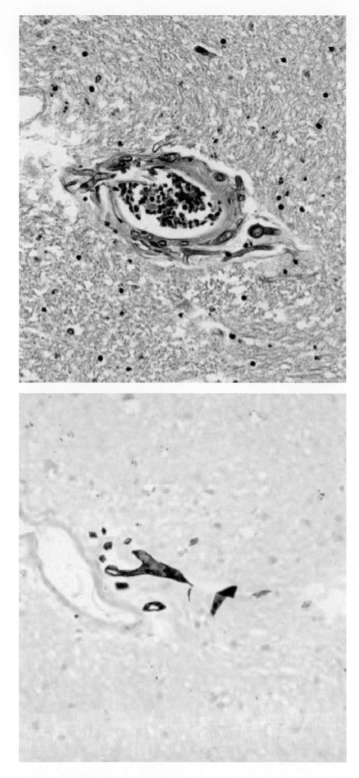

Figures 11.82 and 11.83 Zygomycosis infection. Zygomycocetes such as *Rhizopus* spp. are frequently aggressive angio-invasive fungi that cause fatal infections. Their broad hyphae can be found within vessel walls. The most common manifestations are rhinocerebral or pulmonary infections.

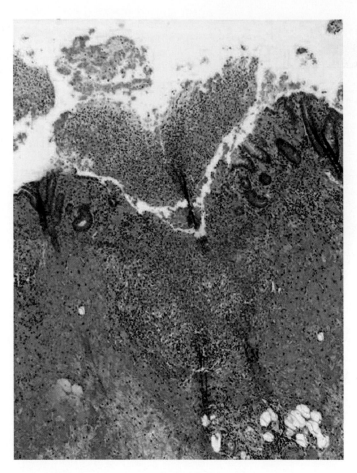

Figure 11.84 Pseudomembranous colitis also known as antibiotic-associated colitis. Pseudomembranous colitis develops following treatment with broad-spectrum antibiotics such as clindamycin. Although many organisms may cause this colitis, *Clostridium difficile* is common. The bowel shows eroded surface epithelium with a mucopurulent exudate that can progress to involve the entire wall thickness with necrosis. Note the pseudomembrane at the top of the image.

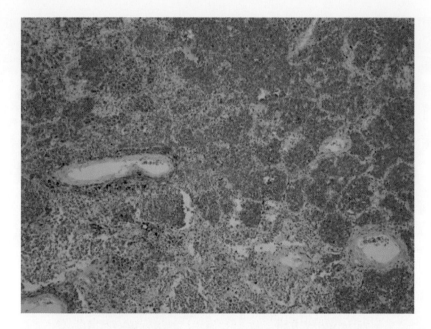

Figure 11.85 Diffuse alveolar hemorrhage is a pattern of injury with diffuse hemorrhage and hemosiderin-laden macrophages within the alveolar spaces. This process can occur in collagen vascular disorders, Goodpasture syndrome, toxin exposure such as crack, and other conditions.

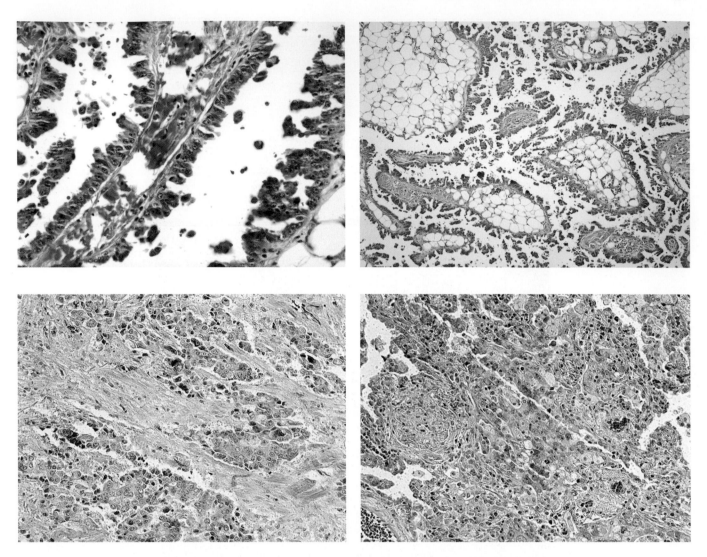

Figures 11.86–11.89 Mesothelioma (H&E, low and high power). The main histologic subtypes of pleural mesothe-lioma are epithelioid, sarcomatoid, biphasic, and desmoplastic. Epithelioid is the most commonly encountered and may respond to some chemotherapeutic agents. Immunohistochemical stains are positive for calretinin, D2-40, CK 5/6, and WT-1 and negative for BerEp4, MOC-31, CEA, and B72.3. The diagnosis of mesothelioma requires stromal invasion. Mesothelial cells in lymph node sinuses are not diagnostic and may represent benign mesothelial inclusions.

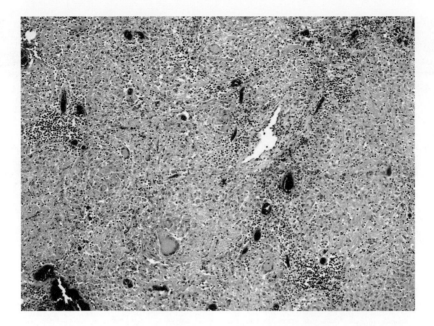

Sarcoid 4×

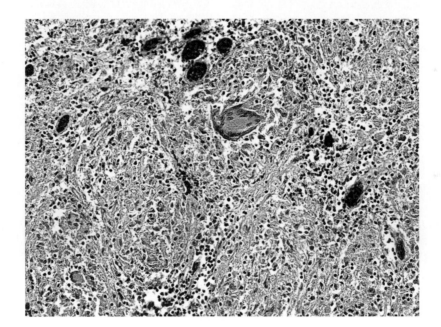

Sarcoid 10×

Figures 11.90 and 11.91 Aspiration Pneumonia vs. Sarcoidosis: Aspiration pneumonia is characterized by an inflammatory response to aspirated materials such as food particles and bacteria, leading to an immune response similar to acute bronchopneumonia with foreign material consisting of food. This can lead to a chronic immune response with foreign body giant cells and numerous macrophages engulfing the foreign debris. In contrast to sarcoidosis, aspiration pneumonia is usually diffuse with ill-defined borders, may have necrosis, and is less likely to form individual nodules. Sarcoidosis are typically has Langhan's type giant cells.

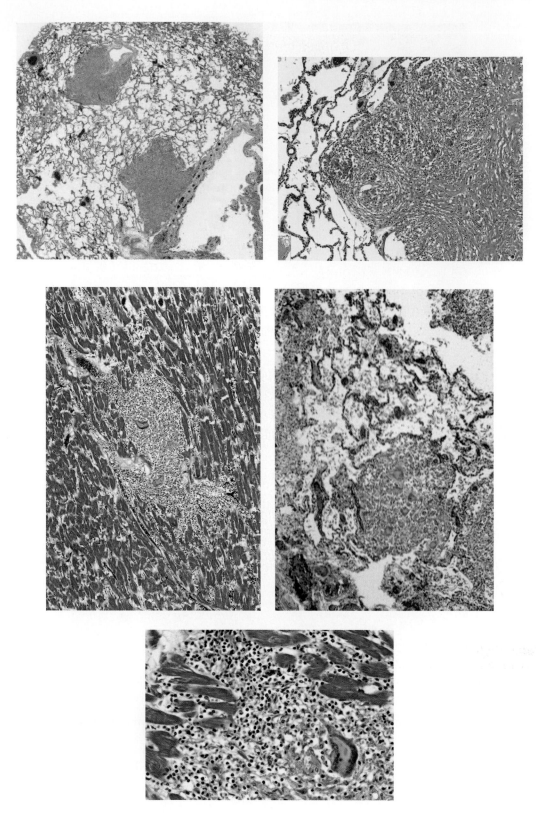

Figures 11.92–11.96 Sarcoid (heart and lung), H&E, low to high power. Pulmonary sarcoid shows perivascular and bronchiolar distribution with hyalinized non-necrotizing granulomas with giant cells. When granulomas involve vessels, necrosis can be seen and must be distinguished from infectious and autoimmune conditions. Sarcoid may be associated with sudden death especially in cases that involve the cardiac conduction regions. Note the chronic inflammation, epithelioid cells, lymphocytes, and giant cells. These nodularities may be found anywhere but are most commonly seen in the perihylar lymph nodes.

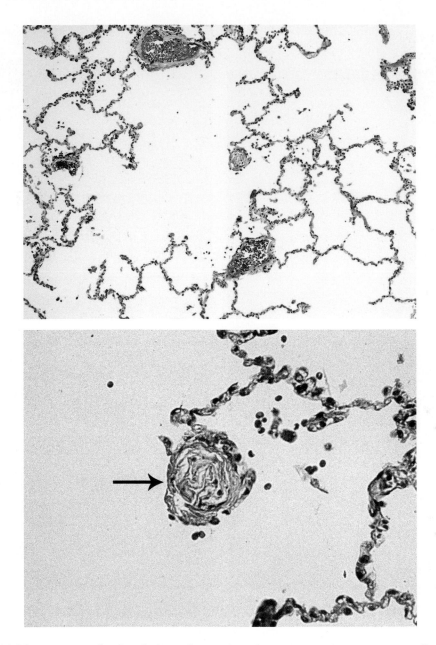

Figures 11.97 and 11.98 Amniotic fluid embolism, low and medium power, H&E. Amniotic fluid, composed of squamous cells, mucus, lanugo, and possibly meconium, found within the pulmonary vessels as demonstrated by the arrow. Thrombi may be seen as well. This can cause death by triggering an allergic reaction.

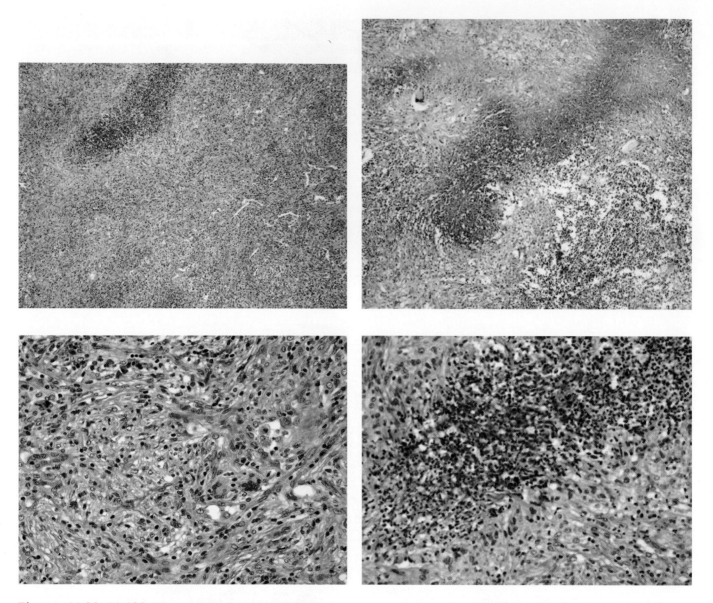

Figures 11.99–11.102 Wegner granulomatosis, also known as granulomatosis with polyangiitis, is a destructive disease frequently affecting the lung, nasal cavity, and kidneys, characterized by a lymphocytic and granulomatous vasculitis of small- to medium-sized vessels with resulting bionecrosis and parenchymal destruction.

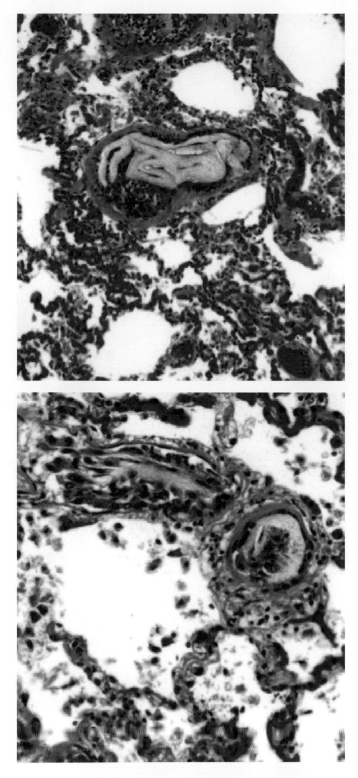

Figures 11.103 and 11.104 Hydrophilic polymer emboli from intravenous catheters. Basophilic, lamellated, nonpolarizable material can fragment from the surface of intravascular catheters and embolize, causing parenchymal infarction. This has been reported in the lung, brain, and heart.

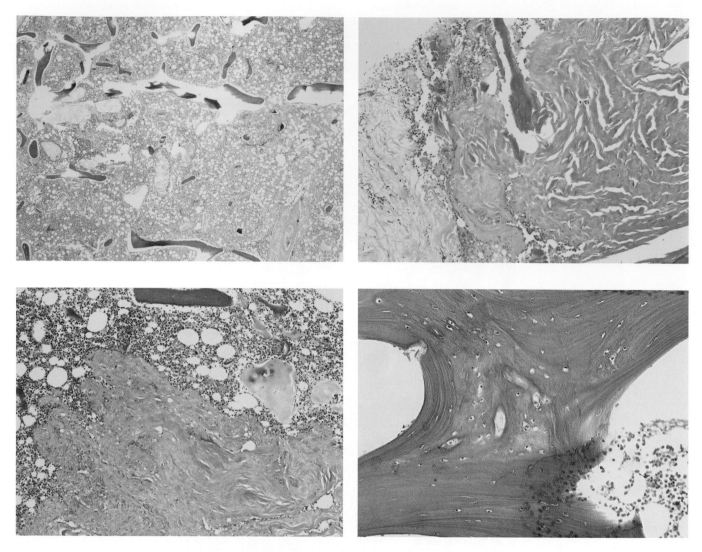

Figures 11.105–11.108 Osteogenesis imperfecta is a common congenital bone disease with variable penetrance and forms with variable severity that affects Type 1 collagen. The most severe Type II shows woven bone with crowded osteocytes. This condition is associated with blue to gray discoloration of the sclera and more easily fractured bones.

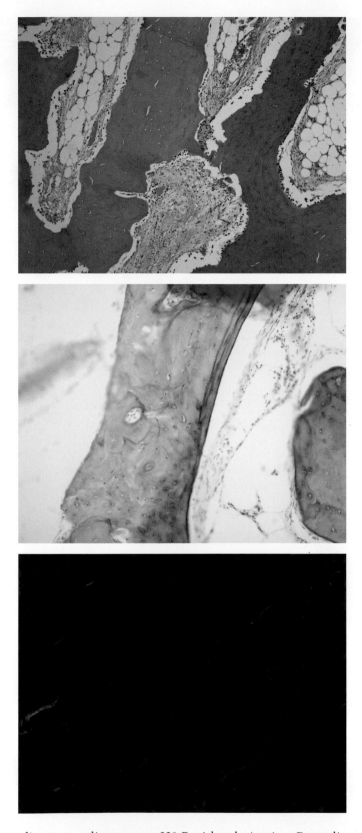

Figures 11.109–11.111 Paget disease, medium power, H&E with polarization. Paget disease of the bone is typically an incidental finding at autopsy; however, fractures can occur, especially in the spine and femur. In the mixed phase, there is a mosaic pattern of intersecting cement lines in thickened trabeculae along with thinned bone and increased osteoclasts. There is excessive breakdown and formation of bone, followed by disorganized remodeling. Histology may appear as a jigsaw puzzle, mapping, or mosaic pattern. Increasing hat size is a common presenting feature due to a thickened skull. See Figures 1.34–1.36 in Chapter 1. Polarized light examination highlights the abnormal collagen layering in woven bone. Sarcomas developing in the setting of polyostotic Paget are uniformly fatal.

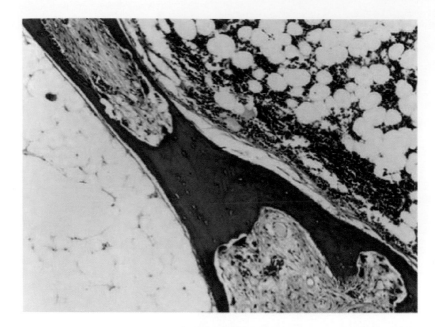

Figure 11.112 Dissecting osteitis, H&E. Typically in patients with secondary hyperparathyroidism and renal failure, there is dynamic bone loss. Initially, the bones of the hands are affected and show subperiosteal bone loss. Within the trabeculae of the bone there is tunneling of fibroblast-rich granulation tissue.

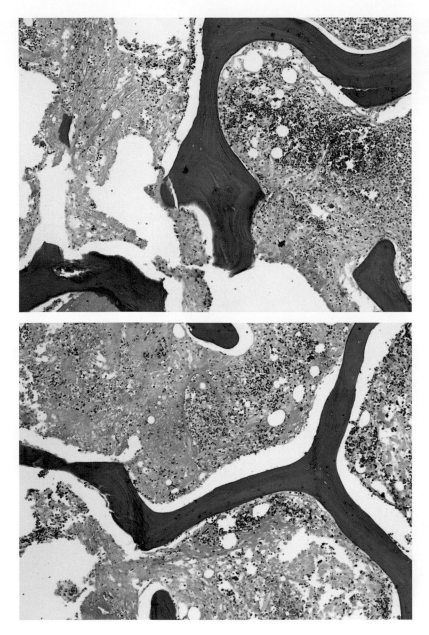

Figures 11.113 and 11.114 Early fracture, low and medium power, H&E. The bone marrow shows edema, hemorrhage, fibrin, and fat necrosis with necrotic bone trabeculae (loss of osteocyte nuclei).

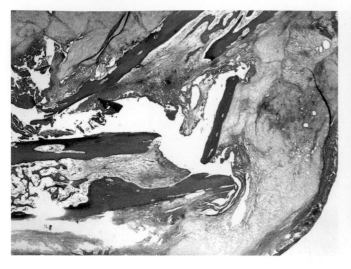

Figure 11.115 Fracture at 3 weeks at 2×.

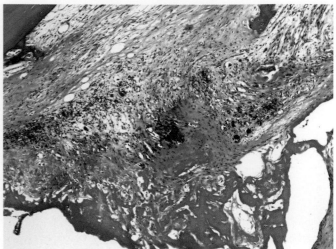

Figure 11.116 Fracture at 3 weeks at 10×.

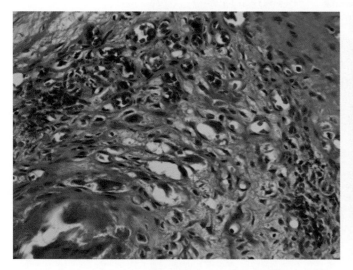

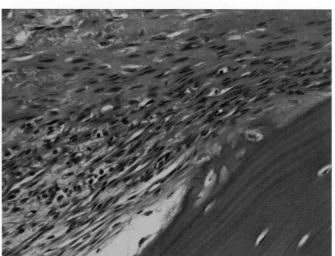

Figures 11.117 and 11.118 Fracture at 3 weeks at 40×.

Figure 11.119 Bone, callus, low power, H&E. After a period of weeks following a fracture, a bony callus forms with granulation tissue abating and fibrocartilage replaced by woven bone.

Figure 11.120 Craniotomy site with bone and scar tissue.

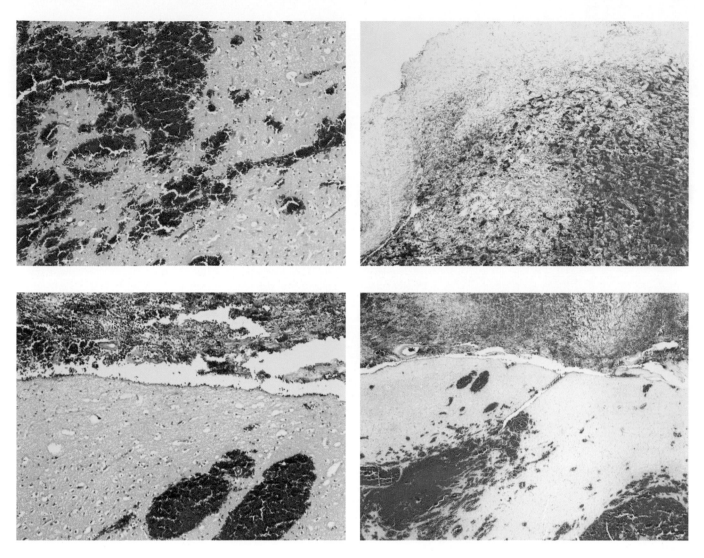

Figures 11.121–11.124 Subdural hematoma.

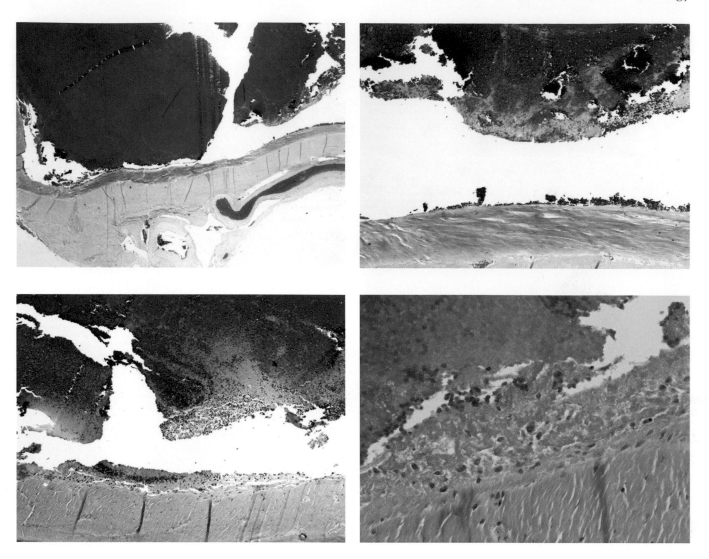

Figures 11.125–11.128 Subdural hematoma 2–4 days.

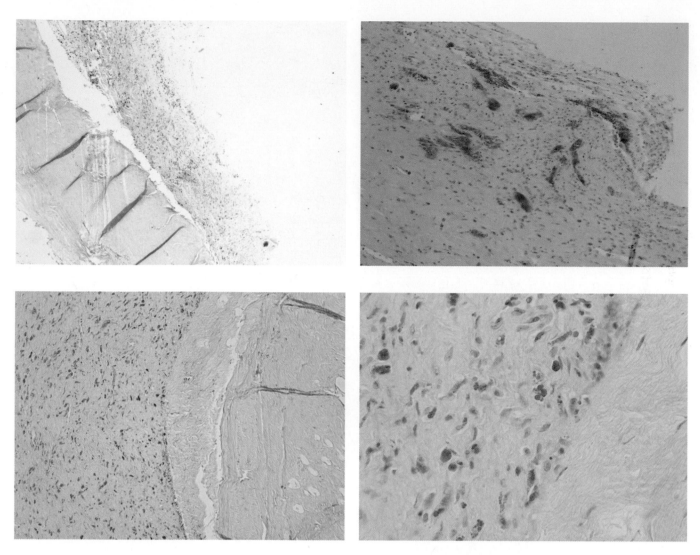

Figures 11.129–11.132 Subdural hematoma status post 1 month, H&E, low and medium power. The dural membrane is thickened with developed neomembrane, which is now combined less than two times the thickness of the normal dura. The neomembrane is collagenized, and there is no apparent clot, but there are numerous pigment-laden macrophages. Capillaries and small vessels continue to vascularize the neomembrane.

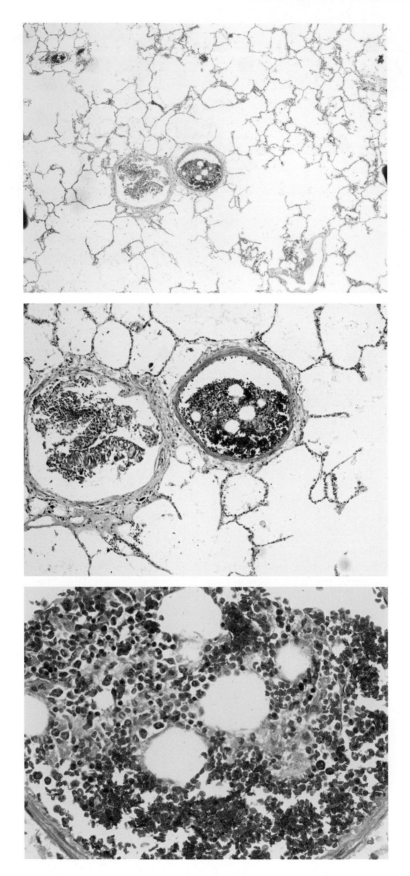

Figures 11.133–11.135 Lung with bone marrow embolus. Most bone marrow emboli are incidental and related to resuscitation efforts. In fat embolism syndrome related to trauma and bone fractures or in the context of sickle cell anemia, the lung parenchyma surrounding the marrow emboli should show a vital reaction such as hemorrhage or infarction.

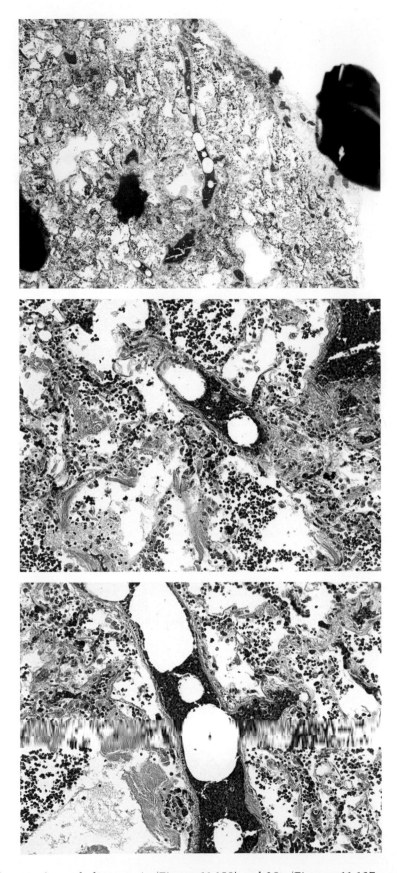

Figures 11.136–11.138 Lung fat embolism at 4× (Figure 11.150) and 20× (Figures 11.137 and 11.138). Note the white spaces within the blood vessel due to fat that was dissolved away during slide processing. This can be seen with skeletal fractures, crush injury to fatty tissue, burns, and even liposuction. This stage may be rapidly fatal if the embolized fat quantity is large enough and is dispersed into blood vessels quickly, even before it passes through to affect the brain.

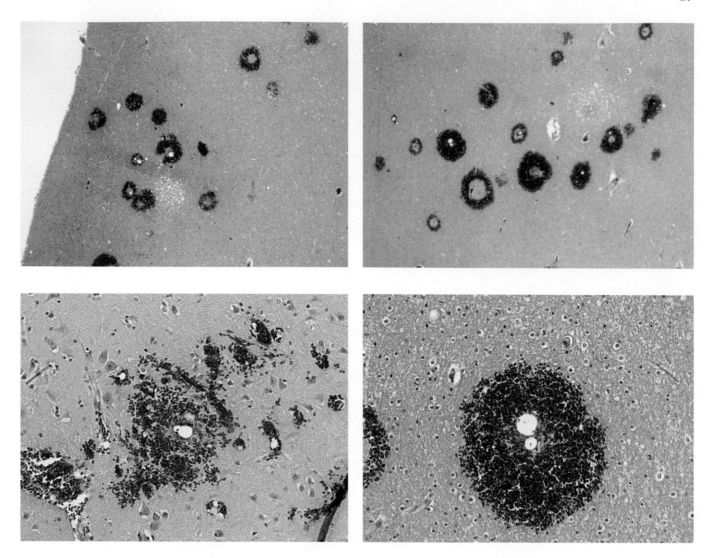

Figures 11.139–11.142 Fat embolism, brain, medium and high power, H&E. Diffusely there are perivascular "ring" hemorrhages with intravascular empty spaces that compress the adjacent cells and tissues corresponding to the intravascular fat globules dissolved during processing. Oil red O or osmium staining can be performed on fresh sections. Intravascular fat globules without hemorrhages are nonspecific. Fat embolism syndrome usually presents between 1 and 3 days after trauma with shortness of breath, neurological changes, and petechial rash. This syndrome may be fatal.

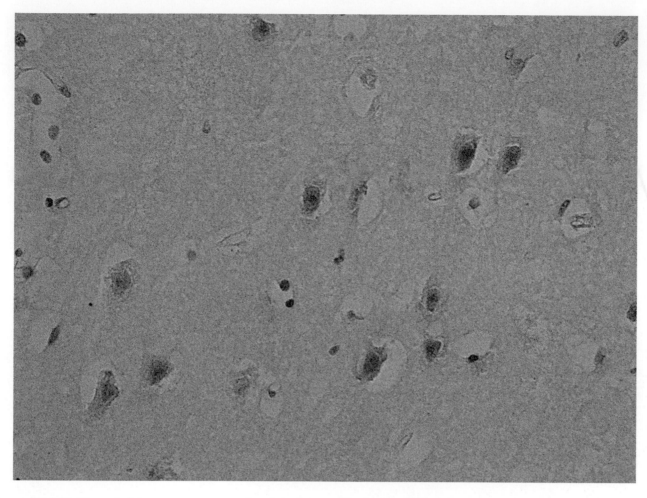

Figure 11.143 Hypoxic hippocampus. Note the shrunken eosinophilic neurons.

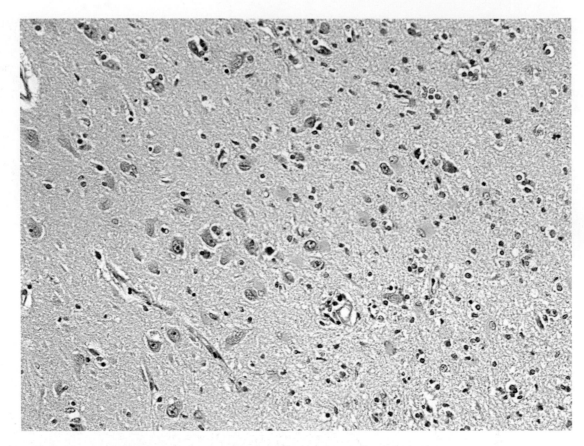

Figure 11.144 Cerebral anoxia 20×. Note the anoxic eosinophilic neurons and neuronophagia with edema.

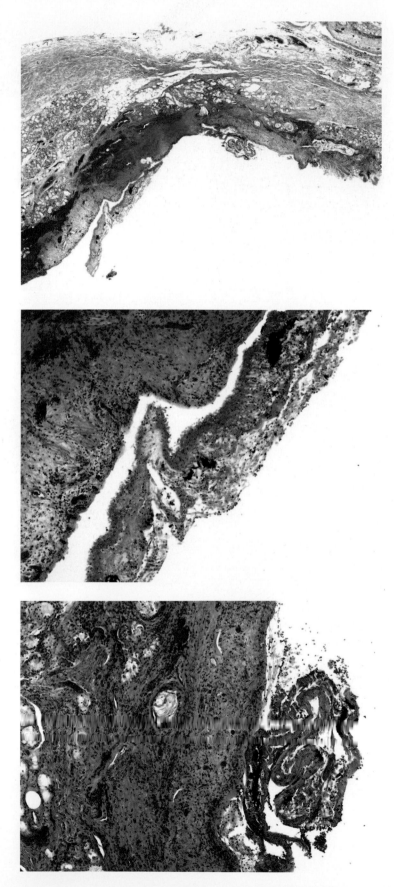

Figures 11.145–11.147 Trachea with soot 2× (Figure 11.145) and 10× (Figures 11.146 and 11.147). This individual died of smoke inhalation during a house fire.

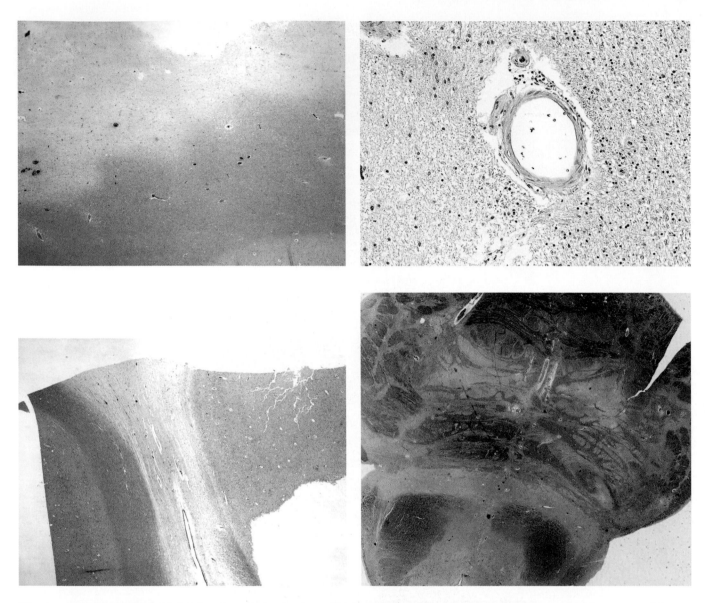

Figures 11.148–11.151 Multiple sclerosis 2×. Both on H&E and Luxol fast blue, pale areas correspond to areas of demyelination, typically in a perivascular distribution with lymphocytes and macrophages. In the pons this is to be contrasted with the midline demyelination found in central pontine myelinolysis.

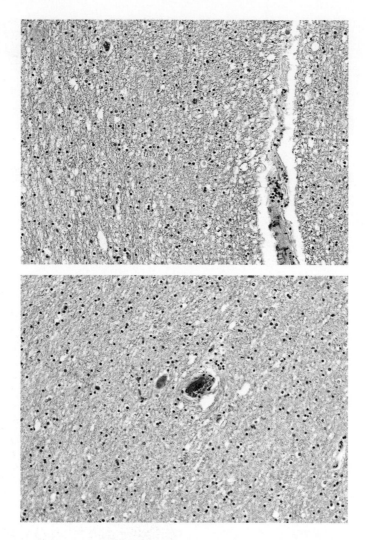

Figures 11.152 and 11.153 Multiple sclerosis 20×.

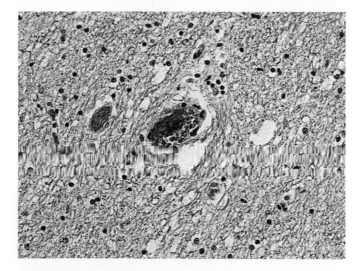

Figure 11.154 Chronic inflammation of blood vessels in multiple sclerosis 40×.

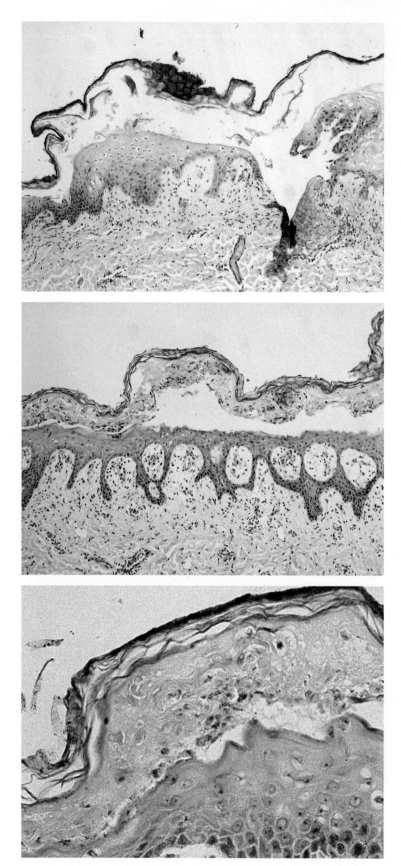

Figures 11.155–11.157 Toxic epidermal necrolysis (TEN) or Stevens–Johnson syndrome (SJS), H&E, medium power. Usually a result of hypersensitivity drug reaction, especially sulfonamides. The TEN is the SJS variant with full epidermal necrosis, typically showing epidermal–dermal separation with necrotic keratinocytes at the point of cleavage. TEN is fatal 30%–40% of the time and is considered a rare occurrence.

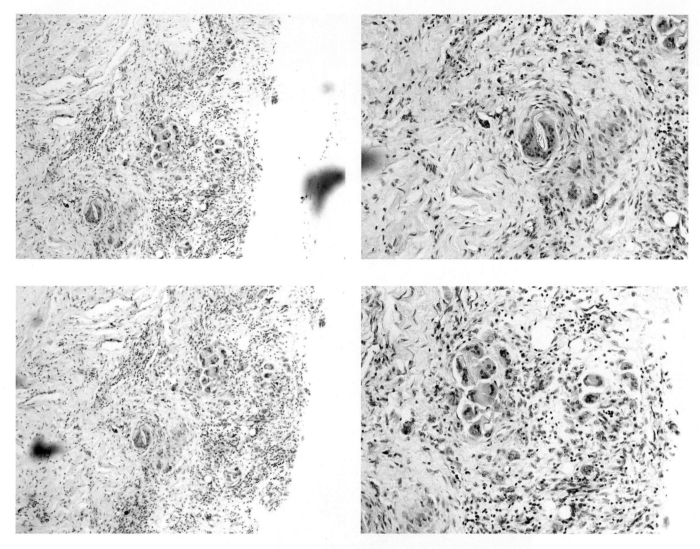

Figures 11.158 and 11.159 Skin intravenous drug abuse tract mark 10×.

Figures 11.160 and 11.161 Skin intravenous drug abuse tract mark w/ foreign body and granuloma 20×.

Figures 11.162–11.164 This individual died as a result of intravenous injection of crushed hydrocodone pills. Note the polarizable debris within and around the pulmonary blood vessels.

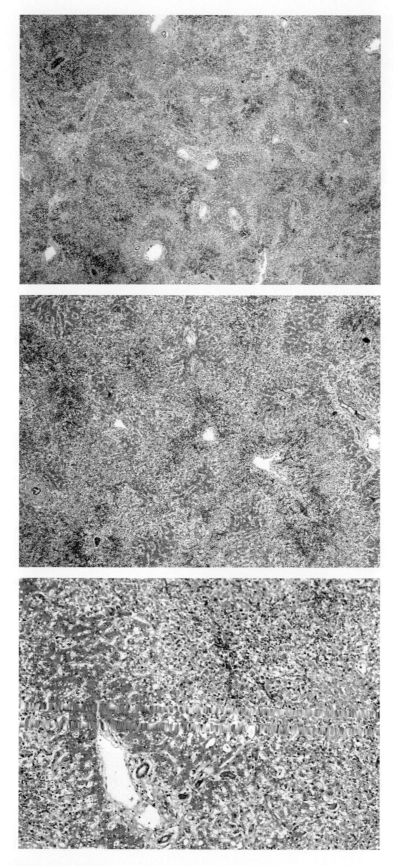

Figures 11.165–11.167 Hepatic acetaminophen toxicity 2×. Centrilobular necrosis in acetaminophen overdose 4×. Dead and dying hepatocytes in acetaminophen overdose 10×. There are typically no symptoms in the first 24 hours following overdose, leading to massive liver necrosis between 3 and 5 days.

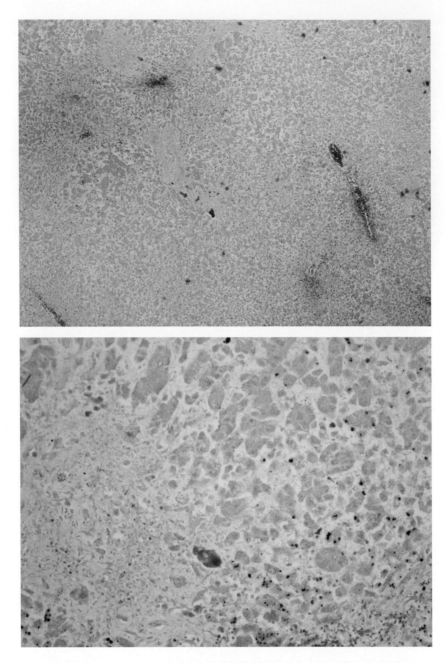

Figures 11.168 and 11.169 Halothane is an inhalational halogenated general anesthetic that may cause significant liver damage. The image demonstrates extensive necrosis in this fatal case. The spectrum leading up to this may include mild lymphocytic infiltrates of the portal tracts and partial sparing of periportal hepatocytes.

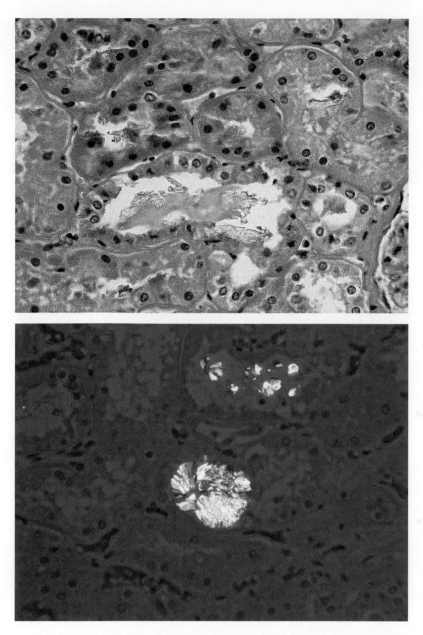

Figures 11.170 and 11.171 Ethylene glycol, pegylated, H&E/polarized, medium power. Following ingestion of ethylene glycol, there is hepatic metabolism to glycolic acid and eventually to oxalic acid. Glycolic acid is responsible for the metabolic acidosis in ethylene glycol poisoning. The increased oxalic acid excretion results in the formation of calcium oxalate crystals in the renal tubules and the foamy appearance of the tubules. The oxalate crystals can be visualized under polarized light examination. The presence of oxalate crystals is not pathognomonic for ethylene glycol poisoning.

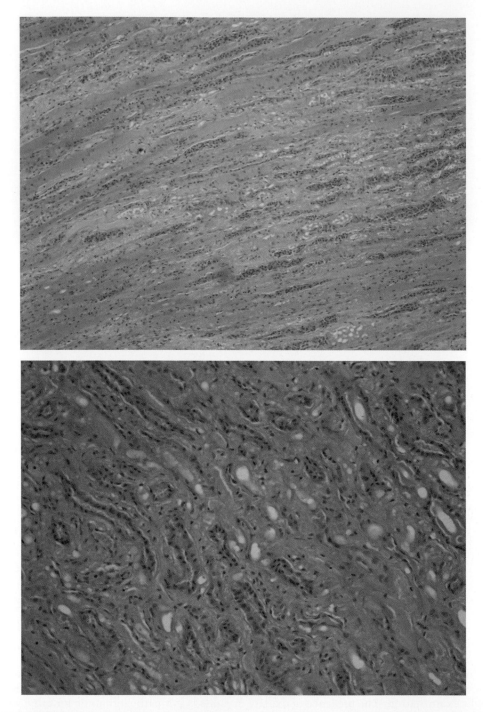

Figures 11.172 and 11.173 Freeze artifact in the kidney demonstrating autolysis and empty clefts from expanding ice crystals. These clefts may lead to accelerated putrefaction in a thawed body. Figure 11.172, 10×; Figure 11.173, 20×.

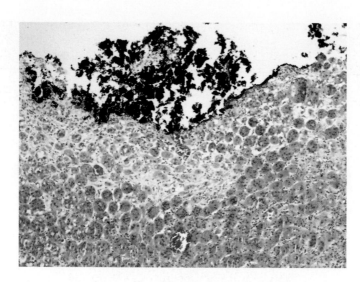

Figure 11.174 Stomach with charcoal debris, high power, H&E. Activated charcoal is an absorbent powder used for gastrointestinal decontamination following a toxic ingestion. Histologically, it appears as a black amorphous substance similar to soot.

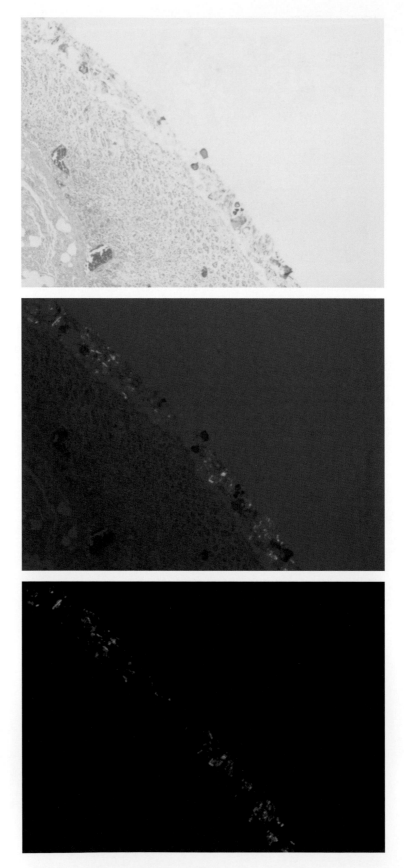

Figures 11.175–11.177 Suicidal overdose by oral pill ingestion. Note the gastric mucosal pill fragments that are demonstrated in different degrees of polarization.

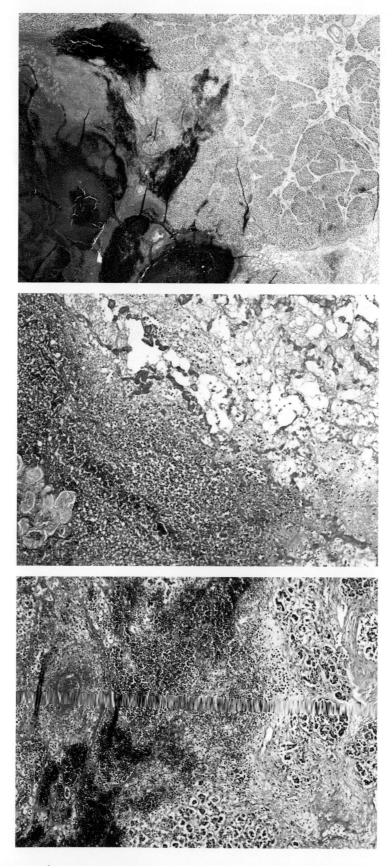

Figures 11.178–11.180 Hemorrhagic pancreatitis, low and medium power, H&E. Low power shows the frank hemorrhage (Figure 11.178) into the pancreas with retained lobulation. Progressively, there is acute inflammation with parenchymal and fat necrosis (Figure 11.179) and secondary vasculitis (Figure 11.180). Frequent causes include alcohol abuse, gallstones, metabolic disorders, infections, and endoscopic retrograde cholangiopancreatography.

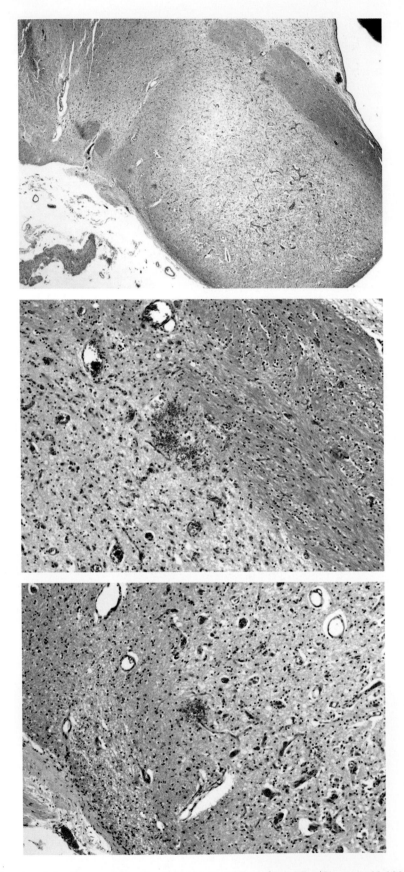

Figures 11.181–11.183 Wernicke hemorrhage 2× (Figure 11.181) and at 10× (Figures 11.182 and 11.183). Wernicke–Korsakoff encephalopathy occurs in alcoholics with thymine (vitamin B1) deficiency. Characteristics include anterograde amnesia, confabulation, and hallucinations. The mammillary bodies are affected as depicted.

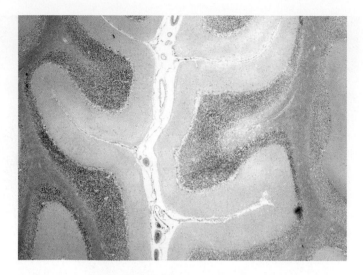

Figure 11.184 Cerebellum with chronic alcohol (ethanol).

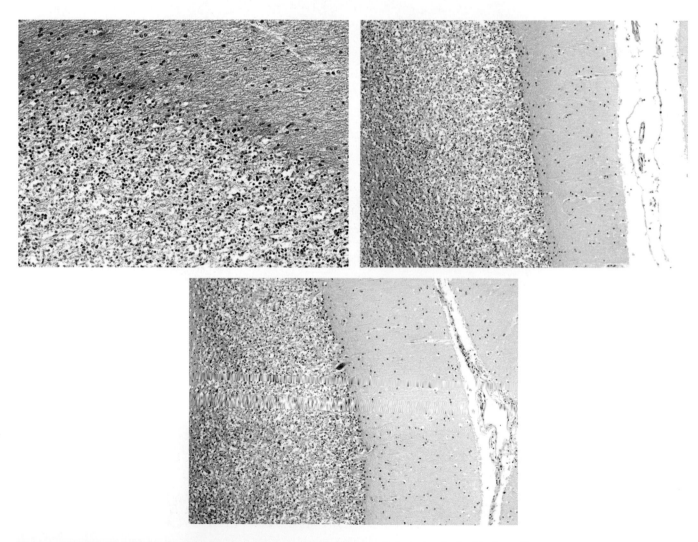

Figures 11.185–11.187 Purkinje cell with presence and absence of chronic alcohol (ethanol).

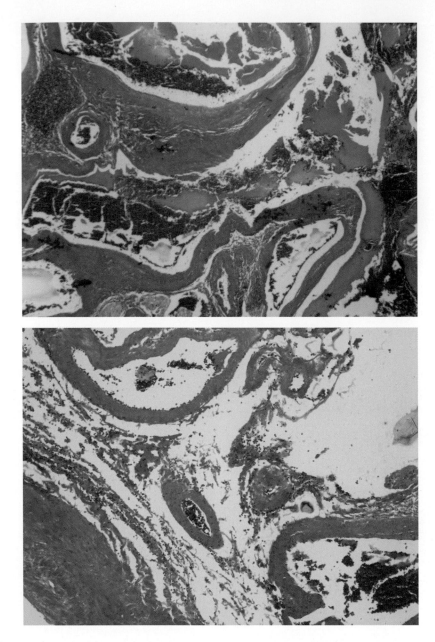

Figures 11.188 and 11.189 This ruptured cerebral arteriovenous (AV) malformation led to rapidly fatal subarachnoid hemorrhage. Grossly these malformations may appear as red spongy masses or may be too small to identify easily.

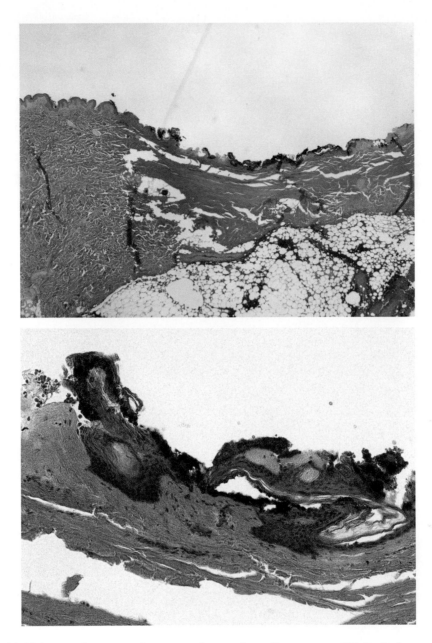

Figures 11.190 and 11.191 Gunshot wound, contact, low and medium power, H&E. At low power, the eosinophilic contraction of the dermis is apparent. At high power, there is nuclear streaming and condensation epidermis embedded with black soot.

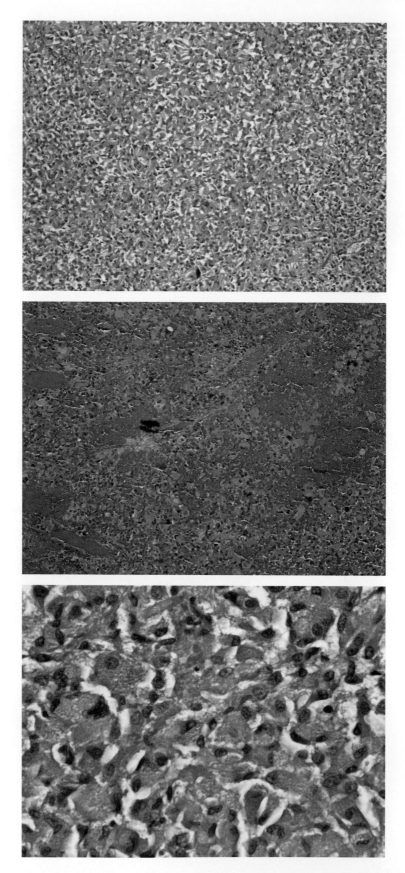

Figures 11.192–11.194 Pheochromocytomas are usually benign tumors of the adrenal medulla originating from neuroendocrine chromaffin cells. Symptoms include those associated with sympathetic hyperactivity including fluctuations in blood pressure, heart rate, weight loss, and anxiety. Death may occur by fatal arrhythmia. The highly vascular nature will lead to some degree of red to brown discoloration.

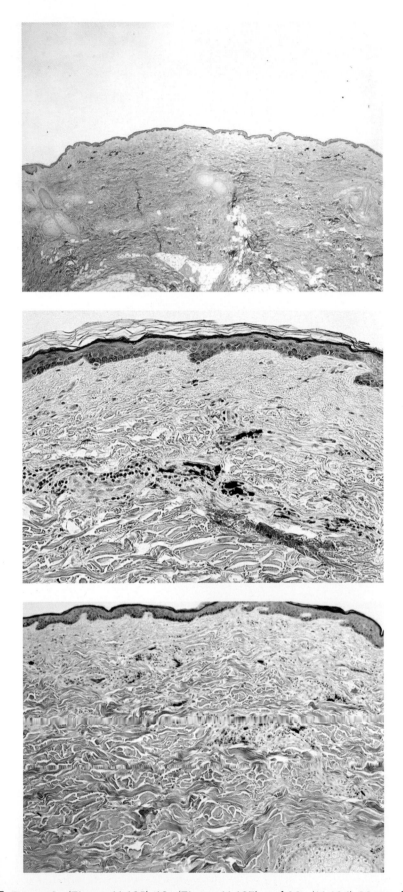

Figures 11.195–11.197 Tattoo 2× (Figure 11.195), 10× (Figure 11.197), and 20× (11.196). Macrophages with phagocytized colored pigments.

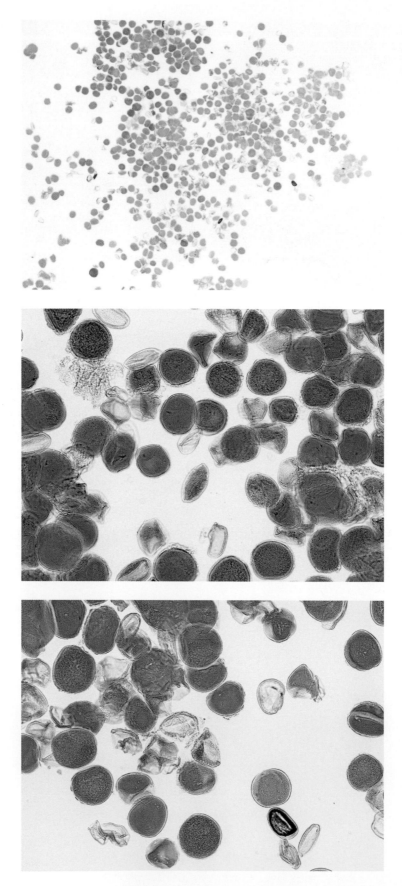

Figures 11.198–11.200 Pollen can take a variety of forms but, in general, has a mean size of 25 mm. Palynology is the study of pollen and has many forensic applications.

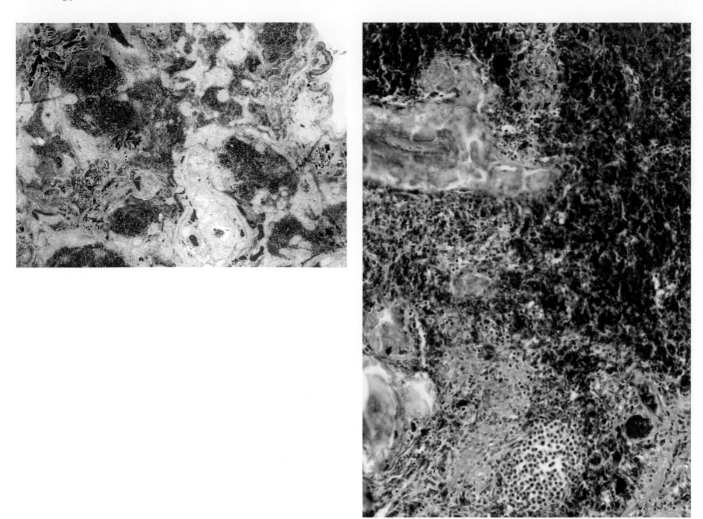

Figures 11.201 and 11.202 Autoinfarction of spleens from adult individuals with sickle cell anemia. These spleens are typically shrunken and firm. Note the histopathology sections with marked congestion, fibrosis, and Gamna–Gandy bodies from iron pigments with calcium salts. Gamna–Gandy bodies are not pathognomonic for sickle cell disease.

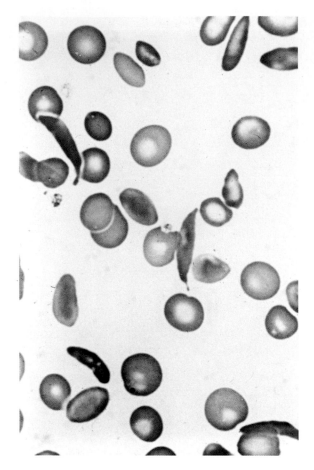

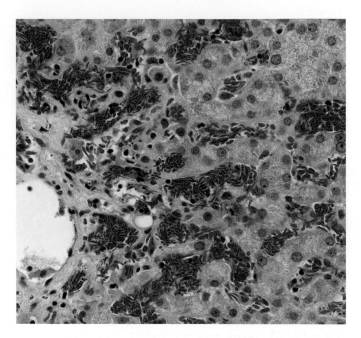

Figure 11.204 Sickle cell anemia, liver, high power, H&E. The sinusoidal spaces are diffusely congested and filled with sickle-shaped red blood cells. Hemosiderosis may be concomitantly found. Isolated sickled red blood cells may occur in patients without sickle cell anemia.

Figure 11.203 Sickle cell anemia. Peripheral blood smear showing sickled cells.

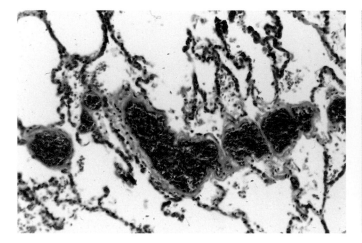

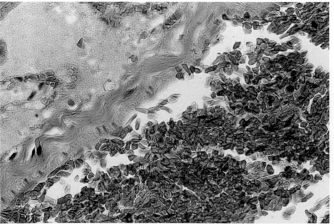

Figures 11.205 and 11.206 Sickle cell anemia with crisis. Lung with marked congestion and pulmonary edema. Hemoglobin crystallization leading to malformed sickle-shaped red blood cells may be perpetuated by hypoxia acidosis and dehydration from activities such as vigorous exercise. Sickled cells create blood flow obstruction, further sickling, and further hypoxia with hemolysis. This is associated with severe pain and possibly tissue infarction that may lead to death. Even individuals with sickle cell trait, under severe conditions, have been known to go into crisis and die.

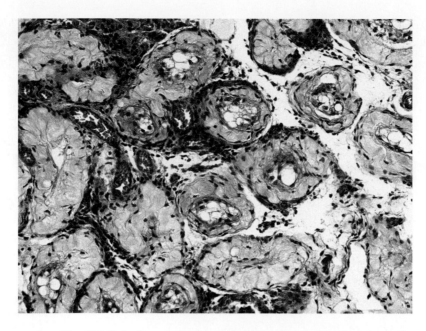

Figure 11.207 Testis, atrophy, 20×, H&E. In low-androgen states in a postpubertal male such as chronic ethanol abuse and anabolic steroid use, the seminiferous tubules show hyalinization with atrophy of the germ cells leaving only Sertoli and Leydig cells.

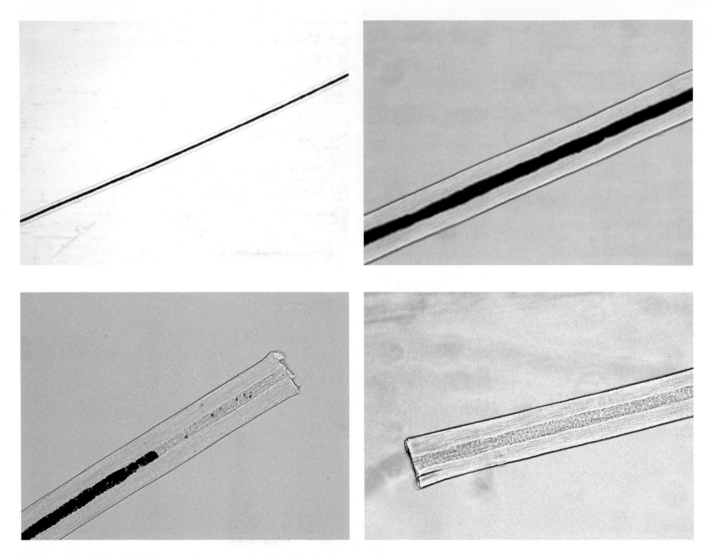

Figures 11.208–11.211 Dog hair, unstained.

Figures 11.212–11.215 Brown human hair.

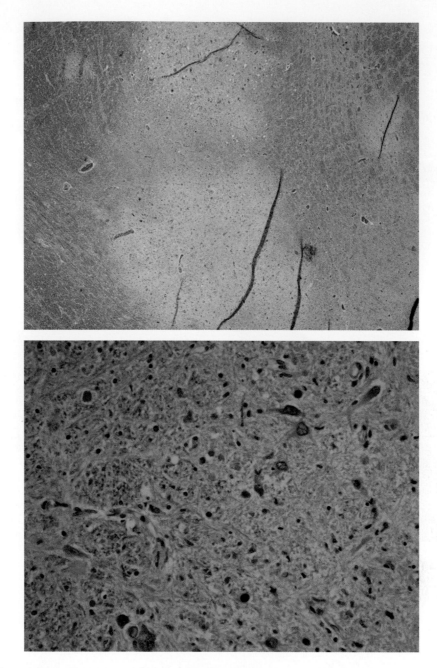

Figures 11.216 and 11.217 Progressive multifocal leukoencephalopathy is typically the result of infection with JC virus in the central nervous system. The infected glial cells are can appear bizarre and pleomorphic with glassy nuclear inclusions. The lesions are centered in the white matter and produce demyelination.

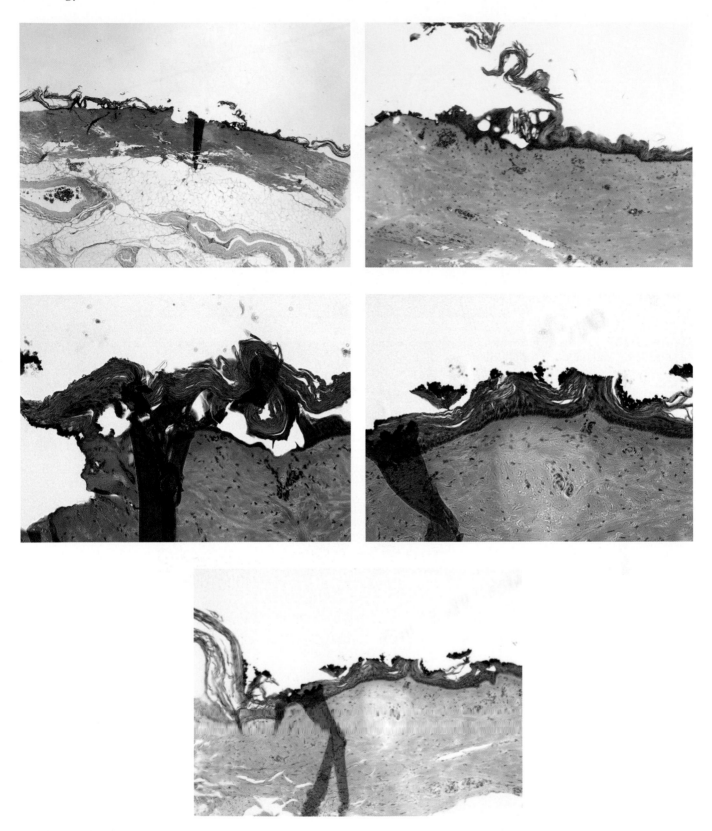

Figures 11.218–11.222 Burn of skin. In a thermal burn, the epidermis and dermis are contracted with hypereosino-philia and nuclear streaming.

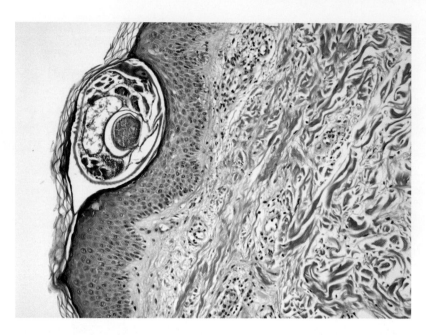

Figure 11.223 The scabies burrow is mostly in the epidermis and contains the mite. The inflammatory infiltrate can be significant and include eosinophils.

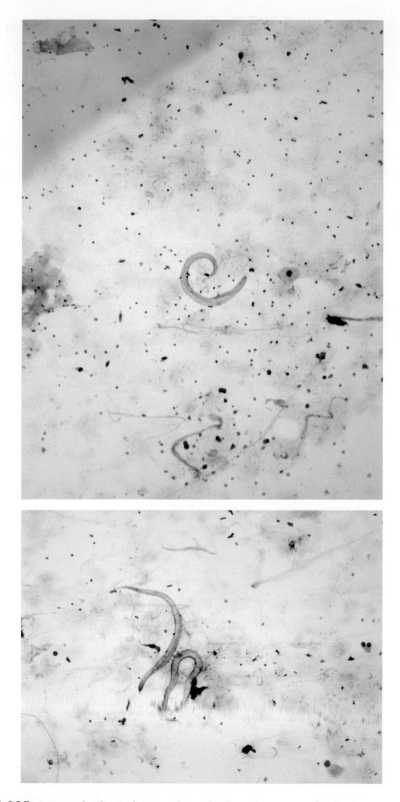

Figures 11.224 and 11.225 *Strongyloides* infection, bronchial wash. *Strongyloides* is an intestinal parasite that can cause pulmonary infections, mostly in immunocompromised hosts. Strongyloidiasis can present with acute respiratory insufficiency/failure or pulmonary embolism.

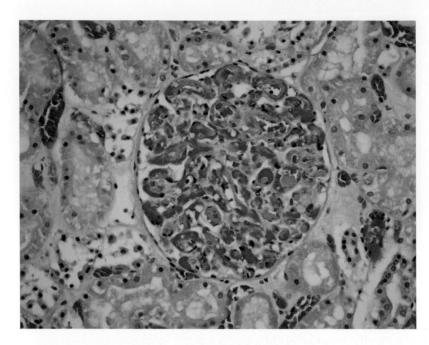

Figure 11.226 Idiopathic thrombocytopenia (ITP). ITP is caused by antibodies to platelet antigens, which can develop as a primary or secondary disease process. The presentation is varied and can include minor bleeding or major hemorrhage. In the kidney, the glomerular capillary loops contain fibrin thrombi, similar to thrombotic thrombocytopenic purpura (TTP).

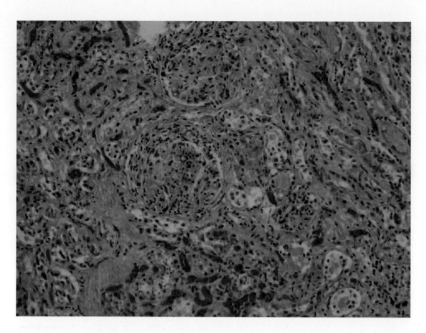

Figure 11.227 Crescentic or rapidly progressive glomerulonephritis. A crescent is the result of marked basement membrane injury and characterized by epithelial cells, macrophages, fibrin, and debris within Bowman space. The degree and amount of glomerular crescents generally correspond to the degree of renal injury. The etiology can be vasculitis (immune), collagen vascular disease, or antiglomerular basement membrane disease.

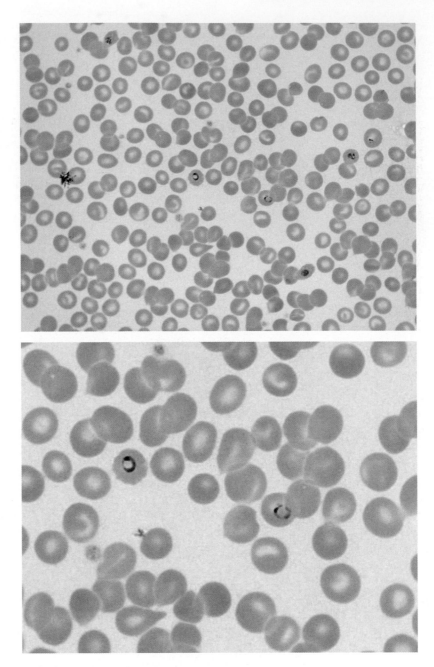

Figures 11.228 and 11.229 *Plasmodium falciparum* infection. The immature trophozoite (ring) forms are seen within the mature red blood cells on this smear.

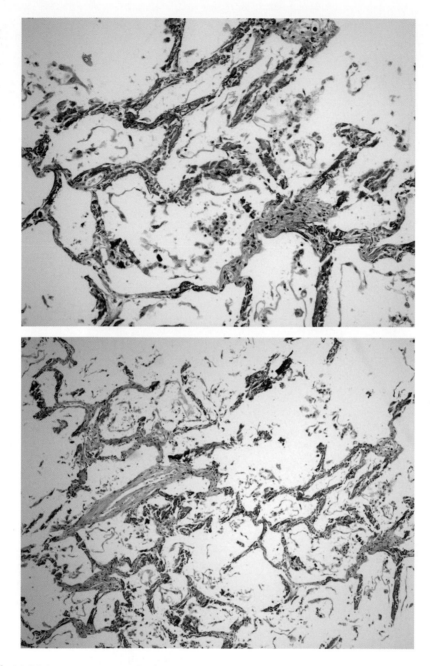

Figures 11.230 and 11.231 Metastatic calcification typically occurs in patients with chronic renal insufficiency undergoing hemodialysis. In the lung, the basophilic calcification appears within the alveolar walls and is positive with von Kossa staining. In some patients, widespread calcification can result in significant pulmonary edema, respiratory compromise, and death.

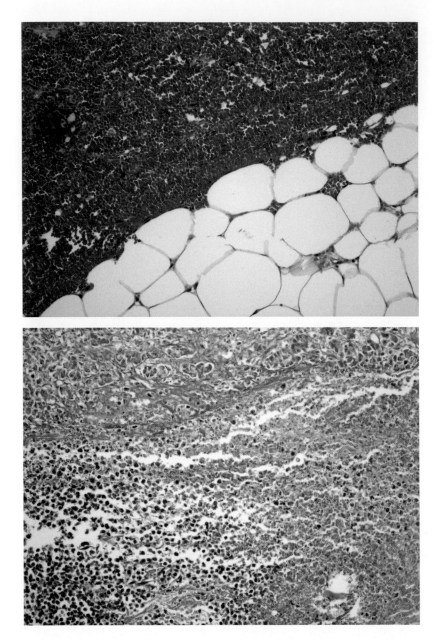

Figures 11.232 and 11.233 Interpretation of the healing response to injury in a given time period may be quite variable depending on the immune response, adjacent intact vasculature, amount of hemorrhage, the presence of infection, and the location in the body. Relative to skin, first there is blood clot formation with scab consisting mostly of dried blood, platelets, and fibrin. After the first 4 hours or so there is generally edema, blood vessel margination of neutrophils, and progression of acute inflammation. Neutrophils peak in 1–3 days. Figure 11.232 depicts mostly hemorrhage, which will generally be present for the first several hours. Figure 11.233 depicts a large acute inflammatory response with clearing of damaged tissue, which would be seen in typically about 2–3 days.

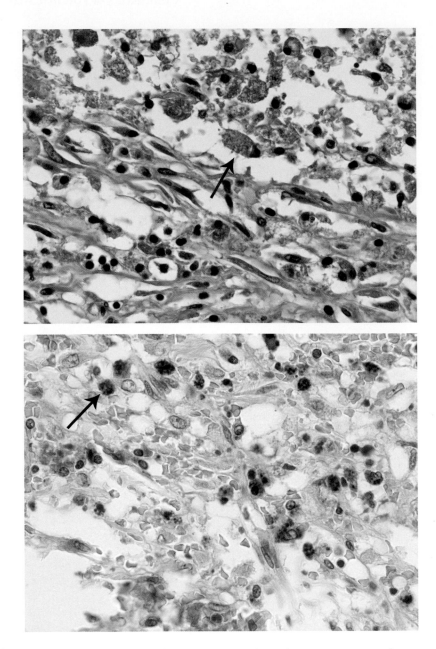

Figures 11.234 and 11.235 Wound healing. After approximately 16 hours monocytes first appear consisting of lymphocytes and macrophages. Macrophages with hemosiderin first appear as early as 24 hours after injury. Hemosiderin from red blood cell absorption and iron accumulation can be demonstrated by iron stain (in Figure 11.235 Prussian blue, which is indicated by the blue intramacrophage granules demonstrated by the arrows in the photographs).

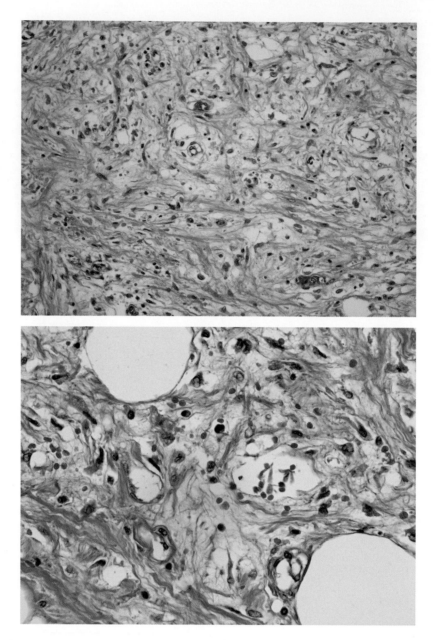

Figures 11.236–11.237 Wound healing. While the inflammatory response is going on, granulation tissue begins to form at about 24–72 hours and continues for up to 7 days or more. Note the loose connective tissue with early blood vessel formation, plump fibroblasts, and early collagen deposition. It generally takes weeks for full healing with scar formation and wound contraction to occur. It is also important to note that a scar is always weaker than normal skin.

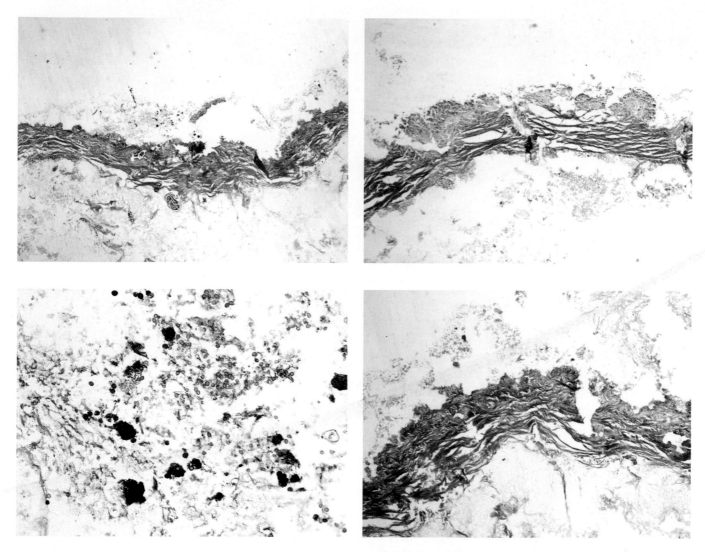

Figures 11.238 and 11.239 Decomposed skin 2×.   **Figures 11.240 and 11.241** Decomposed skin 4×.

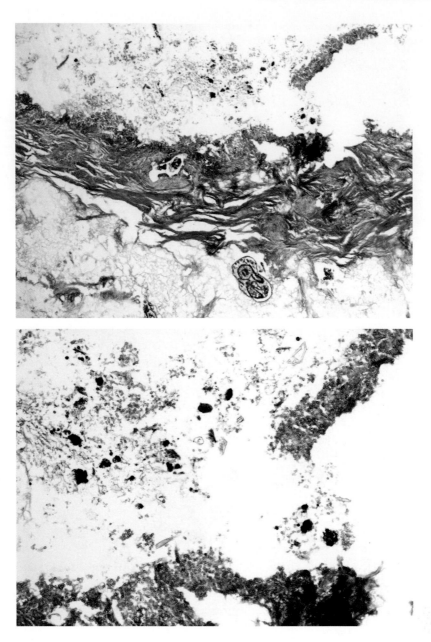

Figures 11.242 and 11.243 Decomposed skin 10×.

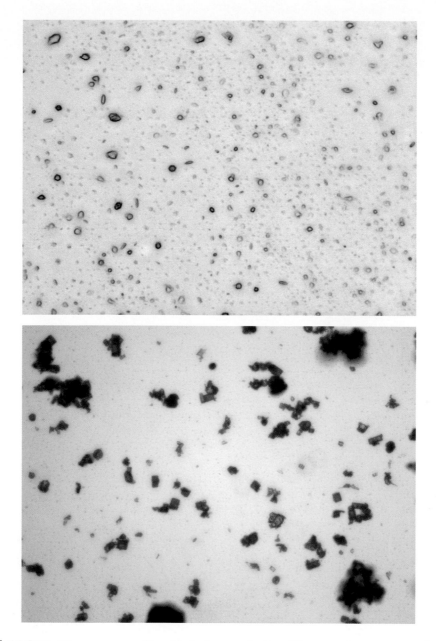

Figures 11.244 and 11.245 Diatoms are cell-walled algae and plant-like aquatic organisms found in water or soil. When found in lungs and organs of nondecomposed bodies retrieved from fresh water, they support drowning as a cause of death and may be useful in determining the location of death as well.

Forensic Photography

12

GINA SANTUCCI, CHARLES A. CATANESE,
AND BRUCE LEVY

Contents

Introduction

Forensic photography is used to document evidence at a scene or at an autopsy for use by a pathologist or presented in court. It is important to accurately document each step of the investigation. To do this one must first understand how photography works, then devise a system that is consistent from scene to scene and from autopsy to autopsy. A shot list with accurate angles, scales, and tools will provide a formula that will cover all the photographic evidence needed for the investigation. Without a minimal shot list of photographs, the viewers not present at the scene could misinterpret evidence. Although each scene or autopsy may require additional photographs, it is good to have a basic shot list for the average scenario. This chapter will provide a simple system that breaks down scene and autopsy photography

into three easy sections: overalls, midrange, and close-ups. These three sections will cover all the photography skills needed to properly document forensic evidence and create a fast, consistent workflow. Before we begin, though, we will review the legal and regulatory environment, as well as how a camera works and how to accurately acquire images with as little distortion as possible.

Legal and Regulatory Considerations

The American legal system regularly uses photographic and digital images obtained during a forensic death investigation as evidence. The Federal Rules of Evidence defines the legal requirements for the use of these images in federal court, and has helped shape state laws regarding use of these images in state courts (although it is important to learn your state's rules as they may differ significantly from the Federal Rules). The legal standards for inclusion of images include:

- The image has to be relevant to the issue before the court (Federal Rules of Evidence 401).
- The image has to be authentic, presenting a fair and accurate representation of the actual injury, scene, or other evidence (Federal Rules of Evidence 901).
- The image cannot be overly prejudicial, meaning its probative value is greater than its prejudicial value (Federal Rules of Evidence 403).

In addition, there are a plethora of guidelines regarding the use of digital images in forensics. The Scientific Working Group on Imaging Technology (SWGIT) created most of these guidelines. It is critical to understand the difference between the two distinct categories of images defined by SWGIT, as these categories are universally recognized by other imaging guidelines. Most images obtained in the course of a forensic death investigation fall under Category 1. However, if these images are used for any type of analysis, then the more stringent Category 2 applies. Analysis in the realm of forensic death investigation would include patterned injuries, pattered evidence, or matching of an injury to an implement/mechanism, such as a bite mark or shoe imprint. Regardless of the SWGIT category, any editing of the images must be performed on a copy of the image. The original image must remain forever unaltered. Basic processing techniques defined by SWGIT and commonly used by forensic pathology include brightness and contrast adjustment, resizing, cropping, positive-to-negative inversion, image rotation/inversion, conversion to grayscale, white balance, basic image sharpening and blurring, and de-interlacing.

Category 1 Images

- Most images obtained through a death investigation.
- Requires documentation of available processing techniques in a standard operating procedure.
- Documentation of specific steps performed on an image is NOT required.

Category 2 Images

- Any images used for analysis, such as pattern matching.
- Use and sequence of any processing technique should be documented in every instance.
- Goal is to allow another investigator to exactly follow steps using another copy of the original image and arrive at the exact same processed copy of the image.

Basic Photography for Forensics

How to Hold a Camera Properly

- Place left hand under the lens.
- Prop left elbow against chest for support.
- Wrap right hand around right side of camera.
- Keep right elbow down toward chest (see Figure 12.1a and b).

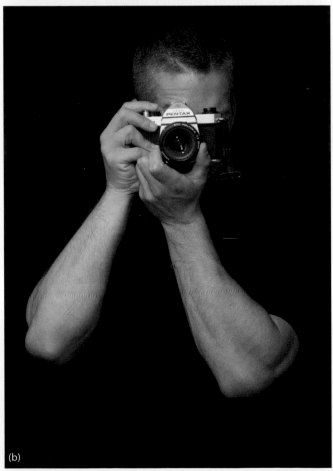

Figure 12.1

Figure 12.2

Why One Should Hold a Camera This Way
- Depressing the shutter button pushes down on the camera and can cause it to move, creating motion blur.
- Left arm acts as a tripod for the camera.
- Support of the arm under the lens and against body stabilizes the camera.

Holding a Camera Vertically
- When holding the camera vertically, still support the lens with your left hand and press the left arm firmly against your body.
- Use your right hand to control the camera settings (see Figure 12.2).

Tripods and Monopods

Sometimes scenes are very dark. To prevent motion blur, one may want to use a tripod or monopod. These items will stabilize the camera during long exposures to prevent motion blur.

Timer

Another option is to set the timer on the camera and set it on a flat surface. The surface should be at least at the level of the waist. Make sure the angles in the photo are not compromised.

Using Auto Focus

Although all cameras are slightly different, most function the same. Almost all point-and-shoot and single lens reflex (SLR) cameras have an auto focus feature that functions in a similar fashion. Surprisingly, most people are never taught how to use auto focus in a similar fashion. Of course, this is an important skill in forensics. If one is pointing the camera at a subject and pressing the shutter release button down, then the picture will be taken before the camera has had time to focus. To focus, do the following:

Focusing

- Depress the shutter-release button halfway.
- Wait for the camera to focus.
- Do not let go of the shutter-release once the lens is focused.
- Fully depress the shutter-release without moving camera.
- Stay still while photo is being taken.

How One Will Know the Lens Is Focused

- Make sure your camera is set on auto focus (AF) before focusing.
- Most cameras have a small square that lights up in the viewfinder when it is in focus
- Some cameras make a beeping sound.
- Both of these settings as well as the area of focus can be changed on SLR and point-and-shoot cameras.

AF-Assist Illuminator

If the subject is too dark, some cameras have an AF-assist illuminator that will light up to assist focus operation. An AF-assist illuminator is a small light usually on the front upper right- or left-hand side on the camera. The light will illuminate automatically when working in an auto setting once the shutter button is depressed halfway.

Flashlights

Scene investigators should carry flashlights to aid investigating in dark environments. Flashlights can be used to help focus when using a camera without an AF-assist illuminator; however, once the camera is in focus it is better to turn the flashlight off before taking the picture to prevent hot spots within the photo. To do this, depress the shutter halfway down, turn off the flashlight, then continue to fully depress the shutter-release button without moving the camera. Proper technique necessitates the need for a tripod or an assistant to help control the flashlight.

Troubleshooting Auto Focus

Auto focus does not perform well under certain conditions. If the camera cannot focus automatically, do one of four things: focus the camera manually, focus on another object at the same distance, relight the scene, or recompose the photograph.

Focus relies on distance. If one focuses on something that is 4 feet away, then everything on that same plane will be in focus. When the shutter button is depressed halfway, the auto focus is locked. Therefore, if you focus on something 4 feet away then move the camera after focusing, only objects at the same distance will be in focus. This can work to your advantage or disadvantage. If one wants to focus on an object but the camera will not focus, try focusing on an object at the same distance, keep the shutter depressed halfway, and move the camera over to the desired subject. Conversely, if one depresses the shutter halfway and moves the camera to a subject that is not at the equivalent distance, the subject will be out of focus.

If the camera still is not focusing, it may be due to one of five common problems:

- **Low Contrast:** If there is little or no contrast between the subject and the background, the camera will have a hard time focusing when set on auto focus. *Example: the subject and background are the same color.*
- **Depth of Field:** If focusing on a subject behind or in something and there are objects at different distances from the camera, the auto focus may have difficulty focusing on the desired subject.
- **Sharp Contrast:** If the focus area contains sharp contrast, the camera may have trouble focusing when using auto focus. *Example: if the subject is half in shade.*
- **Patterns:** If there is a repeating pattern, the auto focus may not know what to focus on.
- **Lack of Light:** If the lighting is too dark, the AF-illuminator should light up to help focus, but one may still need a flashlight or external ambient light to help focus. Always use as much light as possible (see Figure 12.3).
- **Flat Surfaces:** If the lens does not have an edge to focus on, it will not focus automatically. If there is no edge to focus on, pick an object at the same distance as your subject, focus, keep the shutter release depressed halfway, and recompose the picture before pushing the button.

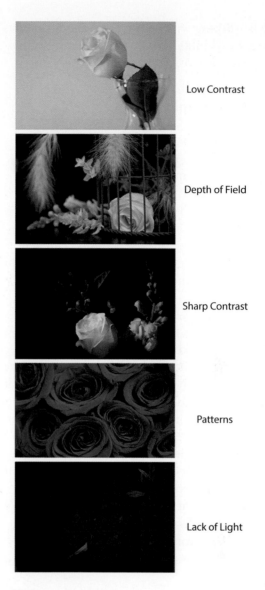

Low Contrast

Depth of Field

Sharp Contrast

Patterns

Lack of Light

Figure 12.3

Using Manual Focus

When auto focus does not suffice, it is best to manually focus. Working in forensics requires efficiency; work must be done quickly and correctly. Auto focus is preferred; however, if one is working with an SLR or a point-and-shoot that has a manual lens, the lens can always be focused manually. On SLRs, there is a switch on the side of the lens that usually reads AF/M, or something similar. AF enables auto focus, while M enables manual focus. To use manual focus, do the following:

- Push the switch on the lens over to M.
- Rotate the dial on the end of lens with the left hand while supporting the camera. Use right hand to control camera settings and the shutter release button.
- Once the subject is focused through viewfinder, depress shutter release button.

If one is working with a point-and-shoot that has manual focus capability, check the camera manual to see how to change to manual mode.

Basic Photography

There are three elements that control exposure:

- F-Stop/Aperture
- Shutter Speed
- ISO

Understanding these three settings is critical in order to control exposure and to understand what is happening when shooting in the Auto setting.

F-Stop/Aperture

The f-stop, also known as the aperture, affects the amount of light hitting the sensor. The aperture functions much like the pupil of an eye: it regulates the amount of light hitting the retina. In a dark room, the pupil opens to let light in. Similarly, in dark environments, the aperture should be opened wide to permit more light to hit the sensor. Conversely, in bright settings, the aperture should be narrow as to limit the amount of light hitting the sensor.

The diameter of the aperture is expressed in a series of standard numbers.

The change from one setting to the next is called a "stop." So, f2.8 to f4 is one stop, f2.8 to f5.6 is two stops, etc.

The f-stop also controls the **depth of field** in the photograph. Depth of field is the distance from the nearest to the farthest objects that are in focus in the image. The depth of field is synonymous with **focal length**. When the aperture is wide open, there is very little depth of field (see Figure 12.4).

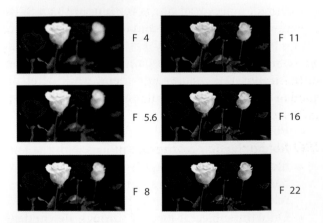

Figure 12.4

How F-Stop Affects Depth of Field

- If camera is set to f2.8 (large diameter), and you are focusing on something in the foreground, background will be out of focus.
- If camera is set to f22, (small diameter), and you focus on something in the foreground, both the foreground and background will be in focus.
- In summary, the aperture diameter and the depth of field are inversely proportional (i.e., as diameter increases, depth of field decreases and vice versa).

F-Stop for Forensic Photography

- Best apertures for crime scene: f8–f22

Houses and apartments are often poorly lit. It is hard to shoot between these f-stops because a lot of light is needed for such a small aperture. If the aperture falls below f8, adjust other settings to keep it from going any lower or add light to the scene. When doing close-ups, one can use f11 through f22 because the flash will light the subject, giving enough light for small apertures. It is important to keep the f-stop as close to the 22 as possible to get maximum depth of field.

Shutter Speeds

The shutter determines the duration the sensor is exposed to light. It also controls the motion of the subject being photographed.

The settings that determine how long the shutter is open are divided into seconds or fractions of seconds. Each setting change is called a "stop," just like f-stops.

Changing from 1/30th of a second to 1/60th of a second is one stop. Changing from 1/30 to 1/125 is two stops (1/30th to 1/60th then to 1/125th).

Controlling Motion

Fast shutter speeds (1/125–1/2000) freeze motion. These shutter speeds need a lot of light and are usually taken outside in bright sunlight, with a flash, or with studio lights.

Slow shutter speeds (below 1/30) are usually taken in medium/low-light situations to maximize the amount of light reaching the sensor.

When using a handheld camera, do not go below 1/60th of a second. This will help prevent motion blur. Below 1/60, the motion of the subject or the person shooting the photo can cause blurring of the image. Since scenes are usually still, one can put the camera on a tripod for stabilization. This will allow you to use long shutter speeds such as 1/30 and below, allowing light

1/125th of a second

ISO 100

ISO 6400

Figure 12.6

Choosing the Correct ISO

- Use a low ISO in bright light.
- Use a high ISO in low light.
- Example: ISO of 100 in bright outdoor scene.
- Example: ISO of 3,200 in shadowy hallway scene.

ISO usually ranges from 100 to 3,200, although some cameras go lower or higher. The ISO settings are usually as follows: 100, 200, 400, 800, 1600, and 3200. Newer digital cameras are capable of going much higher than 3,200. This gives you the ability to shoot in very low light situations; however, a high ISO compromises the quality of the image. High ISOs tend to make the image pixilated or "noisy." To prevent noise in your image use low ISO (see Figure 12.6a and b).

ISO for Forensic Photography

- Outside: 100 or 200 ISO for scene photography.
- Inside: 200 or 400 for scene photography, 100 or 200 for autopsy photography.
- Do not go over 400 ISO if possible; the picture will become too noisy.

1/15th of a second

Figure 12.5

into the camera for brighter exposures. This is the ideal way to shoot at a scene; however, during autopsy one will need to shoot handheld and keep the shutter speed above 1/60th (see Figure 12.5a and b).

ISO

The ISO setting controls the light sensitivity of the image sensor. A low-ISO setting decreases the sensor's sensitivity to light. Conversely, a high-ISO setting increases the sensor's sensitivity to light.

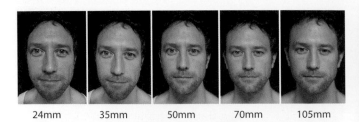

24mm   35mm   50mm   70mm   105mm

Figure 12.7

Figure 12.8

Lens

In forensics, it is very important to have accurate angles with as little distortion as possible in your images.

- 50-mm lens when possible to minimize distortion

The width of a lens can change the shape of an object. Knowing what millimeter lens you have and what type of distortion it may cause is imperative. Anything below 35 mm is considered a wide-angle lens. Wide-angle lenses cause bowing along the edges of the frame. 50-mm to 60-mm lenses are usually used as portrait lenses because they have the least distortion at close range. Although some crime scene photographers believe it is better to use 100-mm lens for face shots, there can be magnification distortion with longer lenses. Additionally, one must get too far away from the subject for it to be practical to use at a scene or in an autopsy environment. 60-mm to 1200-mm lenses are considered telephoto lenses. Telephotos are used for photographing distant objects and can introduce magnification distortion.

In small spaces, it is difficult to avoid shooting with a wide-angle lens. Try shooting with a 50-mm lens whenever possible to reduce distortion. When shooting outdoors, shoot with a 50-mm lens. This lens gives the viewer the proper distance between photographer and subject, making it easier to tell the distance between objects within the photo correctly (see Figure 12.7).

Flash Photography

Most of the time when the camera is handheld, one will be using flash photography both in the field and at autopsy. It is a necessity to learn how a flash works, when to use a flash, and how to control the outcome. Flashes are a very useful tool in low-lighting situations and in mixed light. They help even out contrasting values in a picture and prevent motion blur when the light is too low by adding light. Here are some ways to control your flash.

Fill Flash

If the primary subject is in mixed bright light and shadows, use a fill flash to even out the difference between highlights and shadows. The flash will bring the shadowed parts of the exposure up to the same value as the highlights or will override both, thus creating a new even exposure (see Figure 12.8).

Flash Compensation

The flash output can be increased to make the main subject appear brighter or can be reduced to prevent unwanted highlights or reflections. Flash compensation can be used to alter flash output from –3EV to greater than +3EV depending on the flash; the output is adjusted in increments of 1/3EV on most flashes. This function is controllable on both external flashes as well as some built-in flashes. Even if you have a point-and-shoot, you may be able to change the flash output. Check the manual to change the flash output settings on point-and-shoots and external flashes. Flash compensation is one of the most useful tricks for controlling light in your photographs (see Figure 12.9).

Flash Reflections

If you can see the flash in a reflective surface, take the flash off the camera and move it out of the way. This can be done with a sync cord that attaches your flash to your camera or a remote slave. If you do not have a cord or a slave, shoot on a slight diagonal.

EV–1   EV 0   EV+1

Figure 12.9

No reflector

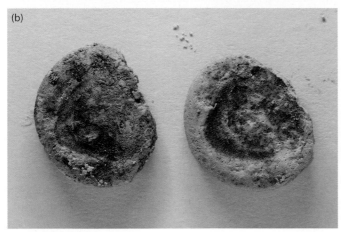

With reflector on the bottom

Figure 12.10

Flash Dissipation/Reflection and Absorption

When shooting a whole room, light from a flash spreads and dissipates; however, when shooting a close-up, the light concentrates. This can cause a harsh spotlight that goes dark toward the bottom of the frame. This is due to the lens being lined up with the subject, so light from the flash passes too high resulting in hot spots on the top and dark spots on the bottom. There are a few ways to fix this problem (see Figure 12.10a and b).

- Step back and zoom in. This allows the light to dissipate.
- Use a reflector. White reflects light, and black absorbs it. White foam core is often used as a reflector to even out the light when working with an on-camera flash.
- Use a ring flash. Ring flashes are circular flashes that go around the end of the lens. They are extremely useful in decreasing shadows, macro photography, and shooting into concave objects such as mouths.

When working with on-camera flash, one will often have to reflect light to fill in harsh shadows. Use reflectors adjacent to your flash to ameliorate the shadows. Reflectors will bounce the light coming from the flash back to fill in harsh shadows. A cheap and accessible reflector is foam core. Foam core allows you to build supports so you can use it hands-free, plus it can be cut to multiple sizes.

It is important to be aware that if white reflects light, then black absorbs it. This may come into play with clothing or at scenes. Black can change your light reading dramatically or cause harsh shadows. If this occurs and you are aware of why it is occurring, you can accurately correct for it.

Bouncing Flash

If an external flash with a pivoting head is used, one can bounce the light off the ceiling or corners of a room. This works nicely in small room like bathrooms that may have reflective surfaces or mirrors. Bouncing light will help light the entire room instead of a single subject (see Figure 12.11a and b).

Flash bounced off ceiling

Direct flash

Figure 12.11

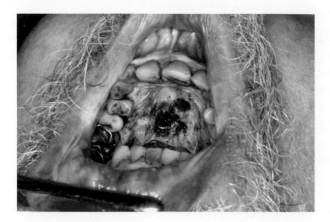

Figure 12.12

Ring Flash

- Macro photography
- Convex surfaces
- Concave surfaces

Ring flashes are used in forensics for macro photography and both convex and concave surfaces. When shooting into a hole, bring the flash down to the level of the lens. This will allow the light to go exactly where the lens is aimed. On convex surfaces, the ring flash brings the light to the middle, allowing more even lighting. For example, if you were photographing a face, you would turn the camera vertically. This would bring your external flash to one side of the face. For example, say the flash is on the right. Because the face is convex, the right side of the face would appear bright and the left side would appear dark. There are two ways to fix this. One would be to put a reflector on the left side to reflect the light back. The other would be to use a ring flash. This would bring the flash to the center of the face for even lighting. The same applies when you are working up close with a subject. An external flash may be too high up and will not be able to dissipate while working in a macro setting. A ring flash will allow you to get very close and surround your subject with light (see Figure 12.12).

Metering

Most cameras have a center-weighted in-camera meter that reads for middle gray. When pointing the camera toward an object and focusing on it, the camera also takes a light reading. On the viewfinder of an SLR, there is a meter that displays whether the setting is resulting in overexposure or underexposure.

Overexposed

- Overexposed means the picture is too bright or washed out.
- Overexposed photos lose detail.

Underexposed

- Underexposed pictures are too dark.
- More detail can be obtained from an underexposed photo than an overexposed photo when shooting on digital.

How to Read a Meter

One side of the meter has a plus sign; the other has a minus sign. Each large slash represents a full stop. If the meter is lit at the first slash on the plus side, it represents +1; the camera settings are one stop overexposed, and the picture will be too bright. If the meter is reading the first slash on the minus side, the picture is underexposed by one stop and will be too dark. Note: this exposure is for ambient light, not the flash.

18% Gray (Middle Gray)

The camera's meter reads the light reflecting off the object in focus and assumes that it is a neutral tone to set the exposure. Middle gray is a tone exactly halfway between perfect white and perfect black. Middle gray reflects approximately 18% of the light that hits it. Therefore, the camera is metering for 18% gray. The 18% gray card was developed to mimic a perfect scene with the tone balanced halfway between white and black. When focusing on an 18% gray card in any light condition, you are getting the middle exposure between blacks and highlights. If you then focus on an object that is black, the camera will think it is gray. Gray now assumes the value of white, and anything white will be blown out (see Figure 12.13a, b, and c).

Metering on white

Figure 12.13   *(Continued)*

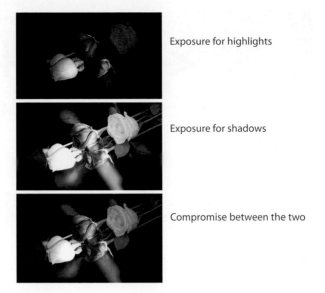

Exposure for highlights

Exposure for shadows

Compromise between the two

Metering on gray

Metering on black

Figure 12.13 (*Continued*)

Metering on White

When metering on white, the camera will make the white subject the middle value. With the camera thinking that white is 18% gray, gray becomes black and black becomes nonexistent.

Problems with Metering

Metering on white can become problematic. Assume you are photographing someone wearing a white shirt. If you meter off their shirt without knowing it, their skin will become extremely dark. It is always better to meter off a person's skin, since you want that to be your middle value. If you cannot meter for a person, meter off a neutral-toned object that would be closest to middle gray.

Compromised Exposure

If the desired image has both shadows and highlights in it and a fill flash is not being used, one may have to

Figure 12.14

compromise between the two. Take a meter reading for the highlights and one for the shadows. Choose an exposure between the two to get both in the exposure range (see Figure 12.14).

Reciprocal Exposure

The final meter reading will determine what f-stop, shutter speed, and ISO will be used. These three elements affect one another and create the exposure. Changing one of the three aforementioned settings may result in changing the others to compensate.

Camera Reading

Say one takes a camera reading and it reads f22 at 1/15th of a second. The camera is telling you this is the exposure that will give you enough light in your picture; however, it does not take into account how much motion blur or how much depth of field there will be.

Going below 1/60th of a second without the aid of a tripod increases the risk of getting motion blur. When changing the shutter speed to 1/60th of a second, for every stop faster the shutter speed gets, the aperture must be opened up one stop to let more light in. This ensures the exposure remains the same.

Say the camera meters at a shutter speed of 1/15 and an f-stop of f8. 1/15 is too slow so you change it to 1/60th of a second, but now that puts the f-stop at f4 (see Figure 12.15a) and there is no depth of field. There are two ways to remedy this situation. The first solution is to change the ISO (see Figure 12.15b). Every increase in ISO will give you more light. The second solution is to add more light by turning up the flash output or adding ambient light.

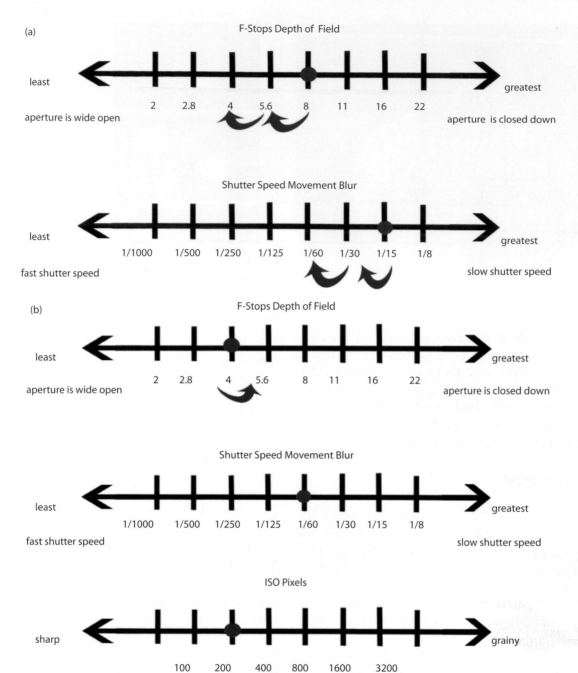

Figure 12.15

Color Temperature

Daylight

Most photography will be shot in daylight or with daylight-balanced light. When a light is daylight-balanced, it has a cool tone or blue hue. Flash photography, studio strobes, and afternoon sunlight are daylight-balanced.

Tungsten Light

Tungsten light is a household light bulb (the old round kind, not the new curly ones). They give off an orange

light that is often dim. The camera will have a setting to balance this light. When the camera is set to daylight balance while shooting in tungsten light, the light will appear orange in the photograph. This setting can be changed under white balance (WB) on the camera's menu settings.

Fluorescent Light

Fluorescent lights are the long lights seen in hallways of public buildings. The light they emit appears green if the camera is set to daylight balance (see Figure 12.16).

| Tungsten | Daylight | Fluorescent |

Figure 12.16

Kelvin Scale

The Kelvin scale is a scale of light temperatures. Knowing where the light falls on the Kelvin scale will help control the look and feel of the photograph. Often bulbs will have the Kelvin number listed on the box. More advanced cameras will let you type this number into the custom white balance to get the correct color temperature. Some cameras can photograph a white area and automatically adjust the white balance.

Almost all cameras, including point-and-shoots, have a white balance menu that can be changed.

Scene Photography

Scene photography can be quite complex. Scenes are often dark, dirty, cramped spaces. They do not always offer much natural light when they are indoors nor a lot of space to put equipment down. Investigators often find themselves shooting photos with one hand so they can carry their equipment in the other. In low-light situations, this can lead to a number of problems with motion blur and getting the photographs needed for the medical examiner to do a proper investigation. The best way to approach any forensic photography is to have a set plan in place. This plan should consist of a shot list that can be broken down into three parts.

- Overall photographs
- Midrange photographs
- Close-range photographs

These three categories will assure that everything needed for an investigation is covered. Overshooting can be just as confusing to people who are not at the scene as undershooting. The goal is to walk the viewer through a story. If the story is incomplete, they may not understand it. If the story gets sidetracked consistently, it may be confusing. The best plan is the story outline. It should be consistent from scene to scene, with only slight variations tailored toward highlighting various components of homicides, suicides, accidents, and natural deaths.

Overall Photographs

Overalls are an overview of the scene and its surroundings. These photos acclimate the viewer to the scene and what is around it.

Before shooting overalls, a photo identifier must be established. This may be a sheet of paper with the decedent's claim number and personal information or a card with the case number on it. This will help both you and others viewing the images identify which case they are looking at.

The purpose of overall photographs is to answer the question, "Where am I?" If you are outside, then shoot the street sign closest to you or the milepost marker on the highway. Subsequently, shoot in all four directions with the body in the frame. This will show the environment around the body. Shooting in all four directions will eliminate any possible doubt as to the placement of the body at the scene and the surrounding environment. Proper scene photography can change the way people perceive an incident; therefore, it is paramount to carefully and thoroughly document a scene using photography (see Figure 12.17).

Figure 12.17

35mm close up   50mm lens from distance

Figure 12.18

If you are shooting a scene inside, the first step should be to take a photograph of the building you are entering. This should be shot at standing height with a 50-mm lens to exclude distortion. When shooting these photos, step back as far as possible until the building fills the frame. The composition should always fill the frame, taking care to omit as much extraneous information as possible. Keep the back and the front of the camera as level as possible so there is no perspective distortion (see Figure 12.18a and b).

Overlap Photos

If the scene cannot fit into one picture, take several photos that overlap. This will capture the entire scene.

Show the entrances, hallway, and all the rooms in the house or apartment. This may seem excessive, but in natural deaths and suicides, it is commonplace to find blood or evidence in rooms the decedent was not found in. Someone may see something in these photos that can change the course of the investigation or the investigation may change on its own later on (see Figure 12.19a and b).

Figure 12.19

How to Document a Room

Four Corners There are two ways to photograph a room upon entrance. The first is from each corner of the room. No matter what view a picture is taken from, you always want a view looking back to where you entered. Taking a picture from all four corners will capture the entire room.

The same principle applies to shooting an outdoor scene. The body will be seen at autopsy the next day but the scene will not be; therefore, it is important to show the body in the scene and its surrounding environment. Shoot in all four directions around the body (see Figure 12.20a, b, c, and d).

From Each Wall The second way to photograph a room is from each flat wall straight out. This is much harder to do, but it reduces distortion. If you are unable to photograph an entire wall in one shot, make sure to overlap from one photo to the next; this will ensure that nothing is missing and will serve to orient the viewer (see Figure 12.21a, b, c, and d).

Using Tripods and Monopods

It is advantageous to use a tripod or monopod at a scene if possible. Using a tripod or monopod will permit longer shutter speeds while eliminating motion blur in dark spaces. Sometimes it is hard to find space or time to set up a tripod. A monopod is a good compromise in this situation, although not as efficient. A tripod is the number one piece of equipment needed to properly shoot a scene.

Shooting with Other People

Most of the time there will be a lot of people at a scene, especially a crime scene. Compose your photograph and politely ask people to step out of the frame. Family members and investigators should not be walking around in the scene photographs.

Midrange

A midrange photograph shows the orientation of evidence in relation to its environment. If one was to photograph a room and then had a close-up of a knife, one might question where the knife is in the room. The midrange shot is the orientation shot. It tells you the knife is on the roof next to the fire escape ladder. The ladder is portrayed in the overall. To tell this story, both the knife and part of the ladder must appear together in the photograph. The composition should only include the information needed to tell the story. Crop out distracting objects that do not pertain to this story and may cause confusion or clutter. Do not move objects at a scene without first

Figure 12.20

Figure 12.21

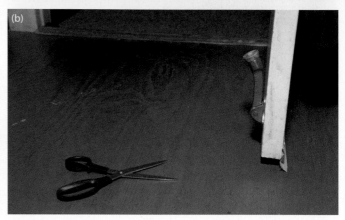

Figure 12.22

Figure 12.23

photographing the scene the way it was found. If a piece of evidence is behind a box, first photograph the box in relation to a fixed object, then move the box and take the same photo again. Moving objects at a scene could be considered tampering with evidence. The original position of the objects may be pertinent to the scene investigation (see Figure 12.22a and b).

Linear Viewpoint

Make sure the evidence and the fixed object at the scene are not overlapping as this can distort the perspective. Only photograph the objects parallel to the camera, drawing an imaginary line between them. Try to keep both subjects equidistant from the camera and keep the camera level (see Figure 12.23a and b).

Shooting across from a Reflective Surface

You never want to see yourself, your equipment, or the flash in a reflective surface. If you are shooting across from a mirror, a window, or a reflective surface, you may have to shoot on a slight diagonal. If this is the case, shoot the picture from both sides so nothing is missing. Keep the sensor plane parallel to the evidence.

Shadows

When shooting outside, try to avoid having your own shadow or coworkers' shadows in the shot. While shooting close-ups, if your shadow is unavoidable, try to place it over the entire frame of the photo or use a flat surface to cover the light and meter for the shadow.

Lens Flare

Try not to point the camera toward the sun if possible. The subject being photographed is backlit and spots across the photo will appear. These spots are known as lens flare. If this is not possible, use a lens hood or cover the top of the lens with your hand (see Figure 12.24a and b).

Three-Dimensional Impressions and Raised Evidence

When lighting three-dimensional impressions such as tire marks or footprints or raised evidence such as raised patterns, take care to show the depth of the impression or the height of the concave pattern. Light the subject from a low angle by removing the flash from the camera with a sync cord or remote slave to cast a short shadow; make sure the shadow is not covering up any evidence. Use a reflector on the opposite side of the flash to lighten harsh shadows so everything is visible (see Figure 12.25).

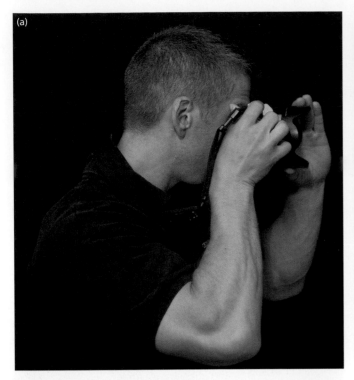
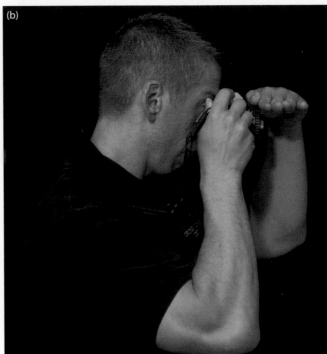

Figure 12.24

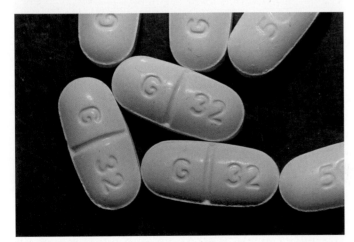

Figure 12.25

Close-Ups

Close-ups show the detail of the evidence you are documenting. Fill the frame with the evidence, keeping the camera parallel to the sensor plane. Do not tilt the camera, as tilting will cause perspective distortion (see Figure 12.26).

Labeled Scales

It is standard practice to include a labeled scale in each of the close-ups. This label should have the same information as your photo identifier plus a ruler. Scales should be photographed on the same plane as the evidence for accuracy.

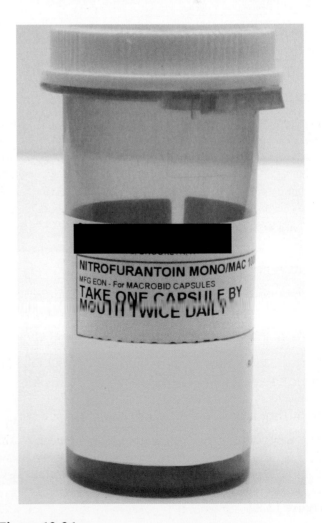

Figure 12.26

Medications and Small Evidence

When shooting small evidence up close at a scene, your flash may blow your subject out. Step back and zoom in to let you flash dissipate.

Photographing Bodies

When photographing a body at a scene, first establish where the body is in the room by taking overalls of the room (see Figure 12.27a and b). Proceed by taking a midrange photograph of a section of the body in relation to a fixed object.

After the scene is established, continue with overalls of the body, photographing it in three or four sections down both sides using a 50-mm lens and making sure to crop out the background. Take the photos from standing height and ensure the photos overlap slightly. If the body fits in one shot with a 50-mm lens, do this as well. If possible, shoot the body from both sides in this manner. Overhead shots are also needed if possible (see Figure 12.28a, b, and c).

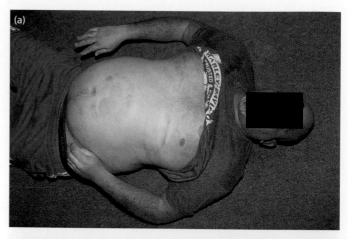
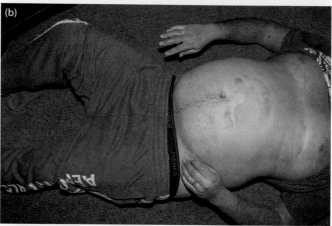
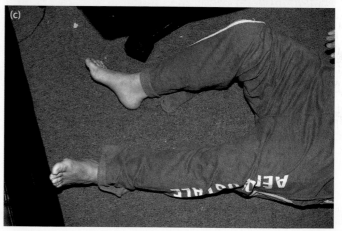

Figure 12.28

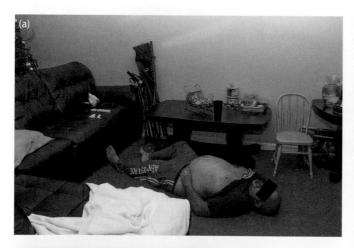

Figure 12.27

Face Photo

Document the face close-up, from the neck to the top of the head only. Shoot vertically as long as the face is longer than it is wide (see Figure 12.29).

Remain Parallel

Make sure your lens remains parallel to the surface plane. Try not to shoot up from the chin or down from the forehead. This will create distortion.

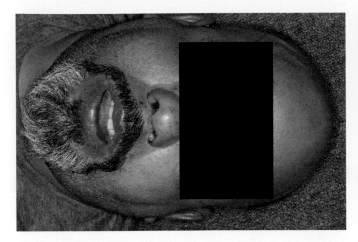

Figure 12.29

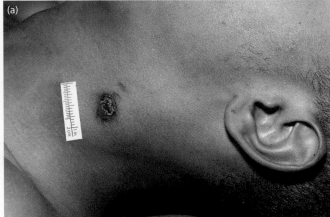

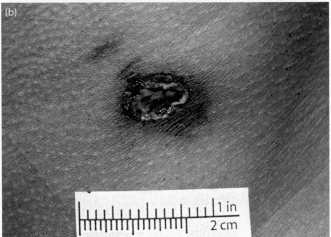

Figure 12.31

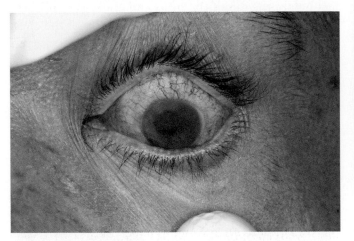

Figure 12.30

Eyes

During routine investigation of the eyes at a scene, one may see petechial hemorrhages. These hemorrhages should be photographed if present. Photograph them the same way you shoot small evidence. Make sure your flash is on; step back and zoom in to let the flash dissipate, unless a ring flash and a macro lens are being used. If a ring flash is being used with a macro lens, get close-up. The flash may need to be angled as to minimize the reflection of it in the pupil (see Figure 12.30).

Photographing Wounds

Before taking a close-up of a wound or evidence on the body, locate its position on the body by taking a mid-range shot showing a reference point such as a belly button, nipple, or armpit. Follow by shooting the close-up with the label parallel to the floor as if the decedent was standing. Doing this will ensure everyone knows where

the decedent's head and feet are in relation to the wound (see Figure 12.31a and b).

Perspective

Keep the camera parallel to the sensor plane when shooting overalls. Shooting on an angle distorts perspective and becomes confusing to the viewer.

Set the lens at 50 mm and fill the entire frame with the subject. However, there are some cases where it is more important to see the injuries than to shoot at 50 mm or have your camera lens parallel to the surface plane. In these situations you may have to compromise to get the best photo. Keep the integrity of the photo by keeping it as close as possible to the correct settings.

Autopsy Photography

Much like scene photography, autopsy photography can be broken down into three sections: overalls, midrange, and close-up photos.

Overalls

Overalls in autopsy photography are contained to the body. Show the entire body from head to foot to document the condition the body arrived in or the condition it is in after clothing and hospital therapy are removed.

"As Is" Overalls

A request may be made to photograph the body "as is." This means as soon as the body bag is opened, photograph the body the way it arrived from the scene. "As is" photographs help the medical examiner understand whether there were changes made to the body in transit to the morgue. For example, assume the body arrives at the morgue with a laceration on his or her head, but in the scene photos there was no laceration. This tells the medical examiner that the laceration occurred during transit. Also, personal effects may be removed from the body at the scene. The body may have been photographed wearing a ring at the scene but may not have the ring on when it arrived at the morgue. There are many different situations where documenting the body on arrival may be useful. The most important of these is a homicide. All homicides should be photographed "as is" when they arrive. This gives the M.E. the opportunity to review the body and the condition it arrived in (see Figure 12.32).

Clean Overalls

It is very important to have clean, dry overalls of the body in all cases. Blood, dirt, and feces may cover injuries that need to be properly documented. Clean photographs are only taken after all the evidence needed is collected by the doctor on staff (see Figure 12.33).

How to Shoot Overalls

Overalls are shot in two ways, from the side and overhead. Use the flash sync speed for your shutter speed and a midrange f-stop such as f11. Aim to use an ISO of 200 or lower. If an external flash is being used, you may want to spread the light by programming the flash to a wider setting than the lens diameter.

Shooting Overalls from the Side The first way is to shoot from the side of the body at standing height. These photographs should be taken with a 50-mm lens to reduce distortion, and should be broken down into three or four overlapping sections. The body should fill the frame, making sure that all sections of the body are within the frame. The first section should be from the head to chest, with the end of the frame starting just before the top of the head and ending somewhere around the armpit. Keep the arm and top of the chest in frame, taking care to include little to no extraneous material. The next section should slightly overlap the first section so nothing is missing in sequential photos. Continue this down the body. Each photograph should have labels with the case number in it, and should be facing the foot of the photographer, orienting the photograph so the body is lying down. Shoot both sides.

Backgrounds

When shooting from the side, it is good to have a sliding background to put behind the body. This allows the photographer to shoot without having distractions behind the body (technicians, doctors, other bodies, etc.) The background should be durable, washable, and

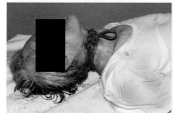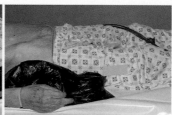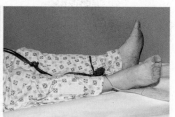

Figure 12.32

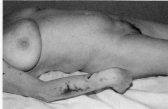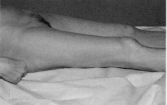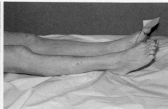

Figure 12.33

on wheels. You can make backgrounds out of Formica and PVC piping. Also, the background should be a neutral color; 18% gray is the best choice for accurate light readings.

Shooting Overalls from Overhead In photography the human body is like a rectangular box. If the photograph is taken from the side, the top area will be omitted; however, if you photograph it only from the top looking down, you may be missing injuries on the lateral aspects of the body. Which way the overalls are shot may be based on the injuries present. Lateral and top-down shots must be done to get a complete overview of the body. This may not be necessary in most cases, though. Sometimes the photos are taken to get a general idea of the weight, height, and condition of the body and only one view may be needed. To take overalls from overhead, one will need either a ladder or an overhead camera stand. Overhead photos should also be taken in three or four sections, keeping the lens as true to 50 mm as possible and the perspective plane level as possible. Overlap each photo to make sure nothing is missing in sequential photographs. Overhead photos come in handy for decedents who have been crushed in events such as MVAs or pedestrian versus vehicle accidents. These photos may show tire marks or crushing injuries. They are also necessary for homicides that may have injuries such as gunshot wounds or stab wounds on the surface (see Figure 12.34).

Photographing the Back of a Body

There are two ways to photograph the back of a body, on the side or prone.

On the Side You can roll the body onto its side, which reveals the flat surface of the back. Photograph the back in three or four overlapping sections. These images also require labels with the case number facing the foot of the photographer in each photograph. It is best if a background is included for these pictures to cut out distractions (see Figure 12.35).

Prone You may want to orient the decedent so he/she is prone. Prone shots would be useful if injuries extend from the back to the side or to document injuries that may be under the lateral aspect of the body. Regarding homicides, it is good practice to roll the decedents over in the prone position as to not miss any injuries. This is also helpful in severe trauma cases for proper documentation. Once the body is prone, it can be shot overhead with necessary side photos or both from the side and overhead (see Figure 12.36).

Face Photograph

The face photograph is always included in the overall series. This photograph should be framed from the top of the head to the chin, filling the frame entirely. Do not tilt the camera in any way, and use a 50-mm lens to minimize distortion. When using a camera flash, keep the camera away from the body to let the flash dissipate. This will help in creating softer, more even lighting. If possible,

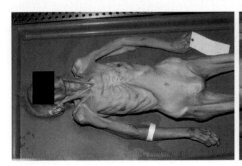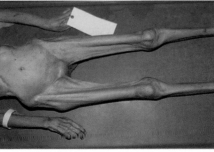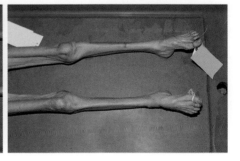

Figure 12.34

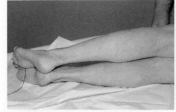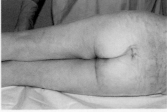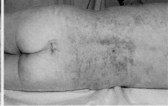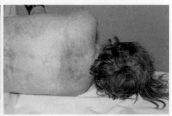

Figure 12.35

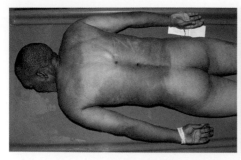
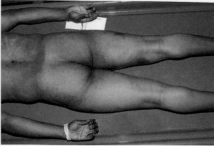
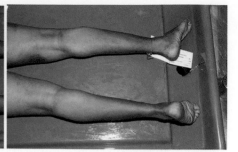

Figure 12.36

use a bounce card on the flash and a reflector opposite the flash to even out the light. A 35-mm frame is slightly longer than it is wide. Line the long end of the frame up with the long end of the face to get the best results. If a ring flash is available, use it. This will place the flash in the center of the face instead of off to one side. When the camera is vertical and the flash is set to the right or left side, shadows will form on the opposite side. This is why reflectors and ring flashes are useful. The shutter speed can stay the same as the overall; however, if too much falls off with f11, the f-stop can be raised to f16 if there is enough flash output (see Figure 12.37).

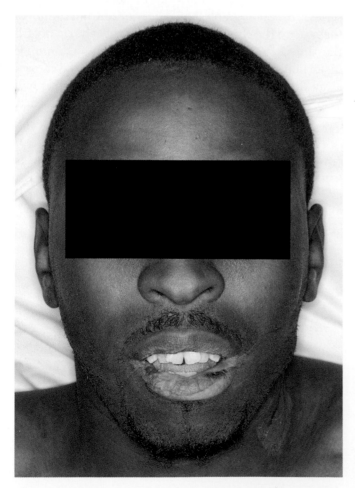

Figure 12.37

Midrange Photographs

Midrange photographs are the orientation shots. This time the photographs will show where something is on or in the body, or how injuries relate to one another. For example, if there is a gunshot wound, before taking a close-up, a midrange photograph would be taken to show where the gunshot wound is. This photograph should show the gunshot wound and an identifiable part of the body. Following sufficient midrange photos, the close-ups would be next. If you are showing a relationship between wounds, you are telling a story about what may have happened. For example, you might show an entrance gunshot wound on an arm, an exit wound on the same arm, and an entrance wound on the body together. This implies the bullet may have gone through the arm and into the body.

These photos should be taken with a 50-mm lens with the label oriented toward the foot of the decedent. The label should face this direction to help orient the doctor when the area is unidentifiable. If the label is always facing the foot of the decedent, then the doctor knows where the head is and where the feet are without seeing them. Forensic photographers should always be consistent with this unless otherwise requested by the doctor.

Midrange photographs also include isolated body parts, such as a single foot or hand. Forensic photographers should always photograph all aspects of the hands on a homicide before evidence is collected. If the decedent has injuries on the hands, then you would photograph them again once they are clean (see Figure 12.38). The camera sync speed for these photos should be between f11 and f16.

Close-Ups

When shooting close-ups, fill the frame with the desired subject matter. The label again should always face the foot of the decedent, especially now that there is nothing to orient the viewer. When shooting close-up, a higher f-stop is necessary since the focal length drops off quicker. It is recommended to use f16–22 when shooting close-up. Keep the sync speed the same as the shutter speed (see Figure 12.39a and b).

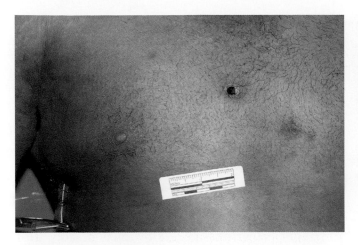

Figure 12.38

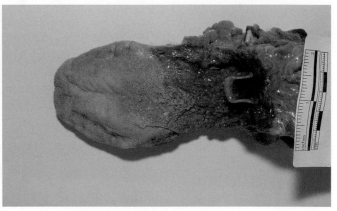

Figure 12.40

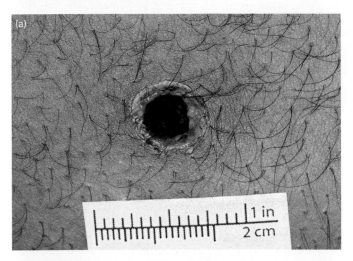

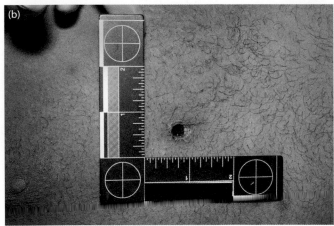

Figure 12.39

placed on a clean background. Specimen photographs usually consist of an overall and a close-up of a specific area. The label should always face the bottom of the specimen for orientation (see Figure 12.40).

Copy Stands

If you have a budget and room for a copy stand, they are highly advantageous. They are great for shooting small to medium-sized flat evidence, such as money, identification, credit cards, and so on. They are also good for shooting slices of cut organs, which can be very shiny and troublesome when shot with a flash. Although bullets are not flat, they are small enough to shoot on the copy stand as well. They can appear less reflective this way. When using a copy stand, make sure the lights are daylight-balanced for good color correction. Since the camera is mounted, slower shutter speeds can be used; however, staying above 1/50 of a second shutter speed is recommended. Slower shutter speeds can let too much ambient light in and disturb the color balance. For most photos, an ISO of 400, 1/60 of a second shutter speed and an f-stop of f11 are sufficient. (See Figure 12.41).

Specimen Photography

Specimen photography is an integral part of autopsy documentation. For example, injured organs due to an accident or homicide will be photographed. Internal organs are often photographed to document pathology also. These photographs may occur *in situ* or *ex situ*. If the specimen is removed from the body, it should be

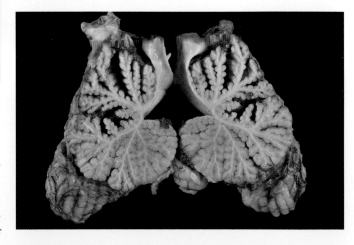

Figure 12.41 Cerebella atrophy due to chronic alcoholism.

Evidence

In forensic photography, you will shoot everything from a bullet to a pair of jeans. Each piece of evidence, based on its size, is photographed differently.

When photographing homicide clothing, use overalls and midrange photographs to illustrate where defects are in the clothing. It helps to use arrows or paper under the defects to show where the defect is, especially on dark clothing. First, shoot a photograph showing the entire garment with the defects highlighted. Then, take a midrange photograph showing the defect in proximity to an identifying part of the clothing, such as a collar. The label should always face the bottom of the garment (see Figure 12.42a and b).

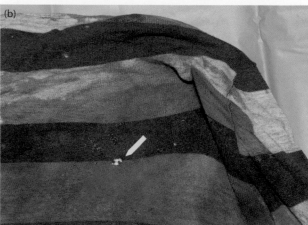

Figure 12.42

Index